SEX DIFFERENCES AND SIMILARITIES IN COMMUNICATION

LEA's COMMUNICATION SERIES

Jennings Bryant and Dolf Zillmann, General Editors

Selected titles in Interpersonal Communication (Rebecca G. Rubin, Advisory Editor) include:

Allen/Preiss/Gayle/Burrell • *Interpersonal Communication Research: Advances Through Meta-Analysis*

Cupach/Spitzberg • *The Dark Side of Interpersonal Communication*

Kalbfleisch/Cody • *Gender, Power, and Communication in Human Relationships*

Petronio • *Balancing the Secrets of Private Disclosures*

Stafford • *Maintaining Long-Distance and Cross-Residential Relationships*

SEX DIFFERENCES AND SIMILARITIES IN COMMUNICATION

Second Edition

Edited by

Kathryn Dindia
University of Wisconsin–Milwaukee

Daniel J. Canary
Arizona State University

Lawrence Erlbaum Associates
Taylor & Francis Group

New York London

Library of Congress Cataloging-in-Publication Data
Sex differences and similarities in communication / edited by Kathryn Dindia, Daniel J. Canary.– 2nd ed.
p. cm. — (LEA's communication series)
Includes bibliographical references and index.
ISBN 0-8058-5141-0 (casebound : alk. paper) — ISBN 0-8058-5142-9 (pbk. : alk. paper)
1. Communication—Sex differences. I. Dindia, Kathryn. II. Canary, Daniel J. III. Series.

P96.S48S49 2006
155.3′3—dc22 2005030783

Books published by Lawrence Erlbaum Associates are printed on acid-free paper, and their bindings are chosen for strength and durability.

Printed in the United States of America
10 9 8 7 6 5 4 3 2

Contents

Preface

A science teacher in Baltimore, Md., was offering lessons in anatomy when one of the boys in class declared, "There's one less rib in a man than in a women." The teacher pulled out two skeletons—one male, the other female—and asked the student to count the ribs in each. "The next day," the teacher recalls, "the boy claimed he told his priest what happened and his priest said I was a heretic."

—Gibbs (2005, p. 40)

Of course, men and women differ in many ways. Some biological differences, for instance, are undeniable in that no one seriously considers an examination of sex differences in reproductive roles (pregnancy, childbirth, and breast-feeding). However, some biological similarities are undeniable in that no one seriously considers an examination of sex differences in number of ribs. In addition to sex differences, sex inequalities are clearly evident in the division of labor, unequal pay for men and women, and the sex composition of the highest levels of corporate and government offices. For instance, women working outside the home continue to struggle to achieve equal pay in the workforce and a fair division of labor in the home. Less, clear, however, are the differences in men's and women's communicative behaviors in professional, social, and personal relationships.

Scholarly opinions about the differences between men and women are more than academic; opinions about sex differences have personal, professional, and political implications. Given the seriousness of the implications, it is no wonder that scholars often advocate their academic positions on the issue of sex differences and similarities with passion and zeal.

This book examines the social scientific literature regarding how men and women communicate. Readers who are interested in the scientific literature on communication, social psychology, and related fields should find this anthology an important resource. Students in advanced undergraduate classes and graduate classes, and practitioners interested in research-based conclusions regarding sex differences in communicative behavior, should be especially informed. People who seek support for the point of view that men and women are divided into dichotomous or polarized groups will probably want to look elsewhere.

This is the second edition of *Sex Differences and Similarities in Communication*. The first edition was published in 1998. Since then, far more research has been conducted, and by scholars across disciplines such as communication, social psychology, sociology, linguistics, organizational behavior, and other literatures, on sex differences and similarities in communication. Several of the authors contributing to this volume were not included in the first edition. Some of the chapters present new perspectives on sex or gender and communication; some present substantially revised versions of earlier chapters. All are more theoretically oriented and based on a wider range of empirical data than the first edition.

We are especially pleased by the breadth of scholarship evidenced in this volume, breadth across not just the field of communication but also social psychology, sociology, and organizational behavior. Communication is not solely studied by communication researchers. It is important that communication anthologies represent the diversity of communication theory and research found in other disciplines, just as it is important that other disciplines recognize the scholarship being carried out in the field of communication.

As the title implies, chapters in this book present sex similarities as well as sex differences in communication. The primary reason we examine sex similarities in addition to sex differences stems from our desire to present a balanced scientific anthology on the topic. In our view, another book that polarizes men and women would move the corpus of knowledge backward, making us less informed than we should be at this point in time. Instead, this book advances the idea that, with respect to communicative behavior, men and women are similar in some domains and different in others. The task, then, is to juxtapose similarities and differences.

We believe that sex similarities provide a context, a backdrop, for sex differences. This backdrop offers ways to contrast communicative differences between men and women, yet the backdrop metaphor represents more than an ideological frame of reference. More precisely, using similarities to contextualize and clarify differences between men and women allows researchers to look for differences only in places where we theoretically and empirically hypothesize them to be, as opposed to everywhere. The scientific study of how sex similarities might contextualize and inform the study of sex differences is largely a novelty. Most of the time, researchers want to see differences, not similarities; researchers seek confirmation of the research hypothesis, not support for the null. Only when they find no significant differences do scientists tend to admit that similarities appear plausible.

This book specifically aims to uncover sex and gender differences within the context of similarities. Neither of the editors presumes that omnipresent sex differences exist. Our view is that men and women are different. However, men and women are more alike than different, and focal points that connect similarities to differences theoretically as well as methodologically constitute a critical juncture for speculation and study.

Critically, the chapters in this volume vary in terms of the authors' positions. Most of the authors theoretically or empirically elaborate sex similarities and sex differences, whereas a few take positions on either end of the similarity–difference continuum. These alternative points of view provide a sense of freedom not found in other books that aim to limit views about men's and women's communication; one does not have to presume sex differences or sex similarities to be politically correct (PC) or scientifically correct (SC) in this book. Accordingly, this volume provides various models regarding how scholars can recalibrate categorical thinking to discover where sex differences and similarities lie.

Most of the chapters provide innovative alternatives to categorical thinking about men and women. As editors, we were pleased by the variation in scope and evidence used to develop ideas. Contributors characteristically offer in-depth, state-of-the art reviews of the scientific literature. These are organized into four thematic parts.

In Part I, the chapters frame the conversation regarding the extent to which sex differences are found in social behavior. In the first chapter, "Men are From North Dakota; Women are from South Dakota," Kathryn Dindia uses this deviant and wry metaphor to reflect that men and women are more similar that different. In terms of this metaphor, men and women are not from different planets, or different cultures, but rather from adjacent states. Likewise, Elizabeth Aries persuasively argues that one should take account of context and other factors when examining sex or gender differences. Paul Wright extends this theme in his excellent chapter on friendship. Wright notes that instrumental and communal behaviors influence the extent to which sex differences are important. Next, Judith Hall takes a comparative approach by examining how nonverbal sex differences compare with other sex differences in psychology and how nonverbal sex differences compare with other correlates of nonverbal behaviors. Following Hall, Gary Powell and Laura Graves review the research on leadership perception. They acutely note that stereotypical thinking on leadership styles does not reflect current reality, and that women enact behaviors that reflect leadership effectiveness. Part I closes with an examination by Mike Allen and Kathleen Valde of how the sex difference–similarity debate should lead to a discussion of ethics in sex and gender research.

The chapters in Part II emphasize different theoretical perspectives on the topic. This part begins with a provocative argument for a social evolutionary approach. In chapter 7, Peter Andersen notes how human evolution has led to sex differences in nonverbal sensitivity and use of space. Next, Brant Burleson and Adrianne Kunkel boldly challenge the view that women and men inhabit different cultures. They report on several studies demonstrating that men and women appreciate the same forms of social support. Continuing on the issue of support, Alice Eagly and Anne Koenig highlight how we might understand helping behavior from the perspective of social role theory. Eagly and Koening's analysis is persuasive in showing that the direction of sex differences changes depending on what type of helping behavior is under consideration (e.g., helping someone in need vs. helping someone who wants help). Then Mary Crawford and Michelle Kaufman "discuss ways in which gender is constructed through language and how this creates and maintains a hierarchy of power" (their words). These authors passionately argue for a social constructionist approach to the examination of gender and language. Finally, Vince Waldron and Lesley Di Mare remind us that the discussion of sex differences cannot occur without the consideration of culture. These scholars consider how sex differences compare with and interact with cultural differences in their examination of the United States and Japan.

Part III examines how sex differences and similarities can be seen in various verbal and nonverbal communicative behaviors across contexts. Anthony Mulac begins this section with a summary of research on the "gender-linked language effect." His research indicates that sex differences and similarities exist in various dimensional properties of language. Next, the reader will find the chapter by Laura Guerrero, Susanne Jones, and Renee Boburka on emotional differences. Using both bioevolutionary and socialization perspectives, the authors insightfully examine how and why sex differences emerge in four types of emotions (positive affect, anger, sadness or depression, and jealousy). Then Judee Burgoon and associates evaluate the evidence related to deception—its enactment and detection—and they report some intriguing findings with regard to the behaviors that men and women attend to in episodes involving deception. Following that chapter, Elizabeth Lindsay and Walter Zakahi explore what happens when people deviate from sex-role stereotypes in initial interactions. Again, their findings suggest that violating stereotypes leads to perceptions that are not entirely predictable. Pamela Kalbfleisch and Anita Harold conclude this section with an examination of recent research that compares power or status to sex differences in communicative behaviors, and they then focus on leadership behaviors. Although this analysis initially indicates that women engage in less powerful behaviors, they also note a twist on the issue that makes the power–sex link more complex than originally thought.

Part IV focuses on communication behavior in romantic relationships. Melanie Trost and Jess Alberts leverage evolutionary theory to discuss differences in men's and women's attraction. Their findings are compelling reminders that biology matters. Paul Mongeau and colleagues then provide an excellent overview of romantic relationship development in terms of sex differences that occur during various transition points, specifically, first dates, first significant self-disclosure, and first sexual encounter. Their analysis also implies some intriguing ideas about the changing landscape of relational development. Next, Dan Canary and Jodi Wahba ask whether women work harder than men at maintaining their romantic relationships. As with other chapters, the answer to their question is not a simple one. Linda Sagrestano, Christopher Heavey, and Andrew Christensen present an insightful analysis of alternative ways to think about the conflict interaction and social influence behavior of men and women. The authors provide empirical evidence for and against individual difference and social structural approaches from research on the demand–withdraw pattern in marital conflict and the use of social influence strategies in peer and marital relationships. Finally, Julia Wood offers a nuanced and carefully crafted portrayal of violence in romantic relationships. Her use of both quantitative and qualitative data is insightful as well as unexpected.

Janet Shebly Hyde concludes the book with a critical overview of the issues that she believes are salient in this anthology. Her analysis provides insight regarding future research as well as the research that is summarized here. The reader might want to read the Epilogue first.

We sincerely hope that you find this anthology as intriguing as we have. We think that the chapters will interest you and kindle new ways to think about sex differences and similarities in communicative behavior. We believe that scholarly interest in sex differences in communicative behavior will continue to be advanced by also paying attention to sex similarities.

We want to thank many people who helped to make this second edition a reality. First and foremost, we thank the contributors to this edition. As the reader can see, the scholars contributing to this book are first-rate researchers. What the reader cannot see is that these people provided excellent drafts and revised them in a timely manner. Linda Bathgate at Lawrence Erlbaum Associates was especially instrumental. The first edition of this book was Linda's first communication series project at LEA, and we marvel at her skill in promoting our book and others in the discipline. We want to acknowledge the help of Karin Wittig Bates, also at LEA. In addition, we thank the editors of the LEA Communication Series (Jennings Bryant and Dolf Zillmann) as well as Dennis Gouran for his advice regarding the inclusion of the first edition in that series. Finally, we thank our spouses, whose generosity and consideration allowed us to pursue this project with zeal.

Daniel J. Canary
Kathryn Dindia

REFERENCE

Gibbs, N. (2005, February 21). Parents behaving badly. *Time, 165*, 40–49.

Contributors

Jess K. Alberts, PhD, Hugh Downs School of Human Communication, Arizona State University, Tempe, AZ.

Mike Allen, PhD, Department of Communication, University of Wisconsin–Milwaukee, Milwaukee, WI.

Peter Andersen, PhD, School of Communication, San Diego State University, San Diego, CA.

Elizabeth Aries, PhD, Department of Psychology, Amherst College, Amherst, MA.

J. P. Blair, PhD, Criminal Justice, University of Texas at San Antonio, San Antonio, TX.

Renee Reiter Boburka, PhD, Department of Psychology, East Stroudsburg University, East Stroudsburg, PA.

David Buller, PhD, Cooper Institute, Denver, CO.

Judee Burgoon, PhD, Department of Communication, University of Arizona, Tucson, AZ.

Brant R. Burleson, PhD, Department of Communication, Purdue University, West Lafayette, IN.

Daniel J. Canary, PhD, Hugh Downs School of Human Communication, Arizona State University, Tempe, AZ.

Andrew Christensen, PhD, Department of Psychology, University of California at Los Angeles, Los Angeles, CA.

Mary Crawford, PhD, Department of Psychology, University of Connecticut, Storrs, CT.

Kristin Leigh Davis, MA, Hugh Downs School of Human Communication, Arizona State University, Tempe, AZ.

Lesley Di Mare, PhD, Communication Studies, Arizona State University West, Phoenix, AZ.

Kathryn Dindia, PhD, Department of Communication, University of Wisconsin–Milwaukee, Milwaukee, WI.

Alice H. Eagly, PhD, Department of Psychology, Northwestern University, Evanston, IL.

Laura M. Graves, PhD, Graduate School of Management, Clark University, Worcester, MA.

Laura K. Guerrero, PhD, Hugh Downs School of Human Communication, Arizona State University, Tempe, AZ.

Judith A. Hall, PhD, Department of Psychology, Northeastern University, Boston, MA.

Christopher L. Heavey, PhD, Department of Psychology, University of Nevada at Las Vegas, Las Vegas, NV.

Mary Lynn Miller Henningsen, PhD, Department of Communication, Northern Illinois University, DeKalb, IL.

Anita L. Herold, MA, School of Communication, University of North Dakota, Grand Forks, ND.

Janet Shibley Hyde, PhD, Department of Psychology, University of Wisconsin–Madison, Madison, WI.

Susanne M. Jones, PhD, Department of Communication, University of Minnesota, Twin Cities, MN.

Pamela J. Kalbfleisch, PhD, School of Communication, University of North Dakota, Grand Forks, ND.

Michelle R. Kaufman, MA, Department of Psychology, University of Connecticut, Storrs, CT.

Anne M. Koenig, MA, Department of Psychology, Northwestern University, Evanston, IL.

Adrianne Kunkel, PhD, Department of Communication, University of Kansas, Lawrence, KS.

A. Elizabeth Lindsey, PhD, Department of Communication, New Mexico State University, Las Cruces, NM.

Paul A. Mongeau, PhD, Hugh Downs School of Human Communication, Arizona State University, Tempe, AZ.

Anthony Mulac, PhD, Department of Communication, University of California at Santa Barbara, Santa Barbara, CA.

Gary N. Powell, PhD, Department of Management, University of Connecticut, Storrs, CT.

Mary Claire Morr Serewicz, PhD, Human Communication Studies, University of Denver, Denver, CO.

Patti Tilley, MA, Management Information Systems, Florida State University, Tallahassee, FL.

Lynda M. Sagrestano, PhD, Department of Psychology, Southern Illinois University, Carbondale, IL.

Melanie R. Trost, PhD, Anaconda, MT.

Kathleen S. Valde, PhD, Department of Communication, Northern Illinois University, DeKalb, IL.

Vincent Waldron, PhD, Communication Studies, Arizona State University West, Phoenix, AZ.

Jodi Wahba, MA, Hugh Downs School of Human Communication, Arizona State University, Tempe, AZ.

Julia, T. Wood, PhD, Department of Communication Studies, University of North Carolina at Chapel Hill, Chapel Hill, NC.

Paul H. Wright, PhD, Department of Psychology, University of North Dakota, Grand Forks, ND.

Walter R. Zakahi, PhD, Department of Communication, New Mexico State University, Las Cruces, NM.

SEX DIFFERENCES AND SIMILARITIES IN COMMUNICATION

I

Framing Sex Differences and Similarities

1

Men are From North Dakota, Women are From South Dakota

Kathryn Dindia
University of Wisconsin–Milwaukee

Julia Wood and I opened the first edition of *Sex Differences and Similarities in Communication* with a gentle debate on the topic of similarities and differences between women and men (Wood & Dindia 1998). Julia's interests have changed since then, and she writes about her current passion in this edition. My passion remains unchanged. My professional and personal life is dominated by the three questions we addressed in the first edition of this book: First, are women and men different? Second, if so, what is the cause of these differences? Third, what should be the focus of research on sex and gender differences and similarities in communication?

In preview, I believe that sex differences exist but that they are overwhelmed by similarities. When there are differences, in general they are small, although there are some instances of moderate (which may include nonverbal communication) and large differences. Differences between women and men are differences of degree, not kind. Sex or gender differences are the result of the interaction of biology and culture. Finally, differences between women and men should be studied along with similarities, and we need to focus more on theoretical explanations for sex or gender differences. This chapter presents an opportunity for me to re-present these views and to further elaborate the anecdotal and empirical support for them.

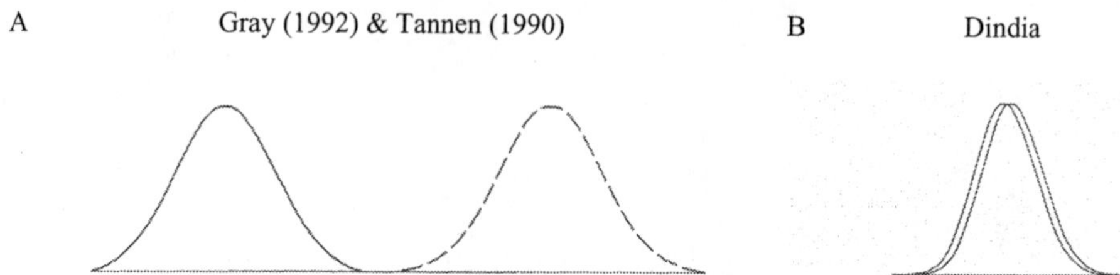

FIGURE 1.1. Representations of the Degree of Overlap between Women and Men.

ARE WOMEN AND MEN DIFFERENT?

The popular press would have us believe that women and men are radically different. Indeed, in his book *Men Are From Mars, Women Are From Venus*, John Gray (1992) used this metaphor to represent differences between women and men. Gray argued that "men and women differ in all areas of their lives. Not only do men and women communicate differently but they think, feel, perceive, react, respond, love, need, and appreciate differently. They almost seem to be from different planets, speaking different languages and needing different nourishment" (p. 5).

Deborah Tannen (1990) is more modest in her claims; she argued that women and men are from different cultures. She stated that "boys and girls grow up in what are essentially different cultures, so talk between women and men is cross-cultural communication.... Women speak and hear a language of connection and intimacy, while men speak and hear a language of status and independence" (pp. 18 and 42). Thus, according to Gray and Tannen, the difference between women and men would look something like that shown in Figure 1.1A.

Unlike Gray (1992) and Tannen (1990), who have argued that women and men are radically different, I argue that women and men are not radically different and in fact are strikingly similar. The metaphor I use to represent differences between women and men is this: Men are from North Dakota, women are from South Dakota. According to this metaphor, women and men do not come from different planets or different cultures; they come from neighboring states. The empirical evidence indicates that differences between women and men in psychological variables, including communication behaviors, are minimal by any measure, and these minimal differences do not warrant the labeling of women and men as different. Figure 1.1A represents what I believe to be the difference between women and men. In my opinion, the men are from North Dakota, women are from South Dakota metaphor more aptly reflects the degree of difference between women and men.

Girls and boys are neither from different planets (Gray, 1992) nor raised in different cultures (Tannen, 1990). In my opinion, North American girls and boys are raised in the same culture, but that culture teaches them that they different. In spite of this, they turn out remarkably similar. For example, my 13-year-old son recently returned from a week at overnight camp. At the dinner table, he was telling us about his camp experiences and proceeded to tell us about a camp event in which only the boys, not the girls, were allowed to be leaders. He explicitly labeled the event as "sexist" and communicated his disdain for the practice. My reaction was mixed. I was overjoyed that my son had acquired a value I had sought to teach him, that is, the recognition of and disdain for sexism. I was equally saddened by the fact that, as of the year 2004, we still insist on inculturating differences between women and men.

As a parent of a 13-year-old son and a 12-year-old daughter, I can tell you that this is not an isolated event. I could fill up this entire book with stories of the sexism my children have encountered in day care, schools, camps, organized sports, and so on, without ever mentioning the sexism portrayed on children's television. So often have I witnessed differences in how girls and boys are treated today, and think back to how much more sexist my upbringing was, not to mention my mother's, that instead of asking the question, Why are women and men different? I often end up asking the question, Why are women and men similar? The fact that women and men are similar, given how differently they are treated in our culture, is a testament to the underlying similarity of women and men.

Sex–Gender Differences Are Small

Meta-analyses of sex differences in communication behavior generally indicate that there are small differences between women and men in their communication behaviors, and that these differences are moderated by other variables. A meta-analysis is a quantitative summary of the results from multiple quantitative studies (for an excellent anthology of meta-analyses applied to communication behavior, see Allen, Preiss, Gayle, & Burrell, 2002). In a meta-analysis, the quantitative studies on a given topic, such as sex differences in self-disclosure (Dindia & Allen, 1992), are located and the results (differences between women and men) for each study are converted to a common statistic such as $d (d = M1 - M2/SD)$, which tells us how far apart the means for women and men are in units of standard deviation. The mean effect size across studies is calculated and represents the average difference between women and men for this group of studies. An effect size represents the amount of variance that is explained in the dependent variable by the independent variable, for example, how much one can predict self-disclosure from sex (female–male). A meta-analysis also examines the variability of effect sizes across studies. A homogeneity statistic is often used to determine whether the effect size across studies varies more than one would expect as a result of sampling error.

Effect sizes in the social sciences, when measured in d, range in absolute value from zero (no effect or no difference) to over 1.0. Cohen (1969) offered the following guidelines for interpreting d: $d = 0.20$ is small, $d = 0.50$ is moderate, and $d = 0.80$ is large. An effect size of $d = 0.2$ indicates that sex accounts for 1% of the variance in the dependent variable and represents an 85% overlap in the

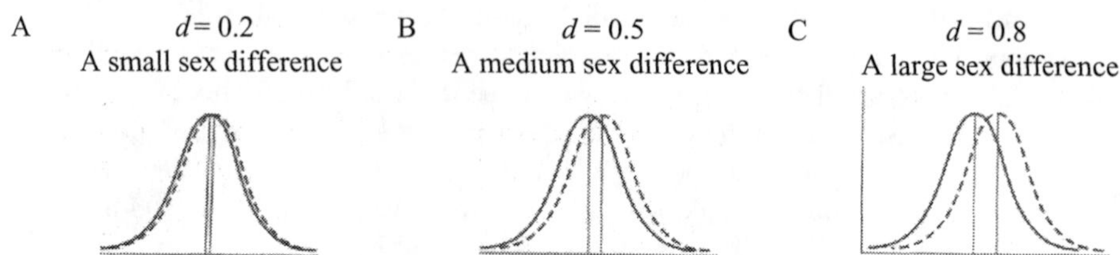

FIGURE 1.2. Degree of Overlap between Women and Men for Different Effect Size.

distributions of women and men on the dependent variable. Thus, an effect size of $d = 0.2$ means that 85% of women and men overlap in their scores on the dependent variable (see Fig. 1.2A); alternatively, 15% of women and men do not overlap in their scores on the dependent variable. For example, the result of a meta-analysis on sex differences in self-disclosure (Dindia & Allen, 1992) was a small effect size ($d = 0.18$), indicating that approximately 85% of women and men overlap in their self-disclosure and that approximately 15% of women and men differ in their self-disclosure, with women disclosing more than men.

Cohen labeled a value of $d = 0.5$ as a medium effect size. When $d = 0.5$, there is a 67% overlap in the distribution of women and men on the dependent variable. Alternatively, one third of women and men do not overlap in their scores on the dependent variable (see Fig. 1.2B).

Finally, Cohen labeled a value of $d = 0.8$ as a large effect size. A large effect accounts for 14% of the variance in the dependent variable. When $d = 0.8$, there is a 53% overlap in the scores of women and men on the dependent variable. Accordingly, slightly less than half of women and men do not overlap in their scores on the dependent variable (see Fig. 1.2C).

Several researchers have attempted to summarize the results of meta-analyses of sex differences in communication and psychology. For instance, Canary and Hause (1993) reviewed 15 meta-analyses of sex differences in communication variables and concluded that sex differences are small and moderated by a number of factors. Canary and Hause found an average weighted effect size of $d = 0.24$, which indicates that sex or gender accounts for about 1% of the variance in communication variables and that about 85% of women and men overlap in their behavior on these variables. In addition, all the meta-analyses reported significant moderating variables (sex interacts with another variable to affect the dependent variable, so the effect of sex is not consistent across studies).

Hall (1984) conducted a number of meta-analyses of sex differences in nonverbal communication. Hall summarized the results of the meta-analyses in a table (p. 142) titled "Average Sex Differences (r) for Nonverbal Skills and Behaviors." This table is included here in an adapted form (see Table 1.1, first four columns). Hall reported effect sizes as Pearson product–moment correlation coefficients (so I translated r to d).

TABLE 1.1
Average Sex Differences (r) for Nonverbal Skills and Behaviors

Variable	*Age Group*	*High r*	*No. of Studies Associated With High r*	*Low r*	*No. of Studies Associated With Low r*
Decoding skill	All ages	.21	64	.11	125
Face recognition skill	Children & adolescents	.15	5	.06	12
	Adults	.17	12	.08	28
Expression skill	All ages	.25	35	.19	49
Facial expressiveness	Adults	.45	5	?	6
Social smiling	Children	−.02	5	.00	20
	Adults	.30	15	.20	23
Gaze	Infants	.20	8	.06	33
	Children	.19	10	.08	25
	Adults	.32	30	.16	61
Receipt of gaze	Adults	.31	6	.12	16
Distance of approach to others					
Naturalistic	Adults	−.27	17	−.08	59
Staged	Adults	−.06	8	−.02	19
Projective	Adults	−.07	11	−.03	26
Distance approached by others					
Naturalistic	Infants	−.44	5	−.44	5
	Adults	−.43	9	−.21	20
Staged	Adults	−.30	5	−.25	6
Projective	Adults	−.39	7	−.24	12
Body movement & position					
Restlessness	Adults	−.34	6	−.14	14
Expansiveness	Adults	−.46	6	−.46	6
Involvement	Adults	.16	7	.06	18
Expressiveness	Adults	.28	7	.13	15
Self-consciousness	Adults	.22	5	.10	11
Vocal behavior					
Speech errors	Adolescents & adults	−.33	6	−.17	14
Filled pauses	Adolescents & adults	−.51	6	−.51	6
Total speech	Adults	−.05	12	−.01	22
Weighted averages		.25 (d = .53)	312	.12 (d = .24)	651

Note: Low r and number of studies associated with low r were added to the table. Studies in which the results were reported as not statistically significant and no statistics were provided from which to calculate an effect size were set to 0 for calculations of low r. Positive correlations mean higher values on named behavior by women. Average weighted r was calculated by use of absolute values of r. High r and number of studies associated with high r are taken from *Nonverbal Sex Differences: Communication Accuracy and Expressive Style* (p. 142, Table 11.1), by J. A. Hall, 1984, Baltimore: The Johns Hopkins University Press. Reprinted with permission.

The average weighted effect size across Hall's studies is $r = 0.25$ or $d = 0.53$ (see Table 1.1, columns labeled "High *r*" and "Number of Studies Associated With High *r*"). This is quite a bit higher than the average weighted effect size found by Canary and Hause ($d = 0.24$). One might conclude that sex differences in nonverbal communication are higher than sex differences in other communication variables. However, the average effect sizes reported in Hall's table include only those studies (312 out of 651, or slightly less than half) in which the effect size was reported or could be calculated. A number of studies (339) in which the effect size was not reported and could not be calculated were not included in the calculation of the effect sizes in Hall's table. These are primarily studies in which the results were nonsignificant and the authors did not report the nonsignificant statistic (they simply reported that the results were *ns*) or other statistical information from which an effect size could be calculated (such as means and standard deviations). The consequence of this is that a substantial number of nonsignificant effect sizes were not included in the calculation of the average effect sizes, and the average effect sizes are therefore over estimates. Hall acknowledged this, stating that "these effect sizes may be somewhat larger than actual nonverbal sex differences are because smaller effect sizes may often have failed to reach statistical significance and not been reported" (1984, pp. 141–142). Thus, the column labeled "High *r*" in Table 1.1 represents the highest possible values of *r*.

I recalculated Hall's effect sizes, including the 339 studies that reported no significant differences and did not include information from which to calculate an effect size (see Table 1.1, columns labeled "Low *r*" and "Number of Studies Associated with Low *r*"). I set the effect size for these studies to zero. Zero is the lowest possible value for these effect sizes. The true value lies somewhere between zero and the minimum value that is associated with statistical significance. The average effect size across these studies was $r = 0.12$ or $d = 0.24$. The effect size is lower than that which would be obtained had the actual effect sizes for the studies that reported no significant differences and did not include information from which to calculate an effect size been included. Thus, the true effect size for nonverbal sex differences in the studies reviewed by Hall (1984) lies somewhere between $d = 0.24$ and $d = 0.53$, or a small to moderate effect.

The reviews by Canary and Hause and by Hall are purposefully limited to communication variables. They do not include the broader domains of social, personality, and cognitive psychology (see Ashmore, 1990; Hyde & Frost, 1993; and Hyde & Plant, 1995 for reviews of meta-analyses of sex differences in psychology). For instance, Hyde and Plant analyzed effect sizes found in 171 meta-analyses of psychological gender differences and found that 25% of them found women and men to be similar ($d = 0$–0.10), 35% found small effect sizes ($d = 0.11$–0.35), 27% found medium effect sizes ($d = 0.36$–0.65), and 13% found large effect sizes ($d = 0.66$ and above; see Table 1.2). Thus, Hyde and Plant concluded that there are more null to small sex differences but also some large differences. I calculated the average weighted effect size across these 171 studies and it was $d = 0.26$, which

TABLE 1.2
Results from Hyde and Plant's (1995) Summary of Meta-Analyses of Psychological Gender Differences

	$d = 0–0.10$	$d = 0.11–0.35$	$d = 0.36–0.65$	$d = 0.66–1.0$	$d > 1.0$
No. of studies ($N = 171$)	43	60	46	17	5
% of studies	25	35	27	10	3

is very close to the value found by Canary and Hause ($d = 0.24$) and the lowest estimate of effect sizes calculated for nonverbal sex differences ($d = 0.24$).

The magnitude and variability of sex differences can be compared with the magnitude and variability of other effects. Hyde and Plant (1995) compared effect sizes for psychological gender differences with effect sizes for various psychological, educational, and behavioral treatments. They found that the distribution of effect sizes for gender was significantly different from the distribution of effect sizes for treatments. In particular, there were more close-to-zero effect sizes for gender (25%) than for treatments (6%). Treatment effect sizes probably are not representative of psychological effect sizes in general. A better comparison would be the effect size of sex differences in social psychological variables with social psychological effects in general.

Richard, Bond, and Stokes-Zoota (2003) compiled the results from 322 meta-analyses (involving more than 25,000 studies and 8 million people) of social psychological effects (categorized into 18 topics: aggression, attitudes, attribution, expectancy effects, gender roles, group processes, health psychology, helping behavior, intergroup relations, law, leadership, methodology, motivation, nonverbal communication, personality, relationships, social cognition, and social influence). This appears to be the largest social psychological database of effect sizes ever assembled. It allows the most rigorous generalizations to date about the magnitude and variability of social psychological effects.

Richard et al. (2003) found that social psychological effects yield a mean effect size of $r = 0.21$ or $d = 0.43$. They also found that social psychological effects vary in size (r units, $SD = 0.15$, d units, $SD = 0.30$). The largest mean effects were found in the study of attitudes ($d = 0.56$) and group processes ($d = 0.68$). The smallest were found in the study of attributions ($d = 0.28$) and social influence ($d = 0.26$). The distribution of effect sizes was positively skewed; 30% were less than $d = 0.20$, 46% were between $d = 0.20$ and $d = 0.50$, 19% were between $d = 0.50$ and $d = 0.80$, and 5% were greater than $d = 0.80$ (See Table 1.3).

Richard et al. (2003) included 83 meta-analyses of sex differences, with 16 in attribution, 14 in relationships, 10 in nonverbal communication, and 43 on other topics. Overall, sex differences in social psychological variables were small, $r = 0.12 (d = 0.24)$. The distribution of effect sizes for sex differences was even more positively skewed than the distribution of effect sizes for social psychological

TABLE 1.3
Results from Richard et al.'s (2003) Summary of Meta-Analyses in Social Psychology

	$d < 0.2$ *or* $r < 0.10$	$d = 0.20–0.50$ *or* $r = 0.10–0.30$	$d = 0.50–0.80$ *or* $r = 0.30–0.50$	$d > 0.80$ *or* $r > .50$
Social psychological effects (%)	30	46	19	5
Sex differences in social psychological effects (%)	49	43	8	0

effects; 48% of the effect sizes for sex differences were less than $d = 0.20$, 43% were between $d = 0.20$ and $d = 0.50$, 9% were between $d = 0.50$ and $d = 0.80$, and none were greater than $d = 0.80$ (See Table 1.3). Sex differences were not especially variable across studies (d units, $SD = 0.20$, vs. $SD = 0.30$ for all social psychological effects). Richard et al. included 10 meta-analyses of sex differences in nonverbal communication. The average effect size across these studies was $r = 0.14 (d = 0.28)$, which is close to the low-end estimate of average effect size that I calculated for nonverbal sex differences in the studies reviewed by Hall in 1984 ($r = 0.12, d = 0.24$). Thus, the results of this compilation of meta-analyses of social psychological effect sizes indicate that social psychological effects are, on average, close to medium in size ($d = 0.42$), although there are many small and some large effects, and that sex differences are small ($d = 0.24$), in particular, smaller than other social psychological effects.

On the basis of the evidence just given, we can conclude that sex differences in communication variables in particular and social psychological and psychological variables in general are, on average, small (Canary & Hause, 1993, $d = 0.24$; Hyde & Plant, 1995, $d = 0.26$, Richard et al., 2003, $d = 0.24$, respectively), although sex differences for nonverbal communication may be larger ($d = 0.24–0.53$). However, given the fact that science has a long-standing tradition of not publishing nonsignificant results, it is possible that the effect sizes are even lower. Thus, the average woman is not that much different from the average man. Sex differences are also smaller than other social psychological effects. Moreover, the evidence indicates that sex differences vary across studies (that is, sex differences are moderated by other variables), although not as much as social psychological effects in general.

From this evidence we can see that a high degree of overlap exists in the distributions of women's and men's communicative, social psychological, and psychological variables. According to the average effect size found, approximately 85% of women and men overlap in their scores across the various psychological variables, whereas approximately 15% of women and men do not overlap. Therefore, differences between women and men in communicative, social psychological, and psychological variables are small. Scholars as well as laypeople are not justified in labeling women and men as different, at least insofar as psychological variables and communication behaviors are concerned. For the most part (approximately 85%), women and men are similar. This does not mean that there are not medium and large differences between women and men on certain communicative, social psychological, and psychological variables. As demonstrated by Hyde and Plant, approximately 13% of sex differences in psychological variables are large.

I draw the conclusion that there are small differences between women and men in psychological variables on the basis of the results of quantitative research on sex differences, fully realizing that this research is imperfect. Among other things, much of the quantitative research on sex differences relies on perceptual data (Ragan, 1989)—when observational data are employed, research generally occurs in artificial laboratory situations—and college student samples, which may or may not generalize to the larger population. Thus, the quantitative research on sex differences is flawed in a number of ways; meta-analyses of this research are only as valid as the original studies. Regardless of these limitations, the preponderance of empirical evidence suggests that sex differences in psychological variables are generally small.

Differences of Degree Versus Kind

The evidence just presented indicates that differences between women and men reflect differences of degree, not kind. Women and men would differ in kind if women either have certain characteristics or perform certain behaviors that are not present in men, or vice versa (Adler, 1975). For example, if all women are communal and no men are communal, women and men differ in kind with respect to communion. Similarly, if all men are agentic and no women are agentic, men and women differ in kind with respect to agency. Thus, differences in kind would be represented by Figure 1.1A. Women and men differ in degree if both possess the same trait or display the same behavior but one possesses or displays more of it (Adler). Thus, if both women and men are agentic and communal, but women are more communal and men are more agentic, then, with respect to agency and communion, they differ in degree, not kind. Differences in degree would be represented by Figure 1.1B.

At least one perspective on gender differences, the different cultures perspective, portray gender differences as being differences *in kind*. Tannen (1990) and Gray (1992) presented women and men as members of radically different cultures. I disagree. As indicated in the preceding section, the empirical research indicates that although statistically significant mean differences exist between women and men in a number of communication behaviors, the small effect sizes and the overlap in distributions of women and men on these variables are not consistent with the kind of difference that would be expected if women and men represented different cultural groups (see Burleson & Kunkel, chap. 8, this volume). If women and men represented different cultures, then we would expect large effect sizes and little overlap in the distributions of women and women.

Why Women and Men Are Polarized

If differences are small and reflect differences of degree rather than kind, why are women and men portrayed as dichotomous groups (Thorne, 1993), or as two separate and homogeneous categories (Crawford, 1995) that are polar opposites (Canary & Hause, 1993)? In my opinion, this is the result of gender stereotyping, which is reinforced by the scholarly and popular press.

One cause of this false dichotomy is the failure to report effect sizes in the scholarly literature. Thousands of studies have been published that report statistically significant results for sex differences. The authors of these studies conclude that women and men differ with respect to a dependent variable. Similar to placing individuals into dichotomous groups labeled *women* and *men*, researchers dichotomize statistical results into groups labeled *significant* or *nonsignificant*, failing to realize the variability within statistically significant findings or the variability within nonsignificant findings. As stated by Hunter (1996a, 1996b), "the conventional significance test provides NO direct information about effect size." Conventional significance tests indicate only whether women and men differ; they do not indicate the size of the difference. The difference has to be measured quantitatively and the magnitude of the difference reported. We should not just ask, Does sex have an effect? We should also ask, How large is the effect? (Hunter, 1996a, 1996b).

Unfortunately, few studies on sex differences report effect sizes. This practice is no longer excusable, though it might remain normative in some disciplines. Cohen's (1969) book on power analysis was published more than 30 years ago. It is time researchers stopped dichotomizing research results on sex differences into significant and nonsignificant groups and instead started reporting the magnitude of these effects, which tells us the extent to which there are differences.

Fortunately, research on sex differences is so popular that meta-analyses have been performed on a number of different dependent variables. Meta-analysis provides a remedy for the failure to report effect sizes. One of the major benefits of meta-analysis is that it indicates not only whether a significant difference exists, but also how large it is (Hyde & Frost, 1993).

Nonetheless, the magnitude of sex differences should be reported in empirical studies that report significant results. To ensure that this happens, journal editors should require researchers to report effect sizes when they find statistically significant results regarding sex differences. However, as noted by Eagly (1995), if this is done, it should be done for all effects. Eagly argued that reporting effect sizes for sex differences alone would trivialize sex differences, because most readers are unaware that the percentage of variance accounted for by any one variable is typically small in psychological research. Although Richard et al. (2003) demonstrated that psychological effect sizes are moderate, the argument is still valid. In this volume, we have asked authors to report effect sizes.

The popular press is also responsible for portraying women and men as fundamentally different. Gender stereotypes are pervasive in this culture—more pervasive than racial or ethnic stereotypes. As stated by Kahn and Yoder (1989), "one of the core beliefs of our society is that women and men are basically different—the 'opposite' sexes" (p. 422). As a communication scholar who believes in the power of words to shape perceptions, I have stopped using the term *opposite sex*, and instead refer to the *other sex* because it is less polarizing. The stereotype that women are feminine (i.e., attractive, deferential, unaggressive, emotional, nurturing, and concerned with people and relationships) and men are masculine (i.e., strong, ambitious, successful, rational, and nonemotional; Wood, 1997) is propagated by the popular press.

John Gray, author of the highest-selling work of nonfiction in the 1990s (6.6 million copies sold between 1990 and 1999), *Men are From Mars, Women are From Venus*, is making a fortune selling the message that women and men are different. He has written several other bestsellers capitalizing on supposed sex differences; hundreds of thousands of people attend his seminars and buy his audiotapes and videotapes. He has conducted world tours promoting his videos, Web sites, counseling centers, movies, and TV shows. He would not be rich if he were saying that women and men were both from the same planet, Earth: Not only does sex sell, but sex differences sell.

However, Gray (1992) does more than reflect gender stereotypes; he reproduces them (amplifies them to the level of intergalaxy differences). Canary and Hause (1993) made a similar observation about Tannen (1990). Gray propagates the myth that men and women are fundamentally different (e.g., that men want to go to their cave and women want to talk). Gray portrays all problems between the sexes as the result of these differences. He provides simple solutions to complex problems, thus providing poor, and, some may say, unethical, advice to laypersons. His prescriptions are sexist (e.g., he tells men to listen to women, and women to leave men alone). He provides an excuse for bad behavior (e.g., I'm a man and men go to their caves). The *New York Times* called Gray inept but harmless. I disagree. What Gray argues is nothing less than biological determinism or the idea that men and women are intrinsically different.

ARE DIFFERENCES BETWEEN WOMEN AND MEN MATTERS OF SEX OR GENDER?

Sex differences have been explained by biology (e.g., evolutionary psychology), culture (broadly defined as the external, societal, and structural factors, including social, historical, political, and cultural forces, that shape and reinforce certain patterns of behavior in women and men; see Kahn & Yoder, 1989), and the interaction of biology and culture (e.g., the biosocial perspective; see Wood & Eagly, 2002).

The most popular explanation of sex differences is the different cultures perspective originated by Maltz and Borker (1982) and popularized by Tannen (1990). According to this perspective, "American men and women come from different sociolinguist subcultures, having learned to do different things with words in a conversation, so that when they attempt to carry on conversations with one another, ... cultural miscommunication results" (Maltz & Borker, p. 200). The primary cause of cultural differences in communication is that boys and girls are socialized in gendered speech communities. According to Maltz and Borker, children play in sex-segregated groups; boys' play is group oriented, competitive, and status oriented and girls' play is dyadic, cooperative, and egalitarian. Boys and girls learn to use communication as they play with same-sex others; consequently, girls and boys develop different styles of communication, which carry over into adulthood. Girls learn to create and maintain relationships of closeness and equality through talk, to criticize others in socially acceptable ways, and to interpret accurately the verbal and nonverbal communication of other girls. Boys learn to verbally exercise dominance, to attract and maintain an audience, and to assert themselves when others speakers have the floor (Maltz & Borker).

I am not persuaded by the different cultures explanation of gender differences (see Burleson & Kunkel, chap. 8, this volume, for a more thorough critique of the different cultures perspective). It may be true that girls and boys play in sex-segregated groups and girls' play may be different from boys' play. However, the bottom line is that, in this culture, girls and boys are raised together, a point Maccoby (1988) made at the end of her review of the sex-segregation hypothesis. Crawford (1995) also made the common culture of girls and boys clear: "They share the use of common space in their homes; eat, work and play with their siblings of both sexes; generally attend co-educational schools in which they are aggregated in many classes and activities; and usually participate in religious meetings and activities together" (pp. 87–88).

Elizabeth Aries (1996) made a similar observation:

> Boys and girls have daily interactions with members of the opposite sex, with siblings, parents, relatives, friends in the neighborhood, or teachers at school. While people of different classes or racial groups may have little opportunity to interact with people outside their group, this is not true for males and females. Although boys and girls tend to select same-sex peers as their primary companions, their daily interactions are by no means limited to people of the same sex. (p. 141)

I am also not persuaded by biological explanations of sex differences, in particular those offered by evolutionary psychology (see Andersen, chap. 7, and Trost & Alberts, chap. 17, both this volume). Wood and Eagly (2002) persuasively demonstrated how sex differences in mate preferences, the "signature finding" (Eagly & Wood, 1999) of evolutionary theory, can be better explained by social role theory (Eagly & Wood; Wood & Eagly). According to evolutionary psychology, women value mates' resources and men value mates' youth and physical attractiveness because of the different parental investment of the sexes. Women, as the more investing sex, seek older mates and mates with resources that can support their offspring. Men, because women's reproductive capacity is time limited, seek mates with attributes that suggest reproductive capacity (youth and physical attractiveness). Using a social role perspective, Eagly and Wood predicted that sex differences in mate preferences become smaller as the traditional division of labor weakens and societies become more egalitarian. (To test these predictions, Eagly and Wood reanalyzed data from Buss' well-known study of mate selection (Buss, 1989; Buss et al., 1990) and found that women's preferences for older mates and mates with resources, and men's preferences for younger mates and mates with housekeeping and cooking skills, became less pronounced as the traditional division of labor weakened and societies became more egalitarian, thus supporting the predications of social role theory.

The bottom line is that there are rival hypotheses to evolutionary explanations of sex differences. Sex differences predicted by evolutionary psychology can be alternatively explained by culture. As a personal example, in my late twenties to early thirties, I began thinking about having children for the first time in my life. I just assumed my "biological clock" started ticking, the stereotypical explanation for this phenomenon. The more I thought about it, though, the more I realized all the messages I was receiving from our culture about having kids. Even *Friends*, the most popular sitcom in recent years, based on the lives of six single people in their twenties, portrayed all the main characters (except one who was arguably still a child—Joey) as having children or trying to have children. Thus, maybe it wasn't biology (my biological clock); could it have been my environment?

I find Wood and Eagly's biosocial perspective (2002), which argues that sex differences are best explained by the interaction of biological factors (specifically, men's size and strength and women's reproductive activities) and culture (the economic and social structural aspects of societies), very persuasive. Wood and Eagly reviewed the cross-cultural evidence on women's and mens' behavior in nonindustrial societies' particularly activities that contribute to the sex-typed division of labor and patriarchy. Their review identified sex-differentiated behaviors that emerged universally or near-universally in nonindustrial societies, along with sex-differentiated activities that varied considerably across societies. All of the cultures revealed a division of labor between women and men, which appeared to be organized to enable mothers to bear children and nurse and care for infants and to take advantage of men's size, strength, and speed. The specific tasks that were performed by women and men varied with the local ecology and socioeconomic structure, with the result that task characteristics of men were performed by women under circumstances that reduced the constraints of women's reproductive activities (e.g., women hunted in societies in which hunting did not unduly restrict women's reproductive and child care activities). Social and environmental factors also moderated the impact of reproductive constraints. "The findings suggest that biology, social structure, and the environment interact reciprocally to produce the sex-typed roles that constitute a society's division of labor" (Wood, & Eagly, p. 718).

Although I believe that culture explains more of the variance in psychological differences between women and men than biology does, I do not think that cultural explanations alone can explain these differences. Cultural conventions, including gender roles, the division of labor, patriarchy, and so on, arise as a result of biological differences between women and men and the perceived limits these biological differences place on women and men. If there were no biological differences between women and men, cultural differences would not emerge.

WHAT IS THE VALUE OF STUDYING SEX DIFFERENCES?

There is value in studying sex differences as long as we accurately report the size of these differences and also report sex similarities (i.e., nonsignificant sex differences). Julia Wood, in the first edition of this volume, made this statement:

> [R]esearchers have spotlighted differences between the sexes, often at the cost of neglecting substantial similarities between them.... [H]ighlighting differences fosters falsely dichotomous thinking, risks reinforcing gender stereotypes that can be detrimental to both sexes, and fuels division between women and men.... Historically, claims of sex and gender differences consistently have been used against women. (pp. 32–33)

The undue scholarly attention to sex differences—to the exclusion of sex similarities—has perpetuated stereotypes of women and men and, consequently, inequities between women and men. The emphasis on gender differences has blinded us to gender similarities (Hyde, 1985). In fact, we have studied sex differences and ignored sex similarities. It is time to start studying sex differences and similarities. This, in part, is the reasoning behind this volume.

We have an ethical responsibility to inform the scholarly and lay communities about sex differences and similarities. The most pervasive stereotype in our culture is that women and men are different. It is our duty as social scientists to correct this stereotype. It is our ethical responsibility to conduct and publish research that provides evidence of the overwhelming similarities between men and women.

Moreover, it is important to disseminate this information outside scholarly books and journals, to textbooks and the popular press. Textbooks have to be more circumspect in how they report sex differences. I have seen a number of authors of textbooks state that Dindia and Allen (1992) found sex differences in self-disclosure, without mentioning the fact that the difference was small ($d = 0.18$) and that these small differences accounted for approximately 1% of the variance in self-disclosure and that approximately 85% of men and women overlapped in their self-disclosure. The inaccurate reporting of results of studies raises concerns not only about what our students are reading but also about the ethical responsibility of authors to accurately report the findings and conclusions. Combating ignorance is difficult enough when the truth or facts are told, but when authors do not take the time to check their assumptions and carefully read and report results, the task becomes impossible. However, if accurate information penetrates beyond the traditional boundaries of academic journals and volumes to textbooks and the public domain, it can reduce rigid adherence to gender stereotypes and sexism. If we can provide accurate information on the degree and variability of sex differences to students and the general public, perhaps the camp counselors at my son's camp will allow girls to be leaders.

Mary Crawford and Michelle Kaufman argue that there is too much emphasis on describing gender differences (chap. 10, this volume). Although I agree, the goals of science are to describe, predict, explain, and, ultimately, control. We must describe and isolate differences and similarities between women and men before we can predict and explain them. Research on the kinds and degree of differences between women and men narrows the potential explanations. For example, evolutionary psychology cannot account for declining sex differences over a short period of time, as has been found in a range of attributes including the value that women place on job attributes in comparison with men; the career aspirations of female university students in comparison with male students; the amount of risky behavior in which women engage in comparison with men; the tendency for men rather than women to emerge as leaders in small groups; women's self-reports of assertiveness, dominance, and masculinity in comparison with men; and the tendency of men to score higher than women on math and science (Wood & Eagly, 2002). Thus, we must describe sex and gender differences and their extent before we can begin to explain them.

However, scholarship on sex and gender differences in communication, like all research, has to be theoretically driven (for an excellent example in the broader domain of psychology, see Eagly, Biell, & Sternberg, 2004), and many of the contributors to this volume have relied on theory. Unfortunately, theory lags behind descriptive research in the literature on sex and gender in communication. There are too many studies of sex differences in communication in which there is no theoretical rationale for testing sex differences. Is it necessary to examine every variable ever studied in communication for sex differences? Quantifying sex and gender differences and similarities is preliminary to explaining differences and similarities we find in women's and men's communication. Thus, quantifying sex and gender differences and similarities is important work that must continue, but it should not be the end result of this pursuit.

As already stated, communication scholars must concern themselves with the dissemination of their findings beyond academia to the popular press. One of the many stereotyped differences discussed in Gray's (1992) book is that "men go to their caves and women talk" (p. 29). Gray tells women that they "need to learn that when a man is upset or stressed he will automatically stop talking and go to his 'cave' to work things out" (p. 69). He advises women to let men hide in their cave.

In contrast, he tells men that "when a woman is stressed she instinctively feels a need to talk about her feelings and all the possible problems that are associated with her feelings" (p. 36). He advises men to listen to women. These are sexist prescriptions based on traditional sex roles in which the man works outside the home and the woman works within the home. I have asked thousands of women who work outside the home whether they would like to come home from work and "go to their cave," and they overwhelmingly say yes. This has nothing to do with whether you are a man or a woman. It is a matter of whether you work outside the home. When you have been interacting all day long with others, you want to come home and be left alone; when you have been home alone (or home with the kids) all day, you want to engage in some (adult) interaction.

It is oversimplified to advise women to let men go to their caves and to advise men to listen to women. Communication is more complicated than this. The key to effective communication is being able to perceive when your partner wants to be left alone versus when he or she wants to talk, and then to respond accordingly. I realize that this message is too complicated for a best-selling self-help book; but we should at least get it right in our textbooks.

CONCLUSION

Men and women are not from different planets or different cultures, and they do not speak different languages. Men and women are from the same planet, the same culture; they communicate by using the same language. Indeed, the empirical research indicates that the average man is not that much different from the average woman. For many communicative, social psychological, and psychological variables, sex differences are small, and approximately 85% of men and women overlap in their scores on these variables. Men are not from Mars; women are not from Venus. The metaphor that more accurately represents the differences between men and women is that men are from North Dakota, and Women are from South Dakota.

REFERENCES

Adler, M. J. (1975). The confusion of the animalists. In R. M. Hutchins & M. J. Adler (Eds.), *The great ideas today 1975* (pp. 72–89). Chicago: Encyclopedia Brittanica.

Allen, M., Preiss, R. W., Gayle, B. M., & Burrell, N. (2002). *Interpersonal communication: Advances through meta-analysis*. Mahwah, NJ: Lawrence Erlbaum Associates.

Aries, E. (1996). *Men and women in interaction: Reconsidering the differences*. New York: Oxford University Press.

Ashmore, R. D. (1990). Sex, gender, and the individual. In L. A. Pervin (Ed.), *Handbook of personality: Theory and research* (pp. 486–526). New York: Guilford.

Buss, D. M. (1989). Sex differences in human mate preferences: Evolutionary hypotheses tested in 37 cultures. *Behavioral and Brain Sciences*, *12*, 1–14.

Buss, D. M., Abbott, M., Angleitner, A., Biaggo, A., Blanco-Villasenor, A., Bruchon Schweitzer, M., et al. (1990). International preferences in selecting mates: A study of 37 cultures. *Journal of Cross-Cultural Psychology, 21*, 5–47.

Canary, D. J. & Hause, K. S. (1993). Is there any reason to research sex differences in communication? *Communication Quarterly, 41*, 129–144.

Cohen, J. (1969). *Statistical power analysis for the behavioral sciences.* San Diego, CA: Academic Press.

Crawford, M. (1995). *Talking difference: On gender and language*. London: Sage.

Dindia, K., & Allen, M. (1992). Sex-differences in self-disclosure: A meta-analysis. *Psychological Bulletin, 112*, 106–124.

Eagly, A. H. (1995). The science and politics of comparing women and men. *American Psychologist, 50*, 145–158.

Eagly, A. H., Biell, A. E., & Sternberg, R. J. (Eds). (2004). *The psychology of gender* (2nd ed.). New York: Guilford.

Eagly, A. H., & Wood, W. (1999). The origins of sex differences in human behavior: Evolved dispositions versus social roles. *American Psychologist, 54*, 408–423.

Eagly, A. H., Wood W., & Johannesen-Schmidt, M. C. (2004). Social role theory of sex differences and similarities: Implications for the partner preferences of women and men. In A. H. Eagly, A. E. Biell, & M. C. Johannesen-Schmidt (Eds.), *The psychology of gender* (2nd ed., pp. 269–295). New York: Guilford.

Gray, J. (1992). *Men are from Mars, Women are from Venus.* A practical guide to improving communication and getting what you want in your relationships. New York: HarperCollins.

Hall, J. A. (1978). Gender effects in decoding nonverbal cues. *Psychological Bulletin, 85*, 845–857.

Hall, J. A. (1984). *Nonverbal sex differences: Communication accuracy and expressive style*. Baltimore: Johns Hopkins University Press.

Hunter, J. (1996a, June/July). *Significance tests.* Debate held at the meeting of the American Psychological Society, San Francisco.

Hunter, J. (1996b, August). *Significance tests.* Debate held at the meeting of the American Psychological Association, Toronto.

Hunter, J. S. (1997). Needed: A ban on the significance test *Personal Relationship Issues, 4*, 4–6.

Hyde, J. S. (1985). *Half the human experience: The psychology of women* (3rd ed.). Lexington, MA: Heath.

Hyde, J. S., & Frost, L. (1993). Meta-analysis in the psychology of women. In F. Denmark & M. Paludi (Eds.), *Psychology of women: A handbook of issues and theories* (pp. 67–103). Westport, CT: Greenwood.

Hyde, J. S., & Plant, E. A. (1995). Magnitude of psychological gender differences: Another side to the story. *American Psychologist, 50*, 159–161.

Kahn, A. S. & Yoder, J. D. (1989). The psychology of women and conservatism: Rediscovering social change. *Psychology of Women Quarterly, 13*, 417–432.

Maccoby, E. E. (1988). Gender as a social category. *Development Psychology, 24*, 755–765.

Maltz, D., & Borker, R. (1982). A cultural approach to male-female miscommunication. In J. J. Gumpertz (Ed.), *Language and social identity* (pp. 196–216). Cambridge, England: Cambridge University Press.

Ragan, S. L. (1989). Communication between the sexes: A consideration of sex differences in adult communication. In J. F. Nussbaum (Ed.), *Life-span communication: Normative processes* (pp. 179–193). Hillsdale, NJ: Lawrence Erlbaum Associates.

Richard, F. D., Bond, C. R., & Stokes-Zoota, J. J. (2003). One hundred years of social psychology quantitatively described. *Review of General Psychology, 7*, 331–363.

Tannen, D. (1990). *You just don't understand: Women and men in conversation.* New York: Morrow.

Thorne, B. (1993). *Gender play: Girls and boys in school.* New Brunswick, NJ: Rutgers University Press.

Wood, J. (1997). *Gendered lives: Communication, gender and culture*, (2nd ed). Belmont, CA: Wadsworth.

Wood, J. T., & Dindia, K. (1998). Whats the difference? A dialogue about differences and similarities between women and men. In D. J. Canary & K. Dindia (Eds.), *Sex differences in Communication* (pp. 19–39). Mahweh, NJ: Erlbaum.

Wood, W., & Eagly, A. H. (2002). A cross-cultural analysis of the behavior of women and men: Implications for the origins of sex differences. *Psychological Bulletin, 128*, 699–727.

2

Sex Differences in Interaction: A Reexamination

Elizabeth Aries
Amherst College

The study of sex differences in interaction has drawn the attention of numerous researchers from the disciplines of psychology, sociology, linguistics, communication studies, women's studies, and organizational behavior. Across a wide variety of subject populations, interaction settings, and research methodologies, researchers typically report that men are more likely than women to emerge as leaders, to be directive and hierarchical, to dominate in groups by talking more and interrupting more, and to be orientated toward solving problems. Women, in contrast, are found to be more expressive, supportive, facilitative, egalitarian, and cooperative than men, to focus more on relationships, and to share more personally with others (Aries, 1987, 1996).

By taking a different perspective on this data, however, these well-established "truths" about men and women in interaction may be called into question. The prevailing picture that has emerged is based on the fact that we have not paid careful attention to five important questions:

1. Do our stereotypes describe most men and women or only selected samples of men and women?
2. What is the magnitude of the differences we have found?
3. To what extent does the appearance of sex differences depend on the situational context?

4. Are the sex differences we have found attributable to other variables that covary with sex such as status and social roles?
5. To what extent are sex differences in conversation due to stereotype effects?

If we reframe our thinking around these five questions, we come to see that knowledge of a person's sex gives us little ability to make an accurate prediction about how a person will behave, and that variables that covary with sex may be responsible for many of the sex differences we have observed.

RELIANCE ON WHITE MIDDLE-CLASS PARTICIPANTS

Research findings regarding sex differences in interaction are based primarily on White middle-class samples of individuals. What we have taken to be the characteristics of men and women in interaction may pertain only to the selected individuals we have studied. Neither men nor women form homogeneous groups. Members of the same sex differ from one another in age, race, ethnicity, social class, sexual orientation, variables that affect self-definition, and patterns of interaction. Because we have based our findings on men and women who are White and middle class, we have exaggerated the coherence within male and female styles of communication and failed to appreciate the extent to which members of the same sex differ, thereby making comparisons between men and women problematic.

The extension of research to diverse subject populations has already begun to challenge the accuracy of traditional gender stereotypes. Sex-role prescriptions that hold for mainstream Americans may not be identical for minority groups (De Leon, 1995). African American participants have reported masculine characteristics (e.g., assertiveness, independence, and self-reliance) to be as desirable for women as for men (Harris, 1994). Black women have attributed more masculine traits to themselves than have White women (Binion, 1990; De Leon). Black women, in their capacity as wives, mothers, providers, and heads of households, have had to exhibit more so-called masculine qualities in order to be successful in the performance of their multiple roles (De Leon). When describing the communication style that characterizes their friendships with people of their own race, Black participants used terms such as *quick-tempered* and *confrontive* whereas White participants used terms such as *nonconfrontive*, *tactful*, and *withdrawn* (McCullough, 1987, cited in Kramarae, 1990).

As we begin to pay attention to the differences that exist in communication styles among members of the same sex who differ in race, ethnicity, class, or sexual orientation, the clarity of our conception of sex differences diminishes. What we see instead is that there may be multiple sex-role systems that differ in their prescriptions for the behavior of men and women.

THE MAGNITUDE OF SEX DIFFERENCES

One criterion that has been widely used to determine whether men and women differ is statistical significance. Several limitations exist to the use of statistical significance as the sole criterion for the interpretation of research evidence. A statistically significant difference may not be a large or substantial difference. When sample sizes are large, a very small mean difference can be statistically significant (at $p < .05$).

To take a research example from the literature on role differentiation in mixed-sex groups, Anderson and Blanchard (1982) examined the extent to which men and women differed in their focus on task behavior, and the social-emotional aspects of interaction. These researchers assessed the magnitude of the differences found in studies of sex and role differentiation and found in the studies they reviewed that men on average were 8 percentage points higher than women on the use of task behavior, and women were 8 percentage points higher than men on use of positive social-emotional behavior. These differences were statistically significant yet small in magnitude. We describe men as task oriented and women as social-emotional in orientation when in fact *both* men and women devote the majority of their behavior to the task and the difference in their behavior is not even moderate. We have tended both to overlook the considerable overlap between the behavior of men and women and to misrepresent small differences as mutually exclusive differences.

Researchers have begun to look to other criteria to assess research findings, such as the percentage of variance in behavior that can be accounted for or explained by knowledge of a person's sex. Sex generally accounts for less than 10% of the variance in social behavior, and typically less than 5% (Canary & Hause, 1993; Eagly, 1987; Hyde & Linn, 1986). For example, in a study of interruptions, Michael Natale and his colleagues found that, in dyads, the speaking time of the conversational partner predicted 63% of the variance in interruptions whereas the sex of the speaker accounted for only 7% of the variance (Natale, Entin, & Jaffe, 1979). Thus, to make an accurate prediction of how frequently a person will interrupt, knowledge of the speaker's sex has relatively little predictive value in comparison with other variables. As Unger has argued, sex is not "particularly important in comparison to all the independent variables that influence any particular human behavior" (Unger, 1990, p. 115).

A related piece of information that can be used to assess research findings is the magnitude of the difference or the effect size—that is, the degree to which sex differences are manifested. Effect size can be conceptualized in terms of how much overlap there is between the distributions for men and women: The smaller the overlap between the distributions for men and women, the larger the effect size. An effect size of zero, as measured by Cohen's d (Cohen, 1977), reflects a 100% overlap between the distributions of men and women. Cohen considers an effect of $d = 0.20$ to be small (with an 85% overlap between the distributions for men and women), an effect of $d = 0.50$ to be moderate (with a 67% overlap), and an effect of $d = 0.80$ to be large (with a 53% overlap). A small effect accounts for 1% of the variance in behavior, a medium effect for 6% of the variance, and a large effect 14% of the variance.

Effect sizes can be used to assess the results not only of single studies but also of whole domains of research through a statistical technique called meta-analysis. Meta-analysis enables researchers to combine effect sizes found in individual studies to assess the overall magnitude of effect size across all studies in a given area.

Let us review some of the effect sizes that have been found for meta-analyses that have been carried out in the area of sex and communication. Dindia and Allen did a meta-analysis of self-disclosure, covering 205 published studies and 51 dissertations. They found women to be more disclosing than men but the effect size to be small ($d = 0.18$). They concluded that, "Whether the magnitude of sex differences in self-disclosure is theoretically meaningful and practically important is debatable.... It's time to stop perpetuating the myth that there are large differences in men's and women's self-disclosure" (Dindia & Allen, 1992, p. 118).

Two meta-analyses have been carried out in the area of biological sex and leadership behavior. Eagly and Johnson (1990) carried out a meta-analysis of 162 studies of sex differences in leadership style. In that study, male leaders did not differ from female leaders on task orientation ($d = 0.00$), and female leaders did not show more of an interpersonal orientation than male leaders ($d = 0.04$). Women showed a more democratic style than did men ($d = 0.22$), but the effect size was small. In this meta-analysis, sex differences were found in the laboratory studies but not in the field studies. Eagly and Johnson concluded that the criteria used by organizations for selecting and socializing managers into their roles minimizes any tendencies that men and women might bring to lead or manage with distinctly different styles. Eagly and Karau (1991) conducted a meta-analysis of 58 studies of leadership emergence in mixed-sex, initially leaderless, task-oriented groups. In that study, men emerged more frequently as leaders than women when task leadership was assessed ($d = 0.41$) and women emerged more as leaders when social leadership was assessed ($d = -0.18$).

Although there are numerous narrative reviews of the literature on sex differences in language, the magnitude of these differences has not been assessed. Initial analyses from a report of a meta-analysis of sex and language that aggregated results from studies using different language forms revealed no consistent sex differences in language use (Smythe & Schlueter, 1989).

Thus, effect sizes found for sex differences in communication style range from very small to moderate, accounting for less than 6% of the variance in behavior at best, and generally less than 1% of the variance in communication behavior. The review by Canary and House (1993) of meta-analyses on sex differences in communication activities suggests that only 1% of variance is accounted for by sex. When we look beyond statistical significance and attend to effect size or percentage of variance explained, the data suggest that the overlap in the behavior of men and women is considerable, and that polarized depictions of interaction styles are not warranted.

THE SITUATIONAL CONTEXT OF INTERACTION

Sex differences are not manifested in all situational contexts. As Deaux and Major have argued, "Because perceivers, individual selves, and situations all vary in the content and salience of gender-linked expectations, we expect a wide range in observed female and male behaviors, from virtual identity of the sexes in some circumstances to striking differences in others" (Deaux & Major, 1987, p. 382).

A review of the literature on sex differences in interaction reveals that the appearance of sex differences is inconsistent from one study to the next. In a 1993 review of the literature on interruptions, James and Clarke reported that, in the majority of studies, no significant sex differences were found. In an analysis of 64 data sets looking at power and prestige in mixed-sex task groups, Lockheed (1985) found that 70% showed more male activity, influence, or leadership, 17% showed no difference due to biological sex, and 12.5% favored women. In a review of sex differences in amount of talk, James and Drakich (1993) found men to talk more in 43% of the studies, no sex differences in 28.6% of the studies, 27% of the studies to have equivocal results, and women to talk more than men in 3.6% of the studies. Wheelan and Verdi (1992), in a review of 28 studies of task behavior, found men to be more task oriented than women in 19 studies, whereas 9 studies showed no sex difference. In their review of 20 studies of social-emotional behavior, Wheelan and Verdi (1992) also found that 16 studies reported women to be higher than men, and 4 studies reported no sex difference.

Although many studies find sex differences that fit the stereotypes, numerous studies report no sex differences, and some report findings in the opposite direction. We may not even be aware of all the findings of no sex difference, for two reasons. Findings of no difference are often considered to be unworthy of publication. In addition, in studies that use multiple dependent variables, the lack of sex differences on many of those variables is rarely cited by later reviewers while only the few significant differences are highlighted.

We must look to the situational context of the interaction in each study to explain why it is that sex differences are manifested in some studies but not in others. How people behave depends on such moderating variables as the demands of the task, the length of the interaction, the sex composition of the group, and the relationship between the participants; these are variables that may effect the salience of gender-linked expectations for behavior.

Nature of the Task

If tasks draw on roles, interests, or expertise assumed to be more typically acquired by men, men are more likely to show higher levels of task activity than women in groups (Aries, 1996). For instance, when the task was taken into consideration in Eagly and Karau's (1991) meta-analysis of biological sex and leadership emergence, men were found to be much more likely to emerge as leaders in initially leaderless task groups when tasks were masculine ($d = 0.79$) than when tasks were feminine ($d = 0.26$), or when tasks required greater social complexity, such as interpersonal problem solving, extensive sharing of ideas, and negotiation ($d = 0.23$). Even in online groups, men dominate more often when the task is masculine (vs. feminine; see Postmes, 2002).

Some researchers have found women to be more self-disclosing than men to same-sex partners (Dindia & Allen, 1992; Hill & Stull, 1987). However, whether men are disclosing depends on the context. When men and women were asked to bring a same-sex best friend to the laboratory to have an intimate conversation, and to reveal thoughts and feelings, Reis, Senchak, and Solomon (1985) found no sex differences in self-disclosure. Thus, when self-disclosure was legitimized between men, their behavior was similar to that of women.

Length of the Interaction

Sex differences tend to be greater in groups that are engaged in very brief or one-time encounters than they are in groups that meet over time. As members get to know the relative task-relevant competencies and attributes of other members, sex becomes less important as a determinant of behavior. Because so many of our studies involve short encounters, the tendency for men to emerge as leaders has been exaggerated. The meta-analysis of sex and leadership emergence by Eagly and Karau (1991) showed that men were more likely to emerge as leaders when groups lasted less than 20 minutes ($d = 0.58$) than when interaction lasted more than a single session ($d = 0.09$). In their review of the literature on sex and role differentiation, Wheelan and Verdi (1992) found few studies of groups that met for extended periods. In their own study of a 4-day group-relations conference, Wheelan and Verdi found that sex differences emerged initially in expressive and goal-directed activity, but these differences disappeared over time.

Sex Composition of the Speakers

Another factor that affects the expression of sex differences is the sex composition of the speakers (see, e.g., Karakowsky & Siegel, 1999). In many cases, sex differences have been found to be greater in single-sex than in mixed-sex interaction (Aries, 1996). The sex of one's conversational partner has been found to affect the amount that a person is willing to disclose. The highest levels of self-disclosure are found to occur between women, and the lowest between men; cross-sex disclosure falls between the two. Meta-analytic findings reveal sex differences in self-disclosure to be greater in single-sex interaction ($d = 0.31$) than in mixed-sex interaction ($d = 0.08$; see Dindia & Allen, 1992). Men's lower level of disclosure to other men does not mean that men cannot be self-disclosing, but rather that men may be more likely to choose women as the target for their disclosures. Indeed, Dindia and Allen found equal disclosure to men by men and women ($d = 0.00$).

When comparisons are made of all-male and all-female groups, researchers have found men to place a greater emphasis on displays of dominance than women (Aries, 1976; Ellis, 1982; Miller, 1985). In one meta-analysis, Mast (2002) reported that the correlation between dominance and speaking time was greater for men than for women. However, researchers have also found men to place less emphasis on dominance in their interactions with women than with other men (Aries, 1976; McCarrick, Manderscheid, & Silbergeld, 1981). For example, Mast found the association between dominance and speaker time to be greatest in all-male versus mixed-sex groups. In addition, Karakowsky, McBey, and Miller (2004) found that both men and women expressed more verbal interruptions in groups in which men were the majority (vs. groups in which women were the majority).

The sex composition of the group has also been found to affect leadership behavior. In studies of dominance and leadership behavior involving interaction with strangers, women who are high in dominance assumed leadership over women low in dominance, but not over men low in dominance (Carbonell, 1984; Davis & Gilbert, 1989; Megargee, 1969; Nyquist & Spence, 1986). Leadership is associated with masculinity, and women are aware of sex-linked expectations for their behavior, making them reluctant to assume overt leadership over men. Some evidence suggests that women use more qualifications of speech in mixed-sex task groups than in single-sex groups (Carli, 1990; McMillan, Clifton, McGrath, & Gale, 1977). Carli found that women in mixed-sex dyads who prefaced remarks with such phrases as "I'm no expert, I may be wrong" frequently had greater influence over their male partners. Thus, women may adopt stereotypic deferent behavior with men in order to be effective.

We can see from these studies that men and women do not display a single style of interaction; interaction style varies with the social context. Situations place different pressures on individuals to display gender-stereotypic behavior (Deaux & Major, 1987). Contextual variables play an important role in determining the magnitude of sex differences that are found in our studies.

STATUS AND SOCIAL ROLES

For decades, feminists have argued that the differences we have been attributing to sex can be accounted for by differences in social roles and social status (Henley, 1973–1974, 1977; Kramarae, 1981; Spender, 1980; Thorne & Henley, 1975; Unger, 1976, 1979). Despite the profound social change that has occurred in American society over the past 25 years, men and women are still positioned differently in society, with men holding more power and status than women. Women have indeed entered the labor force in greater numbers, but they are still paid less for the same work and, on average, hold jobs with lower status than men.

A great deal of evidence demonstrates that the dominance and leadership we attribute to men is displayed more often by high-status than low-status individuals, and that when status is controlled for, sex differences are diminished. For example, in a study of dominance displayed at work, Moskowitz, Jung Suh, and Desaulniers (1994) found that dominance was predicted by participants' social roles. Less dominance was displayed toward coworkers and supervisors than toward people being supervised. However, dominance was not predicted by the sex of the participant.

High-status and powerful individuals have been found to interrupt more than low-status, less powerful individuals (Eakins & Eakins, 1983; Greif, 1980; Kollock, Blumstein, & Schwartz, 1985; West & Zimmerman, 1977; Woods, 1988). In discussions among intimate heterosexual couples, speaking time was related to the amount of power each person held in the relationship in decision making. The more powerful person spoke more in discussions. When men and women enjoy equal power, men do not speak significantly more than their female partners in discussions (Kollock et al.). When we place men and women in equal-status positions, sex differences are reduced. When dominance and leadership are legitimized for women in organizational settings, the behavior of male and female leaders is quite similar (Eagly & Johnson, 1990).

Similarly, many of the characteristics we attribute to women, such as their interpersonal sensitivity, their politeness, and their use of "women's language" (e.g., tag questions, qualifications of speech), are found more often in low-status individuals than in high-status individuals. In two studies of interaction in dyads in which one person was the leader and the other the follower, subordinates showed more sensitivity to the way the leaders felt about them than the leaders showed to the subordinates' feelings; however, there were no sex differences (Snodgrass, 1985, 1992). People who hold power show less politeness than do those who hold low power (McLachlan, 1991). People mitigate their requests when speaking to superiors (Baxter, 1984; Johnson, 1976; Sagrestano, 1992; Steil & Hillman, 1993). Women's language appears to be used more frequently by people who are unemployed, are housewives, or hold lower status jobs than by well-educated and professional people (O'Barr & Atkins, 1980). Subordinates have shown higher rates of speech associated with women than managers (Johnson, 1994). Risman (1987) found that the behavior of men who were single fathers and had primary responsibility for the care of young children was more similar to the behavior of working or single mothers than it was to married fathers. Men are capable of providing nurturance and do so when placed in the traditionally female role.

We have not always given sufficient attention to the importance of social, political, and economic contexts in examining sex differences. The sex differences we observe are produced in a context in which men hold positions of power over women. Many have argued that gender is not simply a matter of difference but must be understood as a matter of power and dominance (Henley, 1977; Kramarae, 1981; Spender, 1980; Thorne & Henley, 1975, Torres, 1992). Our reliance on laboratory studies masks the effect of these variables by taking people out of their current roles and context. When status and social roles are built into our studies as independent variables along with sex, then sex differences are mitigated.

STEREOTYPE EFFECTS AND SELF-FULFILLING PROPHECIES

In interaction, we immediately recognize the sex of our conversational partners on the basis of discernable visible cues. To the extent that we hold stereotyped beliefs about men and women, these beliefs can lead us to differential expectations about how people will behave based on their sex and can cause us to perceive sex differences even when they are not present (Aries, 1996). Even perceptions of the task's being a stereotypically masculine or feminine one can affect people's assessments of their own skills and their career-relevant aspirations, even when their skill sets are identical (e.g., women do not do as well at math; Correll, 2004).

Broad consensus has existed about the characteristics presumed to be typical of each sex. Men are described as leaders, as dominant, aggressive, independent, and competitive. Women are described as emotional, subjective, and aware of the feelings of others (Broverman, Vogel, Broverman, Clarkson, & Rosenkrantz, 1972). These stereotypes have remained relatively stable over the past 20 years (Bergen & Williams, 1991; Werner & LaRussa, 1985). Male speakers are believed to be louder, more forceful, dominating, and aggressive, whereas female speakers are believed to be more friendly, open, self-revealing, emotional, and polite, and to show more concern for the listener (Kramer, 1977). Women (vs. men) are thought to use more indirect influence strategies (Johnson, 1976) and to use more tag questions (Siegler & Siegler, 1976), whereas men are thought to interrupt more than women (Hawkins, 1988).

Stereotypes are not always accurate depictions of group members. Research shows that African American and Puerto Rican women attribute more masculine characteristics to themselves than White women attribute to themselves and do not fit traditional stereotypes of femininity (Binion, 1990; De Leon, 1995). In a similar manner, men are perceived as leaders. Yet, in a test of the accuracy of people's beliefs, Swim (1994) found the perceived effect size for leadership emergence by men to be quite large ($d = 1.04$), whereas actual meta-analytic findings were much smaller ($d = 0.49$). Women are believed to use tag questions more than men do, but women have not consistently been found to do so (Aries, 1996).

Studies show that, even when men and women behave in an identical manner, they may be perceived differently. Listeners bend their perceptions in the direction of expectation. When participants heard tape recordings of conversation in which male and female speakers used tag questions and qualifiers equally, women were perceived to use these speech forms more frequently than did men (Newcombe & Arnkoff, 1979). When participants read transcripts of speech believed to be spoken by a woman, speech was rated higher on aesthetic quality (pleasing, nice, sweet, and beautiful); when speech was believed to be spoken by a man, it was rated higher on dynamism (strong, active, aggressive, and loud; see Mulac, Incontro, & James, 1985). This occurred regardless of whether the actual speaker from whom the transcript was based was male or female or whether there were actual speech differences. In a follow-up study, when participants believed a speaker to be male, they rated the speaker higher on dynamism than if the speaker was believed to be female, but the effect held for only two out of four conversations (Lawrence, Stucky, & Hopper, 1990). Thus, stereotype effects, like sex differences, may be evoked to different degrees, depending on specific speakers or specific conversational contexts.

Male and female speakers may not only be perceived differently but be evaluated differently when displaying identical behavior. Bradley (1981) observed 24 experimental groups with a male or a female confederate in each who posed as a subject. The confederates were instructed to argue a position contrary to the other group members. Half the confederates advanced their cases without proof, and the other half advanced arguments by giving evidence and factual data. Half the confederates in each condition used tag questions and disclaimers; half did not. Women who advanced arguments without support were evaluated as less intelligent, knowledgeable, and influential than men who argued without support. Women who used tag questions and disclaimers were rated as less intelligent and knowledgeable than men who used these speech forms. Whether or not men used tag questions or disclaimers hardly affected their ratings, whereas women were perceived as less intelligent and knowledgeable when they used tag questions and disclaimers. Thus the sex of the speaker contributes to the *impression* the speaker makes beyond actual behavior differences, if any. Similarly, women who used forceful language in job interviews were seen as more aggressive than men who used similar language (Wiley & Eskilson, 1985).

In a meta-analysis of 61 studies of sex and the evaluation of leaders, Eagly, Makhijani, and Klonsky (1992) found a small tendency for female leaders to be evaluated less favorably than male leaders ($d = 0.05$), but the effect was more pronounced for leaders using an autocratic style ($d = 0.30$). The further women departed from sex-role expectations, the more negatively they were evaluated. Women are caught in a double bind. When they use behavior associated with women, they are perceived as lacking in instrumental competency; when they use behavior associated with men, they are seen as aggressive.

Two theories put forth to account for sex differences in interaction emphasize the importance of stereotypes in shaping these differences. The theory of status characteristics and expectation states holds that, when direct information about the relative competency of group members is not available, members will rely on external status to form expectations (Berger, Cohen, & Zelditch, 1972; Berger, Fisek, Norman, & Zelditch, 1977). Higher expectations will be formed for men because of their higher status in society, and these expectations will become self-fulfilling prophecies for behavior. Men will be given more opportunities to participate and their contributions will be more highly valued. Research shows that, when no expectations are given about the competency of group members, men are believed to be more competent than women, but that these sex differences are reduced when women are believed to possess more task-related competency than men (Pugh & Wahrman, 1983, 1985; Wood & Karten, 1986).

Social role theory contends that, because men and women are assigned to different roles in work and in the family, men and women will be expected to possess different characteristics that suit them for those roles. Men will be expected to be more agentic and task oriented and women will be expected to be more communal and emotionally expressive (Eagly, 1987), in accordance with their social roles. These expectations furnish guidelines for how men and women ought to behave; people are expected to behave in a manner consistent with their roles.

Thus gender stereotypes have both a descriptive and a prescriptive component. They indicate what group members are like but also what group members *should* be like, that is, what behavior is appropriate for members of the group. People do not necessarily perform gender-related behaviors because they are internalized in personality. Eagly contends that "people often conform to gender-role norms that are *not* internalized, because of the considerable power that groups and individuals supportive of these norms have to influence others' behavior through rewards and punishments of both subtle (e.g., nonverbal cues) or more obvious (e.g., monetary incentive, sexually harassing behavior) varieties" (Eagly, 1987, p. 19).

As both expectations states theory and social role theory predict, sex stereotypes have the power to become self-fulfilling prophecies for behavior. Rice, Bender, and Vitters (1980), in a study of West Point cadets, demonstrated that the attitudes that group members held about women's roles could affect the behavior of women leaders. In all-male groups in which members held liberal attitudes toward women, women leaders initiated more structure and played a more important role than they did in groups in which men held traditional attitudes toward women's roles. Thus men's attitudes toward women were reflected in their behavior toward women, which in turn affected the ability of those women to be effective leaders.

In summary, research shows that sex stereotypes play an important role in setting expectations for our own behavior and that of others. Stereotypes dictate what we notice. They may cause us to see sex differences even when they are not present and to respond differently to individuals on the basis of sex. Sex stereotypes also have the power to become self-fulfilling prophecies for behavior. However, it is important to note that stereotype effects are evoked to a different degree depending on the situational context, and they are most pronounced when sex is a salient issue in an interaction (Aries, 1996). Sex stereotypes have a larger impact in shaping the expectations and perceptions of speakers in initial encounters when more personal information about participants is not yet available. The magnitude of sex stereotypes has not been assessed. Like sex effects, it is likely that stereotype effects are statistically significant but not large.

CONCLUSIONS

A review of the research on conversational interaction reveals many sex differences. A polarized depiction of men and women has emerged from these findings that has been widely popularized by best sellers such as Deborah Tannen's *You Just Don't*

Understand: Women and Men in Conversation (Tannen, 1990) and John Gray's *Men Are From Mars, Women Are From Venus* (Gray, 1992). Gray goes so far as to claim that "not only do men and women communicate differently but they think, feel, perceive, react, respond, love, need, and appreciate differently. They almost seem to be from different planets, speaking different languages" (p. 5).

The research evidence, however, permits multiple interpretations. We have tended to focus on men and women as groups, overlooking individual differences between members of the same sex. The findings for samples of individuals that are not White and middle class do not always support popular stereotypes. We have tended to polarize differences, misrepresenting small differences as mutually exclusive differences. We have failed to pay sufficient attention to situational variability in behavior, to the fact that sex differences do not appear consistently across situational contexts and are not found in many studies. We have overlooked the importance of social roles, status, and sex stereotypes as alternative explanations for sex differences.

Those who take an essentialist position have argued that the differential socialization of men and women leads to the development of contrasting styles of communication. Women learn to be polite and expressive and to assume an interpersonal orientation, whereas men learn to be assertive and direct. These differences need not be biologically based, but they are assumed to reside within the individual. The data reviewed in this chapter suggest, however, that we must move beyond the essentialist model to explain why there is so much within-sex variability, why the appearance of sex differences in interaction is situationally variable, why no sex differences are found in many contexts, and why people use behaviors associated with the opposite sex in certain roles and contexts. We can only begin to make an accurate prediction of the particular behaviors speakers will choose if we know something about their role and status, the type of conversation in which they are engaged, their conversational partners, and the goals they are trying to achieve. Knowledge of the sex of the speaker will give us little predictive power.

Many researchers, such as West and Zimmerman (1987), are beginning to move toward an understanding of sex as something that people do in social interaction. West and Zimmerman have argued that "a person's gender is not simply an aspect of what one is, but, more fundamentally, it is something that one *does*, and does recurrently, in interaction with others" (p. 140). The display of feminine or masculine behavior depends on the situational context. As Bohan (1993) has contended, "thus, none of us is feminine or is masculine or fails to be either of those. In particular contexts, people do feminine; in others, they do masculine" (p. 13).

We need to move beyond the conception that the interaction styles of men and women reside within individuals. We should return gender to its larger social context, taking into consideration other social forces that shape the expression of gendered behavior. We must weigh carefully not only how we choose to understand the sex differences we have found, but also how much importance we choose to give to these sex differences. Our construction of polarized conceptions of men and women in interaction helps to sustain current realities and keep inequalities in place.

REFERENCES

Anderson, L. R., & Blanchard, P. N. (1982). Sex differences in task and social-emotional behavior. *Basic and Applied Social Psychology, 3*, 109–139.

Aries, E. (1976). Interaction patterns and themes of male, female, and mixed groups. *Small Group Behavior, 7*, 7–18.

Aries, E. (1987). Gender and communication. In P. Shaver & C. Hendrick (Eds.), *Sex and gender* (pp. 149–176). Newbury Park, CA: Sage.

Aries, E. (1996). *Men and women in interaction: Reconsidering the differences.* New York: Oxford University Press.

Baxter, L. A. (1984). An investigation of compliance-gaining as politeness. *Human Communication Research, 10*, 427–456.

Bergen, D. J., & Williams, J. E. (1991). Sex stereotypes in the United States revisited: 1972–1988. *Sex Roles, 24*, 413–423.

Berger, J., Cohen, B. P., & Zelditch, M. (1972). Status characteristics and social interaction. *American Sociological Review, 37*, 241–255.

Berger, J., Fisek, M. H., Norman, R. Z., & Zelditch, M. (1977). *Status characteristics and social interaction.* New York: Elsevier.

Binion, V. J. (1990). Psychological androgyny: A Black female perspective. *Sex Roles*, 22, 487–507.

Bohan, J. S. (1993). Regarding gender: Essentialism, constructionism, and feminist psychology. *Psychology of Women Quarterly, 17*, 5–21.

Bradley, P. H. (1981). The folk-linguistics of women's speech: An empirical examination. *Communication Monographs, 48*, 73–90.

Broverman, I. K., Vogel, S. R., Broverman, D. M., Clarkson, F. E., & Rosenkrantz, P. S. (1972). Sex-role stereotypes: A current appraisal. *Journal of Social Issues, 28*, 59–78.

Canary, D. J., & Hause, K. S. (1993). Is there any reason to research sex differences in communication? *Communication Quarterly, 41*, 129–144.

Carbonell, J. L. (1984). Sex roles and leadership revisited. *Journal of Applied Psychology, 69*, 44–49.

Carli, L. (1990). Gender, language, and influence. *Journal of Personality and Social Psychology, 59*, 941–951.

Cohen, J. (1977). *Statistical power analysis for the behavioral sciences.* New York: Academic Press.

Correll, S. J. (2004). Constraints into preferences: Gender, status, and emerging career aspirations. *American Sociological Review, 69*, 193–113.

Davis, B. M., & Gilbert, L. A. (1989). Effect of dispositional and situational influences on women's dominance expression in mixed-sex dyads. *Journal of Personality and Social Psychology, 57*, 294–300.

Deaux, K., & Major, B. (1987). Putting gender into context: An interactive model of gender-related behavior. *Psychological Bulletin, 94*, 369–389.

De Leon, B. (1995). Sex role identity among college students: A cross-cultural analysis. In A. M. Padilla (Ed.), *Hispanic psychology: Critical issues in theory and research* (pp. 245–256). Thousand Oaks, CA: Sage.

Dindia, K., & Allen, M. (1992). Sex differences in self-disclosure: A meta-analysis. *Psychological Bulletin, 112*, 106–124.

Eagly, A. H. (1987). *Sex differences in social behavior: A social-role interpretation.* Hillsdale, NJ: Lawrence Erlbaum Associates.

Eagly, A. H., & Johnson, B. T. (1990). Gender and leadership style: A meta-analysis. *Psychological Bulletin, 108*, 233–256.

Eagly, A. H., & Karau, S. J. (1991). Gender and the emergence of leaders: A meta-analysis. *Journal of Personality and Social Psychology, 60*, 685–710.

Eagly, A. H., Makhijani, M. G., & Klonsky, B. G. (1992). Gender and the evaluation of leaders: A meta-analysis. *Psychological Bulletin, 111*, 3–22.

Eakins, B., & Eakins, R. G. (1983). Verbal turn-taking and exchanges in faculty dialogue. In B. L. Dubois & I. Crouch (Eds.), *Proceedings of the Conference on the Sociology of the Languages of American Women* (pp. 53–62). San Antonio, TX: Trinity University.

Ellis, D. G. (1982). Relational stability and change in women's consciousness-raising groups. *Women's Studies in Communication, 5*, 77–87.

Gray, J. (1992). *Men are from Mars, women are from Venus. A practical guide to improving communication and getting what you want in your relationships.* New York: HarperCollins.

Greif, E. B. (1980). Sex differences in parent–child conversations. *Women's Studies International Quarterly, 3*, 253–258.

Harris, A. C. (1994). Ethnicity as a determinant of sex role identity: A replication study of item selection for the Bem Sex Role Inventory. *Sex Roles, 31*, 241–273.

Hawkins, K. (1988). Interruptions in task-oriented conversations: Effects of violations of expectations by males and females. *Women's Studies in Communication, 11*, 1–20.

Henley, N. (1973–1974). Power, sex, and nonverbal communication. *Berkeley Journal of Sociology, 18*, 1–26. Reprinted in B. Thorne & N. Henley, Eds., 1975, *Language and sex: Difference and dominance* (pp. 184–203). Rowley, MA: Newbury House.

Henley, N. M. (1977). *Body politics: Power, sex and nonverbal communication.* Englewood Cliffs, NJ: Prentice-Hall.

Hill, C. T., & Stull, D. E. (1987). Gender and self-disclosure: Strategies for exploring the issues. In V. J. Derlega & J. H. Berg (Eds.), *Self-disclosure: Theory, research, and therapy* (pp. 81–100). New York: Plenum.

Hyde, J. S., & Linn, M. C. (Eds.). (1986). *The psychology of gender: Advances through meta-analysis.* Baltimore: Johns Hopkins University Press.

James, D., & Clarke, S. (1993). Women, men, and interruptions: A critical review. In D. Tannen (Ed.), *Gender and conversational interaction* (pp. 231–280). New York: Oxford University Press.

James, D., & Drakich, J. (1993). Understanding gender differences in amount of talk: A critical review. In D. Tannen (Ed.), *Gender and conversational interaction* (pp. 281–312). New York: Oxford University Press.

Johnson, C. (1994). Gender, legitimate authority, and leader–subordinate conversations. *American Sociological Review, 59*, 122–135.

Johnson, P. (1976). Women and power: Toward a theory of effectiveness. *Journal of Social Issues, 32*, 99–110.

Karakowsky, L., McBey, K., & Miller, D. L. (2004). Gender, perceived competence, and power displays: Examining verbal interruptions in a group context. *Small Group Research, 35*, 407–439.

Karakowsky, L., & Siegel, J. P. (1999). The effects of proportional representation and gender orientation of the task on emergent leadership behavior in mixed-gender work groups. *Journal of Applied Psychology, 84*, 620–631.

Kollock, P., Blumstein, P., & Schwartz, P. (1985). Sex and power in interaction: Conversational privileges and duties. *American Sociological Review, 50*, 34–46.

Kramarae, C. (1981). *Men and women speaking.* Rowley, MA: Newbury House.

Kramarae, C. (1990). Changing the complexion of gender in language research. In H. Giles & W. P. Robinson (Eds.), *Handbook of language and social psychology* (pp. 345–361). Chichester, England: Wiley.

Kramer, C. (1977). Perceptions of female and male speech. *Language and Speech, 20*, 151–161.

Lawrence, S. G., Stucky, N. P., & Hopper, R. (1990). The effects of sex dialects and sex stereotypes on speech evaluations. *Journal of Language and Social Psychology, 9*, 209–224.

Lockheed, M. F. (1985). Sex and social influence: A meta-analysis guided by theory. In J. Berger & M. Zelditch (Eds.), *Status, rewards and influence* (pp 406–429). San Francisco: Jossey-Bass.

Mast, M. (2002). Dominance as expressed and inferred through speaking time: A meta-analysis. *Human Communication Research, 28*, 420–450.

McCarrick, A. K., Manderscheid, R. W., & Silbergeld, S. (1981). Gender differences in competition and dominance during married-couples group therapy. *Social Psychology Quarterly, 44*, 164–177.

McCullough, M. (1987, November). Women's friendships across cultures: Black and White friends speaking. Paper presented at the meeting of the Speech Communication Association, Boston, MA.

McLachlan, A. (1991). The effects of agreement, disagreement, gender and familiarity on patterns of dyadic interaction. *Journal of Language and Social Psychology, 10*, 205–212.

McMillan, J. R., Clifton, A. K., McGrath, D., & Gale, W. S. (1977). Women's language: Uncertainty or interpersonal sensitivity and emotionality. *Sex Roles, 3*, 545–559.

Megargee, E. I. (1969). Influence of sex roles on the manifestation of leadership. *Journal of Applied Psychology, 53*, 377–382.

Miller, J. B. (1985). Patterns of control in same-sex conversations: Differences between women and men. *Women's Studies in Communication, 8*, 62–69.

Moskowitz, D. S., Jung Suh, E., & Desaulniers, J. (1994). Situational influences on gender differences in agency and communion. *Journal of Personality and Social Psychology, 66*, 753–761.

Mulac, A., Incontro, C. R., & James, M. R. (1985). Comparison of the gender-linked language effect and sex role stereotypes. *Journal of Personality and Social Psychology, 49*, 1098–1109.

Natale, M., Entin, E., & Jaffe, J. (1979). Vocal interruptions in dyadic communication as a function of speech and social anxiety. *Journal of Personality and Social Psychology, 37*, 865–878.

Newcombe, N., & Arnkoff, D. B. (1979). Effects of speech style and sex of speaker on person perception. *Journal of Personality and Social Psychology, 37*, 1293–1303.

Nyquist, L., & Spence, J. T. (1986). Effects of dispositional dominance and sex role expectations on leadership behaviors. *Journal of Personality and Social Psychology, 50*, 87–93.

O'Barr, W., & Atkins, B. (1980). "Women's language" or "powerless language"? In S. McConnell-Ginet, R. Borker, & N. Furman (Eds.), *Women and language in literature and society* (pp. 93–110). New York: Praeger.

Postmes, T. (2002). Behavior online: Does anonymous computer communication reduce gender inequality? *Personality and Social Psychology Bulletin, 28*, 1073–1083.

Pugh, M. D., & Wahrman, R. (1983). Neutralizing sexism in mixed-sex groups: Do women have to be better than men? *American Journal of Sociology, 88*, 746–762.

Pugh, M. D., & Wahrman, R. (1985). Inequality of influence in mixed-sex groups. In J. Berger & M. Zelditch (Eds.), *Status, rewards, and influence* (pp. 142–162). San Francisco: Jossey-Bass.

Reis, H. T., Senchak, M., & Solomon, B. (1985). Sex differences in the intimacy of social interaction: Further examination of potential explanations. *Journal of Personality and Social Psychology, 48*, 1204–1217.

Rice, R. W., Bender, L. R., & Vitters, A. G. (1980). Leader sex, follower attitudes toward women, and leadership effectiveness: A laboratory experiment. *Organizational Behavior and Human Performance, 25*, 46–78.

Risman, B. J. (1987). Intimate relationships from a micro-structural perspective: Men who mother. *Gender and Society, 1*, 6–32.

Sagrestano, L. (1992). Power strategies in interpersonal relationships. *Psychology of Women Quarterly, 16*, 481–495.

Siegler, D. M., & Siegler, R. S. (1976). Stereotypes of males' and females' speech. *Psychological Reports, 39*, 167–170.

Smythe, M., & Schlueter, D. W. (1989). Can we talk? A meta-analytic review of the sex differences in language literature. In C. M. Lont & S. A. Friedley (Eds.), *Beyond boundaries: Sex and gender diversity in communication* (pp. 31–48). Fairfax, VA: George Mason University Press.

Snodgrass, S. E. (1985). Women's intuition: The effect of subordinate role on interpersonal sensitivity. *Journal of Personality and Social Psychology, 49*, 146–155.

Snodgrass, S. E. (1992). Further effects of role versus gender on interpersonal sensitivity. *Journal of Personality and Social Psychology, 62*, 154–158.

Spender, D. (1980). *Man made language*. London: Routledge & Kegan Paul.

Steil, J. M., & Hillman, J. L. (1993). The perceived value of direct and indirect influence startegies: A cross-cultural comparison. *Psychology of Women Quarterly, 17*, 457–462.

Swim, J. K. (1994). Perceived versus meta-analytic effect sizes: An assessment of the accuracy of gender stereotypes. *Journal of Personality and Social Psychology, 66*, 21–36.

Tannen, D. (1990). *You just don't understand: Women and men in conversation*. New York: Morrow.

Thorne, B., & Henley, N. (1975). Difference and dominance: An overview of language, gender and society. In B. Thorne & N. Henley (Eds.), *Language and sex: Difference and dominance* (pp. 5–42). Rowley, MA: Newbury House.

Torres, L. (1992). Women and language: From sex differences to power dynamics. In C. Kramarae & D. Spender (Eds.), *The knowledge explosion: Generations of feminist scholarship* (pp. 281–290). New York: Teacher's College Press.

Tracy, K., & Eisenberg, E. (1990–1991). Giving criticism: A multiple goals case study. *Research on Language and Social Interaction, 24*, 37–70.

Unger, R. K. (1976). Male is greater than female: The socialization of status inequality. *Counseling Psychologist, 62*, 2–9.

Unger, R. K. (1979). *Female and male: Psychological perspectives*. New York: Harper & Row.

Unger, R. K. (1990). Imperfect reflections of reality: Psychology constructs gender. In R. T. Hare-Mustin & J. Marecek (Eds.), *Making a difference: Psychology and the construction of gender* (pp. 102–149). New Haven, CT: Yale University Press.

Werner, P. D., & LaRussa, G. W. (1985). Persistence and change in sex role stereotypes. *Sex Roles, 12*, 1089–1100.

West, C., & Zimmerman, D. H. (1977). Women's place in everyday talk: Reflections on parent–child interaction. *Social Problems, 24*, 521–529.

West, C., & Zimmerman, D. H. (1987). Doing gender. *Gender and Society, 1*, 125–151.

Wheelan, S. A., & Verdi, A. F. (1992). Differences in male and female patterns of communication in groups: A methodological artifact? *Sex Roles, 27*, 1–15.

Wiley, M. G., & Eskilson, A. (1985). Speech style, gender stereotypes and corporate success: What if women talk more like men? *Sex Roles, 12*, 993–1007.

Wood, W., & Karten, S. J. (1986). Sex differences in interaction style as a product of perceived sex differences in competence. *Journal of Personality and Social Psychology, 50*, 341–347.

Woods, N. (1988). Talking shop: Sex and status as determinants of floor apportionment in a work setting. In J. Coates & D. Cameron (Eds.), *Women in their speech communities: New perspectives on language and sex* (pp. 141–157). New York: Longman.

3

Toward an Expanded Orientation to the Comparative Study of Women's and Men's Same-Sex Friendships

Paul H. Wright
University of North Dakota

C. S. Lewis, a literary scholar of acknowledged depth and versatility, once observed that women and men enjoy laughing at one another (Lewis, 1960). Among other things, women often exchange comments of bemusement and amusement about the golf games, fishing trips, car talk, sports talk, and shoptalk they assume form the core of men's activity-centered, goal-directed and wholly depersonalized friendships. Men, likewise, exchange comments of bemusement and amusement about the phone conversations, coffee dates, personal talk, soul baring, and emotional give-and-take they assume form the core of women's relationship-centered, mutually supportive, and wholly personalized friendships. These polarized conceptions of women's and men's friendships are, of course, caricatures. Or are they?

The essence of a caricature is that, while recognizing it as a gross exaggeration, most people see in the exaggeration highlights of the distinctive features of the subject portrayed. In other words, caricatures embody some elements of truth. How good, then, are the caricatures people draw of the typical friendships of women and men? Literally scores of studies suggest that they embody large elements of truth, leading some scholars to say that the so-called caricatures are not exaggerations at all but provide essentially valid portrayals of the friendships of women and men. Other scholars disagree. For the latter group, a discerning look at the same studies reveals enough exceptions and qualifications to persuade them that differences in women's and men's friendships are not notably large or pervasive. The caricatures, they believe, are indeed caricatures, and broad or definitive statements about differences in women's and men's friendships are unwarranted.

Carried to its logical extreme, the controversy over the nature of women's and men's friendships raises a basic question: Should relationship scholars be working toward one theory or model of friendship, or do we need two—one applicable to women's and another applicable to men's friendships? This question is not, as I once suggested, hyperbolic (Wright, 1998). At issue is whether we regard sex differences in friendship as a manifestation of fundamental dispositional differences between women and men as opposed to variations on themes that are fundamental to the friendships of both women and men. The former view would foster the development of separate models of friendship for women and men, and the latter the development of a single, overarching model applicable to both. Friendship scholars have not, to the best of my knowledge, explicitly addressed this issue. As a result, research on sex differences in friendship has been designed, executed, and reported in ways that leave unstated or unclear how those differences fit in to a reasonably well-articulated conception of either sex differences or friendship. This leaves us with a residue of ambiguity concerning what and how much (or how little) to make of those differences. In the face of this ambiguity, scholars with opposing views persist in exchanges of the "yes—but" kind, with each side conducting research (and interpreting that of the other side) in ways that support their respective positions.

This chapter argues for the necessity of expanding our orientation by exploring sex differences in friendship within a broader conceptual and empirical context. The subsequent review will show, I believe, that research on this topic clearly favors a single model of friendship rather than separate models for women and men. The proposed expansion entails exploring and interpreting sex differences in friendship within the context of friendship as a whole. I further propose that sex differences in friendship are better understood if we take into account the influence of sociostructural as well as dispositional influences, a point strongly argued some time ago by Fischer & Oliker (1983).

I open this chapter with a discussion and a critique of the "classical" view that women's friendships are personal, expressive, and socioemotionally oriented whereas men's friendships are depersonalized, instrumental, and activity oriented. I follow this by reexamining some key studies of sex differences in friendship, intending to provide an overall empirical picture and its implications. I close the chapter with a proposal for an expanded orientation to the study of women's and men's friendships.

THE CLASSICAL VIEW OF SEX DIFFERENCES IN FRIENDSHIP AND ITS VARIATIONS

In 1981, Bell asserted broadly and boldly, "When we look at friendship in society, we can see many variations. But there is no social factor more important than that of sex in leading to friendship differences" (1981, p. 55). A great deal of research conducted both before and since 1981, taken as a whole and more or less uncritically, seems to substantiate Bell's claim. Just what are those important sex-linked variations? The classical consensus holds that (a) women's friendships are affectively richer than those of men (Booth, 1972); (b) women's friendships emphasize reciprocity, whereas men's emphasize agreement and similarity (Weiss & Lowenthal, 1975; (c) women's friendships are reciprocal, men's associative (Reisman, 1981); (d) women have complex and holistic friendships with partners who have relevance for many areas of experience, whereas men have focused and circumscribed friendships with special-purpose partners who have relevance for limited areas of experience (see, e.g., Barth & Kinder, 1988).

Sex Differences in Friendship as Dichotomous

The foregoing litany of sex differences in friendship is by no means exhaustive. Several investigators have undertaken reviews of the voluminous literature on this topic (e.g., Fehr, 1996; Sherrod, 1989; Wright, 1989). These reviews clearly show that the interrelated matters of intimacy, self-disclosure, expressiveness, and mere talk versus nonintimacy, inexpressiveness, and activity-centeredness are pivotal. Women's friendships are characterized by the former, men's by the latter. At one time, I epitomized these differences metaphorically, describing women's friendships as *face to face* and men's friendships as *side by side.* On a more conceptual level, the entire pattern of differences is encapsulated in Bakan's (1966) distinction between *communion* and *agency*. Scholars adopted the convention of characterizing women's friendships as communal and men's friendships as agentic.

A Challenge to the Dichotomy and a Response

Eventually, a number of friendship scholars began scrutinizing the empirical underpinnings of this essentially dichotomous view and concluded that the frequency, strength, and ubiquity of the modal pattern of sex differences in friendship were not as great as typically assumed (see, e.g., Wright, 1988). Whereas such scrutinies generally supported the overall robustness of the modal pattern, an appreciable number of studies failed to show the usual sex differences. Moreover, when sex differences were found, they were often quite small (despite being statistically significant), generally characterized by considerable within-sex variance, and often attenuated by organismic or subject variables other than sex of participants (e.g., sex-role orientations, intimacy motivation, power motivation).

Such observations did not go unheeded by friendship scholars, some of whom continued to emphasize the opposition of communality and agency even as they became less dichotomous in their orientations. For instance, as recently as 2002, Brehm, Miller, Perlman, and Campbell took a "weight of evidence" stance that acknowledged but minimized findings that failed to show the usual sex differences in friendship, epitomizing the respective personalized versus activity-centered nature of women's and men's friendships as follows: "Terms used roughly 20 years ago by Wright (1982) seem to remain pithy and accurate descriptors of two different, gender-related approaches. Women's friendships are 'face to face' whereas men's are 'side by side'" (p. 212).

In a similar weight of evidence vein, Fehr (1996) devoted a book chapter to a painstaking review of the issue of sex differences in friendships, coming down rather heavily in favor of large and pervasive differences.

Sex Differences in Friendship as Continuous, not Dichotomous

Viewing sex differences in friendship less dichotomously involves a shift to viewing them more continuously. The orientation implied in such a shift may take one of two forms. One possibility would be to view friendship communality and friendship agency as a single bipolar continuum, with sex differences in friendship varying bimodally (with minimal overlap) along that continuum. Women's friendships would be concentrated toward the communal and men's toward the agentic pole, as illustrated in the hypothetical distributions shown in Figure 3.1.

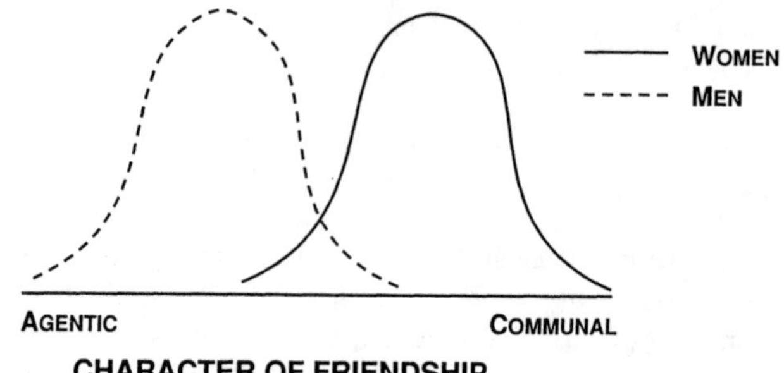

FIGURE 3.1. Hypothetical distribution of women's and men's friendships along an agentic–communal continuum as implied in the first nondichotomous orientation in the classical view.

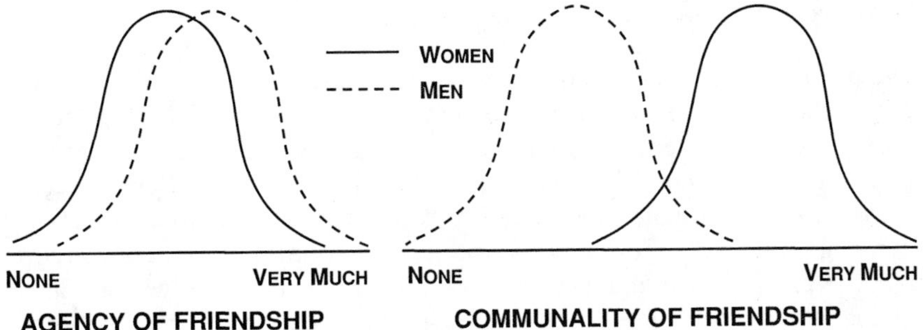

FIGURE 3.2. Hypothetical distribution of women's and men's friendships along separate agentic and communal continua as implied in the second nondichotomous orientation in the classical view.

This orientation seems most consistent with the highly polarized stance suggested by Brehm et al. (2002).

In view of findings that sex differences in friendship agency are neither as large nor as consistently found as those in friendship communality, a second possibility would be to view communality and agency as separate continua. This orientation would depict communality and agency as two separate continua, each ranging from *none* to *very much*. For the communality dimension, the hypothetical distributions for women and men would overlap slightly; the central tendency would be considerably higher for women. For the agency dimension, the distributions would overlap to a greater extent; the central tendency would be somewhat, but not 'considerably,' higher for men (see Fig. 3.2).

THE QUESTIONABLE STATUS OF THE CLASSICAL VIEW AND THE NEED FOR A CLOSER LOOK

The third of the orientations within the classical view is, in my opinion, an improvement over the other two in that it allows for flexibility and compromise in interpreting the comparative degree of communality and agency in the friendships of women and men. Nevertheless, there is cause to doubt whether any of these orientations—that is to say, the classical view as a whole—provides a sound framework within which to organize and interpret research on sex differences in friendship. The reason for this is that interpretations of data supporting the classical view involve four problematic predilections that, if examined closely, indicate that the opposition of women's communality and men's agency in friendships is markedly exaggerated.

Four Problematic Predilections

One predilection among friendship scholars is to highlight and expand on research results showing differences between women's and men's friendships and to disregard or downplay results showing extensive similarities. In a report of an early diary study, for example, Wheeler and Nezlak (1977) elaborated on the finding that women classified a significantly greater percentage of interactions with friends as "sharing"—defined as "exchanges of perceptions or feelings about one's self or others" (p. 747)—than did men (12% vs. 3%). They also noted without further discussion that about 70% of both women and men classified their interactions as "conversation" (See also Reis, Lin, Bennett, & Nezlak, 1993). This does not, of course, negate the opposition of communion and agency in women's and men's friendships, but it does diminish its prominence.

A second predilection is to assess communality in terms of various talk-related interactions such as amount and intimacy of self-disclosure and explicit emotional supportiveness, and to assess agency broadly and simply, in terms of shared activities. That is, if friends focus their interactions primarily on activities, they are ipso facto being impersonal and instrumental. Therefore, researchers infer from the commonly reported finding that female friends more often engage in talk and male friends in shared activities that women's friendships are personal and expressive (communal) whereas men's friendships are impersonal and instrumental (agentic). As I shall note in more detail later, several problems accompany this inference. For now it will suffice to note that activities, as well as different kinds of talk and emotional sharing, vary widely in communality and that, as several researchers have proposed, men are inclined to express personalness and intimacy more through activities than through talk (Hays, 1984, 1985; Swain, 1989; Wood, 1994; Wood & Inman, 1993).

A third predilection is to interpret and report research findings on friendship communality and agency separately and in a noncontextualized manner. That is, attention is devoted neither to how these characteristics relate to one another nor to how they fit into a broader conception of friendship. This predilection becomes problematic when we consider virtually any of the formal (and detailed) conceptions of friendship currently available. Although each conception has its own set of distinctives, they agree that the development of friendships from casual to deeper levels is marked by an increase in all the beneficial aspects of friendship, including both those that are agentic and communal. Moreover, these beneficial aspects covary positively in fully developed friendships. Empirical support for this positive covariation abounds (e.g., Duch & Wright, 1993; Lea, 1989). Simply put, friendships involving high levels of communality also involve high levels of agency, and vice versa. Here, then, is another reason for suspecting that sex differences in friendship communality and agency may be exaggerated.

A fourth predilection is to explain sex differences in friendship in dispositional terms to the relative exclusion of structural terms. That is, such differences are explained in terms of how women and men differ, in general, with respect to internalized and presumably stable personal characteristics such as nuturance, interpersonal sensitivity, competitiveness, intimacy motivation, and power motivation. Moreover, it is not uncommon for investigators to focus on dispositional characteristics that inhibit expressiveness in men's friendships instead of—or in addition to—those that enhance it in women's friendships (see, e.g., Bank & Hansford, 2000, regarding male homophobia, emotional restraint, and masculine identity). In contrast to this dispositional emphasis, Fischer and Oliker (1984) argued that structural factors influence both the number and kinds of friendships that women and men form and maintain. I will look at the implications of the structural emphasis in greater detail later. For now, I need only note that it allows for more situational variability in women's and men's friendships than one would expect on the basis of dispositionally determined communal and agentic inclinations. For example, in at least two studies of friendship in the workplace (Furman, 1987; Markiewicz, Devine & Kausilas, 2000), the usual sex differences were not found.

The Need for a Closer Look

The preceding points suggest the need for a reexamination of key studies of sex differences in friendship and a closer look at some of the data. In the three sections that follow, I undertake such a review and the implications of that closer look. The first section considers friendship characteristics for which women and men were found to be clearly alike. The second considers the major friendship characteristics for which sex differences were found and, where warranted, qualifies the nature or extent of those differences. The third section presents a perspective on the comparative empirical picture concerning women's and men's friendships, highlighting its implications for what friendship per se is "really like," and what friendship differences between women and men "really signify." This discussion sets the stage for a proposed expansion in our orientation to sex differences in friendship based on an overall conception that includes an adaptation of Hess's (1972) early but apparently little noted proposal for incorporating social influences into the study of friendship in general.

WOMEN'S AND MEN'S FRIENDSHIPS: FUNDAMENTAL SIMILARITIES

Women and men are clearly similar on four aspects of friendship: conceptions and values of friendship, friendship agency–instrumentality, the prominence of talk for talk's sake, and the importance accorded fun and relaxation. Collectively, these similarities may be considered fundamental in the sense that they (a) identify what women and men alike regard as ideal (and presumably aspire to) in friendships, (b) specify an important category of friendship rewards on which women and men are similar, (c) document what friends do most of the time when they get together, and (d) highlight an easily overlooked facet of friendship that is nonetheless associated with friendship strength, intimacy, and satisfaction.

Conceptions and Values of Friendship

Sapadin (1988) concluded from her study of professional women and men that, despite differences in the actual experience of friendship, "both sexes viewed the characteristics of an ideal friendship in similar ways" (p. 400). In support of this conclusion, an impressive array of studies with somewhat varying emphases found that both women and men considered the most valued characteristics of friendship (or of an ideal friend) to be those generally identified as the modal pattern for women, that is, intimacy, trust, interpersonal sensitivity, emotional expressiveness, and authenticity (e.g., Monsour, 1992). Similarly, Caldwell and Peplau (1982) found that a large majority of both women and men indicated a preference for a few intimate friends rather than many good but less intimate friends.

Friendship Agency–Instrumentality

Despite the commonly accepted generalization that women's friendships are communal whereas men's are agentic, there is, in fact, no compelling evidence that women's friendships are any less agentic than those of men. On the contrary, there is evidence that women's and men's friendships do not differ in this respect. Duck and Wright (1993; see also Wright & Scanlon, 1991) noted that, within levels of friendship, women's friendships were significantly higher on communal characteristics but that women's and men's friendships did not differ on agentic characteristics. Similarly, Bank (1995) found that women's friendships were more expressive or intimate than those of men but found no sex difference in friendship instrumentality.

Talk for Talk's Sake

Diary techniques tapping daily interactions reveal that, when friends get together, they most often engage in casual conversation or talk for talk's sake. Women and men do not differ in this regard. In studies reported by Wheeler and Nezlak (1977) and Reis et al. (1993), women and men classified 66.3% and 61.3% (respectively) of their interactions with friends as conversation. By way of contrast, none of the other classifications of interaction used in these studies exceeded 20%. Similarly, in three sets of data utilizing the Iowa Communication Record (Duck & Wright, 1993), with some minor variation across sets, both women and men rated talk as the most frequent purpose of interactions with their friends and working on a task as second.

Fun and Relaxation

Fehr (2000) recently noted that two intertwined and heretofore unheralded aspects of friendship, fun and relaxation, are beginning to capture the attention of relationship scholars. She cited several studies showing that fun and relaxation are common and highly valued features of friendship for both women and men. Specifically, they are an indication that a mere acquaintanceship has progressed to a friendship, and they are strongly related to friendship intimacy and friendship satisfaction.

WOMEN'S AND MEN'S FRIENDSHIPS: EMBEDDED DIFFERENCES

Studies of women's and men's friendship have yielded sex differences on several specific topics, pointing to the general conclusion that women's friendships are, on the average, more communal than those of men. The following review covers the major characteristics for which sex differences have been found and suggests that most of those differences, although robust and generally noteworthy, are embedded in a context of broad similarities.

Talk Versus Activity

Female friends talk; male friends do. This common conclusion seems to be supported by scores of studies, yet it is inconsistent with the observation, already noted, that conversation is the predominant focus of interaction in the friendships of both women and men. The apparent inconsistency disappears, however, when we consider variations in methodology. Female–male similarity in the prominence of talk is found in studies using diary techniques. Differences in talk versus activities are found in studies using retrospective interviews and self-reports that sometimes solicit preferences rather than estimated occurrences. For example, in a study often cited as attesting to women's talk-centered and men's activity-centered friendships, Caldwell and Peplau (1982) found that more women than men preferred just talking with friends than doing some activity. The opposite held true for men (for a cross-cultural replication, see Aukett, Ritchie, & Mill, 1988). What Caldwell and Peplau actually found was that 57% of the women preferred talk, leaving 43% who preferred an activity. The comparison for men was more impressive, with 84% preferring an activity. What this outcome indicates is that men more likely emphasize activities with their friends, whereas women are about equally divided in their preferences for talk and activities. In other words, women do not greatly emphasize talk at the expense of activities.

The work of Caldwell and Peplau does not, of course, stand alone. Numerous studies using interviews and self-report measures generally confirm the typical talk versus activity differences. Within this literature, however, researchers often tacitly and sometimes explicitly recognize that female friends do, in fact, participate in varied activities and that male friends talk quite a bit (e.g., Pukalos, 1989). Whereas this latter observation should raise some doubts about the generality of the talk–activity dichotomy, it does not. Women's activities are regarded as vehicles for interaction in which talk remains focal (Johnson & Aries, 1983a; Pukalos); men's talk centers on impersonal topics such as sports, work, hobbies, and shared activities (Johnson & Aries, 1983b). This conclusion introduces two different points for further consideration. The first has to do with the balance of talk and activities in women's and men's friendships, and the second with sex differences in a category of talk that shades into intimacy per se, in other words, self-disclosure.

Talk About Talking Versus Talk About Doing

Concerning the balance of talk and activities, the overall body of relevant research suggests that both women and men friends talk a lot and do a lot, with both placing more emphasis on talking than doing (see the earlier subsection on talk for talk's sake). However, when reflecting on their friendships, as in responses to interview questions, women more often talk about talking and men more often talk about doing. This impression finds support in a study by Walker (1994), who found that women and men responded initially to broad questions about friendship with the usual talk versus activity difference. When asked more focused questions about friendships, however, women's reports of involvement in activities increased, as did men's reports of involvement in talk.

Self-Disclosure

Concerning self-disclosure, reviews of work on sex differences in friendship typically note that women, on average, self-disclose more broadly and more intimately than do men. This is exemplified in the Wheeler and Nezlak (1975) study cited previously. Recall that women classified a significantly higher percentage of interactions with friends as sharing than did men, and that the comparative percentages were, respectively, 12 and 3. In addition to the significant female–male difference, this finding indicates that explicit self-disclosure occurs infrequently in the interactions of either female or male friends. Indeed, some investigators (Dindia, Fitzpatrick, & Kenny, 1989; Duck, Rutt, Hurts, & Strejc, 1991) have reported that expressiveness, including self-disclosure, occurs only about 2% of the time in everyday talk between relational partners. Moreover, Dindia and Allen (1992) concluded from a meta-analysis of 205 studies that there are sex differences in self-disclosure, but such differences are so small as to be of questionable practical or theoretical importance. On balance, the preponderance of the evidence suggests that female friends engage in expressive and self-disclosing talk more than do male friends, but that neither do so very much.

Friendship Intimacy

Women's friendships are characterized by high levels of intimacy, whereas men's friendships are not. This generalization expresses what many researchers consider the core distinction between women's communal and men's agentic friendships. Numerous studies support the conclusion that women's friendships are, on the average, more intimate than those of men (e.g., Bank & Hansford, 2000; Reis, 1998). The tacit (and sometimes explicit) conclusion from these studies is that men's friendships are nonintimate. This conclusion is implied in the common and largely unquestioned acceptance of the appellations "inexpressive male" and "male deficit model." However, the body of research on this issue suggests a different conclusion: Men's friendships are, in general, at least moderately and sometimes impressively intimate although not, on the average, as intimate as those of women. I base this conclusion on two considerations. First, mean differences in women's and men's friendship intimacy scores are usually small, with the mean for men typically falling in the moderate range and that for women in the moderately high range (e.g., Bank & Hansford). Sometimes men's friendship intimacy means, although lower than those of women, are nonetheless in the moderately high range (Duck & Wright, 1993; Wright & Scanlon, 1991).

Second, as noted earlier, researchers show a predilection to regard shared activities (as opposed to talk) as nonintimate. From our earlier discussion, recall Hays' (1984, 1985) observation that activities as well as talk vary in their degree of intimacy. Some relationship scholars (Swain, 1989; Wood, 1994; Wood & Inman, 1993) take this to mean that men's friendships are just as intimate as women's but that men express intimacy differently, that is, through activities. I believe there is a serious flaw in this argument. I agree that, as a result of the emphasis on intimacy as talk, the intimacy of men's friendships has been underestimated. However, there is no reason to believe that women's friendships involve intimate activities any less than do those of men. In fact, my conjecture is that women's friendships involve intimate activities somewhat more. I arrive at this conjecture by combining Hays' (1985) observation that activities vary in the degree to which they are intimate (socioemotional) with the assumption that, traditionally, women have been more involved than men in activities that are intrinsically socioemotional. Joining a partner in shingling a roof would normally be less socioemotional than, for example, going with a partner to a mutual acquaintance's baby shower. Intimacy, then, appears to be an essential aspect of the close friendships of both women and men. It is, however, typically somewhat stronger in the friendships of women, regardless of how it is identified.

Holistic Versus Circumscribed Friendships and Friendship Closeness

Several scholars have found that women are more likely than men to relate to their friends in global and multifaceted ways as opposed to relating to them with respect to distinct, relatively isolated attributes (Auhaugen, 1991; Barth & Kinder, 1988). Even though such holistic friendships are more common among women than men, it is generally assumed that holistic friendships are relatively rare for both.

This assumption is reflected in the work of Gouldner and Strong (1987). These researchers found that upper-middle-class working women made a clear distinction among talk friends, activity friends, work friends, and close friends. Beyond these categories, women identified a special class of friendships characterized by high levels of both personalism or expressiveness and mutual involvement in a variety of activities and personal pursuits. Such friendships were so rare as to be designated the "extraordinary relationship." Metaphorically, one might well think in terms of a friendship for all seasons or (nonmetaphorically) as one that is extremely close.

Another and perhaps more parsimonious way of framing the sex difference in holistic versus circumscribed friendships is to say, simply, that women's friendships tend to be stronger and more intense than those of men. This greater strength and intensity is reflected in two closely related (but not identical) ways. First, there is evidence that, when assessed by independent measures of friendship strength, women's best friendships are (on the average) stronger than those of men (Duck & Wright, 1993; Wright & Scanlon, 1991). Second, as implied in the sex difference in holistic friendships, women are more likely to form friendships that are extremely close.

Sex Differences in Friendship Satisfaction

Given, as we have seen, that women and men alike value depth and intimacy in friendships and that women, on average, experience more of it, it should follow that women will generally find their friendships more enjoyable and satisfying. Available evidence indicates, not surprisingly, that this is the case (e.g., Bank, 1995; Reisman, 1990).

THE EMPIRICAL PICTURE: SUMMARY AND IMPLICATIONS

Taken as a whole, our empirical picture of women's and men's friendships points to two sets of implications, one of which has relevance for what friendship in general is really like and the other for what sex differences in friendship really signify. Concerning the former, friendships that develop beyond the formal or casual levels, whether between women or men, provide the partners with both socioemotional and instrumental rewards and, in addition, involve partners in such apparent banalities as talk for talk's sake, fun, and relaxation. Indeed, inasmuch as such banalities characterize most of partners' interactions, friendship is to an appreciable degree a celebration of the mundane. Mundane, however, does not mean inconsequential. Although space does not permit a full discussion of the significance of the trivial in friendship, it is worth noting that the studies cited by Fehr (2000) indicate that fun and relaxation are associated with friendship strength, intimacy, and satisfaction. In any case, the closer the friendship, the more all of its positive aspects will be in evidence, and the more satisfying and enjoyable the friendship will be. Finally, friendships—even best friendships—among both women and men range in strength or intensity between moderate and extremely close levels. In sum, considering the broad spectrum of friendship characteristics, women's and men's friendships are more similar than different.

Concerning what sex differences in friendship actually signify, our empirical picture suggests two disarmingly simple conclusions about the number and magnitude of those differences. First, women form friendships that are closer, on average, than those of men. Second, even with friendship closeness held constant, women's friendships are generally more communal than men's. Women's greater friendship communality is evident in two ways.

First, although the actual talk–activity balance is similar in the friendships of women and men, women are more likely to talk about talk, and men are more likely to talk about activities. Thus, judging from the ways they reflect on and discuss them, talk is an experientially more salient aspect of women's than men's friendships. Second, the friendships of women are typically more person centered, expressive, and intimate at all levels than those of men.

All this suggests that the key to understanding sex differences in friendship reduces to the answer to one question: Why are the friendships of women so often observed to be closer and more communal than those of men? As noted in some detail previously, researchers' answers to this question have favored dispositional explanations. Whereas there is little question that dispositional variables contribute to the difference in women's and men's friendship communality, it is likely that structural variables influence this difference at least as much, and possibly more. Our empirical picture provides several reasons for believing that dispositional differences do not tell all, or even most, of the story about sex differences in friendship.

First, women and men alike hold conceptions of the ideal friendship that emphasize communal characteristics, and both women and men value (and presumably aspire to) friendships that have those characteristics. Second, women find their friendships more satisfying and enjoyable than do men. Third, in studies equating women's and men's friendships with respect to their broader settings (e.g., the workplace), the usual sex differences are often not found.

The foregoing considerations suggest that the comparative study of women's and men's friendships would be enhanced by an expanded orientation based on an overall conception of friendship. The following section presents a modest beginning toward such an orientation. In brief, I propose first that, as a result of the preferential and unconstrained character of friendship, the development and expression of friendship communality is affected at least as much by activity-centered as by conversation-centered interactions. I propose second that, for the same reason, the development and enactment of friendships (including their communal nature) is more at the mercy of factors within the overall social milieu than are more highly structured relationships. Taking these factors into account in our studies should both eliminate or moderate (probably the latter) observed sex differences in friendship communality and refine our understanding of what those differences really signify.

TOWARD AN EXPANDED ORIENTATION

Some time ago (Wright, 1978), I proposed a preliminary theory of friendship. This theory finds consensual validation in a number of other conceptions of friendship published both before and since its introduction. These conceptions would agree on two propositions. First, friendship growth involves increasing amounts of contact between partners in a growing variety of settings and activities. Second, such growth takes place within a relationship that is preferential, nonobligatory, and relatively unstructured with respect to specific role requirements and normative regulations. The first of these points has implications for the development and expression of communality in friendships; the second has implications for the impact of structural variables on friendship communality. Ultimately, each has implications for the comparative study of sex differences in friendship.

The Development and Expression of Communality and Friendship in General

Interactions that increase in both amount and variety in a developing friendship carry with them the opportunity, if not the inevitability, that each partner will be exposed to more facets of the other. In addition, with growing familiarity and security, the partners likely become increasingly spontaneous (i.e., less guarded and less self-monitoring) in how they act and what they say. Such behavioral self-exposure and (usually implicit) verbal self-disclosure will normally enhance each partner's awareness of what the other regards as important and self-involving as well as enable each to see the other with respect to what is genuine rather than superficial or affected.

To the degree that each partner in a friendship considers the other unfeigned and genuine, and responds to that partner with respect to what the partner regards as important and self-involving, the partners are, in a basic sense, expressing communality. From this point of view, explicit and self-conscious verbal expressions of communality are no more important in friendship than expressions of communality implicit in the kinds of activities close friends share, and in the ways friends engage in those activities. Both flow from the familiarity, trust, and personalized interest and concern that are characteristic in close friendships. Thus, if we distinguish between communality expressed through talk and communality expressed through activity, we should note that they likely unfold in a closely parallel fashion in developing friendships. In fact, in light of the findings noted herein, that explicit self-disclosures make up an extremely small percentage of the talk friends exchange in everyday interactions, intimacy expressed through activities may be a more sensitive index of friendship closeness.

The Expression of Communality in Women's Versus Men's Friendships

If researchers were to define and measure friendship communality in a way that included communal acts and activities along with self-disclosure, would they still find female friends, on the average, scoring higher than male friends? The answer to this question, of course, awaits the outcome of relevant research. The relevancy of such research would hinge on the use of procedures that tap intimacy levels of acts and activities with as much differentiation and precision as those used to tap the intimacy levels of self-disclosure.

Studies should give due recognition to three points concerning intimacy levels of activities. First, as already noted and exemplified, some activities are intrinsically more intimate than others. Second, a given reported activity may involve more or less intimacy, depending on its broader setting. To use a hackneyed example, two men may report fishing together. A fishing trip that entailed canoeing into the deep woods for a 3-day campout would be more intimate than one that entailed a short drive to a nearby lake for an hour or so of angling. Third, a given activity may involve more or less intimacy, depending on the way the partners interact and, especially, their primary reason for participating in it. Two people may play chess simply because they love the game and welcome any and all comers. However, they may be good friends who use their mutual enjoyment of chess as one of perhaps several ways of expressing their friendship. The game just wouldn't be the same with anyone else.

What would such relevant research show about the comparative communality of women's and men's friendships? Evidence suggests that women's friendships would still show higher levels of communality, but the difference would be reduced in size and observed less consistently. This impression, however, presupposes research that, like most, does not equate women's and men's friendship with respect to such things as friendship settings or situational constraints. In other words, controlling for the influence of structural variables may greatly reduce sex differences in friendship communality. But would they eliminate them completely? Given that such differences are influenced to at least some degree by sex-linked dispositional variables, probably not. However, just how large and how ubiquitous remaining differences would be is a question awaiting the outcome of relevant research.

Structural Factors in Friendship

For some time after the late 1960s, when friendship started gaining popularity as a research topic, scholars emphasized dispositional factors in the study of friendship in general as well as sex differences in friendship in particular. More recently, some scholars have begun to emphasize structural factors (e.g., Adams & Allen, 1998). A detailed examination of relevant social structures is beyond the scope of this chapter. My own efforts to articulate the direct impact of sociobehavioral environments on friendship have been sporadic and incomplete (Wright, 1982b, 1989), but even these call for more elaboration and documentation than I can render here.

In brief, my present position is this: Friendship is largely preferential and nonobligatory, that is, the least normatively regulated, role-bound, legalistic, and programmed of any important personal relationship (Paine, 1974; Suttles, 1970; Wright, 1978). Two implications follow. First, the impact of structural factors is largely permissive rather than promotive: Friendships probably will not flourish in sociobehavioral environments with strong normative restraints against free, unstructured interaction. They may or may not flourish in those without such restraints. Second, in the absence of normative constraints, friendship carries with it much less prescription and urgency than more clearly regulated personal and social relationships. Therefore, friendships are relatively easy to put on hold, and often to forego completely, in the face of expectations from more structured relationships and role obligations.

The preceding considerations suggest the usefulness of analyzing the general impact of structural factors on friendships in terms of the individual's overall pattern of roles and obligations. Some time ago, Hess (1972) provided a starting point for such an analysis. Beginning with the observation that structural factors determine the individual's total cluster of roles, she proposed that this cluster of roles, in turn, influences the number and kinds of friendships an individual can establish. At an operational level, however, one may bypass a delineation of the cluster of roles and identify the broad characteristics of a given friendship in terms of the primary type of connection that exists between that friendship and the person's other roles. Hess specified four such connections. These connections are *fusion*, *substitution, complementarity*, and *competition*. Only the connections of fusion and competition are directly relevant to this chapter.

In the fusion connection, a friendship is formed and maintained in conjunction with the performance of one or more other roles. Examples are coworker associations, mentor–protégé relationships, mutual involvement in interest groups, and the like, when interaction goes beyond formal role enactment into the voluntary and personalized relating definitive of friendship.

In competition, a friendship and other roles impose conflicting demands on the individual's time or value allegiances. For instance, a person's involvement in career development may be so intense as to limit the time and resources that she or he can devote to friendships.

Implication for Communality in Friendships in General

With the addition of two points beyond those Hess highlighted, her typology has clear implications for the development of communal friendships. The first is that the connections she identifies do not necessarily exclude one another. A friendship may, and often does, stand in both a fused and a competitive connection with an individual's other roles. Second, fused and competitive connections, either alone or in combination, between a friendship and other roles can have a strong bearing on the communal character (or its lack) of that friendship. Specifically, both fused and competitive connections often impose restraints against the development of communal friendships. There are three reasons for this.

First, fused friendships most often occur with respect to roles structured around specific time constraints, relatively well-defined tasks, and often performance standards or tangible output. Examples are involvement in work and career pursuits, political activism, clubs and lodges, civic or philanthropic associations, and religious organizations. In friendships fused with roles associated with such pursuits, the partners must divide their efforts between enacting the roles and pursuing the friendships. This, of course, constitutes a competitive connection, limiting both the time and flexibility necessary for the development of communal friendships.

Second, concerning competitive connections, the greater the number of roles one adopts and the more effort one expends on them, the less time and energy one has to devote to any friendships, including those that are fused with the roles. Therefore, busy people may (or may not) have a relatively large number of fused friendships, but it is unlikely that many of those friendships will be communal in nature.

Third, roles that are structured around time constraints and circumscribed activities often (but not always) encourage competition in its more general connotation. Thus, in friendships fused with such roles, the partners may find themselves vying for unshareable resources or outcomes such as raises, promotions, a place on the starting lineup, the political party's endorsement of candidacy, or the choice part in a dramatic production. We would normally expect this kind of competitive situation to constitute an obstacle to developing a communal friendship.

Implication for Sex Differences in Friendship Communality

The greater overall communality of women's than men's friendships may be due partly, perhaps mostly, to the total cluster of roles that impose stronger restraints against men's developing communal friendships. The issue of concern is the degree to which differences in the friendships of women and men—or, for that matter, girls and boys through childhood and adolescence—are influenced by differences in the number and kinds of activities in which they are permitted, encouraged, or pressured to participate. More specifically, do such patterns of activity relate to roles that are more conducive to the development of fused friendships for men than for women, and of freestanding friendships for women than for men? Do these roles, either in number or their degree of preemptiveness, encourage more competitive connections between friendships and other roles for men than for women? Do women's total cluster of roles entail activities that are more intrinsically socioeomotional than those of men? Or, to put it another way, do men's total cluster of roles, more often than those of women, involve competition in the general sense—that is, competition with others for unshareable resources or outcomes?

Summarizing the impact of structural variables in terms of differing types of connections may not provide a complete answer to questions of the foregoing kind, but it provides a workable place to start. Pertinent research would entail developing techniques for assessing connections between a given friendship and the individual's other roles, especially with respect to fusion and competition. Such techniques would enable investigators to augment participants' reports of the more immediate dyadic characteristics of a given friendship with data concerning an important aspect of the overall structural context of the friendship. Then researchers could easily use matching or regression procedures to examine the extent to which the sex difference in friendship communality is due to structural versus dispositional influences. Such an approach would provide valuable information about friendship, about sex differences, and about sex differences in friendship.

CONCLUSION

Some time ago (Wright, 1988), I capped a plea for moderation and caution in the way we interpret research on sex differences in friendship as follows: "Our research should move us toward valid and increasingly applicable conceptualizations of personal relationships. Let us avoid stereotypes or, worse yet, caricatures" (p. 372). Obviously, my sentiment in this regard persists. However, I no longer agree with the implication that caricatures are worse than stereotypes. *Au contraire*: People who hold and act on stereotypes are seldom aware that they do so and are insidiously affected by them. People who create and respond to caricatures are aware that they are exaggerations and generally enjoy them.

However, are the caricatures of women's and men's friendships presented at the opening of this chapter really caricatures? In light of the rest of the chapter, definitely. Are such caricatures a bad thing? Not necessarily. It is probably healthy that women and men laugh at not only one another's friendships, but at their own as well—as when comedienne Rita Rudner described her husband's response to her plea that he get in touch with his feminine side. "I tried," he said, "but she was always on the phone talking to her friend." And perhaps, as Lewis (1960) quipped, "no one ever really appreciated the other sex—just as no one really appreciates animals or children—without at times thinking them funny. For, indeed, both sexes are" (p. 111).

Granted, the goal of our research is to arrive at increasingly valid insights into sex similarities and differences in friendship, but our increased understanding is unlikely to make whatever differences exist either disappear or seem any less funny. Perhaps we should expect healthy laughter. Let us hope, however, that our increased understanding will keep us from taking our laughter too seriously.

REFERENCES

Adams, R. G., & Allen, G. (1998). Introduction: Contextualising friendship. In R. G. Adams & G. Allen (Eds.), *Placing friendship in context: Structural analysis in the social sciences* (pp. 1–14). New York: Cambridge University Press.

Auhaugen, A. E. (1991). *Freundschaft im Alltag: Untersuchung mit dem Doppeltagebuch* (Everyday friendship: Research with the Double Diary). Bern: Hans Huber.

Aukett, R., Ritchie, J., & Mill, K. (1988). Gender differences in friendship patterns. *Sex Roles, 19*, 57–66.

Bakan, D. (1966). *The duality of human existence*. Boston: Beacon.

Bank, B. J. (1995). Friendships in Australia and the United States: From feminization to a more heroic image. *Gender and Society, 9*, 79–98.

Bank, B. J., & Hansford, S. L. (2000). Gender and friendship: Why are men's best same-sex friendships less intimate and supportive? *Personal Relationships, 7*, 63–78.

Barth, R., & Kinder, B. N. (1988). A theoretical analysis of sex differences in same-sex friendships. *Sex Roles, 19*, 349–363.

Bell, R. R. (1981). *Worlds of friendship*. Beverly Hills, CA: Sage.

Booth, A. (1972). Sex and social participation. *American Sociological Review, 37*, 183–192.

Brehm, S. S., Miller, R. S., Perlman, D., & Campbell, S. M. (2002) *Intimate relationships* (3rd ed.). New York: McGraw-Hill.

Caldwell, M. A., & Peplau, L. A. (1982). Sex differences in same-sex friendships. *Sex Roles, 8*, 721–732.

Dindia, K. & Allen, M. (1992). Sex differences in self disclosure: A meta-analysis. *Psychological Bulletin, 112*, 106–124.

Dindia, K., Fitzpatrick, M. A., & Kenny, D. A. (1989, May). *Self disclosure in spouse and stranger interactions: A social relations analysis*. Paper presented at the annual convention of the International Communication Association, New Orleans, LA.

Duck, S., Rutt, D. J., Hurts, M. H., & Strejc, H. (1991). Some evident truths about everyday conversation: All communication is not created equal. *Human Communication Research, 18*, 228–267.

Duck, S., & Wright, P. H. (1993). Re-examining gender differences in friendship: A close look at two kinds of data. *Sex Roles, 28*, 709–727.

Fehr, B. (1996). *Friendship processes*. Newbury Park, CA: Sage.

Fehr, B. (2000). The life cycle of friendship. In C. Hendrick & S. S. Hendrick (Eds.), *Close relationships: A sourcebook* (pp. 70–82). Thousand Oaks, CA: Sage.

Fischer, C. S., & Oliker, S. J. (1983). A research note on friendship, gender and the life cycle. *Social Forces, 62*, 124–133.

Furman, L. G. (1987). *Cross-gender friendships in the work place: Factors and components*. Unpublished doctoral dissertation, Fielding Institute. Santa Barbara, CA.

Gouldner, H., & Strong, M. S. (1987). *Speaking of friendship: Middle-class women and their friends*. New York: Greenwood.

Hays, R. B. (1984). The development and maintenance of friendship. *Journal of Social and Personal Relationships, 1*, 75–98.

Hays, R. B. (1985). A longitudinal study of friendship development. *Journal of Personality and Social Psychology, 48*, 909–924.

Hess, B. B. (1972). Friendship. In M. W. Riley, M. Johnson, & A. Foner (Eds.), *Aging and society* (pp. 357–393). New York: Sage.

Johnson, F. L., & Aries, E. J. (1983a). The talk of women friends. *Women's Studies International Forum, 6*, 353–361.

Johnson, F. L., & Aries, E. J. (1983b). Conversational patterns among same-sex pairs of late-adolescent close friends. *Journal of Genetic Psychology, 142*, 225–238.

Lea, M. (1989). Factors underlying friendship: An analysis of the Acquaintance Description Form in relation to Wright's friendship model. *Journal of Social and Personal Relationships, 6*, 275–292.

Lewis, C. S. (1960). *The four loves*. New York: Harcourt Brace.

Markiewicz, D., Devine, I., & Kausilas, D. (2000). Friendships of women and men at work: Job satisfaction and resource implications. *Journal of Managerial Psychology, 15*, 161–184.

Monsour, M. (1992). Meanings of intimacy in same-and cross-sex friendships. *Journal of Social and Personal Relationships, 9*, 277–295.

Paine, R. (1974). An exploratory analysis in "middle-class" culture. In E. Leyton (Ed.), *The compact: Selected dimensions of friendship* (pp. 117–137). St. John's, New Found Land (NFLD): Institute for Social and Economic Growth.

Pukalos, J. (1989). Young adult relationships: Siblings and friends. *Journal of Psychology, 123*, 237–244.

Reis, H. T. (1998). Gender differences in intimacy and related behaviors: Context and process. In D. J. Canary & K. Dindia (Eds.), *Sex differences and similarities in communication* (pp. 203–231). Mahwah, NJ: Lawrence Erlbaum Associates.

Reis, H. T., Senchak, M., & Solomon, B. (1985). Sex differences in intimacy of social interaction: Further examination and potential explanations. *Journal of Personality and Social Psychology, 48*, 1204–1217.

Reis, H. T., Lin, Y. C., Bennett, E. S., & Nezlak, J. (1993). Change and consistency in social participation during early adulthood. *Developmental Psychology, 29*, 633–645.

Reisman, J. M. (1981). Adult friendships. In S. Duck & R. Gilmour (Eds.), *Personal relationships: Vol. 2. Developing personal relationships* (pp. 91–103). London: Sage.

Reisman, J. M. (1990). Intimacy in same-sex friendships. *Sex Roles, 23*, 65–82.

Sapadin, L. A. (1988). Friendship and gender: Perspectives of professional men and women. *Journal of Social and Personal Relationships, 5*, 387–403.

Sherrod, D. (1989). The influence of gender on same-sex friendships. In C. Hendrick (Ed.), *Review of personality and social psychology: Vol 10. Close relationships* (pp. 164–186). Newbury Park, CA: Sage.

Suttles, G. D. (1970). Friendship as a social institution. In G. J. McCall (Ed.), *Social relationships* (pp. 95–135). Chicago: Aldine.

Swain, S. (1989). Covert intimacy: Closeness in men's friendships. In B. J. Risman & P. Schwartz (Eds.), *Gender and intimate relationships* (pp. 71–86). Belmont, CA: Wadsworth.

Walker, K. (1994). Men, women and friendship: What they say, what they do *Gender and Society, 8*, 246–265.

Weiss, L., & Lowenthal, M. F. (1975). Life-course perspectives on friendship. In M. Thurnher & D. Chiraboga (Eds.), *Four stages of life* (pp. 48–61). San Fransico: Jossey-Bass.

Wheeler, L., & Nezlak, J. (1977). Sex differences in social participation. *Journal of Personality and Social Psychology, 35*, 742–754.

Wood, J. T. (1994). *Gendered lives: Communication, gender and culture*. Belmont, CA: Wadsworth.

Wood, J. T., & Inman, C. C. (1993). In a different mode: Masculine styles of communicating closeness. *Journal of Applied Communication Research, 21*, 279–295.

Wright, P. H. (1978). Toward a theory of friendship based on a conception of self. Human *Communication Research, 4*, 196–207.

Wright, P. H. (1982a). Men's friendships, women's friendships and the alleged inferiority of the latter. *Sex Roles, 8*, 1–20.

Wright, P. H. (1982b, February). *The development and selected applications of a conceptual and measurement model of friendship*. Paper presented at the Texas Tech University Conference on Families and Close Relationships, Lubbock, TX.

Wright, P. H. (1988). Interpreting gender differences in friendship: A case for moderation and a plea for caution. *Journal of Social and Personal Relationships, 5*, 367–373.

Wright, P. H. (1989). Gender differences in adults' same- and cross-gender friendships. In R.G. Adams & R. Blieszner (Eds.), *Older adult friendships: Structure and process* (pp. 197–221). Newbury Park, CA: Sage.

Wright, P. H. (1998). Toward and expanded orientation to the study of sex differences in friendship. In D. J. Canary & K. Dindia (Eds.), *Sex differences and similarities in communication* (pp. 41–63). Mahwah, NJ: Lawrence Erlbaum Associates.

Wright, P. H., & Scanlon, M. B. (1991). Gender role orientations and friendship: Some attenuation but gender differences abound. *Sex Roles, 24*, 551–566.

4

How Big Are Nonverbal Sex Differences? The Case of Smiling and Nonverbal Sensitivity

Judith A. Hall
Northeastern University

Any sensible perspective for judging the magnitude of research findings requires that magnitude be regarded as a relative matter.

—Eagly (1995, p. 150)

According to common stereotypes, women smile more and are more interpersonally sensitive than men (Briton & Hall, 1995). These beliefs are consistent with the popular notion that women are warm, affiliative, and attuned to others (Spence, Helmreich, & Stapp, 1975). These beliefs are also accurate in that the empirical evidence shows that women do, in fact, exceed men on both smiling and interpersonal sensitivity, where sensitivity is defined as accuracy in identifying others' states or traits on the basis of nonverbal cues such as those conveyed by the face, body, or voice tone. This conclusion is based on meta-analytic reviews that reveal quite consistent differences for both of these traits (Hall, 1978, 1984; Hall & Halberstadt, 1986; LaFrance, Hecht, & Levy Paluck, 2003; McClure, 2000).

The meta-analytic summary of sex differences has greatly advanced our understanding of overall differences in men's and women's psychology as well as variables that moderate those differences (Eagly, 1987; Eagly & Wood, 1991; Hyde & Frost, 1993; Hyde & Linn, 1986). However, although it is possible for us to express such differences precisely by using effect-size estimates such as the point-biserial correlation or Cohen's measure of effect size (Cohen's *d*; see Cohen, 1988), both of which will be explained later, the interpretation of the size of the differences remains an ambiguous, sometimes contentious, task (Eagly, 1995; Hyde & Plant, 1995). Because there is no universal standard by which to appraise magnitude, it is easy to conclude either that sex differences are substantial or that they are trivial, depending on one's theoretical preference and methodological approach. Although the present chapter cannot provide a final answer, in it I attempt to inform the debate with a more comprehensive analysis than has been undertaken thus far. I picked differences between the sexes in smiling and sensitivity to nonverbal cues as demonstration cases for this exercise.

One approach to understanding the magnitude of a sex difference is to treat the effect size in an absolute manner by calculating the proportion of variation accounted for by sex. Thus, one might determine that sex accounts for, say, 5% of the variation in some psychological variable. A related approach emphasizes the degree of overlap between the male and female distributions. When these approaches are applied to sex effects as well as nearly all effects in social-personality psychology, they tend to yield the following conclusion: The effects are trivial because so little variation is explained (or, equivalently, because there is such a great overlap between the distributions).

Although these approaches do not lack descriptive correctness, they remain mute with respect to an understanding of the practical impact of sex, and they lack a contextual perspective. Rosenthal and Rubin (1982) used their binomial effect-size display to argue that a relatively small correlation can make for an impressive difference when expressed in terms of standardized population proportions. To illustrate, one would start with a given sex difference expressed in terms of the point-biserial correlation between sex and the variable in question. The point-biserial correlation is the Pearson correlation (r) between a dichotomous variable (sex, in this case, which is given arbitrary numerical values such as 0 for men and 1 for women) and a continuous variable (let us say say frequency of smiling). A point-biserial correlation's sign (positive or negative) reveals the direction of the sex difference (for the sex coding given here a positive correlation would mean that women smiled more than men and a negative correlation would mean the reverse). The magnitude of the correlation reveals the strength of the effect on the correlation scale (-1.0 to $+1.0$), and the p value is identical to that which would result from comparing men and women by use of an ordinary independent-samples t test. In terms of the binomial effect size display of Rosenthal and Rubin, a correlation of $r = .30$ between sex and smiling would mean that, although only 9% of the variance in smiling is accounted for by sex (because squaring .30 yields .09), when smiling and sex are expressed as dichotomies with standardized (equal) overall population frequencies, this correlation translates into a rate of smiling of 65% among women but only 35% among men. Expressed in this manner, the modest correlation invites new attention.

Although an awareness of the limits of the variance-accounted-for approach can help prevent the trivialization of sex differences (Eagly, 1995), a comparative approach is still needed. It is hard to know what to make of this or any effect in isolation. I will consider two comparative questions in detail. First, how do the nonverbal sex differences compare with other sex differences in psychology? Second, how do the nonverbal sex differences compare with other correlates of the same nonverbal behaviors? These two questions pose the comparative question in orthogonal directions and allow a good triangulation regarding the "how big?" question.

To set the stage for these comparisons, it is very helpful to consider the size of experimental and other (not just sex-difference) effects in social-personality psychology in general. It appears that most effects in social-personality psychology, many of which have been subjected to meta-analytic summary, are in the small to medium range according to Cohen's (1988) conventions, being roughly $r = .20$–$.30$ (Eagly, 1995), accounting for 4% to 9% of the variance. Expressed in terms of units of standard deviation (Cohen's measure of effect size, d, defined as the difference between male and female means divided by the pooled within-groups standard deviation), a difference like this would correspond to $d = 0.40$–0.60. According to Cohen, this is an expected upper limit to obtainable effects, given the poor control of extraneous variation typical of studies in social-personality psychology. (Cohen's d and the point-biserial r are reexpressions of each other, such that for values of r below .24, $d = 2r$. For values of r greater than this, d has an accelerated function in relation to r such that the larger the r, the even larger the d. This means that d "stretches out" the scale for higher values of r; see Cohen.)

Two major reviews of research have provided quantitative evidence on the question of how big typical effects are in social-personality psychology. Richard, Bond, and Stokes-Zoota (2003) summarized over 450 meta-analyses of social psychological phenomena, a research base encompassing more than 25,000 studies and 8 million people. The overall average effect size was $r = .21$, and the range of average effect sizes over 18 topic areas ranged from $r = .13$ to $r = .32$. Lipsey and Wilson (1993) performed a similar, nonoverlapping summary of the efficacy of psychological, educational, and behavioral treatments across 302 meta-analyses. The overall effect size was $r = .24$, a figure remarkably like that of Richard et al. Both results fit with the theoretical range of effects proposed by Cohen (1988).

Thus, speaking very broadly, we can say that effects in social-personality psychology (both basic and applied) are of small to medium magnitude according to Cohen's guidelines and account for about 5% of variation in the many phenomena investigated. Against this backdrop, we now turn to the two comparative questions identified earlier.

How does one sex difference compare with other sex differences? Here the "how big" question is focused on comparisons among sex differences. To answer this question with respect to sex differences in nonverbal communication, Hall (1984) compared nonverbal sex differences with sex differences for other psychological variables for which meta-analytic summaries were available. Hall concluded that "although nonverbal sex differences are not large in absolute magnitude, they are as large or larger than those found for most of the psychological variables that have been summarized so far" (p. 148). At the time Hall reached this conclusion, not many other sex differences had been summarized meta-analytically, which could limit the accuracy of the conclusion. Currently, the situation is very different because many more meta-analyses of sex differences exist. Later in this chapter, sex differences for smiling and nonverbal sensitivity will be compared with sex differences for a much longer list of traits and behaviors (cf. Hyde & Frost, 1993).

How does the magnitude of a particular sex difference compare with the magnitudes of other correlates of that same trait or behavior? To my knowledge, this comparative question has not been asked with respect to any sex differences. Therefore, my final major goal in this chapter is to compare the magnitude of sex differences in smiling and nonverbal sensitivity with the magnitude of *other* correlates of smiling and nonverbal sensitivity. Thus, this approach examines the same psychological variables that are at issue in the sex difference evaluations.

SEX DIFFERENCES IN SMILING AND NONVERBAL SENSITIVITY

Smiling

For children, Hall (1984) found no overall effect in the meta-analytic summary. For adults smiling in social interaction, Hall concluded that, in the 15 studies for which the effect size could be calculated, the average point-biserial correlation between sex (0 = male, 1 = female) and amount of smiling was $r = .30$ (Table 4.1). Over 90% of the studies showed more female than male smiling, and over 50% found this difference to be statistically significant. If one adds 8 studies for which the effect size could not be calculated, entering the estimated effect as $r = 0$, the average effect was $r = .20$. Thus, the real value is somewhere between .20 and .30. Hall (1984) and Hall and Halberstadt (1986) also found that the

TABLE 4.1
Sex Differences in Smiling and Nonverbal Sensitivity (Meta-Analyses)

Behavior and Source	*No. of Studies*	*Mean (or Median) r*
Smiling		
Hall (1984)	15	.30
LaFrance et al. (2003)	418	.20
Nonverbal sensitivity		
Rosenthal et al. (1979)	133	.20
Hall (1978)	46	.20
Hall (1984)	18	.25
McClure (2000)	60	.09

smiling difference was greatly reduced in less social situations (e.g., when people were observed alone or passing on the street).

LaFrance, Hecht, and Levy Paluck (2003) performed a much larger meta-analysis of sex differences in smiling. They found an overall effect of $r = .20$ (Table 4.1), and, like Hall (1984), found that age was a moderator of the effect. LaFrance et al. found the largest effect among teenagers ($r = .27$), with a progressive decline in magnitude as the age of the individuals in the samples increased. In fact, the overall age effect appears to be curvilinear, with a peak in adolescence and a decline at both younger and older ages. LaFrance et al. also found a variety of situational moderators.

Nonverbal Sensitivity

By the term *nonverbal sensitivity*, I refer to people's ability to infer the meanings of nondeceptive nonverbal cues conveyed in the face, body, and vocal channels. In one extensive analysis, Rosenthal, Hall, DiMatteo, Rogers, and Archer (1979) compared male and female scores on the Profile of Nonverbal Sensitivity (PONS), a well validated, standardized test of accuracy in judging nonverbal affective cues that consists of two hundred and twenty 2-s clips of silent video, content-masked speech, or combined video and content-masked speech of a young woman enacting 20 different interpersonal scenarios (for validity data, see Rosenthal et al.). For 133 samples of participants from third grade through adulthood, tested mostly in the United States but also in numerous countries around the world, Rosenthal et al. analyzed sex differences. Female participants scored higher 80% of the time and the median effect size (point-biserial correlation) was $r = .20$ (see Table 4.1), a figure close to the correlation of $r = .23$ found in a large normative sample of U.S. high school students tested with the PONS. Analyses demonstrated no Age × Sex interaction, meaning that, across the ages tested, the sex difference had approximately the same magnitude.

Because the PONS test measures accuracy in judging just one stimulus person, it was important to ascertain whether other instruments showed similar effects. More extensive meta-analytic summaries of the published literature on sex differences in nonverbal sensitivity were therefore conducted and published by Hall (1978, 1984). In these summaries, care was taken to include only a small number of studies based on the PONS so that a nonredundant analysis could be made. The nonverbal sensitivity tests included in Hall (1978, 1984) were conceptually similar to the PONS: They used drawings, photographs, silent video, or content-masked speech (or combinations thereof) in testing the accuracy of people's inferences about (mainly affective) nonverbal cues.[1] For 46 studies located up through 1978 with known effect sizes, the average point-biserial correlation was $r = .20$; for an

[1]The test developed by Costanzo and Archer (Interpersonal Perception Task, 1989) includes both verbal and nonverbal cues. However, because the verbal cues are intentionally ambiguous, test takers must rely primarily on nonverbal information in answering test items.

additional 18 studies with known effect sizes published between 1978 and 1984, the average correlation was $r = .25$ (Table 4.1). Again, there was no Age × Sex interaction. When one adds in studies with unknown effect sizes in both of these reviews (estimating the unknown effects each to be $r = 0$), the average effects were $r = .12$ (75 studies) and $r = .09$ (50 studies), respectively. When the overall trend favors one group, of course it is probably overly conservative to estimate the unknown effects to average zero in magnitude. For the analysis of the 133 samples of participants that took the PONS test, there were no unknown effects and the overall effect was $r = .20$.

McClure (2000) performed a meta-analysis of sex differences in affect recognition of facial expressions, measured in 60 studies of children ages 2 to 17 years (Table 4.1). Although the overall effect size was smaller for this age range than that in Hall's earlier meta-analyses (which did not include many studies of children), McClure did not find that age was a moderator. Thus, McClure's review found smaller average effects than did Hall's reviews, but among McClure's studies, age did not make a difference.

Although the overall sex difference is clearly evident and statistically significant in all of the reviews, there are qualifications to the tendency of women to judge nonverbal cues more accurately than men. First, among adults, the female advantage is most evident when participants judge the face as opposed to other nonverbal channels (Rosenthal & DePaulo, 1979a). Second, among adults, the female advantage decreases when discrepant, very brief, or deceptive cues are being judged (Rosenthal & DePaulo, 1979b; Zuckerman, DePaulo, & Rosenthal, 1981). Third, a task developed by Ickes (2001) that measures "empathic accuracy," defined as a person's accuracy at identifying the thoughts and feelings of a target person, sometimes shows an adult female advantage but often shows no difference (Ickes, Gesn, & Graham, 2000). Ickes et al. proposed that the sex difference is present only when perceivers are asked to evaluate their own performance on each test item. However, Thomas and Fletcher (2003) found significant sex differences on this task even without that instruction. The empathic accuracy paradigm is different in several respects from standard nonverbal cue-decoding measures; most notably, it draws much more on verbal cues than nonverbal cues (Gesn & Ickes, 1999). Future research will have to investigate further whether, and when, sex differences appear on instruments of that type.

OTHER SEX DIFFERENCES

As I explained earlier, one way to appraise the magnitude of sex differences in smiling and nonverbal sensitivity is to compare them with sex differences that have been documented for other psychological variables. Richard et al. (2003) gave insight into this question by isolating 83 meta-analyses of sex differences from their larger collection of studies on social-personality topics. For these studies the average effect size was $r = .12$, a figure smaller than that found for smiling and sensitivity.

Table 4.2 presents a list that I assembled of psychological (not just social-personality) sex differences. All of the sources are meta-analytical reviews. For convenience, I group studies into the domains of nonverbal communication, cognition, personality, small-group or organizational behavior and attitudes, and other social behaviors and attitudes. The appendix provides information on inclusion criteria and other methodological decisions.

A comparison of Tables 4.1 and 4.2 allows us to ask how the sex differences for smiling and nonverbal sensitivity compare with other sex differences. The absolute values of the correlations (r) within each category are used as the indicator of magnitude (the absolute value is used because directionality of effects is not an issue here). Table 4.2 reveals that sex had a median absolute r of .32 with other nonverbal communication variables, which is somewhat larger than the smiling and nonverbal sensitivity differences.

Sex differences in the cognitive domain were smaller (Table 4.2). For ability or achievement (the first five entries in the cognitive domain), the median absolute $r = .17$; for attitudes about academic performance (the remaining entries), the median absolute $r = .12$. For personality, the differences were smaller still (Table 4.2), with median absolute $r = .08$. However, the range was much greater than in the cognitive domain; the effects for assertiveness, masculinity, femininity, and tendermindedness were the largest. Interestingly, the first three of these variables, like smiling and nonverbal sensitivity, all imply interpersonal communication style.

Behavior and attitudes in small groups and organizations (Table 4.2) had median absolute $r = .10$; only two effects (task and socioemotional contributions in groups) had appreciably larger magnitudes. These two variables reflect communication style, like a number of the other variables showing larger sex differences. Other social behaviors and attitudes, admittedly a heterogeneous collection, had median absolute $r = .14$.

The median effect across all the variables in Table 4.2 is $r = .11$, which is, not surprisingly, nearly identical to that of the Richard et al. (2003) review of sex differences, considering that many studies were included in both reviews. On balance, then, we can reach the broad conclusion that sex differences in smiling and nonverbal sensitivity, like sex differences for other nonverbal communication variables, exceed most of the sex differences found in other domains of psychology. This is consistent with my earlier conclusion (Hall, 1984).

CORRELATES OF SMILING AND NONVERBAL SENSITIVITY

The next approach to assessing the magnitude of the smiling and nonverbal sex differences is addressed in Tables 4.3 and 4.4, which present correlations of smiling and nonverbal sensitivity, respectively, with other psychological variables besides sex. This represents the final comparative approach described earlier. The tables include only adolescent and adult Western, nonclinical samples. The table

TABLE 4.2
Other Sex Differences (Meta-Analyses)

Source	*Behavior*	*No. of Studies*	*Mean r*
Nonverbal communication			
Hall (1984)	Face-recognition skill	12	.17
	Expression accuracy[a]	20	.31
	Expression accuracy[a]	15	.18
	Facial expressiveness	5	.45
	Gazing	30	.32
	Distance of approach to others	17	−.27
	Restlessness of body	6	−.34
	Expansive movements	6	−.46
	Nods or forward lean	7	.16
	Gestural expressiveness	7	.28
	Self-touching	5	.22
	Speech errors	6	−.33
	Filled pauses	6	−.51
Cognitive domain			
Hyde, Fennema, & Lamon (1990)	Math performance	143	−.17
Voyer et al. (1995)	Spatial ability	212	−.20
Fleming & Malone (1983)	Science achievement	17	−.08
Hyde & Linn (1988)	Verbal ability	17	.06
Hyde (1981)	Field independence	14	−.24
Hyde, Fennema, Ryan, et al. (1990)	Math confidence	26	−.12
	Math anxiety	43	.08
Fleming & Malone (1983)	Positive science attitudes	15	−.06
Rosen & Maguire (1990)	Computerphobia	19	.15
Hembree (1988)	Test anxiety	39	.14
Personality			
Cohn (1991)	Ego development	63	.16
Thoma (1986)	Moral judgment	53	.10
Hattie (1979)	Self-actualization	6	.08
Feingold (1994)	Self-esteem	39	−.07
Hall (1984)	Self-esteem	10	−.06
Feingold (1994)	Internal locus of control	20	−.03
Hall (1984)	Internal locus of control	16.	−.12
Feingold (1994)	Anxiety	24	.10
Hall (1984)	Anxiety	14	.16
Feingold (1994)	Anxiety	25	.14
	Assertiveness	25	−.24
	Assertiveness	22	−.09
Hall (1984)	Social poise, dominance, assertiveness	14	−.06
Feingold (1994)	Gregariousness	22	.08
Hall (1984)	Extraversion	17	.02
	Fear of success	11	.03
	Achievement motivation/values	13	−.05
	Masculinity	12	−.25
	Femininity	12	.37

TABLE 4.2
(Continued)

Source	*Behavior*	*No. of Studies*	*Mean r*
	Loneliness	6	−.08
	Depression	5	.08
	Neuroticism	14	.16
	Psychoticism	8	−.14
Feingold (1994)	Impulsiveness	14	−.03
	Activity	13	−.04
	Openness to ideas	12	−.02
	Trustingness	11	.12
	Tendermindedness	18	.44
	Conscientiousness	7	.06
Rosenthal & DePaulo (1979a)	Self-monitoring	10	−.11
Behavior in small groups or organizations		76	.01
Eagly et al. (1995)	Leader effectiveness		
Eagly & Karau (1991)	Emergence as a task leader	34	−.20
	Emergence as a social leader	15	.09
	Interpersonal leadership style	136	.02
	Task leadership style	139	.00
Wood (1987)	Performance in groups	19	−.19
Eagly et al. (1994)	Motivation to manage	51	−.11
Dobbins & Platz (1986)	Leadership style:		
	Initiating structure	8	.02
	Initiating consideration	8	.02
Eagly & Carli (1981)	Persuasibility	33	.08
	Conformity under group pressure	46	.16
	Conformity in other situations	11	.14
Carli (1982)	Socioemotional contributions in small groups	9	.28
	Task contribution in small groups	10	−.28
	Divides rewards equally	17	.05
	Divides rewards equitably	10	−.10
	Takes smaller rewards for self	11	.14
	Behaves cooperatively in mixed-motive games	47	−.04
Other social behaviors or attitudes	Helping behavior	99	−.17
Eagly & Crowley (1986)			
Eagly & Steffen (1986)	Aggression	50	−.15
Dindia & Allen (1992)	Self-disclosure	205	.09
Hall (1984)	Liberal sex-role attitudes	6	.25
	Liking/emotional closeness with others	10	.22
Warr (1971)	Attributing positive traits to people	6	.21
Lirgg (1991)	Self-confidence in physical activities	27	−.23
Wood et al. (1989)	Subjective well-being	18	.02
Martocchio & O'Leary (1989)	Occupational stress	19	−.01

(Continued)

TABLE 4.2
(Continued)

Source	*Behavior*	*No. of Studies*	*Mean r*
Oliver & Hyde (1993)[b]	Positive attitudes toward:		
	Premarital sexual intercourse	46	−.18
	Sexual permissiveness	39	−.27
	Amount of intercourse experience	28	−.06
	Younger age at first intercourse	135	−.16
	Masturbation frequency	26	−.43
Whitley & Kite (1995)		91	.13
Frieze et al. (1982)	Attributes successful performance to:		
	Ability	13	−.10
	Effort	9	.06
	Task	9	.00
	Luck	12	.14
	Attributes unsuccessful performance to:		
	Ability	12	−.11
	Effort	9	−.11
	Task	8	−.01
	Luck	12	.18
Hall & Dornan (1990)	Satisfaction with medical care	19	−.01
Feingold (1992)	Valuing the following in a mate:		
	High socioeconomic status	15	.33
	Ambition	10	.32
	Character	13	.17
	Intelligence	15	.15
	Humor	7	.07
	Personality	5	.04
Zuckerman et al. (1981)	Ability to deceive	9	−.02
	Ability to detect deception	14	.08

Note: All variables are scaled so that the named behavior describes the high end of the scale. Effect sizes are the point-biserial correlation (*r*) coded so that higher values signify higher scores for women.

[a] Includes studies of children.

[b] Because Oliver and Hyde (1993) presented many variables, only those that were measured in 25 or more studies are included here.

for smiling excludes physiological measures and electromyographic studies (i.e., studies of electrical activity in the facial muscles). The table for sensitivity excludes physiological variables, comparisons across cultures, and correlations with other nonverbal sensitivity tests.

I located the results in the tables through PsycLIT searches and bibliographic searches of textbooks and articles. Although I made a sincere effort to locate results, there are undoubtedly many studies reporting correlates of smiling and nonverbal sensitivity that I did not retrieve, and for that reason these tables do not purport to represent all published correlates of smiling and nonverbal sensitivity. Moreover, for a small number of studies that reported numerous results, only a subset of the results are displayed in the present tables. My purpose is not to present

TABLE 4.3
Correlates of Smiling

Source	*Correlate*	*r*
Cognitive domain		
Mehrabian & Williams (1969)	Vocabulary	−.18
Personality		
Frances (1979)	Sociability	.51
	Wants inclusion	.43
	Affiliation	.39
	Nurturance	.34
	Deference	.37
	Abasement	.34
	Toughmindedness	−.39
LaFrance & Carmen (1980)	Femininity	.47
Rosenfeld (1966a)	Need for social approval	.29
Ruch (1994)	Extraversion	.40
Interpersonal behavior		
D'Augelli (1974)	Nodding	.20
	Interpersonal skill	.22
	Warmth	.18
Fairbanks et al. (1982)	When talking to a more mentally ill patient	−.29
Halberstadt et al. (1988)	Talking on happy topic (vs. sad)	.52
	While talking (vs. listening)	.25
Hill et al. (1981)	Counselor's empathy or positive regard	.31
	Satisfaction of one's counselees	.13
Kraut & Johnston (1979)	Friend as target (vs. bowling pins)	.50
	Greeting–conversing (vs. not)	.55
Lee et al. (1980)	Nonverbal sensitivity	−.20
Lee & Hallberg (1982)	Better counseling skill	.10
McAdams et al. (1984)	Speaking time	−.10
	Laughing	.56
	Eye contact	.49
	Intimacy motivation	.30
Mehrabian (1971)	Verbal facilitators	.32
	Positive verbal messages	.38
	Hand–arm gestures	.30
	Positive voice tone	.33
Rosenfeld (1966a)	When seeking approval	.40
	Nodding (2)	.46
	Self-touching	−.56
	Posture shifts	−.22
	Gesticulating	.58
Rosenfeld (1966b)	When seeking approval	.32
	Self-touching	−.53
	Positive evaluation by other	.15
Zuckerman & Driver (1985)	Act of deception (19)	−.04
Chaikin et al. (1974)	Positive expectancies for pupils	.75
Coutts & Schneider (1976)	Friend as target (vs. stranger)	.32
	While gazing	.43

(Continued)

TABLE 4.3
(Continued)

Source	*Correlate*	*r*
Cupchik & Leventhal (1974)	Effect of canned laughter	.31
	Effect of canned laughter	.32
Other		
Cupchik & Leventhal (1974)	Subjects' own ratings of cartoon funniness	.50
	Objective ratings of cartoon funniness	.80
Kraut & Johnston (1979)	Better weather	.12
Hall & Horgan (2003)	Self-reported happy affect (19)	.20
Hall et al. (in press)	Status or dominance (22)	−.03
Deutsch (1990)	Perception of control	−.39
	Feelings of dominance	−.26

Note: If the result is based on more than one sample or study, the number of summarized results is given in parentheses and the value in the correlation column is the mean over those results.

an exhaustive compilation of correlates of these nonverbal variables, but rather to present a reasonably representative and extensive array of results that can provide a basis for comparison with their respective sex differences shown in Table 4.1. Although Tables 4.3 and 4.4 were not limited to meta-analytic summaries as Tables 4.1 and 4.2 were, inspection reveals that a substantial number of the findings in Table 4.4 are based on multiple results. This is especially the case for findings based on the PONS test (Rosenthal et al., 1979).

Other Correlates of Smiling

Studies in Table 4.3, showing correlations of smiling with other variables, are grouped into the categories of cognition, personality, interpersonal behavior, and other. The one study in the cognitive domain showed a correlation of $r = -.18$. Studies of personality had median absolute $r = .39$, and studies of social interaction had median absolute $r = .32$. The "other" category of correlates had median absolute $r = .26$. Over all of the results in the table, the median correlation was $r = .32$ (52 results). Thus, smiling shows many substantial correlations with other psychological and situational variables. These relations tend to be somewhat larger than the sex difference in smiling.

Other Correlates of Nonverbal Sensitivity

Table 4.4 presents correlates of sensitivity to nonverbal cues, with the correlates divided into the categories of cognition, personality, interpersonal behavior, ratings by acquaintances, and other. In the cognitive domain, the median absolute $r = .16$. Within this category, all the correlations for cognitive abilities were closely grouped around this value, but two correlations were larger: for cognitive complexity (a measure of cognitive style, not ability) and for amount learned during a teaching session. Because the latter involved face-to-face communication, it carries

TABLE 4.4
Correlates of Nonverbal Sensitivity

Source	*Correlate*	*r*
Cognitive domain		
Barnes & Sternberg (1989)	Mental ability	.19
	School performance	.15
Bernieri (1991)	Amount learned from teacher	.51
Rosenthal et al. (1979)	IQ (6)	.15
	Scholastic Aptitude Test (6)	.15
	Field independence (3)	.16
	Greater cognitive complexity (2)	.28
Personality		
Funder & Harris (1986)	Empathy	.21
Barnes & Sternberg (1989)	Empathy	.18
	Self-monitoring	.14
	Social competence	.24
Costanzo & Archer (1989)	Machiavellianism	.17
	Self-monitoring	.25
DiMatteo (1979)	Self-monitoring	.07
Hall (1979)	Empathy (10)	.01
Hall et al. (1997)	Dominance (11)	.14
	Capacity for status (11)	.15
Rosenthal et al. (1979)	California Psychological Inventory:	
	Sociability (5)	.10
	Social presence (5)	.26
	Self-acceptance (5)	.31
	Well-being (5)	.24
	Responsibility (5)	.18
	Socialization (5)	.30
	Self-control (5)	.01
	Tolerance (5)	.26
	Communality (5)	.50
	Achievement by means of conformance (5)	.27
	Achievement by means of independence (5)	.31
	Intellectual efficiency (5)	.32
	Psychological mindedness	.23
	Flexibility (5)	.31
	Femininity (5)	.13
	Personality Research Form:	
	Impulsivity (3)	−.03
	Change (2)	−.02
	Harm avoidance (3)	−.07
	Order (3)	.11
	Cognitive structure (2)	.12
	Achievement (3)	.07
	Endurance (3)	.05
	Play (3)	.09
	Succorance (2)	.00
	Autonomy (3)	−.10
	Understanding (3)	−.02

(Continued)

TABLE 4.4
(Continued)

Source	*Correlate*	*r*
	Sentience (2)	−.19
	Dominance (3)	−.05
	Abasement (2)	−.16
	Affiliation (3)	.08
	Nurturance (3)	.18
	Exhibition (3)	−.07
	Social recognition (3)	.04
	Aggression (3)	−.08
	Defendence (2)	−.14
	Dogmatism (2)	−.20
	Need for social approval	.00
	Machiavellianism (4)	−.08
	Values	
	Theoretical	−.29
	Economic	−.20
	Aesthetic	−.02
	Social	.22
	Political	−.17
	Religious	.35
	Extraversion (3)	−.02
	Self-monitoring (6)	−.08
Sabatelli et al. (1983)	Internal locus of control	−.04
	Interpersonal trust	.26
Schroeder (1995)	Shyness	−.33
	Sociability	.27
	Public self-consciousness	.39
	Private self-consciousness	.01
	Social anxiety	−.23
	Self-monitoring	−.03
Simon et al. (1990)	Masculinity	.14
	Machiavellianism	−.23
Hodgins & Koestner (1993)	Mother's ratings of easy childhood temperament	.32
Interpersonal behavior		
Lee & Hallberg (1982)	Better counseling skill	−.03
Lee et al. (1980)	Smiling	−.20
Rosenthal et al. (1979)	Eye contact	.31
Littlepage et al. (1983)	Skill in detecting deception	.16
Firth et al. (1986)	Ability to judge others' social competence	.27
Fingeret et al. (1985)	Behavioral anxiety	−.52
	Skill in role playing	.54
Cooper & Hazelrigg (1988)	Greater susceptibility to experimenter expectancy effect (10)	.11
Hazelrigg et al. (1991)	Greater susceptibility to experimenter expectancy effect	.12
Rosenthal et al. (1979)	Teacher's observed encouragingness to pupils (2)	.76

(Continued)

TABLE 4.4
(Continued)

Source	*Correlate*	*r*
Acquaintance ratings		
Costanzo & Archer (1989)	Other-rated sensitivity	.48
Funder & Harris (1986)	Other-rated hostility	−.35
	Other-rated manipulativeness	−.32
	Other-rated assertiveness	−.27
	Other-rated seeks reassurance from others	.50
	Other-rated warmth	.35
	Other-rated perfectionism	.29
	Other-rated dependability	.29
Rosenthal et al. (1979)	Other-rated clinical skill (13)	.21
	Other-rated quality as a foreign service officer	.30
	Other-rated nonverbal sensitivity (22)	.16
	Other-rated popularity (2)	.20
DiMatteo (1979)	Satisfaction of one's patients (2)	.14
Other		
Hall et al. (1997)	Higher socioeconomic status (17)	.15
Blanck et al. (1980)	Sibling's nonverbal sensitivity	.09
Buller & Aune (1988)	Liking for fast speech	.18
Keeley-Dyreson et al. (1991)	Experimenter-induced stress while taking decoding test	−.08
Rosenthal et al. (1979)	Age (third grade through adulthood; 124)	.34
	Better interpersonal judgment (paper and pencil)	.26
	Self-rated interpersonal success (3)	.06
	Self-rated nonverbal sensitivity	.08
	Task orientation as a leader	.21
	Democratic attitudes as a teacher (2)	.24
Smith et al. (1991)	Self-rated accuracy on decoding test	.08
Zuckerman & Larrance (1979)	Self-rated nonverbal sensitivity	.13
	Spouse's nonverbal sensitivity	.14
	Advantage of decoding familiar other	.40
	Better school adjustment in one's child	.25

Note: If the result is based on more than one sample or study, the number of summarized results is given in parentheses and the value in the correlation column is the mean over those results.

a flavor of social interaction that might justify placing it in the social interaction category rather than the cognitive one.[2] For the personality variables in Table 4.4, there was a median absolute $r = .15$ with nonverbal sensitivity, but this was associated with a wide range of correlations. Interpersonal behavior and acquaintance ratings were both larger, with median absolute $r = .24$ and median absolute $r = .29$,

[2]When the cognitive ability variables are considered, the distinction between convergent and discriminant validity becomes relevant. Whereas most, and possibly all, of the other variables in Tables 4.3 and 4.4 are ones for which the original investigators likely expected nonzero correlations with the nonverbal variables, the cognitive variables are different. Rosenthal et al. (1979) clearly treated cognitive ability in the context of discriminant validity, meaning specifically that no, or at least negligible, correlations with nonverbal sensitivity were predicted.

respectively. Finally, the "other" category of correlates had median absolute $r =$ .15. Over all results in the table, the median absolute $r = .18$ (112 results).

Thus, it appears that the effect size for the sex difference in nonverbal sensitivity (for adults, which is comparable with the studies in the present comparison) falls within the range of other correlates of nonverbal sensitivity—being somewhat smaller than the two interpersonal categories but larger than the cognitive, personality, and "other" categories.

DISCUSSION

On the basis of this comparison among effect sizes, I find it justified to conclude that sex differences for smiling and nonverbal sensitivity are not trivial. I base this conclusion on three kinds of evidence. First, sex differences for smiling and nonverbal sensitivity, as well as for several other nonverbal variables, are larger than many other social psychological effects. Second, the nonverbal sex differences are larger than most other psychological sex differences. Of course, I cannot reach a conclusion about psychological sex differences that have not been measured or included in these summaries. I can only say that, provisionally, sex differences in the nonverbal domain appear to be larger than sex differences for many other attitudes, behaviors, abilities, and traits, and they are comparable in magnitude with a number of others.

The third line of evidence supporting the conclusion that the smiling and nonverbal sensitivity sex differences are relatively large is based on comparisons between these effects, on the one hand, and correlations of smiling and nonverbal sensitivity with other psychosocial variables, on the other. This comparison yielded more mixed results, in that the sex difference for smiling is somewhat smaller than the average relations of other variables besides sex with smiling, whereas the sex difference for nonverbal sensitivity is of comparable magnitude with other correlates of nonverbal sensitivity, although these are clearly generalizations because the range was very wide. These findings indicate that, although sex does not account for a large amount of variation in smiling and nonverbal sensitivity, its predictive validity is not dramatically different from that of many other personal and situational variables. This greatly bolsters confidence that the nonverbal sex effects are worth discussion.

Of course, documenting a sex difference is much easier than explaining it. For neither smiling nor nonverbal sensitivity is there consensus on the roots of the sex differences. There is similarly no consensus for any of the other nonverbal communication variables described here, nor for any other psychological variables, for that matter (Eagly, 1987, 1995; Hall, 1984; Hall, Carter, & Horgan, 2000; Hall & Halberstadt, 1994; Hall, Halberstadt, & O'Brien, 1997; LaFrance et al., 2003; LaFrance & Henley, 1994; Noller, 1986). Many psychological sex differences are clearly associated with sex stereotypes (Briton & Hall, 1995; Hall & Carter, 1999;

Swim, 1994), but this may be as much a reflection of the observable nature of the actual differences as an explanation for their existence.

In an effort to understand possible sources of the gender differences discussed in this chapter, students at Northeastern University were asked to rate the traits and behaviors shown in Tables 4.1 and 4.2 on their centrality to their own gender identity (Hall & Carter, 1996). There was a high degree of within-sex consensus on how central the traits and behaviors were, and the male and female centrality ratings were positively, but not strongly, correlated with each other. This means that men and women did not regard the traits and behaviors as equally relevant to their gender self-concepts. When the averaged centrality ratings were correlated, within sex, with the actual sex differences from Table 4.2, it was found that, for men, the more they said the traits and behaviors were central to their gender identity, the more the actual sex difference favored men. Similarly, the more the women said the traits and behaviors were central, the more the actual sex differences favored women. The correlation between the differences between men's and women's centrality ratings and the actual sex differences was $r = .68$ ($p < .0001$), indicating that sex differences parallel, to an impressive degree, people's assessments of how important those behaviors are to their gender identity. For this sample, only the traits of liking–emotional closeness to others, femininity, masculinity, and liberal sex-role attitudes showed bigger male–female differences in centrality than did smiling. This suggests that smiling is indeed very important to men's and women's basic conceptions of themselves, and it may provide some insight into the relative strength of this sex difference.

Of course, such findings could merely signify that people are aware of both the sex stereotypes and the actual differences (see, e.g., Briton & Hall, 1995; Swim, 1994; Zuckerman & Larrance, 1979), and that they structure their own gender role values to conform to these stereotypical and actual differences. If this is the case, the gender-role centrality ratings may again be more a consequence than a cause of the sex differences. Because of the power of expectations to shape behavior, any such beliefs and expectations could in turn shape men's and women's actual behavior (Eccles, Jacobs, & Harold, 1990; Hall & Briton, 1993).

Moving beyond smiling and nonverbal sensitivity in particular, the present chapter reveals that the entire nonverbal domain stands out in terms of the size of sex differences. It may be that, developmentally, as sex-role identity is shaped and maintained, the interpersonal realm is much more important to this process than is the more intrapsychic realm (which would include cognitive skills and attitudes, and many personality traits). Consistent with this speculation, some of the larger sex effects reviewed here were for behaviors that strongly implied social communication style even if they were not specifically nonverbal. In the quest for sex-role identity, feedback about acceptance and rejection by others is much more likely to shape behavior and self-concept than are the more intrapsychic processes. Thus, face-to-face interactions in which one can display one's sex identification and receive reactions from others may be crucial for sex-role development. In this light, it would not be surprising if the development of a sex-consistent repertoire of interpersonal behaviors holds high priority for individuals and is related to the development of rather pronounced between-sex differences in this domain. This idea is reminiscent of Birdwhistell's (1970) conceptualization of male–female differences in nonverbal communication as tertiary sexual characteristics—sexual characteristics that are learned and social-behavioral in form, unlike primary and secondary sexual characteristics (e.g., breast budding). Such tertiary sexual characteristics would likely be crucial for mating, division of labor, and maintenance of gender roles in general.

ACKNOWLEDGMENTS

Preparation of this chapter was supported by the National Science Foundation under Grant SBR-9311544. The comments of Amy Halberstadt on this chapter are greatly appreciated.

APPENDIX: INCLUSION CRITERIA FOR STUDIES SHOWN IN TABLE 4.2

The table includes (a) the meta-analyses to which Hall (1984) compared nonverbal sex differences, which are identifiable by their dates (prior to 1984); (b) personality differences collected from four journals over a 9-year period by Hall (1984), referred to in the table as Hall (1984); (c) meta-analyses located by PsycLIT searches, using the terms *gender and meta-analysis*. and *sex and meta-analysis* (for the years 1974–1997); and (d) other meta-analyses in my files. Any psychological variable (observed behavior, attitude, or self-reported trait) is included, but not physiological or motor variables or IQ. Results were expressed as the point-biserial correlation (r) or in a form that was easily transformed into that metric (e.g., a standardized two-group comparison such as Cohen's d or means and standard deviations; Rosenthal, 1991). Mean effect sizes reported are based on summaries of known effect sizes wherever possible (i.e., summaries that included unknown effect sizes as having an effect size of $r = 0$ were avoided). Mean effect sizes were based on at least five studies. When possible, the mean effect size weighted by sample size is reported. Only sex main effects are included, and typically only the main result of a meta-analysis (i.e., secondary results and moderated effects are not always included). A meta-analysis is not included if it was substantially superseded by a later meta-analysis of the same behavior. Meta-analyses of the same behavior shown in the table are based on nonoverlapping groups of studies. Results for adolescents and adults only are included; to achieve this end, mean effect sizes were recalculated from data supplied in a meta-analysis when necessary. Samples were nonclinical and were from Western countries (except for the second entry, which included some non-Western groups). Finally, the book or journal containing the meta-analysis had to be available in my university library or in my own possession.

REFERENCES

Barnes, M. L., & Sternberg, R. J. (1989). Social intelligence and decoding of nonverbal cues. *Intelligence, 13,* 263–287.

Bernieri, F. J. (1991). Interpersonal sensitivity in teaching interactions. *Personality and Social Psychology Bulletin, 17,* 98–103.

Birdwhistell, R. L. (1970). *Kinesics and context.* Philadelphia: University of Pennsylvania Press.

Blanck, P. D., Zuckerman, M., DePaulo, B. M., & Rosenthal, R. (1980). Sibling resemblances in nonverbal skill and style. *Journal of Nonverbal Behavior, 4,* 219–226.

Briton, N. J., & Hall, J. A. (1995). Beliefs about female and male nonverbal communication. *Sex Roles, 32,* 79–90.

Buller, D. B., & Aune, R. K. (1988). The effects of vocalics and nonverbal sensitivity on compliance: A speech accommodation theory explanation. *Human Communication Research, 14,* 301–332.

Carli, L. L. (1982). *Are women more social and men more task oriented? A meta-analytic review of sex differences in group interaction, reward allocation, coalition formation, and cooperation in the Prisoner's Dilemma Game.* Unpublished manuscript, University of Massachusetts at Amherst.

Chaikin, A. L., Sigler, E., & Derlega, V. J. (1984). Nonverbal mediators of teacher expectancy effects. *Journal of Personality and Social Psychology, 30,* 144–149.

Cohen, J. (1988). *Statistical power analysis for the behavioral sciences* (2nd ed.). New York: Academic Press.

Cohn, L. D. (1991). Sex differences in the course of personality development: A meta-analysis. *Psychological Bulletin, 109,* 252–266.

Cooper, H., & Hazelrigg, P. (1988). Personality moderators of interpersonal expectancy effects: An integrative research review. *Journal of Personality and Social Psychology, 55,* 937–949.

Costanzo, M., & Archer, D. (1989). Interpreting the expressive behavior of others: The Interpersonal Perception Task. *Journal of Nonverbal Behavior, 13,* 225–245.

Coutts, L. M., & Schneider, F. W. (1976). Affiliative conflict theory: An investigation of the intimacy equilibrium and compensation hypothesis. *Journal of Personality and Social Psychology, 34,* 1135–1142.

Cupchik, G. C., & Leventhal, H. (1974). Consistency between expressive behavior and the elevation of humorous stimuli: The role of sex and self-observation. *Journal of Personality and Social Psychology, 30,* 429–442.

D'Augelli, A. R. (1974). Nonverbal behavior of helpers in initial helping interactions. *Journal of Counseling Psychology, 21,* 360–363.

Deutsch, F. M. (1990). Status, sex, and smiling: The effect of role on smiling in men and women. *Personality and Social Psychology Bulletin, 16,* 531–540.

Dindia, K., & Allen, M. (1992). Sex differences in self-disclosure: A meta-analysis. *Psychological Bulletin, 112,* 106–124.

DiMatteo, M. R. (1979). Nonverbal skill and the physician–patient relationship. In R. Rosenthal (Ed.), *Skill in nonverbal communication: Individual differences* (pp. 104–134). Cambridge, MA: Oelgeschlager, Gunn & Hain.

Dobbins, G. H., & Platz, S. J. (1986). Sex differences in leadership: How real are they? *Academy of Management Review, 11,* 118–127.

Eagly, A. H. (1987). *Sex differences in social behavior: A social-role interpretation.* Hillsdale, NJ: Lawrence Erlbaum Associates.

Eagly, A. H. (1995). The science and politics of comparing women and men. *American Psychologist, 50*, 145–158.

Eagly, A. H., & Carli, L. L. (1981). Sex of researchers and sex-typed communications as determinants of sex differences in influenceability. *Psychological Bulletin, 90*, 1–20.

Eagly, A. H., & Crowley, M. (1986). Gender and helping behavior: A meta-analytic review of the social psychological literature. *Psychological Bulletin, 100*, 283–308.

Eagly, A. H., & Johnson, B. T. (1990). Gender and leadership style: A meta-analysis. *Psychological Bulletin, 108*, 233–256.

Eagly, A. H., & Karau, S. J. (1991). Gender and the emergence of leaders: A meta-analysis. *Journal of Personality and Social Psychology, 60*, 685–710.

Eagly, A. H., Karau, S. J., & Makhijani, M. G. (1995). Gender and the effectiveness of leaders: A meta-analysis. *Psychological Bulletin, 117*, 125–145.

Eagly, A. H., Karau, S. J., Miner, J. B., & Johnson, B. T. (1994). Gender and motivation to manage in hierarchic organizations: A meta-analysis. *Leadership Quarterly, 5*, 135–159.

Eagly, A. H., & Steffen, V. J. (1986). Gender and aggressive behavior: A meta-analytic review of the social psychological literature. *Psychological Bulletin, 100*, 309–330.

Eagly, A. H., & Wood, W. (1991). Explaining sex differences in social behavior: A meta- analytic perspective. *Personality and Social Psychology Bulletin, 17*, 306–315.

Eccles, J. S., Jacobs, J. E., & Harold, R. D. (1990). Gender role stereotypes, expectancy effects, and parents' socialization of gender differences. *Journal of Social Issues, 46*(2), 183–201.

Fairbanks, L. A., McGuire, M. T., & Harris, C. J. (1982). Nonverbal interaction of patients and therapists during psychiatric interviews. *Journal of Abnormal Psychology, 91*, 109–119.

Feingold, A. (1992). Gender differences in mate selection preferences: A test of the parental investment model. *Psychological Bulletin, 112*, 125–139.

Feingold, A. (1994). Gender differences in personality: A meta-analysis. *Psychological Bulletin, 116*, 429–456.

Fingeret, A. L., Monti, P. M., & Paxson, M. A. (1985). Social perception, social performance, and self-perception: A study with psychiatric and nonpsychiatric patients. *Behavior Modification, 9*, 345–356.

Firth, E. A. Conger, J. C., Kuhlenschmidt, S., & Dorcey, T., (1986). Social competence and social perceptivity. *Journal Social and Clinical Psychology, 41*, 85–100.

Fleming, M. L., & Malone, M. R. (1983). The relationship of student characteristics and student performance in science as viewed by meta-analysis research. *Journal of Research in Science Teaching, 20*, 481–495.

Frances, S. J. (1979). Sex differences in nonverbal behavior. *Sex Roles, 5*, 519–535.

Frieze, I. H., Whitley, B. E., Hanusa, B. H., & McHugh, M. C. (1982). Assessing the theoretical models for sex differences in causal attributions for success and failure. *Sex Roles, 8*, 333–343.

Funder, D. C., & Harris, M. J. (1986). On the several facets of personality assessment: The case of social acuity. *Journal of Personality, 54*, 528–550.

Gesn, P. R., & Ickes, W. (1999). The development of meaning contexts for empathic accuracy: Channel and sequence effects. *Journal of Personality and Social Psychology, 77*, 746–761.

Halberstadt, A. G., Hayes, C. W., & Pike, K. M. (1988). Gender and gender role differences in smiling and communication consistency. *Sex Roles, 19*, 589–604.

Hall, J. A. (1978). Gender effects in decoding nonverbal cues. *Psychological Bulletin, 85*, 845–857.

Hall, J. A. (1979). Gender, gender roles, and nonverbal communication skills. In R. Rosenthal. (Ed.), *Skill in nonverbal communication: Individual differences* (pp. 32–67). Cambridge, MA: Oelgeschlager, Gunn & Hain.

Hall, J. A. (1984). *Nonverbal sex differences: Communication accuracy and expressive style.* Baltimore: The Johns Hopkins University Press.

Hall, J. A., & Briton, N. J. (1993). Gender, nonverbal behavior, and expectations. In P. D. Blanck (Ed.), *Interpersonal expectations: Theory, research, and applications* (pp. 276–295). Cambridge, England: Cambridge University Press.

Hall, J. A., & Carter, J. D. (1996). Unpublished data, Northeastern University, Boston.

Hall, J. A., & Carter, J. D. (1999). Gender-stereotype accuracy as an individual difference. *Journal of Personality and Social Psychology, 77,* 350–359.

Hall, J. A., Carter, J. D., & Horgan, T. G. (2000). Gender differences in the nonverbal communication of emotion. In A. H. Fischer (Ed.), *Gender and emotion: Social psychological perspectives* (pp. 97–117). Paris: Cambridge University Press.

Hall, J. A., Coats, E. J., & Smith LeBeau, L. (in press). Nonverbal behavior and the vertical dimension of social relations: A meta-analysis. *Psychological Bulletin.*

Hall, J. A., & Dornan, M. C. (1990). Patient sociodemographic characteristics as predictors of satisfaction with medical care: A meta-analysis. *Social Science & Medicine, 30,* 811–818.

Hall, J. A., & Halberstadt, A. G. (1986). Smiling and gazing. In J. S. Hyde & M. C. Linn (Eds.), *The psychology of gender: Advances through meta-analysis* (pp. 136–158). Baltimore: The Johns Hopkins University Press.

Hall, J. A., & Halberstadt, A. G. (1994). "Subordination" and sensitivity to nonverbal cues: A study of married working women. *Sex Roles, 31,* 149–165.

Hall, J. A., & Halberstadt, A. G. (1997). Subordination and nonverbal sensitivity: A hypothesis in search of support. In M. R. Walsh (Ed.), *Women, men, and gender: Ongoing debates* (pp. 120–133). New Haven, CT: Yale University Press.

Hall, J. A., Halberstadt, A. G., & O'Brien, C. E. (1997). "Subordination" and nonverbal sensitivity: A study and synthesis of findings based on trait measures. *Sex Roles, 37,* 295–317.

Hall, J. A., & Horgan, T. G. (2003). Happy affect and smiling: Is their relation moderated by interpersonal power? *Emotion, 3,* 303–309.

Hattie, J. (1979). Stability of results across many studies: Sex differences on the Personal Orientation Inventory. *Journal of Personality Assessment, 43,* 627–628.

Hazelrigg, P. J., Cooper, H., & Strathman, A. J. (1991). Personality moderators of the experimenter expectancy effect: A reexamination of five hypotheses. *Personality and Social Psychology Bulletin, 17,* 569–579.

Hembree, R. (1988). Correlates, causes, effects, and treatment of test anxiety. *Review of Educational Research, 58,* 47–77.

Hill, C. E., Siegelman, L., Gronsky, B. R., Sturniolo, F., & Fretz, B. R. (1981). Nonverbal communication and counseling outcome. *Journal of Counseling Psychology, 28,* 203–212.

Hodgins, H. S., & Koestner, R. (1993). The origins of nonverbal sensitivity. *Personality and Social Psychology Bulletin, 19,* 466–473.

Hyde, J. S. (1981). How large are cognitive gender differences? A meta-analysis using ω^2 and *d*. *American Psychologist, 36,* 892–901.

Hyde, J. S., Fennema, E., & Lamon, S. J. (1990). Gender differences in mathematics performance: A meta-analysis. *Psychological Bulletin, 107,* 139–155.

Hyde, J. S., Fennema, E., Ryan, M., Frost, L. A., & Hopp, C. (1990). Gender comparisons of mathematics attitudes and affect: A meta-analysis. *Psychology of Women Quarterly, 14,* 299–324.

Hyde, J. S., & Frost, L. A. (1993). Meta-analysis in the psychology of women. In F. L. Denmark & M. A. Paludi (Eds.), *Psychology of women: A handbook of issues and theories* (pp. 67–103). Westport, CT: Greenwood.

Hyde, J. S., & Linn, M. C. (Eds.). (1986). *The psychology of gender: Advances through meta-analysis.* Baltimore: The Johns Hopkins University Press.

Hyde, J. S., & Linn, M. C. (1988). Gender differences in verbal ability: A meta-analysis. *Psychological Bulletin, 104,* 53–69.

Hyde, J. S., & Plant, E. A. (1995). Magnitude of psychological gender differences: Another side to the story. *American Psychologist, 50,* 159–161.

Ickes, W. (2001). Measuring empathic accuracy. In J. A. Hall & F. J. Bernieri (Eds.), *Interpersonal sensitivity: Theory and measurement* (pp. 219–241). Mahwah, NJ: Lawrence Erlbaum Associates.

Ickes, W., Gesn, P. R., & Graham, T. (2000). Gender differences in empathic accuracy: Differential ability or differential motivation? *Personal Relationships, 7,* 95–109.

Keeley-Dyreson, M., Burgoon, J. K., & Bailey, W. (1991). The effects of stress and gender on nonverbal decoding accuracy in kinesic and vocalic channels. *Human Communication Research, 17*, 584–605.

Kraut, R. E., & Johnston, R. E. (1979). Social and emotional messages of smiling: An ethological approach. *Journal of Personality and Social Psychology, 37*, 1539–1553.

LaFrance, M., & Carmen, B. (1980). The nonverbal display of psychological androgyny. *Journal of Personality and Social Psychology, 38*, 36–49.

LaFrance, M., Hecht, M. A., & Levy Paluck, E. (2003). The contingent smile: A meta-analysis of sex differences in smiling. *Psychological Bulletin, 129*, 305–334.

LaFrance, M., & Henley, N. M. (1994). On oppressing hypotheses: Or differences in nonverbal sensitivity revisited. In H. L. Radtke & H. J. Stam (Eds.), *Power/gender: Social relations in theory and practice* (pp. 287–311). London: Sage.

Lee, D. Y., & Hallberg, E. T. (1982). Nonverbal behaviors of "good" and "poor" counselors. *Journal of Counseling Psychology, 29*, 414–417.

Lee, D. Y., Hallberg, E. T., Kocsis, M., & Haase, R. F. (1980). Decoding skills in nonverbal communication and perceived interviewer effectiveness. *Journal of Counseling Psychology, 27*, 89–92.

Lipsey, M. W., & Wilson, D. B. (1993). The efficacy of psychological, educational, and behavioral treatment: Confirmation from meta-analysis. *American Psychologist, 48*, 1181–1209.

Lirgg, C. D. (1991). Gender differences in self-confidence in physical activity: A meta-analysis of recent studies. *Journal of Sport and Exercise Psychology, 13*, 294–310.

Littlepage, G. E., McKinnie, R., & Pineault, M. A. (1983). Relationship between nonverbal sensitivities and detection of deception. *Perceptual and Motor Skills, 57*, 651–657.

Martocchio, J. J., & O'Leary, A. M. (1989). Sex differences in occupational stress: A meta-analytic review. *Journal of Applied Psychology, 74*, 495–501.

McAdams, D. P., Jackson, R. J., & Kirshnit, C. (1984). Looking, laughing, and smiling in dyads as a function of intimacy motivation and reciprocity. *Journal of Personality, 52*, 261–273.

McClure, E. B. (2000). A meta-analytic review of sex differences in facial expression processing and their development in infants, children, and adolescents. *Psychological Bulletin, 126*, 424–453.

Mehrabian, A. (1971). Verbal and nonverbal interaction of strangers in a waiting situation. *Journal of Experimental Research in Personality, 5*, 127–138.

Mehrabian, A., & Williams, M. (1969). Nonverbal concomitants of perceived and intended persuasiveness. *Journal of Personality and Social Psychology, 13*, 37–58.

Noller, P. (1986). Sex differences in nonverbal communication: Advantage lost or supremacy regained? *Australian Journal of Psychology, 38*, 23–32.

Oliver, M. B., & Hyde, J. S. (1993). Gender differences in sexuality: A meta-analysis. *Psychological Bulletin, 114*, 29–51.

Richard, F. D., Bond, C. F., Jr., & Stokes-Zoota, J. J. (2003). One hundred years of social psychology quantitatively described. *Review of General Psychology, 7*, 331–363.

Rosen, L. D., & Maguire, P. (1990). Myths and realities of computerphobia: A meta-analysis. *Anxiety Research, 3*, 175–191.

Rosenfeld, H. M. (1966a). Instrumental affiliative functions of facial and gestural expressions. *Journal of Personality and Social Psychology, 4*, 65–72.

Rosenfeld, H. M. (1966b). Approval-inducing functions of verbal and nonverbal responses in the dyad. *Journal of Personality and Social Psychology, 4*, 597–605.

Rosenthal, R., & DePaulo, B. M. (1979a). Sex differences in accommodation in nonverbal communication. In R. Rosenthal (Ed.), *Skill in nonverbal communication: Individual differences* (pp. 68–103). Cambridge, MA: Oelgeschlager, Gunn & Hain.

Rosenthal, R., & DePaulo, B. M. (1979b). Sex differences in eavesdropping on nonverbal cues. *Journal of Personality and Social Psychology, 37*, 273–285.

Rosenthal, R., Hall, J. A., DiMatteo, M. R., Rogers, P. L., & Archer, D. (1979). *Sensitivity to nonverbal communication: The PONS test.* Baltimore: The Johns Hopkins University Press.

Rosenthal, R., & Rubin, D. B. (1982). A simple, general purpose display of magnitude of experimental effect. *Journal of Educational Psychology, 74*, 166–169.

Ruch, W. (1994). Extraversion, alcohol, and enjoyment. *Personality and Individual Differences, 16*, 89–102.

Sabatelli, R. M., Buck, R., & Dreyer, A. (1983). Locus of control, interpersonal trust, and nonverbal communication accuracy. *Journal of Personality and Social Psychology, 44*, 399–409.

Schroeder, J. E. (1995). Interpersonal perception skills: Self-concept correlates. *Perceptual and Motor Skills, 80*, 51–56.

Simon, L. J., Francis, P. L., & Lombardo, J. P. (1990). Sex, sex-role, and Machianellianism as correlates of decoding ability. *Perceptual and Motor Skills, 71*, 243–247.

Smith, H. J., Archer, D., & Costanzo, M. (1991). "Just a hunch": Accuracy and awareness in person perception. *Journal of Nonverbal Behavior, 15*, 3–18.

Spence, J. T. Helmreich, R., & Stapp, J. (1975). Ratings of self and peers on sex-role attributes and their relation to self-esteem and conceptions of masculinity and femininity. *Journal of Personality and Social Psychology, 32*, 29–39.

Swim, J. K. (1994). Perceived versus meta-analytic effect sizes: An assessment of the accuracy of gender stereotypes. *Journal of Personality and Social Psychology, 66*, 21–36.

Thoma, S. J. (1986). Estimating gender differences in the comprehension and preference of moral issues. *Developmental Review, 6*, 165–180.

Thomas, G., & Fletcher, G. O. (2003). Mind-reading accuracy in intimate relationships: Assessing the roles of the relationship, the target, and the judge. *Journal of Personality and Social Psychology, 85*, 1079–1094.

Voyer, D., Voyer, S., & Bryden, M. P. (1995). Magnitude of sex differences in spatial abilities: A meta-analysis and consideration of critical variables. *Psychological Bulletin, 117*, 250–270.

Warr, P. B. (1971). Pollyanna's personal judgements. *European Journal of Social Psychology, 1*, 327–338.

Whitley, B. E., Jr., & Kite, M. E. (1995). Sex differences in attitudes toward homosexuality: A comment on Oliver and Hyde (1993). *Psychological Bulletin, 117*, 146–154.

Wood, W. (1987). Meta-analytic review of sex differences in group performance. *Psychological Bulletin, 102*, 53–71.

Wood, W., Rhodes, N., & Whelan, M. (1989). Sex differences in positive well-being: A consideration of emotional style and marital status. *Psychological Bulletin, 106*, 249–264.

Zuckerman, M., DePaulo, B. M., & Rosenthal, R. (1981). Verbal and nonverbal communication of deception. In L. Berkowitz (Ed.), *Advances in experimental social psychology* (Vol. 14, pp. 1–59). New York: Academic Press.

Zuckerman, M., & Driver, R. E. (1985). Telling lies: Verbal and nonverbal correlates of deception. In A. W. Siegman & S. Feldstein (Eds.), *Multichannel integrations of nonverbal behavior* (pp. 129–147). Hillsdale, NJ: Lawrence Erlbaum Associates.

Zuckerman, M., & Larrance, D. T. (1979). Individual differences in perceived encoding and decoding abilities. In R. Rosenthal (Ed.), *Skill in nonverbal communication: Individual differences* (pp. 171–203). Cambridge, MA: Oelgeschlager, Gunn & Hain.

Zuckerman, M., & Przewuzman, S. J. (1979). Decoding and encoding facial expressions in preschool-age children. *Environmental Psychology and Nonverbal Behavior, 3*, 147–163.

5

Gender and Leadership: Perceptions and Realities

Gary N. Powell
University of Connecticut

Laura M. Graves
Clark University

Management's face has changed dramatically over the past three decades. That face is now female almost half of the time. What are the implications of this change for the practice of management? How well do gender stereotypes, which represent stereotypical views of male–female differences in general, apply to the managerial ranks in particular? Do female and male leaders (or *managers*; we use the terms interchangeably) differ in their basic qualities and overall effectiveness? If there are sex differences in leadership qualities, which sex has more of the qualities that organizations need to thrive?

In this chapter, we examine stereotypes and behaviors associated with the managerial role. First, we compare stereotypes of leaders with gender stereotypes and examine whether leader stereotypes have changed over time. Second, we investigate whether (and if so, how) female and male managers differ in their behavior and effectiveness as leaders. Traditionally, men have been regarded as having the "right stuff" to be leaders. More recently, it has been argued that women have the right stuff. We examine exactly what kind of so-called stuff leaders need and whether men or women are more likely to have it.

LEADER AND GENDER STEREOTYPES

Studies of the relationships among sex, gender stereotypes, and leader stereotypes were first conducted in the 1970s (Butterfield & Grinnell, 1999). Virginia Schein

(1973, 1975) compiled a list of 92 characteristics that people commonly believe distinguish between men and women, the basis for gender stereotypes. She then asked a sample of U.S. middle managers to describe how well each of the characteristics fit women in general, men in general, or successful middle managers in general. Schein hypothesized that because the vast majority of managers were men, the managerial job would be regarded as requiring personal attributes thought to be more characteristic of men than women. In support of her hypothesis, she found that both male and female middle managers believed that a successful middle manager possessed personal characteristics that more closely matched beliefs about the characteristics of men in general than those of women in general.

In more recent studies (e.g., Brenner, Tomkiewicz, & Schein, 1989), U.S. women have been less inclined to view management as the domain of men. They now associate the characteristics of successful managers equally with those of women in general and men in general. U.S. men continue to associate the characteristics of successful managers more with those of men in general than women in general. This tendency is reduced when men's descriptions of successful middle managers are compared with their descriptions of female and male managers rather than with their descriptions of women and men in general. Nonetheless, male managers in the United States still link the managerial role more with men than women. Men and women in Great Britain, Germany, Japan, and China hold views similar to those of U.S. men: They believe that men are more similar to successful managers than women are. Although these results are from a narrow range of countries, they suggest that international beliefs about managers, except for those of U.S. women, may be expressed as "think manager—think male" (Schein, 2001).

Gary Powell and Tony Butterfield (1979) undertook a different approach to the analysis of leader stereotypes. Their approach was based on Sandra Bem's (1974, 1977) pioneering work on the concept of androgyny, which represents a combination of high levels of masculine and feminine characteristics. Bem believed that androgyny was more flexible than the dual standards of masculinity for men and femininity for women and thus offered androgyny as a new unisex standard of psychological health. Powell and Butterfield began to explore whether Bem's notions about the superiority of androgyny were consistent with individuals' beliefs about effective management. They asked part-time MBA students in the United States, most of whom were full-time workers, and undergraduate business students to describe both themselves and a "good manager" by using the Bem Sex-Role Inventory (BSRI; Bem, 1974), which provides separate masculinity and femininity scores. They later rescored the results by using only the items that belonged to the Short BSRI (Bem, 1981), an abbreviated version of Bem's original instrument.

When Powell and Butterfield (1979) began their data collection in 1976, the proportion of women in management positions in the United States was 21%, an increase from 16% in 1970. On the basis of Bem's work and the recent increase in the proportion of women in management, they hypothesized that a good manager

TABLE 5.1
Descriptions of a Good Manager

Sample/Gender Identity	*1976–1977* (%)	*1984–1985* (%)	*1999* (%)
Male undergraduates			
Androgynous	26	25	29
Masculine	54	62	44
Feminine	4	2	8
Undifferentiated	16	11	19
Female undergraduates			
Androgynous	26	24	31
Masculine	54	70	52
Feminine	5	3	4
Undifferentiated	15	3	13
Male part-time MBAs			
Androgynous	30	16	16
Masculine	62	63	57
Feminine	0	3	4
Undifferentiated	8	18	23
Female part-time MBAs			
Androgynous	20	25	19
Masculine	75	60	56
Feminine	0	0	0
Undifferentiated	5	15	25

Note: All results are based on items included in the Short Bem Sex-Role Inventory.

Table information taken from "Gender and Managerial Stereotypes: Have the Times Changed?", G. N. Powell, D. A. Butterfield, & J. D. Parent, 2002, *Journal of Management, 28*, pp. 177–193.

would be seen as androgynous. As shown by the data reported in the first column of Table 5.1, this hypothesis was not supported. A good manager was seen as possessing predominantly masculine characteristics by a majority of respondents in all groups, including undergraduate and part-time graduate male and female students. Powell (1978) obtained similar results in a separate study of actual managers' stereotypes of a good manager. Thus, the idea of think manager—think masculine prevailed in these studies.

Powell and Butterfield (1989) conducted a replication of their original study during the period from 1984 to 1985. The proportion of women in management in the United States was 35% in 1984, which was a considerable increase from 21% in 1976. Powell and Butterfield hypothesized that this increase in the proportion of women in management since their earlier study would lead to good managers' being viewed as androgynous. However, their new results (second column of Table 5.1) were consistent with their earlier results. A good manager was still seen as possessing predominantly masculine characteristics by the majority of respondents in all groups.

By the end of the 20th century, the proportion of female managers in the United States was 45%, a further substantial increase from 35% in 1984. The proportion of female managers had more than doubled since 1976, when it was 21%, and women now accounted for almost half of all managers. Management was no longer a male-intensive occupation, making it possible that the managerial role was no longer associated with predominantly masculine characteristics. Accordingly, Powell and Butterfield, now with Jane Parent (2002), replicated their original study once again in 1999 with samples of undergraduate business students and part-time MBA students. The latest results appear in the third column of Table 5.1. The proportion of respondents from different groups that described a manager as possessing predominantly masculine characteristics was reduced. However, men and women still described a good manager in predominantly masculine terms.

In summary, in studies conducted in three different decades, men and women at different career stages, including undergraduate business students preparing to enter the workplace, part-time MBA students preparing for managerial careers, and practicing managers, described a good manager as higher in stereotypically masculine traits than stereotypically feminine traits. Support for the masculine stereotype of the good manager has diminished somewhat over time but remains strong. Support for the stereotype of men as more suited for the leader role than women is also strong, except in the views of U.S. women. Overall, managerial stereotypes continue as think manager—think masculine and think manager—think male.

Are these leader stereotypes important? The answer to this question is a resounding yes. Leader and gender stereotypes put aspiring female leaders at a distinct disadvantage by forcing them to deal with the perceived incongruity between the leader role and their gender role (Eagly & Karau, 2002). If women conform to the female gender role by displaying predominantly feminine characteristics, they fail to meet the requirements of the leader stereotype. However, if women compete with men for leadership positions and conform to the leader role by displaying predominantly masculine characteristics, they fail to meet the requirements of the female gender role, which calls for feminine niceness and deference to the authority of men (Rudman & Glick, 2001).

This incongruity between the leader role and the female gender role may affect women's aspirations to seek management positions. In all of the studies conducted by Powell and his colleagues, undergraduate business students exhibited stereotypical sex differences in their self-descriptions, with male students seeing themselves as more masculine and less feminine than female students. Female and male undergraduates agreed on a description of the good manager as highly masculine. As a result, undergraduate women tended to describe a good manager as less like themselves than undergraduate men did. Undergraduate women who do not see themselves as fitting the stereotype of a good manager may not develop management skills and may be diverted from pursuing managerial careers. Those who see themselves as fitting the stereotype may be the ones who go on to graduate business programs and eventually attain managerial positions.

When women decide to pursue management positions, they may encounter barriers in the selection process. Given leader stereotypes that focus on masculine characteristics and men, women may be less likely than men to be hired for management positions. Moreover, once women assume leader roles, leader stereotypes act as constraints on their behavior. Many organizations exert strong pressures on their members to conform to standards of behavior dictated by those in power. As long as men remain in the majority in the top ranks of management, the masculine leader stereotype is likely to prevail, and women throughout the organization will be expected to behave as men. Thus a masculine stereotype of the good manager is self-reinforcing and inhibits the expression of femininity by women in management positions.

In addition, the mismatch between the leader role and the female gender role constrains the advancement of female managers (Eagly & Karau, 2002). When performance evaluations are conducted, women may receive lower ratings than men for similar levels of performance. Women may also be subjected to discrimination when decisions are made about promotions into higher leadership positions, making it difficult for them to rise in managerial hierarchies. As a result, being competent does not ensure that a female manager will have the same amount of organizational success as her male equivalent (Eagly & Karau, 2002; Heilman, 2001).

Research results regarding leader stereotypes raise as many questions as they answer. The first question is this: Do leader stereotypes depend on sex ratios in management ranks? If the proportion of female managers rises more, will there be some point at which stereotypes of managers no longer agree with the masculine gender stereotype? Probably not. Support for gender stereotypes has not diminished over time, despite considerable changes in women's and men's roles in the workplace and in society (Deaux & Kite, 1993; Eagly, Wood, & Diekman, 2000). Similarly, stereotypes of leaders have remained essentially the same despite the substantial increase in female managers in recent years. There is little reason to believe that these stereotypes will change if even more women become managers. The upper levels of management remain a male bastion, despite the overall increase in the proportion of female managers; the proportion of women in top management positions in Fortune 500 corporations, although higher than in the 1970s, is only 16% (Catalyst, 2002). If stereotypes of leaders are influenced at all by sex ratios, they may be influenced most by the sex ratio of top executives.

The second question is this: Are stereotypes of leaders dependent on the racial and ethnic composition of the management ranks? Women currently hold slightly less than half of U.S. managerial positions. However, the vast majority of both female and male managers are non-Hispanic Whites. Thus, stereotypes of male and female leaders in general may largely reflect beliefs about the characteristics of leaders from the dominant racial and ethnic group in the managerial ranks and ignore the characteristics of leaders from other groups (Parker & ogilvie, 1996).

The third and final question raised by leader stereotypes is this: How well do they apply to the practice of management? Stereotypes are resistant to change and do not necessarily reflect current realities. Widely held stereotypes that men are better managers and that better managers are masculine may not reflect what makes good managers. Instead, these stereotypes could reflect only that most managers have been men and that most men have been expected to live up to the masculine stereotype.

LEADER BEHAVIOR AND EFFECTIVENESS

Are men and masculine behaviors really best in leadership positions, as suggested by leader stereotypes? We now review the extent to which perceptions of leadership match current realities. First, we consider how the major theories of leadership regard the merits of stereotypically feminine or masculine behaviors. Next, we examine research evidence on sex differences in leader behavior and effectiveness.

Theories of Leadership

Early theories of what leaders do and what does and does not work well were based almost entirely on studies of male managers. Stogdill (1974) discovered few studies that examined female leaders exclusively or even included female leaders in their samples. When female managers were present in organizations being studied, they were usually excluded from the analysis because their inclusion might lead to distorted results. It was as if female managers were less legitimate or less worthy of observation than male managers. Although management researchers no longer exclude female managers from their samples, many of the existing theories of leadership were developed with male managers in mind. However, most theories refer to feminine and sex-neutral as well as masculine characteristics.

There are two distinct types of behavior that managers may use to influence the actions of their subordinates (Eagly & Johnson, 1990). The first type, task style or task accomplishment, refers to the extent to which the manager initiates and organizes work activity and defines the way work is to be done. The second type, interpersonal style or maintenance of interpersonal relationships, refers to the extent to which the manager engages in activities that tend to the morale and welfare of people. Task and interpersonal styles of leadership are typically regarded as independent dimensions.

Managers may also exhibit different decision-making styles. A leader who exhibits democratic leadership allows subordinates to participate in decision making, whereas a leader who exhibits autocratic leadership discourages such participation (Eagly & Johnson, 1990). These are generally considered to be opposite styles.

Some theories regard one type or combination of behaviors as best in all situations. For example, Managerial Grid Theory (Blake & Mouton, 1964) proposes that the best manager is one who is high in both task style and interpersonal style in all situations. Collins (1997) argued that a democratic decision-making style is superior to an autocratic style for ethical reasons, much as democracy is superior to authoritarianism as a political system. In Western societies, management is seen as the last bastion of the autocratic style.

Other theories regard different types of leader behavior as appropriate for different situations. For example, situational leadership theory (Hersey, Blanchard, & Johnson, 2000) recommends that managers adopt high task–low interpersonal, high task–high interpersonal, low task–high interpersonal, and low task–low interpersonal styles in that order as their subordinates' maturity increases. More mature subordinates are more willing and able to take responsibility and have greater education and experience relevant to the task at hand. Furthermore, Tannenbaum and Schmidt's (1973) leadership theory recommends that managers become more democratic and less autocratic in decision making as subordinates display a greater need for independence, readiness to assume responsibility, and ability to solve problems as a team.

In recent years, leadership theories have become more dynamic and holistic by distinguishing among transformational, transactional, and laissez-faire leadership (Bass, 1998; Bass, Avolio, & Atwater, 1996). Transformational leaders are regarded as superior. They motivate followers to transcend their own self-interests for the good of the group or organization by setting exceptionally high standards for performance and then developing subordinates to achieve these standards. In this way, they turn followers into leaders. Transformational leaders exhibit four types of behavior: (a) charisma, by displaying attributes that induce followers to view them as role models and by communicating values, purpose, and the importance of the mission; (b) inspirational motivation, by exuding optimism and excitement about the mission and its attainability; (c) intellectual stimulation, by encouraging followers to question basic assumptions and consider problems and tasks from new perspectives; and (d) individualized consideration, by focusing on the development and mentoring of followers and attending to their individual needs (Bass, 1998; Bass et al., 1996).

In contrast, transactional leaders focus on clarifying the responsibilities of subordinates and then responding to how well subordinates execute their responsibilities. They exhibit two kinds of behavior: (a) contingent reward, by promising and providing suitable rewards if followers achieve their assigned objectives; and (b) management by exception, by intervening to correct follower performance either in anticipation of a problem or after a problem has occurred. Transactional leaders who engage in active management by exception systematically monitor subordinate performance for mistakes, whereas those who engage in passive management by exception wait for subordinate difficulties to be brought to their attention before intervening. Transformational leaders may be transactional when it is necessary to achieve their goals. However, transactional leaders are seldom transformational (Bass, 1998; Bass et al., 1996).

Distinct from both transformational and transactional leadership is laissez-faire leadership. Laissez-faire leaders avoid taking responsibility for leadership altogether. Such leaders refrain from giving direction or making decisions and do not involve themselves in the development of their followers (Bass, 1998; Bass et al., 1996).

The call for transformational leadership has occurred partly in recognition of the changing economic environment in which organizations operate. As global environments become more turbulent, highly competitive, and reliant on new technologies, they call for organizations with decentralized authority, flexible structures, and few managerial levels (Drucker, 1988; Hitt, Keats, & DeMarie, 1998). Individuals who are able to articulate and rally followers behind a unified vision, stimulate creativity in achieving the vision, and develop rewards, recognition, and career opportunities for high-performing specialists are best suited for leader roles in such organizations. In addition, participatory management approaches that emphasize open communication and delegation are most conducive to the rapid innovation and response to customers that organizations need to survive in such environments. As a result, organizations are shifting away from an authoritarian model of leadership and toward a more transformational and democratic model (Lawler, Mohrman, & Ledford, 1995). If management is the last bastion of the autocratic style as Collins (1997) claimed, fewer organizations appear to be choosing this style.

Gender Stereotypes and Leadership Theories

Several linkages may be made between gender stereotypes and leadership theories (Powell & Graves, 2003). A high propensity to exhibit task-oriented behaviors such as setting goals and initiating work activity is associated with the masculine stereotype. The feminine stereotype is associated with a high propensity to exhibit interpersonally oriented behaviors such as showing consideration toward subordinates and demonstrating concern for their satisfaction. When individuals tend to exhibit both task-oriented and interpersonal-oriented behavior, they adopt the profile of an androgynous leader (Sargent, 1981). However, when individuals are low in the propensity to exhibit either type of behavior, they can be regarded as undifferentiated (Bem, 1974, 1977). Thus, Managerial Grid Theory suggests that an androgynous leader will be effective in all situations. In contrast, situational leadership theory suggests that leaders should be masculine, androgynous, feminine, and finally undifferentiated in turn as followers increase in maturity.

The autocratic style of decision making is more associated with the masculine stereotype, reflecting a greater emphasis on dominance and control over others. In contrast, the democratic style of decision making is more associated with the feminine stereotype, reflecting a greater emphasis on the involvement of others

(Eagly & Johnson, 1990). Tannenbaum and Schmidt's (1973) leadership theory suggests that leaders behave in an increasingly feminine manner as their followers gain independence, responsibility, and the ability to work well as a team.

Although much of what makes a leader transformational does not pertain to either gender stereotype, the ability to offer individualized consideration to subordinates is more associated with the feminine stereotype because of its greater concern with relationships and the needs of others. In contrast, the primary activities of transactional leaders, including the granting of contingent rewards and active or passive management by exception, reflect a high task orientation that is more associated with the masculine stereotype. Thus, the argument that transformational leaders are superior to transactional leaders is more consistent with the notion that feminine characteristics are desirable in leaders than the notion that masculine characteristics are desirable (Bass et al., 1996).

Recall that leader stereotypes place a high value on masculine characteristics. Even though early leadership theories were developed at a time when there were far fewer women in leader roles, the review of major leadership theories does *not* support these stereotypes. Leadership theories also do not endorse feminine characteristics exclusively. The recent calls for transformational leadership over transactional leadership and democratic leadership over autocratic leadership place somewhat more emphasis on feminine characteristics than masculine characteristics. Other theories, however, recommend that leaders either act in an androgynous manner (Managerial Grid Theory) or vary the amount of masculine and feminine characteristics they display according to the situation (situational leadership theory; Tannenbaum & Schmidt's leadership theory). Thus, leadership theories do not suggest that either stereotypically feminine or stereotypically masculine behaviors are the key to leader effectiveness.

Evidence on Sex Differences in Leader Behavior and Effectiveness

Although leadership theories do not exclusively promote either masculinity or femininity, researchers have devoted a great deal of attention to sex differences in leader behavior and effectiveness. Three distinct perspectives have emerged regarding these differences:

1. Stereotypical differences favoring men: Female and male managers differ in ways predicted by gender stereotypes as a result of early socialization experiences that make men better suited as managers (e.g., Hennig & Jardim, 1977).
2. Stereotypical differences favoring women: Female and male managers differ in accordance with gender stereotypes as a result of early socialization experiences, but femininity is particularly needed by managers to be effective in today's workplace (e.g., Helgesen, 1995; Rosener, 1990).

3. No differences: Women who pursue the nontraditional career of manager do not adhere to the feminine stereotype and behave similarly to men who pursue managerial careers (e.g., Morrison, White, Van Velsor, & The Center for Creative Leadership, 1992).

Sex differences have been examined in several types of leader behaviors recommended by various theories. Eagly and Johnson (1990) conducted a meta-analysis of studies that examined sex differences in task style, interpersonal style, and democratic versus autocratic decision-making style. They divided studies included in the meta-analysis into three types: (a) laboratory experiments, which compare the behavior of male and female leaders in group simulations; (b) assessment studies, which compare the behavioral inclinations of men and women who do not currently hold leadership roles, such as business students; and (c) organizational studies, which compare the actual behavior of men and women in equivalent leadership roles.

As gender stereotypes would predict, women tended to be higher in interpersonal style than men (Eagly & Johnson, 1990). This sex difference, however, appeared only in laboratory experiments and assessment studies, not in organizational studies. That is, it was present only for individuals who participated in laboratory experiments and for nonleaders who were assessed on how they would behave if they actually were leaders. There was no sex difference in the interpersonal style of actual managers. In addition, contrary to gender stereotypes, men and women did not differ in task style in any type of study.

A consistent sex difference emerges in individuals' tendencies to adopt a democratic versus autocratic style of decision making (Eagly & Johnson, 1990). In support of gender stereotypes, women tended to be more democratic and less autocratic leaders than men. This sex difference was present for individuals in all settings and circumstances—actual leaders, nonleaders, and participants in laboratory experiments.

Eagly, Johannesen-Schmidt, and van Engen (2003) conducted a meta-analysis of sex differences in transformational and transactional leadership. Their results suggested that female leaders are more transformational than their male counterparts. Women rated higher than men on all dimensions of transformational leadership: charisma (especially attributes that motivate pride and respect), inspirational motivation, intellectual stimulation, and individualized consideration. Women also rated higher than men on the contingent reward dimension of transactional leadership. In contrast, men rated higher than women on two dimensions of transactional leadership: active management by exception and passive management by exception. Men also rated higher than women in laissez-faire leadership.

Other evidence suggested that all of the dimensions of transformational leadership and the contingent reward dimension of transactional leadership are positively associated with leader effectiveness as reflected in individual, group, and organizational performance (Lowe, Kroeck, & Sivasubramaniam, 1996). In contrast, passive management by exception and laissez-faire leadership are negatively associated with leader effectiveness. Thus, the aforementioned results suggest that women rate higher than men in behavior that contributes to their effectiveness as leaders and lower than men in behavior that would detract from their effectiveness.

A separate meta-analysis by Eagly, Karau, and Makhijani (1995) on sex differences in leader effectiveness found that women and men overall did not differ in their effectiveness as leaders. Most of the studies included in this meta-analysis were conducted in organizational settings. Men were more effective than women in military settings, which are extremely male intensive, whereas women were more effective than men in education, government, and social service settings, which are less male intensive. Neither men nor women were more effective in business settings. Men were more effective than women when the particular leader role examined was more congruent with the male gender role, and there was a larger proportion of men as both leaders and subordinates. Further, men were more effective than women in lower-level management positions, whereas women were more effective than men in middle-level management positions. The position of middle manager is often regarded as requiring heavy use of interpersonal skills to wield influence, which would favor women according to gender stereotypes. Not enough studies of men and women in top management positions allow a comparison of the sexes by use of meta-analysis.

In summary, the bulk of evidence regarding sex differences in leader behavior suggests the existence of stereotypical differences. As gender stereotypes predict, women are higher in interpersonal style than men in laboratory experiments and assessment studies (but not organizational studies), and they are higher in democratic decision-making style than men in all types of studies. Women are also higher than men in the individualized consideration dimension of transformational leadership, which is associated with the feminine stereotype, and lower than men in active and passive management by exception, which are associated with the masculine stereotype. Contrary to gender stereotypes, women are higher than men in the contingent reward dimension of transactional leadership. Offering some support for the "no differences" perspective, women and men do not differ in task style in any type of study.

However, the stereotypical differences in leader behavior that were found favor women, not men. Women are higher than men in dimensions of transformational and transactional behavior that contribute to leader effectiveness and lower than men in dimensions of transactional behavior that detract from leader effectiveness. Women's greater use of a democratic decision-making style aligns them with what business ethicists regard as a superior approach to management. Moreover, trends in the economic environment seem to call for a transformational and democratic leadership style that is associated more with women than men.

Studies that directly measure leader effectiveness, however, rate women as no more or less effective than men. Additional evidence suggests that situational factors influence whether men or women are more effective as leaders. These factors include the nature of the organizational setting and leader role, the proportions of male leaders and followers, and the managerial level of the position. As a result, some leader roles are more congenial to male leaders, whereas other leader roles are more congenial to female leaders.

Thus, the evidence clearly refutes the stereotypes that men are better leaders and that better leaders are masculine. Effective leadership today requires a combination of behaviors that are masculine (contingent rewards), feminine (individualized consideration), and sex neutral (charisma, inspirational motivation, and intellectual stimulation). Women exhibit more of these behaviors than do men. However, situations differ in whether they favor women or men as leaders.

IMPLICATIONS FOR PRACTICE

Sandra Bem (1978, p. 19) declared that "*behavior* should have no gender." To amend Bem's statement, *leader behavior* should have no gender. That is, the sex of individuals who hold leader roles should be of little concern. What should matter is how well individuals, male and female, respond to the demands of the particular leader role that they occupy. However, the sex of leaders does make an emphatic difference to others. Individuals describe leaders in stereotypical terms that favor men over women. They also hold attitudes that make it more difficult for female leaders to be effective in their roles.

What is required to create a working environment in which members of both sexes have an equal chance to be effective in the leader role? For this objective to be achieved, prejudices against women as leaders must be confronted (Eagly & Karau, 2002; Yoder, 2001). Such prejudices are most likely to be exhibited in highly masculinized work settings where the majority of both leaders and followers are men and the leader role is associated with the male gender role. To give women a greater chance of being effective in such settings, organizations have to consider the ways in which leaders are evaluated. When leaders are evaluated on the basis of whether they promote group cohesiveness and develop subordinates for future roles as well as accomplish tasks, female leaders, who rank higher in individualized consideration than male leaders, have more of an opportunity to be seen as effective. To take advantage of this opportunity, female leaders need to have resources to promote subordinate development.

Male leaders in settings that are more congenial to women face somewhat different issues. Because men have more societal status than women, they are likely to be granted higher status in a feminized work setting than female leaders are granted in a masculinized work setting. However, male leaders may still be subjected to negative attitudes. Male leaders do not deserve to be the target of sexist attitudes any more than female leaders do. When sexist attitudes are directed toward male as well as female leaders, they have to be addressed.

No matter what the setting, organizations have to be ready to act when their members embrace stereotypical views or display prejudices toward members of one sex as leaders. Although beliefs (e.g., leader stereotypes) and attitudes (e.g., prejudice against women as leaders) are difficult to change, organizations may take steps to counteract problematic beliefs and attitudes through diversity-training programs. Such programs should be designed to make individuals aware of the ways in which biases related to sex (as well as race, ethnicity, age, sexual orientation, etc.) can affect their decisions, and to teach them how to move beyond their own biases. Organizations should also encourage employees to engage in the most effective kinds of behavior, whatever their beliefs or attitudes may be.

IMPLICATIONS FOR RESEARCH

There is still more to be learned about the linkage between gender and leadership. The persistence of the perceived linkages among being a leader, being male, and being masculine has several implications for research. First, researchers should examine whether leader stereotypes result in sex differences in how the behavior of male and female leaders is perceived and evaluated. For example, given that leader stereotypes devalue women, are women and men who engage in equal levels of transformational leadership viewed as behaving in the same manner? Are female transformational leaders evaluated less favorably than male transformational leaders because individuals expect them to be less successful?

In addition, researchers should explore how the link between leader and gender stereotypes can be reduced. For instance, evidence suggests that increasing the proportion of women in top management positions reduces gender-based categorization and increases the legitimacy of female leaders (Ely, 1994). Researchers might examine whether it also reduces reliance on leader stereotypes. In addition, the literature on improving intergroup relations (e.g., Brewer & Miller, 1984) suggests that cooperative interaction has the potential to reduce reliance on stereotyping. Thus, researchers might explore whether positive interactions with female managers weaken the association between leadership and gender. The influence of other factors, such as the diversity culture of the organization (Powell & Graves, 2003), might also be examined.

In conclusion, we note that evidence increasingly suggests that women are better suited than men to serve as leaders in the ways required in the global economy. This is not to say that organizations should choose women for leader roles on the basis of their sex. The challenge for organizations is to take advantage of and develop the capabilities of all individuals in leader roles and then create conditions that give leaders of both sexes an equal chance to succeed. The proper goal for leadership-training programs is neither to teach men how to behave more like women, nor to teach women how to behave more like men. Instead, the goal should be to enhance the likelihood that all people, women and men, will bring the right stuff to leader roles.

REFERENCES

Bass, B. M. (1998). *Transformational leadership: Industry, military, and educational impact.* Mahwah, NJ: Lawrence Erlbaum Associates.

Bass, B. M., Avolio, B. J., & Atwater, L. (1996). The transformational and transactional leadership of men and women. *Applied Psychology: An International Review, 45*, 5–34.

Bem, S. L. (1974). The measurement of psychological androgyny. *Journal of Consulting and Clinical Psychology, 42*, 155–162.

Bem, S. L. (1977). On the utility of alternative procedures for assessing psychological androgyny. *Journal of Consulting and Clinical Psychology, 45*, 196–205.

Bem, S. L. (1978). Beyond androgyny: Some presumptuous prescriptions for a liberated sexual identity. In J. A. Sherman & F. L. Denmark (Ed.), *The psychology of women: Future direction in research* (pp. 1-23). New York: Psychological Dimensions.

Bem, S. L. (1981). *Bem Sex-Role Inventory: Professional manual.* Palo Alto, CA: Consulting Psychologists Press.

Blake, R. R., & Mouton, J. S. (1964). *The managerial grid.* Houston: Gulf.

Brenner, O. C., Tomkiewicz, J., & Schein, V. E. (1989). The relationship between sex role stereotypes and requisite management characteristics revisited. *Academy of Management Journal, 32*, 662–669.

Brewer, M. B., & Miller, N. (1984). Beyond the contact hypothesis: Theoretical perspectives on desegregation. In N. Miller & M. B. Brewer (Eds.), *Groups in contact: The psychology of desegregation* (pp. 281–302). Orlando, FL: Academic Press.

Butterfield, D. A., & Grinnell, J. P. (1999). "Re-viewing" gender, leadership, and managerial behavior: Do three decades of research tell us anything? In G. N. Powell (Ed.), *Handbook of gender and work* (pp. 223–238). Thousand Oaks, CA: Sage.

Catalyst. (2002). *Census of women corporate officers and top earners.* New York: Author.

Collins, D. (1997). The ethical superiority and inevitability of participatory management as an organizational system. *Organization Science, 8*, 489–507.

Deaux, K., & Kite, M. (1993). Gender stereotypes. In F. L. Denmark & M. A. Paludi (Eds.), *Psychology of women: A handbook of issues and theories* (pp. 107–139). Westport, CT: Greenwood.

Drucker, P. F. (1988). The coming of the new organization. *Harvard Business Review, 88*(1), 45–53.

Eagly, A. H., Johannesen-Schmidt, M. C., & van Engen, M. L. (2003). Transformational, transactional, and laissez-faire leadership styles: A meta-analysis comparing women and men. *Psychological Bulletin, 129*, 569–591.

Eagly, A. H., & Johnson, B. T. (1990). Gender and leadership style: A meta-analysis. *Psychological Bulletin, 108*, 233–256.

Eagly, A. H., & Karau, S. J. (2002). Role congruity theory of prejudice toward female leaders. *Psychological Review, 109*, 573–598.

Eagly, A. H., Karau, S. J., & Makhijani, M. G. (1995). Gender and the effectiveness of leaders: A meta-analysis. *Psychological Bulletin, 117*, 125–145.

Eagly, A. H., Wood, W., & Diekman, A. B. (2000). Social role theory of sex differences and similarities: A current appraisal. In T. Eckes & H. M. Trautner (Eds.), *The developmental social psychology of gender* (pp. 123–174). Mahwah, NJ: Lawrence Erlbaum Associates.

Ely, R. J. (1994). The effects of organizational demographics and social identity on relationships among professional women. *Administrative Science Quarterly, 39*, 203–238.

Heilman, M. E. (2001). Description and prescription: How gender stereotypes prevent women's ascent up the organizational ladder. *Journal of Social Issues, 57*, 657–674.

Helgesen, S. (1995). *The female advantage: Women's ways of leadership* (Paper ed.). New York: Currency Doubleday.

Hennig, M., & Jardim, A. (1977). *The managerial woman.* Garden City, NY: Anchor/Doubleday.

Hersey, P., Blanchard, K. H., & Johnson, D. E. (2000). *Management of organizational behavior: Utilizing human resources* (8th ed.). Englewood Cliffs, NJ: Prentice-Hall.

Hitt, M. A., Keats, B. W., & DeMarie, S. M. (1998). Navigating in the new competitive landscape: Building strategic flexibility and competitive advantage in the 21st century. *Academy of Management Executive, 12*(4), 22–42.

Lawler, E. E., III, Mohrman, S. A., & Ledford, G. E., Jr. (1995). *Creating high performance organizations: Practices and results of employee involvement and total quality management in Fortune 1000 companies.* San Francisco: Jossey-Bass.

Lowe, K. B., Kroeck, K. G., & Sivasubramaniam, N. (1996). Effectiveness correlates of transformational and transactional leadership: A meta-analytic review of the MLQ literature. *Leadership Quarterly, 7,* 385–425.

Morrison, A. M., White, R. P., Van Velsor, E., and The Center for Creative Leadership. (1992). *Breaking the glass ceiling: Can women reach the top of America's largest corporations?* (Updated ed.). Reading, MA: Addison-Wesley.

Parker, P. S., & ogilvie, d. t. (1996). Gender, culture, and leadership: Toward a culturally distinct model of African-American women executives' leadership strategies. *Leadership Quarterly, 7,* 189–214.

Powell, G. N. (1978, March). *Management styles.* Address to Allstate Insurance Company, Farmington, CT.

Powell, G. N., & Butterfield, D. A. (1979). The "good manager": Masculine or androgynous? *Academy of Management Journal, 22,* 395–403.

Powell, G. N., & Butterfield, D. A. (1989). The "good manager": Did androgyny fare better in the 1980s? *Group & Organization Studies, 14,* 216–233.

Powell, G. N., Butterfield, D. A., & Parent, J. D. (2002). Gender and managerial stereotypes: Have the times changed? *Journal of Management, 28,* 177–193.

Powell, G. N., & Graves, L. M. (2003). *Women and men in management* (3rd ed). Thousand Oaks, CA: Sage.

Rosener, J. B. (1990). Ways women lead. *Harvard Business Review, 68*(6), 119–125.

Rudman, L. A., & Glick, P. (2001). Prescriptive gender stereotypes and backlash toward agentic women. *Journal of Social Issues, 57,* 743–762.

Sargent, A. G. (1981). *The androgynous manager.* New York: AMACOM.

Schein, V. E. (1973). The relationship between sex role stereotypes and requisite management characteristics. *Journal of Applied Psychology, 57,* 95–100.

Schein, V. E. (1975). Relationships between sex role stereotypes and requisite management characteristics among female managers. *Journal of Applied Psychology, 60,* 340–344.

Schein, V. E. (2001). A global look at psychological barriers to women's progress in management. *Journal of Social Issues, 57,* 675–688.

Stogdill, R. M. (1974). *Handbook of leadership.* New York: The Free Press.

Tannenbaum, R., & Schmidt, W. H. (1973). How to choose a leadership pattern. *Harvard Business Review, 51* (3), 162–180.

Yoder, J. D. (2001). Making leadership work more effectively for women. *Journal of Social Issues, 57,* 815–828.

6

Researching a Gendered World: The Intersection of Methodological and Ethical Concerns

Mike Allen
University of Wisconsin–Milwaukee

Kathleen S. Valde
Northern Illinois University

The examination of sex and gender differences continues to receive attention by social science and generates a large and intense atmosphere of controversy. The importance of gender to the lives of individuals and the practice of social science reflects the real concerns of individuals and social institutions about the importance of a sex–gender identity. Although the research community emphasizes the concept, the current and historical reservoir of empirical research findings fails to provide evidence justifying continued reliance on this variable as a means of fundamentally understanding human communication. Given a background of disappointment in establishing large and routine empirical sex and gender differences, this chapter examines questions about the future of sex and gender research considering both methodological and ethical implications.

In this chapter, we argue that the lack of empirical evidence to support gender or sex differences means that social scientists need to develop more focused approaches for conducting research. We make this argument on the basis of (a) an examination of the current state of empirical evidence, (b) an assessment of the methodological and statistical issues that emerge when gender is measured, and (c) a review of the ethical implications of continuing or changing the research practices of investigating sex and gender differences given the existing empirical evidence. The challenge of an existing corpus of research that fails to sustain claims of widespread large gender differences requires changes in theoretical and methodological approaches to the continued study of sex and gender differences.

CURRENT STATE OF EMPIRICAL KNOWLEDGE

Despite the level of theoretical argument about gender as a variable and the importance of this variable, little empirical data support the widespread value of this individual difference as a means to explain fundamental communication differences between persons (see reviews by Canary & Hause, 1993; Goldsmith & Fulfs, 1999; Hyde & Frost, 1993; Hyde & Plant, 1995). The problem is that, despite many investigations of gender, few large differences are supported by existing meta-analyses. The perception of the existence of enormous and frequent gender and sex differences remains probably the most widely accepted myth in social sciences.

The popular culture version of gender differences, the separation of male and female cultures based on conversational content and styles (Tannen, 1990), receives little support from the scientific community (Goldsmith & Fulfs, 1999). The problem resembles the one faced by the character Mulder in the *X-Files*, who tried to justify his belief in extraterrestrials and other things that go bump in the night: "I want to believe." However, the empirical evidence simply fails to justify the continued faith that biological sex or socialized gender provides a great deal of explanation for communication differences. The size of the difference remains small ($r = .10$), and it is not always consistent with the hypothesis derived from theoretical argument. Although individual difference models are popular and continue to receive attention, the continued reliance on gender as an important element for individual difference becomes problematic.

Although sex differences exist, they are probably far smaller in size and in number than most people would probably believe. For example, differences observed in self-reported preference for conflict styles between men and women exist, consistent with the argument that men prefer competition and women prefer collaboration (Gayle, Preiss, & Allen, 2002). However, when the scenarios used to elicit self-reports are covaried on the basis of whether the situation is more likely to be encountered by a man or woman, gender differences vanish (Gayle, Preiss, & Allen, 1998, 2002). This finding indicates that the observed gender differences reflect a methodological artifact related to scenario construction used to elicit responses and may not indicate a fundamental difference related to gender or sex. Instead, the argument requires a more sophisticated view relating to stereotypes and potential social expectations rather than a simple model dealing with behavioral preferences related to biological sex.

A popular press example is the argument that girls are lower in self-esteem than boys. A meta-analysis (Sahlstein & Allen, 2002) indicated no general difference in self-esteem between boys and girls. However, when the various subscales are referred to (social, cognitive, and body image), a difference on one factor becomes evident—girls express a lower esteem about body image than boys. This finding undermines the general approach to gender differences in self-esteem and provides a possible indictment of the contribution of the media to the development of women's lower positive evaluation of body image (Han, 2003; Herrett-Skjellum & Allen, 1996; Wolf, 1991). What the popular culture portrays as a general gender difference in self-esteem receives little or no support from the scientific evidence. However, in some important areas and limited areas or contexts (like conversations about safer sex in the context of HIV; see Allen, Emmers-Sommer, & Crowell, 2002), important gender differences emerge.

The problem becomes one of taking theoretical positions and examining those positions in comparison with empirical data. The current approaches to the study of sex or gender endorse or create monolithic stereotypes that assume various kinds of global distinctions. The empirical picture emerging reveals relatively small differences; however, in some well-defined and articulated contexts or measures, the differences are larger. The findings point to the need for a theoretical brush that requires less broad strokes, providing a set of theoretical arguments more limited in scope with fewer universal claims. The difficulty of generating and evaluating theoretical claims of this kind represents a challenge, because the nature of the academic marketplace of ideas encourages and rewards scholars who are willing to make broad and sweeping claims. The contrast between less panoramic but precise theories supported by empirical findings and more elegant but less accurate theoretical systems requires consideration.

METHODOLOGICAL AND STATISTICAL ISSUES

A number of particular existing considerations require examination when gender plays a role in ongoing research. The first section on methodological and statistical issues examines how gender or sex as a variable operates in most investigations as a marker variable. For many empirical investigations, the inclusion of gender represents the addition of a demographic characteristic of the sample, easy to measure but with no primary theoretical utility. The second section examines how any difference or lack of difference is represented statistically. A subtle phrasing of the results can radically change the (mis)interpretation of the findings. The final section considers how gender stereotypes develop, and it considers the implications for measurement and theory as well as the paradox that the results of empirical investigations often provide when researchers are trying to generate a conclusion. The analysis of the presented methodological and statistical approaches to gender and sex suggest the need for closer attention to measurement issues when researchers study gender as well as more focused theories.

Using Sex as a Marker Variable for Gender

The usual measurement of sex involves a self-report instrument with a choice between (a) male and (b) female. Usually, most participants complete the question by marking the item that matches their biological sex. The measure is quick and convenient and highly reliable (most persons know their biological sex and have little difficulty with confidently, consistently, reliably, and accurately completing the item). The measure is a demographic characteristic convenient to measure and easy to analyze in almost any social scientific setting. More importantly, an analysis focusing on gender issues remains relatively easy to publish in the social sciences, making the inclusion of the measure extremely attractive for practical reasons. From a methodological standpoint of measurement, the indication is both easy and provides a lot of possibilities for analysis.

The problem comes at the theoretical level, where scholars seldom hypothesize a difference based on a biological factors. Instead, biological sex serves as a "marker" variable. A marker variable is a means of indirectly measuring a variable of interest. For example, when a person's temperature exceeds 98.6 °F many people would say the person is sick or probably has the flu. Even though no direct test for a virus is made, the existence of a fever provides a marker for the existence of a viral infection (when it is combined with other markers such as muscle ache and weakness, few people would question the diagnosis). Biological sex is believed to mark a difference in socialization of two groups (male and female). The measurement is indirect, as it does not directly measure developmental indicators related to gender; the assumption is that the biological measure of sex represents gender. The rationalization is that direct measurement of the issues of gender is extremely difficult or impossible, and therefore convenience (as well as scientific tradition) makes this biological marker more attractive (similar to why a thermometer to measure temperature is used rather than a blood test for a virus). The challenge is that the scholar must assume that the level of homogeneity in the gender socialization process within the biological groups is smaller than the believed corresponding heterogeneity between the biological groups (a central assumption of both the analysis of variance and the t test). The assumption of relatively homogenous social development within a biological group can be challenged fairly directly and may independently provide explanation for the disappointing findings for indirect gender measurement relying on the biological marker.

Society contains a great deal of variability of socializing agencies and models. Factors such as region of the country, religion, family size, and dissolution will all impact the gender socialization of the person. Recent movie heroines in films such as *Laura Croft: Tomb Raider* and *Kill Bill* (Vols. 1 and 2) portray women as action-adventure heroes wielding weapons of violence in what would be considered traditional masculine roles. However, it remains unclear if these female images truly represent independence and assertiveness or simply create new expectations for additional womanly duties (subservient to men). Even *Buffy: The Vampire Slayer* ends with Buffy, supposedly a strong heroine who protects the world from evil, finally freeing herself from the set of rules (developed by men) that condemn her to a life of servitude of killing. For researchers, the difficulty is that the social processes believed to generate the differences between men and women are never directly examined or compared (either between or even within groups) when a biological marker is used rather than direct measurement. Essentially, the very foundation for the research (e.g., impact of socialization practices) never receives attention and development. Further, researchers lack a theoretical means for characterizing the findings based on the use of marker variables. This lack of theory creates problems because findings from studies using marker variables frequently become part of the ideological battle over the existence and interpretation of social mores and social images.

The problem is not empirical but rather theoretical. At the current time, no scientific theory about gender differences emerges that handles the paradox of plenty of data (and now meta-analyses) and the lack of a clear and consistent method for characterizing the emerging set of findings. The development of a theory that articulates and hypothesizes about differences in a testable manner (making the underlying processes methodologically accessible) becomes a requirement. Eventually, a theory that handles both the sex or gender differences and lack of sex or gender differences will emerge that provides coherence to the plethora of findings. The current apparent inconsistency in findings represents the lack of a general theoretical approach that provides for a relationship between measurement and outcome. The current state of scholarship is a set of empirical data generated by a methodology that is inconsistent with the theoretical arguments used to justify the investigations. Simply asking persons to state whether they are male or female provides a crude biological marker about issues of gender development.

The Middle Versus the Tail of the Curve

Social science operates on an assumption about the central tendencies or the distribution of values for a variable: The distribution forms a normal, bell-shaped curve. The normal or bell-shaped curve illustrates a defined distribution (for a formula and some of the implications, see Glass, McGaw, & Smith, 1981). The usual comparison between groups uses the mean level of the distribution, and when associations or differences emerge, the statement really is about (in most circumstances, but not all) comparing the "average" man to the "average" women. Most gender or sex research characterizes or compares the central tendency (arithmetic mean) of the two groups.

Consider the meta-analysis (Gayle, Preiss, & Allen, 2002) examining the comparison of men and women on the self-reported use of conflict strategies that concludes that men use more competitive strategies ($d = 0.20$ or $r = .10$). The effect size is relatively small; when the score of the average man and the average woman is compared, the differences would not be very large. Many persons would probably square the correlation of .10 and get .01 and conclude that a 1% variance accounted for is irrelevant. Rosenthal (1985) pointed out that this conclusion is often inaccurate—a point echoed by Eagly (1995a) and Abelson (1985). This section demonstrates that what most scholars would consider small effects sometimes generate important implications for the social sciences. One method of demonstrating the potential importance of so-called small effects is to change the perspective or wording of the conclusion. Instead of comparing the average man to the average woman, suppose one wants to compare extremely competitive men to extremely competitive women; then one is examining a different part of the data distribution (the area of the curves).

A comparison of normal curves operates by using the typical z tables found in most textbooks on statistics or quantitative research methodology. The z table provides a percentage of the normal curve between the mean and the particular score (as represented in terms of z, or the standardized score). The standard normal curve provides a representation of what percentage of scores should be greater or less than any particular score on the curve. One way to compare the impact of gender is to ask how many (what percentage) of men or women score past a particular cutoff point (or below a particular score as well).

At the level of curves, consider the following: Suppose men score a mean score of 100 with $SD = 10$ on some measure of competitiveness conflict strategy use and women score 98 with $SD = 10$ on the same scale. The difference between the male and female means would be $d = 0.20$ ($r = .10$). A cutoff score divides the curve of scores into a percentage of area on each side of the curve (the percentage reflects the number of scores on each side of the cutoff value). There are 50% of men who score above the mean for men, whereas 42.07% of women who score above the mean for men. This is based on a z score of 0.00 for men and 0.20 for women. Table 6.1 demonstrates that the ratio of men to women over this particular score is 50 : 42—for every woman scoring greater than that score, there are 1.19 men. To put it another way, the meta-analysis by Gayle et al. (1994) suggested that 19% more men score above the self-reported male mean competitiveness strategy score than women at that particular cutoff point. That difference indicates that more men report higher use of competitive strategies than women. The difference is

TABLE 6.1
Binomial Effect Size Display for Interpreting Results

	Percentage of Persons Past the Cutoff Score			
Cutoff Score	*Men*	*Women*	*Ratio of Men to Women*	*Percentage Increase*
Greater than the mean; above average	50.00	42.07	1.19:1	19
Greater than 1 *SD* above the mean; mildly competitive	15.87	11.51	1.38:1	38
Greater than 2 *SD* above the mean; very competitive	2.28	1.39	1.64:1	64
Greater than 3 *SD* above the mean; extremely competitive	0.13	0.06	2.16:1	116

statistically significant, but the statement that the average man and average woman are different would probably violate what most people believe such a statement implies (that there is a large difference between men and women on reported use of conflict strategy preference). The key is that statistical significance (particularly in a meta-analysis with a sample size in the thousands) does not indicate a finding that supports a theoretical argument. The question is one of characterization: Is a 19% increase in the number of men scoring above the male average an important substantive finding or not?

Consider higher levels of competitiveness strategy use and examine the ratio at 1 *SD* over the male mean (a score of 110). At this point, 15.87% of the men will score greater than the cutoff score. At this cutoff score, only 11.51% of the women score this high or higher. The ratio of men to women at this score is 15.87:11.51 or 1.38. This value indicates that, for every woman above that point, there is 1.38 men or an increase of 38%. That is, 38% more men would endorse more competitive strategy use than women. The more extreme the cutoff score, the larger the difference in the ratio.

Suppose we use a cutoff score of 120, or 2 *SD* above the mean. At this point, approximately 2.28% of the men and 1.39% of the women will score equal to or above this value (a raw score of 120 or a *z* score of 2.00). This is a ratio of 2.28:1.39 or 1.64, indicating 64% more men above this value. What is important to note is that most persons would probably characterize a 64% increase as a significant and important finding. However, only 2.28% of the men score past this cutoff and only 1.39% of women. The finding is only important if the question of substance considers highly competitive individuals and then examines the ratio of gender for that population. The ratio or finding for the average man and the average woman remains the same.

Finally, suppose we use a cutoff score of 130 (or 3 *SD* above the male mean). At this point approximately 0.13% of the men and 0.06% of the women would score at or above this point. The ratio is now 0.13 : 0.06 or 2.16 : 1, indicating that 116% more men than women score past this point on self-reports of competitive strategy use.

The farther the distance from the mean and the more extreme the score, the greater the ratio between the two groups. The larger the cutoff score, the greater the number of men to women. Correspondingly, going the other direction, we find that the lower the cutoff score, the greater the number of women relative to men. That relative ratio may indicate the practical outcomes of selection requirements on the basis of sex. If we compare groups on the basis of the overall average score, the distinctions between men and women seem small. However, as we go to more extreme values for a cutoff or selection score, that difference in the ratio based on biological sex becomes greater and greater.

Here is the paradox. The statement that extremely competitive persons are most likely male is true at the same time as the statement that there is little difference between men and women on competitiveness. The problem in the paradox lies in the fact that the first part of the statement compares men and women at the extreme end of the scale. The second part of the statement really wants to compare average men with average women. The problem is that both statements have potentially important ramifications, and both statements are true. That is why the results of any empirical investigation or meta-analysis should be examined carefully to determine what kind of claim the investigator makes. Is the claim advanced to compare the average man and woman, or is the comparison about some type of person (highly competitive)?

A statement of comparison is all about what you are comparing and on what basis. Consider a dependent variable that is (fortunately) extremely rare—serial killers. We know from experience that serial killers are men (not 100%, but probably a ratio of something like 50:1 or 60:1). Not all men are serial killers. If we could magically create a scale that was 100% accurate in classifying serial killers, we would probably find that the mean difference on this scale between men and women would be very small (possibly of the order of $r = .001$). Such a small mean difference between groups, however, when we go out 50 or 100 *SD* might easily produce a ratio of 50:1 or 60:1. The key is that the comparison is not about gender (because such a small percentage of persons are serial killers); when we go that far out on the curve, we are talking about serial killers, not gender. So it may be true that believing that serial killers are men is justified by such data, but it would be inaccurate to characterize men as serial killers.

Explanation for Stereotypes

Stereotypes come from a process of prototype development that applies examples drawn from the extremes. The assertion usually is structured in the following way: All of *X* possess the quality *Y*. The assertion designates an undesirable characteristic (*Y*) that members of the group (*X*) possess. This section considers how social science contributes to the formation and promulgation of stereotypes. The stereotype developed is wrong, but the data used to develop the stereotype are correct.

The work by Gayle et al. (1994, 1998, 2002) on conflict styles indicates that there are probably twice as many extremely competitive men than women (i.e., at 3 *SD* above the mean). The stereotype that men are more competitive than women is probably based on exposure to extremely competitive persons. If we consider asking a person about whether men or women are more competitive, the probability is that the person will recall the more extreme elements. It would also be accurate to say that we are twice as likely to encounter a highly competitive man as we are to encounter a highly competitive woman. A person stating that men are more competitive simply is searching a memory that contains a biased sample of extreme values that are dominated by male individuals. The result is a representation about gender differences that is inaccurate when we are comparing the average man and woman but not inaccurate when we are considering the ratio of extreme cases.

Accordingly, the stereotype has a basis in fact (and perhaps experience), but the information is misapplied when we are developing the stereotype as applied to the particular person.

ETHICAL IMPLICATIONS OF (DIS)CONTINUING THE CURRENT RESEARCH PRACTICES

The general public reads about differences based on extreme values and misapplies that to a general difference existing between men and women. Given the social implications of the findings, the ways in which the general public uses social scientific findings raises questions about the future conduct of research involving gender or sex. The challenge facing scientists is to determine whether to continue the current practices or not. Empirical evidence disputes the widely held view of massive sex or gender differences, but for science to abandon consideration of these issues undermines the massive concerns about discrimination and inequity. Ignoring the popular belief in the existence of such fundamental differences separates science from the everyday lives of the population (like letting the population believe the world is flat when the scientific community believes otherwise). Therefore, it is important to explore the ethical implications of maintaining and changing the status quo.

Two general principles of research ethics become relevant to the discussion of continuing the study of gender differences. First, general principles of ethical research suggest that researchers have a responsibility to the larger community (Anderson, 1987). Reynolds (1982) suggested that social scientists are concerned with improving the human condition. So, research agendas should be developed with the larger community in mind (how society will benefit from the research), and researchers should present findings honestly and fairly (Anderson). Second, researchers should be concerned with the ethical implementation of knowledge (Reynolds). Researchers' responsibilities continue after the publication of their findings; researchers should be concerned with the implications of findings for public policy and other applications.

Ethical Issues Related to Continuing the Study of Sex or Gender Differences

One ethical issue that arises in discussing the continued study of sex or gender differences is looking at the extent to which the study of difference is going to support and perpetuate the very stereotypes that feminists and others challenge. Canary and Hause (1993) argued that researchers perpetuate stereotypes by interpreting research findings in light of stereotypes. They demonstrate that skillful researchers can interpret data that both supports and contradicts stereotypes in ways that reinforce the existence of stereotypes. Canary and Emmers-Sommer (1997) pointed out that the problem is not with stereotypes in and of themselves, because stereotypes provide a means for predicting behaviors and establishing baseline expectations when we are interacting with unfamiliar persons. For Canary and Emmers-Sommer, the issue is the extent to which researchers utilize stereotypes uncritically as scientific explanations and predictors of difference. They go on to suggest that existing stereotypes are outdated, distorted, and unreflective of communication in most personal relationships.

Although Canary and Emmers-Sommer (1997) pointed out that researchers often utilize stereotypes unknowingly, they also noted that researchers' use of stereotypes often reflects the difficulty that the researchers have in letting go of ideological frameworks. Even when confronted with findings that contradict belief systems, researchers find it difficult to let go of beliefs about gender, and they interpret such findings in light of belief systems or ideological frameworks. Political beliefs and ideological frameworks color the way in which researchers see and interpret research findings. Anderson (1987) argued that some researchers become caught in complex systems in which they learn to play particular games that serve the wrong interests. Although interpreting data in ways that support ideological beliefs about sex and gender may be, in the short term, beneficial to the politics of challenging gender discrimination, in the long term such practices may not meet the aims of good science or the interests of the larger community.

Stereotypical views of men and women polarize men and women (Canary & Hause, 1993). Eichler (1991) argued that researchers should not dichotomize behaviors into male and female when such behaviors are part of the human condition. She suggested that dichotomization constitutes gender insensitivity. The polarization of men and women has received much attention in the popular press (i.e., Tannen, 1990; Gray, 1992). However, research (i.e., Goldsmith & Fulfs, 1999) challenges the claims of the two-cultures view presented both in the popular press and in communication textbooks. MacGeorge, Graves, Feng, Gillihan, and Burleson (2004) asserted that "the mythical status of the different cultures thesis is now so evident, especially with respect to supportive communication, that we believe it is, henceforth, inappropriate (and irresponsible) for authors of textbooks, self-help books, and similar publications to feature favorably this thesis or leading statements of it" (p. 173). They go on to argue that such texts are meant to inform and instruct people; therefore, teaching the different cultures perspective constitutes the presentation of misinformation. Essentially, they argue that it is unethical to perpetuate the idea that men and women live in distinct cultures. Following the claims of MacGeorge et al., we find it unethical to continue to suggest that men and women live in two cultures. Researchers have a responsibility to try to see that the findings that contradict popular works (e.g., Tannen and Gray) are incorporated into textbooks to show the limitations of these perspectives and open a dialogue as to what the findings might mean (e.g., Goldsmith & Fulfs, 1999). Further, researchers have a responsibility to use findings to generate theories that appeal to both the scholarly and the lay community. Researchers need to test their theories of gender to ensure they work in practice (Wood & Dindia, 1998).

Ethical Issues Related to Discontinuing Gender Difference Research

Three issues of concern arise when we consider the ethics of discontinuing the practice of examining gender differences in communication. These issues examine the potential harms that might occur if the community stopped studying gender differences. If part of research is improving the human condition (Reynolds, 1982), then we should be concerned with what harm might arise if a set of questions and concerns simply disappears from the research agenda.

The two-cultures view of gender receives a lot of attention (both scientific and popular), but the social scientific evidence amassed demonstrates similarity and small differences essential to debunking the popular myths and stereotypes of gender differences. Ceasing research constitutes an irresponsible decision that would prevent scholars from offering evidence that would challenge misinformation presented in the popular press. The acceptance of a conclusion in the scientific community does not automatically end the discussion in society or result in widespread acceptance of that conclusion. The need to continue to demonstrate that the findings remain consistent represents a continued challenge to the scientific community. The fact that scientific consensus may exist does not automatically confer popular or public consensus. The separation in discourse between the public and technical spheres of argument reflects the gap between what is known versus what is accepted.

A second ethical issue emerges from concerns about what might be lost in terms of research equality if the study of gender differences in communication were stopped. Criticisms of androcentric practices of science made by feminists such as Harding (1986) were seminal in challenging research practices. Prior to feminist critiques of androcentrism in science, much of the theoretical research assumed a male standard for judging the behaviors of both men and women (Canary & Emmers-Sommer, 1997). The criticisms have raised attention to the use of a male standard, and some of the practices have begun to change. However, Eichler (1991) suggested that degrees of androcentrism continue in social scientific research. Particularly, she pointed to practices such as using a male frame of reference to evaluate events, treating men as social actors and women as passive, maintaining male interests over female interests, and rendering women invisible. Thus, one potential concern is that decreased attention to gender differences might result in changes in research practices that would make researchers less vigilant to decreasing androcentric practices.

A related concern is ensuring that scholars do not use androcentric practices to interpret findings that support differences of degree or skill. Dindia has argued that many of the communication differences between men and women are differences of degree, not kind (Wood & Dindia, 1998). MacGeorge et al. (2004) made a similar claim in looking at differences in social support. They found that men and women are similar in the kinds of support that they provide, and they noted that differences in providing social support are differences in skill, with women exhibiting more skill in providing emotional support. Although research findings suggest similarities in the ways in which men and women communicate, the prevailing emphasis on two cultures leads to the possibility that differences, even differences in degree but not kind, will be emphasized over similarity. Further, a focus on difference could perpetuate andocentric views. Jaggar (1990) noted the social tendency to value male attributes as assets and female attributes as deficits. Thus, focusing on differences could perpetuate stereotypes in which the behaviors of one gender (male) are valued over the behaviors of the other (female).

A third concern emerges from considerations of the ways in which ceasing to look at gender might alter policy decisions. The reasonable-woman standard used to determine or judge what counts as sexual harassment is based on research findings suggesting that there are gender differences in perceptions of sexual harassing behaviors. Research suggests that men and women have differing perceptions of what counts as sexually harassing behaviors; thus, the policy is based on what women (not men) would see as sexually harassing. As noted earlier, researchers have a responsibility to work at integrating research in ethical and appropriate ways (Reynolds, 1982). The connection between research and practice raises two important questions. First, to what extent are communication researchers responsible for ensuring that they are doing research that will lead to good policy? Second, if the research community stops examining gender differences, will it have a negative affect on policy development and implementation? Consideration of the impact of any restriction on gender research that might contribute to misinformation and lack of information that will produce bad policy should remain a fundamental issue for social scientists.

CONCLUSIONS

The problem facing the social science community concerns the transition from acceptance of gender differences as a basis for empirical examination to, instead, a more focused (nuanced) and theoretically based set of assumptions and thinking about gender and sex. The next generation of practices requires a greater emphasis on the relationship between theoretical argument about the substance of gender or sex differences and the operational methods of examining the differences.

The reliance on simple biological sex as a marker variable of social differences should simply be considered a failure. Methodologically, this marker simply lacks enough differentiation to substantiate the widely held beliefs in such differences. However, methodological problems should be considered an opportunity for more sophistication in the measurement and greater emphasis on theoretical development. The focus on the development of measures of gender starts to unpack the theoretical implications or assumptions of gender and should promote a wider discussion as well as more developed thinking.

Rather than viewing the end of the discussion of gender differences, this essay would argue that the scientific community operates at the beginning of the process of understanding gender differences. The challenge to the community requires the creation of some type of theoretical scheme to provide interpretation for the growing database. The problem that Harding (1986, 1991) identified is that, without the availability of an alternative conceptualization to challenge the existing thinking, change will not occur. If the current scientific approaches are not up to the task, then new approaches and theories must be developed. Whether successful development of an empirical theory will come from feminist, biological, or traditional approaches remains to be seen. Even once an acceptable approach emerges, that theory will eventually be replaced by a more comprehensive and accurate theory. Despite a plethora of calls made starting 20 years ago for a reconceptualization of gender issues (Putnam, 1982, Rakow, 1986; West & Zimmerman, 1987), a dearth of fully developed and articulated alternatives exist.

The generation of scientific theoretical positions fully articulated and testable eventually resolves the problem. Any scientific theory should provide the means for its own demise by stating testable sets of assumptions. Scientists intend to provide the most reasonable explanation and interpretation of existing data. However, one problem that negatively affects the scientific study of gender is the existence of polemic attitudes toward the issue. Sommer (1994) provided a catalogue of examples with the problems that exist when scientific evidence is disregarded or distorted in the effort to advance propositions. Therefore the challenge is to not get caught in the political or polemic arguments about gender in society. Science has a poor track record of uncovering and ascertaining accurate representations when the fundamental driving force behind the research advances a particular social agenda. The tension remains between those scholars wishing things to be true to justify particular actions (e.g., Frey, Pearce, Pollock, Artz, & Murphy, 1996) and those scientists using a method to seek and find the truth (e.g., Wood, 1996).

Eagly (1995a, 1995b) pointed out the paradox and perils that exist when scholars and activists wish to use social scientific findings to promote particular social and political agendas. One set of feminist scholars hopes to find no gender differences as a basis for promoting equity, whereas another set of feminist scholars would like to emphasize differences between men and women as a basis for social change to promote equitable practices. Relying on scientific data as a basis for political action ignores the real moral and ethical requirements for public action. Science provides information, and scientists should advocate and work to promote social welfare. However, the ethics of research require us to eventually be bound by the results of our investigations and the theories that guide us, rather than what we would like to find.

Examining sex or gender differences and similarities is not a simple case of concluding that men and women are different or similar. Certainly there are differences in physiology, psychology, and sociology. One cannot simply say that men and women are different. Men and women do share an astoundingly large number of physiological, psychological, and sociological characteristics. The challenge is to create, articulate, and then test a scientific theory differentiating the basis of those similarities and differences. In the long term, relying on a single-item measure that reflects no explicit theoretical premise is doomed to produce useless and meaningless scientific data while at the same time the application to social agendas and actions represents a fundamental problem for the responsible use of scientific information. This chapter articulates only some of the measurement and statistical issues encountered when we are considering such endeavors. These issues should be addressed in any ongoing program of research comparing gender or sex.

REFERENCES

Abelson, R. (1985). A variance explanation paradox: When a little is a lot. *Psychological Bulletin, 97*, 129–133.

Allen, M., Emmers-Sommer, T., & Crowell, T. (2002). Couples negotiating safer sex behaviors: A meta-analysis of the impact of conversation and gender. In M. Allen, R. Preiss, B. Gayle, & N. Burrell (Eds.), *Interpersonal communication research: Advances through meta-analysis* (pp. 263–280). Mahwah, NJ: Lawrence Erlbaum Associates.

Anderson, J. A. (1987). *Communication research: Issues and methods*. New York: McGraw-Hill.

Canary, D. J., & Emmers-Sommer, T. M. (1997). *Sex and gender differences in personal relationships*. New York: Guilford.

Canary, D. J., & Hause, K. (1993). Is there any reason to research sex differences in communication? *Communication Quarterly, 41*, 129–144.

Eagly, A. (1995a). The sciences and politics of comparing women and men. *American Psychologist, 50*, 145–158.

Eagly, A. (1995b). Reflections of the commenter's views. *American Psychologist, 50*, 169–171.

Eichler, M. (1991). *Nonsexist research methods: A practical guide*. New York: Routledge.

Frey, L., Pearce, W. B., Pollock, M. A., Artz, L., & Murphy, B. O. (1996). Looking for justice in all the wrong places: On a communication approach to social justice. *Communcation Studies, 47*, 110–127.

Gayle, B., Preiss, R., & Allen, M. (1994). Gender differences and the use of conflict strategies. In L. Turner and H. Sterk (Eds.), *Differences that make a difference: Examining the assumptions in gender research* (pp. 13–26). Westport, CT: Bergin & Garvey.

Gayle, B., Preiss, R., & Allen, M. (1998). Embedded gender expectations: A covariate analysis of conflict situations and issues. *Communication Research Reports, 15*, 379–387.

Gayle, B., Preiss, R., & Allen, M. (2002). A meta-analytic interpretation of intimate and nonintimate interpersonal conflict. In M. Allen, R. Preiss, B. Gayle, & N. Burrell (Eds.), *Interpersonal communication research: Advances through meta-analysis* (pp. 345–369). Mahwah, NJ: Lawrence Erlbaum Associates.

Glass, G., McGaw, B., & Smith, M. (1981) *Meta-analysis in social research*. Beverly Hills, CA: Sage.

Goldsmith, D., & Fulfs, P. (1999). "You just don't have the evidence": An analysis of claims and evidence. In M. Roloff (Ed.), *Communication yearbook 22* (pp. 1–50). Thousand Oaks, CA: Sage.

Gray, J. (1992). *Men are from Mars, Women are from Venus. A practical guide to improving communication and getting what you want in your relationships*. New York: HarperCollins.

Han, M. (2003). Body image dissatisfaction and eating disturbance among Korean college female students: Relationships to media exposure, upward comparison, and perceived reality. *Communication Studies, 54*, 65–78.

Harding, S. (1986). *The science question in feminism.* Ithaca, NY: Cornell University Press.

Harding, S. (1991). *Whose science? Whose knowledge? Thinking from women's lives.* Ithaca, NY: Cornell University Press.

Herrett-Skjellum, J., & Allen, M. (1996). Television programming and sexual stereotypes: A meta-analysis. In B. Burleson (Ed.), *Communication yearbook 19* (pp. 157–186). Thousand Oaks, CA: Sage.

Hyde, J., & Frost, L. (1993). Meta-analysis in the psychology of women. In F. Denmark & M. Paludi (Eds.), *Psychology of women: A handbook of issues and theories* (pp. 185–207). Wesport, CT: Greenwood.

Hyde, J., & Plant, E. (1995). Magnitude of psychological gender differences: Another side to the story. *American Psychologist, 50*, 129–161.

Jaggar, A. M. (1990). Sexual difference and sexual equality. In D. L. Rhode (Ed.), *Theoretical perspectives on sexual differences* (pp. 239–254). New Haven, CT: Yale University Press.

MacGeorge, E. L., Graves, A. R., Feng, B., Gillihan, S. J., & Burleson, B. R. (2004). The myth of gender cultures: Similarities outweigh differences in men's and women's provision of and responses to supportive communication. *Sex Roles, 50*, 143–175.

Putnam, L. (1982). In search of gender: A critique of communication and sex roles research. *Women's Studies in Communication, 5*, 1–9.

Rakow, L. (1986). Rethinking gender research in communication. *Journal of Communication, 76*(4), 11–26.

Reynolds, P. D. (1982). *Ethics and social science research*. Englewood Cliffs, N.J.: Prentice-Hall.

Rosenthal, R. (1985). *Meta-analysis procedures for social researchers.* Newbury Park, CA: Sage.

Sahlstein, E., & Allen, M. (2002). Sex differences in self-esteem: A meta-analytic assessment. In M. Allen, R. Preiss, B. Gayle, & N. Burrell (Eds.), *Interpersonal communication research: Advances through meta-analysis* (pp. 59–72). Mahwah, NJ: Lawrence Erlbaum Associates.

Sommer, C. (1994). *Who stole feminism? How women have betrayed women.* New York: Simon & Schuster.

Tannen, D. (1990). *You just don't understand: Women and men in conversation.* New York: Ballantine.

West, C., & Zimmerman, D. (1987). Doing gender. *Gender & Society, 1*, 125–151.

Wolf, N. (1991). *The beauty myth.* New York: Morrow.

Wood, J. T. (1996). Social justice research: Alive and well in the field of communication. *Communication Studies, 47*, 128–134.

Wood, J. T., & Dindia, K. (1998). What's the difference? A dialogue about differences and similarities between women and men. In D. J. Canary & K. Dindia (Eds.), *Sex differences and similarities in communication: Critical essays and empirical investigation of sex and gender in interaction* (pp. 19–39). Mahwah, NJ: Lawrence Erlbaum Associates.

II

Approaches to Sex Differences and Similarities

7

The Evolution of Biological Sex Differences in Communication

Peter A. Andersen
San Diego State University

During the past decade, communication scholars have engaged in a heated debate about sex differences in communication. Whereas one group of scholars suggests that sex differences are large and culturally based, another group maintains that sex differences are small and overblown (Wood & Dindia, 1998). Virtually lost in this debate is a serious consideration of whether sex differences are partly biological in nature and have evolutionary origins, regardless of the magnitude of these differences. Based on an examination of the communication literature on sex differences, Andersen (1998) suggested that the field of communication is in biological denial. This chapter is an effort to restore some intellectual balance by examining research that shows that a number of sex differences may, indeed, have a biological basis.

The fact that biologically based sex differences exist in human communication does not mean that culturally based sex and gender differences do not exist; quite the contrary. Sex and gender differences are affected by both nature and nurture and the interaction between these two forces over time. By denying evolutionary differences in male–female communication behavior the rich interplay between biology and culture can never be fully examined. In this chapter I briefly review five bodies of research that demonstrate biological sex differences between men and women in communication. First, I explore a plethora of evidence that demonstrates the innate superiority of women in nonverbal receiving ability, a vital component of social skill. Next, I explore the corresponding advantage of men in navigational skill and spatial ability. Third, I examine the effect of evolutionary forces on the physical appearance of men and women. Fourth, I examine differences in sexual communication behavior that are attributable to social-evolutionary forces. Last, I briefly review research on the interpersonal and relational preferences and behaviors of men and women.

Years ago, Birdwhistell (1970) discussed three types of sex differences. In this taxonomy, primary sexual characteristics relate to basic reproductive functions and behaviors such as the production of ova or spermatozoa and the ability to ejaculate, gestate, and lactate (Andersen, 1999). Secondary sexual characteristics, which are the indirect result of reproductive roles, are often anatomical but can be behavioral as well. Physical differences such as differences in body hair or muscle mass are secondary sexual characteristics, but so are behaviors that are genetically sex linked. Tertiary characteristics are patterns of social behaviors that are learned, culturally based, and situationally produced.

Primary, reproductive differences are the least amenable to change based on gender roles (even sex-change operations do not give the patient the ability to produce eggs or sperm) and are least influenced by the sociocultural climate. As Halpern (1986) stated, "the different roles that men and women play in reproduction are incontrovertible" (p. 68). Because human beings have spent hundreds of thousands of years evolving as men and women, a fruitful place to search for the most stable differences in communication would be in primary and secondary behaviors that are most closely related to a person's reproductive role.

In the field of communication, textbooks on sex (or gender) and communication can still be characterized as being in biological denial. Few books have a forthright discussion of genetic or biological differences in the communication behavior of men and women. Denying or suppressing the biological basis of behavior stifles intellectual and scholarly progress, which leads to outrageous claims that cannot be countered. Academics should not suppress findings that fail to meet current standards for political correctness. Realizing the political minefield that navigating this literature entails, I begin my discussion of biological differences with one of the most consistent differences in communication research: the superior social and nonverbal sensitivity of women.

DIFFERENCES IN SOCIAL AND NONVERBAL SENSITIVITY

Several published meta-analyses, such as those by Canary and Hause (1993) and Wilkins and Andersen (1991), show little or no differences in male and female communication behavior. Unfortunately, neither of these meta-analyses included the hundreds of studies that have examined sex differences in nonverbal receiving ability. Both folk wisdom and a considerable body of current communication research indicate that women are more engaged, sensitive, and skilled communicators than men (e.g., see Burleson & Kunkel, chap. 8, this volume). Though some of these differences may emerge from differences in the socialization of men and women, these differences are too geographically, historically, and developmentally pervasive to be primarily social.

Hall (1979) suggested that "if there is a key feature of women's mystique, it is probably some kind of special social sensitivity or social ability that they are believed to possess... detection of emotional cues is surely a part of what is called 'women's intuition'" (p. 32). Similarly, women are better able to express themselves, particularly in the realms of emotional and nonverbal communication (see other chapters in this volume). As a male communication scholar, it is hard to summarize this body of research without feeling a degree of envy for the communication skill and connection that women experience.

Studies have shown that women are better decoders and encoders of nonverbal and emotional communication (Hall, chap. 4, this volume; Guerrero, Jones, & Boburka, chap. 13, this volume). Women also have generally superior verbal skills that emerge in infancy (Collaer & Hines, 1995; Halpern, 1986), are more skillful and connected listeners (Ivy & Backlund, 1994; Tannen, 1990), and are more engaged, empathic communicators (Pearson, West, & Turner, 1995). In the area of social sensitivity, and of nonverbal sensitivity in particular, research suggests that women have justifiably earned their reputation for enhanced social skill and intuition (Burleson & Kunkel, chap. 8, this volume; Hall, this volume).

Nonverbal Receiving Ability

One of the clearest and most consistent sex differences in communication concerns women's superior nonverbal receiving or decoding ability. This difference has been consistently detected for people at a variety of ages and across numerous cultures (Knapp & Hall, 1992).

Some of the research has used the Profile of Nonverbal Sensitivity (PONS; Rosenthal, Hall, DiMatteo, Rogers, & Archer, 1979), a test with notoriously poor reliability (e.g., Buller & Aune, 1992). Despite the insensitivity of the PONS, it consistently picks up sex differences. Rosenthal et al. found that female individuals have approximately a 0.5 *SD* advantage in nonverbal sensitivity. This was true of the short PONS, the long PONS, and the still-photo (nonverbal sensitivity) NS, and it was consistent across age. Moreover, the size of the effect was slightly larger for grade-school children, which suggests either early developmental or biological differences. Rosenthal et al. pondered, "are females biologically programmed to have or to develop superior nonverbal skill (perhaps because such skill enhances the survivability of offspring) or do female children develop superior skill as a result of social learning?" (p. 165). These researchers did not take a position on this issue but cited research studies that have shown that, for infants 1 to 3 days old, girls tended to cry more than boys in response to another infants' cries but not to other sounds, suggesting a biological difference. Additionally, Rosenthal and DePaulo (1979) reported meta-analytic research across 11 nations showing consistently higher scores for women than for men on the PONS.

Meta-analyses of sex differences using a variety of measures of nonverbal sensitivity also demonstrate the superior skill of women in this domain. Hall (1978) summarized 75 studies on this topic and found 80% of them showed a female advantage. The effect size across all of the studies was moderate ($d = 0.40$) or slightly less than 0.5 *SD*. The combined probability of the female advantage in nonverbal sensitivity all of the studies was 3 in 10,000, suggesting chance can be ruled out as an explanation. Hall (1979) also demonstrated that these results are stable across the decades when the study was conducted. Moreover, Hall (1978) showed no effect for the sex or age of the senders or the age of the receivers, suggesting this is not likely to be a cultural or developmental phenomenon. When other factors have so little impact on a phenomenon, biological forces would seem to be indicated. Hall (1979) came to this conclusion: "Even the youngest ages tested, the female advantage is at least what it is found among older groups. If females' advantage is learned it must be learned very early indeed" (p. 42).

The Evolution of Women's Receiving Ability Advantage

Alternatives to a biological explanation for women's greater nonverbal sensitivity seem implausible. It has been suggested that sex differences in nonverbal sensitivity really reflect gender differences in sex-role orientation. If so, the masculinity or femininity scores of individuals, regardless of biological sex, should better predict nonverbal sensitivity than does biological sex. However, this is not the case. Based on a meta-analysis of 11 studies that associated masculinity and femininity with nonverbal sensitivity, Hall (1979) concluded that "overall the correlations of masculinity or femininity measured on unipolar scales with nonverbal decoding ability were small and nonsignificant" (p. 52). Greater femininity does not result in greater nonverbal sensitivity. Indeed, according to Hall, when masculinity and femininity were partialed out, the effects for sex differences in decoding were not appreciably changed. In her commentary on Hall's results, Wietz (1979) concluded that "Hall says she does not wish to speak about the possible biological roots of what has been loosely termed 'women's intuition,' but perhaps it is time that we did speak of this factor. The difficulty of doing so without an excess of political baggage is the problem, but should not blind us to the need for discussion" (p. 135).

Similarly, it has been frequently proffered that women are more socially sensitive because they live in an oppressive, patriarchal society in which sensitivity to subtle cues is necessary for survival. No serious student of sex roles can deny that many women have lived and continue to live in an oppressive patriarchal society. However, little support exists for the hypothesis that oppression causes increased sensitivity. Hall (1978) demonstrated that there is no age effect for sex differences in nonverbal sensitivity. She concluded "that young girls should be better judges of nonverbal communication than young boys are is inconsistent with this hypothesis, unless one seriously believes that young girls as well as women are oppressed in our society" (p. 354). Early oppression of girls is a possibility, but other evidence suggests that oppression is not linked to sensitivity. Hall (1979) reported results that show that, when equalitarian attitude scales were correlated with nonverbal sensitivity, no significant association was obtained for men. For women, equalitarianism was actually *positively* associated with nonverbal decoding. Hall summarized this finding: "These positive correlations indicate that females with more equalitarian, 'liberated' views on women's role in society were better decoders than more conservative females, over two age levels" (pp. 5–6). This is exactly the opposite result predicted by the oppression hypothesis. Similarly, Hall (1979) found that women who subscribed to traditional sex roles had lower sensitivity scores than more liberated women.

An alternative explanation for sex differences in social sensitivity is that women are genetically and biologically predisposed to greater sensitivity to social and nonverbal cues. Hall (1978) came to this conclusion:

> Another kind of explanation in its simplest form, would hold that females are "wired" from birth to be especially sensitive to nonverbal cues or especially quick learners of such cues. This would make evolutionary sense, because nonverbal sensitivity on a mother's part might enable her to detect distress in her youngsters or threatening signals from other adults, thus enhancing the survival chances of her offspring. (p. 854)

In fact, several sets of studies show that females are particularly sensitive to negative affective cues (Hall, 1978; Rosenthal et al., 1979). Such increased nonverbal sensitivity would help in selecting a mate that displays little negative affect or hostility. But what are the specific processes that could impart superior social sensitivity to women?

One explanation is based on sex differences in brain lateralization. Considerable research has shown that men have more specialized, lateralized brain functions, whereas women have more symmetrical, integrated brain functions (Andersen, Garrison, & Andersen, 1979; Halpern, 1986). Hall (1979) summarized research suggesting that the more efficient communication between the brain hemispheres of women enable logical, verbal information to be coordinated with nonverbal information to produce greater intuition and social sensitivity. Stacks and Andersen (1989) suggested that interhemispheric cooperation is a primary form of intrapersonal communication that has a number of benefits, including enhanced processing of complex information and analysis of emotional content and imagery.

A second explanation for gender-linked differences in social sensitivity may be a sex-linked difference at the chromosomal level. Sensitivity, as is discussed in greater detail later, has greater benefits for women because women have significantly greater parental investment (Goldsmith, 1991; Symons, 1987; Trost & Alberts, 1998). Women have a finite number of reproductive opportunities because of relatively long periods of gestation and lactation; men have many potential reproductive opportunities because their only necessary biological role in reproduction is insemination. Thus, skills that result in child protection, mate retention, and successful parenting, such as social sensitivity and other communication skills, would be relatively more important from a genetic standpoint for women than for men. Eagly (1987) suggested that the centrality of childrearing in women fosters communal orientation, affectional qualities, interpersonal sensitivity, emotional expressiveness, and social orientation. Evidence suggests that, for thousands of years, social life was primarily matrilineal and the life in sites of human habitation centered on women and their offspring (Miller, 1998).

A third process that may produce sex differences is based on the presence of hormones at critical stages of development. Although little evidence directly links hormone levels to greater or lesser social sensitivity, girls exposed to prenatal male hormones are described as tomboyish—more interested in so-called male activities and less interested in female activities that are arguably more social in nature (Serbin & Sprafkin, 1987).

SEX DIFFERENCES IN SPATIAL SKILLS

Although research has shown that women generally have greater nonverbal communication skills than do men, the reverse is true for spatial and navigational skills. Studies consistently show a robust male advantage in spatial skills of all types. Spatial skills were historically key survival skills that kept the group intact and coordinated hunting, gathering, and the location of mates. Today they are key proxemic skills, as affiliation on dominance displays. Dozens of studies show a moderate to large (d = 0.45–0.96), probably innate sex differences in the spatial skills of men compared with women (e.g., Buffery & Gray, 1972; Gaulin, 1992; Geary, 1998; Hyde, 1990, Rogers, 2001; Voyer, Nolan, & Voyer, 2000; Voyer & Sullivan, 2003). In the communication literature, which is generally oblivious to genetics as a field, Stewart, Cooper, and Friedley (1986) discussed male excellence in visuospatial ability as one of only four well-established primary sex differences. In a major review of the evolution of sex differences in spatial ability, Gaulin noted that, among well-documented psychological sex differences, a male advantage on spatial tasks is the most reliable. He stated that "such explanations can only be evolutionary. When the psychological features under study are widely distributed across human societies and are also present in nonhuman mammals the argument that they are cultural epiphenomenona is substantially weakened" (p. 127).

The largest male advantage is for mental rotation and visualization of objects (Linn & Petersen, 1985, Putz, Gaulin, Sponter, & McBarney, 2004; Voyer et al., 2000; Voyer & Sullivan, 2003). Men excel at tasks that involve the rotating of solid objects, the unfolding of solid objects, and the folding of flat objects (Halpern, 1986). Halpern came to this conclusion:

> Males score considerably higher on novel tests that require spatial visualization. The largest between sex differences are found on tests that require subjects to mentally rotate a two-dimension representation of a three-dimensional object in space. It is highly unlikely that anyone of either sex would have any experience with three-dimensional mental rotations. (p. 152)

Recent meta-analyses conclude that, by conventional status standards, the advantage for men on three-dimensional rotation tasks constitutes a large ($d = 0.96$) effect size (Collaer & Hines, 1995; Hyde, 1990; Linn & Petersen, 1985).

Similar male advantages appear for other spatial tasks. Halpern (1986) reviewed research that men have an advantage on an orientation factor that includes the ability to detect spatial relationships among objects and to perceive spatial patterns accurately. This ability may have evolved as a navigational skill to locate mates (Gaulin, 1992) or to detect movement of enemies or predators.

Men also excel at field independence—the ability to separate a stimulus from its environmental setting in a surrounding visual field—and in various tests of adjusting objects to their vertical position (Buffery & Gray, 1972). These results have been replicated in the United States, England, Holland, Italy, France, Hong Kong, and Sierra Leone (Buffery & Gray). Men exceed women at a host of related spatial perception tasks, for which they display a moderate to large effect size in the available meta-analyses ($d = 0.50$–0.96; Collaer & Hines, 1995; Hyde, 1990; Linn & Petersen, 1985).

Men exceed women across numerous studies of water-tipping tasks in which participants are shown a bottle or glass of water and asked to predict where the water will be when the glass is tilted (Halpern, 1986; Hyde, 1990; Linn & Petersen, 1985; Voyer et al., 2000; Voyer & Sullivan, 2003). The ability of boys exceeds that of girls at every grade throughout childhood and as adults on water-tipping tasks. Halpern concluded that "it does not seem likely that males have more or better experience with a tipped glass of water. In fact, one could argue that females, the primary cooks and dishwashers in many homes, might have more related experience with tipped glasses of water and other liquids than males" (p. 151).

Male advantage is observed across numerous other spatial tasks, motor skills, tracking tests, and spatial memory measures. Men and women employ different mental strategies in attempting to perform spatial tasks. Men usually visualize the entire pattern, whereas women are more likely to use verbal labels (Halpern, 1986). When finding directions or solving mazes, women employ landmarks, whereas males are more sensitive to overall spatial geography and geometry (Gaulin, 1992). Interestingly, just as women appear to be better able to see the entire picture or gestalt in social relations, men seem to be able to visualize the entire pattern or geography in spatial tasks. It appears that the right-brain hemisphere has developed different specializations for which each sex is predisposed. Of course, all of these generalizations are based on group means, and any individual of either sex may have relatively poor or excellent spatial abilities or nonverbal abilities.

What is striking about spatial ability research is how consistent the findings are across the developmental life span and across diverse cultural groups (Hyde, 1990; Linn & Petersen, 1985, Voyer et al., 2000). Similarly, the findings show remarkable cross-cultural consistency (Buffery & Gray, 1972; Gaulin, 1992; Halpern, 1986). Halpern maintained that, "even in countries with more equal participation between the sexes with respect to higher education it is rare to find a study that does not report a male advantage on spatial ability tests" (p. 148). Of course, environment is not irrelevant; several studies suggest that the male advantage can be reduced by education and experience in such tasks for women (Quaiser-Pohl & Lehmann, 2002; Voyer et al.).

EXPLAINING SEX DIFFERENCES IN SPATIAL ABILITY

A primary explanation for the robust sex differences in spatial ability is based on hemispheric brain lateralization. Women have more symmetrical, integrated hemispheric functions, whereas men are more lateralized or specialized for each function (Andersen et al., 1979; Halpern, 1986). Success at some types of tasks such as spatial navigation may be enhanced by extreme lateralization that minimizes linear cognition from the left hemisphere, which may interfere with successful, holistic processing. Other tasks such as human conversational abilities may benefit from integration of information from the verbal, left hemisphere and the nonverbal, right hemisphere. Biologically, men are very left-hemispherically lateralized for language; women have more linguistic functionality in both hemispheres. In men, the right hemisphere is highly specialized for spatial tasks, allowing the right hemisphere to focus on spatial perceptions (Andersen et al.; Halpern).

A second explanation is that gender-linked differences in spatial ability are transmitted through sex-linked chromosomes. Studies have shown that spatial abilities are highly heritable (Buffery & Gray 1972, Linn & Petersen, 1985). Men's superior spatial abilities may be a sex-linked characteristic transmitted through sexual selection. According to Gaulin (1992, p. 125), "sexual selection is a type of disruptive selection that favors one phenotype in females and a different phenotype in males." Of course, physical traits such as hemophilia and color blindness represent precisely this type; they virtually always appear in male but only rarely in female individuals. A daughter receives two X chromosomes, one from each parent. A son receives only one, from his mother; the Y chromosome from his father carries little information. According to genetic theory, "the high spatial ability gene is recessive; therefore this trait will occur more frequently in males than in females because males have no other gene to mask the effects of the recessive gene" (Halpern, 1986, p. 71). Empirical results testing this model have been highly supportive (see Buffery & Gray; Halpern).

A third process that produces sex-linked differences in spatial abilities is based on hormones. Studies have shown that increased androgen levels produce greater spatial ability in both male, *and* female individuals, and estrogen suppresses spatial ability (Browne, 2002; Gaulin, 1992). Sex hormones influence the development of numerous adaptive sex differences, including secondary sexual characteristics at puberty. Hormones, acting during critical developmental periods, have a major effect on spatial abilities (Browne; Gaulin). Women who are masculinized with increased androgens from their own adrenal glands or who receive male hormones prior to a sex-change operation show superior visuospatial skills on a variety of tests (Collaer & Hines, 1995, Hampson, 2000; Van Anders & Hampson, 2005). Similarly, men with chronic androgen deficiencies or androgen insensitivity show many feminine behaviors and deficient visuospatial skills on a variety of tasks, such as object rotation and navigation (Browne; Collaer & Hines).

Thus, three separate but interrelated mechanisms—the degree of hemispheric lateralization, recessive sex-linked chromosomes, and hormonal abnormalities—have each been shown to produce sex-linked variation in spatial ability. What forces in the evolutionary history of humankind have produced females with such superior social abilities and males with such superior spatial abilities?

ORIGINS OF SEX DIFFERENCES IN NONVERBAL AND SPATIAL SKILLS

For most members of the human species, growing old was a luxury few enjoyed. For hundreds of thousands of years, the mean life expectancy was less than 30 years (Kenrick & Keefe, 1992b; Swedlund & Armelagos, 1976). Even by the 17th century, life expectancy barely climbed over 30. As Whicker and Kronenfeld (1986) reported, "life in the agrarian period was indeed short, nasty, and brutish. Life expectancy was short and stresses were great, especially on women. Average life expectancy in England in 1690 was 32" (p. 24). Except for the past several generations, throughout thousands of generations of human history, the typical adult woman had no more than a dozen years to bear children. Given the high infant mortality rate and maternal mortality rates, high fertility levels were necessary to replace the human population each generation.

As we are well aware, the human population grew and continues to grow. Fewer than 1 million humans populated the earth in 35,000 BCE, growing to perhaps 4 to 8 million in 10,000 BCE, to 80 million during the agrarian revolution in 5,000 BCE, to nearly a billion by the end of the 18th century (Jacquard, 1984). Stevens (1992) summarized that "throughout most of human history, people lived in small societies, often hunting and gathering societies typified by high rates of mortality and high rates of fertility" (p. 112). Although women's reduced fertility while nursing and postpartum taboos against sexual intercourse may have decreased fertility (Swedlund & Armelagos, 1976), overall fertility was high throughout human history. Likewise, prior to the modern era, women nursed their babies for several years. The result was this: Women spent much of their short lives pregnant with, nursing, and carrying small infants. Most importantly, women were leaders of the camp or the village, societies were matrilineal, and men hovered at the periphery of the camp or village, often venturing out for mating opportunities, exploration, hunting, and gathering (Andersen, 1998; Browne, 2002; Dunbar, 1988; Miller, 1998). As Miller noted, it is hard for a male scientist to appreciate that men were peripheral characters in human evolution except as bearers of traits sexually selected by women for their amusement or utility.

Women's parental investment and role in the family is far more important than men's role. Buss (1987) stated that "in our species, for example, a male copulation that is trivial in terms of investment can produce a nine-month investment by the female that is substantial in time, energy and foreclosed alternatives" (p. 339). Nursing and childcare add to that investment. Obviously, pregnant or lactating mothers, particularly with children, have major constraints on their physical activities. Activities such as foraging, hunting, scouting, combat, and searching for new mating opportunities were more likely to have been male activities that had significant survival value and were naturally selected as important male characteristics (Andersen, 1998; Hampson, 2000; Rogers, 2001).

Women most likely were leaders of the primary group and spent their time caring for the sick, aphasics with head injuries, and preverbal children. Archeological evidence shows that male combat and resultant injuries, especially head injuries, were common throughout history (Ferrill, 1997; Keeley, 1996; Keegan, 1993; O'Connell, 1989; Venel, 1984). Violence and murder were common both in *Homo sapiens* and Neanderthals, 40% of whom suffered severe head injuries (Ferrill; Keeley, 1996). Studies show that cranial fractures, particularly of adult males, were common (Keeley, 1996). Large numbers of injuries to the left forearm and the left side of the head suggest that hand-to-hand combat with clubs or rocks occurred frequently (Keeley; Wendorf, 1968). Likewise, accidental injuries, including head injuries, were quite common. Accordingly, many male adults experienced head injuries and were nonlinguistic aphasics.

As leaders of the primary group, women had to develop superior social skills, particularly nonverbal communication skills, to communicate with brain-injured adults, preverbal children, and people that spoke other languages. The success of women in using these nonverbal and social skills was essential to their survival and to the existence of subsequent generations. Similarly, the strength, speed, navigational skills, and spatial abilities of male hunters, explorers, and combatants were critical for their survival. As natural selection occurred, these became sex-linked skills. In contemporary society, culture and education can compensate for these biological characteristics to some degree. Nonetheless, as a group, women have retained superior social skills, especially nonverbal skills, and men have maintained superior visuospatial skills and athletic abilities. The differential evolution that produced differential genetic visuospatial and social abilities in men and women also produced other biological sex differences relevant to communication scholars: differences in physical appearance, differences in sexual behavior, and differences in relational behavior.

SEX DIFFERENCES IN PERSONAL APPEARANCES

Initial impressions during interaction are first and foremost a function of physical appearance (Andersen, 1999; 2004); a person's sex is one of the most salient physical features. Biological differences in the physical appearance of men and women are generally apparent to any observer. Biologists classify human beings as a moderately dimorphic species. On average, men attain greater height, muscle mass, upper body strength, higher metabolic rates, more facial and body hair, deeper voices, later sexual maturity, higher mortality, and shorter life spans than woman (Miller, 1998). Women are shorter, manifest the hourglass figure, have wider hips, larger breasts, little facial or bodily hair, and higher voices. This moderate dimorphism in size and other characteristics is consistent with what is found in species that evolved in a polygynous mating system with intense sexual competition among males (Miller; Paul, 2002). These biological sex differences evolved as a result of sexual selection. Humans also augment such cues (not necessarily in healthy ways). For example, men may lift weights or take supplements to increase body size and muscle mass. Women may increase their femininity by removing hair and dieting to maintain an hourglass figure.

In addition to his theory of natural selection, Darwin (1859, 1871) proposed a theory of sexual selection, a process by which men and women disproportionally select features of mates that favor those physical qualities that are attractive to a person of the opposite sex. Sexual selection has been demonstrated in almost every species, including human beings (Miller, 1998). Throughout our evolutionary history, humans have used various criteria to choose mates that are not random; instead they are conscious and unconscious mating choices made systematically by individual females and males.

Sexual dimorphism like that found in human beings occurs in species where males seek multiple opportunities to mate with females. According to Gaulin (1992, pp. 125–126), "in most species of primates, including *Homo sapiens*, the sexes differ in the maximum reproductive rates. In these species sexual dimorphism in anatomy, physiology, and behavior is the norm."

Over the millennia, male preferences for female mates have shaped female physical appearance. Compared with women, men are far more preoccupied with the physical appearance of potential mates (Andersen, 1999). Research suggests that men select mates based on a fairly universal set of physical characteristics that are unconsciously associated with cues to fertility. Over the years, men have selected women for their hourglass figures, large eyes, symmetrical faces, and large breasts and buttocks. Larger, more rounded breasts and buttocks, which contain body fat, functioned as indicator of both fertility and good nutritional status (Miller, 1998).

Similarly, female mate choice influenced the development of physical appearance in men (Ryan, 1998). Females of all species can generally resist copulation attempts by unwanted males and solicit mating from desired males (Miller, 1998). Because females have far greater parental investment than males, they tend to be "pickier" sexual partners, especially in the human species, so women have also had a larger role than men in shaping the appearance of the opposite sex. By picking strong, high quality, attractive, healthy male mates, the chance of having attractive, healthy offspring is increased and the likelihood of a woman's genes surviving is increased (Geary, Vigil, & Byrd-Craven, 2004; Miller). The larger penises of human males compared with other primates, for example, was likely the result of female choice as a sign of male gender, virility, and fertility (Baker & Bellis, 1984; Miller; Ryan). The male gorilla, for example, has only about a 3-inch erect penis.

The very qualities that women find attractive in men are the same qualities that indicate a man's physical and genetic quality (Gangstad & Simpson, 2000). In Hollywood, the traditional male lead is tall, powerful, and handsome. Research suggests that, throughout the world, women tend to select men as mates who have social status and who are large, tall, wide shouldered, physically strong, square jawed, symmetrical, and have a waist to hip ratio of .9 (Browne, 2002; Geary et al., 2004; Hatfield & Sprecher, 1995; Kenrick & Keefe, 1992a). These male physical attributes that provide protection against animal and human predators are also markers of a man's ability to produce strong, healthy offspring. In short, the prototypical attractive male physique is deep within the genes and the psyche of women throughout the world. These deep-seeded genetic predispositions are not always apparent to women but provide the background for the day-to-day choices in what constitutes a physically attractive mate.

DIFFERENCES IN THE SEXUAL BEHAVIOR OF MEN AND WOMEN

A search for biological sex differences in communication should focus where sex differences really do make a difference, in reproductive roles, or what Birdwhistell (1979) labeled primary sex differences. As already indicated, humans are a moderately dimorphic species; that is, males and females are not exactly alike physically or behaviorally (Gaulin, 1992; Goldsmith, 1991; Whicker & Kronenfeld, 1986). In species in which there is no competition for mates and in which animals are monogamous, no dimorphism typically occurs. In species that compete for mates, sexual dimorphism usually results in males becoming larger and more aggressive because these qualities are selected over many generations of competition for mates.

Despite our own cultural values that monogamy and marriage are desirable qualities, the human species is generally polygamous; that is, most humans in most cultures mate with more than one person. Nonetheless, humans also have a paradoxical tendency to pair bond, though these pair bonds are not always exclusive. In his review of literature, Gaulin (1992) maintained that, among 1,154 societies described by ethnographers, 980 (84.9%) practice polygamy. Gaulin maintained the following:

> Many independent sorts of evidence argue that *Homo Sapiens* is a mammal of polygynous ancestry. Certain sex differences are typical of polygynous species but are absent in monogamous species. Relative to female conspecifics, males of polygynous species tend to be larger, more active in courtship, more aggressive, and more susceptible to various perturbations of development. They tend to reach sexual maturity later, to have higher metabolic rates and to be more prone to death at all ages. All of these sex differences are characteristic of human populations. (p. 144)

Considerable evidence suggests that male primates, including humans, are nonmonogamous. Gaulin (1992) concluded that "given the patterns of dimorphism that characterized our hominid ancestry, disruptive selection arising out of polygyny has probably operated for at least four million years in the human lineage" (p. 146). Mating with as many fertile women as possible maximized a man's genetic potential throughout history, whereas a woman's reproduction is constrained by her number of possible pregnancies. Although today's men may mate for other reasons than reproduction (e.g., pleasure, intimacy, and bonding), the biology from which contemporary men evolved remains largely intact. Relational communication researchers should examine this biological basis of sexuality to enhance their understanding of human sexual interaction.

Symons (1987) argued that if a male hunter-gatherer could have four children with his wife during their short life spans, he would increase his reproductive success by 25% if he sired just one child by another woman during his lifetime. For a woman, the reproductive reality is different: She would bear the same number of children whether she has one mate or several (unless of course her primary mate is infertile). Nonmonogamy has lower reproductive or genetic value for women. Men are more likely than women to pursue short-term sexual relationships as an end in and of themselves; and, despite the sexual revolution, this sex difference has remained relatively stable over time (Geary et al., 2004; Symons, 1979).

Men who could travel greater distances and navigate well would have a better opportunity to encounter other groups and potentially sire offspring with women of that group. Size, speed, and increased bone structure of the skull, along with spatial ability, would be selected for men who might encounter other protective male individuals in their ventures, have to navigate long distances, and find their way back (Paul, 2002, Rogers, 2001). Contemporary men have inherited all such qualities by means of natural selection from our long genetic past. According to

Gaulin (1992), "under some kinds of polygynous mating systems, females have small, relatively exclusive ranges while males travel much more widely. In essence, males in these systems compete to increase their access to potential mates by overlapping as many female ranges as possible" (p. 129).

Indeed, this is the typical pattern among many primate species (Gaulin; Gray, 1985). Men pay a price for their size, strength, and mobility. Throughout history, male mortality has been disproportionally higher than female mortality. Nonetheless, according to a biological view, men have been left with the legacy of their ancestors, a legacy that includes superior spatial ability.

According to a biological view, women would be relatively more monogamous, though nonmonogamy may have advantages for them too. Evidence suggests that most female primates, including female humans, are nonmonogamous (Paul, 2002). If a female mates with more than one male, the strongest sperm are most likely to successfully produce an offspring. Research demonstrates that sexual selection can continue after insemination by means of sperm competition (Paul). Such processes would argue that females may not have evolved monogamously and may be a way for females to ensure that they produce the strongest offspring (Paul). Likewise, if a woman became pregnant by another man, she might dupe her unsuspecting mate into raising another man's biological offspring.

Obviously, sexual desire and arousal makes mating a pleasurable, reinforcing activity that facilitates reproduction. However, controversy has long surrounded the female orgasm and its purpose and origins (Symons, 1979). Unlike the male orgasm, which is correlated with the ejaculation of human sperm and has a clear reproductive function, the purpose of the female orgasm is not so clear. It is likely the human female orgasm is multifunctional. First, in all likelihood, the experience of orgasm is sufficiently reinforcing that it will motivate a woman to seek additional sexual episodes. However, a number of female primate species successfully reproduce with no apparent orgasm (Symons). Moreover, sexual intercourse per se may not be the preferred method for achieving orgasm for most women, so sexual behaviors that promote more clitoral contact would seem to be more rewarding than sexual intercourse per se (Rathus, Nevid, & Fichner-Rathus, 1998). A second function may be that orgasmic pleasure strengthens an emotional and relational bond between partners (Symons). If a strong, ongoing pair bond promoted the survival of offspring, then the predisposition for a female orgasm would be selected over time. A final potential set of functions of the female orgasm is to promote male ejaculation during intercourse and pull sperm into the uterus (Baker & Bellis, 1995).

A unique quality of the female human is hidden ovulation. Men, and to some degree women, have no idea when ovulation is occurring. Female humans are potentially sexually receptive throughout adult life, whereas females of other species are only receptive during estrus and ovulation (Buss, 1994). Hidden ovulation enables women to attract greater and more continuous male attention, which leads to more support from men and to more stable pair-bonded relationships, discussed in the next section.

DIFFERENCES IN THE RELATIONAL BEHAVIOR OF MEN AND WOMEN

Sexual selection can also operate to produce gender-linked differences in relational behavior. Throughout the world, women are attracted to somewhat older men, who tend to have higher social status and greater resources (Buss, 1989; Geary 1998; Kenrick & Keefe, 1992a); these are described as culturally successful men (Geary et al., 2004). The prevalence of this preference, for women in their mates but not for men in their mates, throughout the world suggests its evolutionary origins. The ideal situation for a woman is a long-term partner with good genes, reproductive potential, and the willingness to invest in children (Geary et al.). From the Stone Age landscape to the modern inner city, offspring have a better chance of survival if a woman has a male partner. In all cultures that have been studied, the children of culturally successful men have lower mortality and greater psychological and physical health (Geary, 2000). Studies consistently reveal that, when women are forced to make a choice, a marriage partner's cultural success is rated as a necessity and other qualities, including physical appearance, are rated as luxuries (Geary et al.).

Throughout history, men have dominated political, cultural, military, and economic life. Feminists have taken this as an indication of patriarchal male society, but feminist theory usually fails to explain the first cause of this social hegemony by men (Miller, 1998). Alternatively, the classical male trait of striving for power and wealth may be a sexually selected trait actually encouraged by women over thousands of years that became a sex-linked biological trait in men (Miller). The production of art, music, wealth, and power may be genetically engrained male displays designed to attract high-quality females.

The commitments of gestatation and lactation require greater parental investment by females than males of all species, including female humans (Buss, 1994). Men compete intensely for mates, sometimes multiple mates, but most men invest in the well-being of their children. Selecting a dependable man who will add resources to a family means that women are predisposed to seek such men as primary partners. To find mates who are dependable and provide resources, women with superior social nonverbal sensitivity increase their survival advantage if their female offspring inherit these qualities. Women have a preference for men who can protect the home territory, themselves, and their offspring.

Buss (1989) found that, throughout the world, women rated kindness, understanding, and intelligence among the most desired qualities in a husband, even above wealth and cultural success. The ubiquity of this preference suggests it is primarily a biological characteristic of our species, though undoubtedly many cultures may encourage such behavior as well. Researchers who have found that women seek greater intimacy in relationships (Hook, Gerstein, Detterick, & Gridley, 2003) may have inadvertently discovered a biological preference for wanting close, permanent relationships with a stable man. Women have a greater preference for an emotionally intimate relationship (Buss, 1994). According to Parks and Floyd (1996), men also highly value intimacy, just not to the same degree as women. The data strongly suggest that, in relational behavior, women most value stable, trustworthy, intimate, and culturally successful men. These are qualities of the human species that show great cross-cultural similarity and only a slightly different expression in each culture.

CONCLUSION

Human beings evolved from our biological predecessors over the past several million years. Genetic changes proceeded very slowly across many generations (Jacquard, 1984), so humans have experienced relatively little genetic change over the past few hundred generations. Thus, we share a genetic endowment and biological heritage with people who lived thousands of years ago. Culturally, the rate of change is extremely rapid and geometrically accelerating; genetically, however, we still resemble our Stone Age ancestors. Thus, our biological traits evolved under environmental circumstances very different than our present human environment.

Communication researchers, unlike our colleagues in anthropology, biology, and psychology, have largely adhered to the dogma of culture as the nearly exclusive and most powerful cause of sex differences in interaction behavior. This chapter is an effort to reduce this disciplinary myopia. Biological and evolutionary forces significantly impact differences in social skill, spatial ability, appearance, sexual behavior, and relational behavior.

At the same time, none of the arguments offered in this chapter suggest that individuals of either sex cannot be excellent managers, athletes, relational partners, or caregivers. For example, although women may have evolved superior social skills as caregivers, those social skills can be creatively used by women as they become managers, teachers, or doctors. Men no longer need their superior spatial skills for hunting or mate location but may find these skills useful in navigational tasks, sports, or engineering. Biology is not destiny. However, as suggested previously, our evolutionary past has produced some sex-linked group differences in certain abilities, appearance, and behaviors. Only when we account for the origins of sex differences can these variations be understood, accepted, appreciated, or remediated.

REFERENCES

Andersen, P. A. (1998). Researching sex difference within sex similarities: The evolutionary consequences of reproductive differences. In D. J. Canary & K. Dindia (Eds.), *Sex differences and similarities in communication: Critical essays and empirical investigations on sex and gender in interaction* (pp. 83–100). Mahwah, NJ: Lawrence Erlbaum Associates.

Andersen, P. A. (1999). *Nonverbal communication: Forms and functions.* Boston: McGraw-Hill.

Andersen, P. A. (2004). *The complete idiot's guide to body language.* Indianapolis, IN: Alpha Books.

Andersen, P. A., Garrison, J. P., & Andersen, J. F. (1979). Implications of a neuophysiological approach for the study of nonverbal communication. *Human Communication Research, 6,* 74–89.

Baker, R. R., & Bellis, M. A. (1995) *Human sperm competition.* London: Chapman & Hall.

Birdwhistell, R. L. (1970). *Kinesics and context.* Philadelphia: University of Pennsylvania Press.

Browne, K. R. (2002). *Biology at work: Rethinking sexual equality.* New Brunswick, NJ: Rutgers University Press.

Buffery, A. W. H., & Gray, J. A. (1972). Sex differences in the development of spatial and linguistic skills. In C. Ounsted & D. C. Taylor (Eds.), *Gender differences: Their ontogeny and significance* (pp. 123–158). London: Churchill Livingston.

Buller, D. B., & Aune, R. K. (1992). The effects of speech rate similarity on compliance: Application of communication accommodation theory. *Western Journal of Communication, 56,* 37–53.

Buss, D. M. (1987). Sex differences in human mate selection criteria: An evolutionary perspective. In C. Crawford, M. Smith, & D. Krebs (Eds.), *Sociobiology and psychology: Ideas, issues, and applications* (pp. 335–352). Hillsdale, NJ: Lawrence Erlbaum Associates.

Buss, D. M. (1989). Sex differences in human mate preferences: Evolutionary hypothesis tested in 37 cultures. *Behavioral and Brain Sciences, 12,* 1–49.

Buss, D. M. (1994). *The evolution of desire: Strategies of human mating.* New York: HarperCollins.

Canary, D. J., & Hause, K. S. (1993). Is there any reason to research sex differences in communication? *Communication Quarterly, 41,* 129–144.

Collaer, M. L., & Hines, M. (1995). Human behavioral sex differences: A role for general hormones during early development. *Psychological Bulletin, 118,* 55–107.

Eagly, A. H. (1987). *Sex differences in social behavior: A social role interpretation.* Hillsdale, NJ: Lawrence Erlbaum Associates.

Darwin, C. (1859). *On the origin of species by means of natural selection.* London: John Murray.

Darwin, C. (1871). *The descent of man, and selection in relation to sex.* London: John Murray.

Dunbar, M. (1988). *Primate social systems.* London: Croom Helm.

Ferrill, A. (1997). *The origins of war: From the stone age to Alexander the Great.* Boulder, CO: Westview Press.

Gangstad, S. W., & Simpson, J. A. (2000). The evolution of human mating: Tradeoffs and strategic pluralism. *Behavioral and Brain Sciences, 23,* 573–644.

Gaulin, S. J. C. (1992). Evolution of sex differences in spatial ability. *Yearbook of Physical Anthropology, 359,* 125–151.

Geary, D. C. (1998). *Male, female: The evolution of sex differences.* Washington, DC: American Psychological Association.

Geary, D. C. (2000) Evolution and proximate expression of human paternal investment. *Psychological Bulletin, 126,* 55–77.

Geary, D. C., Vigil, J., & Byrd-Craven, J. (2004). Evolution of human mate choice. *Journal of Sex Research, 41,* 27–42.

Goldsmith, T. H. (1991). *The biological roots of human nature.* New York: Oxford University Press.

Gray, J. P. (1985). *Primate sociobiology.* New Haven, CT: HRAF Press.

Hall, J. A. (1978). Gender effects in decoding nonverbal cues. *Psychological Bulletin, 85,* 845–857.

Hall, J. A. (1979). Gender, gender roles, and nonverbal communication skills. In R. Rosenthal (Ed.), *Skill in nonverbal communication: Individual differences* (pp. 31–67). Cambridge, MA: Oelgeschlager, Gunn & Hain.

Halpern, D. F. (1986). *Sex differences in cognitive abilities.* Hillsdale, NJ: Lawrence Erlbaum Associates.

Hampson, E. (2000). Sexual differentiation of spatial functions in humans. In A. Matsumoto (Ed.), *Sexual differentiation of the brain* (pp. 279–300). Boca Rotan, FL: CRC Press.

Hatfield, E., & Sprecher, S. (1995). Men's and women's preferences in marital partners in the United States, Russia, and Japan. *Journal of Cross-Cultural Psychology, 26,* 728–750.

Hook, M. K., Gerstein, L. H. Detterick, L., & Gridley, B. (2003). How close are we? Measuring intimacy and examining gender differences. *Journal of Counseling and Development, 81,* 462–472.

Hyde, J. S. (1990). Meta-analysis and the psychology of gender differences. *Journal of Women in Culture and Society, 16,* 55–73.

Ivy, P. K., & Backlund, P. (1994) Exploring gender speak: Personal effectiveness in gender communication. New York: McGraw-Hill.

Jacquard, A. (1984). *In praise of difference: Genetics and human affairs.* New York: Columbia University Press.

Keegan, J. (1993). *A history of warfare.* New York: Knopf.

Keeley, L. H. (1996). *War before civilization.* New York: Oxford University Press.

Kenrick, D. T., & Keefe, R. C. (1992a). Age preferences in human reproductive strategies. *Behavioral and Brain Sciences, 15,* 75–133.

Kenrick, D. T., & Keefe, R. C. (1992b). Sex differences in age preference: Universal reality or ephemeral construction. *Behavioral and Brain Sciences, 15,* 119–133.

Knapp, M. L., & Hall, J. A. (1992). *Nonverbal communication in human interaction* (3rd ed.). Forth Worth, TX: Hacourt Brace Jovanovich.

Lewis, D. (1985). *Loving and loathing: The enigma of personal attraction.* London: Constable.

Linn, M. D., & Petersen, A. C. (1985). Emergence and characterization of sex differences in spatial ability. *Child Development, 56,* 1479–1498.

Miller, G. F. (1998). A review of sexual selection and human evolution: How mate choice shaped human nature. In C. Crawford and D. Krebs (Eds.), *Handbook of evolutionary psychology: Ideas, issue and applications* (pp. 87–130). Mahwah, NJ: Lawrence Erlbaum Associates.

O'Connell, R. L. (1989). *Of arms and men: A history of war weapons and aggression.* New York: Oxford University Press.

Parks, M. R., & Floyd, K. (1996). Meanings for closeness and intimacy in friendship. *Journal of Social and Personal Relationships, 13,* 85–107.

Paul, A. (2002). Sexual selection and mate choice. *International Journal of Primatalogy, 23,* 887–904.

Pearson, J. C., West, R. L., & Turner, L. H. (1995). *Gender and communication.* Madison, WI: Brown & Benchmark.

Putz, D. A., Gaulin, S. J. C., Sponter, R. J. & McBarney, D. H. (2004). Sex hormones and finger length: What does 2D:4D indicate. *Evolution and Human Behavior*, 25, 187–199.

Quaiser-Pohl, C., & Lehmann, W. (2002). Girls' spatial abilities: Charting the contributions of experiences and attitudes in different academic groups. *British Journal of Educational Psychology, 72,* 245–360.

Rathus, S. A., Nevid, J. S., & Fichner-Rathus, L. (1998). *Essentials of human sexuality.* Boston: Allyn & Bacon.

Rogers, L. (2001). *Sexing the brain.* New York: Columbia University Press.

Rosaldo, M. Z. (1974). Women, culture and society: A rhetorical overview. In M. Z. Rosaldo & L. Lamphere (Eds.), *Women, culture, and society* (pp. 17–42). Stanford, CA: Stanford University Press.

Rosenthal, R., & DePaulo, B. M. (1979). Sex differences in accommodation in nonverbal communication. In R. Rosenthal (Ed.), *Skill in nonverbal communication: Individual differences* (pp. 68–103). Cambridge, MA: Oelgeschlager, Gunn & Hain.

Rosenthal, R., Hall, J. A., DiMatteo, M. R., Rogers, P. L., & Archer, D. (1979). *Sensitivity to nonverbal communication: The PONS test.* Baltimore, MD: Johns Hopkins University Press.

Ryan, M. J. (1998). Sexual selection, receiver biases and the evolution of sex differences. *Science, 281,* 1999–2004.

Serbin, L. A., & Sprafkin, C. H. (1987). A developmental approach: Sexuality from infancy through adolescence. In J. H. Geer & W. T. O'Donahue (Eds.), *Theories of human sexuality* (pp. 163–196). New York: Plenum.

Stacks, D. W., & Andersen, P. A. (1989). The modular mind: Implications for intrapersonal communication. *The Southern Communication Journal, 54,* 273–293.

Stevens, G. (1992). Mortality and age-specific patterns of marriage. *Behavioral and Brain Sciences, 15,* 112–113.

Stewart, L. P., Cooper, P. J., & Friedley, S. A. (1986). *Communication between the sexes: Sex differences and sex-role stereotypes.* Scottsdale, AZ: Gorsuch Scarisbrick.

Swedlund, A. C., & Armelagos, G. J. (1976). *Demographic anthropology.* Dubuque, IA: Brown.

Symons, D. (1979). *The evolution of human sexuality.* New York: Oxford University Press.

Symons, D. (1987). An evolutionary approach: Can Darwin's view of life shed light on human sexuality? In J. H. Geer & W. T. O'Donahue (Eds.), *Theories of human sexuality* (pp. 91–126) New York: Plenum.

Tannen, D. (1990). *You just don't understand: Men and women in conversation.* New York: Morrow.

Trost, M. R., & Alberts, J. K. (1998). An evolutionary view on understanding sex effects in communicating attraction. In D. J. Canary & K. Dindia (Eds.), *Sex differences and similarities in communication: Critical essays and empirical investigations on sex and gender in interaction* (pp. 233–355). Mahwah, NJ: Lawrence Erlbaum Associates.

van Anders, S. M., & Hampson, E. (2005). Testing the prenatal and roger hypothesis: measuring digit ratios, sexual orientation, and spacial abilities in adults. *Harmones and Behavior, 47*, 92–98.

Venel, S. (1984). War and warfare in archeology. *Journal of Anthropological Archeology, 3,* 116–132.

Voyer, D., Nolan, C., & Voyer, S. (2000). The relation between experience and spatial performance in men and women. *Sex Roles, 43,* 891–915.

Voyer, D., & Sullivan, A. M. (2003). *International Journal of Psychology, 38,* 11–23.

Weitz, S. (1979). Commentary: Interactional aspects. In R. Rosenthal (Ed.), *Skill in nonverbal communication: Individual differences* (pp. 135–138). Cambridge, MA: Oelgeschlager, Gunn & Hain.

Wendorf, F. (1968). Site 117: A Nubian final Paleolithic graveyard near Jebel Sabaha, Sudan. In F. Wendorf (Ed.), *The prehistory of Nubia* (pp. 954–995). Dallas, TX: Southern Methodist University Press.

Whicker, M. L., & Kronenfeld, J. J. (1986). *Sex role changes: Technology, politics, and policy.* New York: Praeger.

Wilkins, B. M., & Andersen, P. A. (1991). Gender-differences and similarities in management communication: A meta-analysis. *Management Communication Quarterly, 5,* 6–35.

Wood, J. T., & Dindia, K. (1998). What's the difference? A dialogue about differences and similarities between men and women. In D. J. Canary & K. Dindia (Eds.), *Sex differences and similarities in communication: Critical essays and empirical investigations on sex and gender in interaction.* (pp. 19–39). Mahwah, NJ: Lawrence Erlbaum Associates.

8

Revisiting the Different Cultures Thesis: An Assessment of Sex Differences and Similarities in Supportive Communication

Brant R. Burleson
Purdue University

Adrianne Kunkel
University of Kansas

The notion that men and women constitute different *gender cultures* (Johnson, 2000; Tannen, 1990; Wood, 2000b) has captured both popular and scholarly imaginations in recent decades. One of the core positions of the different cultures thesis (DCT) is that men and women live in different emotional worlds. In particular, proponents of the DCT assert that men and women are fundamentally different with regard to the provision and receipt of emotional support (Bate & Bowker, 1997; Tannen; Wood, 1996). According to the DCT, women tend to value close relationships for their expressive qualities, whereas men value relationships for their instrumental features. Thus, in support situations, women should appreciate efforts that explicitly validate their feelings and perspectives, whereas men should value attempts to fix the problem or shift attention away from upset feelings (Tannen; Wood, 2005). An important corollary is that men and women are supposed to be particularly biased toward, and responsive to, their sex's own way of enacting emotional support.

As we show, the DCT analysis of sex differences in supportive communication has profound implications for both theory and practice. Nevertheless, despite these implications and the wide acceptance of the DCT in both scholarly and popular literatures, the DCT rests on a shallow empirical foundation. Most of the data cited to support the DCT have come from small-scale qualitative studies, personal anecdotes, or examples drawn from novels, movies, and other media (e.g., Maltz & Borker, 1982; Tannen, 1990). Although qualitative and anecdotal evidence can provide compelling illustrations, such data only suggest hypotheses but cannot test them—especially when hypotheses take the form of empirical generalizations about how categories of people (i.e., men and women) frequently or typically behave (Goldsmith & Fulfs, 1999; MacGeorge, Graves, Feng, Gillihan, & Burleson, 2004).

In the late 1990s, the DCT began to receive scrutiny from researchers who employed designs appropriate to testing generalizations about the communicative behavior of women and men (e.g., Burleson, Kunkel, Samter, & Werking, 1996; Michaud & Warner, 1997). In the present chapter we review the now-extensive empirical research evaluating the DCT, particularly its claims about sex differences in supportive communication.[1] We begin by providing a brief overview of claims made by the DCT and detail some of the theoretical, methodological, and practical implications that follow from this thesis. We then derive several predictions from the DCT pertaining to supportive communication and summarize the results of studies that have tested these predictions. In the final section, we interpret these findings and discuss theoretical alternatives to the DCT that are better able to account for the overall pattern of similarities and differences in the supportive communication of men and women.

THE DIFFERENT CULTURES THESIS: PERSPECTIVE AND IMPLICATIONS

The DCT maintains that the differential socialization experiences of boys and girls lead to the articulation and perpetuation of two distinct speech communities or cultures—one male and the other female (Maltz & Borker, 1982; Wood, 1993). Each culture supposedly inculcates in its members a different, although equally valid, set of assumptions concerning the functions of communication (see summary by Kyratzis, 2001). Thus, interaction between members of masculine and feminine

[1]In this chapter, we are principally concerned with the factual accuracy of the DCT rather than its political or ideological status. Numerous writers have criticized the DCT for legitimizing and reinforcing gender-based communicative practices grounded in patriarchal privilege and hegemony (e.g., Crawford, 1995; Henley & Kramarae, 1991; see review by Kyratzis, 2001). These critiques, however, tend to accept the major claims of the DCT as factually accurate (i.e., that men and women do communicate in fundamentally different ways), and they attack this viewpoint primarily on ideological and political grounds.

cultures is believed to proceed along the same lines as interaction between members of any two cultures whose experiences and social milieus differ (Maltz & Borker; Wood, 2005). Hence, communication between men and women is comparable with "cross-cultural communication" (Tannen, 1990, p. 18).

The DCT makes claims about multiple communicative genres (e.g., supporting, informing, persuading, gossiping, and conflict managing; see Tannen, 1990; Wood, 2000a). However, many advocates of the DCT maintain that emotional support or "caring seems to be the principal category that differentiates one sex from the other" (Bate & Bowker, 1997, p. 166; also see Wood, 1994). Moreover, several of the most influential articulations of the DCT (e.g., Maltz & Borker, 1982; Tannen, 1990; Wood, 2000a) focus on claimed gender differences in the disclosure of, and responses to, emotional upset (e.g., so-called troubles talk). Thus, emotional support—the process of providing care, reassurance, and comfort to distressed others (Burleson, 2003a)—represents a critical communicative context for evaluating the merit of the DCT.

The DCT maintains that masculine and feminine ways of caring and providing support, although stylistically different, are functionally equivalent (i.e., equally effective) within their respective cultures. Thus, masculine and feminine support styles are supposedly preferred by members of their respective cultures; according to the DCT, men do not experience feminine support as helpful, and vice versa (Michaud & Warner, 1997; Tannen, 1990; Wood, 1993).

The DCT analysis of sex differences in emotional support has profound implications for theory, research methodology, and practice (e.g., pedagogy, counseling). Theoretically, the DCT implies that social convention determines the effectiveness of particular supportive messages; the DCT suggests that certain message forms become conventionally associated with particular effects in a given community, and this leads those messages to have particular effects (MacGeorge et al., 2004). This notion contrasts with the view that supportive messages have effects through the impact of their features on the psychological processes of recipients (Burleson & Goldsmith, 1998). Further, if men and women come from different cultures, then distinct theories of close relationships, emotion, and communication have to be developed for men and women because they presumably seek different things in their relationships, develop their relationships differently, act differently in those relationships, experience and express emotion differently, and manage relationship issues differently (Burleson, 2003b).

The different cultures view also has important methodological consequences. If men and women are from different cultures, then we should use culturally sensitive methods in conducting research. For example, Cancian (1986) argued that most research on intimacy and emotional support processes suffers from a feminine bias because researchers have used an exclusively feminine "yardstick" to evaluate emotion-related behaviors in relationships (also see Inman, 1996; Swain, 1989). This feminine bias leads scholars (especially researchers in social psychology and communication; see Wood & Inman, 1993) to ignore, devalue, and delegitimize masculine ways of expressing care and support.

The DCT analysis of emotional support has profound practical implications, a point made repeatedly in both scholarly publications (e.g., Wood, 1993) and self-help books (Gray, 1992; Schloff & Yudkin, 1993; see review by Zimmerman, Holm, & Haddock, 2001). Emotional support is one of the most basic provisions of interpersonal relationships and is a central determinant of satisfaction with these relationships. Deficiencies in emotional support received from a partner, such as might arise from the sex differences predicted by the DCT, may be particularly predictive of relationship dissatisfaction (Baxter, 1986) and may even negatively influence health (Ingram, Betz, Mindes, Schmitt, & Smith, 2001; Ingram, Jones, & Smith, 2001). If men and women differ substantially in processes associated with emotional support, they probably need corrective interventions (i.e., counseling, training, and education) to protect and improve their relationships with people of the other sex. According to its proponents, these interventions should strive to increase multicultural awareness of stylistically different but functionally equivalent approaches to communication events such as troubles talk (Wood, 1993), thereby facilitating communication across the cultural divide (Swain, 1989; Tannen, 1990). Thus, counselors, trainers, and educators should, according to the DCT, develop and implement multicultural diversity training that teaches women how to provide masculine support to men and men how to provide feminine support to women.

EVALUATING THE DIFFERENT CULTURES ANALYSIS OF EMOTIONAL SUPPORT

The existence of substantial sex differences in supportive communication processes and preferences is critical to the DCT; thus, researchers have sought to evaluate the extent and magnitude of these differences. Considerable research indicates that there are reliable and sometimes substantial *behavioral* differences in how men and women express care and convey emotional support. Generally, women are more likely than men to seek and provide emotional support; women also are more likely to employ supportive forms of communication that explicitly address feelings, perspectives, and subjective interpretations (e.g., Basow & Rubenfeld, 2003; Cutrona, 1996; Goldsmith & Dun, 1997; MacGeorge, Gillihan, Samter, & Clark, 2003; Oxley, Dzindolet, & Miller, 2002).

In addition to being predicted by the DCT, these sex differences in supportive behavior are predicted by several other theories of sex differences (e.g., biological, evolutionary, social role, and skill specialization). Because these sex differences in supportive behavior are not uniquely predicted by the DCT, their existence does not provide any distinctive support for this account of sex differences. Clearly, adequate tests of a particular theoretical account have to generate and evaluate predictions that follow distinctly from that specific account.[2]

Fortunately, the DCT lends itself to such tests. Both proponents (Johnson, 2000) and critics (Burleson, 1997) of the DCT agree that a culture consists of behavioral practices (e.g., patterns of communication and signification), artifacts, and "abstractions" (e.g., values, meanings, and standards; see Geertz, 1973; Kluckholm, 1951). Abstractions pertaining to significant social activities, such as supportive communication, are an important component of a cultural system (Johnson, 1989). Members of different cultures are regarded as adhering to different systems of abstractions (i.e., as having different beliefs, values, and perceptual schemes). Hence, if men and women constitute distinct cultures, this should be reflected in sizeable sex differences in abstractions (Johnson, 2000), as well as correspondingly large differences in behaviors.[3]

Moreover, the DCT maintains that behavioral differences are *indicative* as well as *constitutive* of cultural differences. This implies that cognitive differences (differences in abstractions) underlie behavioral differences (differences in practices). Thus, the DCT suggests that differences in how supportive communication is enacted reflect underlying cognitive differences, as well as constitute them (Johnson, 1989; Wood, 1993). The cognitive differences are thus crucial to the claim of *cultural* difference; the DCT maintains that men and women (or members of masculine and feminine speech communities) differ in what they think and feel, as well as in how they behave (Wood, 1996, 2000a).

The DCT implies that men and women differ substantially with respect to at least five cognitive variables associated with supportive communication: (a) the value one places on supportive communication skills; (b) the goals pursued when one seeks to provide help in support situations; (c) the criteria used to judge what counts as helpful support; (d) the sex of the person from whom one prefers to seek and receive support; and (e) preferences for the supportive behavioral styles of relationship partners. The DCT predicts the same pattern for each of these five

---

[2]It has sometimes been suggested that the DCT should be evaluated with respect to "masculine" and "feminine" persons rather than with respect to men and women (see Wood, 1997). Burleson (1997) details the logical and empirical problems inherent in any such proposal.

[3]A reasonable question is this: "How big a difference does there have to be between groups to be indicative of a 'cultural' difference?" Any answer to this question necessarily contains an arbitrary element; MacGeorge and her colleagues (MacGeorge et al., 2004, p. 145) propose the following standard, which we find appealing: "We suggest that the degree of non-overlap in group distributions should exceed the degree of overlap on relevant variables (i.e., that Cohen's $U > .50$). This corresponds to a standardized mean difference of $d > 0.87$ (and to r^2 or $eta^2 > .16$). This appears to be a reasonable criterion; if there is not at least this much separation in the two distributions, it is hard to see how a claim of 'cultural' (or even subcultural) difference can be maintained. Obviously, a separation of this (or any other magnitude) does not necessarily mean that there *are* distinguishable cultural (or subcultural) groups; that is always a conceptual decision that must be informed by theoretical as well as measurement considerations."

classes of variables: members of each gender are predicted to be biased toward their own form of providing emotional support.[4] We now examine research relevant to these predictions.

The Value Placed on Supportive Communication Skills

One hypothesis implied by the DCT is that women, who supposedly value the affective and expressive qualities of relationships (Johnson, 1996), should most highly value the supportive and expressive skills of their partners, whereas men, with their more instrumental orientation to social relationships (Inman, 1996), should most highly value the instrumental skills of their relationship partners. This hypothesis has been frequently assessed in research that has employed an instrument developed by Burleson and Samter (1990), called the Communication Functions Questionnaire (CFQ). The CFQ consists of items describing the enactment of several different communication skills, including supportive skills such as comforting and providing ego support, and instrumental skills such as informing and persuading. Participants rate each item for how important they think it is for a partner to possess the depicted skill.

Findings obtained with the CFQ are quite consistent. Specifically, women tend to view the supportive and expressive skills of their relationship partners as slightly more important than do men, whereas men tend to value the instrumental skills of their partners as somewhat more important than do women. However, contrary to the prediction by the DCT, *both* men and women value the supportive and expressive skills of their partners much more highly than they do the instrumental skills of these partners. That is, both men and women assess communication skills such as comforting and providing ego support as much more important than skills such as persuasion and giving information. This pattern has been found to hold for same-sex friendships, opposite-sex friendships, acquaintanceships, best friendships, romantic relationships, and sibling relationships (Burleson et al., 1996; Finn & Powers, 2002; Griffiths & Burleson, 1995; Myers & Knox, 1998; Samter

[4]More specifically, the DCT predicts that men should (a) value instrumental communication skills over expressive skills in most interpersonal relationships; (b) prioritize and pursue problem-focused goals rather than emotion-focused goals when seeking to provide support; (c) view masculine forms of support (e.g., problem-focused advice, minimization of feelings) as more helpful than feminine forms of support (e.g., explicit discussion of feelings and perspectives), (d) prefer other men as sources of support when they are distressed; and (e) most like or be most satisfied with relationship partners who display masculine (i.e., instrumental) skills and orientations in social relationships. In contrast, the DCT predicts that women should (a) value expressive communication skills over instrumental skills in most interpersonal relationships; (b) prioritize and pursue emotion-focused goals rather than problem-focused goals when seeking to provide support; (c) view feminine forms of support as more helpful than masculine forms of support; (d) prefer other women as sources of support when they are distressed; and (e) most like or be most satisfied with relationship partners who display feminine (i.e., expressive) skills and orientations in social relationships.

& Burleson, 2005; Westmyer & Myers, 1996). Similar results have been obtained with an independently developed measure of communication values (Henry, Reed, & McAllister, 1995; Reed, McLeod, & McAllister, 1999).

Wood (1997) criticized most CFQ studies for utilizing samples of college students, arguing that gender differences in college students may be considerably smaller than those in the broader population. In response to this critique, MacGeorge, Feng, and Butler (2003) examined gender differences in the communication values of a sample of 304 adults who ranged in age from 40 to more than 80 years of age. The results of this study largely replicated those obtained with college-aged samples: Both men and women viewed supportive and expressive skills as more important in same-sex friends than instrumental skills, though women valued comforting skill somewhat more highly than did men, and men valued persuasive skill somewhat more highly than did women. Similar findings were obtained by Xu and Burleson (2001), who used a different instrument to assess the value placed by American and Chinese married adults on five types of spousal support (emotional, esteem, network, informational, and tangible). In each national group, both men and women valued emotional support more than any other kind of spousal support, though women viewed this type of support (and, indeed, all types of support) as somewhat more desirable than did men.

In sum, the results of studies assessing communication skill evaluations in close relationships suggest that men and women have substantially similar communication values.[5] Both men and women place the highest value on supportive and expressive communication skills such as providing ego support and comforting, and they place lower value on more instrumental skills such as informing and persuading. These results, obtained with a variety of samples, relationships, and instruments, are clearly inconsistent with predictions derived from the DCT.[6]

---

[5]Samter and Burleson (1990a) suggest that communication skill evaluations provide insight into how people conceptualize their relationships, particularly the perceived provisions of these relationships. Thus, studies assessing communication values indicate that both men and women largely see their close relationships as centered on the exploration, validation, and support of selves. Although relationship partners are also viewed as sources of companionship and instrumental assistance, the lower import accorded to instrumental communication skills by both men and women suggest that both sexes see the instrumental provisions of close relationships as less central than their affective provisions.

[6]The results of studies assessing sex differences in communication values are consistent with studies examining sex differences and similarities in the meaning of concepts such as "intimacy" and "closeness." These studies, most of which have content-analyzed essays describing the experience of intimacy, closeness, and related terms, have found that men and women have quite similar conceptions of these constructs (e.g., Helgeson, Shaver, & Dyer, 1987; D. C. Jones, 1991; Monsour, 1992; Parks & Floyd, 1996). Somewhat similarly, Reis (1990) found no sex differences beyond chance in ratings of the importance of diverse goals in the context of friendship. Comparable patterns of results have been reported in several other studies (see the review by Reis, 1998; e.g., Vangelisti & Daly, 1997). These results are at odds with claims by proponents of the DCT that men and women have substantially, if not fundamentally, different conceptions of intimacy, closeness, and supportiveness (e.g., Inman, 1996; Swain, 1989; Wood & Inman, 1993).

Goals in Support Situations

People's reports concerning the goals they are likely to pursue when others need support can provide information about how they conceptualize support situations and communication as a resource for managing these situations (Burleson, 2003b). According to the DCT, women orient to the affective and relational aspects of support situations and should thus primarily pursue emotion-focused goals, particularly providing solace. In contrast, the DCT contends that men orient to the objective and instrumental aspects of support situations and should thus primarily pursue problem-focused goals such as solving the problem or, alternatively, helping redirect attention away from the troublesome situation and feelings associated with it.

To evaluate these hypotheses, Kunkel and Burleson (1999) had participants rate the importance of emotion-focused and problem-focused goals in support contexts. Contrary to the DCT, both men and women assigned greater priority to emotion-focused goals than to problem-focused goals. Men and women did not differ in the priority given to problem-focused goals, though women did place greater emphasis on emotion-focused goals than did men. Similar results were obtained by Samter, Whaley, Mortenson, and Burleson (1997), whose sample included three different ethnic groups (African Americans, Asian Americans, and European Americans); across ethnicities, both men and women gave greatest priority to emotion-focused goals in support contexts.

Burleson and Gilstrap (2002) asked participants to rate the importance of four support goals: *solace* (providing comfort), *solve* (fixing the problem), *dismiss* (changing the topic), and *escape* (withdrawing from the situation). Both men and women indicated that the solve goal was more important than either escape or dismiss, and that the solace goal was more important than the solve goal. Within this overall pattern, some small sex differences were observed. Specifically, women were somewhat more likely to pursue the goal of solace, and somewhat less likely to pursue the goal of escape, than were men. In contrast, men were somewhat more likely to pursue the goal of solve than were women. Subsequent research (Burleson, Holmstrom, & Gilstrap, in press, Experiment 2) has replicated most of these findings. Other research (MacGeorge, Feng, Butler, Dane, & Passalacqua, 2005) suggests that both men and women may place greater emphasis on providing instrumental than emotional support when it appears that constructive actions can be taken to alleviate the problematic situation.

Though still sparse, research assessing sex differences in goals for support situations provides little support for the DCT. Contrary to the predictions of the DCT, men and women are much more similar than different with regard to their goals in support situations, with their goals in specific situations being influenced more strongly by features of the situation than by gender.

Standards for Helpful Comforting Messages

One of the central claims made by the DCT is that men and women have fundamentally different standards for what counts as sensitive, helpful support (Tannen, 1990; Wood, 1993, 1996, 2000a). According to the DCT, men should respond most favorably to masculine forms of support, whereas women should respond most favorably to feminine forms of support.

Men and women exhibit strong consensus about what constitutes stereotypically feminine and masculine comforting. Researchers (Burleson, et al., in press, Experiment 1; Kunkel & Burleson, 1999) have had participants read several comforting messages that varied in degree of *person centeredness* (the extent to which the feelings and perspective of the distressed target are explicitly acknowledged, elaborated, and legitimized, see Burleson, 1994). Participants then rated each message for how feminine or masculine it seemed. Both men and women perceived highly person-centered (HPC) messages as very feminine and low person-centered (LPC) messages as very masculine. In concert with the results of these gender-typing studies, other research has consistently found that, when attempting to comfort others, women use messages exhibiting somewhat higher levels of person centeredness than do men (Burleson, 1982; Hale, Tighe, & Mongeau, 1997; MacGeorge, Gillihan et al., 2003; Samter, 2002).

Given this collection of findings, the DCT predicts that men and women will respond quite differently to HPC and LPC messages: women should respond positively to feminine HPC comforting messages that explicitly elaborate and explore feelings, and they should respond negatively to masculine LPC messages. Men, in contrast, should exhibit the opposite pattern, responding negatively to feminine HPC messages and positively to masculine LPC messages that avoid discussion of feelings and focus on either fixing the problematic situation or redirecting attention away from that situation.

Kunkel and Burleson (1999) asked participants to rate the sensitivity and effectiveness of 27 comforting messages varying in level of person centeredness. Both men and women evaluated HPC messages as substantially more sensitive and effective than LPC messages (with level of person centeredness explaining 80% of the variance in message evaluations). However, a few small sex differences were also observed: women tended to rate HPC messages slightly more favorably than did men and rated LPC messages slightly less favorably than did men. These findings have been widely replicated in research using (a) a variety of support situations (Burleson & Samter, 1985; S. M. Jones & Burleson, 1997; MacGeorge et al., 2004, Study 3), (b) different methods of presenting message stimuli (Burleson et al., in press, Experiment 1; Samter, Burleson, & Murphy, 1987), (c) samples composed of diverse ethnicities (Samter et al., 1997), (d) samples composed of different nationalities (Burleson & Mortenson, 2003; S. M. Jones, 2004;

Liu, Burleson, & Liu, 2004), and (e) different typologies of comforting strategies (Clark et al., 1998). Contrary to the predictions of the DCT, these studies indicate that men and women have very similar standards about what counts as sensitive and effective verbal comfort.

The results of these message evaluation studies were extended by S. M. Jones and Burleson (2003), who examined whether men and women differed in their actual emotional responses to messages exhibiting different levels of person centeredness. Participants shared a recent upsetting event with either a same-sex or opposite-sex confederate who had been trained to employ comforting messages exhibiting low, moderate, or high levels of person centeredness. Both men and women reported feeling best when exposed to HPC comforting messages, regardless of the sex of the confederate, a result clearly inconsistent with the DCT.[7]

Some claim that experimental evidence affirms the DCT prediction of sex differences in standards for what counts as effective support. For example, Michaud and Warner (1997) asked participants to indicate their likely emotional response to verbal expressions of sympathy and found that women responded more positively than men. However, the sex differences detected by Michaud and Warner were very small, explaining only about 1% of the variance in responses. Moreover, these results were not replicated by Basow and Rubenfeld (2003), who used the same instrument and found no significant sex differences in responses to sympathy. MacGeorge et al. (2004) pointed out that, when viewed more broadly, the data of Michaud and Warner indicate that considerable similarity exists in men's and women's responses to supportive messages, with both sexes responding much more favorably to expressed sympathy than to offered advice—a pattern at odds with the DCT.

In sum, men and women appear to use the same standards in evaluating the helpfulness of comforting messages.[8] Although both sexes view HPC messages as feminine modes of behavior and LPC messages as masculine modes of behavior, both sexes evaluate and experience HPC comforting messages as more helpful than LPC messages. The sex of message recipients occasionally accounts for a small amount of variance (1% to 4%) in how messages are perceived, but the overall pattern in the studies reviewed here is sharply inconsistent with the DCT.

[7]The study by S. M. Jones and Burleson (2003) is also noteworthy for its examination of sex differences in the effects of nonverbal behavior by helpers. Confederates in this study exhibited low, moderate, or high levels of nonverbal immediacy (behaviors such as smiling and eye gaze that reflect warmth and psychological closeness) when responding to distressed participants. Participants of both sexes reported feeling most comforted by confederates displaying high levels of nonverbal immediacy, and this effect was not qualified by sex of the confederate.

[8]Other research (e.g., Reis, Senchak, & Solomon, 1985) indicates that men and women use very similar standards when judging the intimacy of conversational interactions; see the review by Reis (1998).

Preferences for the Gender of Support Providers

Men and women appear to respond similarly to various supportive messages, but who do they want to talk to when they are emotionally upset? The DCT strongly suggests that members of each sex will prefer to seek support from persons of their own sex: men should prefer men as support providers, whereas women should prefer women (Tannen, 1990).

Numerous studies have examined individuals' preferences for the sex of providers of emotional support. For example, Kunkel and Burleson (1999) asked college men and women to indicate whether they would be most likely to seek emotional support from a same-sex or an opposite-sex friend. These researchers found that 71% of the men and 76% of the women indicated a preference for a female comfort provider. Kunkel and Burleson also found that both men and women reported they would feel most comfortable discussing troubles with a female friend and expected a female friend to respond more supportively than a male friend. Clark (1994) found that both female and male adolescents indicated a preference for a female conversational partner when they felt depressed and in need of being cheered up. Many other studies indicate that both sexes see women as generally more supportive than men (e.g., Burda & Vaux, 1987; Hays & Oxley, 1986), and are more likely to seek support, especially emotional support, from female rather than male providers (e.g., Aukett, Ritchie, & Mill, 1988; Barbee, Gulley, & Cunningham, 1990; Buhrke & Fuqua, 1987; Flaherty & Richman, 1989), although one study (Barbee et al.) found that men and women preferred to receive support about both relationship and task problems from people of their own sex.[9]

If men and women are prey to a cultural "clash of conversational styles" (Tannen, 1990), their interactions with members of the opposite sex should be experienced as frustrating and unhelpful when they are in need of emotional support. In contrast, both sexes should find interactions with members of their own sex

[9]The results obtained by Barbee et al. (1990) might be an artifact of the instructions participants received regarding the identification of potential support providers. Specifically, the college students participating in this research were instructed to "choose one close same-sex friend, who was not a current roommate, and one close opposite-sex friend, who was not a current romantic partner" when responding to the study questionnaire (p. 537). It is possible that this instruction confounded relationship closeness with friend sex; that is, it is possible that participants felt closer to the "same-sex friend who was not a current roommate" than they did the "opposite-sex friend who was not a current romantic partner," and thus were more likely to seek support from this closer—and same-sex—person. At many colleges, roommates are assigned by the institution; obviously, both friends and romantic partners are chosen rather than assigned. Thus, the "same-sex friend who was not a current roommate" might very well have been the same-sex individual to whom participants felt closest (i.e., a best friend). In contrast, it is less likely that most participants felt closer to the "opposite-sex friend who was not a current romantic partner" than they did to their current romantic partner. Unfortunately, Barbee et al. did not control for the closeness of helpers. These reflections emphasize the importance of using comparable groups when examining preferences for the gender of support providers.

more rewarding and helpful. This general notion has been examined in several studies (e.g., Mickelson, Helgeson, & Weiner, 1995; Winstead, Derlega, Lewis, Sanchez-Hucles, & Clarke, 1992). Goldsmith, McDermott, and Hawkins (1996) reviewed these studies and concluded that "none of these studies found same-sex pairings provided more effective support than opposite-sex pairings. On the contrary, in several instances opposite-sex pairings were quite successful in providing support" (p. 14). Goldsmith et al. also carried out a study that assessed the influence of dyad composition (same sex vs. opposite sex) on support satisfaction in two different samples, college student intimates (friends or romantic partners) and adult intimates (friends, family members, or romantic partners from the community). These researchers found no clear evidence in either sample that recipients received more satisfying support from people of their own sex.[10]

In sum, contrary to predictions by the DCT, both men and women prefer to seek and receive support, especially emotional support, from women. There are no data consistent with the DCT prediction that men prefer male over female support providers.

Relational Outcomes of Gender-Typical Comforting Behaviors

A fifth general hypothesis derived from the DCT stipulates that members of each sex should have the greatest liking for, be most attracted to, or find relationships to be most satisfying with others who engage in gender-typical forms of comforting behavior (Wood, 1993). One empirically testable consequence of this notion is that men who exhibit masculine (LPC) forms of comforting behavior should be best liked by other men, whereas men who engage in feminine (HPC) modes of comforting should be rejected by same-sex peers. This general hypothesis has been examined in two different studies, one with children (Burleson et al., 1986) and one with adults (Samter & Burleson, 1990b). Both studies employed sociometric methods to assess peer acceptance and rejection. Neither of them yielded results consistent with the DCT. In both studies, male participants who displayed stereotypically masculine comforting behaviors were not better liked by same-sex peers; indeed, they were more likely to be rejected by these peers.

Other studies (e.g., Burleson et al., in press, Experiment 1; Samter et al., 1987) have examined how comforting messages that exhibit different levels of person centeredness influence liking for the message source. In these studies, participants read a support effort by a helper who either used LPC or HPC comforting messages; the participants then completed several scales assessing their

[10]The results of studies assessing preferences for the gender of support providers are consistent with findings reported by Reis and his colleagues (Reis et al., 1985; Wheeler, Reis, & Nezlek, 1983), which indicate that both sexes find interactions with females to be more intimate and meaningful than interactions with men. In concert with these results, Wheeler et al. (1983) found that amount of time spent in interaction with women was negatively associated with self-reported loneliness for both sexes.

liking for the helper and desire to engage in interaction with that person. Liking for the helper was strongly influenced by the person centeredness of the messages used, and sex of the participants did not moderate this effect. In particular, male helpers who employed masculine LPC messages were least liked by both male and female participants.

In sum, both men and women are more attracted to and have more satisfying relationships with people of both sexes when these people exhibit more feminine modes of behavior, especially feminine modes of providing comfort and emotional support. Further, both men and women appear to be repelled by those who engage in highly masculine forms of emotional support. These findings are substantially inconsistent with the DCT.

CONCLUSION: APPRAISAL OF AND ALTERNATIVES TO THE DIFFERENT CULTURES THESIS

The DCT maintains that there should be substantial cognitive, as well as behavioral, differences between men and women. In particular, the DCT suggests that men and women should differ in their values with regard to supportive communication skills, their goals when providing support to others, their judgments about what counts as a helpful support message, their preferences for the gender of a comfort provider, and their attraction to and satisfaction with those who provide masculine and feminine modes of support. We reviewed several studies evaluating these predictions and no support was found for any of them.

Men and women are quite similar in their support-related values, goals, standards, preferences, and patterns of interpersonal liking. Both sexes view emotional support skills as more important than instrumental skills in the context of various personal relationships, and both sexes frequently prioritize emotion-focused goals over problem-focused goals when providing support to distressed others. Even though both sexes indicate that they view HPC comforting messages as feminine forms of behavior, both men and women perceive and experience these messages as the most sensitive and effective forms of support. Moreover, both sexes perceive and experience masculine LPC comforting messages as relatively insensitive and ineffective. Both men and women indicate that they prefer seeking comfort from women in times of trouble and distress. Finally, both men and women are more attracted to, and have more satisfying relationships with, persons who exhibit feminine approaches rather than masculine approaches to providing support.

A few statistically significant sex differences were observed in the studies we reviewed. However, these sex differences were uniformly small in magnitude, rarely accounting for more than 4% of the variance in a dependent variable. The occasional character and small size of observed sex differences is obviously not consistent with the degree of difference that would be expected if men and women really constituted different cultural groups. As Thorne (1993) has suggested, the notion of different cultures implies a sense of dichotomous difference.

Although we found few differences between men and women in the cognitive variables examined in our literature review, it must be remembered that there are important differences between the sexes in aspects of their comforting behavior. As noted previously, women are more likely than men to provide emotional support to others, to seek emotional support from others, to focus on emotions while providing support, and to use HPC comforting messages in the effort to relieve distress. These are important differences. Indeed, the observed gender differences in behavior are comparatively substantial, often accounting for more than 10% of the variance in the examined dependent variables. There is, then, a complex pattern of gender-related similarities and differences with respect to varied features of emotional support. On the one hand, both men and women highly value the ability to provide emotional support, see the same types of messages as providing sensitive comfort, prefer to seek and receive support from women, and respond positively to those who exhibit a feminine mode of providing support. On the other hand, women are more likely than men to provide comfort when needed and to use the message forms experienced as most comforting.

A coherent theory must systematically account for both the similarities and differences in men and women with respect to varied aspects of emotional support. The DCT obviously is not such a theory; it emphasizes and can explain only sex-related differences. An alternative perspective, the skill deficit or skill specialization account (Burleson et al., 1996; Kunkel & Burleson, 1999), appears capable of explaining both the observed similarities and differences.[11]

Like the DCT, the skill specialization account sees gender-related differences in behavior as originating in the socialization experiences of children. According to this view, all cultures are partially composed of a dynamic, but fragmented stock of knowledge (Berger & Luckmann, 1966). All cultures also recognize different types of persons or social categories, with gender being one of the most important distinctions made in any society (Eagly et al., 2000). Over the course of socialization, different types of persons are differentially exposed to various segments of the cultural stock of knowledge. Some portions of the knowledge stock are distributed to all members of the culture (e.g., the linguistic system, certain values), whereas other portions of the knowledge stock are distributed quite narrowly and specifically (e.g., certain skills).

For example, in contemporary American culture, children of both sexes are exposed to many of the same communication practices, cultural artifacts, and value

[11]We view our skill specialization account as a variant of Eagly's social role theory of sex differences in behavior, which maintains that "women and men adjust to sex-typical roles by acquiring the specific skills and resources linked to successful role performance and by adapting their behavior to role requirements. A variety of sex-differentiated skills and beliefs arise from the typical family and economic roles of men and women" (Eagly, Wood, & Diekman, 2000, p. 126).

orientations by socialization agents such as parents, siblings, neighbors, teachers, and the mass media (Golombok & Fivush, 1994; Thorne, 1993). However, to a greater extent than boys, girls in American society are encouraged to express and manage emotions. For example, caretakers talk about feelings and internal states with girls to a greater extent than they do with boys (Dunn, 1998). Moreover, the roles that many women fill in industrial and postindustrial societies lead them to discuss, analyze, and manage feelings somewhat more than do men (Alexander & Wood, 2000). Greater practice at expressing emotions and dealing with the emotions of others leads women to develop more sophisticated skills for nurturing, comforting, and providing support (MacGeorge, Gillihan et al., 2003). In contrast, to a greater extent than girls, boys are encouraged to influence others, direct the activities of others, and amuse others. Greater practice in these activities leads men to develop more sophisticated persuasive and informative skills. Thus, members of each sex tend to specialize in some skills while incurring deficits in other skills. However, what counts as skill in a particular domain (e.g., comforting, persuading) remains the same for both sexes; this is a critical point that differentiates the skill specialization account from the DCT.

Thus, the skill specialization account suggests that men and women seek similar things from their intimate relationships, conduct their intimate relationships through similar forms of behavior, and value the same sorts of communicative skills and abilities in their partners. However, this account also holds that there will be differences in the specific communication skills of men and women as a function of cultural norms that encourage differential patterns of skill development and use. Consequently, the skill specialization account can make sense out of the specific patterns of gender-related similarities and differences observed with respect to comforting and other forms of emotional support.

A growing body of findings provides corroboration for the skill specialization account of sex differences in supportive communication (Burleson, 2002). Competence at supportive communication is theorized to depend on several underlying cognitive abilities and motivational orientations (Burleson & Kunkel, 1996; Feeney & Collins, 2001). Consistent with the skill specialization account, women have been found to possess these abilities and motivational orientations to a greater extent than do men; moreover, these abilities and motivations have been found to mediate sex differences in varied aspects of supportive communication skill (Burleson & Gilstrap, 2002; Kunkel, 2002; MacGeorge, Clark, & Gillihan, 2002; MacGeorge, Feng et al., 2003; MacGeorge et al., 2005; Mortenson, 2002; Samter, 2002).

The skill specialization account has particular virtue in encouraging researchers to adopt a rhetorical perspective, rather than a sociolinguistic perspective, on comforting behavior and similar communication skills. Researchers with backgrounds in linguistics and sociolinguistics (e.g., Maltz & Borker, 1982; Tannen, 1990) tend to treat group-based differences in communicative behaviors as a matter of style. For example, Tannen consistently referred to gender differences in problem talk (i.e., comforting) as a matter of conversational style, and she argued that men and women have "different *but equally valid* styles" (1990, p. 15; emphasis in the original) and that "each style is valid on its own terms" (p. 47). Wood (1993, 1994) also used the *style* terminology in her discussion of male and female differences in emotional support. Moreover, Wood (1993) specifically criticized those who "attach unequal value to masculine and feminine styles, and strive to teach students or clients the 'better' mode" (p. 53). Urging scholars to resist "being 'goaded by hierarchy,'" Wood (1993, p. 53) advocated a neutral evaluative stance with respect to gender differences in patterns of emotionally supportive behaviors.

Taking a neutral evaluative stance toward what is characterized as a matter of conversational style is fully consistent with linguistic and sociolinguistic approaches to communicative phenomena. After all, many (and probably most) differences at the linguistic and sociolinguistic levels of analysis are neutral: it obviously makes no sense to say that the morpheme *tree* is a better representation of a tree than the morpheme *arbor* or that the adjective–noun syntactic pattern is superior to the noun–adjective syntactic pattern. However, many of the communicative phenomena examined by Tannen, Wood, Maltz and Borker, and others are not exclusively subject to analysis from linguistic and sociolinguistic perspectives; indeed, they may not be best analyzed from these perspectives.

Many communicative phenomena, especially functionally directed behaviors such as comforting, are fruitfully considered from a rhetorical perspective. For over 2,500 years, a constitutive assumption of the rhetorical tradition has been that there are not merely different ways of doing things with words; rather, some ways of doing things with words are *better* than other alternatives—more effective, more convincing, more efficient, more sensitive—whatever the particular criterion. Hence, a rhetorical approach to the analysis of gender-linked communication practices, especially functionally directed uses of language such as comforting, diverges significantly from linguistic and sociolinguistic approaches in fundamental assumptions. Research informed by a rhetorical perspective is interested in identifying different strategic options and determining which of these options is better or more effective for the task undertaken. By viewing comforting and related behaviors as social skills, the skill specialization account encourages researchers to adopt a rhetorical perspective.

Important methodological and pedagogical implications follow from our critique of the DCT. Some proponents of the DCT (e.g., Inman, 1996; Swain, 1989) have argued that the way intimacy and emotional closeness have been evaluated by social scientists has been biased by usage of a feminine yardstick, and that many theories of intimacy are "flawed by their exclusion of masculine styles of creating and expressing closeness" (Wood, 1993, p. 45). However, as most of the findings reported in this chapter strongly suggest, men and women tend to use similar, if not identical, yardsticks in evaluating the sensitivity and effectiveness of emotional support. Thus, assessments of comforting behavior in terms of emotion focus (Barbee et al., 1993) or person centeredness (Burleson, 1994) do not unduly rely on an exclusively feminine standard; they use standards that men and women consensually share. Further, the findings summarized in this chapter imply a critique of research designs that exclusively focus on the examination of between-group differences and fail to consider the magnitude as well as the reliability (i.e., statistical significance) of observed differences. A growing literature in the fields of communication and personal relationships suggests that, although some noteworthy differences between men and women exist, when both within- and between-gender comparisons are made, the similarities are as important—if not more important—than the differences (Kyratzis, 2001; MacGeorge et al., 2004). Thus, between-gender differences often must be viewed against the backdrop of more substantial similarities.

Finally, the research reviewed here calls into question the pedagogical advice offered by advocates of the DCT (e.g., Maltz & Borker, 1982; Tannen, 1990; Wood, 1993) that men and women need to become "bilingual" to avoid miscommunication. Rather, our review suggests that men and women speak the same language, although each sex may have certain specialties in the use of that language. Moreover, it would be counterproductive to teach men and women to value the masculine comforting efforts frequently produced by men (i.e., LPC messages). Simply because men typically use less person-centered comforting strategies does not mean that this masculine mode of behavior is, or should be, valued and advocated. In fact, the research findings suggest quite the contrary: more has to be done to enhance the ability of men in the comforting realm – both in schools and in the home. The enhancement of men's comforting skills might help alleviate some of the pressure associated with women's traditional and culturally assigned role of caretaker (Wood, 1994).

To conclude, the DCT, as well as related positions that assert men and women constitute distinct "speech communities" (Wood, 2002), present distorted, misleading views of sex differences in emotional support processes, exaggerating the differences that exist while understating or ignoring the many more substantial similarities. The DCT may have once served a useful function in stimulating research on gender, communication, emotion, and relationships. As the research evidence has accumulated, however, it has become increasingly clear that the DCT is a myth (MacGeorge et al., 2004)—a myth that has lost it narrative force (Thorne, 1993). A myth that has lost its narrative force is a lot like "the emperor's new clothes": Though some may pay homage to these fictions, they lack substance, are largely the product of the imagination, and represent an increasing embarrassment to the good people of the community. The DCT constitutes a deeply flawed basis for theory and practice, and thus it should be rejected by theorists, researchers, practitioners, textbook writers, and others who seek to represent accurately the communication practices of women and men.

ACKNOWLEDGMENTS

Preparation of this chapter was supported, in part, by a fellowship awarded to B. R. Burleson by the Center for Behavioral and Social Sciences, College of Liberal Arts, Purdue University.

REFERENCES

Alexander, M. G., & Wood, W. (2000). Women, men and positive emotions: A social role interpretation. In A. H. Fischer (Ed.), *Gender and emotion: Social psychological perspectives* (pp. 189–210). New York: Cambridge University Press.

Aukett, R., Ritchie, J., & Mill, K. (1988). Gender differences in friendship patterns. *Sex Roles, 19*, 57–66.

Barbee, A. P., Cunningham, M. R., Winstead, B. A., Derlega, V. J., Gulley, M. R., Yankeelov, P. A., & Druen, P. B. (1993). Effects of gender role expectations on the social support process. *Journal of Social Issues, 49*(3), 175–190.

Barbee, A. P., Gulley, M. R., & Cunningham, M. R. (1990). Support seeking in close relationships. *Journal of Social and Personal Relationships, 7*, 531–540.

Basow, S. A., & Rubenfeld, K. (2003). "Troubles talk": Effects of gender and gender-typing. *Sex Roles, 48*, 183–187.

Bate, B., & Bowker, J. (1997). *Communication and the sexes* (2nd ed.). Prospect Heights, IL: Waveland Press.

Baxter, L. A. (1986). Gender differences in the heterosexual relationship rules embedded in break-up accounts. *Journal of Social and Personal Relationships, 3*, 289–306.

Berger, P. L., & Luckmann, T. (1966). *The social construction of reality: A treatise in the sociology of knowledge*. Garden City, NY: Doubleday.

Bruess, C. J. S., & Pearson, J. C. (1996). Gendered patterns in family communication. In J. T. Wood (Ed.), *Gendered relationships* (pp. 59–78). Mountain View, CA: Mayfield.

Buhrke, R. A., & Fuqua, D. R. (1987). Sex differences in same- and cross-sex supportive relationships. *Sex Roles, 17*, 339–352.

Burda, P. C., & Vaux, A. (1987). The social support process in men: Overcoming sex-role obstacles. *Human Relations, 40*, 31–43.

Burleson, B. R. (1982). The development of comforting communication skills in childhood and adolescence. *Child Development, 53*, 1578–1588.

Burleson, B. R. (1994). Comforting messages: Features, functions, and outcomes. In J. A. Daly & J. M. Wiemann (Eds.), *Strategic interpersonal communication* (pp. 135–161). Hillsdale, NJ: Lawrence Erlbaum Associates.

Burleson, B. R. (1997). A different voice on different cultures: Illusion and reality in the study of sex differences in personal relationships. *Personal Relationships, 4*, 229–241.

Burleson, B. R. (2002). Psychological mediators of sex differences in emotional support: A reflection on the mosaic. *Communication Reports, 15*, 71–79.

Burleson, B. R. (2003a). Emotional support skill. In J. O. Greene & B. R. Burleson (Eds.), *Handbook of communication and social interaction skills* (pp. 551–594). Mahwah, NJ: Lawrence Erlbaum Associates.

Burleson, B. R. (2003b). The experience and effects of emotional support: What the study of cultural and gender differences can tell us about close relationships, emotion, and interpersonal communication. *Personal Relationships, 10*, 1–23.

Burleson, B. R., Applegate, J. L., Burke, J. A., Clark, R. A., Delia, J. G., & Kline, S. L. (1986). Communicative correlates of peer acceptance in childhood. *Communication Education, 35*, 349–361.

Burleson, B. R., & Gilstrap, C. M. (2002). Explaining sex differences in interaction goals in support situations: Some mediating effects of expressivity and instrumentality. *Communication Reports, 15*, 43–55.

Burleson, B. R., & Goldsmith, D. J. (1998). How the comforting process works: Alleviating emotional distress through conversationally induced reappraisals. In P. A. Andersen & L. K. Guerrero (Eds.), *Handbook of communication and emotion: Research, theory, applications, and contexts* (pp. 245–280). San Diego, CA: Academic Press.

Burleson, B. R., Holmstrom, A. J., & Gilstrap, C. M. (in press). "Guys can't say that to guys": Four experriments assessing the normative motivation account for deficiencies in the emotional support. provided by men. *Communication Monographs.*

Burleson, B. R., & Kunkel, A. W. (1996). The socialization of emotional support skills in childhood. In G. R. Pierce, B. R. Sarason, & I. G. Sarason (Eds.), *Handbook of social support and the family* (pp. 105–140). New York: Plenum.

Burleson, B. R., Kunkel, A. W., Samter, W., & Werking, K. J. (1996). Men's and women's evaluations of communication skills in personal relationships: When sex differences make a difference–and when they don't. *Journal of Social and Personal Relationships, 13*, 201–224.

Burleson, B. R., & Mortenson, S. R. (2003). Explaining cultural differences in evaluations of emotional support behaviors: Exploring the mediating influences of value systems and interaction goals. *Communication Research, 30*, 113–146.

Burleson, B. R., & Samter, W. (1985). Individual differences in the perception of comforting messages: An exploratory investigation. *Central States Speech Journal, 36*, 39–50.

Burleson, B. R., & Samter, W. (1990). Effects of cognitive complexity on the perceived importance of communication skills in friends. *Communication Research, 17*, 165–182.

Cancian, F. (1986). The feminization of love. *Signs, 11*, 692–708.

Clark, R. A. (1994). Children's and adolescents' gender preferences for conversational partners for specific communicative objectives. *Journal of Social and Personal Relationships, 11*, 313–319.

Clark, R. A., Pierce, A. J., Finn, K., Hsu, K., Toosley, A., & Williams, L. (1998). The impact of alternative approaches to comforting, closeness of relationship, and gender on multiple measures of effectiveness. *Communication Studies, 49*, 224–239.

Crawford, M. (1995). *Talking difference: On gender and language*. Thousand Oaks, CA: Sage.

Cutrona, C. E. (1996). *Social support in couples*. Thousand Oaks, CA: Sage.

Dunn, J. (1998). Siblings, emotion, and the development of understanding. In S. Braten (Ed.), *Intersubjective communication and emotion in early ontogeny* (pp. 158–168). Cambridge, England: Cambridge University Press.

Eagly, A. H., Wood, W., & Diekman, A. B. (2000). Social role theory of sex differences and similarities: A current appraisal. In T. Eckes & H. M. Trautner (Eds.), *The developmental social psychology of gender* (pp. 123–174). Mahwah, NJ: Lawrence Erlbaum Associates.

Feeney, B. C., & Collins, N. L. (2001). Predictors of caregiving in adult intimate relationships: An attachment theoretical perspective. *Journal of Personality and Social Psychology, 80*, 972–994.

Finn, A., & Powers, W. G. (2002). The value of instrumental and affective communication skills in different relational stages. *Communication Quarterly, 50*, 192–203.

Flaherty, J. A., & Richman, J. (1989). Gender differences in the perception and utilization of social support: Theoretical perspectives and an empirical test. *Social Science and Medicine, 28*, 1221–1228.

Geertz, C. (1973). *The interpretation of cultures*. New York: Basic Books.

Goldsmith, D. J., & Dun, S. A. (1997). Sex differences and similarities in the communication of social support. *Journal of Social and Personal Relationships, 14*, 317–337.

Goldsmith, D. J., & Fulfs, P. A. (1999). "You just don't have the evidence": An analysis of claims and evidence in Deborah Tannen's *You Just Don't Understand*. In M. E. Roloff (Ed.), *Communication Yearbook, 22* (pp. 1–49). Thousand Oaks, CA: Sage.

Goldsmith, D. J., McDermott, V. M., & Hawkins, M. (1996, May). *Gender differences in perceived supportiveness of conversations about problems: A prelimrary report of results.* Paper presented at the annual meeting of the International Communication Association Chicago.

Golombok, S., & Fivush, R. (1994). *Gender development.* New York: Cambridge University Press.

Gray, J. (1992). *Men are from Mars, Women are from Venus.* A practical guide to improving communication and getting what you want in your relationships. New York: HarperCollins.

Griffiths, K. M., & Burleson, B. R. (1995, April). *Gender and communication values in friendship: A comparison of gender-related similarities and differences in same-sex and cross-sex friendships.* Paper presented at the convention of the Central States Communication Association, Indianapolis, IN.

Hale, J. L., Tighe, M. R., & Mongeau, P. A. (1997). Effects of event type and sex on comforting messages. *Communication Research Reports, 14*, 214–220.

Hays, R. B., & Oxley, D. (1986). Social network development and functioning during a life transition. *Journal of Personality and Social Psychology, 50*, 305–313.

Helgeson, V. S., Shaver, P., & Dyer, M. (1987). Prototypes of intimacy and distance in same-sex and opposite-sex relationships. *Journal of Social and Personal Relationships, 4*, 195–221.

Henley, N. M., & Kramarae, C. (1991). Gender, power, and miscommunication. In N. Coupland, H. Giles, & J. M. Wiemann (Eds.), *"Miscommunication" and problematic talk* (pp. 18–43). Newbury Park, CA: Sage.

Henry, F., Reed, V. A., & McAllister, L. (1995). Adolescents' perception of the relative importance of selected communication skills in their positive peer relationships. *Language, Speech, and Hearing Services in the Schools, 26*, 263–272.

Ingram, K. M., Betz, N. E., Mindes, E. J., Schmitt, M. M., & Smith, N. G. (2001). Unsupportive responses from others concerning a stressful life event: Development of the Unsupportive Social Interactions Inventory. *Journal of Social and Clinical Psychology, 20*, 173–207.

Ingram, K. M., Jones, D. A., & Smith, N. G. (2001). Adjustment among people who have experienced AIDS-related multiple loss: The role of unsupportive social interactions, social support, and coping. *Omega—Journal of Death & Dying, 43*, 287–309.

Inman, C. (1996). Friendships among men: Closeness in the doing. In J. T. Wood (Ed.), *Gendered relationships* (pp. 95–110). Mountain View, CA: Mayfield.

Johnson, F. L. (1989). Women's culture and communication: An analytical perspective. In C. M. Lont & S. A. Friedley (Eds.), *Beyond boundaries: Sex and gender diversity in communication* (pp. 301–316). Fairfax, VA: George Mason University Press.

Johnson, F. L. (1996). Friendships among women: Closeness in dialogue. In J. T. Wood (Ed.), *Gendered relationships* (pp. 79–94). Mountain View, CA: Mayfield.

Johnson, F. L. (2000). *Speaking culturally: Language diversity in the United States.* Thousand Oaks, CA: Sage.

Jones, D. C. (1991). Friendship satisfaction and gender: An examination of sex differences in contributors to friendship satisfaction. *Journal of Social and Personal Relationships, 8*, 167–185.

Jones, S. M. (2004, October). *Does gender moderate the connections among communication values, interaction goals, and perceptions of comforting messages among Germans and Americans?* Paper presented at the annual meeting of the Organization for the Study of Communication, Language, and Gender, Saint Mary's College, Notre Dame, IN.

Jones, S. M., & Burleson, B. R. (1997). The impact of situational variables on helpers' perceptions of comforting messages: An attributional analysis. *Communication Research, 24*, 530–555.

Jones, S. M., & Burleson, B. R. (2003). Effects of helper and recipient sex on the experience and outcomes of comforting messages: An experimental investigation. *Sex Roles, 48*, 1–19.
Kluckholm, C. (1951). Values and value orientations in the theory of action. In T. Parsons & E. A. Shils (Eds.), *Toward a general theory of action*. Cambridge, MA: Harvard University Press.
Kunkel, A. W. (2002). Explaining sex differences in the evaluation of comforting messages: The mediating role of interaction goals. *Communication Reports, 15*, 29–42.
Kunkel, A. W., & Burleson, B. R. (1999). Assessing explanations for sex differences in emotional support: A test of the different cultures and skill specialization accounts. *Human Communication Research, 25*, 307–340.
Kyratzis, A. (2001). Children's gender indexing in language: From the separate worlds hypothesis to considerations of culture, context, and power. *Research on Language and Social Interaction, 34*, 1–13.
Liu, M., Burleson, B. R., & Liu, Y. (2004, October). *Assessing gender-related (dis)similarities in Chinese people's evaluations of emotional support values, goals, and strategies.* Paper presented at the annual meeting of the Organization for the Study of Communication, Language, and Gender, Saint Mary's College, Notre Dame, IN.
MacGeorge, E. L., Clark, R. A., & Gillihan, S. J. (2002). Sex differences in the provision of skillful emotional support: The mediating role of self-efficacy. *Communication Reports, 15*, 17–28.
MacGeorge, E. L., Feng, B., & Butler, G. L. (2003). Gender differences in the communication values of mature adults. *Communication Research Reports, 20*, 191–199.
MacGeorge, E. L., Feng, B., Butler, G. L., Dane, J. L., & Passalacqua, S. A. (2005). Sex differences in goals for supportive interactions. *Communication Studies, 56*, 23–46.
MacGeorge, E. L., Gillihan, S. J., Samter, W., & Clark, R. A. (2003). Skill deficit or differential motivation? Accounting for sex differences in the provision of emotional support. *Communication Research, 30*, 272–303.
MacGeorge, E. L., Graves, A. R., Feng, B., Gillihan, S. J., & Burleson, B. R. (2004). The myth of gender cultures: Similarities outweigh differences in men's and women's provision of and responses to supportive communication. *Sex Roles, 50*, 143–175.
Maltz, D. N., & Borker, R. A. (1982). A cultural approach to male-female miscommunication. In J. J. Gumperz (Ed.), *Language and social identity* (pp. 196–216). Cambridge: England: Cambridge University Press.
Michaud, S. L., & Warner, R. M. (1997). Gender differences in self-reported response to troubles talk. *Sex Roles, 37*, 527–540.
Mickelson, K. D., Helgeson, V. S., & Weiner, E. (1995). Gender effects on social support provision and receipt. *Personal Relationships, 2*, 211–224.
Monsour, M. (1992). Meanings of intimacy in cross- and same-sex friendships. *Journal of Social and Personal Relationships, 9*, 277–295.
Mortenson, S. T. (2002). Sex, communication values, and cultural values: Individualism-collectivism as a mediator of sex differences in communication values in two cultures. *Communication Reports, 15*, 57–70.
Myers, S. A., & Knox, R. L. (1998). Perceived sibling use of functional communication skills. *Communication Research Reports, 15*, 397–405.
Oxley, N. L., Dzindolet, M. T., & Miller, J. L. (2002). Sex differences in communication with close friends: Testing Tannen's claims. *Psychological Reports, 91*, 537–544.
Parks, M. R., & Floyd, K. (1996). Meanings for closeness and intimacy in friendship. *Journal of Social and Personal Relationships, 13*, 85–107.
Reed, V. A., McLeod, K., & McAllister, L. (1999). Importance of selected communication skills for talking with peers and teachers: Adolescents' opinions. *Language, Speech, and Hearing Services in the Schools, 30*, 32–49.
Reis, H. T. (1990). The role of intimacy in interpersonal relations. *Journal of Social and Clinical Psychology, 9*, 15–30.

Reis, H. T. (1998). Gender differences in intimacy and related behaviors: Context and process. In D. J. Canary & K. Dindia (Eds.), *Sex differences and similarities in communication* (pp. 203–232). Mahwah, NJ: Lawrence Erlbaum Associates.

Reis, H. T., Senchak, M., & Solomon, B. (1985). Sex differences in the intimacy of social interaction: Further examination of potential explanations. *Journal of Personality and Social Psychology, 48*, 1204–1217.

Samter, W. (2002). How gender and cognitive complexity influence the provision of emotional support: A study of indirect effects. *Communication Reports, 15*, 5–16.

Samter, W., & Burleson, B. R. (1990a). Evaluations of communication skills as predictors of peer acceptance in a group living situation. *Communication Studies, 41*, 311–326.

Samter, W., & Burleson, B. R. (1990b June). *The role of affectively oriented communication skills in the friendships of young adults: A sociometric study.* Paper presented at the International Communication Association, Dublin, Ireland.

Samter, W., & Burleson, B. R. (2005). The role of communication in same-sex friendships: A comparison among African Americans, Asian Americans, and European Americans. *Communication Quarterly, 53*, 265–283.

Samter, W., Burleson, B. R., & Murphy, L. B. (1987). Comforting conversations: Effects of strategy type on evaluations of messages and message producers. *Southern Speech Communication Journal, 52*, 263–284.

Samter, W., Whaley, B. B., Mortenson, S. R., & Burleson, B. R. (1997). Ethnicity and emotional support in same-sex friendship: A comparison of Asian-Americans, African-Americans, and Euro-Americans. *Personal Relationships, 4*, 413-430.

Schloff, L., & Yudkin, M. (1993). *He & she talk: How to communicate with the opposite sex.* New York: Plume Books.

Swain, S. (1989). Covert intimacy: Closeness in men's friendships. In B. J. Risman & P. Schwartz (Eds.), *Gender in intimate relationships: A microstructural approach* (pp. 71–86). Belmont, CA: Wadsworth.

Tannen, D. (1990). *You just don't understand: Women and men in conversation.* New York: Morrow.

Thorne, B. (1993). *Gender play: Girls and boys in school.* New Brunswick, NJ: Rutgers University Press.

Vangelisti, A. L., & Daly, J. A. (1997). Gender differences in standards for romantic relationships. *Personal Relationships, 4*, 203–219.

Westmyer, S. A., & Myers, S. A. (1996). Communication skills and social support messages across friendship levels. *Communication Research Reports, 13*, 191–197.

Wheeler, L., Reis, H., & Nezlek, J. (1983). Loneliness, social interaction, and sex roles. *Journal of Personality and Social Psychology, 45*, 943–953.

Winstead, B. A., Derlega, V. J., Lewis, R. J., Sanchez-Hucles, J., & Clarke, E. (1992). Friendship, social interaction, and coping with stress. *Communication Research, 19*, 193–211.

Wood, J. T. (1993). Engendered relations: Interaction, caring, power, and responsibility in intimacy. In S. Duck (Ed.), *Social context and relationships* (pp. 26–54). Newbury Park, CA: Sage.

Wood, J. T. (1994). *Who cares? Women, care, and culture.* Carbondale, IL: Southern Illinois University Press.

Wood, J. T. (1996). She says/he says: Communication, caring, and conflict in heterosexual relationships. In J. T. Wood (Ed.), *Gendered relationships* (pp. 149–164). Mountain View, CA: Mayfield.

Wood, J. T. (1997). Clarifying the issues. *Personal Relationships, 4*, 221–228.

Wood, J. T. (2000a). *Relational communication* (2nd ed.). Belmont, CA: Wadsworth.

Wood, J. T. (2000b). Relational culture: The nucleus of intimacy. In J. T. Wood (Ed.), *Relational communication: Continuity and change in personal relationships* (2nd ed., pp. 76–100). Belmont, CA: Wadsworth.

Wood, J. T. (2002). A critical response to John Gray's Mars and Venus portrayals of men and women. *Southern Communication Journal, 67*, 201–210.

Wood, J. T. (2005). *Gendered lives: Communication, gender, and culture* (6th ed.). Belmont, CA: Wadsworth.

Wood, J. T., & Inman, C. (1993). In a different mode: Masculine styles of communicating closeness. *Journal of Applied Communication Research, 21*, 279–295.

Xu, Y., & Burleson, B. R. (2001). Effects of sex, culture, and support type on perceptions of spousal social support: An assessment of the "support gap" hypothesis in early marriage. *Human Communication Research, 27*, 535–566.

Zimmerman, T. S., Holm, K. E., & Haddock, S. A. (2001). A decade of advice for women and men in the best-selling self-help literature. *Family Relations, 50*, 122–133.

9

Social Role Theory of Sex Differences and Similarities: Implication for Prosocial Behavior

Alice H. Eagly
Anne M. Koenig
Northwestern University

Most people would agree that men and women behave differently under some circumstances and similarly under others. To account for this variable quality of sex differences and similarities, social role theory proposes both distal and proximal causes (see Fig. 9.1; also see Eagly, 1987; Eagly, Wood, & Diekman, 2000).[1] The distal, or ultimate, causes of sex differences consist of (a) the physical characteristics of the sexes and (b) features of social structures and local ecologies. The interactions between these two sets of distal variables produce a male–female division of labor from which the more proximal, or immediate, causes of sex differences emerge. These proximal causes consist of gender roles, or general expectations about women and men, and socialization processes that correspond to the division of labor. In this chapter, we apply this theory to prosocial behavior.

Prosocial behavior includes actions such as helping, comforting, and rescuing that are intended to benefit one or more people other than oneself (Batson, 1998). Prosocial acts can serve a variety of motives and are not necessarily motivated solely to increase another's welfare. Consistent with the complexity in the motives underlying prosocial behavior, there is not one sex that is generally more helpful

[1] In this chapter, the terms *sex* and *sexes* denote the grouping of people into female and male categories. The terms *sex differences* and *similarities* are applied to describe the results of comparing these two groups. The term *gender* refers to the meanings that societies and individuals ascribe to these female and male categories.

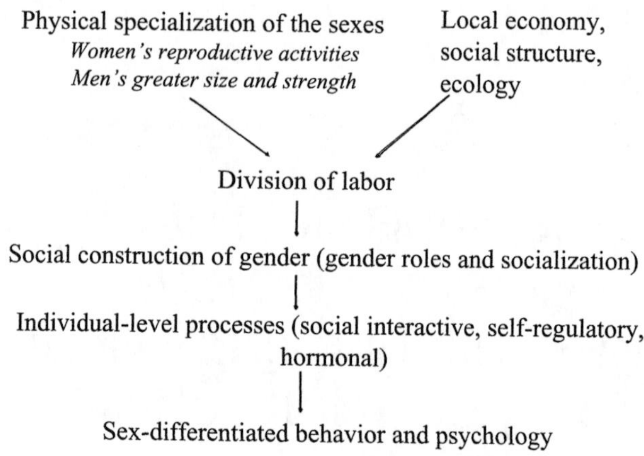

FIGURE 9.1. Social role theory of sex differences and similarities.

than the other sex, although sex differences often emerge in specific types of situations. In this chapter, we examine these complexities in the research literatures on helping behavior, social support, and heroism.

SOCIAL ROLE THEORY: AN OVERVIEW

According to social role theory, the ultimate origins of sex differences in behavior derive mainly from physical sex differences, especially women's capacity for reproduction and men's greater size and strength, in interaction with the demands of socioeconomic systems (Wood & Eagly, 2002). This interaction yields constraints whereby one sex can more efficiently perform certain tasks in particular environments. Some of these constraints follow from women's reproductive activities of pregnancy and lactation, which give women the responsibility of gestating, nursing, and caring for infants. These activities can make it difficult for women to participate as fully as men in tasks that require speed of locomotion, uninterrupted periods of activity, or long-distance travel away from home (e.g., hunting, warfare). In addition, men's greater size and strength yield greater potential for the successful execution of activities that benefit from these qualities, including hunting large animals, plowing, and engaging in warfare. Therefore, a division of labor reflects the specialization of each sex in activities for which they are physically better suited under the circumstances afforded by their society.

Because the implications of each sex's physical attributes depend on the demands of the environment, considerable cross-cultural variability occurs in the particular activities allocated to women and men (Wood & Eagly, 2002). Although patriarchal social arrangements whereby men have more power than women are very common in more complex world societies, the division of labor does not universally produce gender hierarchy. In decentralized, nonhierarchical foraging or pastoral societies with limited technology, relatively egalitarian relations between the sexes are common (Hayden, Deal, Cannon, & Casey, 1986; Salzman, 1999). However, in socioeconomically more complex societies, the physical attributes of the sexes interact with economic and technological developments to enhance men's power and status by giving them roles that can yield decision-making authority (e.g., in warfare) and access to resources (e.g., through intensive agriculture and trade). Men have traditionally garnered most of the social and economic capital that derives from these activities.

Under modern conditions, both the division of labor and gender hierarchy have lessened. These shifts reflect the declining importance of physical sex differences as a result of (a) lower birthrates and less reliance on lactation for feeding infants and young children, and (b) decreased reliance on male size and strength in productive activities. These fundamental changes have set in motion political, social, and psychological transformations whereby women have gained moderate access to roles that yield authority and resources. To the extent that men and women occupy similar roles, they act and behave in a similar manner.

Gender Roles

According to social role theory, sex-typed social roles underlie gender roles, which are consensually shared expectations about men and women (Eagly, 1987). These expectations emerge from observations of male and female behavior. To the extent that social perceivers observe men and women engaging in different types of activities, they infer differing inner dispositions that match these activities. For example, if observations of women commonly include their nurturing activities in caretaking roles, people assume that women tend to be nurturing and caring. The tendency to infer corresponding dispositions from behavior is a well-documented principle of social psychology, known as *correspondent inference* or *correspondence bias* (D. T. Gilbert, 1998). By these processes, activities common to groups of people produce beliefs about the attributes that are typical of group members.

Evidence for the existence of gender roles comes most directly from research on gender stereotypes, which has consistently found that people have differing beliefs about men and women (e.g., Diekman & Eagly, 2000; Newport, Jones, Saad, & Carroll, 2001). These stereotypes constitute *descriptive norms*—that is, beliefs about the actual characteristics of women and men. Like other roles, gender roles also include *injunctive, or prescriptive, norms*, which are beliefs about what women and men should do (Cialdini & Trost, 1998). Both types of norms foster sex-typical behaviors.

Gender roles are diffuse because they apply in virtually all circumstances, regardless of the individual's occupancy of specific roles associated with family relationships and occupations. In contrast to diffuse roles associated with sex and other characteristics such as age, race, and social class, specific roles are relevant primarily to certain settings in the sense that occupational roles are relevant primarily to work settings. Gender roles coexist with these other roles and thus can affect behavior even when these other roles constrain behavior (Ridgeway, 2001). For example, managerial roles and gender roles both influence expectations for managers' workplace behaviors (Eagly & Karau, 2002).

Content of Gender Roles

Studies of gender stereotypes consistently demonstrate that the content of gender roles is heavily saturated with beliefs about communion and agency, with more minor themes pertaining to physical characteristics, cognitive abilities, and other qualities (e.g., Deaux & Lewis, 1984; Diekman & Eagly, 2000; Newport et al., 2001; Spence & Helmreich, 1978; Williams & Best, 1990). Communal traits include characteristics such as being friendly, unselfish, concerned with others, and expressive—qualities ascribed to women. Agentic traits include characteristics such as having mastery, assertiveness, independence, and instrumental competence—qualities ascribed to men. This communal versus agentic divide is consistent with the overall division of labor that gives women disproportionate responsibility in the private sphere of family obligations and men disproportionate responsibility in the public sphere of career and status striving.

Some gender-stereotypical qualities are especially relevant to prosocial behavior. For women, these qualities include kindness, compassion, unselfishness, nurturance, and devotion to others. For men, these qualities include willingness to take risks, adventurousness, assertiveness, and calmness in a crisis. Consistent with these feminine and masculine characteristics are stereotypes that people hold about emotional experience and expression. Among the 19 emotions (e.g., pride, contempt, shame, and happiness) examined by Plant, Hyde, Keltner, and Devine (2000), the largest gender stereotypes consisted of the ascription of more sympathy to women and less fear to men. These gender stereotypes about personality and emotions likely derive from the predominance of women in roles such as teachers, nurses, social workers, and homemakers and of men in roles such as firefighters, law enforcement officers, military personnel, and business executives. Therefore, each gender role encompasses expectations for qualities that are consistent with sex-typical social roles.

The male gender role also features more complex themes prescribing that benevolent protectiveness and politeness should be directed toward women. Deriving from the rules prescribed for medieval knights, conceptions of ideal male behavior in Western society encompass a chivalry theme (see also Felson, 2002). Despite modern ambivalence about chivalry stemming from the recognition of these rules' paternalism and their contribution to the subordination of women (Glick & Fiske, 2001), many such rules have survived in modern etiquette books. For example, even recent etiquette books suggest that men should hold doors open for women and let women go first through doorways and on escalators but lead them over rough ground or on steep, slippery slopes (Post, 1997).

Similar themes relevant to prosocial behavior have emerged in the writings of social scientists who have theorized about gender roles. For example, with respect to the female role, Gilligan (1982) maintained that women's moral reasoning displays a logic that is based on caring and responsibility to others. In addition, many feminist scholars have emphasized that women, especially mothers, are expected to place the needs of others before their own (e.g., Chodorow, 1978; Miller, 1976). With respect to the male gender role's ties to prosocial behavior, David and Brannon (1976) maintained that the essential themes of masculinity encompass the idealization of "daring exploits, and bold excesses of all kinds" (p. 30), and Levant and Kopecky (1995) included risk taking and the ability to remain calm in the face of danger as aspects of the male role.

Influence of Roles on Behavior

After correspondent inference from roles to dispositions has shaped perceivers' beliefs about men and women and these beliefs are shared to become aspects of culture, these beliefs influence the behavior of both sexes, in part through the mediation of parents and other socializing agents who prepare children to occupy sex-typical adult roles. In general, people tend to behaviorally confirm others' gender-stereotypical expectancies by acting in accordance with gender norms, therefore validating others' expectations. People also regulate their behavior to correspond with their own gender-stereotypical self-construals.[2]

Underlying the tendency of people to behaviorally confirm gender stereotypes are tendencies to penalize women and men for deviating from their gender roles (see Eagly et al., 2000). Behavior inconsistent with gender roles often elicits negative sanctions, which may be overt (e.g., losing a job) or subtle (e.g., being ignored, receiving disapproving looks). These sanctions make it easier for men and women to follow their gender roles than to disregard them.

Gender roles also affect the self-concepts of women and men (Cross & Madson, 1997; Gardner & Gabriel, 2004). The internalization of gender-stereotypic qualities results in the adoption of sex-typed norms by people as personal standards for judging their own behavior. Both men and women tend to evaluate themselves favorably to the extent that they conform to these standards and unfavorably to the extent that they deviate from them. In a demonstration of such processes, Wood, Christensen, Hebl, and Rothgerber (1997) showed that to the extent that participants personally endorsed gender role norms, experiences that were congruent with these norms yielded positive feelings about the self and brought participants' actual self-concepts closer to the standards represented by their ideal or morally desirable selves.

[2]In addition, biological processes, especially hormonal changes, provide another mechanism through which gender role norms influence behavior (see Wood & Eagly, 2002).

Important Qualifications

The processes implicated by social role theory allow for nontraditional as well as traditional behaviors. For example, some children have parents who avoid conveying gender-stereotypical norms and instead encourage nontraditional behaviors. In addition, girls and women may become politically activated through the feminist movement, which encourages nontraditional behavior in women and men. Given such environments, some adults have self-concepts that are not conventionally masculine or feminine in agreement with their biological sex, and therefore they behave consistently with less traditional norms. By stressing processes that underlie sex-differentiated behavior in lieu of regarding roles as immutable properties of the social structure, social role theory allows for variability in behavior within each sex.

Another qualification of our presentation relates to its portrayal of the causal direction of social role theory as flowing from physical sex differences within societal contexts to a division of labor, which then leads to the social construction of gender through gender roles and socialization, which in turn foster sex-differentiated behavior (see Fig. 9.1). However, the various causes of the model can influence one another in a reciprocal fashion, allowing for a backward sequence as well. For example, gender- stereotypical behaviors can strengthen gender roles and gender-specific socialization, which then channel men and women into different social roles. Furthermore, to the extent that any causes of sex differences not mentioned in this chapter (e.g., inherited differences in cognitive tendencies or temperament) have some influence, they would also act on gender roles and role distributions.

PROSOCIAL BEHAVIOR

Social role theory predicts that gender roles shape prosocial behavior, leading women and men to specialize in different types of prosocial behavior, with women being more helpful in some situations and men in others. To understand this contextual variation of sex differences in prosocial behavior, we find it useful to distinguish between the direct effects of specific roles on role occupants and the indirect effects of typical role occupancies on all men and women through the mediation of gender roles.

These direct effects refer to the consequences of role occupancy for the people who occupy the role. Specific roles that are occupied predominately by one sex produce sex differences in behavior of the role occupants. For example, women are more likely to be primary caretakers of children and therefore are in a position to perform a range of prosocial actions vis-à-vis their children, including tending, comforting, and feeding them and interceding for them in various situations. Similarly, some sex-typed occupational roles have implications for sex-differentiated prosocial behavior. More women than men are teachers of children, social workers, counselors, and therapists, and, more generally, occupants of a wide range of service roles. Women help others in such roles, albeit in a job that provides an income. Men also help others through their common occupational roles, such as firefighter, police officer, and soldier, which often require acts of service to others in dangerous situations.

The indirect effects of differential occupancy of specific roles by women and men arise from the production of gender roles whereby the characteristics that are required to carry out sex-typical tasks become stereotypical of women and men. Thus, the general expectation that women are and should be sensitive, warm, soft hearted, and compassionate likely arises from their disproportionate occupancy of caring roles, even though a more specific demand for these qualities applies to individuals (primarily women) who actually occupy such roles. The general expectation that men are and should be brave, strong, and calm in a crisis likely arises from their occupancy of roles requiring physical defense of others, even though a more specific demand for these qualities applies to individuals (primary men) who actually occupy such roles. In addition, socialization is shaped to some extent by these more diffuse gender roles. Social roles influence behavior through this indirect route of fostering gender roles and shaping socialization processes, resulting in somewhat different types of prosocial proclivities on the part of women and men, even when they occupy the same specific roles or are in the same situation.

In natural settings, it can be difficult to sort out the direct and indirect effects of role occupancies because social scientists often observe women and men as occupants of different roles (e.g., as husbands and wives). Nonetheless, research often has examined prosocial behavior in situations to which the sexes have relatively equal access or in roles that are not dominated by one sex (e.g., university student, bystander of an emergency in a public setting). Despite relatively equivalent roles and opportunities, men and women are differentially likely to engage in specific prosocial behaviors because of the diffuse social expectations embodied in gender roles and the skills acquired through sex-typed socialization practices.

In general, the socially shared expectations inherent in gender roles suggest that women should be supportive in close relationships and attentive to others' emotional needs. These expectations suggest that men should be helpful in situations entailing serious risks to health and life, requiring assertive intervention, and involving opportunities to direct chivalrous behaviors toward women. As we show, research has supported these predictions.

Helping Behavior

Starting in the 1960s (Darley & Latané, 1968), social psychologists carried out many field and laboratory experiments on helping behavior (see Batson, 1998, for a review). Although the term helping behavior might seem to refer to a wide range of prosocial behaviors, these investigators studied mainly two types of behaviors: (a) interventions in emergency situations in which another person is in need (sometimes called *bystander intervention*), and (b) everyday polite behaviors directed toward another person such as opening a door. Researchers examined these behaviors almost exclusively in brief encounters with strangers in field or laboratory situations and not in long-term role relationships within families or organizations. For example, studies of bystander interventions examined stopping a brutal fight between two individuals and stopping someone from stealing a student's belongings in the library. Studies of polite behaviors examined telling the time to someone who requested it and picking up something a person had dropped and returning it to him or her.

Because most studies in the helping behavior literature involve either bystander interventions or polite, chivalrous behaviors, sex differences in helping behavior should favor men. This assertion follows from the themes of the male gender role, which include assertiveness, courage, boldness, and chivalry. However, features of the setting and the helping act, such as the specific skills required, are likely to affect the direction and magnitude of the sex differences in helping behavior.

A meta-analysis that compared men and women in studies of helping behavior examined social role theory predictions (Eagly & Crowley, 1986). On the basis of 99 male–female comparisons that allowed the computation of effect sizes, the mean effect size was $d = 0.34$ in the direction of men, meaning that, on the average, men's helping exceeded women's by 0.34 *SD*, suggesting a small to moderate sex difference. Despite this robust overall tendency for men to deliver more helping behavior, the effect sizes differed considerably in direction and magnitude. In fact, in 38% of the studies, women helped more than men.

Moderators of Sex Differences

Several characteristics of the studies accounted for the variation in the sex differences in Eagly and Crowley's (1986) meta-analysis. In particular, when women felt less competent to help than men (i.e., when the act was male sex-typed, such as changing a tire), the sex difference was larger in the male direction. In addition, men helped more than women in dangerous situations, especially if women perceived an act as more dangerous than men did (e.g., picking up a hitchhiker).

Another finding was that men tended to be more helpful than women if onlookers were present. In some studies, helpers were alone with the victim or person who requested help; in other studies, the act of helping was more public (e.g., in a subway car or on a city street). The presence of an audience promotes a sex difference in helping behavior because it makes social norms about helping more salient and prescriptive, encouraging people to "do the right thing." Thus, because the male gender role includes expectations of assertive interventions and polite, chivalrous behaviors, an audience fostered men's helping.

The meta-analysis also determined that men were particularly more helpful than women if the opportunity to help came in the form of a need that presented itself rather than an explicit request. A need is present if, for example, a person merely observes someone who seems to be ill or has dropped something. In contrast, a request for help might consist of a person asking for a charitable donation or asking someone to make a phone call. When a need is merely present, a helper has to take some initiative to intervene, whereas when a request is made, the helper can merely acquiesce. It is possible that this tendency for men to be especially more helpful than women in the presence of a need compared with a request may reflect greater assertion on the part of men, consistent with the male gender role's demand for assertiveness.

The tendency of men to help more than women was also more pronounced when the victim or requester was female but absent when the victim or requester was male. The tendency of helping to flow from men to women in this research literature is thus consistent with the norms of chivalry, which prescribe that men direct benevolent acts toward women.

In summary, although men were more likely than women to help overall, under specific conditions this tendency weakened and sometimes reversed. In particular, women tended to help more (sometimes more than men) if they felt competent, if they believed that helping was not dangerous, if the situation was devoid of onlookers, or if the situation included an explicit request to help.

Community Volunteering

Most of the conditions that favor women's prosocial behavior are also met by many forms of community volunteering, which entails freely giving time and services to benefit another person, group, or organization (Wilson, 2000). In the United States, more women than men volunteer (25% of men vs. 32% of women in 2004; see Volunteering in the United States, 2004). Although more women than men volunteer for education or youth-oriented services and health-related organizations, more men than women volunteer for civic, political, and professional organizations. This pattern follows prescribed gender roles whereby women have a greater "ethic of care" that fosters devoting oneself to less fortunate individuals (see Karniol, Grosz, & Schorr, 2003). In contrast, men's volunteering may more often serve their desires for occupational mobility and political influence.

Social Support in Close Relationships

Social support in close relationships is another focus of research on prosocial behavior. Included in gender roles is the expectation that women are more helpful than men in providing personal support and nurturance in close relationships (Wheeler, Reis, & Nezlek, 1983). These beliefs derive from observations of women's role-bound behaviors, for example, as mothers and wives, and encourage women to be empathic, sympathetic, and agreeable toward others, especially in close relationships.

Research has shown that women provide more social support than men to their same-sex friends. In such friendships, women tend to be more cooperative, intimate, and emotionally expressive than men, who tend to focus on events related to careers, sports, and other shared activities (e.g., Caldwell & Peplau, 1982; Duck & Wright, 1993). In line with this difference in friendship, even though men and women may spend equal amounts of time talking with their same-sex friends (Duck & Wright 1993), women often talk about relationships and personal problems, whereas men talk more about current events, work, sports, and politics (e.g., Aries & Johnson, 1983; Bischoping, 1993). Women also self-disclose more to other women than men do to other men (mean $d = 0.37$; Dindia & Allen, 1992). Women's friendship style thus produces greater opportunities for emotional support and informal counseling.

Women also tend to provide more social support in cross-sex relationships. Many, but not all, studies show that men report receiving more acceptance, intimacy, and emotional support from their female than male friends (e.g., Rose, 1985). Furthermore, studies of marital relationships often find that husbands receive more social and emotional support from their wives than wives do from their husbands (Cutrona, 1996). Thus, women give more social support than men, regardless of the sex of the relationship partner (see Burleson & Kunkel, chap. 8, this volume).

Despite the evidence that women convey social support, men may specialize in delivering tangible help to relationship partners, such as helping them solve work or technical problems (see Reis, 1998). Men and women also tend to differ in when and how they offer support (Burleson, 2002). Men may give emotional support mainly under certain circumstances (e.g., times of high stress), but women may give emotional support under a broader set of circumstances (Hale, Tighe, & Mongeau, 1997). Thus, like helping behavior, social support yields sex differences that depend on the situation.

Several researchers have hypothesized that sex differences in social support reflect internalized gender roles (e.g., Barbee et al., 1993; Burleson & Gilstrap, 2002). For example, both men and women who described themselves as relatively feminine were more helpful toward a same-sex confederate who complained of loneliness (Bem, Martyna, & Watson, 1976). These findings, along with the evidence that context affects socially supportive behaviors, are consistent with the social role theory claim that gender roles foster sex-differentiated behavior.

Heroism

Heroism is a form of prosocial behavior whose critical elements are physical risk taking and service to others or to a broader socially valued goal (Becker & Eagly, 2004). The risks faced by heroes are undertaken voluntarily and often are life threatening. Acts that lack the quality of risk (e.g., caring for elderly adults) or service to others (e.g., bungee jumping) are seldom identified as heroic. At a psychological level, such behaviors require both a willingness to take risks and a tendency to feel and act on empathic concern for others' welfare. One of the paradoxical aspects of heroic behavior is that one of these features, willingly taking risks, is culturally masculine, whereas the other feature, showing empathic concern for others, is culturally feminine.

Consistent with stereotypical expectations that men should take risks, there is some evidence for an actual sex difference in risk taking. An inclusive meta-analysis showed that men were somewhat more likely than women to engage in risky behavior (mean $d = 0.13$; Byrnes, Miller, & Schafer, 1999). Although many of the behaviors in this meta-analysis did not involve physical risks, some did (e.g., driving dangerously).

Consistent with culturally shared expectations that women are sympathetic to the needs of others, there is some evidence for an actual sex difference in manifesting empathic concern for others. For example, a relevant meta-analysis confirmed Gilligan's (1982) hypothesis that the moral reasoning of women (vs. men) displays a logic based on caring and a responsibility to others (mean $d = 0.28$; Jaffee & Hyde, 2000). Furthermore, a meta-analysis of personality research showed that women have more tender-minded and nurturant personalities than men (mean $d = 0.75$; Feingold, 1994). Other researchers have found that women have more socially compassionate sociopolitical attitudes than do men (Eagly, Diekman, Johannesen-Schmidt, & Koenig, 2004).

If heroism requires both risk taking and acting on empathic concern for others, heroism should be androgynous in the sense that it is in the domain of both sexes. However, most scholars agree that heroism is culturally defined as masculine (e.g., Lash, 1995). This discrepancy prompted Becker and Eagly (2004) to examine data concerning heroism in settings that have allowed women and men relatively equal access. The relevant data are archival—specifically, archives of Carnegie Hero Medal recipients, the Righteous Among the Nations, living kidney donors, Peace Corps volunteers, and Doctors of the World volunteers.

Archival Data on Extremely Dangerous Heroism

The Carnegie Hero Fund Commission, in operation since 1904, awards medals, scholarships, and financial assistance to Canadian and U.S. heroes, defined as individuals who voluntarily risk their own lives while saving or attempting to save the life of another person (Carnegie Hero Fund Commission, 2002). The commission excludes those who are required by their occupations to perform such actions and those who save family members. The medal recipients are rewarded for their heroic acts in unexpected emergency situations such as fires, potential drownings, attacks by animals, assaults by criminals, and electrocutions. A moderate proportion of Carnegie medals (20%) are awarded posthumously, indicating that considerable risk is associated with such acts.

As of 2003, a substantial majority of these awards (91%) had gone to men. Becker and Eagly (2004) discounted the interpretation that the selection process is biased against women and instead interpreted this finding as a demonstration of a strongly male- dominated form of heroism. Among the reasons for this large sex difference are men's greater size and strength and, possibly, their greater training in emergency intervention. People who intervene in these types of emergency situations are larger in physical size and have more past training dealing with crimes and emergencies than a matched control sample of individuals (Huston, Ruggiero, Cooner, & Geis, 1981).

Another available archive consists of the Righteous Among the Nations, who are non-Jews who have been honored for risking their lives to save Jews during the Nazi holocaust (Becker & Eagly, 2004). The risks that these rescuers took were considerable, because people who helped Jews in occupied countries during World War II were officially or unofficially subject to execution or deportation to concentration camps.

Becker and Eagly (2004) counted the number of men and women on this list of Righteous Among the Nations from Poland, the Netherlands, and France, excluding children and clergy, and compared these counts to the baseline populations of men and women who were present in these countries during World War II. They found that, when all classified individuals were considered, including husband and wife pairs, women and men participated in these rescues in proportions equal to the baseline percentages of each sex who were present in each country. When couples were excluded, slightly but significantly more women and fewer men helped Jews than suggested by the baseline percentages of each sex in each nation. These findings can be enlightened by the research of Oliner and Oliner (1988), who interviewed many rescuers (and nonrescuers). Most rescuers stated an ethical rationale for their risky behavior, primarily having to do with care and compassion. This caring, relational rationale was more prevalent among female than male rescuers (Anderson, 1993).

These example of two different types of heroism show that heroism is not necessarily male dominated. Because both of these situations had high risks of death, men's propensity toward risky behavior does not explain the difference between the two types of heroism. Rather, physical prowess better explains the difference, consistent with the analysis by social role theory of men's greater size and strength and its influence on the roles that men occupy in society (see Wood & Eagly, 2002). Thus, women are less likely to help others in risky situations when strength and skill requirements lessen their ability to intervene effectively (the Carnegie Hero medalists), whereas absent such requirements, women are just as likely if not more likely to help than men (the Righteous Among the Nations).

Another consideration is that the Carnegie medalists engaged in public acts that were immediately labeled as heroic by the rescued and observers of the act and often by the larger community as well. The acts of the Righteous Among the Nations, in contrast, were inherently private because detection of these acts would often have resulted in death. Recognition as a rescuer of Jews came only many years later. This presence of an audience for Carnegie medalists may foster male heroism because it increases the salience of the male gender role's demand for courageous and risky action and of the opportunities that men have to rise in the social hierarchy with public recognition (Baumeister & Sommer, 1997). This explanation is consistent with Eagly and Crowley's (1986) finding that the sex difference in helping behavior was larger in the male direction when the helpers were under surveillance.

The Carnegie medalists also had to act immediately to rescue the victim, whereas the Righteous Among the Nations could often come to their decision to help more gradually as they perceived that friends, neighbors, and colleagues were in danger (M. Gilbert, 2003). This relational aspect of many of the rescues of Jews may also have fostered female heroism, because such acts match cultural expectations of women's sympathetic reactions in close relationships and also correspond to the relational theme in women's self-construals (Cross & Madson, 1997; Gardner & Gabriel, 2004).

Archival Data on Mildly Dangerous Heroism

Becker and Eagly (2004) analyzed several other archives of heroic acts that are less dangerous in terms of risks of death but that still have serious physical consequences. Living kidney donation is one such act. Between 1988 and 2002, more kidneys were donated by women than men (57%), even when other factors were ruled out (e.g., male and female rates of kidney failure and eligibility for donation). The larger number of female donors may be fostered by the more caring attitude that women have about kidney donation, viewing it as an extension of their family obligations (Simmons, Klein, & Simmons, 1977). Indeed, donations to family members constitute the great majority of living donations (e.g., 85.9% in 2000; see the U.S. Organ Procurement and Transplantation Network and the Scientific Registry of Transplant Recipients, 2003). In addition, although cadaveric organ donation is not a risky behavior, women have more positive attitudes toward such donations and are more willing than men to agree to allow their organs to be used after death (e.g., Thompson, Robinson, & Kenny, 2003).

Becker and Eagly (2004) also examined volunteers for the Peace Corps and Doctors of the World. Although service in the Peace Corps is not inherently life threatening, it does entail dangers from serving in poverty-stricken and violence-prone areas of the world and experiencing disease, limited medical care, and (sometimes) assaults against volunteers. Peace Corps volunteers are approximately 60% female in recent years. Overseas volunteers for Doctors of the World, a U.S. organization, are primarily physicians who are stationed around the world to serve vulnerable populations under somewhat risky conditions (e.g., those in Vietnam, Chiapas, Kosovo, and India). These volunteers are also more often women (66% overall and 56% among physicians), compared with the baseline proportions of women and men eligible to serve (e.g., approximately one fourth of physicians are women).

Archival evidence thus shows that not all heroism is male dominated, which is consistent with the argument that heroic acts represent a conjunction of the culturally masculine quality of risk taking and the culturally feminine quality of delivering empathic concern to others. Both men and women can behave heroically, depending on the nature of the heroic act and the situation. As we have shown, the situational variability of sex differences in heroism is for the most part consistent with social role theory.

SUMMARY AND CONCLUSIONS

Prosocial behavior is a complex domain that encompasses different types of behaviors. Because these behaviors relate in differing ways to the demands inherent in gender roles, sex differences are highly variable, sometimes favoring women as the more helpful sex and sometimes favoring men. Although the broad domain of helping encompasses many different types of behaviors, we considered just three types of prosocial behavior that have received the scrutiny of social scientists: everyday acts of helping that occur outside of close relationships in emergency and nonemergency situations, social support in close relationships, and heroic behavior.

We have shown that the observed variability across prosocial behaviors makes sense in terms of the different messages in the male and female gender roles concerning prosocial behavior—that is, the male demand to be courageous, calm in a crisis, and chivalrous, and the female demand to be warm, compassionate, and caring. Some behaviors, such as the heroic behaviors of the rescuers of Jews during the holocaust, required both masculine and feminine qualities and thus were carried out by men and women in almost equal proportions, demonstrating gender similarity in this form of prosocial behavior.

As we have argued, these expectations for sex-typed behavior arise from the actual role occupancies of the sexes, with women specializing more than men in caring roles and men specializing primarily in certain other roles, including occupations such as soldier and firefighter that require physical risk taking. The expectations about men and women arising from these role distributions by correspondent inference create generalized expectancies for helping that act outside of the boundaries of specific roles such as teacher or police officer that require certain forms of helping behavior. Therefore, sex differences in prosocial behavior occur not only when men and women actually occupy different roles but also when they occupy the same role, for example, as a friend or a person who observes a neighbor's house on fire. Men and women thus tend to act prosocially in different contexts in part because of the diffuse cultural expectations that apply to people on the basis of their gender.

REFERENCES

Anderson, V. L. (1993). Gender differences in altruism among holocaust rescuers. *Journal of Social Behavior and Personality, 8*, 43–58.

Aries, E. J., & Johnson, F. L. (1983). Close friendship in adulthood: Conversational content between same-sex friends. *Sex Roles, 9*, 1183–1196.

Barbee, A. P., Cunningham, M. R., Winstead, B. A., Derlega, V. J., Gulley, M. R., Yankeelov, P. S., & Druen, P. B. (1993). Effects of gender role expectations on the social support process. *Journal of Social Issues, 49*, 175–190.

Batson, C. D. (1998). Altruism and prosocial behavior. In D. T. Gilbert, S. T. Fiske, & G. Lindzey (Eds.), *The handbook of social psychology* (4th ed., Vol. 2, pp. 282–316). Boston: McGraw-Hill.

Baumeister, R. F., & Sommer, K. L. (1997). What do men want? Gender differences and two spheres of belongingness: Comment on Cross and Madson (1997). *Psychological Bulletin, 122*, 38–44.

Becker, S. W., & Eagly, A. H. (2004). The heroism of women and men. *American Psychologist, 59*, 163–178.

Bem, S. L., Martyna, W., & Watson, C. (1976). Sex typing and androgyny: Further explorations of the expressive domain. *Journal of Personality and Social Psychology, 34*, 1016–1023.

Bischoping, K. (1993). Gender differences in conversation topics, 1922–1990. *Sex Roles, 28*, 1–13.

Burleson, B. R. (2002). Psychological mediators of sex differences in emotional support: A reflection on the mosaic. *Communication Reports, 15*, 71–79.

Burleson, B. R., & Gilstrap, C. M. (2002). Explaining sex differences in interaction goals in support situations: Some mediating effects of expressivity and instrumentality. *Communication Reports, 15*, 43–55.

Burleson, B. R., & Kunkel, A. W. (2006). Revisiting the different cultures thesis: An assessment of sex differences and similarities in supportive communication. In K. Dindia & D. J. Canary (Eds.), *Sex differences and similarities in communication* (2nd ed.). Mahwah, NJ: Lawrence Erlbaum Associates.

Byrnes, J. P., Miller, D. C., & Schafer, W. D. (1999). Gender differences in risk taking: A meta-analysis. *Psychological Bulletin, 125*, 367–383.

Caldwell, M. A., & Peplau, L. A. (1982). Sex differences in same-sex friendship. *Sex Roles, 8*, 721–732.

Carnegie Hero Fund Commission. (2002). *Requirements for a Carnegie medal.* Retrieved September 11, 2002, from http://www.carnegiehero.org/Require.shtml

Chodorow, N. (1978). *The reproduction of mothering: Psychoanalysis and the sociology of gender.* Berkeley: University of California Press.

Cialdini, R. B., & Trost, M. R. (1998). Social influence: Social norms, conformity, and compliance. In D. T. Gilbert, S. T. Fiske, & G. Lindzey (Eds.), *The handbook of social psychology* (4th ed., Vol. 2, pp. 151–192). Boston: McGraw-Hill.

Cross, S. E., & Madson, L. (1997). Models of the self: Self-construals and gender. *Psychological Bulletin, 122*, 5–37.

Cutrona, C. E. (1996). *Social support in couples: Marriage as a resource in times of stress.* Thousand Oaks, CA: Sage.

Darley, J. M., & Latané, B. (1968). Bystander intervention in emergencies: Diffusion of responsibility. *Journal of Personality and Social Psychology, 8*, 377–383.

David, D. S., & Brannon, R. (1976). The male sex role: Our culture's blueprint of manhood, and what it's done for us lately. In D. S. David & R. Brannon (Eds.), *The forty-nine percent majority: The male sex role* (pp. 1–45). Reading, MA: Addison-Wesley.

Deaux, K., & Lewis, L. L. (1984). Structure of gender stereotypes: Interrelationships among components and gender label. *Journal of Personality and Social Psychology, 46*, 991–1004.

Diekman, A. B., & Eagly, A. H. (2000). Stereotypes as dynamic constructs: Women and men of the past, present, and future. *Personality and Social Psychology Bulletin, 26*, 1171–1188.

Dindia, K., & Allen, M. (1992). Sex differences in self-disclosure: A meta-analysis. *Psychological Bulletin, 112*, 106–124.

Duck, S., & Wright, P. H. (1993). Reexamining gender differences in same-gender friendships: A close look at two kinds of data. *Sex Roles, 28*, 709–727.

Eagly, A. H. (1987). *Sex differences in social behavior: A social-role interpretation.* Hillsdale, NJ: Lawrence Erlbaum Associates.

Eagly, A. H., & Crowley, M. (1986). Gender and helping behavior: A meta-analytic review of the social psychology literature. *Psychological Bulletin, 100*, 283–308.

Eagly, A. H., Diekman, A. B., Johannesen-Schmidt, M. C., & Koenig, A. M. (2004). Gender gaps in sociopolitical attitudes: A social psychological analysis. *Journal of Personality and Social Psychology, 87*, 796–816.

Eagly, A. H., & Karau, S. J. (2002). Role congruity theory of prejudice toward female leaders. *Psychological Review, 109*, 573–598.

Eagly, A. H., Wood, W., & Diekman, A. (2000). Social role theory of sex differences and similarities: A current appraisal. In T. Eckes & H. M. Trautner (Eds.), *The developmental social psychology of gender* (pp. 123–174). Mahwah, NJ: Lawrence Erlbaum Associates.

Feingold, A. (1994). Gender differences in personality: A meta-analysis. *Psychological Bulletin, 116*, 429–456.

Felson, R. B. (2002). *Violence and gender reexamined*. Washington, DC: American Psychological Association.

Gardner, W. L., & Gabriel, S. (2004). Gender differences in relational and collective interdependence: Implications for self-views, social behavior, and subjective well-being. In A. H. Eagly, A. Beall, & R. J. Sternberg (Eds.), *The psychology of gender* (2nd ed., pp. 169–191). New York: Guilford.

Gilbert, D. T. (1998). Ordinary personology. In D. T. Gilbert, S. T. Fiske, & G. Lindzey (Eds.), *The handbook of social psychology* (4th ed., Vol. 2, pp. 89–150). Boston: McGraw-Hill.

Gilbert, M. (2003). *The righteous: The unsung heroes of the holocaust*. New York: Henry Holt.

Gilligan, C. (1982). *In a different voice: Psychological theory and women's development*. Cambridge, MA: Harvard University Press.

Glick, P., & Fiske, S. T. (2001). An ambivalent alliance: Hostile and benevolent sexism as complementary justifications for gender inequality. *American Psychologist, 56*, 109–118.

Hale, J. L., Tighe, M. R., & Mongeau, P. A. (1997). Effects of event type and sex on comforting messages. *Communication Research Reports, 14*, 214–220.

Hayden, B., Deal, M., Cannon, A., & Casey, J. (1986). Ecological determinants of women's status among hunter/gatherers. *Human Evolution, 1*, 449–473.

Huston, T. L., Ruggiero, M., Conner, R., & Geis, G. (1981). Bystander intervention into crime: A study based on naturally-occurring episodes. *Social Psychology Quarterly, 44*, 14–23.

Jaffee, S., & Hyde, J. S. (2000). Gender differences in moral orientation: A meta- analysis. *Psychological Bulletin, 126*, 703–726.

Karniol, R., Grosz, E., & Schoor, I. (2003). Caring, gender role orientation, and volunteering. *Sex Roles, 49*, 11–19.

Lash, J. (1995). *The hero: Manhood and power.* New York: Thames and Hudson.

Levant, R. F., & Kopecky, G. (1995). *Masculinity reconstructed: Changing the rules of manhood—at work, in relationships, and in family life*. New York: Dutton.

Miller, J. B. (1976). *Toward a new psychology of women*. Boston: Beacon Press.

Newport, F., Jones, J. M., Saad, L., & Carroll, J. (2001, February 21). *Americans see women as emotional and affectionate, men as more aggressive*. Retrieved September 6, 2004, from Gallup Brain, http://institution.gallup.com/document View.aspx?tab=document&strID=1978

Oliner, S. P., & Oliner, P. M. (1988). *The altruistic personality: Rescuers of Jews in Nazi Europe*. New York: The Free Press.

Plant, E. A., Hyde, J. S., Keltner, D., & Devine, P. G. (2000). The gender stereotyping of emotions. *Psychology of Women Quarterly, 24*, 81–92.

Post, P. (1997). *Emily Post's etiquette* (16th ed.). New York: HarperCollins.

Reis, H. T. (1998). Gender differences in intimacy and related behaviors: Context and process. In D. J. Canary & K. Dindia (Eds.), *Sex differences and similarities in communication* (pp. 203–231). Mahwah, NJ: Lawrence Erlbaum Associates.

Ridgeway, C. L. (2001). Gender, status, and leadership. *Journal of Social Issues, 57*, 637–656.

Rose, S. M. (1985). Same- and cross-sex friendships and the psychology of homosociality. *Sex Roles, 12*, 63–74.

Salzman, P. C. (1999). Is inequality universal? *Current Anthropology, 40*, 31–44.

Simmons, R. G., Klein, S. D., & Simmons, R. L. (1977) *Gift of life: The social and psychological impact of organ transplantation*. New York: Wiley.

Spence, J. T., & Helmreich, R. (1978). *Masculinity and femininity: Their psychological dimensions, correlates, and antecedents*. Austin: University of Texas Press.

Thompson, T. L., Robinson, J. D., & Kenny, R. W. (2003). Gender differences in family communication about organ donation. *Sex Roles, 49*, 587–596.

U.S. Organ Procurement and Transplantation Network and the Scientific Registry of Transplant Recipients. (2003). Organ donation and utilization in the United States. In *OPRN/SRTR Annual Report* (chap. 3). Retrieved September 3, 2004, from http://www.optn.org/AR2003/Chapter_iii_AR_CD.htm

Wheeler, L., Reis, H., & Nezlek, J. (1983). Loneliness, social interaction, and sex roles. *Journal of Personality and Social Psychology, 37*, 87–96.

Williams, J. E., & Best, D. L. (1990). *Measuring sex stereotypes: A multination study* (rev. ed.). Newbury Park, CA: Sage.

Wilson, J. (2000). Volunteering. *Annual Review of Sociology, 26*, 215–240.

Wood, W., & Eagly, A. H. (2002). A cross-cultural analysis of the behavior of women and men: Implications for the origins of sex differences. *Psychological Bulletin, 128*, 699–727.

Wood, W., Christensen, P. N., Hebl, M. R., & Rothgerber, H. (1997). Conformity to sex-typed norms, affect, and the self-concept. *Journal of Personality and Social Psychology, 73*, 523–535.

Volunteering in the United States. (2004, December 16). *News: Bureau of Labor Statistics*. Retrieved on August 18, 2005, from http:/www.bls.gov/news.release/pdf/volun.pdf

10

Sex Differences Versus Social Processes in the Construction of Gender

Mary Crawford
Michelle R. Kaufman
University of Connecticut

Wanna get rowdy
Gonna get a little unruly
Get it fired up in a hurry
Wanna get dirrty
It's about time that I came to start the party
Sweat drippin' over my body
Dancing getting just a little naughty
Wanna get dirrty
It's about time for my arrival.

When artist Christina Aguilera released this song with her album *Stripped* (2002), she connected her femininity with sexuality, describing it as "dirty" and "sweaty." Coming from the girl-next-door pop star, this song caused much controversy in the pop music world. Aguilera quickly adopted the image of being slutty and risqué. Aguilera's changing image, driven by the words of her song, illustrates the importance of language in gender representation. How an individual presents herself (or himself) as female or male, feminine or masculine, is in large part an accomplishment of language.

Starting in the early 1970s, social scientists' interest in gender grew exponentially, and with it their interest in the communication styles of women and men.

Over time, the field has developed and changed. Today, "there is less emphasis on cataloguing differences in the speech of women and men and more interest in analyzing what people accomplish with talk" (Crawford, 2001, p. 244).

In this chapter, we attempt to develop a dynamic approach to both gender and language, one that is grounded in the theories and methods of our subdiscipline, feminist social psychology. We conceptualize gender as a social system and language as a social process, and we situate our discussion at the intersection of the two. We discuss ways in which gender is constructed through language and how this creates and maintains a hierarchy of power. We argue for the use of a social constructionist perspective and discourse analytic methods as a potentially fruitful direction for future research.

GENDER AS A SYSTEM

Gender has been described as a system of social classification and hierarchy based on social power, whereby control over resources and opportunities are held by a given group (Molm & Hedley, 1992). The possession of social power increases one's status, which is a person's ability to influence or control others (Crawford, 2006).

What does it mean to conceptualize gender as a system? Gender distinctions occur at many levels of society. Gender-related processes influence behavior, thoughts, and feelings in individuals; they affect interactions among individuals; and they help determine the structure of social institutions. How can researchers analyze the workings of this pervasive system of social classification that shapes the relations between women and men? For analytical purposes, it is useful to think of the gender system as operating at three levels: sociocultural, interactional, and individual (Crawford, 2006). These levels are linked and mutually reinforcing. Societal structures create limits within which people must act; interactions between and among individuals reinforce larger structural inequities; and individuals often internalize aspects of their gendered position in society, coming to accept their society's definition of masculinity or femininity as part of the self and identity. In this chapter we focus primarily on the first two of these three levels of gender, looking first at societal structures and then at interactional processes.

Societal Structures Create Gender

Societies can organize hierarchies and allocate resources on the basis of a wide variety of arbitrary distinctions—tribe, religion, caste, skin color, age—distinctions that vary in importance from one society to another. On the basis of these arbitrary distinctions, the dominant group(s) in a society have access to more of what that society values as a scarce resource, be it land, livestock, leisure time, education, or political office. Gender is perhaps the only one of these hierarchical classification schemes that is universal. Every known society makes social distinctions based on gender (Sidanius & Pratto, 1999). "To a greater or lesser degree, most modern societies are patriarchal, a word that literally means 'ruled by the fathers'" (Crawford, 2006).

The sociocultural structuring of gender as a system of relative advantage for men and disadvantage for women can be seen in many areas of contemporary societies. In the political sphere, for example, women account for only about 14% of national parliaments and other governing bodies worldwide (Galliano, 2003). There is no modern society in which women have equal or near-equal control of political decision making, the use of the military or law enforcement, or the technology of warfare (Sidanius & Pratto, 1999).

The gender hierarchy can also be seen in access to education, leisure, and wealth. Worldwide, literacy rates are lower for women than for men (Galliano, 2003). Men control more wealth and have more leisure time in virtually every society in which data are collected by the United Nations (Pratto & Walker, 2004). When women work for pay, they are paid less than men are for similar or comparable tasks. Moreover, women do a great deal more unpaid work than men do in child and elder care, subsistence farming, and housework. Overall, women work longer hours for smaller rewards (Crawford, 2006).

There has been much debate about the origins of male dominance; contemporary theories include psychodynamic, cognitive, evolutionary, social constructionist, and social role approaches (Eagly, Beall, & Sternberg, 2004; Unger, 2001). Although the origins of patriarchy may be unresolved, much is known about how gender-based power imbalances are perpetuated. The power of dominant groups is not static. Rather, power is actively maintained through a variety of social processes. For example, societies create legitimizing myths that justify prejudice and discrimination against subordinated groups (Sidanius & Pratto, 1999). Many of the legitimizing myths of gender come from patriarchal traditions emphasizing that women are different from men. Some of these beliefs are hostile, such as the archetype of women as evil, sexually polluting, and dangerous—the whore stereotype. Others are seemingly benevolent, such as the belief in women as more pure, noble, and self-sacrificing than men—the Madonna stereotype (Glick & Fiske, 2001). Both hostile and benevolent forms of sexism serve as justifications for the social control of the subordinated gender. Whether women are seen as evil (in need of control) or pure (relegated to a pedestal), they are still defined in terms set by the dominant group.

Though larger political and social structures are important in creating and maintaining gender distinctions and inequalities, they are not the only sites where gender is played out. We turn now to interpersonal interactions, examining the salience of gender as a cue and the use of gender in self-representation.

Social Interactions Create Gender

Gender is an important cognitive category used to classify others in social interactions, and many studies have shown that it is highly salient in social perception. For example, in a study in which participants watched a video of a discussion group and later were asked to remember who said what, they were more likely to confuse two people of the same gender than two of the same age, the same race, or even the same name (Fiske, Haslam, & Fiske, 1991). These participants had spontaneously classified the people in the discussion group on the basis of gender. Although they sometimes could not remember which speaker had made a particular statement, they were likely to remember whether the speaker was a woman or a man.

The cognitive salience of gender is problematic because it opens the way for intergroup bias and outgroup homogeneity effects. In other words, people tend to favor their own group and see members of other groups as different from them and "all alike." These biases were demonstrated in a study in which pairs of male or female college students were asked to discuss "American women" or "American men" for 5 minutes (Harasty, 1997). Analyses of the open-ended discussions showed that participants made more generalizations about the gender outgroup than about their own gender group. In other words, female pairs made more global "men are . . . " statements and male pairs more global "women are. . . " statements. When talking about others of their own gender, dyadic members were more specific and less likely to make sweeping generalizations. The more general comments also tended to be more negative. Overall, outgroup members were spoken of as more alike and less worthy than ingroup members.

Not only do individuals classify others on the basis of gender in everyday interaction, they strive to present themselves socially as good examples of their gender. Gender tends to be accompanied by an ascribed status that is created by cultural norms. "Maleness" is associated with greater power, prestige, and social value than "femaleness" (Cohen, Berger, & Zelditch, 1972; Unger, 1976, 1978).

The gender system requires that men "do" being men and women "do" being women (Zimmerman & West, 1975). "Doing gender" is not just a display of the stereotypical differences between the sexes; it is linked to power. When women and men do gender, they are also doing status, and women, in particular, are "doing subordination" (Crawford, 2006). Doing gender is often an unconscious process, and the production of a gendered self seems natural and spontaneous. Nevertheless, this process constitutes the social representation of gender: "There is no such thing as 'being a woman' outside the various practices that define womanhood for my culture—practices ranging from the sort of work I do to my sexual preferences to the clothes I wear to the way I use language" (Cameron, 1996, p. 46).

LANGUAGE AS A SOCIAL PROCESS

Much of research in language, a majority of which has been conducted under the umbrella of linguistics, treats language as an asocial phenomenon (Holtgraves, 2002). The use of language can also be viewed as a social system, whereby word choice, conversational dominance, or tone of voice can be used to express and create a speaker's power and social status in relation to the perceiver. Most psycholinguists focus on an individualist perspective in the analysis of language, in which the production and comprehension of language is assumed to occur in a vacuum outside of the social context. Only recently has cognitive psychology recognized the communicative side of language as it occurs in dyads.

Cognitive Views of Language and Communication

Clark (1996) conceptualized language use as the secondary aim in a joint activity, whereby two people carry out a task. According to Clark, the joint activity is the primary focus of social interaction, and language use is secondary. All joint activities rely on communicative acts, verbal or nonverbal, and discourse is a joint activity in which language plays an important role. Clark has extensively studied language in joint activities and actions. For example, he has investigated the ways in which dyads must establish a "common ground," or what others have called common knowledge (Lewis, 1969), joint knowledge (McCarthy, 1990), or mutual knowledge or belief (Schiffer, 1972), in order to carry out a joint activity successfully.

According to Fillmore (1981), the primary place for language use is in dyadic conversation, and all other uses of language are secondary and derivative to this primary function. Clark built on this position, developing a cognitive psychology of dyadic interaction. He separated a conversation into a hierarchy of parts, including conversation (the introduction, body, and exit of a topic); section (transitions or digressions from the main conversation topic); adjacency pairs (two ordered utterances, such as "thank you," and then "you're welcome"); and turn (who speaks when). Clark described conversation as purposeful but unplanned and therefore analyzed it as a series of utterances between two individuals whose goals are primarily action oriented.

Clark has forcefully argued that language is a distinctively human activity and that the prototype for language is dyadic conversation. Although Clark has looked at language and communication as it occurs within dyads, he and others in the cognitive tradition have not fully conceptualized language as a social production. In cognitively focused research on conversation, speakers are often represented outside their social contexts or in socially trivial settings. As far as the researchers are concerned, the participants' task is to make themselves understood so that they can accomplish a joint venture (e.g., setting a lunch date) as efficiently as possible. Although establishing joint understanding of semantic meaning and joint enactment of an action are important, they are not the only purposes of dyadic communication. Instead, we argue that language use should be thought of as fundamentally social from the beginning. It is in conversation that individuals present themselves to others as members of a social group and seek to establish and maintain social status.

Language and Group Membership

Although the utterances created and the ideas constructed in language come from the individual, the process of conversation and communication is certainly a social behavior and should be evaluated as such. Only recently has social psychology contributed significantly to research on language (Holtgraves, 2002), particularly its role in stereotyping and prejudice (e.g., Maass, Salvi, Arcuri, & Semin, 1989), social reasoning (e.g., Hilton, 1995), and person perception (e.g., Berry, Pennebaker, Mueller, & Hiller, 1997). Group membership may function to activate a particular stereotype, which, in turn, influences evaluations of a target and perceptions of the target's speech style. For example, in an early line of research, Thakerar and Giles (1981) found that when participants were led to believe a speaker was high in status, they perceived the speaker's speech to be more standard than if they believed the speaker was of low status. Similarly, Williams, Whitehead, and Miller (1972) found that participants rated the speech of African American children to be below standard and less confident than that of Caucasian children, even though the same (Caucasian) voices were used in both instances. More recently, in a study by Popp, Donovan, Crawford, Marsh, and Peele (2003), participants were asked to generate dialogue for a fictional college student whose race and gender were varied. Participants then rated the character on a series of adjective pairs that comprised five factors: social appropriateness, dominance, directness, emotionality, and playfulness. Results showed a consistency of stereotyping patterns for Caucasian and African American targets, such that Caucasians were rated significantly more socially appropriate, less direct, lower in emotionality, and more playful in their speech than were African Americans. Stereotyping patterns were also found for the gender of the targets; female targets were rated as less direct in their speech and as possessing higher emotionality than male targets.

In sum, group membership does matter in evaluating the speech style and communication of others. Relationships have been shown in terms of race, status, and other categories. Because gender is one of the most salient cognitive categories in person perception, we can expect that gender stereotypes often affect perceptions of speech and communication. Women and men who show identical behavior in a given situation may be functioning in different social spheres because of others' social reactions to them as women or men, reactions that include how others speak to them and evaluate their speech (Crawford, 1995; Weatherall, 2002).

THE INTERSECTION OF GENDER AND LANGUAGE

Although social psychologists have begun to examine language as a form of social power, and gender researchers have been discussing the construction of gender as a power system, the two fields have not consistently collaborated on how gender and language interact to create a social power structure for men and women. Despite pioneering feminist research on gender, language, and power (Henley, 1977; Thorne & Henley, 1975; Thorne, Kramarae, & Henley, 1983; see also Crawford & Popp, 2003), much research on gender and language has continued to focus on differences between men and women's speech styles. There has been less attention to how these differences are co-constructed in social interaction, and what the consequences are for differences when they are so closely tied to social power.

Gendered Interaction as a Power Process

To begin an examination of the interaction of gender and language as they relate to power structures, one must first evaluate how gender is constructed through language. As mentioned previously, the gender system requires that men "do" being men and women "do" being women. In the context of language, men generally "do" being men by showing dominance in a conversation, and women "do" being women by more commonly assuming the role of a subordinate listener.

The interaction of gender and language, and the subsequent power structure created, has been acknowledged in some previous research. For example, Ruscher (2001) has written about the ways in which people tend to "talk down" to outgroup members. Social categorizations such as gender, race, or age indicate status in social interactions (Berger, Wagner, & Zelditch, 1985). If the speaker in an interaction views the listener to be of lower social status on the basis of these categorizations, the speaker tends to conclude (sometimes unconsciously) that the listener is incompetent. The presumption of incompetence often leads to speech that is patronizing or controlling.

Language addressed to infants, elderly people, mentally retarded people, foreigners, and pets shares certain syntactical and lexical characteristics that linguistically create the effect of patronizing control (Ruscher, 2001). These include lexical simplification, exaggerated pitch changes, and increased repetition. Because speech addressed to elders or babies may have a caring function, it is likely to be more patronizing than controlling. However, speech addressed to other categories of lower status people may have a higher rate of direct imperative (command) forms and efforts to control the conversation, such as ignoring the target's attempts to make a contribution. The controlling aspect of talking down "explicitly functions to keep low-status individuals 'in their place'" (Ruscher, 2001, p. 88).

Talking down was demonstrated with respect to gender in a study by Duval and Ruscher (1994) that began with teaching the Heimlich maneuver to college student participants. (This task was chosen because it was not gender stereotyped and was equally unfamiliar to female and male college students.) The slides showed a male and a female actor demonstrating the maneuver on each other, with male and female voices alternating descriptions of the steps involved in the task. Following the presentation of the slides, the participants were asked to teach the Heimlich maneuver to another student, and they were videotaped while they explained the steps of the maneuver to an opposite-sex or same-sex partner. Results showed that men used more imperative verbs when teaching the maneuver to women than in any of the other teacher–learner combinations, suggesting that the gender difference in status prompted talk that was both patronizing and controlling.

Another example of the use of power in language is to not allow another person to be heard at all by interrupting, controlling the topic discussed, or taking up a majority of the talk time (Crawford, 1995). Many studies show that men use these tactics frequently when engaging in conversation with women more than they do when speaking with other men and more than women do when speaking to each other. For example, in a now-classic study in which researchers listened in on same- and mixed-gender conversations in public places, 96% of the interruptions in conversations between males and females were made by male speakers. In same-gender dyads, the number of interruptions was the same for each speaker (Zimmerman & West, 1975). Not all interruptions are intended to assert conversational dominance. However, in a recent meta-analysis, it was found that men commit more intrusive interruptions, in which an active attempt is made to end a conversation or take over the discussion. This has been found to be more common in naturalistic settings where conversations resemble everyday interaction than in laboratory settings (Anderson & Leaper, 1998).

Despite the stereotype that women are more talkative than men, studies have shown men to take up a majority of the talk time in a variety of settings, including classrooms, business meetings, and informal conversations (Crawford, 1995). In a review of 63 studies conducted over a 40-year span, 34 of the studies showed that men talk more than women, whereas only 2 displayed the opposite finding (the others showed no gender differences in talk time or mixed results; see James & Drakich, 1993). These differences were most robust in formal, task-oriented settings such as committee meetings, classrooms, and problem-solving groups. However, even in less formal social settings, over 37% of the studies showed men talking more than women, whereas only 6% showed women talking more than men. These studies suggest that men dominate conversations, especially in more formal settings where one's status and control over the situation may be more tied to material or social gain.

Subversions of Gendered Power

The classification of women's language as "powerless" and men's language as "powerful" originated in Robin Lakoff's *Language and Woman's Place* (1975). Lakoff suggested that the association of indirect speech with the language of women and direct speech with that of men is a reflection of the power imbalance between men and women in society. Lakoff proposed that a cluster of features characteristic of women's talk (hesitation, tag questions, euphemisms, etc.) constituted a unique speech style. However, Lakoff may have underestimated the flexibility of speech styles, mistakenly equating form with function (Crawford, 1995). In some instances, the use of stereotypically feminine language may function quite differently.

Kira Hall (1995) conducted a series of interviews with phone sex workers, many of whom reported that they used so called women's language—sexy, inviting, and supportive—as a commodity to attract customers. The phone sex workers knew how to create stereotypical female sex objects—such as the nymphomaniac and the lesbian—through the deliberate adoption of a particular speech style. Because phone sex is easily marketable, the study of mixed-gender linguistic exchanges should acknowledge the more seditious aspects of conversational consent. One operator, who was a male posing as a female on the phone service, talked about the importance of a "soft and quiet voice" in order to convince his callers of his womanhood. "It's better to sound soft and quiet than loud and noisy . . . if you're a woman . . . [It's] better to sound soft, you know, softer. You know, like whispering, rather than OH HO HO HO, really *loud*, you know, and *screaming*" (p. 202).

Although phone sex lines may be viewed as offensive or degrading to women, several women Hall interviewed saw the use of their language to gain callers as empowering and their position in the conversation as dominant. They reported being in complete control of every conversation. In fact, many of the phone sex workers felt they were so superior linguistically and socially to the average male caller that they did not view male power as an issue when on the phone lines (Hall, 1995).

In the more mundane realm of communication between relationship partners, there has been much discussion about the ways in which women and men differ in their communication styles. Pop psychologist John Gray (1992) has made a lucrative career out of examining supposed gender differences in communication in his self-help books and television appearances (see Dindia, chap. 1, this volume). Gray preaches the existence of fixed gender differences and instructs his audience to embrace and attempt to understand these supposed differences so that they can enhance their marital relationships. The Mars–Venus therapy omits a discussion as to how women and men could become so different, and instead it relies on gender stereotypes about social roles to reinforce the thought that difference is natural and normal. For example, Gray metaphorically describes how men tend to retreat to their "caves" rather than deal with an issue with their spouse. Gray tells his clients that women should recognize men's entitlement to not become involved in domestic life until they are ready to return from that cave. In this excerpt from a televised couples' discussion group (as cited in Crawford, 2004,[1] p. 70), Gray stands in a family room set next to a large recliner:

JG: See, *whenever a Martian has stress*, on MARS, *we go to our cave.*
This is our cave.
This is our territory.
((Sits in Recliner))
Nobody can tell me what to do. The problem is, women don't understand it's healthy and normal for men to do this, and this is what they

[1] For a description of this annotation, see Crawford, 2004.

need to do. Then you PUNISH *them for going to the cave.* ((Stands. Using exaggerated gestures, points to the family room set)) Let him have his space. Don't take it personally. And if you don't go in, he'll come out. He gets lonely in there.

The Mars–Venus media present a seemingly perfect discourse of essential gender difference. The function of this self-help series is to reproduce and make natural the stereotypical language and communication between men and women, which is usually oppressive to women (Crawford, 2004). Because the women who use this guide seem content in their marriage upon following these steps, the popularity of Mars–Venus is somewhat puzzling and problematic from a feminist perspective. Although some critical responses were made by women during the discussions analyzed by Crawford (2004), the participants are still urged to "accept the fact" that men need their caves. In this excerpt (Crawford, p. 72), a group of women debate the fairness of men's entitlement to caves:

MM: You know (.) *all this* is asking women once again (.) to take the *high road* (.) And that *bothers me* (.) Now I have to *suppress* (.) *I have to sacrifice* (.) Got to *keep it in* (.) And when *he's* ready, *I have to* be ready too.

.

.

SC: But that-that's what *marriage* IS. I mean =

DT: =But it still seems rude to me (.) *I don't get a cave.*

.

.

SC: *He* wants to be in his *cave* ((gestures with hand on table)) and not be bothered by you (.) and *you're* not *doing* that.

DT: Whether it's turning on the TV or running away ((on the part of the husband)) (.) we can *use* this ((the M/V ideology)) so we can *deal* with it so I don't get so RESENTFUL. But the reality I (.) I *still* think it's WRONG ((gestures with hand on table)), and it's not very nice.

Crawford (2004) has speculated that at least some women in unsatisfying heterosexual relationships may use the Mars–Venus discourse to open up areas for discussion and contestation in their marital arrangements. Rather than accepting notions of deep-seated gender differences, they subvert the simplistic metaphors of Mars and Venus in order to voice their own marital agenda. This agenda may include renegotiating an inequitable division of domestic work and childcare. Like the phone sex workers studied by Hall (1995), these women may use beliefs about difference toward their own ends.

MODELS FOR A SOCIAL PSYCHOLOGY OF GENDER AND LANGUAGE

We have argued that the study of gender and language should prioritize the social aspects of language, particularly the social psychology of power and status. Many theoretical models and research programs have aimed to do this. Others have discussed the strengths and weaknesses of well-established models such as speech act theory (Crawford, 1995; Schiffrin, 1994; Turnbull, 2003), ethnomethodology (Crawford, Schiffrin, & Weatherall, 2002), and conversation analysis (Kitzinger, 2000; Kitzinger & Frith, 1999; Turnbull, 2003; Weatherall, 2002), and we will not review those discussions here. All these methods are, broadly speaking, empirical; that is, their data come from people using language, not from hypothetical examples devised by linguists. All conceive of meaning and action in language use as jointly achieved in interaction. All endorse the importance of the immediate social context and the broader cultural framework in shaping language use and speech style (Schiffrin, 1994). However, they vary in the degree to which they view social reality itself as constructed through language. In what follows, we argue for a social constructionist perspective as a fruitful approach to further research in this area.

Social Constructionism

A social constructionist view of language theorizes that language use and communication is the base of and socially constructs power. Social constructionists question several aspects of the conventional sex-gender model: (a) the view of gender as a property of individuals; (b) that gender is a static and enduring set of traits; (c) the separation of sex and gender into a dichotomy; and (d) the claim that biological sex is a foundation that stands apart untouched by culture and language (Marecek, Crawford, & Popp, 2004).

In a social constructionist view, power is possessed by an individual or a group as an effect of discourse (Weatherall, 2002), and relations of power are negotiated through the medium of language (Crawford, 1995; Potter & Wetherell, 1987). For example, the social control of female sexuality may be expressed in religious teachings, moral discourses, and media representations. It is also evident in everyday language, such as slang ("player" vs. "ho"; see Crawford & Popp, 2003). From a social constructionist perspective, these meanings are not fixed, but they are always evident in human interactions. Furthermore, people do not passively perceive cultural messages without awareness. The ongoing flow of meanings about gender is part of the flow of social life.

From a social constructionist perspective, power is a central dimension of social life. However, power is conceptualized not as a fixed property or characteristic of individuals, but rather as a network of social forces that is continually produced, enacted, resisted, and subverted. Therefore, social constructionists prefer research methods that allow close examination and analysis of mundane, naturally occurring social interactions. By analyzing such interactions, they hope to "document the micropolitics of subordination, dominance, and resistance" (Marecek et al., 2004, p. 195).

Social constructionists view language as an extremely flexible tool for creating social reality; they have studied not only the use of rhetorical devices for legitimizing the speaker's claims (Potter & Wetherell, 1987) but also the use of subversive conversational devices such as humor (Crawford, 1995, 2003). Often, social constructionists focus on how people shift strategically among different accounts of themselves, their attitudes, and their behavior in the context of differing settings and relationships. For example, in a naturalistic study of conversation among friends, a woman talked about gender stereotypes in subtly different ways when she was with her female peers than when she was with a mixed-gender group. With women, she spoke directly of the disadvantages that stereotypes create for women; with men, she talked more generally of the disadvantages stereotypes cause for "society" (Stapleton, 2001). Which behaviors reflect her "real" attitudes? A social constructionist would argue that the reality is constructed by—and changes with—the social context (Marecek et al., 2004; Crawford, 2006).

Because social constructionists believe that power relations are negotiated through the medium of language, they view mundane conversational interaction, as well as more formal and public types of speech, as important activities with practical material consequences (Marecek et al., 2004). For this reason, they often prefer qualitative and interpretive methods that permit close analysis of the meaning and function of talk. The term *discourse analysis* refers both to a rapidly evolving field of study and an eclectic group of methods for studying language use and the ideological assumptions underlying it (Schiffrin, Tannen, & Hamilton, 2003). Not all discourse analysis is social constructionist. One of the most distinctive aspects of a discourse analytic approach grounded in social constructionism is that it conceives of gender (including gender identity) not as existing prior to and separate from language, but as being discursively constituted through language (Weatherall, 2002).

Discourse analytic approaches currently are generating a great deal of research; space permits mention of only a few examples to illustrate the range and utility of the methods. Edwards (1998) used interaction from a couples' counseling session to examine how the language deployed by the wife and husband served to justify particular constructions of reality. Is an extramarital sexual encounter an "affair" or a "fling"? Did the encounter take place with a "girl" or "another woman"? The categories used by the couple in counseling did not reflect a preexisting consensual reality. Instead, Edwards argued, they were locally constructed and managed to do particular things—to justify one's own behavior and criticize the partner's behavior, for example. In another recent study, discussed earlier in this chapter, Crawford (2004) used the method of critical feminist discourse analysis to examine the text of *Men are From Mars, Women are From Venus*, as well as couples' strategic use of its faux-psychological rhetoric in negotiating and resisting change in their marriages. In an example from a different domain, Nichter (2000) analyzed the "fat talk" of adolescent girls about their bodies. Regardless of their actual weight or body size, these girls frequently complained of being too fat or having ugly body parts. Nichter analyzed the functions of this talk in creating rapport with others and eliciting support and reassurance about one's body. At the same time as it fulfilled these relatively benign functions, the "fat talk" also reaffirmed the cultural norm that body size is a critical feature on which females should be judged and ranked.

Other researchers have examined the construction and presentation of masculinity in interaction. For example, Wetherell and Edley (1999) used critical discourse analysis to identify three social positions taken by men in talk about what it means to be a man. The "heroic" position aligned itself with hegemonic masculinity: being tough, courageous, emotionally in control, and competitive. In contrast, some men characterized themselves as being normal, average, nonmacho men or as rebelliously flouting conventions of masculinity (e.g., by cooking or knitting). In other words, they positioned themselves in contrast to the heroic ideal. However, Wetherell and Edley argued that the contrary positions nevertheless functioned to reproduce male power much like the heroic position, because the men who characterized themselves as such said that they were different from normal or rebellious other men in being more independent and autonomous—aspects of the heroic ideal.

Because masculinity is so closely linked with social power, studies of masculinity often focus on how men position themselves with respect to less powerful groups (Crawford, 2001). For example, Mulkay (1988) did extensive discursive research on men's humor about women and sexuality. Mulkay argued that such humor objectified women, represented them as sexually available at all times, and contained themes of silencing women's agency and voice. Cameron (1997) analyzed the talk of male college students and described the derogation of other men whom the students characterized as "gay." Within this group of friends, naming others as part of a gay outgroup (regardless of the accuracy of the label) provided a means of generating group solidarity and displaying group members' own heterosexual and dominant masculinity. (For a fuller description of these and other studies using discourse analysis to examine the production of gendered selves, see Crawford, 2001 and Weatherall, 2002).

ON THE SEARCH FOR SEX DIFFERENCES

Although research on the relationship between gender and language is abundant, much of it has focused on decontextualized sex differences. This focus has been the subject of criticism and debate almost since its inception. Barrie Thorne and Nancy Henley, pioneers in the feminist study of gender and language, argued as early as 1975 that this area of research should not be given a high priority. Thorne, Kramarae, and Henley, in their influential 1983 book, contrasted the focus on difference to a (more fruitful, in their view) focus on dominance.

More broadly, some feminists have argued that the study of sex differences in any area of psychology is likely to be a waste of research time and energy, prompting others to defend the utility of such research (Canary & Dindia, 1998; Hare-Mustin & Marecek, 1994; Hyde, 1994; Kitzinger, 1994; Unger, 1979, 1989, 1992). One recurrent viewpoint is that a focus on difference encourages social scientists and laypeople alike to think of women and men as polar opposites; distracts attention from the linkage of gender with power and status; treats gender as a fixed, static attribute of individuals rather than a complex social categorization system; and disregards the diversity of women and men (Crawford, 1995, 2001; Canary & Emmers-Sommer, 1997; Pratto & Walker, 2004).

We have argued for the utility of a social constructionist perspective and described studies that relied on various versions of constructionist-grounded discourse analysis. To devote still more time to researching static and decontextualized gender differences in language use would, in our view, be a mistake. Gender is more fruitfully construed as a process enacted in a cluster of activities such as the division of labor, sexual intimacy, and children's play (Canary & Emmers-Sommer, 1997).

Social constructionism offers rich new prospects for a better understanding of how gender is socially produced and maintained. We propose spending more time focusing on the intersection of gender and language use as it relates to the creation of social power. The most fruitful research path for the future may involve turning the question of sex differences on its head—not asking, How do men and women use language differently? but rather, How are femininity and masculinity produced and maintained through language?

REFERENCES

Anderson, K. J., & Leaper, C. (1998). Meta-analysis of gender effects on conversational interruptions: Who, what, when, where, and how. *Sex Roles, 39*, 225–252.

Berger, J., Wagner, D. G., & Zelditch, M., Jr. (1985). Introduction: Expectation states theory—Review and assessment. In J. Berger, & M. Zelditch, Jr. (Eds.), *Status, rewards, and influence: How expectations organize behavior* (pp. 1–72). San Francisco: Jossey-Bass.

Berry, D. S., Pennebaker, J. W., Mueller, J. S., & Hiller, W. S. (1997). Linguistic bases of social perception. *Personality and Social Psychology Bulletin, 23*, 526–537.

Cameron, D. (1996). Performing gender identity: Young men's talk and the construction of heterosexual masculinity. In S. Johnson, & U. H. Meinhof (Eds.), *Language and masculinity* (pp. 47–64). Oxford, England: Blackwell.

Canary, D. J., & Dindia, K. (Eds.). (1998). *Sex differences and similarities in communication.* Mahwah, NJ: Lawrence Erlbaum Associates.

Canary, D. K., & Emmers-Sommer, T. M. (1997). *Sex and gender differences in personal relationships.* New York: Guilford.

Clark, H. H. (1996). *Using language.* New York: Cambridge University Press.

Cohen, B. P., Berger, J., & Zelditch, M. (1972). Status conceptions and interactions: A case study of developing cumulative knowledge. In C. McClintock (Ed.), *Experimental social psychology.* (pp. 408–411). New York: Holt, Rinehart & Winston.

Crawford, M. (1995). *Talking difference: On gender and language.* London Sage.

Crawford, M. (2001). Gender and language. In R. K. Unger (Ed.), *Handbook of the psychology of women and gender* (pp. 228–244). Hoboken, NJ: Wiley.
Crawford, M. (2003). Gender and humor in social context. *Journal of Pragmatics, 35*, 1413–1430.
Crawford, M. (2004). Mars and Venus collide: A discursive analysis of marital self-help psychology. *Feminism & Psychology, 14*, 63–79.
Crawford, M. (2006). *Transformations: Women, gender, and psychology.* New York: McGraw–Hill.
Crawford, M., & Popp, D. (2003). Sexual double standards: A review and methodological critique of two decades of research. *The Journal of Sex Research, 40*, 13–26.
Crawford, M., & Unger, R. (2004). *Women and gender: A feminist psychology.* Boston: McGraw-Hill.
Duval, L. L., & Ruscher, J. B. (1994, July). *Men use more detail to explain a gender-neutral task to women.* Poster presented at the annual meeting of the American Psychological Society, Washington, DC.
Eagly, A. H., Beall, A. E., & Sternberg, R. J. (Eds.). (2004). *The psychology of gender* (2nd ed.). New York: Guilford.
Edwards, D. (1998). The relevant thing about her: Social identity categories in use. In C. Antaki, & S. Widdicombe (Eds.), *Identities in talk* (pp. 15–34). London: Sage.
Fillmore, C. (1981). Pragmatics and the description of discourse. In P. Cole (Ed.), *Radical pragmatics* (pp. 143–166). New York: Academic Press.
Fiske, A. P., Haslam, N., & Fiske, S. T. (1991). Confusing one person with another: What errors reveal about the elementary forms of social relations. *Journal of Personality and Social Psychology, 60*, 656–674.
Galliano, G. (2003). *Gender: Crossing boundaries.* Belmont, CA: Wadsworth.
Gray, J. (1992). *Men are from Mars, Women are from Venus. A practical guide to improving communication and getting what you want in your relationships.* New York: HarperCollins.
Glick, P., & Fiske, S. T. (2001). An ambivalent alliance: Hostile and benevolent sexism as complementary justifications for gender inequality. *American Psychologist, 56*, 109–118.
Hall, K. (1995). Lip service on the fantasy lines. In K. Hall, & M. Bucholtz (Eds.), *Gender articulated* (pp. 183–216). New York: Routledge.
Harasty, A. S. (1997). The interpersonal nature of social stereotypes: Differential discussion patterns about in-groups and out-groups. *Personality and Social Psychology Bulletin, 23*, 270–284.
Hare-Mustin, R. T., & Marecek, J. (1994). Asking the right questions: Feminist psychology and sex differences. *Feminism & Psychology, 4*, 531–537.
Henley, N. M. (1977). *Body politics.* Englewood Cliffs, NJ: Prentice-Hall.
Hilton, D. J. (1995). The social context of reasoning: Conversational inference and rational judgment. *Psychological Bulletin, 118*, 248–271.
Holtgraves, T. M. (2002). *Language as social action: Social psychology and language use.* Mahwah, NJ: Lawrence Erlbaum Associates.
Hyde, J. S. (1994). Should psychologists study gender differences? Yes, with some guidelines. *Feminism & Psychology, 4*, 507–512.
James, D., & Drakich, J. (1993) Understanding gender differences in amount of talk: A critical review of research. In D. Tannen (Ed.), *Gender and conrversational interaction* (pp. 281–312). New York: Oxford.
Kitzinger, C. (1994). Sex difference: Feminist perspectives. *Feminism & Psychology, 4*, 501–596.
Kitzinger, C. (2000). Doing feminist conversation analysis. *Feminism & Psychology, 10*, 163–193.
Kitzinger, C., & Frith, H. (1999). Just say no? The use of conversation analysis in developing a feminist perspective on sexual refusal. *Discourse and Society, 10*, 293–316.
Lakoff, R. (1975). *Language and woman's place*. New York: Harper & Row.
Lewis, D. K. (1969). *Convention: A philosophical study.* Cambridge, MA: Harvard University Press.
Marecek, J., Crawford, M., & Popp, D. (2004). On the construction of gender, sex, and sexualities. In A. H. Eagly, A. E. Beall, & R. J. Sternberg (Eds.), *The psychology of gender* (2nd ed.), (pp. 192–216). New York: Guilford.

Maass, A., Salvi, D., Arcuri, L., & Semin, G. (1989). Language use in intergroup contexts: The linguistic intergroup bias. *Journal of Personality and Social Psychology, 68*, 116–126.

McCarthy, J. (1990). Formalization of two puzzles involving knowledge. In V. Lifschitz (Ed.), *Formalizing common sense: Papers by John McCarthy* (pp. 158–166). Norwood, NJ: Ablex.

Molm, L. D., & Hedley, M. (1992). Gender, power, and social exchange. In C. L. Ridgeway (Ed.), *Gender, interaction, and inequality* (pp. 1–28). New York: Springer-Verlag.

Mulkay, M. (1988). *On humor.* New York: Basil Blackwell.

Nichter, M. (2000). *Fat talk.* Cambridge, MA: Harvard University Press.

Popp. D., Donovan, R. A., Crawford, M., Marsh, K. L., & Peele, M. (2003). Gender, race, and speech style stereotypes. *Sex Roles, 48*, 317–325.

Potter, J., & Wetherell, M. (1987). *Discourse and social psychology.* London: Sage.

Pratto, F., & Walker, A. (2004). The bases of gendered power. In A. H. Eagly, A. E. Beall, & R. J. Sternberg (Eds.), *The psychology of gender* (2nd ed.), (pp. 242–268). New York: Guilford.

Ruscher, J. B. (2001). *Prejudiced communication: A social psychological perspective.* New York: Guilford.

Schiffer, S. R. (1972). *Meaning.* Oxford University Press.

Schiffrin, D. (1994). *Approaches to discourse.* Malden, MA: Blackwell.

Schiffrin, D., Tannen, D., & Hamilton, H. E. (2003). *The handbook of discourse analysis.* Malden, MA: Blackwell.

Sidanius, J., & Pratto, F. (1999). *Social dominance: An intergroup theory of social hierarchy and oppression.* New York: Cambridge University Press.

Stapleton, K. (2001). Constructing a feminist identity: Discourse and the community of practice. *Feminism & Psychology, 11*, 459–491.

Thakerar, J. M., & Giles, H. (1981). They are—so to speak: Noncontent speech stereotypes. *Language and Communication, 1*, 251–256.

Thorne, B., & Henley, N. (Eds.). (1975). An overview of language, gender and society. In B. Thorne, & N. Henley (Eds.), *Language and sex: Difference and dominance* (pp. 5–42). Rowley, MA: Newbury House.

Thorne, B., Kramarae, C., & Henley, N. (Eds.). (1983). *Language, gender, and society.* Rowley, MA: Newbury House.

Turnbull, W. (2003). *Language in action: Psychological models of conversation.* New York: Psychology Press.

Unger, R. K. (1976). Male is greater than female: The socialization of status inequality. *The Counseling Psychologist, 6*, 2–9.

Unger, R. K. (1978). The politics of gender: A review of relevant literature. In J. Sherman, & F. Denmark (Eds.), *Psychology of women: Future directions of research* (pp. 463–517). New York: Psychological Dimensions.

Unger, R. K. (1979). *Female and male: Psychological perspectives.* New York: Harper & Row.

Unger, R. K. (1989). Explorations in feminist ideology: Surprising consistencies and unexamined conflicts. In R. Unger (Ed.), *Representations: Social constructions of gender* (pp. 203–211). New York: Baywood.

Unger, R. K. (1992). Will the real sex differences please stand up? *Feminism & Psychology, 2*, 231–238.

Unger, R. K. (2001). *Handbook of the psychology of women and gender.* Hoboken, NJ: Wiley.

Weatherall, A. (2002). *Gender, language, and discourse.* New York: Routledge.

Wetherell, M., & Edley, N. (1999). Negotiating hegemonic masculinity: Imaginary positions and psych-discursive practices. *Feminism & Psychology, 9*, 335–356.

Williams, F., Whitehead, J. L., & Miller, L. (1972). Relations between attitudes and teacher expectancy. *American Educational Research Journal, 9*, 263–277.

Zimmerman, D. H., & West, C. (1975). Sex roles, interruptions, and silences in conversation. In B. Thorne, & N. Henley (Eds.), *Language and sex: Differences and dominance* (pp. 105–129). Rowley, MA: Newbury House.

11

Researching Gendered Communication in Japan and the United States: Current Limitations and Alternative Approaches

Lesley Di Mare
Vincent R. Waldron
Arizona State University

A debate exists in communication studies regarding the usefulness of continuing traditional, behaviorally based research on gender differences in interpersonal and organizational settings. It has been argued by a number of quantitative researchers (e.g., Canary & Hause, 1993; Harper & Hirokawa, 1988; Hirokawa, Mickey, & Miura, 1991; Wilkins & Andersen, 1991) that evidence indicates that sex differences in communicative behavior are tiny and contradictory and that many of our views of women's communicative styles reflect stereotypes rather than empirical observations. For example, in their meta-analysis, Wilkins and Andersen found that only 0.5% of the variance in organizational communication behaviors is due to sex differences. More recently, Branzei (2002) found similarly small differences in a study of cross-cultural influence tactics used by Japanese and American managers.

Further complicating the debate is a body of qualitative, ethnographic, and cultural analyses of how men and women communicate. This research indicates that there are decided differences in the overall communicative style and with the specific communication strategies employed by men and women in a variety of contexts (Bass & Avolio, 1994; Belenky, Clinchy, Goldberger, & Tarule, 1986; Darus, 1994; Eagly & Johnson, 1990; Holloway, 1995; Ingersoll-Dayton, Campbell, & Mattson, 1998; Lee, 1994; Lipman-Blumen, 1992; Powell & Graves, 2003; Roesner, 1990; Troemel-Ploetz, 1994; Zellner, 1994). The contradictory finding in these two bodies of research has lead to numerous issues surrounding the study of sex differences in communication.

In this chapter we address that contradiction and highlight the need for discussions surrounding communication and sex differences to include analyses of how gender is manifested in other cultures, specifically Japan. We also argue that the implications such analyses carry for research on the subject of how men and women communicate should be considered. One of our purposes in this chapter is to determine whether it is sex, culture, or a combination of these things that best accounts for differences in communication in Japan and the United States (Waldron & Di Mare, 1998). We caution that imposing Western views of sex differences on other societies is problematic in that sex differences in one culture simply may not operate as an organizing principle in the development of communicative styles in the same way that it does for other cultures. A look at the recent literature supports the validity of our premise and, in fact, suggests that cultural and contextual features such as status, hierarchy, age, power, and region should also be examined more carefully regarding communication styles in Japan.

To achieve these objectives, we begin this chapter with an updated review of the literature that documents Western perceptions of the Japanese. We then move to a review of the quantitative and qualitative literature that examines the relative importance of sex and culture in explaining communication styles of each group.

We believe that comparing Japanese with American communication behavior continues to be useful for several reasons. First, Japan is perceived by academia as well as the general public as an extremely patriarchal and gendered society; indeed it is, to a far greater degree than the United States, as evidenced in popular conceptions and in a number of studies conducted on Japanese culture and communicative styles (Connor, 1985; Powell & Graves, 2003; Saso, 1990). Second, research suggests that fundamental differences exist between Japan and the west concerning assumptions and attitudes about human interaction (Wetzel, 1993). International ties between Japan and America suggest that the continued analysis of communicative interaction between the two cultures is particularly important in view of the developing feminism and equality in Japan, which makes communication between Japan and the United States dynamic and changing (Renshaw, 1999).

WESTERN PERCEPTIONS OF GENDER IN JAPAN

Westerners' perceptions of Asian societies, particularly the Japanese, are that these cultures are extremely gendered, patriarchal, and masculine. For example, Hofstede's (1980) influential analysis of cultures as masculine or feminine defined

Japanese culture as high on masculinity and American culture as high on femininity. According to Hofstede, masculinity predominates in cultures in which there are clearly differentiated sex roles, whereas femininity predominates in cultures in which there are fluid sex roles and androgyny is the ideal.

Although some scholarly research indicates that Japan is a masculine society, recent research indicates that conceptions of the Japanese as a gendered society are, to some extent, stereotypical and more representative of how Westerners perceive the Japanese to behave communicatively. Although the issue of equality of the sexes in Japan appears to be an ongoing one, Tanaka (1990) noted that it is mostly those outside of Japan, for example, who maintain stereotypes of Japanese women as passive and submissive. Connor (1985) argued that the mass media and popular press in America inscribe Japan as the "last bastion of male supremacy" while depicting Japanese women as dependent, docile, deferent, shy, submissive, and subservient. He argued further that Americans' confusion between the concepts of *female* and *mother* in Japan allows us to perpetuate stereotypes of men and women in that culture. Schooler and Smith (1978) showed that Japanese women resist the stereotype of the Japanese wife as "a paragon of domesticity who selflessly and subserviently meets all of her husband's domestic needs" (p. 23). Instead, Japanese women see themselves as equal to their husbands because of the importance of the role of mother and person in Japanese society.

Examples such as this cause us to question to what degree gender remains an important influence on communication practices. Consequently, a systematic review of the quantitative and qualitative research is needed to determine the ways in which sex, gender, and cultural differences affect and create communication patterns in Japan and the United States. A review of the quantitative literature could yield evidence supporting one or more of the following outcomes. First, this body of comparative research may indicate that sex is a significant factor influencing communication in both the United States and Japan. In contrast, it may be culture (defined as nation status) that is the primary source of variation in communication style, without regard to gender (Barnlund & Araki, 1985). Third, some combination of culture and sex might account for differences in communication. Sex may be a consequential determinant of communication style in Japan but not in the United States, or vice versa. Perhaps sex has equally potent but qualitatively different effects in the two nations.

Still, a review of the qualitative literature could find that philosophical and cultural differences rather than sex differences are more likely to explain the ways in which men and women in Japanese and American cultures communicate. Ultimately, an updated review of both quantitative and qualitative research should result in a better understanding of the ways in which sex differences and cultural differences may or may not affect the communicative styles of Japanese and American men and women.

REVIEW OF COMPARATIVE QUANTITATIVE STUDIES OF AMERICAN AND JAPANESE COMMUNICATION STYLES

The amount of research comparing American and Japanese communication styles is enormous (see, e.g., Barnlund, 1975, 1989; Cai & Wilson, 2000; Gudykunst, 1993; Gudykunst, Guzley, & Ota, 1993; Gudykunst & Nishida, 1993; Hirokawa & Miyahara, 1986; Klopf, 1991; Loveday, 1986; Oetzel et al., 2001). However, we necessarily narrowed our focus to studies of adults that had (a) been published in the past 25 years in a journal catalogued in one of the major indexes of communication-related studies in the United States, Japan, or both; (b) included a measure of communication behavior or style as a dependent measure; (c) included sex or gender as an independent variable; and (d) included nationality as an independent variable. We searched six databases (PsychLit, Sociofile, ABI/INFORM, Linguistics and Language Behavior Abstracts, Philosophy Index, and ATLA Religion Database) likely to reference articles by Japanese or American scholars on the topics of gender, communication, and culture. The results of our review are presented in Table 11.1. The results pointed to various topics, which we subsequently review. We use both the earlier studies we read as well as those more recently encountered.

Studies of Communication Tactics

Several studies have examined Japanese and American sex differences at the tactical level of communication. In regard to persuasion and conflict-management tactics, Steil and Hillman (1993) assessed the perceived value of direct and indirect influence tactics. The authors reasoned that cultural concerns for politeness and face saving (Hsu, 1983) might yield a preference by Korean and Japanese students for indirect tactics, such as evasion, avoidance, and use of third-party advocates. In another study of MBA students' reactions to hypothetical influence scenarios, Branzei (2002) found that Japanese and American students differed in their preference for some tactics, including coalition, exchange, ingratiation, and personal appeals. Gender was less important, as the only differences concerned the use of ingratiation. Japanese women used it more frequently.

Other studies concerned face-management tactics. In an early study, Barnlund (1975) found no sex differences in the communication strategies used by men and women to respond to interpersonally threatening communication. A second comparison based on the same descriptive data set found no sex difference in self-disclosure preferences. Later, Cocroft and Ting-Toomey (1994) studied the relationship between culture and facework. The study found that both culture (50%) and sex (10%) accounted for significant amounts of variance in tactic use. In general, members of the U.S. culture used significantly more antisocial and

TABLE 11.1
Summary of Quantitative Studies Measuring the Effects of National Culture and Sex on Communication Variables

Study	Communication Variable	Results		
		Sex	*Culture*	*Interaction*
Communication tactics				
Bransei (2002)	Persuasion	X		
	Ingratiation			X
Steil & Hillman (1993)	Persuasion		X	
Cocroft & Ting-Toomey (1994)	Facework	X	X	
Otio et al. (1996)	Accounts	X	X	X
Barnlund (1975)	Self-disclosure		X	
	Facework		X	
Bresnahan et al. (2002)	Responses to criticism		X	X
	Silence		X	
	Assertiveness		X	X
	Avoidance			X
Barnlund & Araki (1985)	Compliments		X	
Nonverbal speech characteristics and behaviors				
Loveday (1986)	Pitch			X
Miller et al. (1987)	Language intensity			X
Boyer et al. (1990)	Immediacy	X	X	
Barnlund (1975)	Touch			X
Elzinga (1975)	Touch			X
Patterns of meaning				
Higashiyama & Ono (1988)	Demonstratives	(no significant differences)		
Communication traits and styles				
Frymier et al. (1990)	Affect-orientation			X
Thompson et al. (1990)	Assertiveness	X	X	X
	Responsiveness	X	X	X
Bresnahan et al. (2001)	Assertiveness		X	X
Toren et al. (1997)	Interactive leadership		X	X
Harman et al. (1990)	Verbal Aggressiveness	X		

Note: Our summary of results is complicated by the incomplete data and comparatively rudimentary statistical procedures reported in the early studies. We offer our interpretations in these cases. Where effect sizes are available, associated statistics are found in the text.

self-presentation strategies. Similarly, men more than women were likely to threaten the other's face and protect their own face in interaction.

A somewhat similar pattern was found in the accounts (e.g., apologies, excuses, and justifications) offered by Japanese and Americans in response to hypothetical social miscues (Itoi, Ohbuchi, & Fukuno, 1996). Results showed that Japanese participants preferred mitigating tactics such as apologies or excuses whereas they avoided more confrontational approaches. Again, gender played a less substantive role. Women were somewhat less likely to offer justifications for offensive behavior or to simply ignore the offense. Gender differences were most pronounced among the Japanese participants, with women choosing the tactic of apology more than men.

Tactical responses to criticism and compliments have also been examined. In a study of college students in Japan, China, and the United States by Bresnahan, Shearman, Lee, Ohashi, & Mosher (2002), despite expectations to the contrary, men and women used similar levels of assertiveness in response to criticism. Nationality was a better predictor than sex difference, with Americans showing higher levels of assertiveness than either Japanese or Chinese respondents. However, contrary to expectation, Japanese and American participants exhibited similar levels of avoidance. The authors also found that individual traits such as argumentativeness, nationality, and gender interacted in complex ways. For example, Japanese women with high levels of trait aggression were more likely to offer assertive responses to criticism. This pattern was not evident in the American subsample.

Finally, in regard to compliments, the nature and frequency of compliments delivered by American and Japanese men and women were the foci of two studies reported by Barnlund and Araki (1985). In a preliminary interview study, the authors apparently found evidence that members of both cultures believed that women engaged in more compliments than did men. However, men and women showed no differences in their preferences, and people from both cultures preferred indirect strategies. A small cultural difference in preference for type of indirect strategy was reported. Later work found a similarly small female preference for the use of ingratiation in cross-cultural encounters (Branzei, 2002).

Studies of Speech Characteristics and Nonverbal Behavior

Several authors have conducted comparisons based on primarily nonsymbolic, nonstrategic aspects of communication such as speech characteristics and nonverbal behavior. The results suggest that Japanese- and English-speaking men used broadly similar patterns of intonation, as did English-speaking men and women (Loveday, 1986). The most striking difference was found in the comparison of Japanese men and women. Japanese women adopted an extremely high pitch, particularly when expressing Japanese politeness formulae. Similarly, Clark (1996) observed similar uses of pitch and intonation by female Japanese managers, presumably as they balanced power and politeness in their interactions with their employees.

Miller, Reynolds, and Cambra (1987) examined the effects of gender and cultural ancestry on language intensity, which is a message component frequently linked to persuasiveness (e.g., Bradac, Bowers, & Courtwright, 1979). They expected sex differences in language use to be more pronounced among Chinese and

Japanese cultural groups as a result of the sex-based status asymmetries observed in Japanese society by several authors (Buck, Newton, & Muramatsu, 1984; Lebra, 1984). The primary result of this study was a statistical interaction between sex and cultural identity. Specifically, within the Japanese and Chinese cultural groups, men chose more intense language than did women. No sex difference was evident in the statistical comparison of American men and women.

In addition, verbal and nonverbal messages that promote distance or closeness were the focus of one study comparing Japanese and American men and women (Boyer, Thompson, Klopf, & Ishii, 1990). The study found significant main effects for both culture and sex, with Americans reporting greater use of immediacy behaviors than the Japanese and women of both cultures reporting greater use of immediacy behavior. Finally, several older studies examined touching preferences in Japan and the United States and found that touching preferences were similar across the two cultures, though the Japanese appear to initiate less body contact in certain relational contexts but not in others (Barnlund, 1975; Elzinga, 1975). Moreover, Japanese women used more physical touch than Japanese men. On the basis of this data, Elzinga claimed that this difference is greater than that found in the United States, suggesting an interaction of sex with culture.

Studies of Meaning

Some authors have examined the role of sex differences in the meanings associated with symbols and concepts. For example, Higashiyama and Ono (1988) studied how Japanese speakers use the demonstratives of *koko*, *soko*, and *asoko* to divide personal space. In the end, the authors found no differences in the way American or Japanese men and women describe personal space.

Studies of Communication Traits, Tendencies, and Styles

Studies classified here examine individual differences in characteristics directly related to communication, such as affect orientation, assertiveness, responsiveness, and verbal aggressiveness. Affect orientation is the tendency to use emotional rather than logical appeals in persuasion (Booth-Butterfield & Booth-Butterfield, 1990). Frymier, Klopf, and Ishii (1990) studied differences among Japanese and American students in use of affect orientation. Results indicate that, in general, Japanese scored lower than Americans on the affect orientation measure. Sex was also a factor but only among the American students. An analysis of the interaction effect indicates that American women scored significantly higher than American men on affect orientation.

Assertiveness refers to the ability to express opinions strongly and defend oneself verbally without abusing others. Thompson, Klopf, and Ishii (1991) compared Japanese and American students on a self-report measure of social style, which included an assertiveness component. American men reported being more assertive than Japanese men, whereas Japanese women were similar in assertiveness to Japanese men and less assertive then American women. More recently, Bresnahan et al. (2002) reported similar results for trait measures of assertiveness. American and male respondents scored higher than Japanese and female respondents. Different results were reported by Bresnahan, Ohashi, Nebashi, Liu, and Lia (2001). Contrary to expectation, Americans scored lowest in assertiveness in these situations. The authors reasoned that the hierarchical culture experienced in American workplaces might encourage compliance with, rather than resistance to, requests. The study revealed no overall sex differences when countries were combined. Both men and women were likely to be more assertive in response to high-imposition requests. However, sex differences were evident among Japanese respondents. Again, contrary to expectations, women were significantly more likely than men to be assertive. The results of studies on assertiveness suggest that cultural and gender differences vary depending on whether situational (state) or trait measures are used. Certain communicative acts (such as unwanted requests) may be interpreted differently in Japanese and U.S. contexts, and thus they may call for different but culturally appropriate responses.

Lastly, verbally aggressive communicators use personal attacks rather than logical arguments in their interactions with others (Infante, 1984). A comparison of the self-reported verbal aggressiveness of Japanese and American university students was reported by Harman, Klopf, and Ishii (1990). Results show differences that were due to sex. Men were more verbally aggressive then women. American men scored highest on the verbal aggressiveness scale, Japanese men scored substantially lower, and Japanese women and American women scored lowest and nearly identically on the aggressiveness measure.

Summary

Given the limitations of the studies, we are cautious in drawing generalizations about the role of sex and gender in Japan. However, it is interesting that, of the 24 analyses reported in the studies, only 6 (25%) appeared to find main effects for sex. Overall, women of both cultures reported higher levels of verbal and nonverbal immediacy than did men (Boyer et al., 1990), and men of both cultures reported higher levels of verbal aggressiveness (Harman et al., 1990) and face-threatening behaviors than did women (Cocroft & Ting-Toomey, 1994). More than twice as many studies—14 (58%)—reported a main effect for culture. When both culture and sex main effects were found (as with Cocroft & Ting-Toomey, 1994), culture typically accounted for larger amounts of variance.

Fourteen studies (58%) found evidence for statistical interactions between culture and gender. Three of these showed gender differences existing in the United States, but not Japan, on the variables of affect orientation (Frymier et al., 1990), assertiveness (Thompson et al., 1991), and responsiveness (Thompson et al., 1991).

Authors reported sex differences among Japanese respondents, with females scoring higher on measures of apology (Otio et al., 1996), ingratiation (Branzei, 2002), and assertiveness (Bresnahan et al., 2001). Loveday's (1986) study of pitch and intonation also found sex differences in Japan but not in the United States. One study found sex differences in language intensity among participants of Japanese heritage but not among Caucasians (Miller et al., 1987). Elzinga (1975) and Barnlund (1975) found that sex differences in touch were manifested differently in the two cultures.

Still, several studies found interactions between culture and gender. Thus, it appears in this comparative literature that biological sex by itself is not the most important factor in determining patterns of communication in Japan or the United States. However, sex might combine with cultural factors to affect communication patterns. In some cases, Japanese men and women are significantly different, whereas American men and women are not. This seems most obvious in studies of nonstrategic and nonverbal communication. However, in about the same number of cases, gender differences found in the United States are not found in Japan. In contrast to the prevailing American view of Japan as a society in which sex differences are magnified, in these studies it appears that Japanese men and women, like American men and women, are more similar than different in most areas of communication.

REVIEW OF JAPANESE COMMUNICATION STYLES

Given that studies reviewed in the previous section indicate that sex may be manifested somewhat differently in the communication of Japanese and Americans, we looked for additional evidence about the nature of sex differences in Japanese communication. Using the same search procedure described earlier, we located and reviewed studies that compared Japanese men and women only. In general, conflicting results and only minor sex differences were found in these studies. Some of those differences that are reported are different from those found in studies of America. For instance, Nakanishi (1986) examined the effects of level of self-disclosure (high, medium, and low) and sex on perceptions of social attractiveness and found that sex interacted with self-disclosure level, such that Japanese men reported being more at ease with high disclosure than did Japanese women. In contrast, female respondents reported themselves to be more at ease (than the male respondents) in low-disclosure situations. The effects of sex difference might have been confounded by the sexual topic of the high-disclosure dialogues Nakanishi used in her study. More recently, Oguchi (1990) studied the self-disclosure of 199 Japanese men and women to determine the effects of recipient openness on the disclosers' willingness to disclose and liking for the recipient. The only substantive gender difference found was that Japanese female disclosive behavior was more responsive to recipients' willingness to reveal the disclosure to a third party.

On a related matter, Wada (1989) observed the nonverbal behavior of 32 acquaintances and strangers paired in same-sex dyads. In addition to the expected differences caused by relationship type and interpersonal distance, the author reported sex differences on measures of frequency of look, duration of smile, body lean, and eye contact. Sex differences in nonverbal behavior were the focus of Bond and Ho (1978) in their study of interview behavior. Thirty-two Japanese college students, equally divided between men and women, were interviewed by male or female interviewers of high and low social status. Results indicate several sex differences, with women versus men showing longer response latencies, less body lean, shorter glances, and more smiles. According to the authors, the manner in which men and women construed the formality and social distance of the interview situation may be the underlying source of differences in nonverbal behavior. They noted that some of the sex differences (e.g., eye contact) are the exact opposite of those found in studies of Western men and women.

Ide, Hori, Kawasaki, Ikuta, and Haga (1986) explored sex differences in the usage of politeness forms. The authors claimed that language choice in interpersonal interactions was determined in part by male–female differences in the perception of the linguistic forms. However, they found that sex did not directly predict the frequency of use of politeness forms. Some sex differences were found in the ratings of politeness forms and social situations. These in turn predicted (self-reported) frequency of use. This result suggests that individual interpretations of situational and cultural norms, moderated somewhat by gender, could be the most important predictors of politeness behavior in Japan. The situated nature of gender differences may also explain the results of an early study by Ohbuchi and Baba, which reported that Japanese female respondents exhibited a small preference for indirect influence attempts when compared with male counterparts, especially in situations characterized by interpersonal conflict (1988, described in Itoi, Ohbuchi, & Fukuno, 1996).

Finally, two studies compared the linguistic patterns of women and men in Japan. Using a quantitative technique to summarize patterns in linguistic data, Ogino (1986) found that Japanese women used more polite honorifics than their male counterparts. However, in a wider ranging, unpublished study of sociolinguistic behavior, Hibaya (1988; cited by Chambers, 1992) found no significant correlations between linguistic variables and sex.

Summary

This limited body of studies provides only mixed support for the prominence of gender differences in Japanese communication. One study of self-disclosure found that gender differences exist but attributed them to topical taboos imposed on Japanese women in high-disclosure situations. In the self-disclosure study (Oguchi,

1990), sex differences were minimal. The results of the studies correlating sex and linguistic behaviors also conflict. Ide et al. (1986) indicate that sex differences in Japan may be most obvious in the way men and women define social relationships. These perceptual differences may or may not result in observable differences in actual behavior. Only Wada's (1989) study of nonverbal behavior shows a clear pattern of sex differences. Interestingly, some of the sex differences observed here are opposite those found in the West. Perhaps Japanese cultural influences on gender relations are most obviously manifested in the realm of nonstrategic, nonverbal behavior (as was the case with the study by Loveday, 1986). In the remainder of this chapter we look to qualitative studies, which may better address the cultural milieu in which Japanese gender differences and similarities are expressed.

REVIEW OF QUALITATIVE STUDIES

The qualitative research examined in this chapter includes studies on communication styles in the Japanese culture and on communication and gender between Japanese and Americans. These studies utilized open-ended questionnaires, observational data, discourse analysis, and theories of sociolinguistics as frameworks to guide their investigations.

Chambers (1992) explored the notion that the failure to make the distinction between gender and sex in sociolinguistic studies may disguise significant correlations of linguistic variation with gender on the one hand and sex on the other. Chambers posited that the hypothesis of sex-based variability must be added to our study of how men and women interact. Specifically, Chambers argued that sex and gender must be differentiated in studies on sociolinguistics to understand whether differences in language are culturally or biologically based. The terms *sex-based variability* and *gender-based variability* suggest differences in language that are due to sex (biological) or gender (social). Chambers makes this claim specifically in regard to Japanese men and women, about whom she refuted prior research that argues that the sociolinguistic behavior of Japanese men and women is primarily gender specific.

Additionally, Smith (1992) reviewed studies that drew on a general theory of politeness and culturally specific gendered strategies for encoding politeness and authority in Japan. These studies focused on the ways in which the speech of women is equated with powerlessness. Smith compared the linguistic practices of Japanese men and women as they gave directions to subordinates in a variety of situations. In the end, she found that women tend to be more polite than their male counterparts and that this appears to be the case whether Japanese women occupy traditional or nontraditional roles. Smith also suggested that a unified set of linguistic behaviors, directives, in Japanese interaction relates to underlying cultural notions. She indicated that Japanese women who acquire positions of authority in nontraditional domains experience linguistic conflict. However, Smith's research, unlike a previous study that found that Japanese women in positions of authority attempted to defeminize their speech, suggests something rather different. Specifically, Smith said that "women [Japanese] may rather attempt to resolve the conflict by empowering their own speech (by adopting the Motherese Strategy as a public-domain power strategy) and that they are creating new and powerful strategies (e.g., the Passive Power Strategy) on a female power continuum that is distinct from the male power continuum" (p. 79).

Smith explained that Japanese women in positions of authority appear to be finding ways (such as the Motherese strategy) to ameliorate the problematic of choosing power forms of verbs, pronouns, and so on over the more linguistically appropriate female speech forms, which include honorifics. According to Smith, the Motherese strategy reflects Japanese women's ability to blend politeness with authority in issuing directives. This approach is used by Japanese mothers with their children and has been successful in gaining compliance with male subordinates when used in the public domain. An emphasis on solidarity, combined with an informal, less polite style of speech, creates what Smith identified as a special dimension in an emergent female leadership style. Smith also showed that the Japanese usage of rank terms such as *shocho* (director) or *kacho* (section chief) for address may create a sex-blind hierarchy that insulates Japanese men and women from their sexual identities. This differs from the United States, where "sex identity is inseparable from each individual, male or female, precisely due to its egalitarianism and individualism, which does away with a structural insulator" (p. 63).

Utilizing examples from the ethnographic diary of a female U.S. hire, Clark (1996) analyzed daily communication within an organizational hierarchy and power structure and argued that it continues to prevent Japanese women from achieving positions of authority and control. Both features of women's speech and the use of titles contribute to the subordination of Japanese women in Japanese culture and the workplace. Women's speech contains certain verb forms, particle endings, and word choice that, when tied to a particular pitch and rhythm, cause it to differ from men's speech. As well, the use of titles creates a two-tiered system. For example, in Japan, when individuals are referred to by their family names, a particular level of respect is implied. In contrast, use of one's given name signifies more familiarity and less respect. In the organization, whereas men are referred to by their family name, women are addressed by their given names.

Ingersoll-Dayton et al. (1998) extended the analysis of speech differences to the realm of personal relationships in their analysis of the discourse patterns used by older Japanese and American couples. In interview transcripts, the authors found little evidence to support cultural stereotypes. They found more even distribution of talk among the Japanese couples, whereas American wives spend considerable effort "orchestrating" the conversations in an effort to elicit participation by their husbands. Japanese men engaged in direct contradictions of their wives compliments, apparently to create impressions of modesty. American men engaged in indirect speech, apparently to avoid overt emotional displays. Japanese women exhibited more teasing behavior than the authors expected. Ingersoll and colleagues concluded that Japanese and U.S. couples used some behaviors that appeared similar (e.g., teasing, indirect speech) but used it for different purposes and with different interpretations.

Wetzel (1988) examined the striking parallel claims made concerning Japanese communication strategies and female communication strategies in the West. Wetzel posited that miscommunication between Japan and the West resembles miscommunication between the sexes in the West. Wetzel particularly focused on issues of power in both the West and Japan. Referencing Maltz and Borker's (1982) anthropological framework for identifying differences between Western women's and men's rules for interaction, Wetzel compared interaction patterns of Japanese and Western women (i.e., tag questions, hedges, etc.). Her findings indicate that parallel descriptions of communication between the two groups are not coincidental. In fact, in contrast to Hofstede's (1980) claims that the Japanese culture is a masculine one, Wetzel argued that much of Japanese communicative behavior viewed from a Western perspective is identified as feminine and therefore as powerless interaction. Wetzel pointed out that, by Western standards, power is an attribute of the individual rather than of the role, position, or status an individual occupies, whereas in Japan the opposite is true. This perspective reflects the Japanese view of power as relational and emphasizes the importance that Japanese people place on role interaction within the power structure or hierarchy as opposed to the individual.

In her later work, Wetzel (1993) argued that, although the notion of power in the West has been the subject of a great deal of debate and controversy, it has not received the same sort of attention in Japan. According to Wetzel, power in the West is tied to every conceivable dimension of society's infrastructure: political, social, personal, psychological, and linguistic. For instance, she observed that it is difficult to find a lexical item in Japanese that parallels our Western concept of power. In fact, Wetzel noted that, in Japanese, the terms *kenryoku* (power) or *shihai* (control), which might begin to be the linguistic equivalent to the English notion of power, simply do not reflect the behavior that [Western] linguists want to examine as illustrative of power. For the Japanese, the concept of power is not a core concept for native descriptions or analysis of behavior in Japan; this becomes most clear when one notes that "*Japanese writing about Japan in Japanese for a Japanese audience does not focus on* power" (Wetzel, p. 394; italics added). Relationships in Japan, whether male–female or superior–subordinate, rely on Confucian-influenced notions of role and vertical social structure that are tied to a paternalism that is almost maternalistic in nature: nurturing, benevolent, kind, and supportive. These sorts of relationships rely in great part on the Japanese concept of *amae,* which reflects a need for mutual dependency in vertical relationships in Japan. Wetzel made the point that the West's understanding of paternalism in

Japan is to a great degree a Western construct—one that imposes the notions of power, authoritarianism, and domination in a way that simply does not exist in the Japanese culture.

Di Mare (1995) extended Wetzel's (1988, 1993) findings concerning parallel linguistic constructs of the Japanese culture and American women to include the following forms of communicative practices: indirect communication, nonconfrontational communication, nonargumentative communication, information sharing, and consensus reaching in the decision-making process. According to Di Mare, the philosophical concepts of *wa* and amae, which are important in the construction of Japanese communicative practice, are also important in the construction of communicative practices of American women. Di Mare found that the literature on communicative styles of Japanese and American women indicated that styles representative of both groups are undergirded by notions of harmony and interdependence. On the basis of their studies, Wetzel and Di Mare argued that scholars need to consider how culture influences communication and gender roles.

Finally, Kameda's work (2001) has suggested that perceptions of Japanese communicative style as indirect and ambiguous exist because of the Japanese tendency to use an "explanation first style" that places the verb at the end of a sentence. In addition, the use of inference or what Kameda suggested may be viewed as a "non sequitor pattern" style of communication contributes to this perception. Further, Kameda argued that these linguistic characteristics grow out of historical, geographical, and religious factors, which researchers must consider when they analyze communication styles of the Japanese.

Summary

Of the eight qualitative studies reviewed, three examined whether the sociolinguistic behavior of Japanese men and women is influenced by sex or gender. Results indicate that, although sex differences should be considered in our study of how men and women interact, gender differences are equally if not more important in affecting linguistic choices.

Three of the eight studies compared the use of specific linguistic choices—honorifics, titles, and linguistic forms of politeness—by Japanese men and women. The results of these studies indicate that Japanese women tend to be more polite than Japanese men. However, all of these studies found that the use of more polite linguistic structures by women is governed by a number of variables. These variables include role or status of the listener, age of the speaker and listener, the domain where the interaction takes place (employment or private), and the fact that Japanese women assess individual linguistic forms as less polite than do Japanese men.

Finally, two studies compared particular linguistic structures and communicative styles representative of Japanese men and women with those of American women. They found a number of striking similarities between these linguistic structures and communicative practices. Researchers of these studies argued that similarities in the communicative structures of the two groups grow out of parallel sociocultural conditions and philosophical perspectives concerning relationships.

CONCLUSIONS

In reviewing both quantitative and qualitative literature, we found few systematic differences in the communicative styles of Japanese men and women. The few differences that did emerge most clearly reflected the use of linguistic structures of politeness and honorifics. Additionally, there appear to be minor differences involving nonverbal behavior. When studies examined culture (defined as nationality, as in American or Japanese) and sex, culture was the more important variable. In the quantitative studies, the statistical effects of culture were of greater magnitude than sex. Several conclusions can be drawn from the qualitative research concerning Japanese communication styles. First, qualitative studies were more likely to examine the impact of not only sex and gender differences on communication practices of Japan, but also cultural factors that might influence sex and gender, specifically status, age, hierarchy, power, and regional differences. In the qualitative studies, culture emerged as a significant factor in establishing differences in communicative styles.

Second, Western perceptions of sex and gender in Japanese communication styles are largely unconfirmed by the studies we reviewed. For example, the notion that Japanese men exhibit masculine forms of communication and that Japanese women exhibit feminine forms of communication is largely unsupported by the evidence. Another stereotype—that Japanese women are submissive—again is not supported by a preponderance of the evidence. Only a few studies report contrasting results. For example, Smith (1992) found that Japanese women utilize more polite forms of speech. However, Smith indicated that polite forms of speech reflect a power base that is established in Japan through the mothering role. This is in contrast to Western culture, in which the role and communicative behaviors of the mother are often denigrated and devalued.

Third, to the extent that sex differences become clear in Japan, they often manifest differently than they do in the United States. In the quantitative literature, this has been supported by statistical interactions between culture and sex. Differences between men and women in Japan are not the same as differences between men and women in the United States. For example, Elzinga (1975) found that Japanese and American men and women use touch differently. However, the touch preferences of American women are not always the same as those of Japanese women. The same is true for Japanese and American men.

Fourth, the research on sex differences in Japan remains limited. There remain relatively few quantitative and qualitative studies that examine the impact of gender on the communication practices of Japanese and between Americans and Japanese. In contrast, studies of gender in the United States are extremely common, as are studies that compare the citizens of the two nations on psychological, sociological, and business-related variables. In our review, only 25 comparative analyses (Japanese and American communication practices) and 11 intracultural studies (Japanese communication practices) that examined sex or gender were found. This contrast leads us to wonder in what ways gender is prioritized (if at all) in Japan and how that compares with the way in which it is prioritized in the United States. We also suggest that work and family roles, unrelated to sex or gender, may be more of a governing variable in Japan than it is in the United States.

Fifth, methodological problems in the research lead us to be cautious in interpreting the results of the studies. In the quantitative studies, particularly in earlier studies, statistical procedures were often unsophisticated or incomplete. A separate criticism is that much of the research only examined sex, not gender. Often the terms *sex* and *gender* were used interchangeably. Similarly, we are concerned that, in most studies, culture is equated with nationality, thus overlooking the regional, social, political, and historical factors that shape and diversify a culture.

Additional limitations of the research include the use of college students in U.S. samples, which decreases the representativeness of the larger population in regard to role requirements and status hierarchy. In addition, nearly all of the communication variables were operationalized through self-report procedures of some type (but see Loveday, 1986). Although efficient, self-reports measure perceived, rather than behavioral, communication practices. Most of the measures used in these studies required participants to summarize their behaviors across contexts, which creates the possibility that contexts in which gender and cultural differences are strong are canceled out by contexts in which they are weak. Studies that examined specific relational contexts (e.g., Steil & Hillman, 1993; also see Bresnahan et al., 2001) suggest that gender differences were manifested in some contexts but not in others. Finally, most of the studies reviewed were conducted by American or Japanese researchers who utilized Western methodologies. Suzuki (1991) indicated that the study of gender, which began in Japan in the 1970s by some social scientists and government offices, utilized American scales because there was no original scale developed to measure Japanese sex-role attitudes. Thus, research on gender or the measurement of sex-role attitudes of Japanese men and women may be distorted by Western research models that cannot adequately represent cross-cultural viewpoints or constructs. Even recent studies report similar measurement problems (Bresnahan et al.).

Given the updated research we have now included in our study, we suggest, as before, that future research in the area of sex differences, gender, and communication has to be more sensitive to the cultural and contextual factors that can distort gender differences. We also suggest that research focus on additional cultural factors such as status, hierarchy, age, and regional differences as they affect communicative styles in Japan and between Japanese and Americans. In the quantitative studies of communication and sex, the separation of the act of communication from the context of a society's culture is still common. Qualitative research, which is circumscribed by its own cultural context, appears to be more reflexive and more attentive to communication processes in their actual cultural milieu (e.g., Fitzgerald, 2003). Although the qualitative studies considered the cultural milieu out of which communication styles emerged, such research often did not offer descriptions of actual communication behaviors. On the basis of our updated review, we still argue that research in the field has yet to capture the cultural and contextual complexities of sex or gender and how those complexities shape and reinforce communication styles.

We hope that this chapter encourages researchers in the field to consider alternative approaches to the study of gender and communication in Japan and in communication between Japanese and Americans. As long as both quantitative and qualitative research continues to focus on interpersonal interactions and perceptions of interpersonal behaviors regarding communication patterns or styles within Japan and between Japanese and Americans, cultural and contextual factors will remain unexplored. Many if not all of the situational features that affect intercultural encounters are absent from the studies we reviewed. Cultural and contextual factors such as status, age, power, and regional differences, although given some attention in many of the qualitative studies, were given little if any in the quantitative studies. We suggest that, because communicative styles and perceptions of those styles are circumscribed by cultural context, future research should include analyses of social texts and discourses that reflect such contexts (Di Mare, 1990; Fitzgerald, 2003).

ACKNOWLEDGMENTS

We thank the following Japanese officials and representatives for their contributions to an earlier version of this chapter: Nick Kitamura, Senior Trade Advisor to Arizona; Hiro Kanda, JETRO Toyko; and Ichiro Sone, JETRO Los Angeles.

REFERENCES

Atwater, L., Brett, J., Waldman, D., Di Mare, L., & Hayden, M. (2004). Men's and women's perceptions of the gender typing of management subroles. *Sex Roles, 50*, 191–199.

Barnlund, D. C. (1975). *Public and private self in Japan and the United States.* Tokyo: Simul Press.

Barnlund, D. C. (1989). *Communicative styles of Japanese and Americans: Images and realities.* Belmont, CA: Wadsworth.

Barnlund, D. C., & Araki, S. (1985). Intercultural encounters: The management of compliments by Japanese and Americans. *Journal of Cross-Cultural Psychology, 16*, 9–26.

Bass, B. M., & Avolio, B. J. (1994). Shatter the glass-ceiling: Women may make better managers. *Human Resource Management, 33*, 549–560.

Belenky, M. F., Clinchy, B. M., Goldberger, N. R., & Tarule, J. M. (1986). *Women's ways of knowing.* New York: Basic Books.

Bond, M. H., & Ho, H. Y. (1978). The effect of relative status and the sex composition of a dyad on cognitive responses and nonverbal behavior of Japanese interviewees. *Psychologia, 21*, 128–136.

Booth-Butterfield, M., & Booth-Butterfield, S. (1990). Conceptualizing affect as information in communication production. *Human Communication Research, 16*, 451–476.

Boyer, L. M., Thompson, C. A., Klopf, D. W., & Ishii, S. (1990). An intercultural comparison of immediacy among Japanese and Americans. *Perceptual and Motor Skills, 71*, 65–66.

Bradac, J. J., Bowers, J. W., & Courtwright, J. A. (1979). Three language variables in communication research: Intensity, immediacy and diversity. *Human Communication Research, 5*, 257–269.

Branzei, O. (2002). Cultural expectations of individual preferences for influence tactics in cross cultural encounters. *International Journal of Cross Cultural Management, 2*, 203–218.

Bresnahan, M. J., Ohashi, R., Nebashi, R., Liu, W., & Liao, C. (2001). Assertiveness as a predictor of compliance and resistance in Taiwan, Japan, and the U.S. *Journal of Asian Pacific Communication, 11*, 135–159.

Bresnahan, M. J., Shearman, S. M., Lee, S. Y., Ohashi, R., & Mosher, D. (2002). Personal and cultural differences in responding to criticism in three countries. *Asian Journal of Social Psychology, 5*, 93–105.

Buck, E. B., Newton, B. J., & Muramatsu, Y. (1984). Independence and obedience in the United States and Japan. *International Journal of Intercultural Relations, 8*, 279–300.

Cai, D., & Wilson, S. R. (2000). Identity implications of influence goals: A cross-cultural comparison of interaction goals and facework. *Communication Studies, 51*, 307–328.

Canary, D., & Hause, K (1993). Is there any reason to research sex differences in communication? *Communication Quarterly, 41*, 129–144.

Chambers, J. K (1992). Linguistic correlates of gender and sex. *English World-Wide, 13*, 173–218.

Clark, S. (1996). Maintaining Yoshino's traditional hierarchy: The roles of gender and race in Japanese transplant management. *Journal of Organizational Change Management, 9*, 6–17.

Cocroft, B. K, & Ting-Toomey, S. (1994). Facework in Japan and the United States. *International Journal of Intercultural Relations, 18*, 469–506.

Collier, M. J. (1991). Conflict competence within African, Mexican and Anglo American friendships. In S. Ting-Toomey & F. Korzenny (Eds.), *Cross-cultural interpersonal communication* (pp. 132–154). Newbury Park, CA: Sage.

Connor, J. W. (1985). Differential socialization and role stereotypes in Japanese females introduction? *Journal of Psychoanalytic Anthropology, 8*, 29–45.

Craig, T. J. (Ed.). (2000). *Japan pop!: Inside the world of Japanese popular culture.* Armonk, NY: Sharpe.

Darus, H. J. (1994). Argumentativeness in the workplace: A trait by situation study. *Communication Research Reports, 11*, 90–100.

Davis-Blake, A. (2000). Office ladies and salaried men: Power, gender, and work in Japanese companies. *Administrative Science Quarterly, 45*, 164–167.

Di Mare, L. (1990). MA and Japan. *The Southern Communication Journal, 55*, 319–328.

Di Mare, L. (1995, July). *Japanese communication practices and communication styles.* Paper presented at the biannual World Communication Conference, Vancouver, Canada.

Eagly, A. H., & Johnson, B. T. (1990). Gender and leadership style: A meta analysis. *Psychological Bulletin, 100*, 233–250.

Elzinga, R. H. (1975). Nonverbal communication: Body accessibility among the Japanese. *Psychologia, 18*, 205–211.

Fitzgerald, H. G. (2003). *How different are we?: Spoken discourse in intercultural communication: The significance of the situational context.* Clevedon, England: Multilingual Matters.

Frymier, A. B., Klopf, D. W., & Ishii, S. (1990). Japanese and Americans compared on the affect orientation construct. *Psychological Reports, 66*, 985–986.

Gossman, H. M. (2000). New role models for men and women? Gender in Japanese TV dramas. In T. J. Craig (Ed.), *Japan pop!: Inside the world of Japanese popular culture* (pp. 207–221). Armonk, NY: Sharpe.

Gudykunst, W. B. (Ed.). (1993). *Communication in Japan and the United States*. Albany: State University of New York Press.

Gudykunst, W. B., Guzley, R. M., & Ota, H. (1993). Issues for future research on communication in Japan and the United States. In W. B. Gudykunst (Ed.), *Communication in Japan and the United States* (pp. 291–322). Albany: State University of New York Press.

Gudykunst, W. B., & Nishida, T. (1993). Interpersonal and intergroup communication in Japan and the United States. In W. B. Gudykunst (Ed.), *Communication in Japan and the United States* (pp. 149–214). Albany: State University of New York Press.

Gudykunst, W. B., Nishida, T., & Schmidt, K L. (1989). The influence of cultural, relational, and personality factors on uncertainty reduction processes. *Western Journal of Speech Communication, 53*, 13–29.

Harman, C. M., Klopf, D. W., & Ishii, S. (1990). Verbal aggression among Japanese and American students. *Perceptual and Motor Skills, 70*, 11–30.

Harper, N. L., & Hirokawa, R. Y. (1988). A comparison of persuasive strategies used by female and male managers: I. An examination of downward influence. *Communication Quarterly, 36*, 157–168.

Hibaya, J. (1988). A *quantitative study of Tokyo Japanese*. Unpublished doctoral dissertation, The University of Pennsylvania, Philadelphia.

Higashiyama, A., & Ono, H. (1988). "Koko," "soko," and "asoko" ("here" and "there") as verbal dividers of space. *Japanese Psychological Research, 30*, 18–24.

Hirokawa, R. Y., Mickey, J., & Miura, S. (1991). Effects of request legitimacy on the compliance-gaining tactics of male and female managers. *Communication Monographs, 58*, 421–436.

Hirokawa, R. Y., & Miyahara, A. (1986). A comparison of influence strategies utilized by managers in American and Japanese organizations. *Communication Quarterly, 34*, 250–265.

Hofstede, G. (1980). *Culture's consequences: International differences in work-related values*. Beverly Hills, CA: Sage.

Holloway, J. S. (1995). It's time to recognize that both management styles can be effective. *Small Business Forum, 13*, 79–80.

Hsu, J. (1983). Asian family interaction patterns and their therapeutic implications. *International Journal of Family Psychiatry, 4*, 307–320.

Ide, S., Hori, M., Kawasaki, A., Ikuta, S., & Haga, H. (1986). Sex differences and politeness in Japanese. *International Journal of the Sociology of Language, 58*, 25–36.

Infante, D. A. (1984). Aggressiveness. In J. C. McCroskey & J. A. Daly (Eds.), *Personality and interpersonal communication* (pp. 157–192). Beverly Hills, CA: Sage.

Ingersol-Dayton, B., Campbell, R., & Mattson, J. (1998). Forms of communication: A cross cultural comparison of older married couples in the USA and Japan. *Journal of Cross Cultural Gerontology, 13*, 63–80.

Itoi, R., Ohbuchi, K., & Fukuno, M. (1996). A cross-cultural study of preference of accounts: Relationship closeness, harm severity, and motives of account making. *Journal of Applied Social Psychology, 26*, 913–934.

Jansen, S. (2002). *Critical communication theory*. Lanham, MD: Rowman & Littlefield.

Kameda, N. (2001). The implication of language style in business communication: Focus on English versus Japanese. *Corporate Communications, 6*, 144–149.

Klopf, D. W. (1991). Japanese communication practices: Recent comparative research. *Communication Quarterly, 39*, 130–143.

Kuwabara, T., Nishida, K., Ura, M., & Kayano, J. (1989). A examination of conversation process in social context. *Japanese Journal of Psychology, 60*, 163–169.

Lebra, T. S. (1984). *Japanese women.* Honolulu: University of Hawaii Press.

Lee, C. (1994). The feminization of management. *Training, 31,* 25–31.

Lipman-Blumen, J. (1992). Connective leadership: Female leadership styles in the 21st century workplace. *Sociological Perspectives, 35,* 103–203.

Loveday, L. (1986). *Explorations in Japanese sociolinguistics.* Philadelphia: Benjamins.

Maltz, D. N., & Borker, R. A. (1982). A cultural approach to male–female miscommunication. In J. J. Gumperz (Ed.), *Language and social identity* (pp. 196–216). Cambridge, England: Cambridge University Press.

Martinez, D. (Ed.). (1998). *The worlds of Japanese popular culture: Gender, shifting boundaries and global cultures.* Cambridge, England: Cambridge University Press.

Matsuura, H. (1998). Japanese EFL learners' perception of politeness in low imposition requests. *JALT-Journal, 20,* 33–48.

Miller, M. D., Reynolds, R. A., & Cambra, R. E. (1987). The influence on gender and culture on language intensity. *Communication Monographs, 54,* 101–105.

Nakanishi, M. (1986). Perceptions of self-disclosure in initial interaction: A Japanese sample. *Human Communication Research, 13,* 167–190.

Oetzel, J., Ting-Toomey, S., Masumoto, T., Yokochi, Y., Pax, X., Takai, J., & Wilcox, R. (2001). Face and facework in conflict: A cross-cultural comparison of China, Germany, Japan, and the United States. *Communication Monographs, 68,* 235–258.

Ogino, T. (1986). Quantification of politeness based on the usage patterns of honorific expressions. *International Journal of the Sociology of Language, 58,* 37–58.

Oguchi, T. (1990). The effects of a recipient's openness and conveyance to a third party of the self-disclosure on change in the discloser's liking and self-disclosure. *Japanese Journal of Psychology, 61,* 147–154.

Powell, G. N., & Graves, L. M. (2003). *Women and men in management.* Thousand Oaks, CA: Sage.

Renshaw, J. R. (1999). *Kimono in the boardroom.* New York: Oxford University Press.

Roesner, J. B. (1990). Ways women lead. *Harvard Business Review, 68,* 119–125.

Saso, M. (1990). *Women in the Japanese workplace.* London: Shipman.

Schooler, C., & Smith, K. C. (1978). Social structural antecedents of women's role values in Japan. *Sex Roles, 4,* 23–41.

Sinha, D., & Tripathi, R. C. (1994). Individualism in a collectivist culture: A case of coexistence of opposites. In U. Kim, H. C. Triandis, C. Kâgitbâsi, S. Choi, & G. Yoon (Eds.), *Individualism and collectivism: Theory method and applications* (pp. 123–136). Thousand Oaks, CA: Sage.

Smith, J. S. (1992). Women in charge: Politeness and directives in the speech of Japanese women. *Language in Society, 21,* 59–82.

Steil, J. M., & Hillman, J. L. (1993). The perceived value of direct and indirect influence strategies: A cross-cultural comparison. *Psychology of Women Quarterly, 17,* 457–462.

Suzuki, A. (1991). Egalitarian sex role attitudes: Scale development and comparison of American and Japanese women. *Sex Roles, 24,* 245–259.

Tanaka, Y. (1990). Women's growing role in contemporary Japan. *International Journal of Psychology, 25,* 751–765.

Tanaka, K. (1998). Japanese women's magazines: The language of aspiration. In D. P. Martinez (Ed.), *The worlds of Japanese popular culture* (pp. 110–132). Cambridge, England: Cambridge University Press.

Thompson, C. A., Klopf, D. W., & Ishii, S. (1991). Japanese and Americans compared on assertiveness/responsiveness. *Psychological Reports, 66,* 829–830.

Ting-Toomey, S. (1988). Intercultural conflict styles: A face negotiation theory. In Y. Kim & W. B. Gudykunst (Eds.), *Theories in intercultural communication* (pp. 213–238). Newbury Park, CA: Sage.

Toren, N., Konrad, A. M., Yoshioka, I., & Kashlak, R. (1997). A cross-national cross-gender study of managerial task preferences and evaluation of work characteristics. *Women in Management Review, 12,* 234–243.

Troemel-Ploetz, S. (1994). "Let me put it this way, John": Conversational strategies of women in leadership positions. *Journal of Pragmatics, 22*, 199–209.

Wada, M. (1989). Effects of interpersonal relationship, interpersonal distance and gender on nonverbal behavior in dyads of strangers and acquaintances. *Japanese Journal of Psychology, 60*, 31–37.

Waldron, V. R., & Di Mare, L. (1998). Gender as a culturally determined construct: Communication styles in Japan and the United States. In Daniel J. Canary and Kathryn Dindia (Eds.), Sex Difference and similarities in communicaiton, 179–201. London: Lawrence Erlbaum Associates.

Wetzel, P. J. (1988). Are "powerless" communication strategies the Japanese norm? *Language in Society, 17*, 555–564.

Wetzel, P. (1993). The language of vertical relationships and linguistic analysis. *Multilingua, 12*, 387–406.

Wilkins, B. M., & Andersen, P. A. (1991). Gender similarities and differences in management communication: A meta-analysis. *Management Communication Quarterly, 5*, 6–35.

Zellner, W. (1994 April 18). Women entrepreneurs. *Business Week*, 104–110.

III

Sex Differences and Similarities in Communicative Behaviors

12

The Gender-Linked Language Effect: Do Language Differences Really Make a Difference?

Anthony Mulac
University of California at Santa Barbara

There are two abiding truths on which the general public and research scholars find themselves in uneasy agreement: First, men and women speak the same language. Second, men and women speak that language differently. So we have, at one and the same time, gender-linked (or as they are sometimes called, *sex-linked*) similarities *and* differences in language use. What this means for communication between and among men and women, and in fact whether it means anything at all, is the topic of this chapter.

Program of Research

My observations on women's and men's language are based on a program of research conducted at the University of California, Santa Barbara, over the past 25 years. During this time, colleagues and I have collaborated on some 20 empirical investigations of female–male differences in language use and the effects of those differences on observer judgments. Because we have assessed women's and men's language for possible differences, we have at the same time tested for similarities. This is the case because any language variables that fail, in a given communication context, to distinguish between women and men may be viewed as representing similarities of language use.

From the beginning, our research approach has involved a series of theoretical assumptions: First, if men and women do indeed differ in their communication behavior, then such differences would likely be found in microscopic language behaviors. The logical consequence is to look at their word choice. Second, because language is spoken and understood as combinations of language features, rather than individual features, analyses that seek gender-linked differences should assess linguistic features in combination, not one at a time. Accordingly, look at combinations of language. Third, because different communication contexts might lead to shifts in gender differentiators, investigations should be conducted in a variety of communication settings. That being the case, sample language under various circumstances. Fourth, to increase the power and generalizibility of research findings, relatively large numbers of communicators should be assessed. Therefore, sample a lot of people. Fifth, to be meaningful from a communication standpoint, the transcribed language of men and women should lead to differences in psychological judgments rendered by observers. Consequently, see whether people judge them differently. Sixth, it should be shown that transcript raters cannot determine the sex of communicators, to guard against their judgments being influenced by gender stereotypes. Therefore, check whether judges can guess communicator sex. Finally, a predictive link should be demonstrated between raters' judgments of speakers' psychological characteristics, on the one hand, and the speakers' gender-differentiating language use, on the other. Accordingly, check whether language differences play a part in observer judgments.

For our program of research, we implemented a paradigm that was consistent with these theoretical assumptions: Speakers of a particular age group (e.g., fifth graders, university students, or senior citizens) were asked to engage in a particular communication task (e.g., to describe a landscape photograph or to solve a problem with a partner). Their spontaneous speech samples were recorded on audiotape and transcribed for later analysis. The following are examples of transcripts of two speakers, between 30 and 35 years of age, describing the same landscape photograph:[1]

Speaker number 5: This picture I like very much, with the mountains—they dominate the picture—and the yellow trees. There's a lot of . . . there's color in this picture without really having color. There's, there's a force in this picture; it . . . draws you to it, like you really want to be there. And, uh, let's see . . . there's something so removed from the city about it—peaceful and cool—and you'd really like to be there. Uhm, again there's something about the colors—they, they're icy colors and yet the yellow in the forefront, in the foreground, uhm give, or lend, a certain kind of warmth to the picture.

[1]These transcripts were taken from the 12 whose effects were analyzed in Mulac, Incontro, and James (1985).

Speaker number 11: Okay. It looks like a beautiful winter scene, in which we've got lots of very . . . probably fall, maybe the first snowfall of the year. Large groups of tall mountains and partially covered with snow . . . and perhaps some lower hogbacks and such forth . . . and covered with various types of coniferous and deciduous trees. Probably morning time with a low layer of fog just kind of . . . between the ground and the tops of the mountains. Beautiful blue sky up above. Reminds me a lot of the Sierra Nevada's perhaps, maybe the west side.

In several of our investigations, individuals were asked to write essays or descriptions of landscape photographs, and these were printed for assessment. The number of speakers or writers whose language we sampled in various studies has ranged from 12 to 108 individuals, with an average of 40 or more. By assessing a relatively large number of actual language samples, we increased our ability to generalize to other individuals. Linguistic analyses were then conducted by trained coders, who assessed the transcripts for linguistic features that were previously found to distinguish the speech or writing of women, for example, intensive adverbs ("really") or references to emotion ("I felt sad"), or of men, for example, references to quantity ("30 feet tall") or elliptical sentences ("Great picture."). In each study, the actual gender of the speakers or writers was not made available to the language coders. We aggregated the language data across coders and analyzed these data, using stepwise discriminant analysis procedures, to determine whether the female and male communicators had used language differently.

Next, we asked untrained observers to "guess the sex" of the speakers or writers. Their ability, or inability, to accurately identify the sex of the individuals on the basis of language use provided important information, subsequently discussed, on the degree of similarity of women's and men's language. The sex-guess data also informed us of whether other observers could be influenced by gender stereotypes.

In addition, we asked other untrained observers to rate psychological characteristics of each of the speakers (or writers) "as a person," based on the transcripts of what those individuals had said. Ratings were done by use of a 12-item semantic differential, the Speech Dialect Attitudinal Scale (SDAS; Mulac, 1975, 1976), designed to assess the effects of dialect differences. Factor analyses of the SDAS ratings have consistently yielded the following three-factor solution: (a) Sociointellectual Status (e.g., rich–poor, literate–illiterate), (b) Aesthetic Quality (beautiful–ugly, nice–awful), and (c) Dynamism (strong–weak, aggressive–unaggressive). Our analyses of these ratings showed whether the male and female communicators were judged differently.

Finally, we determined, by means of stepwise multiple regression analysis, whether gender-differentiating language could explain the judgments of psychological characteristics. To the extent that male–female language differences could predict psychological ratings, such results demonstrated that language itself was implicated in the effect.

SIMILARITIES IN LANGUAGE

Sex-Guess Accuracy

Our research has shown that the language used by women and men in the United States is remarkably similar. In fact, it is so indistinguishable that native speakers of American English cannot correctly identify which language examples were produced by women and which were produced by men. Support for this claim comes from our empirical investigations of female–male language differences and the effects of those differences. We felt there was a need to learn whether readers could determine the sex of the speakers, because if they could, then other respondents might be influenced by gender stereotypes when they rated the speakers. In other words, if raters could determine that a given speaker was a man, they might rate him higher on strength and aggressiveness, purely because of their stereotypical view that men exhibit these attributes, without regard to how his language use made him appear. In contrast, if they could not correctly identify speaker sex, they could not be influenced by stereotypes.

In our first study that measured sex-guess accuracy (Mulac & Lundell, 1980), we recorded brief landscape photograph descriptions by 48 speakers from each of four age groups (six male and six female speakers from each group): (a) public-school fifth graders, (b) university freshmen and sophomores, (c) university teaching assistants and instructors, and (d) people in their 50s and 60s. We had 1-minute segments from these recordings transcribed orthographically and printed, one to a page, with arbitrary speaker numbers (e.g., "speaker number 24"). We then asked beginning university communication students, for whom English was their first language, to "guess the sex" of the speakers from each of the age groups. Results showed that they were not able to do so with anything better than chance accuracy.

In our second study (Mulac & Lundell, 1982), we recorded 30 students' giving their first speech in a university public-speaking class. On the basis of 1-minute samples of their transcripts, university students were unable to guess the sex of the speakers. Our third study (Mulac et al., 1985) involved the recording of 12 secondary teachers and college instructors from across the country as they described landscape photographs. Once again, university students were unable to distinguish male from female speakers. We found the same result for the essays of 96 4th-, 8th-, and 12th-grade students, who wrote on the topic, "Is it ever all right to tell a lie?" (Mulac, Studley, & Blau, 1990). Finally, in our fourth study (Mulac & Lundell, 1994), we reported a similar finding for 40 university students' impromptu essays describing landscape photographs.[2]

[2]University students were able to guess speaker sex accurately in one study, but it dealt with the language of characters in children's television programs, rather than that of actual female and male individuals (Mulac, Bradac, & Mann, 1985). In that investigation, respondents could correctly identify the sex for over 68% of the 168 characters, all of whom were speaking in carefully scripted dialogues. Therefore, native speakers of American English are able to detect gender-linked differences, when those differences have been produced by television writers who presumably employ

These consistent results provide clear evidence that the spoken and written language used in everyday communication by women and men, as well as by girls and boys, displays a high degree of similarity.

Average Language Feature Use

Results of our studies also point to the high degree of comparability of language in another way. If we view the actual language use in a given investigation, one variable at a time, we are struck more by the similarity of men's and women's language than by the difference. For example, in Mulac, Wiemann, Widenmann, and Gibson (1988), we assessed the language of university students (63 men and 79 women) as they worked to solve problems in same-sex or mixed-sex dyads. If we average men's and women's use of 12 variables across same-sex and mixed-sex dyads, we see that men interrupted their partner an average of 1.15 times per 100 words of their speech, whereas women interrupted 0.78 times per 100 words. Men used directives (e.g., "Write that down") 0.31 times per 100 words and women used directives 0.22 times. In addition, women employed questions an average of 2.06 times per 100 words versus 1.60 times for the men. Women averaged 0.70 intensive adverbs ("really") per 100 words, whereas men averaged 0.46 intensive adverbs. Other variables demonstrate even smaller discrepancies between women and men in these problem-solving interactions. This evidences a substantial degree of *similarity* in their selection of linguistic elements. However, in spite of the obvious comparability of language use, we did find significant differences in a later phase of this study, subsequently discussed, but only by employing a powerful, multivariate statistical procedure.

Given these results, it appears that similarities in language use are consistently found in the sex-guess phase of our investigations and in the average use of specific language features. Both of these results seem to indicate that similarity of language constitutes the rule regarding the communication behavior of women and men in our society. The question that remains is this: If their language use is so similar, why is there so much heated discussion about differences in their linguistic performance? Do women and men *really* use language differently?

DIFFERENCES IN LANGUAGE

Summary of Research on Differences

The answer to the aforementioned question is an unrestrained "Yes!"—meaningful differences in language behavior do exist. This conclusion is supported by a substantial number of empirical investigations of actual male–female language use, conducted in a variety of communication contexts with communicators of different

---

gender-stereotypical language. However, these same respondents cannot identify actual women and men who are communicating in an impromptu fashion.

TABLE 12.1
Results of Literature Review Finding 21 Language Features That Differentiate Gender in Two or More Empirical Studies

Gender–Language Features	*Examples of Features*	*Studies Finding*[b]
Male language features[a]		
References to quantity	"6 ft., 4 in., tall"	5 Male
Judgmental adjectives	"good," "dumb"	3 Male
Elliptical sentences	"Great picture."	2 Male
Directives	"Write that down."	2 Male
Locatives	"in the background"	2 Male
"I" references	"I think . ."	2 Male
Female language features		
Intensive adverbs	"really," "so"	7 Female
References to emotions	"happy," "hurt"	5 Female
Dependent clauses	"where the shadows are"	5 Female
Sentence-initial adverbials	"Actually, it's . . . "	4 Female
Mean length sentence	(relatively long sentences)	5 F; 1 M[c]
Uncertainty verbs	"It seems to be . . . "	3 Female
Oppositions	"It's peaceful, yet full of movement."	2 Female
Negations	"It's not a . . . "	2 Female
Hedges	"kind of"	2 Female
Questions	"What's that?"	2 Female
Equivocal language feature		
Personal pronouns	"we," "she"	5 F; 2 M
Tag questions	"That's not right, is it?"	4 F; 2 M
Fillers	"you know," "like"	3 F; 2 M
Progressive verbs	"melting"	2 F; 1 M
Justifiers	"It's not that, because . . . "	1 F; 1 M

[a] Where the pattern is consistent across studies, the variable is listed under the gender making greater use of it. Variables are listed in decreasing order of gender-predicting effectiveness.

[b] This indicates the number of studies that found this gender using more of this variable.

[c] Fourth-grade boys' use of run-on sentences seems to explain this inconsistent result.

ages. As part of an experimental study in 2001, we summarized the results of over 30 studies, including our own experimental investigations referenced herein, and all found statistically significant differences[3] in the use of language features by male and female communicators (Mulac, Bradac, & Gibbons, 2001). We found 21 linguistic features to distinguish gender in two or more investigations. Table 12.1 summarizes the results of this analysis, indicating 6 variables used more by men, 10 used more by women, and 5 whose use was equivocal. Next to each variable, a "Male" or "Female" is printed along with the number of studies that found that variable to be employed more by male or by female communicators. For example, we discovered 5 studies that reported references to quantity used more by male

[3]Although the number of linguistic comparisons undertaken in these studies varied, roughly one half of the features assessed across them evidenced gender differences.

communicators (and hence we printed "5 Male" next to it) and 7 that indicated intensive adverbs employed more by female communicators. For definitions and examples of each language feature, as well as the research contexts and citations of studies finding these differences, see Mulac et al. (2001).

We located six features that were generally used more by men and boys. They include the following, with examples drawn from our research transcripts: references to quantity ("an 81% loss in vision"), judgmental adjectives ("Reading can be a drag"), and elliptical sentences ("Nice photo."). Men were also more likely to use directives ("Think of some more."), locatives ("The sun is off to the left side"), and "I" references ("I have a lot of meetings").

In addition, we found 10 language features that were generally used more by women and girls. Among them were intensive adverbs ("He's really interested"), references to emotions ("If he really loved you"), and dependent clauses ("which is the type that produces slightly more fuel than it uses."). Women were also more likely to use sentence-initial adverbials ("When the material is too difficult, studying with someone can be beneficial."), uncertainty verbs ("It seems to be . . . "), oppositions ("The tone of it is very peaceful, yet full of movement."), and negations ("Preparation will make you not sound like a fool."). Finally, this analysis showed that women were more likely to use hedges ("We're kind of set in our ways."), questions ("Do you think so?"), and longer mean length sentences.

The remaining five features were found to be equivocal predictors of gender. That is, some studies showed these five to be used more by men, and others, more by women. These included personal pronouns ("Before we go on, do you . . ?"), tag questions ("That's right, isn't it?"), fillers ("It's, you know . . . , it's"), progressive verbs ("watching him"), and justifiers (". . . because that's what I saw.").

Our review indicated that 16 language features distinguish communicator gender with a high degree of reliability across a substantial number of empirical investigations. These findings demonstrate that clear-cut differences are present and must be acknowledged. However, it is obvious that no Gilesian "markers" of gender exist (Giles, Scherer, & Taylor, 1979)—that is, no linguistic forms were found that clearly and unerringly point to the gender of the speaker. Instead we have, as Smith (1985) observed, only gender-linked "tendencies" to favor certain linguistic features over others. If we use these 16 features to analyze the two language samples, presented earlier, of speakers describing a landscape photograph, we can begin to see some of the subtle tendencies indicated in the literature review:

Speaker number 5 (a woman):

> This picture I *like* [reference to emotion] *very* [intensive adverb] much, with the mountains—they dominate the picture—and the yellow trees. There's a lot of . . . there's *color in this picture without really having color* [opposition]. There's, there's a force in this picture; it . . . *draws you* [reference to emotion] to it, like you *really* [intensive adverb] *want* [reference to emotion] to be there. And, uh, let's see . . . there's something

> *so* [intensive adverb] removed from the city about it—peaceful and cool—and you'd *really* [intensive adverb] *like* [reference to emotion] to be there. Uhm, again there's something about the colors—they, *they're icy colors and yet* [opposition] the yellow in the forefront, in the foreground, uhm give, or lend, a certain kind of warmth to the picture.

A summary of the female indicators found in this woman's description is as follows: four intensive adverbs, four references to emotion, and two oppositions. Although she also used some male features, for example "a lot of" [reference to quantity] and "in the foreground" [locative], we left these unmarked for the sake of clarity of presentation.

Speaker number 11 (a man):

> Okay. It looks like a *beautiful* [judgmental adjective] winter scene, in which we've got *lots of* [reference to quantity] very . . . probably fall, maybe the *first* [reference to quantity] snowfall of the year. *Large groups* [reference to quantity and elliptical sentence] of *tall* (reference to quantity) mountains and *partially* covered [reference to quantity] with snow . . . and perhaps some lower hogbacks and such forth . . . and covered with various types of coniferous and deciduous trees. *Probably morning time* [elliptical sentence] with a *low* [locative] layer of fog just kind of . . . *between the ground and the tops* [locative] of the mountains. *Beautiful blue sky* [elliptical sentence] *up above* [locative]. *Reminds me* [elliptical sentence] a lot of the *Sierra Nevada's* [locative] perhaps, maybe the *west side* [locative].

This man's description includes the following male variables: five references to quantity, one judgmental adjective, four elliptical sentences, and five locatives. As indicated earlier, the italicized gender-indicative features should be viewed as linguistic tendencies of male and female communicators. They are not gender markers, because both men and women use them.

Pattern of Gender-Linked Differences

The 16 gender-distinguishing language features can be seen to form a coherent pattern, when viewed from the perspective of verbal styles that distinguish national language cultures (e.g., German vs. French). But what do intercultural style differences have to do with understanding gender differences? Because of the theoretical claim that men and women grow up in separate subcultures and therefore learn to use language differently (Maltz & Borker, 1982; Tannen, 1994), we thought it seemed reasonable to test the utility of this intercultural perspective. Gudykunst and Ting-Toomey (1988) proposed four dimensions of language style that are useful in describing differences between cultures: The first dimension, *direct versus indirect,* represents the extent to which speakers reveal their intentions through explicit verbal reference. The second, *succinct versus elaborate,* focuses on the quantity of talk and the extent to which rich, expressive language is used. *Personal versus contextual* style emphasizes personhood as opposed to role relations. Finally, *instrumental versus affective* represents the extent to which a speaker focuses on things as opposed to people.

We tested this perspective experimentally, on the basis of reader judgments of parallel sentences with and without each language feature (Mulac et al., 2001). The results indicated that the 6 features of men's style fit on one end of these dimensions, and the 10 features of women's style fit on the opposite end. For example, men's higher use of directives ("Think of some more") exemplifies direct style, in contrast to women's indirectness shown by their use of uncertainty verbs ("It seems like I don't have enough time") and questions ("Do you know what I'm saying?"). In addition, men's use of elliptical sentences ("Gorgeous!") represents succinct style, whereas women's intensive adverbs ("The sky is very blue") and longer mean length sentences indicate elaborate style. Furthermore, men's use of "I" references can be seen as exemplifying personal style, as opposed to contextual style; however, no women's features appear to denote contextual style. Finally, men's greater use of references to quantity ("The view is from out at sea, about a football field away") represents instrumental style, and women's references to emotion ("It seems to be eerie and depressing") represents affective style.

Therefore, men's language can be seen as relatively direct, succinct, personal, and instrumental. Woman's features, in contrast, are indirect, elaborate, and affective. It is significant that our experimental results indicated that neither were there any of the 6 male language features located at the women's end of any cultural dimension, nor were there any of the 10 female language features located at the men's end (Mulac et al., 2001). Thus, we see that gender-linked language differences exhibit a coherent pattern, one that is consistent with intercultural expectations.

Maltz and Borker (1982), among others, have argued that women and men use language features differently, in part because they interpret the same feature (e.g., questions) as carrying different meanings. We have found empirical support for this claim, reporting that questions and back channels (*yeah, un-huh*), embedded in conversations, are seen as having different conversational meaning by women as compared to men (Mulac et al., 1998).

Multivariate Assessment of Differences

Unlike the majority of the 31 studies already discussed, we have employed a somewhat different method to determine whether speakers or writers use language in gender-differentiating ways (Mulac, 1998). Like many investigators, we have used trained observers to code language variables (such as intensive adverbs and directives) appearing in the transcripts of naturally occurring language. However, after aggregating across coders, we have analyzed these language data by means of stepwise discriminant analysis procedures. This multivariate statistical method has important advantages over the univariate or variable-by-variable perspective more commonly followed. Because speech and writing are both produced and comprehended as a *combination* of interrelated language features, rather than a series of independent words, it is reasonable to believe that greater construct validity (Kerlinger, 1973, pp. 461–469) can be attained through the use of multivariate procedures. Such procedures identify weighted combinations of variables for purposes of predicting some criterion variable, in this case communicator gender. Although this approach has been followed in only a handful of linguistic studies, we employed it because it more accurately characterizes the way people produce and comprehend language.

We first used this method to analyze the public speeches of 30 university students (Mulac, Lundell, & Bradac, 1986). Eleven trained individuals coded 35 language features selected as potential discriminators of gender. Results of the stepwise discriminant analysis showed that a combination of 20 of these variables permitted 100% accuracy of gender prediction. Language features found to be more indicative of women's speech were sentence-initial adverbials, oppositions, rhetorical questions, and references to emotion. (Remember that university student readers were not able to guess the sex of these speakers; see Mulac et al.). Features more prominent in men's speech were "I" references, present-tense verbs, vocalized pauses, and grammatical errors. This provided clear evidence of gender-linked language differences in public speaking.

Similarly, in Mulac and Lundell (1986), we analyzed oral descriptions of landscape photographs by 48 speakers ranging in age from 11 to 69 years. Here a combination of 17 variables predicted speaker gender with 87.5% accuracy. In Mulac et al. (1988), we applied the same approach to 71 dyadic interactions, coding 12 variables that significantly predicted interactant gender with 76% accuracy across same-sex and mixed-sex pairings.

We used the same method in another study (Mulac et al., 1990) to determine whether 16 girls and 16 boys from each of three public school groups (4th, 8th, and 12th grades) differed in their written essays. Again, significant discriminant analyses indicated that combinations of six to nine variables could be used to accurately predict gender for 84% to 87% of the 32 writers from each grade level. Similar results were uncovered in a study of 40 university students' written photograph descriptions (Mulac & Lundell, 1994), in which 72% accuracy of gender reclassification was established.

We found additional support for gender differences in our analysis of 108 university students' problem-solving interactions in same-sex and mixed-sex pairs (Mulac & Bradac, 1995). In that study, we found that a combination of 12 features could be used to accurately determine interactant gender for 70% of the individuals. Finally, we found significant gender determination in 140 interactions of spouses and strangers (members of 20 couples engaging in seven dyadic interactions) with an identification accuracy of 78% (Fitzpatrick & Mulac, 1995; Fitzpatrick, Mulac, & Dindia, 1995). In all seven of our studies that employed this procedure, speaker or writer gender was predicted by a weighted combination of the language features, with an accuracy substantially better than chance. In these investigations, the computer program was able to "guess" speaker gender, on the basis of language use, with an accuracy of 70% to 100%.

The results of these investigations indicate that trained language coders, working individually in teams of between 5 and 11 members, can provide linguistic data that demonstrate subtle language preferences, when analyzed by sophisticated statistical procedures. Through these means, we have discovered language differences so small that they escape the notice of intelligent, untrained adults who are unable to guess communicator sex. However, the question remains: If scholars have to employ teams of trained observers and high-powered statistical programs to ferret out these discriminators, just how important are these gender-linked language differences? Put another way, the question is this: Do language differences *really* make a difference?

EFFECT OF LANGUAGE DIFFERENCES

The Gender-Linked Language Effect

The answer to this question is a resounding "Yes!" The reason for the declamatory nature of this answer is that women's and men's language use leads them to be judged differently on psychological dimensions that are of consequence. That is, they are judged differently because of differences in their linguistic strategies. We have called this pattern of judgments the *Gender-Linked Language Effect.* This effect is defined as the evaluative consequences of gender-differentiating language use and has been investigated in a substantial number of communication settings.

In our research, we have had women and men of different ages read the female and male communicators' transcripts and then rate each speaker or writer as a person. For this purpose, the participants used a 12-item semantic differential, the SDAS (Mulac, 1975, 1976). Factor analyses of their ratings have consistently yielded the following three-factor structure: (a) Sociointellectual Status (high social status–low social status, white collar–blue collar, literate–illiterate, and rich–poor), (b) Aesthetic Quality (pleasant–unpleasant, beautiful–ugly, sweet–sour, and nice–awful), and (c) Dynamism (strong–weak, active–passive, loud–soft, and aggressive–unaggressive). Reliability coefficients from these investigations have shown that raters are able to use these psychological dimensions in a consistent, stable fashion.

Typical of this research was our investigation of 30 university students' first speech in a public-speaking class (Mulac & Lundell, 1982). We recorded over

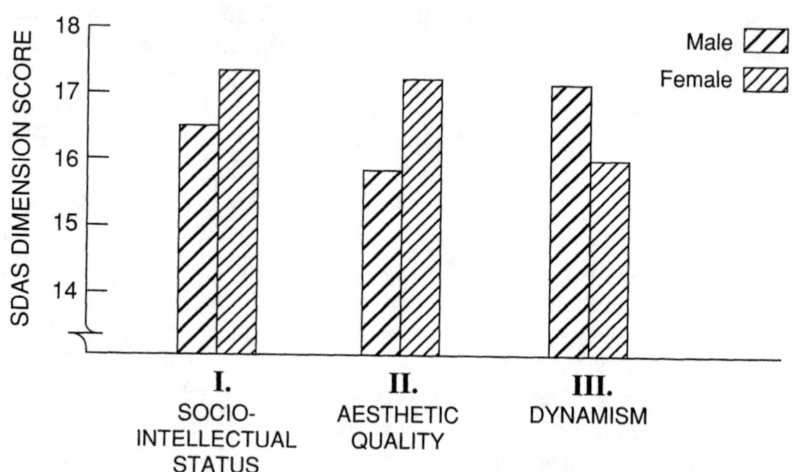

FIGURE 12.1. Mean SDAS dimension scores for male and female speakers, demonstrating the classic pattern of the Gender-Linked Language Effect (Mulac & Lundell, 1982).

one hundred 4- to 5-minute extemporaneous speeches, to inform or persuade, on a topic of the students' choice. To ensure that the speech topics did not reveal the sex of the speakers, we asked graduate teaching assistants to guess speaker sex from the speech topics (e.g., "Euthanasia," and "How to change a flat tire"). We chose for transcription the 15 male and 15 female speeches that yielded the lowest sex-guess accuracy. From these recordings, we produced 1-minute orthographic transcripts that were read by 204 university students, who, as mentioned earlier, unsuccessfully attempted to guess the sex of the speakers.

The 30 transcripts were then evaluated by two other groups of untrained raters, 132 students (median age = 19 years) and 126 older nonstudents (median age = 45), by using the 12-item SDAS (Mulac, 1975, 1976). Results demonstrated what has become the classic pattern of the Gender-Linked Language Effect: The women were generally rated higher on Sociointellectual Status and Aesthetic Quality, whereas the men were evaluated higher on Dynamism (see Fig. 12.1). That is, the women were seen as being more rich, literate, white collar, and high social status, as well as more beautiful, sweet, nice, and pleasant. In contrast, the men were perceived as being more active, strong, loud, and aggressive.

Although this general effect was substantial across the group of 30 speakers, it did not hold for all of them. For example, two of the top five rated speakers on Sociointellectual Status were men, although only one of the lowest five rated speakers on this dimension was a woman. The highest evaluated speaker on Aesthetic Quality was a man, although the next three were women and the bottom five were all men. Finally, on Dynamism, although the top rated three speakers were men (including the man who was judged highest on the first two dimensions), the fourth- and fifth-ranking scores were received by female speakers.

However, in spite of this within-gender variability, the overall effect, an effect that statistically took into account the within-gender variation, was striking in that it could have occurred by chance less than one time in 1,000. The effect sizes of these findings may be interpreted as small to medium for Intellectual Status, large for Aesthetic Quality, and medium for Dynamism (Cohen & Cohen, 1975, pp. 144–152).[4]

We first discovered what was to become the Gender-Linked Language Effect in a study of American dialects (Mulac & Rudd, 1977). In that investigation, we asked raters to evaluate, using the SDAS (Mulac, 1975, 1976), recordings of 12 speakers who represented three regions. In addition, we had another group of raters evaluate printed transcripts of what those speakers said, using the SDAS, in order to control statistically (through analysis of covariance) for the effect of the language used by the speakers. An analysis of reader judgments demonstrated that women's transcripts were rated higher on Aesthetic Quality and men's were judged higher on Dynamism, a partial glimpse at the pattern of effects that we would study in the ensuing program of research.

In a follow-up investigation (Mulac & Lundell, 1980) we sought to establish the effect with rigor and to determine whether it existed equally for different age groups: sixth graders, university freshmen and sophomores, graduate teaching assistants and lecturers, and people in their fifties and sixties. Forty-eight speakers, representing the four age groups, were recorded as they described landscape photographs, and 45-second segments were transcribed. Results demonstrated that the female speakers were rated higher on Sociointellectual Status and Aesthetic Quality, and the male speakers higher on Dynamism. In addition, we found that the male–female disparity was greater for the two older groups of speakers: (a) on Aesthetic Quality, older women were favored more in comparison with older men than were younger women compared with younger men; and (b) on Dynamism, older men were favored more in comparison with older women than were younger men over younger women. The literature on gender stereotypes shows that men are perceived as strong, active, hard, aggressive, and dominating, whereas women are thought to be charming, sensitive, and attractive (Mulac et al., 1985). Therefore, this finding suggests that the language effect measured for older speakers was more consistent with gender stereotypes than it was for younger speakers.

Although the afore mentioned efforts tested the effects of spoken communication, we also investigated consequences of written language. In the first of these studies (Mulac et al., 1990), we assessed the writing of three groups (32 students each) of primary and secondary school children: (a) 4th graders, (b) 8th graders,

[4]The percentage of variance accounted for by speaker gender was as follows, given in the form of eta squared: Sociointellectual Status = .06, Aesthetic Quality = .23, and Dynamism = .15.

and (c) 12th graders. In their English classes, they were asked to write an essay on this topic: "Is it important to tell the truth? Can it ever be better to lie?" Ratings of the 4th graders' transcripts favored girls on Sociointellectual Status and Aesthetic Quality, and boys on Dynamism. However, for the 8th and 12th graders, the only difference was on Dynamism, favoring boys. This showed the existence of the Gender-Linked Language Effect by the time students had reached the 4th grade. It also indicated the effect's modification by the 8th and 12th grades, by which time the boys had learned to write in ways that made them appear to be as literate and pleasant as the girls.

In our second study on the effects of writing, we requested that university students in a communication class write impromptu descriptions of two landscape photographs (Mulac & Lundell, 1994). Ratings of their 40 transcripts demonstrated the Gender-Linked Language Effect for Sociointellectual Status, Aesthetic Quality, and Dynamism. In contrast to the 8th and 12th graders writing philosophical essays in English classes (Mulac et al., 1990), these university students apparently felt less bound to follow formal requirements of essay writing. Interestingly, the judgments of their writing were virtually identical to the ones we found earlier for transcripts of university students' extemporaneous public speeches (Mulac & Lundell, 1982).

The final communication setting we analyzed was same-sex and mixed-sex dyadic interactions. In the first investigation (Mulac et al., 1988), we asked 63 male and 79 female university students to engage in the task of solving a problem, such as, "The five most important ingredients of personal success are . . . ," with a partner whom they did not know well. For same-sex dyads, the results showed support for the Gender-Linked Language Effect on Sociointellectual Status and Aesthetic Quality, but not on Dynamism, for which no differences were found. Faced with an interactive problem-solving task, in which participants were instructed that the quality of their solutions was paramount, the university women and men spoke with the same amount of strength and aggressiveness. As hypothesized on the basis of Speech Accommodation Theory (Giles, Mulac, Bradac, & Johnson, 1987), the results for mixed-sex dyads demonstrated a convergence of ratings for both male and female interactants.

In our latest assessment of language use and effects in paired interactions, we recorded 108 university students (54 men and 54 women) in both same-sex and mixed-sex dyads (Mulac & Bradac, 1995). Their task was to cooperatively solve problems, such as, "What are the best ways to relieve school stress?" and "How will life be different in the year 2000?" This design provided a direct test of potential language convergence and its effects, because the same men and women were measured in both dyad settings. Analyses supported the Gender-Linked Language Effect for all three dimensions, in both same-sex and mixed-sex interactions. That is, no language-effect accommodation was seen. In both dyad compositions, the women were rated higher on Sociointellectual Status and Aesthetic Quality, and the men were rated higher on Dynamism.

These findings are all the more important because, in all eight investigations that found evidence of the Gender-Linked Language Effect, the pattern of judgments provided by female and male raters was identical. That is, purely on the basis of communicators' language samples, women and men both perceive female communicators to be of a higher social status and more literate, as well as nicer and more beautiful, than male communicators. In contrast, both rated male communicators as stronger and more aggressive. This indicates that women and men have similar judgmental standards for gender-differentiating language use.

In three of these studies, we tested the possibility that older nonstudents (median age—older than 40 years) would render judgments that differed from university student raters (median age—younger than 20). These two age groups rated (a) university students' public speeches (Mulac & Lundell, 1982), (b) landscape photograph descriptions of older teachers (Mulac et al., 1985), and (c) essays of 4th, 8th, and 12th graders (Mulac et al., 1990). In all three investigations, the older nonstudents and university students provided virtually identical ratings of the transcript communicators. These results demonstrate that the same effect is perceived by both female observers and male observers, as well as those who are older adults or younger adults. These consistent findings substantiate, in a different way, the broad generalizibility of the consequences of gender-differentiating language.

Prediction of the Gender-Linked Language Effect From Language Features

In keeping with our final theoretical assumption, we examined the extent to which language differences are implicated in the psychological judgments that form the Gender-Linked Language Effect. For this purpose, we utilized stepwise multiple regression analyses to predict Sociointellectual Status, Aesthetic Quality, and Dynamism ratings on the basis of the gender-discriminating language features, such as references to emotion and elliptical sentences. As is the case with discriminant analysis, this multivariate procedure seeks to determine the weighted combination of variables that best explains the predicted, or criterion, variable. We reasoned that if the language features could predict a significant percentage of the variance in psychological judgments, then these features could be seen to be implicated in these judgments. To that extent, they would be truly resulting in the demonstrated outcome. In contrast, if that predictive link was not found, then the judgments would have to be the result of some factor other than gender-linked language.

Typical of this approach was our assessment of the effects of university students' impromptu photograph-description essays (Mulac & Lundell, 1994). Here, we sought to determine the extent to which the nine gender-discriminating linguistic variables found in the first phase of the investigation could predict the psychological ratings rendered by readers in the second phase. The stepwise multiple regression analysis predicting Sociointellectual Status ratings of the writers on the basis of their language use demonstrated a predictive link between the two. The first language feature to enter the predictive equation, and therefore the best overall predictor, was sentence-initial adverbials ("Because there's new snow on the trees and on the ground, this appears to be . . . "). Speakers who employed this form tended to receive higher Sociointellectual Status ratings. References to emotion, the second most important predictor ("There's a mournful quality . . . ") also led to higher ratings of status, and like the first predictor, was used more by female writers. The next two features, in order of importance, were judgmental adjectives ("This is fabulous!") and elliptical sentences ("Winter time."). Both features were displayed more in men's writing, and both were predictive of lower Sociointellectual Status ratings. Because of their use by men and women, and because of their effect on Sociointellectual Status perceptions, these first four features are consistent with the gender-linked language effect. The fifth, however, was not. Uncertainty verbs ("It seems to be early winter"), a female language feature, was found to be predictive of lower ratings of Sociointellectual Status, not higher. Although this was the last variable to enter the predictive equation, and was therefore the least important predictor, its effect was in conflict with the gender-linked language effect. However, use of uncertainty verbs lacked the necessary power to eliminate that effect. In terms of the second psychological dimension, Aesthetic Quality, substantial prediction was also evidenced for a different combination of features. However, in this study, language could not be tied to Dynamism scores, although later investigations were to show that Dynamism could also be predicted by gender-linked language.

In an assessment of oral descriptions of landscape photographs by sixth graders, university freshmen and sophomores, graduate teaching assistants, and people in their 50s and 60s (Mulac & Lundell, 1986), we reported that language differences predicted substantial proportions of the ratings on all three psychological dimensions. Similar results were obtained for university students' public speeches (Mulac et al., 1986), with language features again able to predict meaningful proportions of all three dimensions that distinguished speaker gender. In addition, our analysis of essays by 4th, 8th, and 12th graders showed that differences in language could meaningfully predict psychological ratings in 80% of the analyses (Mulac et al., 1990). Finally, our assessment of university students' same-sex and mixed-sex dyads also demonstrated that interactants' language use could meaningfully predict Sociointellectual Status, Aesthetic Quality, and Dynamism (Mulac & Bradac, 1995).

These five investigations showed that the gender-differentiating language features found in the linguistic analysis phase of the studies could predict 32% to 70% of the variance of the psychological ratings in the same studies. These results support our hypothesis that the effects found for gender differences in ratings are actually the result of the gender-linked language differences located in those same transcripts. Without this link between language and ratings, we could not properly call the phenomenon the Gender-Linked Language Effect.

Comparison of the Gender-Linked Language Effect and Gender Stereotypes

Finally, in a related experimental investigation (Mulac, Incontro, & James, 1985), we tested the correspondence of the Gender-Linked Language Effect and gender stereotypes. This comparison was prompted by our review of literature that demonstrated a startling similarity between these two effects. We therefore tested the extent to which judgments based on gender stereotypes and those based on effects of gender-linked language were (a) *independent* of each other (i.e., could be produced separately or in combination) and (b) *related* to each other (having similar patterns). In this study, we experimentally manipulated the same set of 12 photograph-description transcripts to produce four transcript conditions: (a) language effect only (with speaker sex not indicated and not guessable), (b) language plus stereotype (speaker sex correctly identified 100% of the time), (c) stereotype effect only (50% correct sex identification, balanced for language), and (d) language pitted against stereotype (0% correct identification).

The language effect was produced by transcripts of the 12 speakers, for which speaker sex was not identified and could not be accurately guessed (as indicated by our sex-guess data). The gender stereotype effect was produced by having the same 12 transcripts rated, but with 50% of the six women's transcripts identified as "A WOMAN" and the other 50% indicated as "A MAN." The same manipulation of attributed speaker sex was also accomplished for the six men's transcripts. We found the female stereotype scores by combining all six transcripts' ratings identified as "A WOMAN," one half of which were really those of male speakers. The male stereotype scores combined all six ratings for "A MAN," one half of which were actually spoken by female speakers. In this way, we experimentally controlled the effect of the speakers' language.

Analysis of ratings for the four conditions supported the independence of the two effects: Each consequence could be produced without the other being present, both could be combined congruently to double their effect, and, when pitted against each other, they canceled out each other.

However, in the "look-alike contest" to assess their similarity, the correlation of judgments resulting from stereotypes of men and women, as compared with those resulting from language of men and women, demonstrated an astoundingly high relationship ($r = .93$; see Fig. 12.2). That is, the two effects shared a remarkable 86% of the individual effect variance. Therefore, even though the two effects are independent of each other, their pattern is virtually identical. This implies that the way men and women speak or write reinforces gender stereotypes. It also suggests that gender stereotypes might influence the way people learn to speak, perhaps as a manifestation of cultural expectations.

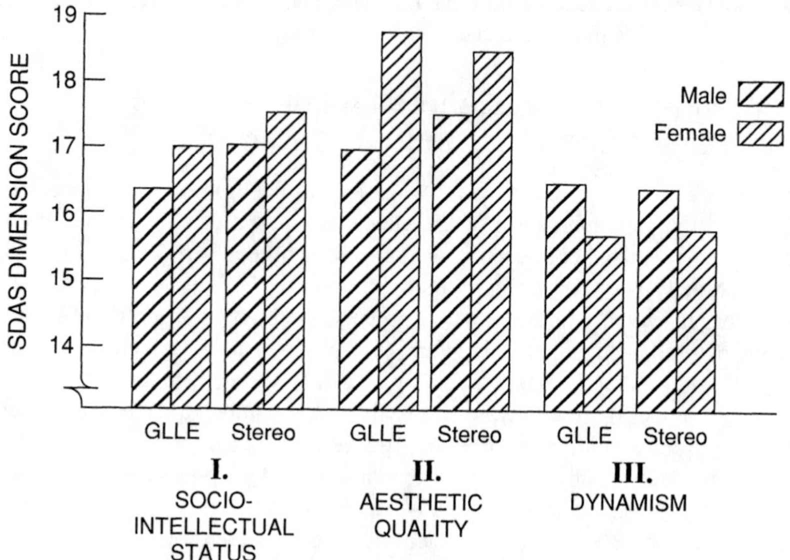

FIGURE 12.2. Mean SDAS dimension scores for the Gender-Linked Language Effect (GLLE) and sex-role stereotype effect for male and female speakers (Mulac et al., 1985).

IMPLICATIONS OF THE FINDINGS

Our findings for women's and men's language use present a curious paradox: We observe, at the same time, similarity *and* difference. Far from appearing as if they come from different planets, the women and men we have studied appear to have come from different sections of the same country. It is obvious that they grew up in different sociolinguistic cultural groups, groups that have subtly different styles and therefore subtly different ways of accomplishing the same communication task.

The findings that support the notion of similarities in language choice are twofold. First, as we have seen, when the communication of men and women, or boys and girls, is transcribed and presented to university students whose first language is American English, the students are not able to guess the sex of the communicators with an accuracy that is any better than chance. This was the consistent finding in all five of our empirical investigations that tested communicators' sex "guessability." Because native speakers of American English cannot identify the sex of these individuals, the communicators must be displaying a high degree of linguistic similarity. In addition to the lack of guessability, we have observed that the summary statistics of how much male and female speakers use particular language features argues more for their similarity than it does for their difference.

In contrast, however, we have related findings that demonstrate significant differences in men's and women's linguistic style. Our summary of over 30 empirical investigations showed 16 variables that generally characterize stylistic differences. Features used more often by male communicators included references to quantity, judgmental adjectives, elliptical sentences, directives, locatives, and "I" references. Those employed more by female speakers and writers were intensive adverbs, references to emotions, dependent clauses, sentence-initial adverbials, uncertainty verbs, oppositions, negations, hedges, questions, and longer mean length sentences. This long list of linguistic preferences certainly weighs in heavily on the side of the difference argument. Moreover, these 16 features provide a consistent and coherent pattern in which male style is perceived by observers as direct, succinct, personal, and instrumental. Female preferences are at the other end of these stylistic dimensions—indirect, elaborate, and affective.

In addition, statistical analyses have located weighted combinations of language features, coded for the transcripts, that accurately determine communicator gender at a precision of 70% to 100%, even though untrained readers cannot. The results of seven investigations have demonstrated the efficacy of this approach for locating clusters of linguistic features that distinguish gender.

Of greatest importance for the difference argument is the fact that, although subtle, the language differences have judgmental consequences. That is, observers perceive the female and male speakers differently, based on their language use. The pattern of these perceptions, the Gender-Linked Language Effect, consists of female communicators being rated higher on Sociointellectual Status (high social status and literate) and Aesthetic Quality (nice and beautiful), whereas male communicators are rated higher on Dynamism (strong and aggressive). The results of eight studies have supported this outcome, in whole or in part. Even though the magnitude of the effect appears to be of moderate size, its pervasive nature amplifies its impact in daily communication. This effect has been found in a variety of communication tasks with people of different ages, as indicated earlier.

In support of another theoretical assumption, we have demonstrated in five investigations that gender-based language differences are implicated in the effect. The findings show that the communicators' gender-distinguishing language use could predict 30% to 70% of their gender-differentiating psychological ratings. Thus we can see that the consistent establishment of the Gender-Linked Language Effect answers the challenge: "*So what* if men and women use language differently?"

Finally, we have shown that the Gender-Linked Language Effect is independent of gender stereotypes. That is, either one can be induced experimentally without the other, they can be joined to double their effect, and they can be pitted against each other to cancel out each other. However, in spite of their demonstrated independence, the results also show that the pattern of judgments emerging from the two effects is overwhelmingly similar—the two manifest an 86% degree of similarity. This finding suggests that societally held norms may play a part in the learning of gender-appropriate language use, and at the same time that stereotypes are reinforced by everyday speech and writing. The mechanism that causes this similarity of effects will require substantial investigation in the future. We have already begun the process by proposing the causal chain, as yet untested, that we believe can provide the explanation (Mulac, Bradac, & Palomares (Nov, 2003).

We are left with a paradox: Our findings indicate that, along with overwhelming similarities in their use of language, women and men produce subtle differences in a wide variety of communication contexts. This is important because observers are responsive to these subtle differences as they make judgments about women and men, judgments that are remarkably similar to those brought about by gender stereotypes. Moreover, these evaluations are the same, whether the observer is female or male, middle-aged or young. No matter who makes the appraisals, the subtle language differences have substantial consequences in how communicators are evaluated. The inescapable conclusion is this: The language differences *really do* make a difference!

ACKNOWLEDGMENTS

A. Mulac acknowledges Sandra L. Thompson's generous and insightful comments on an earlier version of the chapter.

REFERENCES

Cohen, J., & Cohen, P. (1975). *Applied multiple regression/correlation analysis for the behavioral sciences.* Hillside, NJ: Lawrence Erlbaum Associates.

Fitzpatrick, M. A., & Mulac, A. (1995). Relating to spouse and stranger: Gender-preferential language use. In P. J. Kalbfleisch & M. J. Cody (Eds.), *Gender, power and communication* (pp. 213–231). Hillsdale, NJ: Lawrence Erlbaum Associates.

Fitzpatrick, M. A., Mulac, A., & Dindia, K. (1995). Gender-preferential language use in spouse and stranger interaction. *Journal of Language and Social Psychology, 14*, 18–39.

Giles, H., Mulac, A., Bradac, J. J., & Johnson, P. (1987). Speech accommodation theory: The first decade and beyond. In M. L. McLaughlin (Ed.), *Communication yearbook, 10* (pp. 13–48). Newbury Park, CA: Sage.

Giles, H., Scherer, K. R., & Taylor, D. M. (1979). Speech markers in social interaction. In K. R. Scherer and H. Giles (Eds.), *Social markers in speech.* Cambridge, England: Cambridge University Press.

Gudykunst, W. B., & Ting-Toomey, S. (1988). *Culture and interpersonal communication.* Newbury Park, CA: Sage.

Kerlinger, F. N. (1973). *Foundations of behavioral research* (2nd ed.). New York: Holt, Rinehart & Winston.

Lachenbruch, P. A., & Mickey, M. R. (1968). Estimation of error rates in discriminant analysis. *Technometrics, 10,* 1–11.

Maltz, D. N., & Borker, R. A. (1982). A cultural approach to male–female miscommunication. In J. J. Gumperz (Ed.), *Language and social identity* (pp. 196–216). Cambridge, England: Cambridge University Press.

McMillan, J. R., Clifton, A. K., McGrath, D., & Gale, W. S. (1977). Women's language: Uncertainty or interpersonal sensitivity and emotionality? *Sex Roles, 3,* 545–559.

Mulac, A. (1975). Evaluation of the speech dialect attitudinal scale. *Speech Monographs, 42,* 1982–1989.

Mulac, A. (1976). Assessment and application of the revised speech dialect attitudinal scale. *Communication Monographs, 43,* 238–245.

Mulac, A. (1998). Language in combination—does it happen any other way? Multiple-variable analysis of gender-linked language differences. In S. Wertheim, A.C. Bailey, & M. Corston-Oliver (Eds.), *Engendering communication: Proceedings of the fifth Berkeley women and language conference* (pp. 391–402).

Mulac, A., & Bradac, J. J. (1995). Women's style in problem solving interactions: Powerless, or simply feminine? In P. J. Kalbfleish and M. J. Cody (Eds.), *Gender, power and communication* (pp. 83–104). Hillsdale, NJ: Lawrence Erlbaum Associates.

Mulac, A., Bradac, J. J., & Gibbons, P. (2001). Empirical support for the gender-as-Culture hypothesis: An intercultural analysis of male/female language differences, *Human Communication Research, 27,* 121–152.

Mulac, A., Bradac, J. J., & Palomares, N. A. (2003, Nov), A general process model of the gender-linked language effect: Anticedents and consequences of language used by men and women, Meeting of the International Communication Association in San Diago, CA.

Mulac, A., Bradac, J. J., & Mann, S. K. (1985). Male/female language differences and attributional consequences in children's television. *Human Communication Research, 11,* 481–506.

Mulac, A., Erlandson, K. T., Farrar, W. J., Hallett, J. S., Molloy, J. L., & Prescott, M. E. (1998). "Uh-huh. What's that all about?" Differing interpretations of conversational backchannels and questions as sources of miscommunication across gender boundaries. *Communication Research, 25,* 641–668.

Mulac, A., Incontro, C. R., & James, M. R. (1985). Comparison of the gender-linked language effect and sex role stereotypes. *Journal of Personality and Social Psychology, 49,* 1099–1110.

Mulac, A., & Lundell, T. L. (1980). Differences in perceptions created by syntactic-semantic productions of male and female speakers. *Communication Monographs, 47,* 111–118.

Mulac, A., & Lundell, T. L. (1982). An empirical test of the gender-linked language effect in a public speaking setting. *Language and Speech, 25,* 243–256.

Mulac, A., & Lundell, T. L. (1986). Linguistic contributors to the gender-linked language effect. *Journal of Language and Social Psychology, 5,* 81–101.

Mulac, A., & Lundell, T. L. (1994). Effects of gender-linked language differences in adults' written discourse: Multivariate tests of language effects. *Language and Communication, 14,* 299–309.

Mulac, A., Lundell, T. L., & Bradac, J. J. (1986). Male/female language differences and attributional consequences in a public speaking situation: Toward an explanation of the gender-linked language effect. *Communication Monographs, 53,* 115–129.

Mulac, A., & Rudd, M. J. (1977). Effects of selected American regional dialects upon regional audience members. *Communication Monographs, 44,* 185–195.

Mulac, A., Studley, L. B., & Blau, S. (1990). The gender-linked language effect in primary and secondary students' impromptu essays. *Sex Roles, 23,* 439–469.

Mulac, A., Wiemann, J. M., Widenmann, S. J., & Gibson, T. W. (1988). Male/female language differences and effects in same-sex and mixed-sex dyads: The gender-linked language effect. *Communication Monographs, 55,* 315–335.

Smith, P. M. (1985). *Language, the sexes and society.* Oxford: Basil Blackwell.

Tannen, D. (1994). *Gender and discourse.* New York: Oxford University Press.

Theil, H. (1971). *Principles of econometrics.* New York: Wiley.

13

Sex Differences in Emotional Communication

Laura K. Guerrero
Arizona State University

Susanne M. Jones
University of Minnesota, Twin Cities

Renee Reiter Boburka
East Stroudsburg University

Emotions are affective reactions to stimuli that threaten to interrupt, impede, or enhance an individual's goals (Frijda, 1993). Expressions of emotion are shaped by biologically based action tendencies as well as cultural display rules that dictate how an emotion should be communicated within a specific context (Planalp, 1999). In line with this conceptualization of emotional expression, research on sex differences in emotional communication is often guided by bioevolutionary or social learning explanations. Often, biology and socialization are viewed as interactive forces that shape emotional experience and expression (Andersen & Guerrero, 1998b; Brody, 1985; Buck, 1983). For example, Ekman's (1971) neurocultural theory of emotion specifies that men and women are born with innate predispositions for expressing emotions in particular ways, but these natural tendencies are curbed by learned cultural display rules.

In this chapter, we review research on sex differences in emotional communication while advancing the argument that these differences are consistent with both bioevolutionary and social learning explanations. We also contend that sex differences in emotional communication are embedded within a larger pattern of similarities. For purposes of this review, we chose to summarize sex differences in the experience and expression of four emotions—positive affect, anger, sadness or depression, and jealousy. We chose positive affect, which includes emotions such as joy, liking, warmth, and love, because expressing such emotions helps people develop and maintain close relationships (Guerrero & Andersen, 2001). Negative emotions, particularly those related to hostility (such as anger and jealousy) and sadness, can play a role in disrupting relationships (Guerrero & Andersen, 2001). Anger, sadness, and jealousy represent negative emotions with distinct foci. Anger is usually outwardly directed and focuses on external causes; sadness is typically intropunitive, internalized, and self-directed (Brody & Hall, 1993). Jealousy, in contrast, involves a threat to the quality or existence of one's romantic relationship (White & Mullen, 1989). Thus, these three emotions represent unpleasant emotions that are directed at others, the self, or the relationship. Before reviewing literature related to sex differences in communicating these four emotions, we briefly summarize key literature connecting emotion to bioevolutionary and socialization processes.

PERSPECTIVES ON SEX DIFFERENCES IN EMOTIONAL EXPRESSION

Biological and Evolutionary Explanations

Research on the biological bases for sex differences in emotional communication has focused on three main lines of thought: (a) selection processes and evolution; (b) hormones and temperament; and (c) cerebral hemispheric processing. Darwin (1872) was among the first scholars to suggest that the ability to experience and express emotions is passed from generation to generation. According to Darwin, those who are best able to express emotions effectively are more likely to survive and reproduce. In line with the "selection process" explanation, Buck (1983) argued that the ability to encode and decode emotional states has adaptive value. Individuals who express emotion accurately signal their needs and intentions to other group members. Those who are skilled at responding to the emotional states of others are likely to be highly valued members of families and communities. Hall (1978) forwarded a similar argument when she stated that women may be " 'wired' from birth to be especially sensitive to nonverbal cues or to be especially quick learners of such cues. This would make evolutionary sense, because nonverbal sensitivity on a mother's part might enable her to detect distress in her youngsters or threatening signals from other adults, thus enhancing the survival chances of her offspring" (p. 854). In contrast, men may be wired to control certain emotions. For example, controlling fear displays had adaptive value when men were hunting or combating predators. Men may also have an innate ability to encode aggressive, hostile expressions in competitive situations. Thus, being able to decode social emotions may have had more adaptive value for women than men, whereas being able to express anger and control emotions such as fear may have had more adaptive value for men than women.

According to the biological perspective, evolution and natural selection processes, along with genetic heritage, contribute to sex differences in hormones and temperament that lead to sex differences in social behavior, including emotional communication (see also Andersen, chap. 7, this volume). For instance, rising hormonal levels are positively related to sad and anxious affect in adolescent boys (Susman et al., 1987) and girls (Brooks-Gunn & Warren, 1989). Because people are more likely to express intense emotions, Brody (1993) concluded that hormones contribute to the development of emotional expressiveness during adolescence, although less significantly than do social influences. Other research has connected emotional experience to hormones in adults. For example, Cadispoti et al. (2003) found that pleasant stimuli induced increases in prolactin (a hormone that also increases during pregnancy and breastfeeding); unpleasant stimuli decreased prolactin while increasing other hormones related to adrenaline. Because men and women experience different types and levels of hormones, they may experience, and ultimately express, certain emotions differently. In terms of temperament, some theorists have suggested that infant boys express emotion with more intensity than do infant girls (e.g., Malatesta & Haviland, 1982), leading parents to discourage boys from expressing emotion if their affect level is already overly intense (Brody, 1985). This difference in parental behavior, which may have been based initially on temperamental differences between sons and daughters, likely contributes to later sex differences in emotional expressiveness.

Finally, neurological differences between the sexes likely influence emotional communication. For example, some scholars have suggested that men process emotional information by using the more analytic left hemisphere of the brain to a greater extent than do women, and that men's brains work harder than women's when decoding emotion. In contrast, women purportedly use more intuitive right-hemispheric strategies for emotional processing and also use both cerebral hemispheres more symmetrically (e.g., Brody, 1993; Buck, 1982; Witelson, 1976). Although some researchers have cautioned against accepting these conclusions as fact until more research is conducted (e.g., Bleier, 1991; Bryden, 1982), sex differences in cerebral processing are likely to have some effect on emotional functioning.

Socialization Explanations

Although innate, biological forces set the stage for sex differences in emotional functioning, socialization reinforces and solidifies these differences. Research shows that parents play an important role in this differential socialization process. For example, parents discuss emotions more often with girls than boys (except anger, disgust, contempt, and other outwardly negative emotions) and tend to exhibit more facial expressions to girls than to boys (Brody, 1993). Dunn, Bretherton, and Munn (1987) demonstrated that mothers talk more about emotions with their 18- to 24-month-old daughters and, by age 2, girls (relative to boys) produce more emotion words. Similarly, Fivush (1989) found that mothers generally focused more on the emotion state with daughters and, conversely, on the cause and consequence of the emotion state with sons. For example, if a girl falls down and skins her knee, the mother may ask, "How much does it hurt?" If a boy is hurt, she may focus on the action rather than the emotion (e.g., "Did you fall down and go boom?"). Fivush concluded that parents teach their sons control over emotions (with the exception of anger) while teaching daughters to be more sensitive to emotion.

It also appears that boys are raised to be independent and emotionally guarded, whereas girls are raised to seek and give emotional support. Block (1973) found that parents encourage boys more than girls to control affective expression, be independent, and assume personal responsibility, whereas parents encourage girls more than boys to be emotionally expressive but nonaggressive. Conversely, parents encourage sons to be aggressive but unemotional. Thus, parents tend to act in more instrumental, task-oriented, mastery-emphasizing ways with sons and in more expressive, less achievement-oriented, dependency-reinforcing ways with daughters (Block, 1973). This differentiation is hypothesized to contribute to later sex differences in emotional expressiveness and control (Greif, Alvarez, & Ulman, 1981; Malatesta & Haviland, 1982). In one study of adolescents (11 to 17 years old), Stapley and Haviland (1989) found that boys viewed activities and achievement to be particularly emotionally salient, whereas girls viewed affiliation as especially emotionally salient. In another study of adolescents (12 to 18 years old), O'Kearney and Dadds (2004) found that boys were more likely than girls to describe anger by using outwardly directed words related to aggression, whereas girls were more likely than boys to describe anger as controlled and inner directed.

Brody (1985; Brody & Hall, 1993) summarized the implications of prior literature on socialization processes. She argued that boys learn to inhibit the expression of emotions through words or facial expressions, with the exception of outwardly directed negative emotions such as anger and contempt. In contrast, girls are encouraged to express their emotions through words and facial expressions, with the exception of socially unacceptable emotions such as anger, which they learn to inhibit. Various studies have demonstrated that for boys the level of expressiveness for all emotions decreases with age, whereas for girls only the expression of negative affect decreases (Saarni, 1982).

Summary and Extension

The bioevolutionary perspective suggests that different types of emotional expression were adaptive for men and women throughout the ages. Moreover, differences in hormones, temperament, and brain functioning may underlie some sex differences in both the experience and expression of emotion. The social learning perspective suggests that children learn how to display emotions through modeling and reinforcement, with boys taught to inhibit most emotional expressions related to fear and sadness, and girls taught to be emotionally expressive, affiliative, and sensitive while inhibiting emotional expressions related to anger and aggression.

Biology and socialization interact to influence sex differences in social skills related to emotion. On the basis of biology, men and women are predisposed to possess different types and levels of skill related to emotion. These predispositions are strengthened or modified through socialization, with girls and boys learning to express their emotions in socially accepted "feminine" or "masculine" ways, respectively. Indeed, by adulthood, men and women exhibit different profiles of social skills. Women exhibit superior skills in emotional sensitivity and have a slight advantage in accurately decoding nonverbal behaviors (e.g., Guerrero & Reiter, 1998; Hall, 1979, 1984; Hall, Carter, & Horgan, 2000; Riggio, 1986). Women also exhibit more emotional expressivity than men. In fact, Burgoon and Bacue (2003) concluded that findings related to sex differences in emotional expressivity "are highly reliable and are large enough to be socially meaningful" in that the effect size is typically moderate (p. 184).

In general, and consistent with socialization explanations, research suggests that men may have a small advantage when it comes to inhibiting and controlling emotional displays (e.g., Guerrero & Reiter, 1998; Riggio, 1986, 1993). However, these studies only show that men may be better at inhibiting, de-intensifying, or masking emotion than women; they do not suggest that men are better at intensifying or simulating emotion. For example, Riggio's research, as well as Guerrero and Reiter's study, focused specifically on emotional control, which was measured with items such as "I am able to conceal my true feelings from just about anyone" and "I am very good at maintaining a calm exterior, even when I'm upset." The effect sizes associated with sex differences in emotional control are generally small, with sex accounting for only 5% to 10% of the variance. Research focusing on the expression of various emotions (e.g., anger, fear, and sadness) and various types of display rules (e.g., inhibition vs. simulation) may uncover larger effect sizes that are consistent with hypotheses related to evolutionary and socialization explanations. For instance, women may exhibit more skill related to inhibiting angry expressions and simulating or exaggerating positive emotions, whereas men may exhibit more skill related to inhibiting sad or fearful expressions.

SEX DIFFERENCES IN COMMUNICATING SPECIFIC EMOTIONS

In addition to sex differences in emotional skill, bioevolutionary and social learning explanations suggest that men and women should differ in how they express various emotions. Importantly, findings related to specific emotional expressions show that sex differences go beyond *how much* women and men communicate various emotions; they extend to *the ways* in which women and men communicate various emotions. The profiles of sex differences vary on the basis of which emotion is being expressed, but, in general, women tend to focus somewhat more on maintaining interpersonal relationships through emotional expression than do men.

Positive Affect

According to both evolutionary and social learning perspectives, women should express more positive affect than men. Evolutionary theorists have argued that the ability to get along with others is essential for survival (Hohan, 1982; Trivers, 1985). Being able to communicate emotions "such as liking and loving are social adhesives insofar as they bind individuals together in friendships, coalitions, and mating pairs" that help people survive (Dillard, 1998, p. xxiii). The need to affiliate with others may be especially strong for women because of the biological and emotional investments they make in their children. Pregnancy and breastfeeding help bond mothers to their offspring, leading to outward signs of affiliation and attachment. Furthermore, LaFrance and Henley (1994) argued that women may have developed skills related to the expression of positive emotion and the ability to decode the emotional states of others as a survival mechanism that evolved to compensate for their relative lack of physical strength compared with men. Interestingly, research has confirmed that women who are skilled in encoding nonverbal cues associated with happiness tend to be more popular (Coats & Feldman, 1996), which comports with the evolutionary hypothesis that women's expressions of positive affect were adaptive behaviors that enhanced interpersonal relationships and group cooperation. For men, however, the ability to use expressive cues is unrelated to perceptions of friendliness, warmth (Tucker & Friedman, 1993), and popularity (Coats & Feldman, 1996).

Of course, given cultural expectations, the ability to express positive emotion may be a more valuable social skill for women than for men. Research from a socialization perspective has shown that people encourage girls to express more positive affect and be more socially oriented than boys. For example, studies have demonstrated that mothers express more positive affect to their infant and toddler daughters than to their same-age sons (e.g., Malatesta, Culver, Tesman, & Shepard, 1989). Beckwith (1972) contended that, as a result of this differential treatment, girls tend to be more socially oriented during infancy than boys. Klein and Durfee (1978) determined that, by the time children reach their first birthday, girls direct more positive behavior to their mothers than do boys. Cherry and Lewis (1976) showed that, as children grow older, mothers engage in increasingly active verbal interaction with their daughters, but they encourage their sons to seek physical independence and handle problems on their own.

Through socialization, girls learn that people expect them to express positive emotion and engage in affiliative behavior. Indeed, according to Eagly's (1983, 1987) application of social role theory, children learn what constitutes feminine and masculine behavior by observing and modeling adult behavior. Girls are socialized to show femininity through cooperation, affiliation, and the expression of positive emotions. Similarly, LaFrance, Hecht, and Noyes (1994) advanced the expressivity demand theory to explain sex differences in adults' emotional communication. According to this theory, the sex of communicators, their relationship with one another, and the situation they find themselves in work together to influence how much people express emotion. In many situations and relationships, women are expected to be more expressive than men, especially in terms of showing affiliation, so women learn to conform to this expectation. Consistent with sex-role theory and expressivity demand theory, women tend to exhibit more positive emotion and nonverbal immediacy than men (Burgoon & Bacue, 2003). Nonverbal immediacy behaviors include close conversational distances, direct body orientation, forward lean, positive forms of touch, smiling, head nods that indicate agreement, head tilts toward someone, mutual eye contact, a relaxed and open body position, and a warm, expressive voice (Andersen & Guerrero, 1998a).

One of the most consistent findings related to sex differences in nonverbal immediacy is that women tend to smile more and look more facially pleasant than men (Burgoon & Bacue, 2003; Hall, 1984, 1998). On the basis of a meta-analysis of 15 studies, Hall (1984) concluded that the effect size for sex differences in smiling is about .30. Women are more likely than men to smile when experiencing happiness (Coats & Feldman, 1996). Women are also more likely than men to smile as a way of communicating friendliness or politeness even when they are not experiencing any positive affect (LaFrance & Mayo, 1978). Because women are expected to smile more, when a woman fails to smile she may be judged as unfriendly or assumed to be in a bad mood. People are less likely to make such judgments if a man fails to smile. In line with the notion that women smile as a way to show friendliness, Hall and Halberstadt (1986) demonstrated that women only tend to smile more in social situations. When people are observed alone, sex differences in smiling tend to be small or nonexistent (see also Hall, 1984). Relationship type may also affect whether men or women smile more. Guerrero (1997) found that, although women tended to smile and look more facially pleasant than men when interacting with same-sex or opposite-sex friends, there were no sex differences in romantic relationships.

People use nonverbal immediacy to express love as well as general affiliation. Specifically, when people are asked to identify behavior that communicates love, they mention behaviors such as saying "I love you," sitting or standing close to one another, touching, having sex, smiling, using loving gazes, spending time together, using warm vocal tones, giving gifts, giving and wearing rings, and dressing a certain way for one another (Marston & Hecht, 1999; Shaver, Schwartz, Kirson, & O'Connor, 1987). In general, women tend to display more of these affiliative behaviors than do men (Burgoon & Bacue, 2003). For example, women are generally rated as using more eye contact and reinforcing head nods than men (Briton & Hall, 1995; LaFrance & Hecht, 2000), and sex differences in nonverbal immediacy behaviors such as these are relatively stable across age and setting (Hall & Friedman, 1999). However, when specific behaviors are isolated, there are some important exceptions to the general finding that women show more affiliation than men. Some research suggests that men are more likely than women to display resources by giving gifts to romantic partners (e.g., Buss, 1988) or to lean forward during conversations (Guerrero, 1997; Hall, 1985). In addition, relational stage and setting may moderate sex differences in some affiliative behaviors, such as touching and saying "I love you."

In terms of touch, although some studies have found men to touch women more in public, nonintimate settings (Henley, 1973; Major, Schmidlin, & Williams, 1990), this sex difference either vanishes or reverses in intimate, private settings (Major et al.; Stier & Hall, 1984). Indeed, in their summary of the literature, Burgoon and Bacue (2003) concluded that, in general, women touch and are touched more than men. However, three observational studies demonstrate that men are more likely to initiate public touch in the beginning stages of romantic relationships, whereas women are more likely to initiate public touch in marriages (Guerrero & Andersen, 1994; Willis & Briggs, 1992; Willis & Dodds, 1998). Furthermore, Hall and Veccia (1990) found that, although men and women touched one another equally overall, there were differences when age and body part were considered. For touches involving the hand, men tended to touch women more, whereas touches not involving the hand seemed to be initiated slightly more by women. Younger men (under 30 years of age) were also more likely to initiate touch than older men. These findings might be related to sex differences associated with relationship type, rather than age, because people in the under 30 group are less likely to be married or in long-term relationships. Willis and Dodds, who examined both age and relationship type, found that men under 20 years of age who were in the courtship stage of their relationship tended to initiate the most touch, especially to intimate body parts such as the lips, face, and knees. Among the women, those in their forties were more likely to initiate touch than those in their thirties or twenties, or under 20.

A similar pattern emerges for the phrase "I love you." Research suggests that, although nonverbal and verbal behaviors play equivalent roles in communicating love, saying "I love you" may be the single most important way of showing love to a partner (Marston & Hecht, 1999). In a diary study of dating relationships, Owen (1987) demonstrated that men are more likely than women to say "I love you" first. Owen explained this finding by suggesting that men are socialized to be more proactive during courtship than women, whereas women are taught to wait until the partner reveals his feelings before saying "I love you." Once the relationship is committed, women are then freer to say "I love you" more. If this is indeed the case, saying "I love you" first is a good example of a situation in which men are socialized to be more expressive than women. Similar explanations have been given for the finding that men initiate touch more than women in the initial stages of a relationship whereas the reverse is true when partners are married. Willis and

Dobbs (1998) postulated that this sex difference is consistent with evolutionary explanations of courtship behavior, which cast men as interested in initiating sexual relationships, and women as interested in preserving long-term bonds.

Aside from the considerable research indicating that women tend to express positive emotions more often and in different ways than men, research suggests that people decode women's behavior as more affiliative than men's, even when the behavior is similar. For example, a smile is usually perceived as a sign of affiliation, regardless of who shows it. However, a smiling woman is often evaluated as even more affiliative (as well as less dominant) than a smiling man (Jansz, 2000; LaFrance & Hecht, 2000). In other studies, expressions of happiness or pleasantness by women were rated as showing more joy than similar expressions by men (Hess, Blairy, & Kleck, 1997; Wagner, Buck, & Winterbotham, 1993).

Anger and Aggression

Although the ability to express positive emotions is a valued skill for women in the United States, the ability to express anger is not. Research from the evolutionary and social learning traditions suggests that men should more readily express anger through aggression than women. Scholars have argued that competition, as well as the negative emotions that accompany such competition (e.g., anger, jealousy), helped men acquire and maintain resources necessary for survival throughout the ages (Dillard, 1998; Hohan, 1982). Whereas women may have evolved an enhanced ability to obtain and guard resources through cooperation and social affiliation, men may have relied more on the ability to attack and intimidate. Given men's role as hunters and protectors throughout much of human evolutionary history, it makes sense that men would be hardwired to display anger through more aggressive, dominant means than women. Men's hormones (particularly testosterone) are also related to aggressive tendencies (e.g., Sullivan, 2000).

Developmental research indicates that people have different expectations regarding the experience and expression of anger for boys versus girls. In a classic study, Condry and Condry (1976) found that supposed knowledge of an infant's sex affected how adult observers interpreted the infant's emotional state. Adult observers who were told they were watching a baby boy were more likely to label the infant's negative affect as "anger." In contrast, adults who were told they were observing a baby girl were more likely to label the infant's negative affect as "fear." Boys also tend to play with more aggressive toys (such as play guns or military action figures) and to read and watch more aggressive stories. Greif et al. (1981) demonstrated that parents developed different stories with wordless books when interacting with their preschool sons versus daughters. With the exception of anger-related emotions, fathers used more emotion words such as *happy*, *sad*, and *love* when creating stories for their daughters compared with their sons. Mothers used more anger-related words such as *mad* and *hate* when developing stories for their sons compared with their daughters.

Boys are also more likely to receive parental attention when they express anger aggressively, whereas girls are more likely to be punished or ignored (Lemerise & Dodge, 1993). Thus, the aggressive expression of anger is reinforced for boys but discouraged for girls. Mills and Rubin (1992) found that mothers became more tolerant of their sons' aggressive behavior and more punishing of their daughters' aggressive behavior as they moved from preschool to elementary school. Fuchs and Thelen (1988) found that elementary-school-aged girls expected their mothers to act negatively toward them if they displayed anger but positively if they displayed sadness. In contrast, elementary-school-aged boys expected their parents to react negatively if they expressed sadness rather than anger, Perry, Perry, and Weiss (1989) found a similar pattern for adolescents—girls were more likely than boys to report that their aggressive behavior would be viewed as unacceptable and lead to punishment.

Other research on children and adolescents supports the idea that boys exhibit anger more outwardly and aggressively than do girls. Harris and Howard (1987) found that adolescent boys report more intense anger experiences than adolescent girls, which presumably leads to an increased likelihood of expressing anger. Boys also use more retaliation and aggression in response to anger (Fabes & Eisenberg, 1992; Jones, Peacock, & Christopher, 1992), including hitting, whereas girls are more likely to employ both approach and avoidant strategies when coping with anger (Whitesell, Robinson, & Harter,1991).

Research on adults has produced less consistent findings regarding sex differences in anger expression, perhaps because men are better able to curb their aggressive tendencies than boys. Some studies support the hypothesis that women inhibit angry aggression. Shields (1984) found that men and women did not differ in the degree to which they felt anger, but women reported feeling more physiological symptoms of anger, perhaps because they held their anger inside rather than expressing it. Similarly, Buck (1979) argued that in aggressive situations the general trend on internalizing–externalizing is reversed, with women more likely to internalize their anger and men more likely to externalize it. Coats and Feldman (1996) also found that men were more likely to look angry when mad, and that popular men were better at encoding anger than unpopular men. For women, popularity was unrelated to the ability to encode anger. Sharkin (1993) suggested that women control anger expressions because aggression is perceived as incompatible with stereotypes of feminine behavior, whereas men are "generally viewed as emotionally inexpressive with the exception of anger" (p. 386).

Other studies have failed to support the hypothesis that women curb aggressive displays more than men. Burrowes and Halberstadt (1987), for example, failed to find sex differences in anger experience or expression despite analyzing self-reports and reports from family and friends. Similarly, Guerrero (1994; Guerrero & Reiter, 1998) found that men and women did not differ in their self-reports of angry aggression. Thomas (1989) examined both the suppression and expression of anger and found no evidence for sex differences in suppression. However, women reported being more likely to disclose anger than did men.

Some studies suggest that, when women express anger, they may be more likely than men to do so by using passive aggressive strategies, such as giving dirty looks or ignoring a partner (Guerrero, 1994; Guerrero & Reiter, 1998). Similar findings have emerged for African American teenagers, with girls more likely than boys to use passive aggressive strategies, such as crying or giving the silent treatment when angry (Jones et al., 1992). Girls may learn to channel their aggression through indirect channels, such as angrily leaving the scene or giving the silent treatment. Of course, both men and women may underreport their use of directly aggressive behavior. Women, however, may have a tendency to underreport aggression even more than men because they are aware of stereotypes connecting aggression to masculinity rather than femininity (Shields, 1984). Indeed, Guerrero (1994) found that women perceived themselves to use less aggression than their partners perceived them to use.

There may also be subtle sex differences in men's and women's ability to decode anger accurately. Despite women's general superiority in decoding emotions, men may have the advantage when it comes to recognizing angry expressions (Rotter & Rotter, 1988; Toner & Gates, 1985; Wagner, MacDonald, & Manstead, 1986; for an exception, see, Wagner et al., 1993). In some cases, however, men may misattribute anger to the expressions of others. For instance, Larkin, Martin, and McCain (2002) found that men made more mistakes decoding disgust than women, largely because they mistook disgust for anger. Men may also be more likely than women to misinterpret their partner's neutral vocal tones and facial expressions as showing anger, contempt, or other negative emotions (e.g., Gottman, 1994; Noller, 1980).

Sadness and Depression

Interestingly, the tendency to express anger may be inversely related to depression (Newman, Gray, & Fuqua, 1999). Suppressing anger (which women are theorized to do more than men) is associated with experiencing other forms of negative affect, including sadness and fear. Scholars have also theorized that men sometimes transform negative emotions they view as feminine (e.g., sadness, fear) into anger (Newman et al., 1999), and that men tend to express anger aggressively because they are more likely to get to the point where they feel more anger than fear (Campbell, 2003). Campbell suggested that evolution can explain this difference—because women were necessary for the survival of offspring, it was adaptive for them to cope with anger nonaggressively so as not to endanger their safety or the safety of their children.

Consistent with the reasoning that people who express less anger may also experience more depression, considerable evidence shows that women are more likely than men to be sad and depressed (e.g., Harris & Howard, 1987;

Nolen-Hoeksema, 1987; Stapley & Haviland, 1989). This sex difference seems to appear after puberty, with females over 15 years old almost twice as likely to be depressed as males over 15 years old (Nolen-Hoeksema & Girgus, 1994). Studies comparing younger boys and girls have produced mixed results, with some studies showing boys to be more depressed, others showing girls to be more depressed, and still others finding no sex differences (e.g., Nolen-Hoeksema & Girgus, 1994; Nolen-Hoeksema, Girgus, & Seligman, 1991). Some research suggests that hormones may be partially responsible for the finding that adolescent and adult women experience more depression than their male counterparts (e.g., Brooks-Gunn & Warren, 1989; Rondon, 2003) because women's hormone levels change more frequently and rapidly than do men's. Such an explanation is consistent with findings showing that depression is more likely during puberty, post-pregnancy, and the initial stages of menopause (e.g., Rondon, 2003).

Men and women also appear to cope with depression differently. Depressed men tend to engage in activities designed to distract themselves from their depressed state (e.g., engaging in sports) and to withdraw socially (Hammen & Peters, 1977; Oliver & Toner, 1990). Depressed men may refrain from expressing sadness because people stereotypically perceive such expressions as a sign of weakness for men, which could lead men to underreport their level of depression. In contrast, depressed women tend to be less active and to engage in more rumination about their depression (Nolen-Hoeksema, 1987) as well as more interpersonal communication about their problems (e.g., Snell, Miller, Belk, Garcia-Falconi, & Hernandez-Sanchez, 1989; Wallbott, Ricci-Bitti, & Banninger-Huber, 1986). Women also rate themselves as better at expressing sadness to others than do men (Blier & Blier-Wilson, 1989).

There are also sex differences in the specific tactics chosen to cope with sadness and depression. Nolen-Hoeksema (1987) found men to report using the following tactics more often: "I avoid thinking of reasons why I'm depressed," "I do something physical," "I play a sport," and "I take drugs." Similarly, Kleinke, Staneski, and Mason (1982) found that depressed male college students were likely to cope with their sadness by thinking about unrelated items, ignoring their problems, or taking part in a physical activity, whereas Guerrero and Reiter (1998) found men to report dealing with sadness by engaging in dangerous behavior (e.g., driving a car fast) more than women. Although some of these tactics can be problematic because the depressed man does not deal with the source of his depression or engages in potentially harmful behavior, Nolen-Hoeksema argued that some of these responses likely distract men from their current depressive mood and help them avoid ruminating about their problems.

By contrast, women focus more on the sources of their sadness. Nolen-Hoeksema (1987) found that women reported engaging in the following responses more than men: "I try to determine why I'm depressed," "I cry to relieve the tension," and "I talk to other people about my feelings." Similarly, Guerrero and Reiter (1998) found that women report seeking social support more than men when they are experiencing sadness. Women also report decreasing responsibilities and activities, confronting their feelings, and blaming themselves for their depressive state more often than men (Kleinke et al., 1982). According to Nolen-Hoeksema, some of these responses incline women to focus and maintain attention on their depressive mood. Seeking social support, however, can be a highly effective coping strategy.

Similar sex differences in the communication of sadness and depression have been reported for children, suggesting that socialization may affect how people cope with sad emotions. Nolen-Hoeksema et al. (1991) found that depressed boys are more likely than depressed girls to endorse misbehavior (e.g., "I never do what I am told" and "I do bad things"). In contrast, depressed girls are more likely to endorse items indicative of negative self-evaluation and loneliness, such as "I feel alone," "I hate myself," and "I'll never be as good as other kids." Nolen-Hoeksema (1987) concluded that, among elementary school children, depressed boys tend to be more active and outer directed, whereas depressed girls tend to be more contemplative and self-focused. Other studies have come to analogous conclusions, showing that girls tend to appear anxious, internalize their emotions, and seek comfort when dealing with sadness or depression, whereas boys tend to engage in activities that are aggressive, distracting, or constitute misbehavior (Anderson, Williams, McGee, & Silva, 1989; Edelbrock, 1984; Ruble, Greulich, Pomerantz, & Gochberg, 1993).

Jealousy

Research focusing on sex differences in the experience and expression of jealousy has often taken an evolutionary perspective (Guerrero, Spitzberg, & Yoshimura, 2004). One of the most frequently reported findings is that men and women respond to sexual versus emotional jealousy differently. *Sexual jealousy* occurs when people are upset that their partner is (or has been) sexually involved with someone else. *Emotional jealousy* occurs when people are upset because their partner has fallen in love with or has a strong emotional attachment to someone else. Although these forms of jealousy often occur together, there are cases when jealousy is exclusively sexual (e.g., a one-night stand) or emotional (e.g., the partner's love is unrequited). Considerable research has supported the evolutionary hypothesis that men react more strongly than women to sexual infidelity, whereas women react more strongly than men to emotional infidelity (e.g., Buss, Larsen, & Westen, 1996; Buss, Larsen, Westen, & Semmelroth, 1992; see Guerrero et al., 2004, for a review), although some research suggests that both men and women are most bothered by sexual infidelity (e.g., Parker, 1997). According to the evolutionary perspective, men are more upset than women in response to sexual infidelity because they could end up raising another man's child if their mate is unfaithful. Women, in contrast, are more upset than men in response to emotional infidelity because they worry about their mates diverting resources to another love interest.

Other research suggests that women internalize their jealousy through the experience of intropunitive emotions such as anxiety, envy, discomfort, sadness, and confusion while also feeling betrayed (Bryson, 1976; Guerrero, Eloy, Jorgensen, & Andersen, 1993). Presumably, jealous women feel such emotions because they are worried about losing their relationships. Men, in contrast, have been found to get angry at themselves (Bryson, 1976), deny jealous feelings (Buunk, 1982; White, 1981), and focus on threats to self-esteem (Buunk, 1982) more than women. Thus, women may be more likely to contextualize jealous emotions within the context of potential relational loss, whereas men may be more likely to contextualize jealous emotions in terms of self-esteem.

Sex differences in coping strategies and communicative responses to jealousy reflect women's relational concerns. White and Mullen (1989) concluded that jealous women are "more oriented toward solving relationship problems or directly expressing their emotions" (p. 129). Jealous women report using several coping strategies more than men, including (a) inducing counterjealousy in the partner; (b) trying to get even with the partner; (c) improving one's physical appearance; (d) seeking support from others; (e) trying to improve the relationship; (f) demanding increased commitment from the partner; (g) expressing more jealous emotion; and (h) using direct, relatively positive forms of communication focused on self-disclosure and problem solving (Bryson, 1976; Buss, 1988; Guerrero et al., 1993; Guerrero & Reiter, 1998; Parker, 1997; White, 1981). Although many of these strategies focus on solving relational problems and directly expressing emotions, others, such as getting even with the partner, focus on retaliation. Such responses may stem from the feelings of betrayal that jealous women report experiencing or from the belief that such tactics will restore the relationship by igniting jealous passion in the beloved partner.

Jealous men appear to engage in more dangerous, sexually aggressive, and possessive behaviors and to interfere more with the rival relationship (Buss, 1988; White & Mullen, 1989). Men have reported using the following strategies more than women: (a) getting drunk, (b) confronting the rival, (c) keeping the partner away from potential rivals, (d) derogating the partner in front of potential rivals, (e) becoming sexually aggressive or promiscuous with others, (f) getting a friend to talk to the partner about the situation, (g) developing alternatives, (h) breaking off the relationship, and (i) spending money or giving gifts to the partner (e.g., Buss 1988; Guerrero & Reiter, 1998; White & Mullen, 1989). In addition, Buss found jealous men to use sexual inducements (e.g., giving in to sexual requests) and debase themselves (e.g., saying he'll change for her and let her have her way) more than jealous women. Taken together, these findings suggest that men engage in more preemptive behavior designed to guard the primary relationship. If this behavior is unsuccessful, men may either try to preserve their relationship through resource displays (e.g., buying gifts), sexual inducements, or debasement, or they may seek new alternatives and terminate the relationship. Women, in contrast, appear to focus more on directly communicating about the relationship and their jealous feelings. Consistent with the evolutionary perspective, jealous men are more likely to behave competitively toward the rival and to become sexually aggressive or promiscuous than jealous women.

Despite the long lists of findings indicating sex differences in jealous expression, the effect sizes for these differences are generally small. Moreover, the differences listed herein show variations between men and women without always suggesting that a person of a particular sex uses a lot of a certain strategy. For example, men generally confront rivals more than women, but both men and women use this strategy relatively infrequently (Guerrero & Reiter, 1998). Both men and women tend to report using positive forms of communication (such as problem solving) and expressing negative jealous emotion more than they report using responses such as revenge and relationship termination. Thus, although there are a lot of subtle differences in how men and women report responding to jealousy, there is also considerable similarity. The tactic that seems to differ most between men and women is appearance enhancement, with jealous women more likely to attempt to "look good" for their partners than jealous men (Buss, 1988; Guerrero & Reiter, 1998; Salovey & Rodin, 1985).

CONCLUSION

Our review of the literature leads to six conclusions regarding sex differences in emotional communication. First, women generally possess more social skill than men in encoding emotion, decoding emotion, and being emotionally sensitive to others. Second, with the exception of anger, men may be better at inhibiting or controlling most emotions than are women. Third, women generally engage in more immediacy behavior (e.g., smiling, close distancing) than men, although men may be more likely than women to initiate certain immediacy behaviors (e.g., touch) during courtship. Fourth, boys are more likely than girls to show anger aggressively, whereas girls are more likely than boys to engage in passive aggressive behaviors when angry. The results for adults are less consistent, although women do appear to display anger more passive aggressively than men. Fifth, in response to sadness, women are more likely to ruminate about their problems and seek social support than men, whereas men are more likely to engage in distractions or dangerous behavior than women. Finally, in response to jealousy, women are more likely than men to report discussing their thoughts and feelings, expressing emotion nonverbally, and enhancing their physical appearance. Men, in contrast, are more likely than women to report focusing on the rival and buying gifts or spending money on the partner.

From both evolutionary and social learning perspectives, these conclusions make theoretical sense. However, it is important to underscore that natural selection processes are likely to favor an overall profile of emotional communication that generalizes somewhat to both sexes. Thus, sex differences are usually embedded within a larger pattern of similarity. For example, it is adaptive for both men and women to express sadness when they need help and to communicate positive affect in ways that help maintain valued relationships. Socialization processes refine this adaptation process by establishing expectations related to sex differences. For example, in the U.S. culture, boys are often told not to cry in certain situations, whereas girls are probably taught to let a man say "I love you" first. Conforming to these expectations reflects some level of social skill, as does knowing when it is effective to deviate from gender-related expectations. An important next step for researchers is to develop an integrated theoretical framework that incorporates biology and socialization to help explain both differences and similarities between the sexes in emotional communication.

REFERENCES

Andersen, P. A., & Guerrero, L. K. (1998a). The bright side of relational communication: Interpersonal warmth as a social emotion. In P. A. Andersen & L. K. Guerrero (Eds.), *Handbook of communication and emotion: Research, theory, applications, and contexts* (pp. 305–324). San Diego, CA: Academic Press.

Andersen, P. A., & Guerrero, L. K. (1998b). Principles of communication and emotion in social interaction. In P. A. Andersen & L. K. Guerrero (Eds.), *Handbook of communication and emotion: Research, theory, applications, and contexts* (pp. 49–96). San Diego, CA: Academic Press.

Anderson, J., Williams, S., McGee, R., & Silva, P. (1989). Cognitive and social correlates of DSM-III disorders in preadolescent children. *Journal of American Academy of Child Adolescent Psychiatry, 28*, 842–846.

Beckwith, L. (1972). Relationships between infants' social behavior and their mothers' behavior. *Child Development, 43*, 397–411.

Bleier, R. (1991). Gender ideology and the brain: Sex differences research. In M. Notman & C. Nadelson (Eds.), *Women and men: New perspectives on gender differences* (pp. 63–73). Washington, DC: American Psychiatric Press.

Blier, M. J., & Blier-Wilson, L. A. (1989). Gender differences in sex-rated emotional expressiveness. *Sex Roles, 21*, 287–295.

Block, J. H. (1973). Conceptions of sex role: Some cross-cultural and longitudinal perspectives. *American Psychologist, 28*, 512–526.

Briton, N. J., & Hall, J. A. (1995). Beliefs about female and male nonverbal communication. *Sex Roles, 32*, 79–89.

Brody, A. B. (1985). Gender differences in emotional development: A review of theories and research. *Journal of Personality, 53*, 102–149.

Brody, L. R. (1993). On understanding gender differences in the expression of emotion: Gender roles, socialization, and language. In D. Brown (Ed.), Human Feelings: Explorations in affect development and meaning (pp. 87–121). Hillsdales, NJ: Analytic Press.

Brody, L. R., & Hall, J. A. (1993). Gender and emotion. In M. Lewis & J. M. Haviland (Eds.), *Handbook of emotions* (pp. 447–460). New York: Guilford.

Brooks-Gunn, J., & Warren, M. P. (1989). Biological and social contributions to negative affect in young adolescent girls. *Child Development, 60*, 40–55.

Bryden, M. P. (1982). *Laterality: Functional asymmetry in the intact brain.* New York: Academic Press.

Bryson, J. B. (1976, September). *The nature of sexual jealousy: An exploratory paper.* Paper presented at the annual meeting of the American Psychological Association, Washington, DC.

Buck, R. (1979). Individual differences in nonverbal sending accuracy and electrodermal responding: The externalizing–internalizing dimension. In R. Rosenthal (Ed.), *Skill in nonverbal communication* (pp. 140–170). Cambridge, MA: Oelgeschlaeger, Gunn & Hain.

Buck, R. (1982). Spontaneous and symbolic nonverbal behavior and the ontogeny of communication. In R. S. Feldman (Ed.), *Development of nonverbal behavior in children* (pp. 29–62). New York: Springer-Verlag.

Buck, R. (1983). Nonverbal receiving ability. In J. M. Wiemann & R. P. Harrison (Eds.), *Nonverbal interaction* (pp. 209–242). Beverly Hills, CA: Sage.

Burgoon, J. K., & Bacue, A. E. (2003). Nonverbal communication skills. In J. O. Greene & B. R. Burleson (Eds.), *Handbook of communication and social interaction skills* (pp. 179–219). Mahwah, NJ: Lawrence Erlbaum Associates.

Burrowes, B. D., & Halberstadt, A. G. (1987). Self–and family-expressiveness styles in the experience and expression of anger. *Journal of Nonverbal Behavior, 11*, 254–268.

Buss, D. M. (1988). From vigilance to violence: Tactics of mate retention in American undergraduates. *Ethology and Sociobiology, 9*, 291–317.

Buss, D. M., Larsen, R. J., & Westen, D. (1996). Sex differences in jealousy: Not gone, not forgotten, and not easily explained by alternative hypotheses. *Psychological Science, 7*, 373–375.

Buss, D. M., Larsen, R., Westen, D., & Semmelroth, J. (1992). Sex differences in jealousy: Evolution, physiology, and psychology. *Psychological Science, 3*, 251–255.

Buunk, B. (1982). Strategies of jealousy: Styles of coping with extramarital involvement of the spouse. *Family Relations, 31*, 13–18.

Cadispoti, M., Gilberto, G., Ornella, M., Zaimovic, A., Augusta-Raggi, M., & Baldara, B. (2003). Emotional perception and neuroendocrine changes. *Psychophysiology, 40*, 863–868.

Campbell, A. (2003). "I had to smack him one. . . ." *New Scientist, 178*, 50–53.

Cherry, L., & Lewis, M. (1976). Mothers and two-year-olds: A study of sex differential aspects of verbal interaction. *Developmental Psychology, 12*, 278–282.

Coats, E. J., & Feldman, R. S. (1996). Gender differences in nonverbal correlates of social status. *Personality and Social Psychology Bulletin, 22*, 1014–1022.

Condry, J., & Condry, S. (1976). Sex differences: A study of the eye of the beholder. *Child Development, 47*, 812–819.

Darwin, C. (1872). *The expression of the emotions in man and animals*. London: Murray.

Dillard, J. P. (1998). Foreword: The role of affect in communication, biology, and social relationships. In P. A. Andersen & L. K. Guerrero (Eds.), *Handbook of communication and emotion: Research, theory, applications, and contexts* (pp. xvii–xxxii). San Diego, CA: Academic Press.

Dunn, J., Bretherton, I., & Munn, P. (1987). Conversations about feeling states between mothers and their children. *Developmental Psychology, 23*, 132–139.

Eagly, A. H. (1983). Gender and social influence: A social psychological analysis. *American Psychologist, 38*, 971–981.

Eagly, A. H. (1987). *Sex differences in social behavior: A social-role interpretation*. Hillsdale, NJ: Lawrence Erlbaum Associates.

Edelbrock, C. (1984). Developmental considerations. In T. Ollendick & M. Herson (Eds.), *Child behavioral assessment* (pp. 20–37). New York: Pergamon.

Ekman, P. (1971). Universal and cultural differences in facial expressions of emotion. In J. K. Cole (Ed.), *Nebraska symposium on motivation* (pp. 207–283). Lincoln: University of Nebraska Press.

Fabes, R. A., & Eisenberg, N. (1992). Young children's coping with interpersonal anger. *Child Development, 63*, 116–128.

Fivush, R., & Buckner, J. P. (2000). Gender, sadness, and depression: The development of emotional focus through gendered discourse. In A. H. Fischer (Ed.), *Gender and emotion: Social psychological perspectives* (pp. 232–253). New York: Cambridge University Press.

Frijda, N. H. (1993). Moods, emotion episodes, and emotions. In M. Lewis & J. M. Haviland (Eds.), *Handbook of emotions* (pp. 381–403). New York: Guilford.

Fuchs, D., & Thelen, M. (1988). Children's expected interpersonal consequences of communicating their affective state and reported likelihood of expression. *Child Development, 59*, 1314–1322.

Gottman, J. M. (1994). *What predicts divorce? The relationship between marital processes and marital outcomes*. Hillsdale. NJ: Lawrence Erlbaum Associates.

Greif, E., Alvarez, M., & Ulman, K. (1981, April). *Recognizing emotions in other people: Sex differences in socialization.* Paper presented at the biennial meeting of the Society for Research in Child Development, Boston, MA.

Guerrero, L. K. (1994). 'I'm so mad I could screan:' The effects of anger expression on relational satisfaction and communication competence. *The Southern Communication Journal, 59*, 125–141.

Guerrero, L. K. (1997). Nonverbal involvement across interactions with same-sex friends, opposite-sex friends, and romantic partners: Consistency or change? *Journal of Social and Personal Relationships, 14*, 31–58.

Guerrero, L. K., & Andersen, P. A. (1994). Patterns of matching and initiation: Touch behavior and touch avoidance across relational stages. *Journal of Nonverbal Behavior, 18*, 137–154.

Guerrero, L. K., & Andersen, P. A. (2001). Emotion in close relationships. In C. Hendrick & S. S. Hendrick (Eds.), *Close relationships: A sourcebook* (pp. 171–183). Thousand Oaks, CA: Sage.

Guerrero, L. K., Eloy, S. V., Jorgensen, P. F., & Andersen, P. A. (1993). Hers or his? The experience and communication of jealousy in close relationships. In P. Kalbfleisch (Ed.), *Interpersonal communication: Evolving interpersonal relationships* (pp. 109–132). Hillsdale, NJ: Lawrence Erlbaum Associtates.

Guerrero, L. K., & Reiter, R. L. (1998). Expressing emotion: Sex differences in social skills and communicative reasons to anger, sadness, and jealousy. In D. J. Canary & K. Dindia (Eds.), *Sex differences and similarities in communication* (pp. 321–350). Mahwah, NJ: Lawrence Erlbaum Associates.

Guerrero, L. K., Spitzberg, B. H., & Yoshimura, S. M. (2004). Sexual and emotional jealousy. In J. Harvey, A. Wenzel, & S. Sprecher (Eds.), *The handbook of sexuality in close relationships* (pp. 311–345). Mahwah, NJ: Lawrence Erlbaum Associates.

Hall, J. A. (1978). Gender effects in decoding nonverbal cues. *Psychological Bulletin, 85*, 845–857.

Hall, J. A. (1979). Gender, gender roles, and nonverbal communication skills. In R. Rosenthal (Ed.), *Skill in nonverbal communication: Individual differences* (pp. 32–67). Cambridge, MA: Oelgeschlager, Gunn & Hain.

Hall, J. A. (1984). *Nonverbal sex differences: Communication accuracy and expressive style*. Baltimore: Johns Hopkins University Press.

Hall, J. A. (1985). Male and female nonverbal behavior. In S. W. Siegman & S. Feldstein (Eds.), *Multichannel integrations of nonverbal behavior* (pp. 195–225). Hillsdale, NJ: Lawrence Erlbaum Associates.

Hall, J. A. (1998). How big are nonverbal sex differences? The case of smiling and sensitivity to nonverbal cues. In D. J. Canary & K. Dindia (Eds.), *Sex differences and similarities in communication* (pp. 155–177). Mahwah, NJ: Lawrence Erlbaum Associates.

Hall, J. A., Carter, J. D., & Horgan, T. G. (2000). Gender differences in nonverbal communication of emotion. In A. H. Fischer (Ed.), *Gender and emotion: Social psychological perspective* (pp. 97–117). Cambridge, England: Cambridge University Press.

Hall, J. A., & Friedman, G. (1999). Status, gender, and nonverbal behavior: A study of structured interactions between employees. *Personality and Social Psychology Bulletin, 25*, 1082–1091.

Hall, J. A., & Halberstadt, A. G. (1986). Smiling and gazing. In J. S. Hyde & M. C. Linn (Eds.), *The psychology of gender: Advances through meta-analyes* (pp. 136–158). Baltimore, John Hopkins University Press.

Hall, J. A., & Veccia, E. M. (1990). More "touching" observations: New insights on men, women, and interpersonal touch. *Journal of Personality and Social Psychology, 59*, 1155–1162.

Hammen, C. L., & Peters, S. D. (1977). Differential responses to male and female depressive reactions. *Journal of Consulting and Clinical Psychology, 45*, 994–1001.

Harris, I. D., & Howard, K. I. (1987). Correlates of depression and anger in adolescence. *Journal of Child and Adolescent Psychotherapy, 4*, 199–203.

Henley, N. M. (1973). Status and sex: Some touching observations. *Bulletin of the Psychonomic Society, 2*, 91–93.

Hess, U., Blairy, S., & Kleck, R. E. (1997). The intensity of emotional facial expressions and decoding accuracy. *Journal of Nonverbal Behavior*, 21, 241–257.

Hohan, R. (1982). A socioanalytic theory of personality. In M. M. Page (Ed.), *Nebraska symposium on motivation* (pp. 55–89). Lincoln: University of Nebraska Press.

Jansz, J. (2000). Masculine identity and restrictive emotionality. In A. H. Fischer (Ed.), *Gender and emotion: Social psychological perspective* (pp. 166–187). Cambridge, England: Cambridge University Press.

Jones, M. B., Peacock, M. K., & Christopher, K. (1992). Self–reported anger in Black high school adolescents. *Journal of Adolescent Health, 13*, 461–465.

Klein, R. P., & Durfee, J. T. (1978). Effects of sex and birth order on infant social behavior. *Infant Behavior and Development, 1*, 106–117.

Kleinke, C. L., Staneski, R. A., & Mason, J. K. (1982). Sex differences in coping with depression. *Sex Roles, 8*, 877–889.

LaFrance, M., & Hecht, M. A. (2000). Gender and smiling: A meta-analysis. In A. H. Fischer (Ed.), *Gender and emotion: Social psychological perspective* (pp. 118–142). Cambridge, England: Cambridge University Press.

LaFrance, M., Hecht, M. A., & Noyes, A. (1994, October). *Who is smiling now? A meta-analysis of sex differences in smiling*. Paper presented at the annual meeting of the Society of Experimental Social Psychology, Lake Tahoe, NV.

LaFrance, M., & Henley, N. M. (1994). On oppressing hypotheses: Differences in nonverbal sensitivity revisited. In L. H. Radtke & H. J. Stam (Eds.), *Power/gender: Social relations in theory and practice* (pp. 287–311). Thousand Oaks, CA: Sage.

LaFrance, M., & Mayo, C. (1978). *Moving bodies: Nonverbal communication in social relationships*. Monterey, CA: Brooks/Cole.

Larkin, K. T., Martin, R. R., & McCain, S. E. (2002). Cynical hostility and the accuracy of decoding facial expressions and emotions. *Journal of Behavioral Medicine, 25*, 285–292.

Lemerise, E. A., & Dodge, K. A. (1993). The development of anger and hostile interactions. In M. Lewis & J. M. Jeannette (Eds.), *Handbook of emotions* (pp. 537–546). New York: Guilford.

Major, B., Schmidlin, A. M., & Williams, L. (1990). Gender patterns in social touch: The impact of setting and age. *Journal of Personality and Social Psychology, 58*, 634–643.

Malatesta, C., Culver, C., Tesman, J. R., & Shepard, B. (1939). The development of emotion expression during the first two years of life. *Monographs of the Society for Research in Child Development, 54*, 1–104.

Malatesta, C., & Haviland, J. M. (1982). Learning display rules: The socialization of emotion expression in infancy. *Child Development, 53*, 991–1003.

Marston, P. J., & Hecht, M. L. (1999). The nonverbal communication of romantic love. In L. K. Guerrero, J. A. DeVito, & M. L. Hecht (Eds.), *The nonverbal communication reader: Classic and contemporary readings* (2nd ed, pp. 284–289). Prospect Heights, IL: Waveland Press.

Mills, R. S., & Rubin, K. H. (1992). A longitudinal study of maternal beliefs about children's social behaviors. *Merrill-Palmer Quarterly, 38*, 494–512.

Newman, J. L., Gray, E. A., & Fuqua, D. R. (1999). Sex differences in the relationship of anger and depression: An empirical study. *Journal of Counseling and Development, 77*, 198–202.

Nolen-Hoeksema, S. (1987). Sex differences in unipolar depression: Evidence and theory. *Psychological Bulletin, 101*, 259–282.

Nolen-Hoeksema, S., & Girgus, J. S. (1994). The emergence of gender differences in depression during adolescence. *Psychological Bulletin, 115*, 424–443.

Nolen-Hoeksema, S., Girgus, J. S., & Seligman, M. E. P. (1991). Sex differences in depression and explanatory style in children. *Journal of Youth and Adolescence, 20*, 233–245.

Noller, P. (1980). Misunderstandings in marital communication: A study of couples' nonverbal communication. *Journal of Personality and Social Psychology, 39*, 1135–1148.

O'Kearney, R., & Dadds, M. (2004). Developmental and gender differences in the language for emotions across the adolescent years. *Cognition and Emotion, 18*, 913–938.

Oliver, S. J., & Toner, B. B. (1990). The influence of gender role typing on the expression of depressive symptoms. *Sex Roles, 22*, 775–790.

Owen, W. F. (1987). The verbal expression of love by women and men as a critical communication event in personal relationships. *Women's Studies in Communication, 10*, 15–24.

Parker, R. (1997). The influence of sexual infidelity, verbal intimacy, and gender upon primary appraisal processes in romantic jealousy. *Women's Studies in Communication, 20*, 1–25.

Perry, D. G., Perry, L. C., & Weiss, R. J. (1989). Sex differences in the consequences that children anticipate for aggression. *Developmental Psychology, 25*, 312–319.

Planalp, S. (1999). *Communicating emotion: Social, moral, and cultural processes*. New York: Cambridge University Press.

Riggio, R. E. (1986). Assessment of basic social skills. *Journal of Personality and Social Psychology, 51*, 649–660.

Riggio, R. E. (1993). Social interaction skills and nonverbal behavior. In R. S. Feldman (Ed.), *Applications of nonverbal behavioral theories and research* (pp. 3–30). Hillsdale, NJ: Erlbaum.

Rondon, M. B. (2003). Maternity blues: Cross-cultural variances and emotional changes. *Primary care update for OB/GYNs, 10*, 167–171.

Rotter, N. G., & Rotter, G. S. (1988). Sex differences in the encoding and decoding of negative facial emotions. *Journal of Nonverbal Behavior, 12*, 139–148.

Ruble, D. N., Greulich, F., Pomerantz, E. M., & Gochberg, B. (1993). The role of gender-related processes in the development of sex differences in self-evaluation and depression. *Journal of Affective Disorders, 29*, 97–128.

Saarni, C. (1982). Social and affective functions of nonverbal behavior: Developmental concerns. In R. S. Feldman (Ed.), *Development* via *nonverbal behavior in children* (pp. 123–147). New York: Springer-Verlag.

Sabatelli, R. M., Buck, R., & Kenny, D. A. (1986). A social relations analysis of nonverbal communication accuracy in married couples. *Journal of Personality, 54*, 513–527.

Salovey, P., & Rodin, J. (1985). The heart of jealousy. *Psychology Today, 19*(9), 22–25, 28–29.

Shaver, P. R., Schwartz, J., Kirson, D., & O'Connor, C. (1987). Emotion knowledge: Further explorations of a prototype approach. *Journal of Personality and Social Psychology, 52*, 1061–1086.

Sharkin, B. S. (1993). Anger and gender: Theory, research, and implications. *Journal of Counseling and Development, 71*, 386–389.

Shields, S. A. (1984). Reports of bodily changes in anxiety, sadness, and anger. *Motivation and Emotion, 8*, 1–21.

Snell, W. E., Miller, R. S., Belk, S. S., Garcia-Falconi, R., & Hernandez-Sanchez, J. E. (1989). Men's and women's emotional disclosures: The impact of disclosure recipient, culture, and the masculine role. *Sex Roles, 21*, 467–485.

Stapley, J. C., & Haviland, J. M. (1989). Beyond depression: Gender differences in normal adolescents' emotional experiences. *Sex Roles, 20*, 295–308.

Stier, D. S., & Hall, J. A. (1984). Gender differences in touch: An empirical and theoretical perspective. *Journal of Personality and Social Psychology, 47*, 440–459.

Sullivan, A. (2000). The He hormone. *New York Times Magazine, 149*, 46–56.

Susman, E. J., Inoff-Germain, G., Nottlemann, E. D., Loriauz, D. L., Cutler, G. B., & Chrousos, G. (1987). Hormones, emotional dispositions, and aggressive attributes in young adolescents. *Child Development, 58*, 1114–1134.

Thomas, S. P. (1989). Gender differences in anger expression: Health implications. *Research in Nursing and Health, 12*, 389–398.

Toner, H. L., & Gates, G.R. (1985). Emotional traits and recognition of facial expression of emotion. *Journal of Nonverbal Behavior, 9*, 48–65.

Trivers, R. (1985). *Social evolution.* Menlo Park, CA: Benjamin/Cummings.

Tucker, J. S., & Friedman, H. S. (1993). Sex differences in nonverbal expressiveness: Emotional expression, personality, and impressions. *Journal of Nonverbal Behavior*, 17, 103–117.

Wagner, H. L., Buck, R., & Winterbotham, M. (1993). Communication of specific emotions: Gender differences in sending accuracy and communication measures. *Journal of Nonverbal Behavior, 17*, 29–53.

Wagner, H. L., MacDonald, C. J., & Manstead, A. S. R. (1986). Communication of individual emotions by spontaneous facial expressions. *Journal of Personality and Social Psychology, 50*, 737–743.

Wallbott, H. G., Ricci-Bitti, P., & Banniger-Huber, E. (1986). Non-verbal reactions to emotional experiences. In K. R. Scherer, H. G. Wallbott, & A. B. Summerfield (Eds.), *Experiencing emotion: A cross-cultural study* (pp. 98–116). Cambridge, England: Cambridge University Press.

Willis, E. N., & Briggs, L. E. (1992). Relationship and touch in public settings. *Journal of Nonverbal Behavior, 16*, 55–62.

Willis, F. N., & Dodds, R. A. (1998). Age, relationship, and touch initiation. *Journal of Social Psychology, 138*, 115–123.

White, G. L. (1981). Jealousy and partner's perceived motives for attraction to a rival. *Social Psychology Quarterly, 44*, 24–30.

White, G. L., & Mullen, P. E. (1989). *Jealousy: Theory, research, and clinical strategies.* New York: Guilford.

Whitesell, N. R., Robinson, N. S., & Harter, S. E. (1991, April). *Anger in early adolescence: Prototypical causes and gender differences in coping strategies.* Paper presented at the biennial meeting of the Society for Research in Child Development, Seattle, WA.

14

Sex Differences in Presenting and Detecting Deceptive Messages

Judee K. Burgoon
University of Arizona

David B. Buller
Klein Buendel, Inc.

J. P. Blair
University of Texas at San Antonio

Patti Tilley
Central Connecticut State University

Abundant nonverbal and verbal literature tells us that men's and women's nonverbal expressions differ in many ways (Burgoon, Buller, & Woodall, 1996; Hall, 1984; Tannen, 1994). For example, women tend to smile and gaze more, to be more approachable and expressive, but also less relaxed and more closed off posturally than men. Conceivably, these differences could result in different forms of deception displays. Women's pleasant, immediate style might aid them in strategically creating a favorable image. Conversely, their lack of relaxation and greater expressiveness might result in being perceived as nervous or uncomfortable and hence less credible. However, the fact that many studies have failed to find gender differences in actual nonverbal cue displays (Burgoon, 1991; Burgoon, Le Poire, & Rosenthal, 1995; Miller et al., 1981; Riggio & Friedman, 1983) or in general demeanor (Duncan & Kalbfleisch, 1995; Riggio, Tucker, & Throckmorton, 1987) suggests that the extent of sex differences might be overstated.

Examining deceptive practices is useful for several reasons. It serves as a window into self-presentational strategies and tactics intended to further credibility and a favorable public image. It serves as a counterpoint to truthful communication, providing a contrastive benchmark for understanding what message features contribute to actual or perceived veracity in human discourse. Finally, to the extent that deception is an essential component of human survival, close study of deceptive repertoires sheds light on what communication practices contribute to self-preservation. To the extent that men and women differ in these practices, such differences may dispute the claim that deception is part of natural selection, or it may argue for the value of differentiation and complementarity between men's and women's communicative practices.

The question, then, is whether men and women are inevitably and inescapably different in how they deploy and gauge deception. Or might they, as members of the same genotypic family, inhabiting the same earth and subject to the same life-molding experiences, have more in common than a shared rib? Might they, like their primate relatives, having recognized the significant gains to be had from deceit, have honed similar strategies for duping others? Having been subjected throughout history to others' duplicity, might they have become equally adept or inept at recognizing deceit?

The answer we offer in this chapter is a qualified yes. We review published literature and original data from our own experiments that lead to the conclusion that, as regards encoding of deception, similarities between men and women largely prevail, but as regards decoding of deception, some slight differences are evident. We begin by summarizing extant literature on sex differences in how deception is enacted verbally and nonverbally. We follow this by presenting results from five original experiments that we reanalyzed to tease out any differences between male and female deceivers and truth-tellers that had not been analyzed or reported previously. Our rationale for examining these particular experiments is that, unlike much previous deception research, these investigations not only entailed actual, real-time interaction between deceivers and their targets but also generated much lengthier deceptive responses that could be analyzed for dynamic changes in deceptive displays over the course of an interaction. Next, we consider the literature on deception detection, again looking for evidence of male–female differences, and we report reanalyses of three original experiments that shed light on decoding advantages related to sex of sender and sex of judge. We conclude with some speculations on why men and women might be similar or different.

Before we consider the research evidence, a definition is in order. By *deception* we mean a message knowingly transmitted by a sender to foster false beliefs or conclusions by a receiver (Buller & Burgoon, 1996). Deception encompasses far more than just outright lies. It includes everything from white lies and hyperbole, to equivocations and evasions, to concealments and omissions of relevant information. However, deception should not be construed to include every form of misleading communication. It only encompasses intentional acts, not incidental or accidental ones, and those acts must be directed toward deluding another, not the self.

SEX DIFFERENCES IN THE ENCODING OF DECEPTION

A perusal of the wealth of deception research quickly reveals that, for the most part, the primary focus has been on generic deception displays (verbal and nonverbal) rather than on sex differences in those displays. Several meta-analyses and literature summaries (Buller, Burgoon, Buslig, & Roiger, 1994; DePaulo et al., 2003; Zuckerman, DePaulo, & Rosenthal, 1981; Zuckerman & Driver, 1985) support the argument that behavior linked to deception can be characterized as either strategic or nonstrategic. Strategic cues are those that deceivers attempt to control deliberately during deception. Strategies and associated tactics can be classified in a variety of ways, including *information-management* strategies to alter the quantity, quality, relevance, clarity or personalization of verbal contents (Burgoon, Buller, Guerrero, Afifi, & Feldman, 1996); *behavior-management* strategies to convey appropriate levels of conversational involvement and normalcy (Burgoon, Buller, Floyd, & Grandpre, 1996); or strategies that entail alterations in dominance behaviors; and *image-management* strategies that attempt to exude an honest-appearing and pleasant demeanor (Buller & Burgoon, 1994). For example, deceivers may use certain forms of language and nonverbal behavior strategically to convey uncertainty and to weaken their apparent responsibility for, or commitment to, what they are saying.

Although individuals might be able to control certain aspects of their behavior to appear more truthful, often they cannot control all of these aspects at once; thus some nonstrategic "leakage" may occur. Nonstrategic classes of cues are those that arise unbidden and involuntarily, including indicators of arousal, emotional states, cognitive effort, and memory processes (Burgoon, 2005), which together might result in a less than competent communication performance. For example, out of fear of detection, deceivers might overcontrol their behavior, leading to stiff postures, inexpressive faces, and absence of gesturing. It is this leakage or senders' inability to properly control other cues that might lead receivers to believe that deception is taking place. Notwithstanding the voluminous literature on deception displays, very few behaviors have been isolated that reliably distinguish truthful from deceptive messages and that are unconstrained by culture, situation, and other contextual factors.

Not surprisingly, then, sex or gender differences in studies of deception have been mixed and inconclusive. As regards kinesic (body movement) indicators, Cody and O'Hair (1983) reported that leg and foot movements and gestures were the only nonverbal behaviors that differentiated men from women. Male liars showed more leg and foot movements than female liars initially but not over time, and they suppressed these movements and gestures when they had time to prepare their lies in advance. In short, behavior was sensitive to time and sensitive to strategic preplanning. By contrast, Donaghy, Grandpre, and Davies (1994) found that unrehearsed women had the most foot or leg movement, whereas unrehearsed men had the least, contradicting Cody and O'Hair's findings; men and women giving rehearsed lies were very similar. Donaghy et al., also found that women had longer response latencies and more head movement when lying than when telling the truth, whereas men showed just the opposite (longer response latencies, more head movement when telling the truth); deTurck and Miller (1985), however, found no sex differences on leg or foot movement, response latencies, or head movement. These limited and contradictory findings do little to warrant definitive conclusions about kinesic differences between male and female liars.

In terms of vocal differences, O'Hair and Cody (1987) found that women had more vocal stress than men when lying, particularly when telling prepared lies, whereas men showed the same level of vocal stress for truthful and deceptive responses. The authors speculated that women might release (leak) their internal arousal through an increase in vocal stress. DePaulo (1992) contended that women might have more difficulty concealing their deceit because they are more spontaneously expressive than men, which might be evident in women's vocal stress during deception.

Do these meager findings indicate minimal differences between men and women in their deceptive displays? Not necessarily. To address this issue directly, we revisit five of our recent deception experiments to determine if men and women might differ systematically in the ways they produce deception during interpersonal interaction. These investigations were all undertaken as part of a program of research testing interpersonal deception theory (IDT; Buller & Burgoon, 1996) and so included multiple verbal and nonverbal measures designed to assess strategic and nonstrategic activity during interpersonal interactions. Although it would have been ideal to consider not only sex of sender but also sex of receiver and the resultant sex composition of each dyad, an imbalance in the numbers of male–male, male–female, and female–male dyads precluded doing so. Thus, our focus here is strictly on male and female differences in deceptive versus truthful encoding.

REVISITING FIVE DECEPTION EXPERIMENTS

Deceptive Versus Truthful Displays During Interviews

The first experiment (Burgoon & Buller, 1994; see also Burgoon, Buller, Grandpre, & Kalbfleisch, 1998, for more details) employed an interview format during which participants who were randomly assigned to an interviewee (EE) role answered truthfully or deceptively a series of preset interview questions reframed from a social desirability questionnaire (e.g., "If you broke something expensive in a store and no one saw you, would you walk away?" "Do you consider yourself more intelligent than most other people?"). Other participants randomly assigned to an interviewer (ER) role were or were not induced to be suspicious (the suspicion induction is not relevant here). Undergraduate students ($N = 240$) were paired to form 120 pairs who conducted interviews with strangers or friends (but not best friends or romantic partners). Our interest for the moment is in the interviewees, 48 of whom were male and 74 of whom were female. We chose to use interviews as the experimental task because it is ideal for examining behavioral changes over time, is a familiar form of interaction, and provides some experimental control through use of a standard interview protocol.

After completing a true–false survey related to socially desirable, undesirable, or misanthropic attitudes, half of the interviewees were told that "some people, when answering these kinds of questions in actual conversation, tend to misrepresent their true feelings and actions. We want to determine if conversational partners can detect such lies." The interviewees were instructed to answer the first five questions truthfully and then to lie on the remainder. Interviewees in the truthful condition were simply told that we wanted to determine if their partner could detect truthful answers, so they needed to answer each question truthfully. Interviews were conducted in a living room style laboratory with a one-way mirror through which interviews could be videotaped with minimal intrusiveness (all with participant consent). Interviews lasted up to 5 minutes, after which participants completed questionnaires regarding their own and the other participant's interview behavior.

Subsequently, teams of trained coders rated the videotaped interactions on a large number of nonverbal and verbal behaviors. The behaviors were then clustered into 18 composite and individual measures intended to capture multiple strategies and tactics for information, behavior, and image management. Information management consisted of *talk time* (brevity of turns) and *verbal nonimmediacy* (modifiers, levelers, self-references, and group-references). Behavior management consisted of *nonverbal immediacy* (body lean, closeness, facing, and eye gaze), *nervousness* (vocal and kinesic relaxation, object adaptors, self-adaptors, random movement, and rocking and twisting), and *conversational management* (smoothness of turn exchanges and fluency). Image management consisted of *pleasantness* (vocal and kinesic pleasantness and nodding).

We conducted a 2 (truth or deception) × 2 (male or female) × 2 (time periods following onset of deception) mixed model analysis of variance, with time as a repeated factor, for each dependent measure. Results produced very few sex differences and even fewer related specifically to deception. (Relationship did not moderate results.)

In terms of kinesie behavior, four behaviors showed deception differences. Deceptive women ($M = 4.11$) and truthful men ($M = 4.10$) rocked more than deceptive men ($M = 3.51$) and truthful women ($M = 2.88$). Truthful men increased their head nods over time ($M_{t1} = 2.92$, $M_{t2} = 3.37$), whereas deceptive men decreased them ($M_{t1} = 3.08$, $M_{t2} = 2.61$), and women showed very little change over time or between truth and deception (truthful $M_{t1} = 3.25$, $M_{t2} = 3.19$; deceptive $M_{t1} = 3.59$, $M_{t2} = 3.58$). Truthful men increased their number of self-adaptors from Time 1 to Time 2 ($M_{t1} = 2.37$, $M_{t2} = 2.74$), whereas truthful women decreased them slightly from Time 1 to Time 2 ($M_{t1} = 3.31$, $M_{t2} = 3.00$). Deceptive men exhibited fewer self-adaptors and maintained their low number from Time 1 to Time 2 ($M_{t1} = 2.30$, $M_{t2} = 2.21$), whereas deceptive women increased them over time ($M_{t1} = 2.36$, $M_{t2} = 2.81$), although not to the same level as truthful women. Deceptive men, then, were less active physically and more inclined to decrease activity over time relative to truthful men, whereas women tended to show an increase in activity under deception. Additionally, consistent with prior findings of greater immediacy by women than men, women sat closer to interviewers, leaned forward more, and gazed more than did men, regardless of deception condition.

In terms of vocal behavior, deception was more disruptive for women than for men. When deceiving, men increasingly shortened their response latencies over time ($M_{t1} = 4.34$, $M_{t2} = 5.27$, where 7 = very short), whereas women increased their latencies over time ($M_{t1} = 4.61$, $M_{t2} = 4.05$). When telling the truth, both men and women showed little change in their response latencies (men, $M_{t1} = 4.87$, $M_{t2} = 4.90$; women $M_{t1} = 4.82$, $M_{t2} = 5.25$). Regardless of deception, women had smoother turn transitions than men.

Verbally, deceptive women had notably longer turns ($M = 6.29$) than deceptive men ($M = 4.46$). Turn length for deceptive men was similar to that for truthful men ($M = 4.31$) and women ($M = 4.27$).

Overall, the results showed some effects that were due to sex differences on verbal and nonverbal performance in these deceptive conversations. However, the majority of nonverbal and verbal behaviors tested from this experiment showed no interaction between sender sex and sender deceptiveness. The few behaviors manifesting sex differences are suggestive of men strategically restricting their behavior to avoid arousal cues. Curtailed activity by deceptive men has been seen in other studies, especially when men had the opportunity to plan their lies. However, this reduction in activity might have unwittingly eroded male's credibility by making them look overly restrained, stiff, and uninvolved. The reduction in head nodding, for example, which is a common show of attentiveness and interest, might be viewed as an inadvertent and undesirable by-product of an overall suppression of activity. By comparison, women remained more active, in line with DePaulo's (1992) contention that women might do less well at controlling their expressivity. This tendency also might account for why women became more talkative when deceiving, compared with men.

Although these results indicate some sex differences in deceptive encoding, they must be viewed within the context of the large number of cues that did not distinguish men from women during deceptive performances. Comparatively, fewer behaviors showed differences than did not. The effect sizes likewise failed to lend much credence to a claim of substantial differences between male and female deceivers, as η^2 ranged from .04 to .08. Thus, this investigation was more consistent with a sex similarity than a sex differences argument.

Types of Deception During Interviews

A second experiment (Buller, Burgoon, White, & Ebesu, 1994; see also Burgoon et al., 1998, for more details) was similar to that of the first experiment in that participants were assigned to an interview situation as either an interviewee or interviewer. Participants were adults recruited from the local community ($n = 72$), who participated in exchange for training on interviewing, and from a U.S. Army intelligence school ($n = 60$), who participated voluntarily. Among community participants, 18 pairs were acquainted and 18 were stranger dyads; among the military sample, 11 pairs were acquainted and 19 were stranger dyads. We conducted analyses only on senders in the experimental dyads, 41 of whom were male and 25 of whom were female. Interviewees were instructed to strive to "tell the truth, the whole truth, and nothing but the truth" on the first three questions and then to depart from that ideal on the remaining questions by engaging in one of three common types of deception that a pilot study had shown were familiar and easy to enact: falsification (completely untrue answers), equivocation (vague, unclear, indirect, or ambiguous answers), or concealment (withholding or omitting relevant information). Interviewees saw examples and practiced their assigned deception type before the actual interview commenced. Interviews proceeded for 15 minutes or until all questions had been answered. Participants then completed the postinteraction questionnaire. Trained coders assessed 20 different verbal and nonverbal behaviors of interviewees.

Only two measures produced significant interactions between deception and biological sex. Nonverbally, women used more expressive voices than men when telling the truth and on all types of deception (fabrication, $M = 6.78$; equivocation, $M = 6.78$; concealment, $M = 6.74$). Men were especially less expressive when they equivocated ($M = 5.76$) than when they fabricated ($M = 6.61$) or concealed ($M = 6.19$). Women were also generally more pleasant and spoke more rapidly than men, regardless of truthfulness. Verbally, women used more second- and third-person pronouns than men and increased them far more than men when deceiving (female truth, $M = .04$, deception, $M = 4.5$; male truth, $M = 0.2$, deception, $M = 2.0$). Women ($M = 6.06$) were much more formal than men ($M = 5.15$) when telling the truth; they were less so when deceiving (female $M = 5.28$; male $M = 4.89$). Biological sex did not affect any other verbal or nonverbal behaviors, and relationship did not interact with sex or deception.

Once again, the most prominent finding was that biological sex had little influence on behavior when senders dissembled. Tests on global measures of involvement, pleasantness, dominance, kinesic expressiveness, vocal tension, and kinesic tension revealed no moderating effect of sender sex on deception displays. Neither did specific measures of loudness, articulation, fluency, leveling terms, modifiers, self-references, past- and present-tense verbs, and humor. In the instances where sex did alter deception displays, the differences might be seen as reflecting alternate strategic efforts by men and women when deceiving. Men decreased vocal expressivity and lowered their pitch when equivocating, perhaps as part of the general behavior-management strategy of reducing activity and expressiveness to avoid betraying any arousal. As noted earlier, Cody and O'Hair (1983) and Donaghy et al. (1994) reported evidence for a similar strategy by men. Comparatively, women remained more expressive. Although this might be interpreted as support for the contention that women experience greater difficulty controlling such cues during deception, an alternative interpretation is that maintaining expressivity reflects the twin behavior-management strategies of projecting a normal-appearing demeanor and an impression of engagement in the conversation. Similarly, women's increased informality might have been an image-management strategy to appear open and disclosive rather than secretive.

Originally, the tactic of using more second- and third-person pronouns was conceived as part of a larger information-management strategy of verbal nonimmediacy and disassociation designed to attenuate responsibility for one's utterances. However, the fact that pronoun use by women also exceeded that by men during truth-telling implies that it is not a linguistic move associated exclusively with deception. It might not only convey lack of autonomy (or, more pejoratively, greater dependence and powerlessness) so as to attenuate attributed responsibility for what was said, but it also might signal inclusiveness, solidarity, and affiliation. This affiliative function would have the effect of capitalizing on partner sympathies and creating a positive image of oneself as friendly and trustworthy. Given that many linguistic and nonverbal cues carry multiple meanings and can satisfy dual functions simultaneously (Tannen, 1994), use of more "other" pronouns might have been designed to accomplish both image and information management. Alternatively, it might have been a female version of nonstrategic reductions in involvement (Buller, Burgoon, Buslig, & Roiger, 1996). Absent independent corroboration of senders' motivations, either interpretation is tenable. This argues for closer attention to senders' objectives vis-à-vis their actual performance.

Deceptive and Truthful Presentations During Dyadic Discussions

The third investigation (Burgoon, Buller, Floyd et al., 1996; see also Burgoon et al., 1998, for more details) explored the correspondence among sender, receiver, and observer perceptions of sender verbal and nonverbal behavior. It afforded a comparison between senders' intended strategies and their realization in the eyes of coparticipants or third parties. Participants ($N = 36$) were students solicited for a study of how people discuss personal topics and how such discussions differ among strangers and friends. Topics such as "talk about responsibility" or "describe the worst job you ever had" were listed on game cards. Participants randomly assigned to the Person A role were given instructions to deceive on half of the topics. Color-coded numbers on the cards signaled when they were to switch from truth to deception and vice versa. Participants were encouraged to use a variety of options to deceive (e.g., giving clear but completely untrue answers; being vague, indirect, unclear, and ambiguous; withholding, omitting, or avoiding discussion of relevant information) and to rely on their own communication techniques to give answers falling short of being the truth, the whole truth, and nothing but the truth. Participants in the Person B role were told that their main objective was to keep the interaction flowing smoothly. Incentives were offered for succeeding. Discussions took place in the same interaction room as the two previous experiments and continued until participants had discussed three topics: one baseline truthful, one additional truthful, and one deceptive. Order of the truthful and deceptive questions was rotated so that no two dyads would answer the same truthful and deceptive questions in the same order. Observers watched and rated the live interaction. Afterward, Persons A and B viewed videotaped portions of the interaction and rated Person A's truthful and deceptive responding on 28 measures related to information, behavior, and image management.

For the information-management dimensions, no sex differences either related or unrelated to deception emerged. For the nonverbal involvement dimensions, men saw themselves as less immediate while deceiving ($M = 4.25$) than when telling the truth ($M = 5.25$) and less immediate than women (female deception, $M = 6.33$; female truth, $M = 4.71$). Men also reported being more self-focused under deception ($M = 3.75$) than truth ($M = 6.00$). Women, by contrast, reported being more other centered than men and remained so under deception ($M = 6.22$) and truth ($M = 6.54$). For nonverbal dominance, men saw themselves as becoming more dominant when deceiving (male truth, $M = 3.00$; male deceit, $M = 5.00$) and more dominant than women, who saw themselves as becoming less dominant when deceiving (female truth, $M = 3.71$; female deceit, $M = 2.38$). Observers who rated the interactions did not share male senders' perceptions. They saw both men and women as less dominant under deception, and women as especially submissive. In sum, the nonsignificant relationships outnumbered the significant ones by a large margin, and targets of deception saw no differences related to sex of deceiver. The few findings that did emerge again implicated involvement and dominance as key sites for divergent self- and observer perceptions of male and female behaviors.

Changes in Deceptive Versus Truthful Presentations During Interviews

The fourth investigation (Burgoon, Buller, White, Afifi, & Buslig, 1999) was designed to examine interaction dynamics during deceptive episodes. Two hypotheses were that (a) deception displays in interactive contexts only differ from truthful ones at the outset of interaction and converge toward truthful displays over time, and (b) socially skilled deceivers are best able to approximate a truthful-appearing demeanor. We therefore reexamined this study for any sex differences in deceptive displays over time and in skillfulness at conveying a truthful-appearing demeanor. Participants ($N = 122$) were nontraditional undergraduate students (over the age of 25) and community members recruited from the Pima County (AZ) courthouse.

Participants were paired to conduct interviews, during which those assigned the role of Person A (interviewee) alternated between telling the truth and deceiving in either a truth-deception-truth-deception order or a deception-truth-deception-truth order, with three interview questions per block. Prior to the interview, everyone completed a social skills inventory. Afterward, the videotaped interviews were rated by trained coders on overall involvement, specific nonverbal immediacy indicators (proximity, lean, and gaze), turn length, partner turn length, response latencies, vocalized and nonvocalized pauses, other nonfluencies, and the same indicators of verbal immediacy as in the previous study.

Analyses failed to produce sex main effects or interactions of sex with deception or with question on involvement, vocalized pauses, nonvocalized pauses, other nonfluencies, turn-switch pauses, partner turn length, self-references, present-tense verbs, group references, levelers, or modifiers. The only interaction was due to differences between male deceivers and male truth-tellers rather than between men and women. Women did lean forward more and had shorter turns than men, but these relationships did not differ by deception. Thus, as with previous investigations, the results are most consistent with the conclusion that deceptive communication is largely independent of biological sex effects.

Deceptive and Truthful Behaviors During Mock Theft Interviews

The fifth investigation explored, among other things, the impact that modality might have on cognitive, motivational, and affective states underlying deceptive displays. A mock theft paradigm was used in which participants ($N = 194$) were assigned to a guilty (deceptive) condition, in which they were instructed to "steal" a wallet that was left in their classroom on a specific day, or an innocent (truthful) condition, in which they were alerted to a potential theft that would occur in their class on a given day. All were interviewed by a trained interviewer immediately after the class session and were told that their task was to convince an interviewer that they did not steal the wallet. Interviews were either conducted face to face or from separate locales by use of text chat or audio communication. Following the interview, participants rated how hard they tried to control their behavior, how much arousal they felt, how cognitively difficult the task was, and how motivated they were to succeed.

Results revealed that modality and deception significantly affected self-reported behavioral control, arousal, cognitive difficulty, and motivation (Burgoon, Blair & Hamel, 2005); however, there were no significant main effects for sex or interactions between sex and deception on any of the measures. Given that the sample size afforded more than ample power to detect interactions, the lack of any sex-related effects bolsters the conclusion that not only do deception displays generalize to both men and women but also the cognitive, affective, and motivational states associated with them.

Conclusions About Sex Effects in Encoding of Deception

Overall, the evidence from these and prior investigations is not compelling that men and women differ substantially in their deception profiles. A reexamination of all five experiments showed that sex had minimal influence on the verbal and nonverbal demeanor of deceivers in interpersonal exchanges. Although there was some variability in the cues examined in each experiment, where the same measures appeared at least twice, sex failed to consistently alter the same nonverbal and verbal deception displays across those studies. Moreover, in any given study, the number of nonsignificant sex by deception interactions far exceeded the number of significant ones. The fairest conclusion to be drawn is that biological sex plays a very small role in deceptive encoding, or, put differently, men and women share similar motivations, affective responses, and display patterns under deception.

The few main effects that emerged hint at men opting to manage behavior by restricting nonverbal activity, with resultant decrements in apparent expressivity. If this is a strategic ploy for controlling leakage when deceiving by restraining physical activity, it might be an unwise choice, especially when coupled with a tendency to withdraw from the interaction, as the combined tactics run the risk of appearing abnormal and suspicious if overdone. Comparatively, women might leak more arousal when deceiving but might also create more of an appearance of expressivity, immediacy, and engagement. This pattern of greater involvement by women is the most recurrent sex difference across the experiments and is consistent with other research showing greater nonverbal expressivity by women. As an intentional strategy, it also might be the more efficacious, in light of previous findings that higher involvement and the appearance of normalcy while deceiving are most likely to earn high credibility ratings and to evade detection (Burgoon, Buller, Guerrero, & Feldman, 1996). However, the greater activation associated with it risks conveying nervousness. It is also possible that men attempt to become more conversationally dominant than women when deceiving, but their self-assessments are not borne out by observers' perceptions, so this might be more perceived than real.

Women and men were inconsistent in their use of image-management strategies that projected a positive front. In one experiment, men when deceiving were observed to nod more than women, a behavior that typically occurs in the backchannel as a sign of agreement or attentiveness. In another experiment, women adopted a less formal conversational style when deceiving as opposed to telling the truth, and, if our interpretation of personal pronoun use is correct, created a greater sense of inclusiveness and solidarity. It is therefore possible that women and men use different image-management strategies, but we are hesitant to make such a claim on the basis of such limited and inconsistent evidence across these investigations.

SEX AND THE DECODING OF DECEPTION

Extensive research indicating that women are more accurate and skilled in decoding nonverbal communication (Burgoon & Bacue, 2002) implies that women should be superior to men in detecting deceit. But despite the fact that in the past 60 years, over 100 studies have examined humans' abilities to detect deceit, few studies have examined sex differences (see Fay & Middleton, 1941; Marston, 1920, for the earliest work, see Buller & Burgoon, 1994; Burgoon, Buller, Guerrero et al., 1996; Feeley & deTurck, 1995; Feeley, deTurck, & Young, 1995; and Robinson, 1996 for more recent studies). Those that have been conducted have either considered differences between men and women or differences caused by the sex composition of the dyad.

Sex Differences in Overall Accuracy

Two meta-analyses reported that women detect deception better than men. In the earliest meta-analysis, Zuckerman, DePaulo, and Rosenthal (1981) found that women were slightly better at detecting deception than men. In a later meta-analysis that had only four studies in common with the earlier one, Kalbfleisch (1985) similarly reported that women were slightly better able to detect deception (accuracy $M = 61\%$) than men ($M = 59\%$). The small detection advantage enjoyed by women is consistent with women's general superiority at judging nonverbal behavior and their social sensitivity. However, several recent experiments have failed to turn up gender differences in deception detection (Feeley et al., 1995; Millar & Millar, 1995; Vrij & Semin, 1996) or have produced contradictory results. One counterexample by DePaulo, Epstein, and Wyer (1993) found that women were more likely to accept deceptive communicators' praise for another's artwork at face value, whereas men were not. Hence, women were less accurate in their judgments of sender veracity than men. These results might be explained by the accommodation hypothesis (Rosenthal & DePaulo, 1979a), in which women are more inclined to tune into communicators' intentional messages and to overlook unintended cues. However, the greater detection advantage by women implies that women are not routinely accommodating to the deliberate communication of others.

Sex Composition of the Sender–Receiver Dyad

More consistent have been findings of the impact of sex composition of the dyad. Both the Kalbfleisch (1985) and Zuckerman et al. (1981) meta-analyses reported that both men and women are better able to detect female deceit ($M = 54\%$) than male deceit ($M = 51\%$), but this accuracy depends partly on the sex of the judge. Zuckerman et al., found greater accuracy in same-sex than opposite-sex dyads. By contrast, Kalbfleisch found that men had more difficulty judging same-sex actors ($M = 50\%$) than opposite-sex ones ($M = 52\%$), whereas women were more successful judging same-sex targets ($M = 54\%$) than opposite-sex ones ($M = 50\%$). One reason why results might differ between the two meta-analyses is the total number of male versus female actors being judged. Given that men are more difficult to judge, a disproportionate amount of male or female actors in one of the meta-analyses would have produced lopsided accuracy results. Subsequent studies by DePaulo and associates (DePaulo, Stone, & Lassiter, 1985; DePaulo & Tang, 1994) showed that deceptions by opposite-sex senders were more easily detected than those by same-sex senders, that lies told by women were more often detected than those told by men (consistent with the findings from both meta-analyses), and that the lies of female communicators were more accurately detected than the lies of male communicators by men with social anxiety. These results indicate that men as deceptive senders were not easily detected by other men. Finally, Feeley and deTurck (1995) reported that both male and female observers were more accurate when judging the veracity of male deceivers than male truth-tellers; that is, male deceit is more recognizable than male truths.

One reason that sex composition of the dyad alters detection abilities might be that men and women judge the behavior of other men and women differently. O'Hair, Cody, Gross, and Krayer (1988) found that men evaluated male communicators as being more honest when they exhibited high levels of attentiveness; they evaluated female communicators as being more honest when they exhibited high levels of friendliness. In contrast, female observers relied primarily on perceptions of attentiveness when judging the honesty of both men and women; perceptions of friendliness were secondary predictors of these honesty judgments. The different verbal and nonverbal cues that factor into male versus female judgments of veracity appear to warrant more investigation, especially as to whether they explain differences in detection that are due to sex composition of the dyad.

Reactions to Detected Deception

The only other tangentially related literature concerns how men and women differ in their responses to deception. Camden, Motley, and Wilson (1984) reported that women consider deception to be less permissible and more reprehensible than do men, which fits with women's tendency to be more accommodating than men (Rosenthal & DePaulo, 1979a, 1979b). Women, because they choose to believe what others say to them, might consider deception to be a more serious violation of the conversational expectation or maxim for honesty. This might be why women said that they would more vigorously pursue serious lies when they suspect they are being duped than did men (DePaulo et al., 1993). Their pursuit supposedly would include scrutinizing behavior, looking for additional evidence, and expressing their suspicions to others. Further, women reported being angry and upset by serious lies to a much greater degree, and for a longer period of time, than men. These intense reactions to deception might account for the detection advantage that women enjoy. That they do not translate into far greater decoding accuracy may be attributable to the mix of factors noted earlier, including a proclivity to favor senders' intended signals and to overlook unintended ones. These differences can also be overcome by training (deTurck, 1991).

Tests of Detection Accuracy from Our Experiments

Three experiments from our research program on interactive deception examined accuracy in detection. The first, reported in Burgoon, Buller, Ebesu, and Rockwell (1994), is the same experiment already described examining different types of deception during interviews. Senders gave truthful answers to the first three questions and then falsified, equivocated, or concealed relevant information on the remainder. Accuracy scores were computed by taking the absolute difference between receivers' estimates of sender truthfulness and senders' reports of actual truthfulness in answering each of the interview questions; higher scores represent less accuracy.

Reanalysis of this experiment for sex effects showed that the deceptions of women ($M = 2.66$) were more easily detected than those of men ($M = 3.17$), thus bolstering the results from prior research as well as expanding generalizability of those results beyond outright lies to different types of deception. Also consistent with most past research, a near-significant interaction between sex of sender, sex of receiver, and deception type showed that men lying (fabricating) to men were the least detectable ($M = 4.14$), and women lying to women were the most detectable ($M = 1.43$). In other words, male receivers had the most difficulty judging same-sex senders, whereas female receivers were highly accurate in judging same-sex senders.

The second experiment, already reported as looking at dynamic changes in deception displays (Burgoon et al., 1999), included Person B's estimates of Person A's truthfulness for each of the 12 questions and Person A's estimate of his or her success in conveying truthfulness for each question. These ratings were obtained after each question was asked. Reanalysis of these data for gender effects found no main effects or interactions with deception on either the honesty ratings by Persons B or the success ratings by Persons A. Sex, then, failed to affect detection in this case.

A third experiment (Tilley, George & Marett, 2005) entailed resume faking. Research has shown that from 25% to 67% of applicants lie on their resumes and defend these lies in job interviews (Prater & Kiser, 2002). Participants ($N = 156$) were students from upper division MIS courses who received extra course credit and $10 gift certificates for participating in a study using computer-mediated communication. Applicants brought resumes to the interview. They were asked to enhance their resumes as much as possible to make themselves look like the best candidate. The applicants were then interviewed for up to 20 minutes by means of one of four media types of electronic media: e-mail, Internet relay chat (IRC), IRC with audio, and audio only over IRC. Research assistants compared original with enhanced resumes to identify instances of deception. Afterward, interviewers were asked to identify what, if any, answers seemed dishonest.

Results showed a difference for detection success by sex. Again, women ($M = 0.16$) were better at deception detection than men ($M = 0.06$). However, because the detection accuracy rate was so low (less than 8%) in the aforementioned study, sex differences were slight. Detection differences by modality were unrelated to biological sex.

CONCLUSION AND SUMMARY

Research on sex differences and similarities reported in the deception and detection literature is relatively sparse, considering the volume of research available on encoding and decoding deceptive and truthful messages. It appears that few researchers looking at deception have considered sex differences, or else they have failed to find such differences and tests of sex effects have been relegated to the "file drawer."

However, as the preceding reviews and original data show, although there are some reliable differences between men and women in nonverbal and verbal conversational behavior, there are few consistent or strong differences on deceptive performances. Where there are hints of differences, they might reflect subtle variations in tactics rather than massive departures from overall deception strategies. That is, both men and women might generally attempt to control physical activity and to convey a normal level of conversational involvement, but men might be more inclined to emphasize the former and women, the latter. Consequently, men might opt for reduced nonverbal immediacy and greater physical restraint than women (resulting in less apparent other-centeredness), for shorter response latencies and more nodding to manage the conversation and counteract other noninvolvement cues, and for briefer turns, which may provide greater information control. Women might opt for maintaining a normal appearance through greater immediacy and expressivity (with risks of concomitant leakage of arousal) and displays of informality and affiliation that minimize personal responsibility for their discourse. These depictions, of course, are tentative and deserve further investigation. In many other respects, men and women appear to behave similarly, especially in terms of appearing pleasant, nondominant, and involved in a global sense.

Regarding sex and decoding of deception, the claim of an overall superiority for women continues to garner support, in line with findings in other domains of greater female sensitivity to social information. However, these effects are modest and moderated by the sex composition of the interacting pair such that women's deceits are more readily detected than men's deceits. Whether same-sex or opposite-sex detection is superior remains open to question. We would welcome serious attempts to sort out these conflicting findings as part of an increasing shift from emphasis on individual variables to dyadic ones and to greater attention to the dynamic interplay between individual communicators as deceptive episodes unfold.

ACKNOWLEDGMENTS

Preparation of this manuscript was supported by funding from the U.S. Air Force Office of Scientific Research under the U. S. Department of Defense University Research Initiative (Grant F49620-01-1-0394). The views, opinions, or findings in this report are those of the authors and should not be construed as an official Department of Defense position, policy, or decision.

REFERENCES

Buller, D. B., & Burgoon, J. K. (1994). Deception: Strategic and nonstrategic communication. In A. Daly & J. M. Wiemann (Eds.), *Strategic interpersonal communication* (pp. 191–223). Hillsdale, NJ: Lawrence Erlbaum Associates.

Buller, D. B., & Burgoon, J. K. (1996). Interpersonal deception theory. *Communication Theory, 6*, 203–242.

Buller, D. B., Burgoon, J. K., Buslig, A., & Roiger, J. (1994). Interpersonal deception: VIII. Nonverbal and verbal correlates of equivocation from the Bavelas et al. (1990) research. *Journal of Language and Social Psychology, 13*, 396–417.

Buller, D. B., Burgoon, J. K., Buslig, A., & Roiger, J. (1996). Testing interpersonal deception theory: The language of interpersonal deception. *Communication Theory, 6*, 268–289.

Buller, D. B., Burgoon, J. K., White, C., & Ebesu, A. S. (1994). Interpersonal deception: VII. Behavioral profiles of falsification, concealment, and equivocation. *Journal of Language and Social Psychology, 13*, 366–395.

Burgoon, J. K. (1991). Relational messages interpretation of touch, conversational distance, and posture. *Journal of Nonverbal Behavior, 15*, 233–260.

Burgoon, J. K. (2005). Nonverbal measurement of deceit. In V. Manusov (Ed.), *The source book of nonverbal measures: going beyond words* (pp. 237–250). Hillsdale, NJ: Lawrence Erlbaum Associates.

Burgoon, J. K., & Bacue, A. (2003). Nonverbal communication skills. In B. R. Burleson & J. O. Greene (Eds.), *Handbook of Communication Skills* (pp. 179–219). Mahwah, NJ: Lawrence Erlbaum Associates.

Burgoon, J. K., & Buller, D. B. (1994). Interpersonal deception: III. Effects of deceit on perceived communication and nonverbal behavior dynamics. *Journal of Nonverbal Behavior, 18*, 155–184.

Burgoon, J. K., Buller, D. B., Ebesu, A., & Rockwell, P. (1994). Interpersonal deception: V. Accuracy in deception detection. *Communication Monograph, 61*, 303–325.

Burgoon, J. K., Buller, D., Floyd, K., & Grandpre, J. (1996). Deceptive realities: Sender, receiver, and observer perspectives in deceptive conversations. *Communication Research, 23*, 724–748.

Burgoon, J. K., Buller, D., Guerrero, L., Afifi, W., & Feldman, C. (1996). Interpersonal deception: XII. Information management dimensions underlying deceptive and truthful messages. *Communication Monographs, 63*, 50–69.

Burgoon, J. K., Buller, D. B., Guerrero, L., & Feldman, C. M. (1994). Interpersonal deception: VI. Viewing deception success from deceiver and observer perspectives: Effects of preinteractional and interactional factors. *Communication Studies, 45*, 263–280.

Burgoon, J. K., Buller, D. B., Grandpre, J., & Kalbfleisch, P. (1998). Sex differences in presenting and detecting deceptive messages. In D. Canary & K. Dindia (Eds.), *Sex differences and similiarities in communication* (pp. 351–372). Mahwah, NJ: Lawrence Erlbaum Associates.

Burgoon, J. K., Buller, D. B., White, C., Afifi, W., & Buslig, A. (1999). The role of conversational involvement in deceptive interpersonal interactions. *Personality and Social Psychology Bulletin, 25*, 669–685.

Burgoon, J. K., Blair, J. P., & Hamel, L. (2005). *Deception and motivation: Impairment or facilitation?* Paper submitted to the annual meeting of the International Communication Association, Dresden, Germany.

Burgoon, J. K., Buller, D. B., & Woodall, W. G. (1996). *Nonverbal Communication: The Unspoken Dialogue*. New York: McGraw-Hill.

Burgoon, J. K., Le Poire, B. A., & Rosenthal, R. (1995). Effects of preinteraction expectancies and target communication on reciprocity and compensation in dyadic interaction. *Journal of Experimental Social Psychology, 31*, 287–321.

Camden, C., Motley, M. T., & Wilson, A. (1984). White lies in interpersonal communication: A taxonomy and preliminary investigation of social motivations. *Western Journal* of *Speech Communication, 48*, 309–325.

Cody, M. J., & O'Hair, H. D. (1983). Nonverbal communication and deception: Differences in deception cues due to gender and communicator dominance. *Communication Monographs, 50*, 175–192.

DePaulo, B. M. (1992). Nonverbal behavior and self-presentation. *Psychological Bulletin, 111*, 203–243.

DePaulo, B. M., Epstein, J. A., & Wyer, M. M. (1993). Sex differences in lying: How women and men deal with the dilemma of deceit. In M. Lewis & C. Saarni (Eds.), *Lying and deception in everyday life*. New York: Guilford.

DePaulo, B. M., Lindsay, J., Malone, B., Muhlenbruck, L., Charlton, K., & Cooper, H. (2003). Cues to deception. *Psychological Bulletin, 129*, 74–118.

DePaulo, B. M., Stone, J. I., & Lassiter, G. D. (1985). Deceiving and detecting deceit. In B. R. Schlenker (Ed.), *The self and social life* (pp. 323–370). New York: McGraw-Hill.

DePaulo, B. M., & Tang, J. (1994). Social anxiety and social judgment: The example of detecting deception. *Journal of Research in Personality, 28*, 142–153.

deTurck, M. A., & Miller, G. R. (1985). Deception and arousal: Isolating the behavioral correlates of deception. *Human Communication Research, 12*, 181–201.

Donaghy, W. C., Grandpre, J. R., & Davies, L. (1994, February). *Validating deception detection stimuli: Grouped data vs. subject to subject approaches*. Paper presented at the annual meeting of the Western Speech Communication Association, San Jose, CA.

Duncan, V. J., & Kalbfleisch, P. J. (1995, February). *Race, gender, and perceptions of deceptiveness*. Paper presented at the the annual meeting of the Western Speech Communication Association, San Jose, CA.

Fay, P. J., & Middleton, W. C. (1941). The ability to judge truth-telling, or lying, from the voice as transmitted over a public address system. *Journal of General Psychology, 24*, 211–215.

Feeley, T. H., & deTurck, M. A. (1995). Global cue usage in behavioral lie detection. *Communication Quarterly, 43*, 420–430.

Feeley, T. H., deTurck, M. A., & Young, M. J. (1995). Baseline familiarity in lie detection. *Communication Research Reports, 12*, 160–169.

Hall, J. A. (1984). *Nonverbal sex differences: Communication accuracy and expressive style*. Baltimore: Johns Hopkins University Press.

Kalbfleisch, P. J. (1985). Accuracy in deception detection: A quantitative review. *Dissertation Abstracts International, 46*, 4453B.

Marston, W. M. (1920). Reaction-time symptoms of deception. *Journal of Experimental Psychology, 3*, 72–87.

Millar, M., & Millar, K. (1995). Detection of deception in familiar and unfamiliar persons: The effects of information restriction. *Journal of Nonverbal Behavior, 19*, 69–84.

Miller, G. R., Bauchner, J. E., Hocking, J. E., Fontes, N. E., Kaminski, E. P., & Brandt, D. R. (1981). "and nothing but the truth": How well can observers detect deceptive testimony? In B. D. Sales (Ed.), *The trial process* (pp. 0–0). New York: Plenum.

O'Hair, H. D., & Cody, M. J. (1987). Gender and vocal stress differences during truthful and deceptive information sequences. *Human Relations, 40*, 1–14.

O'Hair, H. D., Cody, M. J., Gross, B., & Krayer, K. J. (1988). The effect of gender, deceit orientation and communicator style on macro-assessments of honesty. *Communication Quarterly, 36*, 77–93.

Prater, T., & Kiser, S. B. (2002). Lies, lies, and more lies. *SAM Advanced Management Journal, Spring*, 9–36.

Riggio, R. E., & Friedman, H. S. (1983). Individual differences and cues to deception. *Journal of Personality & Social Psychology, 45*, 899–915.

Riggio, R. E., Tucker, J., & Throckmorton, B. (1987). Social skills and deception ability. *Personality and Social Psychology Bulletin, 13*, 568–577.

Robinson, W. P. (1996). *Deceit, delusion, and detection.* Thousand Oaks, CA: Sage.

Rosenthal, R., & DePaulo, B. M. (1979a). Sex differences in accommodation in nonverbal communication. In R. Rosenthal (Ed.), *Skill in nonverbal communication* (pp. 68–103). Cambridge, MA: Oelgeschlanger, Gunn, & Hain.

Rosenthal, R., & DePaulo, B. M. (1979b). Sex differences in eavesdropping on nonverbal cues. *Journal of Personality & Social Psychology, 37*, 273–285.

Tannen, D. (1994). *Gender and discourse.* New York: Oxford University Press.

Tilley, P., George, J. F., & Marett, K. (2005). Gender differences in deception and its detection under varying electronic media conditions. *Proceedings of the* 38th *Annual Hawaii International Conference on System Sciences Janujary.*

Vrij, A., & Semin, G. R. (1996). Lie experts' beliefs about nonverbal indicators of deception. *Journal of Nonverbal Behavior, 20*, 65–80.

Zuckerman, M., DePaulo, B., & Rosenthal, R. (1981). Verbal and nonverbal communication of deception. In L. Berkowitz (Ed.), *Advances in experimental social psychology* (Vol. 14, pp. 1–59). New York: Academic Press.

Zuckerman, M., & Driver, R. (1985). Telling lies: Verbal and nonverbal correlates of deception. In A. W. Siegman & S. Feldstein (Eds.), *Nonverbal communication: An integrated perspective* (pp. 129–147). Hillsdale, NJ: Lawrence Erlbaum Associates.

15

Perceptions of Men and Women Departing From Conversational Sex-Role Stereotypes

A. Elizabeth Lindsey
Walter R. Zakahi
New Mexico State University

In 1995, Stephanie Glazer filed a $1 million gender bias suit against the New York Rangers hockey franchise. The suit is based on her claim that she was "removed from the hockey arena for using unfeminine language" ("Female Hockey Fan", 1995, p. C2). Even as she was being removed, however, Glazer charges that male hockey fans were yelling obscenities "in an effort to bait the usher," but Glazer quotes a security guard who winked and smiled as saying, "Guys, no bad language." Glazer's suit presents an extreme example of what might happen when people violate sex-role norms. We are all familiar with the feminine stereotype that women should behave like ladies. An important part of this stereotype, apparently even at some hockey games, is that ladies do not use vulgar language. By contrast, one stereotype of men is that they more commonly use vulgar and obscene language (De Klerk, 1991).

The consequences of sex-role violations are not usually as extreme as the one Ms. Glazer claims to have suffered. It is more likely that the sanctions for sex-role violations are implicit. Such subtle sanctions, however, remain common in the context of day-to-day interaction. Nonverbal behaviors such as dirty looks or verbal sanctions such as a request for behavior change are not uncommon. For example, the male author of this chapter recalls being only rarely sanctioned for his occasional use of vulgar language in public, whereas the female author has used the same type of language and received negative comments. Barring overt verbal and nonverbal sanctions, violations of sex-role norms may influence our behavior in more subtle and insidious ways. We may select mating partners and friends, hire, elect club members, and just generally favor some individuals over others based on whether a man or woman conforms or departs from stereotypical masculine or feminine roles.

In this chapter we review the literature on sex-role stereotypes, violations of those stereotypes, and perceptions of the violations. We then describe two of our own experiments designed to examine perceptions and evaluations of sex-role stereotype violations, with an emphasis on the violation of conversational behaviors during initial interaction. We begin the chapter with a discussion of sex-role stereotypes and the implications of sex-role stereotyping, examining particularly three relatively recent and conceptually influential theoretical treatments of sex-role stereotyping by Bem (1993), Eagly (1987), and Deaux and Major (1987, 1990).

SEX-ROLE STEREOTYPES

Researchers have questioned the value of positing differences between the sexes, arguing that research on sex differences has failed to reveal meaningful differences between men and women (e.g., Canary & Hause, 1993; MacGeorge, Graves, Feng, & Gillihan, 2004; Shibley Hyde & Plant, 1995; but see Eagly, 1987; Shibley Hyde & Frost, 1993). The population of the United States, however, seems to be blissfully unaware that sex differences are supposed to be only minimal and may continue to operate under the assumptions of sex-role stereotypes. Scholars have described the use of sex-role stereotypes as extensive (Eagly; Norris & Wylie, 1995; Ruble, 1983; Smith & Midlarsky, 1985) and even pervasive (Broverman, Vogel, Broverman, Clarkson, & Rosenkrantz, 1972; Heilman, 1997; Deaux & Major, 1987; Williams & Best, 1982). A fairly recent survey of 224 male managers, sampled from a variety of industries and departments, illustrates this pervasiveness (Heilman, Block, & Martell, 1995). When asked to rate either men or women on seven work-relevant characteristics, the managers demonstrated several stereotypical views of both men and women: they tended to perceive men, for example, as more competent, stable and potent than women, both generally and more specifically, when the men or women rated were in management positions. Heilman et al., also found that men, in general, were rated by managers as being more independent whereas women were perceived as having more concerns for others.

Several researchers have argued that sex-role stereotypes are not only widespread but persistent (Deal & Stevenson; 1998; Ruble, 1983; Werner & LaRussa, 1985). Werner and LaRussa replicated research conducted by Sherriffs and McKee in 1957 to find little change in sex-role stereotypes over time. Borisoff and Merrill (1992) argued that male and female stereotypes "have been with us for centuries" (p. 16), and Bem (1993) contends that the roots of sex-role stereotypes can be traced to some of our oldest institutions and ways of thinking (e.g., theology, Greek philosophy).

At a broad level, the content of sex-role stereotypes ascribes an agentic quality to men and a communal quality to women (Deaux & Kite, 1993; Eagly, 1987; Smith, 1985). Described more specifically, the agentic stereotype of men includes qualities such as "self-assertion (e.g., aggressive, ambitious, dominant, forceful, acts as a leader) and independence from other people (e.g., independent, self-reliant, self-sufficient, individualistic)" (Eagly, p. 16). The communal stereotype describes women as nurturing, affectionate, helpful, and emotionally expressive. Generally, women are portrayed as being "concerned for the welfare of other people" (Deaux & Kite, p. 113).

The agentic and communal stereotypes of men and women are typified by several communication behaviors. Women tend to be more inclusive and encouraging of others during conversation. For example, women are more likely than men to invite and encourage the participation of others in conversation (Fishman, 1978; McMillan, Clifton, McGrath, & Gale, 1977; Wood, 1996). Women smile, provide more attentiveness signals, and make more eye contact than do men (Basow, 1986; Duncan & Fiske, 1977). The agentic and controlling stereotype of men may manifest in communication behaviors such as talking for longer periods of time than women, particularly during opposite-sex interactions (Borisoff & Merrill, 1992). Nonverbally, men tend to be less facially expressive, use a loud voice, and invade space (Ortega Murphy & Zorn, 1996). Theoretical approaches by Eagly (1987), Deaux and Major (1987), and Bem (1993) provide a framework for understanding how agentic and communal stereotypical behaviors become manifest during interaction.

An Interaction-Based Model of Sex-Role Stereotypes

Deaux and Major (1987) provided an explanation for sex-role behavior at the level of the conversation. In their model, gender-related behavior is a product of a dynamic process in which each participant's gender belief system (including sex-role stereotypes) influences his or her partner's behavior as well as his or her own behavior. Deaux and Major argued that gender behavior is a product of negotiations that occur during interaction. This negotiation process is a product of two competing forces. First, a person's sex-role stereotypes can influence his or her partner's behavior through the expectancies that he or she communicates. Sex-role stereotypes operate as expectations for the appropriate behavior of men and women in interaction. Sex-role stereotypes, like other behavioral expectations, tend to be confirmed. Deaux and Major highlighted the substantial evidence on expectancy confirmation in general and on sex-role expectations in particular. Acknowledging the powerful influence of expectations to influence behavior, Deaux and Major recognized that expectations do not operate independently of the target's own self-concept and self-expectancies.

The second contributor to this process is the target's self-concept. The target's sex- role stereotypes will tend to influence his or her own behavior so as to construct a particular self presentation (Deaux & Major, 1990). The target holds a self-schema that includes a gender identity; this identity is partially a product of the actor's own sex-role stereotypes. Activation of the sex-role schemata constitutes a significant part of the model by Deaux and Major (1987). Sex-role schemata only matter if they have been raised to an awareness level for the actors in a conversation. Deaux and Major did not assume that all interaction results in activation of sex-role schemata. Certain situations are more likely to activate schemata than others. For example, a target's personal attributes may activate a schemata. Conversing with a petite woman or a rugged-looking man may stimulate the sex-role schemata. The situation also activates the sex-role schemata. A school-sponsored dance may make sex-role beliefs more salient, or conversing with the only man or women working for your company may activate the sex-role schemata.

Of particular interest to us is the uncertainty of an initial interaction between men and women and how it is likely to activate the sex-role schemata. According to Bierhoff (1989), schemata and stereotypes in general are likely to be employed during initial social encounters because they allow perceivers to reduce uncertainty quickly and simply. It is noteworthy that such activation can occur below the perceiver's level of awareness. Schneider, Hastorf, and Ellsworth (1979) noted that people can be responsive to the behavior of a person even when they are not consciously aware of the other person's behavior.

Social Role Interpretations of Sex-Role Stereotypes

Eagly (1987) offered social roles as an alternative to socialization or biology as explanations for sex differences. Eagly borrowed the concepts of structural and cultural approaches from House (1981) to explain her approach. Cultural approaches explain group differences as an outgrowth of socialization. Children learn cultural beliefs and values that later help to account for their behavior as adults. By contrast, structural explanations, such as Eagly's role theory, argue that group differences occur because "members of social groups experience common situational constraints because they tend to have the same or similar social positions within organizations and other structures such as families" (Eagly, 1987, p. 9). Sex-role stereotypes are an important part of Eagly's explanation of sex differences. Sex roles and sex-role stereotypes are a product of the social roles generally held by men or women. For Eagly, social roles explain the communal stereotype of women and the agentic stereotype of men.

For Eagly (1987), social roles can be a product of sex-role stereotypes. We hold stereotypes of men and women that become expectations. Because these expectations are shared by the community, they form social norms. Because members of the community consistently hold expectations for men and women, they are especially potent. As with Deaux and Major (1987), Eagly noted that evidence supports the idea that expectations result in behavioral confirmation. Eagly contended that some of the strongest evidence for behavioral confirmation of stereotypes resides in research dealing with sex stereotypes.

If sex-role stereotypes contain the power to create expectations for the behavior of others, it should be no surprise that these stereotypes are also internalized and have an influence on the target independent of the expectations of a particular perceiver. Eagly's (1987) argument appears similar to Deaux and Major's (1987) position: Sex-role stereotypes have the power to shape the behavior of a target both externally (other expectancies) and internally (self-expectancies).

Enculturated Lens Theory

Bem's (1993) enculturated lens theory is a direct outgrowth of her earlier work on androgyny and gender schema theory. Bem argued that there are three lenses that influence our day-to-day experience of gender: biological essentialism, androcentrism, and gender polarization.

The lens of biological essentialism imparts a view that sex differences between men and women can be reduced to base biological differences. The contemporary application of biological essentialism can be seen in sociobiology. For sociobiologists, sex differences are understood in evolutionary terms. For example, the genes of men who are more aggressive and promiscuous (among other things) are more likely to be passed on to successive generations. For women, genetic survival is the result of stereotypical feminine behavior such as selectivity in choosing a mate (e.g., being attracted to power or wealth) and nurturing. Certain aspects of the agentic stereotype can be seen in biological essentialism as described by Bem (1993).

The lens of androcentrism presumes that experiences are best understood from a male perspective. In other words, male experience is privileged because it is central to whatever is happening, whereas female experience is treated "as specific deviation from the allegedly universal standard" (Bem, 1993, p. 41). Bem has argued that this androcentric lens is exemplified in the practice of using masculine pronouns to describe the experiences of both men and women. She has also argued that this androcentrism is visible in Judeo-Christian theology, Greek philosophy (which she argued has had a strong influence on American culture), Freudian psychoanalysis, and the American legal system.

Simply put, the lens of gender polarization organizes our daily social experiences so that they can be performed and experienced as male or female. This is what Bem (1993) referred to as "mutually exclusive scripts" (p. 81). That is, behavior or activities are labeled as either masculine or feminine. Initiation to gender polarization begins early in life. In the United States, we easily associate the color blue with boys and the color pink with girls. Boys and girls learn through observation or through direct instruction what they can and cannot do in terms of gendered behavior. For example, if a man inspects his fingernails he does so by folding his fingers over his palms. A woman who inspects her nails does so by extending her fingers out and looking down at the back of her hand (Kenneth

Colby, as cited by Payne, 2001). A man who inspects his nails incorrectly risks being labeled feminine, or, as Bem (1993) noted, a "sissy." Gender polarization provides an entire range of behaviors and interests that are appropriate for men but not for women and for women but not for men. Bem argued, however, that the consequences of violating gender norms are a much bigger problem for men and boys than for women and girls. A much more negative connotation accompanies being labeled a "sissy" than a "tomboy."

Unlike Deaux and Major (1987) and Eagly (1987), Bem (1993) did not comment directly on how these lenses operate at the level of a conversation. Although all of the lenses would play a role in conversation, it appears to us that the lens of gender polarization would have the most direct impact on conversation. Because the lens of gender polarization implies how behavior is performed, we would expect that communication and specifically conversation would succumb to the gendered expectations described by Bem's construct of gender polarization.

VIOLATIONS OF SEX-ROLE STEREOTYPIC EXPECTATIONS FOR COMMUNICATION

The results of several studies support Bem's (1993) prediction of negative consequences for sex-role violations. Three studies by Costrich, Feinstein, Kidder, Marecek, and Pascale (1975), for example, demonstrated that popularity ratings of men and women were adversely affected when women were described as acting aggressively and men passively. Similarly, Sadalla, Kenrick, and Vershure (1987) found in three studies that men who engaged in less dominant behaviors were rated as less attractive than men who acted in a dominant manner. Addressing specifically violations of communication sex-role norms, M. Burgoon, Birk, and Hall (1991) found that female physicians communicating in an aggressive manner are rated as less persuasive in their messages than are female physicians who are more affiliative in their style of communication and use of language. Burgoon and his coauthors (M. Burgoon; M. Burgoon & Klingle, 1998) employ language expectancy theory (M. Burgoon & Miller, 1985) to explain that these latter results are due to violations of the cultural expectations we have "about appropriate persuasive communication behavior that are gender specific" (M. Burgoon & Klingle, p. 263). Similarly, communication theories such as cognitive valence theory (Andersen, 1985, 1999), discrepancy-arousal theory (Cappella & Greene, 1982), and J. Burgoon and Hale's (1988) nonverbal expectancy violations theory suggest that communication violating expectations can be perceived negatively, as determined by *characteristics of the person perceived*, *characteristics of the perceiver*, and/or *characteristics of the relationship* between the perceived and the perceiver.

As suggested by Bem (1993), an important characteristic of the person perceived is biological sex. Biological sex first and foremost triggers perceiver expectations for sex-role stereotypical communication behavior. Second, and equally importantly, biological sex can influence the extent to which departures from sex-role norms are evaluated negatively. Likewise, Sandberg, Meyer-Bahlburg, Ehrhardt, and Yager (1993) have maintained that there is less social tolerance for men's sex-role atypical behavior than there is for women's (c.f. M. Burgoon & Klingle, 1998). Selcuk, McCreary, and Mahalik (2004) similarly stated that men who act discordantly with expectations based on sex-role stereotypes are likely to be evaluated more negatively than are women who do so, and Seljuk et al., offered several possible reasons for this phenomenon. One reason is that feminine behavior, generally, is perceived as having lower status and power than is masculine behavior; a man who violates sex-role norms by acting in a feminine manner is thus seen as having less status and power than a woman who demonstrates masculine behavior. A second reason is that feminine men are more likely to be perceived as having dissimilar values to those of the perceiver than are masculine women, particularly if the perceiver is from a masculine culture that places high value on achievement and independence. A man who behaves in a feminine fashion would be perceived as having departed from these values more so than a masculine woman.

A characteristic of the perceiver relevant to perceptions of behavior that runs counter to sex-role stereotype concerns the degree to which the perceiver is *gender schematic* (Deaux & Major, 1987). Gender schematic individuals tend to adhere to traditional conceptions of male and female behavior (Deaux & Major; Martin, 1987) and may be more sensitive to and less tolerant of the violation of gender stereotypes than are *gender aschematics*, who tend to hold fewer if any sex-role expectations for individuals. According to Deaux and Major, gender schematic individuals hold descriptive and prescriptive beliefs about men and women: Gender schematics believe that traits such as instrumentality, dominance, and assertiveness are and should be associated with men, whereas affiliation, warmth, and concern are and should be associated with women. Martin proposed that these beliefs are founded on actual characteristics of men and women, although gender schematics tend to exaggerate the differences in characteristics between men and women. Accurate or not, the beliefs provide consistent and, more important, specific expectations for gender-appropriate behavior (Deaux & Major). Not only do schematics tend to hold specific expectations for male and female behavior, but their *schemata* are easily triggered by situations potentially eliciting the use of stereotyping (Deaux & Major; Martin; McKenzie-Mohr & Zanna, 1990). Initial interactions, situations in which biological sex is observable, and situations that are sex linked (especially interactions with heterosexual overtones) trigger the use of sex-role stereotyping but are particularly likely to do so for schematics (Deaux & Major). As a result, schematics tend to gender stereotype others (Martin), particularly members of the opposite sex (e.g., Anderson & Bem, 1981; Park & Hahn, 1988).

A last factor to affect the evaluations of behavior departing from gender norms concerns the level of intimacy in the relationship—a characteristic of the relationship between the target and the perceiver. Generally, people show less tolerance for deviations from expectations during initial interaction than in developed relationships (Cappella & Greene, 1982). This suggests that the violation of sex-role norms will be perceived more negatively during initial interaction than in the context of a developed relationship.

Violations of Sex-Role Expectations for Asking Questions and Talking About the Self

The influences of biological sex, degree of gender schematicity, and context were the focus of our own first investigation into others' perceptions of sex-role atypical communication (Lindsey & Zakahi, 1996; 1998). Specifically, we were interested in comparing participants' perceptions of men's and women's *question asking versus talking about themselves*, in a context in which sex-role stereotypes would be triggered: an opposite-sex, initial interaction. Although both communication behaviors constitute methods for the reduction of uncertainty in interaction (Berger, 1979; Berger & Bradac, 1982; Douglas, 1990), we argued that part of the communal stereotype for women would be asking questions during initial interaction, whereas men would be more likely to talk about themselves. Our argument was based on previous literature proposing certain functions for question asking and self-disclosure, and on previous observations that women tend to ask more questions during conversation and that men tend to self-disclose, particularly to strangers, more so than do women. We reasoned, as did Deaux and Major (1987) and Eagly (1987), that behaviors frequently observed for men and women were likely to be indicative of sex-role stereotypes (see also Eagly & Karau, 2002; Heilman, Wallen, Fuchs & Tamkins, 2004).

Question asking during conversation has been widely established as a behavior more characteristic of women than of men (e.g., Deaux, 1977; Fishman, 1978; Harding, 1975; Lakoff, 1975, McCloskey, 1987; Roby, Canary, & Burggraf, 1998; Spender, 1980), and Mulac (1998) recently concluded that questions are one of 10 linguistic features consistently found to be employed more by women and girls than by men and boys. Question asking may be especially pronounced when women are interacting with men. Brouwer, Gerritsen, and Dehaan (1979) reported that women asked more questions than men when purchasing a train ticket, and this pattern was most evident when the person selling the ticket was male. McMillan et al. (1977) found the same pattern in mixed- and same-sex problem-solving groups. Conversational analyses have suggested that one function of women's question asking is to elicit self-disclosure, as illustrated by Roby et al.'s finding that the conversational turns of wives contained significantly more non-hostile questions did those of their husbands. Roby et al., defined 'nonhostile' questions as noncritical questions designed to elicit self-disclosure. A second suggested function is to facilitate conversation (Fishman; McCloskey; Spender). Deaux suggested that, generally, women's question asking serves as a self-presentational strategy for bonding or creating affiliation during interaction and, as such, question asking would certainly seem to be consistent with the communal stereotype of women. Question asking is a conversational involvement behavior, and Coates (1986) argued directly that asking questions reflects societal expectations for women.

Societal expectations for men are reflected in a complementary behavior to question asking: talking about the self. According to Mulac (1998), the use of "I" references is one of six linguistic features generally found to distinguish men's communication from that of women. Research has further demonstrated that men talk about themselves more than do women during interactions with strangers or acquaintances (Davis, 1978; Derlega, Winstead, Wong, & Hunter, 1985; Lockheed & Hall, 1976; Stokes, Childs, & Fuehrer, 1981; Stokes, Fuehrer, & Childs, 1980), and the talk may serve one or both of two purposes. The first, as suggested by Davis, is to control the intimacy level of conversation during initial interaction. Derlega et al., argued that this strategy allows men to take advantage of reciprocity norms, so that "a man can select relatively intimate topics to disclose to a woman in order to get the woman to disclose more intimately about herself in return" (p. 27). A second function of talking about the self is to present oneself favorably. Derlega, Metts, Petronio, and Margulis (1993) noted that men are selective when talking about themselves and, more specifically, may withhold information about their vulnerabilities; men tend to talk more often about their successes (Aries, 1987). Both functions appear consistent with the male *stereotype* of control and assertiveness.

We hypothesized that conversational behavior violating sex-role norms (women who talked about themselves and men who asked questions) would be potentially evaluated less positively by perceivers than would behavior following sex-role norms (women asking questions and men who talked about themselves), depending on the extent to which perceivers had the tendency to be gender schematic. We expected gender-schematic individuals to respond less positively to sex-role norm-violating behavior during opposite-sex interactions than to behavior following norms; we did not expect a similar difference in response from gender-aschematic individuals. Second, we expected gender schematics to have less positive responses to norm-violating behavior than would gender aschematics.

We paired male and female strangers together in opposite-sex pairs for a 5-minute "getting to know you" conversation, each participant having been randomly assigned the status of either perceiver or the target perceived. Immediately prior to interaction, targets had been randomly assigned either to ask or to tell conditions. In the ask condition, targets were told to ask as much as they could about their partner during a 5-minute conversation. In the tell condition, targets were instructed to tell as much about themselves as they could to their partner during the interaction. In all, our instructions created four experimental conditions, two that would be considered sex-role typical (female ask and male tell) and two that were sex-role opposite (female tell and male ask). We assessed the gender schematicity of perceivers by using Martin's (1987) ratio measure of sex stereotyping, which they completed before arriving to the study. We measured the degree to which the perceiver felt positively during the interaction and the perceiver's ratings of the target's social attractiveness by using items from Watson, Clark, and Tellegen's (1988) Positive and Negative Affect Schedule and McCroskey and McCain's Interpersonal Attraction Scale (1974, 1979), which we requested that perceivers complete directly following the interaction.

Results from statistical analyses of the collected data indicated, first, that opposite-sex, gender schematic perceivers felt significantly less positively during their interactions with women in the tell condition than they did with women who asked questions.[1] Gender-aschematic perceivers, however, did not experience a similar difference in positive affect under the same conditions. Neither gender schematic nor gender-aschematic opposite-sex perceivers reported differences in the positive affect they experienced between the male tell and ask conditions. In comparison with gender aschematics, however, gender schematics experienced significantly less positive affect when men asked questions. Both of these results provided evidence that gender schematics were more likely than gender aschematics to be bothered by gender norm-violating behavior during opposite-sex interactions.

Although the results for positive affect were consistent with our hypotheses, almost opposite results were produced in the analysis of targets' social attractiveness. Results indicated that opposite-sex, gender schematic perceivers made no significant distinction in their social attraction toward women who asked versus women who talked about themselves. Gender schematic participants also did not find their female partners who primarily talked about themselves to be any less socially attractive than did their aschematic counterparts. Gender schematics had different perceptions of men who asked versus men who told, perceiving the sex-role norm-violating behavior of asking questions to be significantly more socially attractive than they did the behavior of tell. Further, gender schematics found the male target asking questions to be more, not less, socially attractive than did gender aschematics.

An overview of the results from the analysis of social attractiveness suggested, first, that gender schematics are not necessarily likely to be put off by behavior departing from sex-role appropriate communication, although overall they had stronger responses to the sex-role opposite targets than did gender aschematics. The results also indicated that some perceptions of violators may be less than negative, and even indeed actually positive. These results were contrary to our hypothesis, and to previous propositions that deviations from sex-role stereotypes are perceived negatively, particularly men's deviations (Bem, 1993; Sandberg et al., 1993). Last, the results are almost opposite to those we found for positive

[1]Means, effects, effect sizes and levels of statistical significance obtained from the analyses conducted have been previously reported and can be found in Lindsey and Zakahi (1996) and in a previous version of this chapter (Lindsey & Zakahi, 1998).

affect. Why would schematics find men who ask questions during an opposite-sex interaction to be more socially attractive, while feeling less positively during those interactions? Why would schematics indicate no preference between female ask and tell when it came to social attractiveness, while reporting less positive affect when they interacted with the female tell?

One explanation is that gender schematics experienced less positive affect as a result of not knowing how to interact with norm violators. Although they may like the other individual, they may experience less pleasure because of their uncertainty. Another explanation may be that the patterns reflect a difference in how the participants felt about themselves versus how they felt about the target. Perceptions of norm violators were positive, but perceptions of the self may have been less so. We suggest, as do Smith-Lovin and Robinson (1992) and Deaux and Major (1987), that behavior departing from sex-role norms is as disconfirming of the perceiver's gender identity as it is of the target's—and perhaps more so. Although the perceivers may not feel particularly that norm-violating behavior reflects negatively on the violator, it may reflect negatively on the self. Thus, a gender schematic woman may find men asking questions to be attractive while also feeling as if she's not fulfilling her gender role obligations. A gender- schematic man may not care whether a woman acts like a traditional woman beyond how it makes him feel about his own traditional role. A recent study examining self-disclosure during unstructured conversations between unacquainted college men and women (Clark et al., 2004) proposed this same explanation for their finding that the men in their study were more strongly inclined than the women to believe that higher levels of self- disclosure led to more positive perceptions of themselves.

The Catch-22: Simultaneous Positive and Negative Perceptions of Sex-Role Violations

Following our first study on perceptions of sex-role stereotypical versus atypical communication, we designed and executed a second study allowing us to examine both same- and opposite-sex perceptions of behavior more stereotypical of the opposite sex. We further examined perceptions of competence, as well as social attraction (Lindsey & Zakahi, 1998). The study was intended in part to test Tannen's (1995) claim that women should consider using a more masculine style of communication if they want to be perceived as more competent. We were also interested in comparing perceptions of competency to those for social attractiveness, based on the previous work of Bradley (1980, 1981). In one study, Bradley (1980) found that women who, themselves, did not communicate in a stereotypically feminine manner were perceived as more competent than both men and women who engaged in sex-role typical communication. Ratings of their social attractiveness, however, were not similarly more favorable, leading Bradley (1981) to conclude that although women violating communication sex-role stereotype may "succeed in being influential or are credited with intelligence and knowledge, their interpersonal relationships may yet not flourish" (p. 89).

Bradley's conclusion foreshadowed a phenomenon most recently described as a "backlash effect," a "Catch-22" (Rudman & Glick, 1999, 2001) or a "double bind" (Kawakami, White, & Langer, 2000) for women who demonstrate masculine attitudes or behaviors. The Catch-22 is that, whereas women may be perceived as more competent and effective when they demonstrate masculine or even androgynous behavior, they are otherwise judged negatively for having departed from a traditional feminine sex role. The results of our first study suggested similar simultaneous positive and less-than-positive evaluations, held toward not only women but also men.

The male and female college-aged participants in our second study were randomly assigned to one of four different conditions in which they would view a videotape of a woman asking a man questions (female ask), a woman talking about herself to a man (female tell), a man asking questions of a woman (male ask), or a man talking about himself to a woman (male tell) during a fairly brief interpersonal interaction. The same man and woman were used for each of the four videotapes. In both ask conditions, the man and woman asked similar questions ("How many classes did you have today?" "What are you studying?" "Do you get to go out much?") and smiled and nodded in response to their conversational partner's answers. In both tell conditions, the same man and woman disclosed similar items of information about the self (both had five classes that day, both were studying electrical engineering, and both were seniors with little free time) and were nonverbally nonresponsive to their conversational partner. Only the person asking or telling (target) was seen on the videotape, although his or her interactional partner's contributions to the conversation could be heard offscreen. We assessed participants' social attraction to a videotaped target by using McCroskey and McCain's (1974) Interpersonal Attraction Scale. We measured communication competence by using items from a competency scale designed by Gonzales, White, and Spitzberg (1995). Both measures were completed by participants immediately after viewing their videotape.

Our analysis of ratings for social attraction revealed, first, that participants were more socially attracted to the female target talking about herself, the female target asking questions, and the male target asking questions than they were to the male target talking about himself.[2] Results also indicated that there were no differences in this social attraction that were due to the sex of the perceiver. The former result is consistent with those found for the gender schematic perceivers in the first study, who indicated no differences in the attraction they felt toward a woman based on whether she communicatively violates sex-role stereotype, but a greater

[2]Means, effects, effect sizes and levels of statistical significance obtained from the analyses conducted have been previously reported in the previous version of this chapter (Lindsey & Zakahi, 1998).

attraction toward a man demonstrating the sex-role opposite, rather than sex-role norm, communication behavior. The latter result extends our previous findings for social attraction to same- as well as opposite-sex perceivers.

An analysis of the competency data produced a different pattern of results than those for social attraction. Unlike perceptions of social attraction, perceptions of competency were affected by the sex of our participants, although only in relation to the sex of the target; whereas there was no difference in how female perceivers rated the competency of the male and female target, male perceivers rated the female target as more competent than the male. Other results indicated that, regardless of perceiver sex, there were no differences in the perceived competence of the male target according to whether he was asking questions versus talking about himself. The female target, however, was perceived as more communicatively competent when she engaged in the sex-role opposite, tell behavior than when she asked questions. She was also judged as more competent when talking about herself than was the male target in either ask or tell conditions. These findings were not only similar to that of Bradley (1980), but consistent with Bradley's (1980, 1981) idea that a woman engaging in gender-opposite communication is positively violating expectations for lower competency.

An overview of ratings for both social attraction and communication competency prompted us to two tentative conclusions. One is that the data of this second study probably lend more credence to Tannen's (1995) suggestion that women adopt men's sex-role behavior than it provides evidence of a Catch-22. We did find that a woman who talks about herself rather than asking questions was perceived as more competent than when she was maintaining her sex-role norm. We did not find, however, a simultaneous negative evaluation of her social attractiveness. Rather, ratings suggested that a woman may benefit from talking like a man in at least this one way, with little corresponding risk to her social attractiveness. A second and similar conclusion is that men may benefit from asking questions with little corresponding risk to their perceived competence. Our sex-role violating man was viewed as more socially attractive, but no less communicatively competent, than when he was communicating stereotypically like a man.[3]

CONCLUSIONS

Results from our own and others' studies indicate that responses to persons engaging in sex-role opposite behavior are often different from those taken toward individuals conforming to their stereotypical sex-roles. Some results suggest that men will be perceived negatively for behavior more stereotypically feminine than

[3]We note these conclusions as "tentative" because our use of only one female and one male target limits our ability to generalize our results to perceptions of all women and all men.

masculine, such as acting passively (e.g., Selcuk et al., 2004). Other results support negative perceptions of women displaying a more stereotypically masculine aggression while interacting with others (e.g., M. Burgoon et al., 1991), or argue for the idea that a woman will "hang if she does, hang if she doesn't" demonstrate sex-role atypical behavior (Bradley, 1981; Rudman & Glick, 1999, 2001). Our own examination of sex-role violations suggests that, rather than being uniformly negative, responses can be negative, positive, or even neutral, depending on the dimension of evaluation and sometimes the gender schematicity of the perceiver. For example, whereas the results from the second study indicate that women who talk about themselves are seen as more competent, the first study suggests they may still engender less positive affect in schematic men. The results of both studies indicated that men who ask questions are regarded as more socially attractive, though the first study suggests that they may also elicit less positive affect in gender schematic women. On some dimensions there were no differences in perceptions; both studies indicate that women who talk are not significantly more or less socially attractive than women who ask questions.

Because perceivers' responses to sex-role atypical behavior in our studies varied, we cannot make the broad statement that violations are necessarily perceived negatively. Rather, we and other researchers investigating the violation of sex-role norms need to consider why some departures may be regarded positively whereas others are regarded as less so. As already noted, one possible explanation is the dimension of evaluation. Other possible explanations may reside in the type of sex-role behavior investigated or the context in which the behaviors were portrayed. For example, whereas Rudman and Glick (2001) examined the expressed attitudes of male and female candidates during job interviews, our own investigations focused on conversational behaviors occurring in an interpersonal context. Bradley (1981) examined conversational behavior but focused on the use of tag questions and disclaimers rather than question asking and self-disclosure. Differences between our results and those of Selcuk and his colleagues (2004) may be due to their study of passive versus assertive communication, whereas our own study examined communal versus agentic communication. Just as we cannot make broad statements about perceptions engendered by sex-role atypical behavior, we cannot yet make broad statements about departures from all sex-role behaviors, even sex-role conversational behaviors. Nonetheless, and although we are reluctant to make any sweeping conclusions about perceptions of men and women who depart from conversational sex-role stereotype, we believe that, for everyday social interaction, it can be beneficial to depart selectively from those stereotypes.

ACKNOWLEDGMENTS

We acknowledge the research assistance of Miranda Miller and the comments and contributions of the editors during the preparation of this chapter.

REFERENCES

Andersen, P. A. (1985). Nonverbal immediacy in interpersonal communication. In A. W. Siegman & S. Feldstein (Eds.), *Multichannel integrations of nonverbal behavior* (pp. 1–36). Hillsdale, NJ: Lawrence Erlbaum Associates.

Andersen, P. A. (1999). *Nonverbal communication: Forms and functions.* Mountain View, CA: Mayfield.

Anderson, S., & Bem, S. L. (1981). Sex typing and androgyny in dyadic interaction: Individual differences in response to physical attractiveness. *Journal of Personality and Social Psychology, 41*, 74–86.

Aries, E. (1987). Gender and communication. In P. Shaver & C. Hendrick (Eds.), *Sex and gender* (pp. 124–148). Newbury Park CA: Sage.

Basow, S. (1986). *Gender stereotypes: Traditions and alternatives* (2nd ed.). Pacific Grove, CA: Brooks/Cole.

Bem, S. L. (1993). *The lenses of gender: Transforming the debate on sexual inequality.* NewHaven, CT: Yale University Press.

Berger, C. R. (1979). Beyond initial interaction: Uncertainty, understanding, and the development of interpersonal relationships. In H. Giles & R. St. Clair (Eds.), *Language and social psychology* (pp. 122–144). Oxford, England: Blackwell.

Berger, C. R., & Bradac, J. J. (1982). *Language and social knowledge: Uncertainty reduction in interpersonal relations.* London: Edward Arnold.

Bierhoff, H. W. (1989). *Person perceptions and attribution.* Berlin: Springer- Verlag.

Borisoff, D., & Merrill, L. (1992). *The power to communicate: Gender differences as barriers.* Prospect Heights, IL: Waveland Press.

Bradley, P. (1980). Sex, competence and opinion deviation: An expectation states approach. *Communication Monographs, 47*, 101–110.

Bradley, P. (1981). The folk-linguistics of women's speech: An empirical examination. *Communication Monographs, 48*, 73–90.

Brouwer, D., Gerritsen, M. M., & Dehaan, D. (1979). Speech differences between women and men: On the wrong track? *Language in Society, 8*, 33–50.

Broverman, I. K., Vogel, S. R., Broverman, D. M., Clarkson, F. E., & Rosenkrantz, P. S. (1972). Sex-role stereotypes: A current appraisal. *Journal of Social Issues, 28*, 59–78.

Burgoon, J. K., & Hale, J. L. (1988). Nonverbal expectancy violations theory: Model elaboration and application to immediacy behaviors. *Communication Monographs, 55*, 58–79.

Burgoon, M., & Klingle, R.S. (1998). Gender differences in being influential and/or influenced: A challenge to prior explanations. In D. J. Canary & K. Dindia (Eds.), *Sex differences and similarities in communication* (pp. 257–286). Mahwah, NJ: Lawrence Erlbaum Associates.

Burgoon, M., Birk, T., & Hall, J. R. (1991). Compliance and satisfaction with physician–patient communication: Expectancy theory interpretation of gender differences. *Human Communication Research, 18*, 177–208.

Burgoon, M., & Miller, G. R. (1985). An expectancy interpretation of language and persuasion. In H. Giles & R. St. Clair (Eds.), *Recent advances in language, communication and social psychology* (pp. 199–229). Hillsdale, NJ: Lawrence Erlbaum Associates.

Canary, D. J., & Hause, K. S. (1993). Is there any reason to research sex differences in communication? *Communication Quarterly, 41*, 129–144.

Cappella, J., & Greene, J. (1982). A discrepancy-arousal explanation of mutual influence in expressive behavior for adult and infant-adult interaction. *Communication Monographs, 49*, 9–114.

Clark, R. A., Dockum, M., Hazeu, H., Huang, M., Luo, N., Ramsey, J., & Spyrou, A. (2004). Initial encounters of young men and women: Impressions and disclosure estimates. *Sex Roles, 50*, 699–709.

Coates, J. (1986). *Women, men and language.* New York: Longman.

Costrich, N., Feinstein, J., Kidder, L., Marecek, J., & Pascale, L. (1975). When stereotypes hurt: Three studies of penalties for sex-role reversals. *Journal of Experimental Social Psychology, 11*, 520–530.

Davis, J. D. (1978). When boy meets girl: Sex roles and the negotiation of intimacy in an acquaintance exercise. *Journal of Personality and Social Psychology, 36*, 684–692.

Deal, J. J., & Stevenson, M. A. (1998). Perceptions of female and male managers in the 1990s plus ca change. *Sex Roles, 38*, 287–300.

Deaux, K. (1977). Sex differences. In T. Blass (Ed.), *Personality variances in social behavior* (pp. 357–377). Hillsdale, NJ: Lawrence Erlbaum Associates.

Deaux, K., & Kite, M. (1993). Gender stereotypes. In F. L. Denmark & M. A. Paludi (Eds.), Psychology of women: A handbook of issues and theories (pp. 107–139). Westport, CT: Greenwood.

Deaux, K., & Major, B. (1987). Putting gender into context: An interactive model of gender-related behavior. *Psychological Review, 94*, 369–389.

Deaux, K., & Major, B. (1990). A social-psychological model of gender. In D. L. Rhode (Ed.), *Theoretical perspectives on sexual difference* (pp. 89–99). New Haven, CT: Yale University Press.

De Klerk, V. (1991). Expletives: Men only? *Communication Monographs, 55*, 156– 169.

Derlega, V., Metts, S., Petronio, S., & Margulis, S. T. (1993). *Self disclosure*. Newbury Park, CA: Sage.

Derlega, V., Winstead, B., Wong, P., & Hunter, S. (1985). Gender effects in an initial encounter: A case where men exceeded women in disclosure. *Journal of Social and Personal Relationships, 2*, 25–44.

Douglas, W. (1990). Uncertainty, information-seeking, and liking during initial interaction. *Western Journal of Speech Communication, 54*, 66–81.

Duncan, S., & Fiske, D. W. (1977). *Face-to-face interaction: Research, methods and theory*. Hillsdale, NJ: Lawrence Erlbaum Associates.

Eagly, A. H. (1987). *Sex differences in social behavior: A social role interpretation*. Hillsdale, NJ: Lawrence Erlbaum Associates.

Eagly, A. H., & Karau, S. J. (2002). Role congruity theory of prejudice toward female leaders. *Psychological Review, 109*, 573–598.

Female hockey fan files suit for equal right to swear a blue streak (1995, September 18). *The San Diego Union-Tribune*, p. C2.

Fishman, P. M. (1978). Interaction: The work women do. *Social Problems, 25*, 397–406.

Gonzales, F., White, C., & Spitzberg, B. H. (1995, February). *Is humor all that funny? The functions of humor in interpersonal relationships*. Paper presented at the WSCA conference, Portland, OR.

Harding, S. (1975). Women and words in a Spanish village. In R. Reiter (Ed.), *Toward an anthropology of women* (pp. 294–368). New York: Monthly Review Press.

Heilman, M. E. (1997). Sex discrimination and the affirmative action remedy: The role of sex stereotypes. *Journal of Business Ethics, 16*, 877–889.

Heilman, M. E., Block, C. J., & Martell, R. F. (1995). Sex stereotypes: Do they influence perceptions of managers? *Journal of Social Behavior and Personality, 10*, 237–252.

Heilman, M. E., Wallen, A. S., Fuchs, D., & Tamkins, M. M. (2004). Penalities for success: Reactions to women who succeed at male gender-typed tasks. *Journal of Applied Psychology, 89*, 416–427.

House, J. (1981). Social structure and personality. In M. Rosenberg & K. Turner (Eds.), *Social psychology: Sociological perspectives* (pp. 525–561). New York: Basic Books.

Kawakami, C., White, J. B., & Langer, E. J. (2000). Mindful and masculine: Freeing women leaders from the constraints of gender roles. *Journal of Social Issues, 56*, 49–69.

Lakoff, R. (1975). *Language and women's place*. New York: Harper & Row.

Lindsey, A. E., & Zakahi, W. R. (1996). Women who tell and men who ask: Perceptions of men and women departing from gender stereotypes during initial interaction. *Sex Roles, 34*, 767–786.

Lindsey, A. E., & Zakahi, W. R. (1998). Perceptions of men and women departing from conversational sex-role stereotypes during initial interaction. In D. J. Canary & K. Dindia (Eds.), *Sex differences and similarities in communication* (pp. 393–412). Mahwah, NJ: Lawrence Erlbaum Associates.

Lockheed, M. E., & Hall, K. P. (1976). Conceptualizing sex as a status characteristics: Applications to leadership training strategies. *Journal of Social Issues, 32*, 111–124.

MacGeorge, E. L., Groves, A. R., Feng, B. & Gillihan, S. J. (2004). The myth of gender cultures: Similarities outweight differences in men's and women's provisions of and responses to supportive communication. *Sex Roles: A Journal of Research, 50*, 143–176.

Martin, C. L. (1987). A ratio measure of sex stereotyping. *Journal of Personality and Social Psychology, 52*, 489–499.

McCloskey, L. A. (1987). Gender and conversation: Mixing and matching styles. In D. B. Carter (Ed.), *Current conceptions of sex roles and sex typing: Theory and research* (pp. 139–153). New York: Praeger.

McCroskey, J. C., & McCain, T. A. (1974). The measurement of interpersonal attraction. *Speech Monographs, 41*, 216–266.

McCroskey, J. C., & Richmond, V. P. (1979, May). *The reliability arid validity of scales for the measurement of interpersonal attraction and homophily*. Paper presented at the meeting of the Eastern Communication Association, Philadelphia, PA.

McKenzie-Mohr, D., & Zanna, M. P. (1990). Treating women as sexual objects: Look to the (gender schematic male who has viewed pronography. *Personality and Social Psychology Bulletin, 16*, 296–309.

McMillan, J. R., Clifton, A. K., McGrath, D., & Gale, W. S. (1977). Uncertainty or interpersonal sensitivity and emotionality? *Sex Roles, 3*, 545–559.

Mulac, A. (1998). The gender-linked language effect: Do language differences really make a difference? In D. J. Canary & K. Dindia (Eds.), *Sex differences and similarities in communication* (pp. 127–154). Mahwah, NJ Lawrence: Erlbaum associates.

Norris, J. M., & Wylie, A. M. (1995). Gender stereotyping of the managerial role among students in Canada and the United States. *Group and Organizational Management, 20*, 167–183.

Ortega Murphy, B., & Zorn, T. (1996). Gendered interaction in professional relationships. In J. Wood (Ed.), *Gendered relationships* (pp. 233–252). Mountainview, CA: Mayfield.

Park, B., & Hahn, S. (1988). Sex-role identity and the perception of others. *Social Cognition, 6*, 61–87.

Payne, K. E. (2001). *Different but equal: Communication between the sexes*. Westport, CT: Praeger.

Roby, E. B., Canary, D. J., & Burggraf, C. S. (1998). Conversational maintenance behavior of husbands and wives: An observational analysis. In D. J. Canary & K. Dindia (Eds.), Sex differences and similarities in communication (pp. 373–392). Mahwah, NJ: Lawrence Erlbaum Associates.

Ruble, T. L. (1983). Sex stereotypes: Issues of change in the 1970s. *Sex Roles, 9*, 397–402.

Rudman, L. A., & Glick, P. (1999). Feminized management and backlash toward agentic women: The hidden costs to women of a kinder, gentler image of middle-managers. *Journal of Personality and Social Psychology, 77*, 1004–1010.

Rudman, L. A., & P. Glick (2001). Prescriptive gender stereotypes and backlash toward agentic women. *Journal of Social Issues, 57*, 743–763.

Sadalla, E. K., Kenrick, H. T., & Vershure, B. (1987). Dominance and heterosexual attraction. *Journal of Personality and Social Psychology, 52*, 730–738.

Sandberg, D. E., Meyer Bahlburg, H. F. & Yager, T. J. (1993). The prevalence of gender-atypical behavior in elementary school children. *Journal of the American Academy of Child and Adolescent Psychiatry, 32*, 306–314.

Schneider, D. J., Hastorf, A. H., & Ellsworth, P. C. (1979). *Person perception* (2nd ed). Reading, MA: Addison-Wesley.

Selcuk, R. S., McCreary, J. R., & Mahalik, J. R. (2004). Differential reactions to men and women's gender role transgressions: Perceptions of social status, sexual orientation and value dissimilarity. *The Journal of Men's Studies, 12*, 119–132.

Sherriffs, A. C., & McKee, J. P. (1957). Qualitative aspects of beliefs about men and women. *Journal W Personality, 25*, 451–464.

Shibley Hyde, J., & Frost, L. A. (1993). In F. L. Denmark & M. A. Paludi (Eds.), *Psychology of women: A handbook of issues and theories* (pp. 67–103). Westport, CT: Greenwood.

Shibley Hyde, J., & Plant, E. A. (1995). Magnitude of psychological gender differences: Another side to the story. *American Psychologist, 50*, 159–161.

Smith, P. A., & Midlarsky, E. (1985). Empirically derived conceptions of femaleness and maleness: A current view. Sex *Roles, 12*, 313–328.

Smith, P. M. (1985). *Language, the sexes and society*. Oxford, England: Basil Blackwell.

Smith-Lovin, L., & Robinson, D. T. (1992). Gender and conversational dynamics. In C. L. Ridgeway (Ed.), *Gender, interaction, and inequality* (pp. 122–156). New York Springer-Verlag.

Spender, D. (1980). *Man made language*. London: Routledge & Kegan Paul.

Stokes, J., Childs, L., & Fuehrer, A. (1981). Gender and sex roles as predictors of self-disclosure. *Journal of Counseling Psychology, 28*, 510–514.

Stokes, J. Fuehrer, A., & Childs, L. (1980). Gender differences in self-disclosure to various target persons. *Journal of Counseling Psychology, 27*, 192–198.

Tannen, D. (1995). *Communicating from 9 to 5*. New York: Morrow.

Watson, D., Clark, L. A., & Tellegen, A. (1988). Development and validation of brief measures of positive and negative affect: The PANAS scale. *Journal of Personality and Social Psychology, 54*, 1063–1070.

Werner, P. D., & LaRussa, G. W. (1985). Persistence and change in sex-role stereotypes. *Sex Roles, 12*, 1089–1100.

Williams, J. E., & Best, D. L. (1982). *Measuring sex stereotypes: A thirty- nation study*. Beverly Hills, CA: Sage.

Wood, J. T. (1996). Gender, relationships, and communication. In J. T. Wood (Ed.), *Gendered relationships* (pp. 3–19). Mountainview, CA: Mayfield.

16

Sex, Power, and Communication

Pamela J. Kalbfleisch
Anita L. Herold
University of North Dakota

If power was an illusion, wasn't weakness necessarily one also?

—Bujold (1999, p. 401)

It is not the wrongness of her views, but her insolence in proclaiming them.

—Ruskin (1876, cited in Larson, 2003, p. 99)

Power often defines who we are and who others think we are. As early as 1938, Russell remarked that "The fundamental concept in social science is Power, in the same sense that Energy is the fundamental concept in physics" (p. 10). The power others perceive us to have is so important that we might not need to be physically present to influence social interaction and actions taken. Statements such as, "What would Michael say?" and "We can't do that; Sarah wouldn't like it" reflect that the perceived consequences of decisions or actions may be far more influential than any actual reaction from a more powerful other.

More specific to the purposes of this anthology, we must ask the following: Are men more powerful than women or are women more powerful than men? Of course, it is possible that both sexes are equally powerful in some contexts. In reviewing the literature on sex, we find many differences between men and women; in reviewing the literature on power, we find many differences between those who are more and less powerful. We have seen similar descriptions of powerful communication and male communication (such as more staring behavior and less smiling and self-disclosure), and similar descriptions of female communication styles and less powerful behavior (such as more eye contact aversion and more smiling and self-disclosure; see Henley, 1977, 1995).

Does the overlap in these descriptions of powerful individuals and men mean that men are more powerful than women? Does this imply that masculine communication style is more powerful than feminine communication style? Or does this imply that the communication styles are related to power and that sex may enter the equation simply because people who occupy powerful roles in our society are more often men? Henley (1977, 1995) has argued that the differences in power between men and women can be described as power differences and not necessarily sex differences in the enactment of power.

Continuing research endeavors exploring additional communication style differences support Henley's perspective. Furthermore, differences occur in the effectiveness of leaders on the basis of their sex and leadership style. As the enactment of power, leadership is a context in which we can observe similarities and differences in sex and power. Interpersonal relationships and sexual relationships are also contexts for examining sex and power.

In this chapter we review research on power and sex, beginning with definitions of power and sex, an elaboration of Henley's earlier work, and a review of the recent research examining power and sex. We then turn to a consideration of leadership as a context in which power differences and similarities are played out and how the sex of the leader plays a role in leader effectiveness. Leadership literature will also be considered in terms of a possible avenue that can address power differences and sex differences and how to establish an environment where both women and men can be successful.

DEFINITIONS CONSIDERED

For the purpose of this chapter, the term *power* refers to the ability to pursue one's own objectives through a variety of means and to facilitate or prevent others from carrying out their goals. This definition is drawn from the perspective of Keltner, Gruenfeld, and Anderson (2003) that power is "an individual's relative capacity to modify others' states by providing or withholding resources or administering punishments" (p. 265), as well as several other definitions of power (see Kalbfleisch & Cody, 1995, for a more comprehensive review of power).

For this chapter, *sex* refers to the biological differences between men and women. *Gender* concerns the social experiences of being male or female. We do not address transgender sexual differences because of the lacuna of literature on sex differences, including this particular expression of sex.[1]

[1]We also did not consider transgendered, gay, and lesbian use of powerful and less powerful communication in this chapter because so little is known about this issue. Dean (2004) found that female leaders who were lesbian felt their sexual orientation was a hindrance to their career success and therefore gaining positions of power. However, we do not yet know how differences in sexual orientation enter the equation of sex and power.

POWER AND SEX: WHAT THE SCHOLARS KNOW

In her 1977 book, *Body Politics*, Henley reviewed the scholarly research on sex, power, and nonverbal communication, and she advanced several hypotheses based on her literature review. In 1995, Henley, reviewed the research addressing her theses that had been conducted in the years since her book. The thesis that is most central to our chapter is Henley's hypothesis that "the behaviors expressing dominance and subordination between nonequals parallel those used by males and females in the unequal relation of the sexes" (Henley, 1995, p. 28). The research supporting this hypothesis found that people with superior status use familiar address when speaking to subordinates; have an informal demeanor and relaxed posture; may touch others, use close personal space, or a long use of time; may stare at or ignore others; may not smile; and may hide emotional expression and not use self-disclosure (Henley, 1977, 1995). Henley also found that men have an informal demeanor when speaking to women; they use relaxed posture and close personal space; they touch, stare, and ignore; and they hide emotional expression, do not smile, and do not use self-disclosure. Research was not available for sex differences on familiar or polite address or the use of time.

The research reviewed by Henley (1977, 1995) found that subordinates use polite address when speaking to superiors, are prudent in demeanor, have tense posture, use distant personal space and short use of time, don't touch others, avert eyes, watch others, smile, show emotional expression, and use self-disclosure. In parallel fashion, Henley found that women are prudent in demeanor when speaking to men, have tense posture, use distant personal space, do not touch others, avert eyes, watch others, smile, show emotional expression, and use self-disclosure. In brief, the similarity in behavior between male communicators and superior communicators and the similarity in behavior between female communicators and subordinate communicators support Henley's hypothesis regarding the similarity of superior behavior and male behavior, and the similarity of subordinate behavior and female behavior.

In performing a broad-based review of the research on power and sex since Henley's 1977 and 1995 reviews, we also found similarities in communication styles and attributes of powerful individuals and of male communicators, and similarities in communication styles and attributes of less powerful individuals and of female communicators. Our search included the years 1995 through 2004.

From this review of research published since Henley (1995), we found a number of documented characteristics of the communication styles and attributes of powerful individuals. Powerful communicators, as opposed to less powerful communicators, display a composite of approach behaviors, such as extraversion (Anderson, John, Keltner, & Kring, 2001), impulsivity, and disinhibited communication (Keltner et al., 2003). Powerful people are more stereotypical in their evaluations of others and less observant of others' verbal and nonverbal behavior and cues than are less powerful communicators (Anderson & Berdahl, 2002; Keltner & Robinson, 1996, 1997). In addition to being more dominating and more attentive to social rewards, powerful people tend to be more aggressive and are willing to tease their companions and colleagues (Keltner et al., 2003; Tiedens, Ellsworth, & Mesquita, 2000). In addition, those with power tend to have more elevated moods (Anderson, Langner, & Keltner, as cited in Keltner et al.) and higher self esteem (Anderson & Berdahl; Operario & Fiske, 2001) than do the less powerful.

Less powerful communicators are more aware of the potential losses of resources and status than are powerful communicators (Keltner et al., 2003), and they are subject to more threats of resource loss (Hall & Halberstadt, 1994). The less powerful are more likely to display speech hesitations (Holtgraves & Lasky, 1999), and they smile more than their more powerful counterparts (Cashdan, 1998, Hall & Friedman, 1999, Hecht & LaFrance, 1998). Additionally, the less powerful are not as happy as the powerful, experiencing more negative emotions, more negative affect, and more frequent depressed moods (Ebenbach & Keltner, 1998; Hecht, Inderbirtzen, & Bukowski, 1998). It could be argued that the generalized situation of not having power affects mood and emotion rather than being a specific personality trait, just as constricted body movements, speech hesitations, and fewer smiles may be related to low power rather than personality.[2]

Differences in male and female communication style are enumerated in many research articles and scholarly volumes. Male communication style runs the gamut from the general, such as men talk more (Athenstaedt, Haas, & Shwab, 2004), particularly about nonpersonal topics (Brownlow, 2003). To the more specific, for example, men interrupt more (Athenstaedt et al.), give more directives (Athenstaedt et al.; Redeker & Maes, 1996), use fewer pronouns (Brownlow), and tend to be more direct, forceful, judgmental, and opinioned (Brownlow; Mehl & Pennebaker, 2002; Mulac, 1998). Men also communicate differently than women nonverbally. For example, Di Biase and Gunnoe (2004) found that men tend to touch women more often than women touch men.

Female communication, in contrast, tends to be characterized as more attentive to others (Athenstaedt et al., 2004; Basow & Rubenfeld, 2003). Women use more tags, hedges, and disclaimers (Brownlow, 2003; House, Dallinger, & Kilgallen, 1998), and generally women are better interpreters of nonverbal signals (Andersen, chap. 7, this volume; Cashdan, 1998; Di Biase, & Gunnoe, 2004; LaFrance &

---

[2]The finding illustrated in Table 16.1, that being more powerful is associated with heightened mood state and less depression and sadness (and that being less powerful is associated with lower mood state and depression) is also intriguing when one considers that being biologically male is also associated with heightened mood state and less depression and that being female is associated with lowered mood state and more sadness and depression. The finding that being powerful may actually make us feel better and being powerless may make us feel worse brings interesting implications for the mood-altering drug industry as well as our consideration of sex and power. The implication is that perhaps men's elevated mood is due less to their sex than to the fact that they are more likely to have power.

TABLE 16.1
Behavior Comparison Between More and Less Powerful Communicators and Male and Female Communicators.

	Power		*Sex*	
Behavior	*High*	*Low*	*Male*	*Female*
1. Approach	+	−	+	−
2. Inhibition	−	+	−	+
3. Interrupt more	+	−	+	−
4. Give directives	+	−	+	−
5. Talk more in groups	+	−	+	−
6. Other directed	−	+	−	+
7. Show anger more	+	−	+	−
8. Elevated mood	+	−	+	−
9. Sadness or depression	−	+	−	+
10. Stereotype more	+	−	+	−
11. Display more nonverbal cues	+	−	+	−
12. Better at interpreting nonverbal cues	−	+	−	+
13. Aware of potential loss of status and resources	−	+	−	+
14. Engage in self-censorship	−	+	−	+

Note: Plus symbol denotes more enactment of behavior; minus symbol denotes less enactment of behavior. Positive and negative signs indicate increased or decreased likelihood of behavior as reported in studies reviewed (see footnote 3).

Hecht, 1999; LaFrance, Henley, Hall, & Halberstadt, 1997; Schmid Mast & Hall, 2004; Schwarzwald, & Koslowsky, 1999).

Table 16.1 displays the similarities between characteristics of the powerful and less powerful and male and female characteristics as documented in the scholarly research from 1995 through 2004.[3] We can see from this table that many of the characteristics found to be related to being more powerful are also related to being

[3]The behaviors listed in Table 16.1 were compiled from articles found in a search of the databases listed in the text of the chapter; behaviors central to the chapter were listed if they appeared in an article reviewed. The behaviors enumerated in the table are compiled from the following articles: Anderson and Berdahl (2002), Behaviors 1, 2, 5, 7, 8, 9, 13, and 14; Athenstaedt, Haas, and Schwab (2004), Behaviors 3 and 4; Basow and Rubenfeld (2003), Behaviors 2, 6, and 14; Brownlow (2003), Behaviors 3 and 5; Cashdan (1998), Behaviors 5 and 11; Di Biase and Gunnoe (2004), Behavior 11; Ellyson and Dividio (1985), Behaviors 2 and 11; Hecht and LaFrance (1998), Behaviors 8 and 11; House, Dallinger, and Kilgallen (1998), Behaviors 1 and 2; Keltner, Capps, Kring, Young, and Heery (2001), Behaviors 1 and 10; Keltner, Gruenfeld, and Anderson (2003), Behaviors 1, 2, 3, 4, 5, 6, 7, 8, 9, 10, 12, 13, and 14; Keltner and Robinson (1996), Behaviors 10 and 12; Keltner and Robinson (1997), Behaviors 10 and 12; Keltner, Young, Heery, Oemig, and Monarch (1998), Behaviors 1 and 10; LaFrance and Hecht (1999), Behaviors 11 and 12; Mehl and Pennebaker (2002), Behavior 7; Redeker and Maes (1996), Behaviors 3 and 5; Snodgrass, Hetch, and Ploutz-Snyder (1998), Behaviors 6, 11, and 12; Tiedens, Ellsworth, and Mesquita (2000), Behaviors 6 and 9; Van Gundy (2002), Behavior 9; Young and Sweeting (2004), Behaviors 1, 8, and 10. These articles are individual studies and not meta-analyses.

male. We can also see that the characteristics related to being less powerful are similar to those related to being female.

Table 16.1 implies a clear relationship between male communicative style and the communication of those in power versus female communication style and the communication styles of those who do not have power. The early nonverbal communication and power research reviewed by Henley in 1977 and updated in 1995 and the communication and power research from 1995 through 2004 reviewed in this chapter show this pattern.

This review provides additional support for Henley's hypothesis from the recent literature on sex, communication, and power. In reviewing the literature, there are relatively few studies that directly compare powerful and less powerful males and females within the same study. The work that is available suggests there may be some difference in behavior associated with power for both men and women; however, there is not a consistent body of research that examines differences and similarities in this manner. The work that is available shows interesting patterns but is somewhat limited. For example, Gonzaga and Keltner (2001, as cited in Keltner et al., 2003) found that men were generally more disinhibited in flirting behavior than women (provocative eye contact, forward leans, and touching), with men with high power being much more disinhibited than lower power men. High-power women, although displaying less disinhibited flirting than low-power men, were slightly more likely to use disinhibited flirted than women with low power. Ward and Keltner (1998, as cited in Keltner et al., 2003) found that powerful women were more likely to take an extra cookie in a group setting where there were limited cookies than were less powerful women. Men were generally more likely to take extra cookies than were less powerful women but not as likely as were powerful women.

One area that would clearly indicate whether differences between men and women are due to power or biological sex concerns leadership style. In particular, if sex differences exist in leadership styles, then one could draw a stronger inference regarding sex differences versus power differences. Finding out whether men and women in positions of power engage in similar leadership behaviors will help to sort out whether differences between men and women are due to sex or power. The following section considers sex and power in the context of leadership.

SEX DIFFERENCES IN LEADERSHIP STYLE

How do sex differences and similarities play out when communicators of both sexes are in positions of power? Several meta-analyses by Eagly and associates (e.g., Eagly, Johannesen-Schmidt, & van Engen, 2003; Eagly & Johnson, 1990; Eagly, Makhinjani, & Klonsky, 1992) suggested that the answer may depend on the style of leadership employed by men and women in powerful positions. In general, men use agenic leadership styles that tend to be more directive and authoritarian in nature, and women are more likely to use more participatory democratic leadership styles (mean weighted effect size, $d = 0.22$; Eagly & Johnson). In fact, the democratic leadership style is often associated with female leadership, and the authoritarian leadership style is associated with male leaders.

In their early study, Sargent and Miller (1971) described autocratic or authoritarian leaders as being concerned with efficient group productivity, fast action, control, achieving their own personal outcomes, representing their own views, and control of knowledge. Democratic leaders are described as being concerned that group members have the opportunity to influence decisions, reach decisions, stimulate thinking, make evaluations, clarify goals, have positive affect within group, and maintain group relations.

When women adopt an authoritarian style, a violation of expectations works against them, which can lead perceivers to classify them as poor leaders (Eagly & Karau, 2002). In their 1992 meta-analysis, Eagly, Makhijani, and Kolinsky found that men have more latitude in the leadership style they use and are rated more favorably than women when they use the autocratic leadership style (mean weighted effect size, $d = 0.30$). When using the democratic style, men are only slightly less favorably rated than women using the same style (mean weighted effect size, $d = -0.02$).

Although men can adopt the more directive and obviously powerful authoritarian or autocratic leadership styles, or the less directive participative democratic style, it would appear that women may not be able to as successfully adopt the characteristics of the more powerful autocratic style of leadership. However, Cellar, Sidle, Goudy, and O'Brien (2001) found that the perceivers themselves make a difference on the perceived successfulness of men and women adopting differing leadership styles. Cellar and associates found that more agreeable perceivers are more likely to favorably rate a woman who is autocratic and a man who is democratic than are less agreeable perceivers. One reason for these differences is that individuals high in agreeableness would be described as good natured, cooperative, and trustful, and individuals low in agreeableness would be described as intolerant and authoritarian as measured by the short version of the Big Five personality dimensions, NEO-FFI, developed by Costa & McCrae (1992, cited in Cellar et al.). It may be the case that greater willingness to cooperate is needed by the followers of male and female leaders rather than the leader's adopting one particular leadership style to be successful. In other words, one of the components of being successful in positions of power is that the perceivers need to be more willing to adapt to different types of people's holding positions of power and different ways of communicating power. This is in contrast to the perspective that the leader must be of a particular sex and leadership style. It may well be the case that the old prose "think leader think male" (Sczesny, 2003; Willemsen, 2002) no longer applies. It follows that both sexes are powerful leaders in new and exciting ways existing in a complex environment.

A popular leadership style that is now being taught in management classes and encouraged for men and women to adopt is *transformational leadership*. Bass and Avolio (1994) noted that transformational leadership occurs when the leader "stimulates the interest among colleagues and followers to view their work from a new perspective" to "look beyond their own interests towards the needs of the group" (p. 2). According to Judge and Piccolo (2004), the dimensions of transformational leadership are (a) charisma or idealized influence, (b) articulating vision to which followers can relate, (c) intellectual stimulation, and (d) individualized consideration. Transformational leadership behaviors of charisma or idealized influence include demonstrating "high standards for moral and ethical conduct" (Bono & Judge, 2004, p. 901). Inspirational motivation or vision articulation includes "stimulating enthusiasm, building confidence, inspiring followers using symbolic actions and persuasive language" (Bono & Judge, p. 901). Intellectual stimulation suggests "challenging organizational norms, encourage divergent thinking... push followers to develop innovative strategies" (Bono & Judge, p. 901). Individualized consideration is articulated through "recognizing the unique growth and developmental needs of followers, mentoring and coaching followers" (Bono & Judge, p. 901).

The behaviors advocated by this leadership style change the perspective of what a leader is and allows women to gain legitimate power, because it shifts the leadership style enough that expected leadership norms are no longer violated by having a woman in power and the group sees greater benefits from the outcome. Transformational leaders empower their followers to make decisions and to take responsibility for outcomes. Because followers are motivated, the focus is less on the leader and what the leader will do for the group. Followers are a vital part of accomplishing a shared vision with the leader. Transformational leadership is characteristically directional while also being participatory and motivational (Mandell & Pherwani, 2003). Transformational leaders direct and reward their followers while also inspiring them to work toward the good of the group. The follower's behavior is tied to success and directives—not the leader.

The Eagly et al. (2003) meta-analysis on sex and likelihood of using transformational leadership found that women are more likely to be transformational leaders than men ($d = 0.19$), and that women are perceived as being more successful than male leaders when they use this style. Female leaders were rated higher than male leaders in terms of extra effort ($d = 0.09$), satisfaction ($d = 0.14$) and effectiveness ($d = 0.22$). There appears to be benefits for both sexes to using this leadership style in the successfulness of the group. Use of the transformational leadership style shifts the focus from whether men or women are more powerful, and it presents the idea that if we change our approach as a society to a transformational approach, then we can begin to lessen the effects of high or low autocratic style power behavior that has traditionally been seen as only appropriate for men toward leadership behavior that empowers followers and directs them toward excellence.

Findings about transformational leaders, sex, and follower characteristics indicate that the relationship between sex and power may be more complex than seeing one sex as advantaged over the other, as early research suggests (Carli, 1999; Eagly & Karau, 2002; Sczesny, 2003), because the findings show that, through the use of transformational leadership behaviors, sex makes less of a difference. Thus, it is a combination of other factors, not simply that women are disadvantaged, that influences power differences and similarities for men and women. Additionally, researchers such as Wilson, Lizzio, Zauner, and Gallois (2001) have found strategies, such as male and female leaders' being status consistent as opposed to gender-role consistent, as more important to evaluations of leader effectiveness, suggesting further complexities in the analysis of leadership and sex.

COMPLEX ENVIRONMENT AND CHANGE

If we look at Table 16.1 and the differences in power and differences in biological sex, it appears that those perceived to be powerful are those with authoritarian leadership styles. These authoritarian leadership styles, characterized by giving directives to others, talking more in groups, and using approach behaviors, are similar to the male communicator behaviors listed in Table 16.1. Those perceived to be less powerful have characteristics that may be found in other leadership styles, such as the democratic style, which is being other directed, giving fewer directives, and talking less in groups. These styles are similar to some of the perceived behaviors of women listed in Table 16.1. It may be that women actually do have power and are leading; it is just that they are doing so in a nonauthoritarian manner. The research on power may not be picking up these more subtle uses of power, such as the ability to empower others, creating an environment where scholars perceive that women are less powerful than men. It may well be the case that achieving goals and helping or hindering others from achieving their goals can be done through a variety of means other than the leader's directly "providing or withholding resources or administering punishments." (Keltner et al., 2003, p. 265), such as the direct autocratic approach to leadership. With a change in perception of leadership style, resources can be achieved or lost by the group rather than being administered by an external source such as the leader.

Perceptions of power and effective leadership style may also change, as more women become a part of the executive leadership of organizations. For example, Dean (2004) found that, in 25 years, the number of female college presidents went from 5% of all college presidents to 20% of all college presidents. In the past 4 years, though, Dean noted a drop in the number of women who were entering the top leadership positions in universities; however, the point is that there are many more female leaders in universities than there were in the 1970s. Perhaps, perceptions of power and powerful behavior will change as more individuals in power positions communicate in different ways.

In looking across the contexts that might affect sex and power, we can look closely at powerful behavior highlighted in Table 16.1 and see that those with high power use aggressive behaviors such as interrupting, showing anger, and stereotyping others. Interestingly, Blunt Bugental and Lewis (1999) found that such behaviors may be linked to issues with self-esteem. In their research, Blunt Bugental and Lewis found that those who felt low self-esteem were more likely to bully others and be aggressive in trying to make others conform to their desires. In other words, feeling powerless may facilitate the expression of aggressive power-related strategies, with individuals who feel powerless actually expressing the most dominating communication. In this research, both men and women displayed this self-esteem and bullying response in communication with others. In other words, people who are not feeling powerful themselves, even those that hold positions of power, may actually enact the most aggressive strategies dependent on withholding rewards and administering punishments.

One example of a domain influencing the relationship between sex and power is that of health care. Aruguete and Roberts (2000) found that male physicians were more controlling and less affiliative in their communication style than were female physicians. However, when it came to patient recall of the information presented by these physicians, patients remembered more from men who were controlling and less from men who were affiliative, while communication style did not affect remembering the information presented by the female physician. In this case, the controlling and more powerful communication style may be effective for men who are more likely to use this style but may not make a difference in the effectiveness of women in getting their patients to remember what they have said. In other words, being perceived as powerful in this context may help men be more effective. Women, in contrast, may not have to engage in powerful behavior to have power.

In the context of mentoring relationships, Kalbfleisch (1997) found that, regardless of mentor sex, female protégés are more likely than men to use a number of communication strategies to try to appease their more powerful mentors in conflict situations. Male protégés were more likely to see more events as conflict producing and more likely to argue with their mentors. However, men were also more likely to make sacrifices for their mentor to maintain the mentoring relationship. In the case of male and female protégés, the actual appeasement strategies used (e.g., working harder, trying to do better) were the most important in repairing a transgression, not the protégés' sex. In this case the verbal strategies of accommodation and appeasement were more important than powerful communication in repairing these relationships.

Upward influence in organizations is another domain for considering sex and power. O'Neil (2004) found that sex did not affect choice of upward influence strategies by subordinates in organizations. She found that situation-bound variables and power affects–moderates influence tactic usage by women and men in organizations. O'Neil suggested that those in more powerful positions in an organization are more likely to use rationality, assertiveness, and coalition-building in attempting to influence their superiors. The position, not the sex of the person occupying the position, was important in achieving success.

In personal relationships, men are perceived to be the most powerful in heterosexual couples (Felmlee, 1994). However, across heterosexual and homosexual couples, the person who makes the most money is perceived as the most powerful (Schwartz, Patterson, & Steen, 1995). Money may further interrelate with sex to affect one's power. Smits, Mulder, and Hooimeijer (2003) reported that women are more likely to move with their spouses when their spouse finds a better job in a different geographical location. Men are less likely to move for their wives unless their wives are making significantly more money and the move would help increase the financial security of their relationship. In this case, the ability to earn more money may be more important than the biological sex of the person with the job offer to the power-based choice to move.

CONCLUSIONS

Sex and power are both important concepts in their own right, but this chapter has shown that the relationship between sex and power may not be as straightforward as we imagine. Although at first blush it appears that men are powerful and women are less powerful, it may be the case that both men and women are powerful and use different influence strategies to achieve desired goals and help or hinder others from achieving their preferred outcomes. Traditional perceptions of men being powerful and women being powerless may hurt women from achieving some positions of power and using some traditional autocratic power strategies; however, other more transformational or democratic communication styles are available to women. Research suggests that women are using these styles to lead and transform their followers. In fact, the currently preferred leadership style of transformational leadership is one that women are excelling at beyond their male counterparts.

This does not mean to say that the glass ceiling does not exist. Women might still have difficulty finding positions of power and influence because of the perception that they will not be powerful leaders. However, research would suggest otherwise. Rather than being less powerful, women may in fact be equally or more powerful than their male counterparts. Their followers may actually be more satisfied and empowered than those working with a more directional autocratic leader.

However, transformational leadership is more likely to be found at the lower levels of executive and management structures (Eagly et al., 2003). This may be because this is where more female leaders are stationed or where newer leaders are approaching leadership from a new perspective. The vision, sharing, charismatic, empowering leadership style of the transformational leader would be a natural for the top leaders of an organization to use to express power and lead their organization or group to success.

The stereotype of power is still the autocratic leader. Quick decisions, demonstrative use of power over others, and control of resources is very much a part of our standard definitions and conceptions of power. However, the literature suggests that those expressing the most control and power over others may be the ones who feel the most powerless (Blunt Bugental & Lewis, 1999). This would suggest that those who truly have power actually are those who give it to others.

The solution to power differences between men and women may be to look beyond the stereotypes of power and sex-role stereotypes and to look toward an environment of empowerment. Working toward helping others gain power, mentoring, coaching, and caring may be the most powerful actions we can do as human beings.

REFERENCES

Anderson, C., & Berdahl, J. (2002). The experience of power: Examining the effects of power on approach and inhibition tendencies. *Journal of Personality and Social Psychology, 83*, 1362–1377.

Anderson, C., John, O. P., Keltner, D., & Kring, A. M. (2001). Who attains social status? Effects of personality and physical attractiveness in social groups. *Journal of Personality and Social Psychology, 81*, 116–132.

Aruguete, M., & Roberts, C. (2000). Gender, affiliation, and control in physician–patient encounters. *Sex Roles, 42*, 107–118.

Athenstaedt, U., Haas, E., & Schwab, S. (2004). Gender role self-concept and gender-typed communication behavior in mixed-sex and same-sex dyads. *Sex Roles, 50*, 37–52.

Basow, S., & Rubenfeld, K. (2003). "Trouble talk": Effects of gender and gender-typing. *Sex Roles, 48*, 183–187.

Bass, B. M., & Avolio, B. J. (1994). *Improving organizational effectiveness through transformational leadership*. Thousand Oaks, CA: Sage.

Blunt Bugental, D., & Lewis, J. (1999). The paradoxical misuse of power by those who see themselves as powerless: How does it happen? *Journal of Social Issues, 55*, pp. 51–64.

Bono, J. E., & Judge, T. A. (2004). Personality and transformational and transactional leadership: A meta-analysis. *Journal of Applied Psychology, 89*, 901–910.

Brownlow, S. (2003). Gender-linked linguistic behavior in television interviews—1. *Sex Roles: A Journal of Research* [Electronic version]. Retrieved May 22, 2004, from Looksmart/FindArticles at www.findarticles.com

Bujold, L. M. (1999). *A civil campaign*. Riverdale, NY: Baen Books.

Carli, L. (1999). Gender, interpersonal power, and social influence. *Journal of Social Issues, 55*, 81. Article A54831711 retrieved May 24, 2004, from InfoTrac.

Cashdan, E. (1998). Smiles, speech, and body posture: How women and men display sociometric status and power. *Journal of Nonverbal Behavior, 22*, 209–228.

Cellar, D., Sidle, S., Goudy, K., & O'Brien, D. (2001). Effects of leader style, leader sex, and subordinate personality on leader evaluations and future subordinate motivation. *Journal of Business and Psychology, 16*, 61–72.

Dean, D. R. (2004). Priming the pump: CAO's move to the college presidency. *Women in Higher Education, 13*, 1–2.

Di Biase, R., & Gunnoe, J. (2004). Gender and cultural differences in touching behavior. *Journal of Social Psychology, 144*, ProQuest Psychology Journals p. 49.

Eagly, A., & Johnson, B. (1990). Gender and leadership style: A meta-analysis. *Psychological Bulletin, 108*, 233–256. Retrieved May 2004, from PsycARTICLES database.

Eagly, A., Johannesen-Schmidt, M., & van Engen, M. (2003). Transformational, transactional, and laissez-faire leadership styles: A meta-analysis comparing women and men. *Psychological Bulletin, 129*, 569–591.

Eagly, A., & Karau, S. (2002). Role congruity theory of prejudice toward female leaders. *Psychological Review, 109*, 573–598. Retrieved May 2004, from PsycARTICLES database.

Eagly, A., Makhijani, M., & Klonsky, B. (1992). Gender and the evaluation of leaders: A meta-analysis. *Psychological Bulletin, 111*, 3–22.

Ebenbach, D., & Keltner, D. (1998). Power, emotion and judgmental accuracy in social conflict: Motivating the cognitive miser. *Basic and Applied Social Psychology, 20*, 7–21.

Ellyson, S., & Dividio, J. (Eds.). (1985). *Power, dominance, and nonverbal behavior*. New York: Springer-Verlag.

Felmlee, D. (1994). Who's on top? Power in romantic relationships. *Sex Roles, 31*, 275–295.

Hall, J., & Friedman, G. (1999). Status, gender, and nonverbal behavior: A study of structured interactions between employees of a company. *Personality and Social Psychology Bulletin, 25*, 1082–1091.

Hall, J., & Halberstadt, A. (1994). "Subordination" and sensitivity to nonverbal cues: A study of married working women. *Sex Roles, 31*, 149–165.

Hecht, D. B., Inderbirtzen, H., & Bukowski, A. (1998). The relationship between peer status and depressive symptoms in children and adolescents. *Journal of Abnormal Child Psychology, 26*, 153–160.

Hecht, M., & LaFrance, M. (1998). License or obligation to smile: The effect of power and sex on amount and type of smiling. *Personality and Social Psychology Bulletin, 24*, 1332–1342.

Henley, N. (1977). *Body politics: Power, sex and nonverbal communication*. New York: Prentice-Hall.

Henley, N. (1995). Body politics revisited: What do we know today? In P. Kalbfleisch & M. Cody (Eds.), *Gender, power, and communication in human relationships* (pp. 27–61). Hillsdale, NJ: Lawrence Erlbaum Associates.

Holtgraves, T., & Lasky, B. (1999). Linguistic power and persuasion. *Journal of Language and Social Psychology, 18*, 196–205.

House, A., Dallinger, J., & Kilgallen, D. (1998). Androgyny and rhetorical sensitivity: The connection of gender and communication style. *Communication Reports, 11*, 11–20.

Judge, T. A., & Piccolo, R. F. (2004). Transformational and transactional leadership: A meta-analytic test of their relative validity. *Journal of Applied Psychology, 89*, 755–768.

Kalbfleisch, P. (1997). Appeasing the mentor. *Aggressive Behavior, 23*, 389–403.

Kalbfleisch, P., & Cody, M. (1995). Power and communication in the relationships of women and men. In P. Kalbfleisch & M. Cody (Eds.), *Gender, power, and communication in human relationships* (pp. 3–10). Hillsdale, NJ: Lawrence Erlbaum Associates.

Keltner, D., Capps, L., Kring, A., Young, R., & Heerey, E. (2001). Just teasing: A conceptual analysis and empirical review. *Psychological Bulletin, 127*, 229–248. Retrieved May 2004, from PsycARTICLES database.

Keltner, D., Gruenfeld, D., & Anderson, C. (2003). Power, approach, and inhibition. *Psychological Review, 110*, 265–284. Retrieved May 2004, from PsycARTICLES database.

Keltner, D., & Robinson, R. (1996). Extremism, power, and the imagined basis of social conflict. *Current Directions in Psychological Science, 5*, 101–105.

Keltner, D., & Robinson, R. (1997). Defending the status quo: Power and bias in social conflict. *Personality and Social Psychology Bulletin, 23*, 1066–1077.

Keltner, D., Young, R., Heery, E., Oemig, C., & Monarch, N. (1998). Teasing in hierarchical and intimate relations. *Journal of Personality and Social Psychology, 75*, 1231–1247. Retrieved May 24, 2004 from PsycARTICLES database.

LaFrance, M., & Hecht, M. (1999). Option or obligation to smile: The effects of power and gender on facial expression. In P. Philippot, R. S. Feldman, & E. J. Coats (Eds.) *The Social Context of Nonverbal Behavior*, pp. 45–70. New York: Cambridge University Press.

LaFrance, Henley, Hall, & Halberstadt (1997). Nonverbal behavior: Are women's superior skills caused by their oppression? In M. R. Walsh's, *Women, men & gender: Ongoing debates.* pp. 101–133. New Haven: Yale University Press.

Larson, J. (2003). Where is the woman in this text? Frances Power Cobbe's voices in *Broken Lights. In Victorian literature and culture* (pp. 99–129).

Mandell, B., & Pherwani, S. (2003) Relationship between emotional intelligence and transformational leadership style: A gender comparison. *Journal of Business and Psychology, 17*, 387–404.

Mehl, M., & Pennebaker, J. (2002, January). Mapping students' natural language use in everyday conversations. Paper presented at the 3rd annual meeting of the Society for Personality and Social Psychology, Savannah, GA.

Mulac, A. (1998). The gender-linked language effect: Do language differences really make a difference? In D. Canary & K. Dindia (Eds.), *Sex differences and similarities in communication* (pp. 127–153). Mahwah, NJ: Lawrence Erlbaum Associates.

O'Neil, J. (2004). Effects of gender and power on PR managers' upward influence. *Journal of Managerial Issues, 16*, pp. 127–144. Retrieved April 2, 2004, from ProQuest database.

Operario, D., & Fiske, S. T. (2001). Effect of trait dominance on powerholders' judgments of subordinates. *Social Cognition, 19*, 161–180.

Redeker, G., & Maes, A. (1996). Gender differences in interruptions. In D. Slobin, J. Gerhardt, A. Kyratzis, & J. Guo (Eds.), Social interaction, social context, and language (pp. 579–612). Mahwah, NJ: Lawrence Erlbaum Associates.

Russell, B. (1938). *Power: A new social analysis*. London: Allen and Unwin.

Sargent, J. F., & Miller, G. R. (1971). Some differences in certain communication behaviors of autocratic and democratic group leaders. *Journal of Communication, 21*, 233–252.

Schmid Mast, M., & Hall, J. (2004). When is dominance related to smiling? Assigned dominance, dominance preference, trait dominance, and gender as moderators. *Sex Roles, 50*, 387–399.

Schwartz, P., Patterson, D., & Steen, S. (1995). The dynamics of power: Money and sex in intimate relationships. In P. Kalbfleisch & M. Cody (Eds.), *Gender, power, and communication in human relationships* (pp. 253–274). Hillsdale, NJ: Lawrence Erlbaum Associates.

Schwarzwald, J., & Koslowsky, M. (1999). Gender, self-esteem, and focus of interest in the use of power strategies by adolescents in conflict situations (Social influence and social power: Using theory for understanding social issues). *Journal of Social Issues, 55*, 15.

Sczesny, S. (2003). A closer look beneath the surface: Various facets of the think-manager-think-male stereotype. *Sex Roles, 49*, 353–363.

Smits, J., Mulder, C., & Hooimeijer, P. (2003). Changing gender roles, shifting power balance and long-distance migration of couples. *Urban Studies, 40*, 603–613.

Snodgrass, S., Hecht, M., & Ploutz-Snyder, R. (1998). Interpersonal sensitivity: Expressivity or perceptivity? *Journal of Personality and Social Psychology, 74*, 238–249. Retrieved May 24, 2004, from PsycARTICLES.

Thompson, M. (2000). Gender, leadership orientation, and effectiveness: Testing the theoretical models of Boleman & Deal and Quinn. *Sex Roles 42*, 969–992.

Tiedens, L., Ellsworth, P., & Mesquita, B. (2000). Stereotypes about sentiments and status: Emotional expectations for high- and low-status group members. *Personality and Social Psychology Bulletin, 26*, 560–574.

van Engen, M., ver der Leeden, R. & Willemsen, T. (2001). Gender, context and leadership styles: A field study. *Journal of Occupational and Organizational Psychology, 74*, 581–598.

Van Gundy, K. (2002). Gender, the assertion of autonomy, and the stress process in young adulthood. *Social Psychology Quarterly, 65*, 346–364.

Willemsen, T. (2002). Gender typing of the successful manager—a stereotype reconsidered. *Sex Roles, 46*, 385–391.

Wilson, K., Lizzio, A., Zauner, S., & Gallios, C. (2001). Social rules for managing attempted interpersonal domination in the workplace: Influence of status and gender. *Sex Roles, 44*, 129–155. Retrieved March 7, 2004, from ProQuest database.

Young, R., & Sweeting, H. (2004). Adolescent bullying, relationships, psychological well-being, and gender atypical behavior: A gender diagnosticity approach. *Sex Roles, 50*, 525–537.

IV

Sex Differences and Similarities in Romantic Relationships

17

How Men and Women Communicate Attraction: An Evolutionary View

Melanie R. Trost
Anaconda, Montana

Jess K. Alberts
Arizona State University

As researchers, we have both examined interpersonal processes because we are fascinated by the basic questions about how people meet and form romantic relationships. For example, "Why do males so often take the initiative in locating and courting mates, and why do females so often reject their suitors?" "Why do males so often fight with one another over females?" "Why do females so often seem to prefer males that have bizarre ornaments and strange behavioral displays?" Bizarre ornaments and strange behavioral displays? Actually, these questions are not ours; they were written by John Alcock (1993, p. 394), an ethologist who studies animal behavior, and he was referring more to peacock plumes and strutting baboons than to human behavior. However, we have asked the same questions about flirting and rejecting in our own species and have, quite frankly, always been a bit mystified by the appeal of puka beads in the 1970s or the body piercings on our students today.

Interest in these relational issues, not only within our own species but across species as well, may be a function of their importance for the proliferation of life. That is, finding a partner and developing an intimate interpersonal bond are critically important tasks for us. Even if our ancestors had been superb at other survival-related tasks—such as foraging and hunting for food, fending off predators and enemies, or building impressive structures to keep out the elements—had they not been able to attract partners and propagate, we would not be here to talk about it. This process of procreation begins with meeting an appropriate partner, a task that often involves flirtation.

Eibl-Eibesfeldt (1975) filmed women's reactions to flirtation in both industrialized cultures and hunter–gatherer cultures (including Samoa, Papua, France, Japan, and several different tribes in South America and Africa) and found a common sequence of motor actions that can easily be observed at the local coffee shop or nightclub. The sequence begins with a quick smile and "eyebrow flash" (eyes opened wide, accompanied by raising the eyebrows), followed by dropping and turning the head, and then a sidelong glance (sometimes referred to as the "coy glance"). It is not so difficult to understand why a behavior that is as elemental as initiating a relationship might have evolved to show cross-cultural similarities in form and expression, given that successfully reproducing and raising offspring was vital for our ancestors' evolution (Mealey, 2000). Although male and female animals (including humans) share the goal of producing offspring, the sexes also differ in the optimal quantity and quality of investment in those offspring, and this chapter gives an updated overview of how a comparative evolutionary perspective can provide insight into and explanations about sex differences and similarities in human courting behaviors, particularly in flirtation.

Since the previous edition of this book, mounting evidence supports the utility of an evolutionary approach to understanding human mating behavior. A systematic pattern across a wide variety of studies indicates that what often appear to be arbitrary cultural expressions of mating behavior actually radiate "honest signals" of reproductive fitness (Mealey, 2000). Men's and women's signals during this process differ in ways that are shaped by their biological functions as well as their cultural environment, however (Kenrick, Trost, & Sundie, 2004). The quest for this chapter is to examine where—and *why*—those signals converge and diverge. This search to understand human behavior has often been characterized as dueling explanations, such as "nature vs. nurture," "culture vs. biology," or even "alpha bias vs. beta bias" (Canary & Dindia, 1998). Such dichotomies do not hold up under careful scrutiny, however, and evolutionary theorists now more accurately emphasize that sex differences and similarities are created by the interplay of biological goals for successful reproduction and the cultural context. That is, it is not nature versus nurture but nature *and* nurture interacting to create adaptive behaviors. From this perspective, we can predict how women's and men's interests in flirting and mating are similar and different. Thus, we specifically address *sex differences* in this chapter, as well as some important *sex similarities*. Canary and Hause (1993) have rightly argued against fishing for sex differences between women and men in communication processes when there is no theoretical reason to expect any. The essays in this book provide a wide variety of perspectives on the contested reality of sex differences, ranging from authors who make claims of no differences to those who argue for significant differences. Our perspective provides one response to Canary and Hause's comment that "We believe there are sex differences in communication, but they are eluding us. Perhaps a definitive answer to the question of sex differences in communication will arrive within the next fifty years" (p. 141). We propose that one overlooked explanation for sex differences in communicative behavior has already been available for over 100 years, ever since Darwin first advanced a theory of human evolution in 1859.

AN EVOLUTIONARY FRAMEWORK

Darwin's (1859) *theory of natural selection* is based in the processes of random variation and selective retention. As a result of the limited resources in any environment, all animals compete for access to food, shelter, and mating partners—the essential elements for survival. Any individual whose genetic characteristics enhance the acquisition of resources will tend to live longer, reproduce for a longer period of time, and enjoy more success in mating. Random variation in genetic characteristics that improve adaptation, survival, and reproduction are therefore more likely to be passed on to ensuing generations. In this way, nature selects certain adaptive characteristics over others. This force is analogous to the artificial selection of desirable characteristics that is exercised by animal breeders, who have used the process to create hairless cats and aggressive pit bull dogs. Darwin (1872) noted that this process of natural selection can also have implications for emotional expression. Snarling conveys an intention to attack, and animals that recognize the signal and avoid a snarling opponent save themselves from potentially deadly encounters, resulting in the selection of natural abilities to both transmit and receive emotional communications.

What do hairless cats and snarling dogs have to do with human relationship formation? Some abilities, such as accurately reading emotional expression, are universally advantageous for all humans, regardless of sex, age, or environmental conditions. For instance, Ekman (1992) has found that basic emotional states, such as anger and joy, show cross-cultural consistency in expression and recognition. Such functional adaptations provided a gene-transmitting advantage to individuals in the environment in which the trait evolved, so they were selected and appear across cultures in subsequent generations (Williams, 1966). However, Darwin (1859) was equally intrigued by the recognition that some animal behaviors seemed maladaptive to individual survival but persisted because they helped attract mates. For instance, during mating season in Australia, the male satin bowerbird builds an elaborate lair simply to lure mates (Borgia, 1986). He decorates an intricate bower of twigs with eye-catching debris, such as parrot feathers, flower petals, and rubberbands (Alcock, 1993). He woos females with this attractive boudoir as well as a loud and varied musical serenade. The females shop around, inspecting a number of bowers before entering the one they find most tempting in order to mate with the owner. Even after the female has mated and left, the male continues to upgrade his abode, inviting more females to hop in. One male was observed to mate with 33 different females, where other males did not mate at all. Thus, constructing a marvelous bower is a highly adaptive behavior that will be selected by the females who choose to mate with the master builders, ensuring that their genes will be passed on to the next generation. However, this flashy mating behavior can be costly to survival. The males' noisy and exposed courtship makes them highly noticeable not only to interested females but also to hungry predators—definitely not a survival-related advantage.

Evolution via Reproductive Fitness

The process by which characteristics evolve that benefit reproduction rather than survival is known as *sexual selection* (Darwin, 1859). Sexual selection operates through two key processes: *intersexual choice*, in which a trait gains an advantage because it is attractive to the opposite sex (like the bowerbird's bower or the flashy tail feathers of a male peacock); and *intrasexual competition*, in which a trait gains an advantage because it helps an individual compete with same-sex rivals for access to opposite-sexed partners (like horns on a male bighorn sheep). Trivers (1972) elaborated on Darwin's notion of selection by means of reproductive fitness in his theory of *differential parental investment*. According to the theory, the sex with the initially higher investment in offspring is a desirable resource for which members of the other sex compete. The term *sex* that differentiates females from males in many species is rooted in the biological production of *gametes*, or reproductive material. Females produce large eggs that are more nutrient rich, fewer, and more costly to produce than males' small but abundant sperm (Alcock, 1993). Because males can produce an almost unlimited numbers of gametes, their lifelong ability to reproduce is greater than females' ability (Mealey, 2000). Females' typical reproductive potential is further limited by gestation time and postpartum lactation, whereas males are limited only by the number of females to whom they have access (Geary, Vigil, & Byrd-Craven, 2004). Consequently, females and males devote different amounts and types of effort into having offspring. This sexual differentiation also means that reproduction is (usually) inherently more costly for females than it is for males, so that females allocate more energy to *parental effort* whereas males expend more energy in *mating effort* (Mealey, 2000; Trivers, 1972). These limitations have a number of implications for mating behavior choices.

One implication of differential parental investment is that the sex with more to lose from a poor mating choice will also demand more before agreeing to mate. Among mammals, the biological reality of *internal gestation* means that females have a much higher initial investment than males in their offspring. Therefore, female mammals should be more selective about choosing mates, as they give their bodies for the gestation and nurturing of the progeny. Most male mammals reproduce with little cost; frequently, the male's direct input into procreation does not extend beyond copulation. For example, dueling male elk demonstrate dominance by bugling, spraying urine, horning the ground, and marching in a parallel line of display; they lunge with their magnificent antlers only as a last resort to ward off competitors for their female harem (Geist, 2002). The potential risk of injury is worthwhile, however, as the females prefer to mate with only the few bulls that prove to be the most powerful (i.e., most genetically fit) through this competition. In such species, males tend to be nonselective about their mates, whereas females tend to be extremely demanding. In the few species in which the male has a larger initial investment than the female, the mating behaviors follow the parental investment model. For instance, seahorses and pipefishes reproduce through internal gestation in the male (Daly & Wilson, 1983); accordingly, the females are more brightly colored and aggressive in courtship. Similarly, when female reproductive capabilities vary by social rank, as in the spotted hyena, males selectively choose to associate with the higher status females that are likely to have higher reproductive success (Szykman et al., 2001).

A second repercussion of female internal gestation gives rise to an important concern for males—the *certainty of paternity.* A female always has complete confidence that any offspring are hers, but a male in natural circumstances can never be certain that they are his, making him more susceptible to the danger of wasting his resources on another male's genetic legacy (Daly & Wilson, 1983). Avoiding cuckoldry (named after the cuckoo bird, who lays her eggs for incubating and hatching in the nest of unwitting "foster" parents) is of paramount importance for males, who lose genetic fitness by investing their precious resources in offspring that are not their own. For this reason, males tend to be very careful about guarding access to their partners and ensuring their fidelity. For instance, a male langur who takes over a new troop of females may kill the infants left by his predecessor (Hrdy, 1981). The infanticide ensures that his protection and resources are not wasted on another male's offspring. For most species, then, the biological facts of disproportionate maternal investment and paternal uncertainty lead to different strategies and sensitivities in the two sexes' mating-related behaviors.

A Qualified Differential Parental Investment Model for Humans

Like other mammals, humans reproduce by means of internal gestation—women conceive and carry the child inside their bodies and men do not. Unlike most other mammals, however, humans tend to be a pair-bonding species, forming long-term, intimate relationships that help ensure the survival of the fragile offspring until self-sufficiency is achieved (Benshoof & Thornhill, 1979; Daly & Wilson, 1983). In this pattern of mostly monogamous pairs within larger social groups, we are unique among mammals (Benshoof & Thornhill). All human societies have some form of marriage (Daly & Wilson), and anthropological evidence indicates that romantic love is present across a wide variety of cultures and mating strategies (Jankowiak & Fischer, 1992). The universality of the marriage bond may appear to interfere with reproductive fitness, especially for men who are required to invest very little physical effort into parenting. The adaptive logic of love is relatively straightforward, however, if not particularly romantic. Evolution occurs at the level of the "selfish gene" (Dawkins, 1976); that is, if a genetic predisposition toward the behaviors of monogamy and fidelity enhances the ability of any single individual's genes to be replicated and survive to produce future offspring, those behaviors will be selected for (Williams, 1966). Therefore, pair-bonding (whether it is monogamous, polygamous, or polyandrous) has to provide advantages in reproductive fitness for both women and men to be selected. Among birds, for instance, pair-bonding is common in those species that incubate the young for long periods of time or that have helpless infants who require extensive parental care (Alcock, 1993). For humans, several factors favor relational bonding beyond simply ensuring paternity (Benshoof & Thornhill, 1979). First, human infants are totally dependent on older humans for survival for months after birth and require constant supervision, making food gathering difficult for any single parent. For most of our evolutionary past, an infant left unattended by a foraging mother would be an easy target for predators. Second, the evolution of hunting enabled a man to contribute to the health and development of his offspring by providing a source of high-energy protein with relatively little effort. Finally, the gradual evolution of a large brain with the capacity for and dependence on cultural transmission of knowledge likely favored infants who received teachings from two parents. Hence the benefits of paternal investment in offspring increased to rival those of the mother, and our hearts were selected to bond with the person who sets them aflutter.

Given that men do invest valuable resources in their offspring, such as time, money, and emotional support, human mating should follow a somewhat modified parental investment model (Kenrick, Groth, Trost, & Sadalla, 1993; Kenrick, Sadalla, Groth, & Trost, 1990). In particular, men's level of selectivity in choosing a long-term, committed partner should approach the selectivity of women. But selectivity based on what qualities? The process of sexual selection would favor mate qualities that maximize one's own reproductive fitness by providing both the unique characteristics that only the opposite sex can contribute to the offspring (such as fertile eggs or healthy sperm) as well as qualities that contribute to successful reproduction in both sexes (Geary et al., 2004). In terms of unique attributes, women's initial and primary contributions to creating children are their physical bodies, whereas men's unique contributions are their genes and indirect resources, such as money and shelter. Both partners have a role in nurturing the child. From an evolutionary perspective, men's and women's preferences should reflect these desirable attributes.

A growing body of research shows that mate choice preferences follow these predictions (see Geary et al., 2004). Both men and women seek honest signals of physical health, but through different characteristics. For instance, evidence indicates that women prefer men who exhibit physical indicators that have been associated with genetic strength and immunocompetence, such as facial and body symmetry (Gangestad & Simpson, 2000); broad shoulders tapering to a more narrow waist; large eyes; and prominent cheek bones and chin (Geary et al.). These characteristics may also reflect a man's ability to provide needed protection and parenting. Consistent with the adaptive flexibility of human evolution, recent evidence indicates that women's preferences for symmetry and masculine characteristics tend to fluctuate over the course of the menstrual cycle (see Geary et al.). Men also look for indicators of genetic health and indicators of fertility in characteristics that we often label "physical attractiveness." For instance, men prefer a waist-to-hip ratio that indicates sexual maturity (with body mass being less important than the 0.7 waist-to-hip ratio; Singh, 1993); body and facial symmetry; and "youthful" features (large eyes, smooth skin, etc.; see Geary et al.). Geary et al. noted that it is not simply the individual's constellation of these characteristics that determines attractiveness, but their match with the partner's characteristics and mate value also influences their appeal.

In addition to these genetic fitness markers, men and women show differences and similarities in their preferred behavioral attributes, as women prioritize social status and men prioritize physical attractiveness. Because women prefer men who can contribute resources, women tend to value socially dominant males (e.g., those with social status, ambition, and acquired wealth; Buss, 1989; Kenrick et al., 1990, 1993), and evidence indicates that the children of such men do have lower mortality rates (Geary et al., 2004). This effect is pancultural, as Buss surveyed 10,000 people in 37 cultures and found that the trait of being a "good financial prospect" was significantly more important for women than for men *in all of the cultures*, as were "ambition and industriousness" in 29 of 37 cultures. Moreover, when forced to consider the importance of a mate's social level versus other desirable characteristics, women rated it as a necessity, whereas others, such as physical attractiveness, were rated as luxuries (Li, Bailey, Kenrick, & Linsenmeier, 2002). However, men's preferences across all of these same studies prioritize physical attractiveness over other traits. Even when the choice of qualities in a partner was constrained by availability, men emphasized the necessity of physical attractiveness over other characteristics (Li et al.). In the midst of these clear differences, the studies have also found important similarities in men's and women's preferences for the qualities of kindness and intelligence in their partners, indicating that characteristics that enhance the ability to be a good parent (e.g., maintain a relationship and problem solve) are also adaptive and desirable qualities (Geary et al.; Li et al.).

Sexual Strategies in Developing Relationships

Recently, evolutionary researchers have focused on the different mating strategies that men and women use to enhance their reproductive fitness. Sexual strategies are "integrated sets of adaptations that organize and guide an individual's reproductive effort" (Gangestad & Simpson, 2000, p. 575). Based on Trivers' (1972) differential parental investment model, most treatments have distinguished between seeking partners for short- and long-term relationships. Research findings indicate that there is no single mating strategy that is used by either sex across all situations; rather, humans adopt different sexual strategies depending on their level of desired involvement and the environmental context (Gangestad & Simpson; Geary et al., 2004). Generally, women's high level of parental investment in procreation favors a monogamous, long-term relational strategy with a committed, socially successful male who exhibits the qualities noted earlier (Buss & Schmitt, 1993; Kenrick et al., 1990, 1993; Li et al., 2004). Therefore, women should be most concerned with finding a partner who will commit to a relationship. Accordingly, women are more likely than men to engage in secret tests of relational commitment, such as piquing men's jealousy (Baxter & Wilmot, 1984). Women also report more distress over imagined threats to the romantic relational bond than to their partner's imagined sexual infidelity, as long as the infidelity does not include a relational attachment to the other woman (Buss, Larsen, Westen, & Semmelroth, 1992). However, women do engage in short-term liaisons when they are reproductively adaptive. For example, some women use "short-term" sexual liaisons to draw men into long-term relationships (Geary et al.). Women who do seek casual sexual partners tend to be very selective—they prefer men who have high social status, are highly physically attractive (Kenrick et al., 1993), and are willing to generously spend money on them (Buss & Schmitt). They are most likely to have short-term extramarital affairs with men whose status exceeds their husband's, and to do so at the point of peak fertility during their monthly cycle (Baker & Bellis, 1995). Emerging evidence also indicates that women are more sensitive to cues of men's fitness when they are ovulating (see Gangestad & Simpson; Geary et al.). These patterns imply that women in short-term relationships may be attempting to increase the genetic fitness of their offspring through a type of "hyper" mate selection. They also imply that women's sexual strategies are flexible and responsive to environmental conditions; for instance, women are more likely to pursue short-term strategies when sex ratios are skewed (fewer available men for long-term pairings; Geary et al.). Mixing long- and short-term strategies can have serious repercussions for women, however; an "unfaithful" partner risks an unwanted pregnancy, the withdrawal of relational resources (Buss, 1999), and even violence (Daly & Wilson, 1988), as men are particularly vigilant against the potential threat of cuckoldry, as described in the paragraphs that follow.

Men have a different set of strategy concerns in maximizing their reproductive fitness. As noted earlier, males' reproductive potential is limited only by the number of females to whom they have access. Given the low level of effort expended by males in mating, they have the ability to sire many children by many partners in a short period of time. Therefore, an important implication of the differential parental investment model is that men, who have little to lose and a great deal to gain from promiscuous mating opportunities, should be more unrestricted in their sexual desires and behaviors—a supposition borne out across a wide variety of research studies and contexts. Men not only want to have sex with more partners during their lifetimes than women (Buss & Schmitt, 1993), but they actually do, on average. They want to have sex sooner in relationships (Buss & Schmitt), and they pursue sexual relationships as ends in themselves (Geary et al., 2004). Men's mate preference standards on qualities such as intelligence and agreeableness are exceedingly low for a one-night stand (with one exception: physical attractiveness)—they are willing to have sex with someone who would not meet their minimum criteria for a date (Kenrick et al., 1993). Men have more extramarital affairs and are more likely to have sex with animals and inanimate objects (Daly & Wilson, 1983). Still, most men want to have a long-term partner, and many men only want a long-term partner (Geary et al.). In that case, men are as choosey as women in preferring high-quality partners (Buss & Schmitt; Kenrick et al., 1990, 1993). Men in long-term relationships are particularly concerned with finding a faithful mate to avoid cuckoldry. The effects of paternal uncertainty are reflected in a variety of ways: men universally value chastity more so than do women (Buss, 1989); they report more distress over their partner's imagined sexual infidelity than to their partner's romantic bond to another man (Buss et al., 1992); and men throughout the world jealously guard access to their partners through seclusion, adultery laws that support the harsh punishment of wives' infidelity (including death) but lenient treatment of husbands' infidelity, and practices such as clitoridectomy that are clearly designed to control female sexuality (Daly & Wilson). Still, men are more likely than women to benefit from a mixed strategy of a long-term relationship with short-term matings on the side (Buss, 1999).

The combined pressures of determining the level of relational interest in a potential partner (and, hence, the partner's level of potential investment) and screening for commitment and faithfulness (among other characteristics) make relationship initiation a particularly challenging endeavor. We now turn to an examination of a particularly important aspect of relationship initiation, flirting, within an evolutionary context.

EVOLUTIONARY THEORY AND COURTSHIP INTERACTION

Because men and women face disparate reproductive realities, they should behave differently during courtship interactions (Grammer, 1990; Moore, 1995). In the remainder of this chapter, we consider how these differential reproductive pressures affect flirting behavior. This review reorganizes findings from the current flirtation literature within an evolutionary framework, even though the research may not have been specifically designed to test evolutionary hypotheses. Our intent is to show not only the adaptive nature of flirtation, but also how our knowledge of interpersonal processes can enrich our understanding of evolutionary processes in humans. We review research on both evolutionary theory and interpersonal relationships indicating that, during courtship, women are generally more discerning than men, find high status men more attractive and desirable, and control the mating process through signaling their proceptivity to appropriate men. This research also reveals that, during courtship, men generally attempt to gain intersexual advantage by overtly displaying their status and dominance, are sensitive to and engage in intrasexual competition, and are more likely to approach women who have selectively signaled proceptivity. As these topics indicate, courtship is a reciprocal process, and the concerns of one sex mirror the concerns of the other. However, how women and men address these concerns differs during the initial stages of courtship, that is, during flirtation.

Predictions From Evolutionary Theory for Women's Courtship Behavior

As noted earlier, the balance between the ultimate costs and benefits of romantic heterosexual involvement predicts differences in men's and women's goals at the initial flirtation stage. For instance, because women have more to lose from a botched pair bond, they should be more discerning about how and with whom they flirt. Thus, contrary to the notion that women are pawns that are played by more socially dominant men, women are generally the more discriminating sex and control the flirting process (Moore, 1985; Perper, 1985; Townsend & Wasserman, 1997). The female's ultimate control over the mating process is dramatically illustrated in the Barbary macaques (Small, 1992). A female in estrus is obvious in that the pink tissues around her hind end swell, indicating to the male that she is ready to mate. She selects her partner, however, by approaching the desired male and swinging her hind end into his face. As noted by Small (p. 149), "if the male is also interested, which he generally is, the two monkeys mate." Human courtship rituals, by nature of our physiology and bonding patterns, may be less sensational but nonetheless interesting in the intricacies of their execution.

The mating process presents different dilemmas for each sex (Grammer, 1990), which influence how men and women flirt. Specifically, women must be capable of distinguishing themselves from the other women in the crowd (Grammer, Renninger, & Fischer, 2004) while signaling their proceptivity clearly, but with a subtlety that borders on ambiguity (Grammer, Kruck, & Magnusson, 1998; Moore, 1995). Because men are sensitive to the threat of intrasexual competition (Buss, 1999), a man may only respond to signals he believes are directed at him to minimize rejection. Therefore, a woman must be clearly available to the desired man, but not to others. One legacy of paternal uncertainty is that a man who is interested in more than a fleeting relationship must also be sensitive to signs that a woman is promiscuous or unfaithful—one who would make him a potential cuckold. Consequently, a woman needs to be able to direct her attentions and avoid appearing as if she is signaling to any and every man in the environment. These pressures both argue for a woman to isolate a desirable man and clearly signal her attraction.

However, women also face the humiliating possibility of rejection. Thus, subtle signals can both minimize the possibility of suffering rejection as well as assure the targeted man of her exclusivity and fidelity. Moreover, while managing this complex and subtle projection of availability and interest, a woman must simultaneously screen the desired man for cues of status, interest, and stability, especially if she is interested in a long-term relationship. Finally, a woman must also be able to clearly but subtly reject undesirable suitors in the environment who might interfere with her ability to attract an appropriate mate, while still protecting the face of the unwanted suitor so as to avoid provoking a violent retaliation (Trost, 1996).

On the basis of evolutionary principles and the dilemmas that women face in the courtship process outlined herein, one can predict that, during flirting interactions, women will (a) be more skillful at encoding and decoding nonverbal behaviors, (b) possess a larger repertoire of flirting or proceptivity behaviors to signal the men they wish to attract, (c) possess a larger repertoire of rejection strategies, and (d) be approached by men when they exhibit behaviors that are interpreted as flirtatious.

Research on Women's Courtship Behavior

Research on flirting and mating behavior supports each of these predictions. First, women would be expected to exhibit more skill at encoding and decoding nonverbal behavior in order to clearly but subtly display availability, as well as to discern male signals of status, interest, and stability. In fact, we know from nonverbal researchers that women are more accurate than men at both encoding and decoding nonverbal communication (Hall, 1998; Hall, Gault, & Kent, 1999; Moore, 2002); even when the differences are not significant, they favor women (Noller, 1986). According to meta-analyses of expression accuracy (Hall, 1984), women are better at expressing their emotions and feelings, with effect sizes ranging from $r = .12$ to $r = .31$. Flirting is typically initiated through visual contact, so it is also relevant to note that women's ability to encode and decode nonverbal signals is typically greater for the visual channel (Drag & Shaw, 1967), particularly the face (Rosenthal & DePaulo, 1979), than for the vocal channel (Noller, 1985). Hall (1998) has conducted several meta-analytic reviews of sex differences in nonverbal sensitivity, or ability to decode nonverbal cues, and found that the effect size consistently favors women, ranging from $r = .20$ to $r = .25$. Perhaps most significantly, women's superiority at nonverbal coding and decoding is most pronounced when the target is a stranger (Noller, 1986). Thus, women are likely to be more skillful than men at delivering and detecting nonverbal cues in the initial flirting context, where the target typically is a stranger or an acquaintance.

The second prediction suggests that women should possess a large repertoire of flirtation strategies to signal interest in men. Once again, research results support such a claim. A number of studies have established that women possess a broad range of proceptivity strategies. For example, Muehlenhard, Koralewski, Andrews, and Burdick (1986) delineated 21 verbal and 15 nonverbal cues that women use to convey interest, whereas Perper and Weiss's (1987) participants identified 22 strategies they used to attract men. In the most comprehensive and naturalistic study of female flirtation behaviors, Moore (1985) conducted observations in singles bars and identified 52 different nonverbal flirtation behaviors exhibited by women. Out of 12 coded behaviors, McCormick and Jones (1989) found that women exhibited a wider variety of and more frequent flirtation gestures than did men, especially early in the flirtation episode. Grammer et al. (2004) found evidence among women at a nightclub that they were aware of the signaling function conveyed by their clothing, and that some had deliberately matched their clothing choice for the evening to fit with their courtship motivation. Others have found that women's signaling is important in initiating a flirtation sequence. On the basis of observations of 70 couples, McCormick and Jones determined that women were more nonverbally active in initiating flirtation and more active in escalating the flirting sequence than were men. In over 900 hours of observation in bars, Perper (1985) also observed that women's signals were most likely to initiate the flirting episode. Grammer et al. (1998) uncovered that women are reluctant to display nonverbal signals, however, until they have developed some interest in a specific man, at which point a very complicated sequence of nonverbal synchronization unfolds that is idiosyncratic to the couple.

The third prediction arising out of evolutionary theory proposes that women will have a larger repertoire of rejection strategies than will men. As noted earlier, men have more to gain from capitalizing on opportunistic mating possibilities than do women, implying that women are more likely to have to reject unsuitable men who approach them. Of course, rejection can simply be the absence of flirtation; but, rejection becomes more than the absence of flirtation when an overt approach by an interested party must be acknowledged and, in some manner, deflated. Consequently, women, who are more likely to be approached than men, should have a wider array of strategies from which to choose. As expected, women do report rejecting men more frequently than vice versa, and women report using significantly more rejection strategies that span a broader range of categories than do men (Trost, 1996).

The fourth and final prediction concerning women's flirtation behavior suggests that women who exhibit flirtatious behaviors will be approached more by men than women who do not. To argue that a behavior has an adaptive function in attracting men indicates that it should be present in those situations in which flirting is possible, and absent in those situations in which flirting is unlikely to occur. In a direct test of the contextual nature of flirtation, Moore (1985) found that women were more likely to exhibit effective flirting behaviors in environments that included a large proportion of men, such as a bar, than in an environment with very few men, such as a women's meeting. Research also demonstrates that the use of flirtation strategies influences the likelihood that a woman actually will be approached by a man. For example, Walsh and Hewitt (1985) found that repeated signaling of more than one type of flirtation gesture significantly influenced a woman's probability of being approached by a man. Moore (1985) found that women who emitted a higher number of nonverbal flirtation displays (in this case 35 or more per hour) received more than 4 approaches per hour. In contrast, women who displayed low levels of nonverbal flirtation behaviors elicited fewer than 0.48 approaches per hour. In addition, women who used a broader range of categories (more than 10) were more likely to be approached by a man. In fact, the correlation between the number of women's proceptivity signals and the number of male approaches across three contexts (bar, library, and snack bar) was 0.89. Although approaches were most frequent in a bar, where displays were most frequent, those women who signaled often were those most often approached, regardless of context. Moore (1995) replicated these findings in adolescent girls' proceptive behavior, whose signals also elicited more approaches by boys. Importantly, these studies have established that a female's courtship signaling was far more instrumental than other factors, including her physical attractiveness, in eliciting male advances (Moore & Butler, 1989).

In sum, a woman who is interested in connecting with a man faces a daunting task that requires a high degree of skill and sensitivity. She must simultaneously transmit availability to the desired man, avoid rejection by him, express fidelity, reject unwanted suitors, and deduce his characteristics and intentions—a process that is fraught with the potential for dangerous miscommunication. The process of connecting is fraught with no little amount of danger for men as well.

Predictions From Evolutionary Theory for Men's Courtship Behavior

The mating dilemmas for men, although equally difficult, are somewhat different from those faced by women. To be successful as targets of women's proceptive behavior, men need to attract a woman's attention by signaling status and willingness to commit while competing successfully with other men in the vicinity. These tasks are intertwined. That is, the first dilemma for men is to advertise their desirability as mates so as to elicit female attention and proceptive behavior. Unfortunately for men, although status and willingness to commit are valuable, they are difficult to signal nonverbally. Second, in most species, intrasexual competition is greater within the sex that makes a lower initial investment into the offspring, i.e., the male (Trivers, 1972). For example, bull elephant seals bite their competition with sharp teeth until one of them retreats, and bighorn sheep run at each other and ram foreheads with a force that would scare most defensive linemen. Because humans do engage in pair bonding, men and women should both attend to and attempt to minimize their competition to a certain extent. Even so, women are the gatekeepers to relationships, and men still will vie with each other for access to the most desirable women. Consequently, men should tend toward overt advertisement of the qualities most desired by women, not only to attract women but to hopefully silence the competition (Buss, 1988). Grammer (1990) proposed that men can deal with these dilemmas by enacting one of two possible strategies: approach only women who signal interest, which reduces the likelihood of rejection and humiliation in front of the competition, or take immediate and fast action to beat the competition to a valuable woman.

Thus, an evolutionary perspective can assist one in making predictions about men's flirting behaviors as well. According to this perspective, men will (a) attempt to signal status, dominance, and willingness to commit; (b) approach women who signal interest; and (c) take immediate and fast action once signaled. Although research does exist to support these predictions, considerably less research has been conducted on men's flirtation behavior than on women's behavior.

Research on Men's Courtship Behavior

In one of the few studies to examine the role of male relational bonding, Greer and Buss (1994) found that the most effective tactics for promoting a sexual encounter for men involved investing time and attention and communicating a willingness to commit. Thus, this study established that, as predicted, women are more likely to select a mate who displays qualities that suggest long-term investment. Studies also have examined male displays of status and dominance during courtship. For example, Buss (1988, 1996) has assessed the role of self-promotion in mate attraction. He found that showing resource potential was judged to be the most effective tactic for men seeking a long-term mate. He also asked both men and women to describe behaviors that they use to make themselves attractive to the opposite sex (Buss, 1988). Some of the behaviors were similar for both men and women, including showing a sense of humor or being sympathetic, being well mannered, and being well groomed—all characteristics that are related to long-term relational stability. In keeping with the expectation that men want to signal status and dominance, however, men reported being significantly more likely to display resources, such as flashing money (an act that has the double advantage of impressing a potential partner and intimidating the competition.) Men were also more likely to exaggerate their display of dominance or resources (the "bizarre ornamentation" noted by Alcock in 1993, such as wearing expensive "label" clothing that was actually beyond their means), brag about their superior intelligence, or exaggerate their level of sexual activity and sexual popularity (Tooke & Camire, 1991). In other words, men's awareness of the need to display dominance and undermine the competition not only extends to accurate reporting of their resources but may also lead to some slight embellishments as well. In keeping with the view that the pair-bonded nature of our species elicits similar attention to competition among women, it is important to note that women also reported elaborating on their mating potential by exaggerating the characteristics most valued by men; namely, they enhance their bodily appearance through behaviors such as dieting, wearing perfume, sun tanning, and walking with a greater swing than normal when around men (Tooke & Camire), and wearing more revealing clothing (Grammer et al., 2004). Display strategies also vary in different contexts: women who do not expect to find men who are willing to invest in their offspring are more likely to wear sexy clothing and engage in sex than women who expect to find high-investment males (Cashdan, 1993).

The second prediction, that men are more likely to approach women who signal their interest, is supported by Moore's (1985) work cited earlier; that is, men are eight times more likely to approach a woman who uses a high number of flirtation signals and are more likely to approach women who use multiple nonverbal channels (Moore, 1985; Walsh & Hewitt, 1985). Grammer et al. (2004) found that women who engaged in signaling through self-described revealing clothing were also more likely to be touched by men. In addition, studies that have asked men about their likelihood of approaching women reveal that men are unlikely to ask a woman for a date unless she provides cues of interest (Muehlenhard & McFall, 1981; Muehlenhard & Miller, 1988).

The final prediction, that men will take immediate and fast action in mating contexts, has not been tested directly. However, this issue has been addressed indirectly in research examining men's motivations for flirting and their interpretations of women's behaviors as friendly versus flirtatious. Grammer (1990) has argued that men outmaneuver the competition by responding quickly to a woman's signals of interest. Although men and women do not appear to differ in their perceptions of what constitutes flirtatious communication, men tend to rate those behaviors as more inviting than do women (Abrahams, 1994; Moore, 2002; O'Farrell, Rosenthal, & O'Neal, 2003). Related research indicates that men are more likely than women to interpret women's nonverbal behavior as flirtatious or sexual than friendly (Abbey, 1982, 1987; Abbey & Melby, 1986; Montgomery, 1987; Saal, Johnson, & Weber, 1989; Shotland & Craig, 1988), perhaps because the flirtation of young men, in particular, appears to be motivated by sexual intentions (Montgomery). Overall, men impute more sexual meaning to heterosexual interaction (Abbey, 1982) and show more interest in returning flirtation (Downey & Vitulli, 1987). In addition, Moore found that men view women's rejection signals as sending a less "potent," or negative, message than do women, suggesting that they are less put off by rejection than are women. Thus, one response to competition and the need to establish dominance is for men to interpret women's nonverbal and conversational cues in a romantic framework (Rytting, 1976) and to discount their rejection cues.

In sum, a framework of evolutionary pressures and adaptations can be useful in predicting how the process of flirtation differs for women and men. In particular, rather than viewing women as passive recipients of men's amorous advances, an evolutionary perspective underscores the importance of female choice in courtship and reproduction (Darwin, 1859). The parental investment model allows one to predict that women, as the more selective sex, should initiate a flirtatious episode by nonverbally signaling their proceptivity, be approached by the targeted man, and then continue escalation of the interaction (if desired) or reject the pursuit (if not). As we have implied throughout, research indicates that women do initiate the flirting process through their nonverbal behavior (McCormick & Jones, 1989; Perper, 1985), men are more likely to physically approach women than vice versa (Trost, 1996), and women use more and more varied rejections strategies (Perper & Weiss, 1987; Trost). Although we have addressed the communication demands on men and women separately in this analysis, it is important to note that neither sex totally commands a successful flirtation episode (Moore, 1995; Perper & Weiss). Continued escalation of the encounter requires a reciprocated sequence of approach behaviors from both parties involved in the interaction. Even though the phases that describe a flirtation episode may appear to be relatively fixed (Perper), the exact combination of behaviors exhibited in the exchange can differ dramatically, enhancing the aura of magic that pervades the experience (Grammer et al., 1998). Moreover, our description has been limited to flirtation that is intended to ultimately result in an intimate relationship, although such intimacy is not always the intended outcome of flirtation (Montgomery, 1987). Certainly other motivations for flirting can be adaptive, as well; however, the evolutionary perspective is particularly relevant to predicting reproductive behaviors.

CONCLUSIONS

Our response to Canary and Hause's (1993) suggestion that the exploration of sex differences is confusing in the absence of theory is that, in fact, an evolutionary framework can be useful in predicting and explaining sex differences and similarities in behavior. From an evolutionary perspective, Mealey (2000) noted that, as humans, men and women have more in common with each other than with any other animal; "it is part of our 'human nature' that we have similar anatomy, similar sense organs, and similar capacities for awareness, feelings, language, and creativity" (p. xi). Therefore, men and women are not truly opposites; they have many common features and concerns that lead to behavioral similarities. The evolutionary perspective, however, also shows that differences in men's and women's mating physiology have affected the adaptive nature of different mating preferences and behaviors. These behavioral differences will only apply to those tasks for which men and women face dissimilar selection pressures, such as finding an appropriate mate. At an ultimate level of analysis, women stand to lose the most from an ill-fated match, and they benefit by being particularly selective in looking for stable men who can provide the resources necessary to raise their offspring. Women, therefore, should generally reflect a strong preference for men who are able to establish dominance, exhibit adequate resources, and show an ability to commit. Men, in contrast, have less physical investment in their offspring and, as their initial investment is lower, must compete with other men for access to desirable and highly discriminating women. As indicated, cross-cultural evidence indicates that there are universals in mate preferences that are consistent with the differential parental investment model (Buss, 1989; Kenrick & Keefe, 1992). Moreover, aspects of women's flirtatious behavior appear to be universal as well (Eibl-Eibesfeldt, 1975). Nonetheless, recent research indicates that women's and men's sexual strategies are also very sensitive to contextual conditions, such as the local sex ratio or a woman's ovulatory cycle (Gangestand & Simpson, 2000; Geary et al., 2004). Cross-cultural evidence is only one way of testing hypotheses based on evolutionary principles (for a fuller discussion, see Buss, 1999; Capella, 1991; and Kenrick et al., 2004). It is hoped that continued examination of how evolutionary adaptiveness may interact with environmental and cultural contexts will provide a more complete picture of the role of sex differences in behavior.

We specifically have examined how women's and men's search behaviors may differ on the basis of their different goals in finding a partner. Taking an evolutionary perspective has led to observations that, in fact, women control the flirtation process (Moore, 1985), even though the behaviors need not always be conscious (Kenrick et al., 2004; Mealey, 2000). The myth of the passive female who patiently waits to be swept away by her Prince Charming has, indeed, been relegated to the status of a fairy tale (Hrdy, 1981; Small, 1992). Daly and Wilson (1983) made this notation:

> Men usually appear to be running the show, but it can be argued with some justice that they are peripheral hangers-on whose posturing and prancing is largely irrelevant to the essential business of human life and procreation. But even if men are not necessarily the prime movers of society, they certainly make themselves conspicuous! Men are everywhere the more political sex. They wheel and deal, bluster and bluff, compete overtly for valuable commodities and for mere symbols. Ultimately, these male machinations reflect a struggle for access to female reproductive capacity. (p. 288)

As people who observe behavior for a living, interpersonal researchers are particularly attuned to the nuances of expressive behavior; it is a topic in which we are naturally interested. However, as biological organisms, we should all be naturally interested in discriminating those who are interested in us from those who are not—for if we fail to successfully negotiate the intricate steps of meeting and mating, we will cease to exist.

ACKNOWLEDGMENTS

We appreciate the helpful comments of Daniel Canary, Kathryn Dindia, and Douglas Kenrick on an earlier version of this chapter. Parts of the chapter were presented at the Western States Communication Association Convention, Pasadena, CA, in February of 1996, and at the International Communication Association Convention, Chicago, IL, in May of 1996.

REFERENCES

Abbey, A. (1982). Sex differences in attributions for friendly behavior: Do males misperceive females' friendliness? *Journal of Personality and Social Psychology, 42*, 830–838.

Abbey, A. (1987). Misperceptions of friendly behavior as sexual interest: A survey of naturally occurring incidents. *Psychology of Women Quarterly, 11*, 173–194.

Abbey, A., & Melby, C. (1986). The effects of nonverbal cues on gender differences in perceptions of sexual intent. *Sex Roles, 15*, 283–298.

Abrahams, M. F. (1994). Perceiving flirtatious communication: An exploration of the perceptual dimensions underlying judgments of flirtatiousness. *Journal of Sex Research, 31*, 283–292.

Alcock, J. (1993). *Animal behavior: An evolutionary approach* (5th ed.). Sunderland, MA: Sinauer Associates.

Baker, R. R., & Bellis, M. A. (1995). *Human sperm competition.* London: Chapman and Hall.

Baxter, L. A., & Wilmot, W. W. (1984). "Secret tests": Social strategies for acquiring information about the state of the relationship. *Human Communication Research, 11*, 171–201.

Benshoof, L., & Thornhill, R. (1979). The evolution of monogamy and concealed ovulation in humans. *Journal of Social and Biological Structures, 2*, 95–106.

Borgia, G. (1986). Sexual selection in bowerbirds. *Scientific American, 254*, 92–100.

Buss, D. M. (1988). The evolution of intrasexual competition: Tactics of mate attraction. *Journal of Personality and Social Psychology, 54*, 616–628.

Buss, D. M. (1989). Sex differences in human mate preferences: Evolutionary hypotheses tested in 37 cultures. *Behavioral and Brain Sciences, 12*, 1–49.

Buss, D. M. (1996). Strategic self-promotion and competitor derogation: Sex and context effects on the perceived effectiveness of mate attraction tactics. *Journal of Personality and Social Psychology, 70*, 1185–204.

Buss, D. M. (1999). *Evolutionary psychology: The new science of the mind.* Boston, MA: Allyn & Bacon.

Buss, D. M., Larsen, R., Westen, D., & Semmelroth, J. (1992). Sex differences in jealousy: Evolution, physiology, and psychology. *Psychological Science, 3*, 251–255.

Buss, D. M., & Schmitt, D. P. (1993). Sexual strategies theory: An evolutionary perspective on human mating. *Psychological Review, 100*, 204–232.

Canary, D. J., & Dindia, K. (1998). Prologue: Recurring issues in sex differences and similarities in communication. In D. J. Canary & K. Dindia (Eds.), *Sex differences and similarities in communication* (pp. 1–17). Mahwah, NJ: Lawrence Earlbaum Associates.

Canary, D. J., & Hause, K. S. (1993). Is there any reason to research sex differences in communication? *Communication Quarterly, 41*, 129–144.

Capella, J. N. (1991). The biological origins of automated patterns of human interaction. *Communication Theory, 1*, 4–35.

Cashdan, E. (1993). Attracting mates: Effects of parental investment on mate attraction strategies. *Ethology and Sociobiology, 14*, 1–23.

Daly, M., & Wilson, M. (1983). *Sex, evolution, and behavior* (2nd ed.). Belmont, CA: Wadsworth.

Daly, M., & Wilson, M. (1988). *Homicide.* New York: de Gruyter.

Darwin, C. (1859). *The origin of species.* London: Murray.

Darwin, C. (1872). *The expression of emotions in man and animals.* London: Murray.

Dawkins, R. (1976). *The selfish gene.* New York: Oxford University Press.

Downey, J. L., & Vitulli, W. F. (1987). Self-report measures of behavioral attributions related to interpersonal flirtation situations. *Psychological Reports, 61*, 899–904.

Drag, R. M., & Shaw, M. E. (1967). Factors influencing the communication of emotional intent by facial expressions. *Psychonomic Science, 8*, 137–138.

Eibl-Eibesfeldt, I. (1975). *Ethology: The biology of behavior* (2nd ed.). New York: Holt, Rinehart & Winston.

Ekman, P. (1992). An argument for basic emotions. *Cognition and Emotion, 6*, 169–200.

Gangestad, S. W., & Simpson, J. A. (2000). The evolution of human mating: Trade-offs and strategic pluralism. *Behavioral and Brain Sciences, 23*, 573–644.

Geary, D. C., Vigil, J., & Byrd-Craven, J. (2004). The evolution of human mate choice [Electronic version]. *Journal of Sex Research, 41*, 27–43.

Geist, V. (2002). Adaptive behavioral strategies. In D. E. Toweill & J. W. Thomas (Eds.), *North American elk: Ecology and management* (pp. 389–433). Washington, DC: Smithsonian Institution Press.

Grammer, K. (1990). Strangers meet: Laughter and nonverbal signs of interest in opposite-sex encounters. *Journal of Nonverbal Behavior, 14*, 209–236.

Grammer, K., Kruck, K. B., & Magnusson, M. S. (1998). The courtship dance: Patterns of nonverbal synchronization in opposite-sex encounters. *Journal of Nonverbal Behavior, 22*, 3–29.

Grammer, K., Renninger, L., & Fischer, B. (2004). Disco clothing, female sexual motivation, and relationship status: Is she dressed to impress? *Journal of Sex Research, 41*, 66–75.

Greer, A., & Buss, D. M. (1994). Tactics for promoting sexual encounters [Electronic version]. *Journal of Sex Research, 31*, 185–201.

Hall, J. A. (1984). *Nonverbal sex differences*. Baltimore: Johns Hopkins University Press.

Hall, J. A. (1998). How big are nonverbal sex differences? The case of smiling and sensitivity to nonverbal cues. In D. J. Canary & K. Dindia (Eds.), *Sex, gender, and communication: Similarities and differences* (pp. 155–178). Mahwah, NJ: Lawrence Erlbaum Associates.

Hall, C., Gaul, L., & Kent, M. (1999). College students' perception of facial expressions. *Perceptual and Motor Skills, 89*, 763–770.

Hrdy, S. B. (1981). *The woman that never evolved*. Cambridge, MA: Harvard University Press.

Jankowiak, W. R., & Fischer, E. F. (1992). A cross-cultural perspective on romantic love. *Ethnology, 31*, 149–155.

Kenrick, D. T., Groth, G., Trost, M. R., & Sadalla, E. K. (1993). Integrating evolutionary and social exchange perspectives on relationships: Effects of gender, self-appraisal, and involvement level on mate selection. *Journal of Personality and Social Psychology, 64*, 951–969.

Kenrick, D. T., & Keefe, R. C. (1992). Age preferences in mates reflect sex differences in reproductive strategies. *Behavioral and Brain Sciences, 15*, 75–133.

Kenrick, D. T., Sadalla, E. K., Groth, G., & Trost, M. R. (1990). Evolution, traits, and the stages of human courtship: Qualifying the parental investment model. *Journal of Personality, 58*, 97–116.

Kenrick, D. T., Trost, M. R., & Sundie, J. M. (2004). Sex roles as adaptations: An evolutionary perspective on gender differences and similarities. In A. H. Eagly, A. E. Beall, & R. J. Sternberg (Eds.), *The psychology of gender* (2nd ed., pp. 65–91). New York: Guilford.

Li, N. P., Bailey, J. M., Kenrick, D. T., & Linsenmeier, J. A. W. (2002). The necessities and luxuries of mate preferences: Testing the tradeoffs. *Journal of Personality and Social Psychology, 82*, 947–955.

McCormick, N. B., & Jones, A. J. (1989). Gender differences in nonverbal flirtation. *Journal of Sex Education and Therapy, 15*, 271–282.

Mealey, L. (2000). *Sex differences: Development and evolutionary strategies*. San Diego, CA: Academic Press.

Montgomery, B. M. (1987, May). *Sociable vs. sensual flirting: The influence of gender*. Paper presented at the annual meeting of the International Communication Association, Montreal, Canada.

Moore, M. M. (1985). Nonverbal courtship patterns in women: Context and consequences. *Ethology and Sociobiology, 6*, 237–247.

Moore, M. M. (1995). Courtship signaling and adolescents: "Girls just wanna have fun"? *Journal of Sex Research, 32*, 319–328.

Moore, M. M. (2002). Courtship communication and perception. *Perceptual and Motor Skills, 94*, 97–105.

Moore, M. M., & Butler, D. L. (1989). Predictive aspects of nonverbal courtship behavior in women. *Semiotica, 3*, 205–215.

Muehlenhard, C. L., Koralewski, M. A., Andrews, S. L., & Burdick, C. A. (1986). Verbal and nonverbal cues that convey interest in dating: Two studies. *Behavior Therapy, 17*, 404–419.

Muehlenhard, C. L., & McFall, R. M. (1981). Dating initiation from a woman's perspective. *Behavior Therapy, 12*, 682–691.

Muehlenhard, C. L., & Miller, E. N. (1988). Traditional and nontraditional men's responses to women's dating initiation. *Behavior Therapy, 12*, 682–691.

Noller, P. (1985). The video primacy effect: A further look. *Journal of Nonverbal Behavior, 9*, 28–47.

Noller, P. (1986). Sex differences in nonverbal communication: Advantage lost or supremacy regained? *Australian Journal of Psychology, 38*, 23–32.

O'Farrell, K. J., Rosenthal, E. N., O'Neal, E. C. (2003). Relationship satisfaction and responsiveness to nonmates' flirtation: Testing an evolutionary explanation. *Journal of Social and Personal Relationships, 20*, 663–674.

Perper, T. (1985). *Sex signals: The biology of love*. Philadelphia: ISI Press.

Perper, T., & Weiss, D. L. (1987). Proceptive and rejective strategies of U.S. and Canadian college women. *Journal of Sex Research, 23*, 455–480.

Rosenthal, R., & DePaulo, B. M. (1979). Sex differences in accommodation in nonverbal communication. In R. Rosenthal (Ed.), *Skill in nonverbal communication: Individual differences* (pp. 68–103). Cambridge, MA: Oelgeschlager, Gunn & Hain.

Rytting, M.B. (1976, May). *Sex or intimacy: Male and female versions of heterosexual relationships*. Paper presented at the annual meeting of the Midwestern Psychological Association, Chicago, IL.

Saal, F. E., Johnson, C. B., Weber, N. (1989). Friendly or sexy?: It may depend upon whom you ask. *Psychology of Women Quarterly, 13*, 263–276.

Shotland, R. L., & Craig, J. M. (1988). Can men and women differentiate between friendly and sexually interested behavior? *Social Psychology Quarterly, 51*, 66–73.

Singh, D. (1993). Adaptive significance of female physical attractiveness: Role of waist- to-hip ratio. *Journal of Personality and Social Psychology, 65*, 293–307.

Small, M. F. (1992). Female choice in mating. *American Scientist, 80*, 142–151.

Szykman, M., Engh, A. L., Van Horn, R. C., Funk, S. M., Scribner, K. T., & Holekamp, K. E. (2001). Association patterns among male and female spotted hyenas (*Crocuta crocuta*) reflect male mate choice [Electronic version]. *Behavioral Ecology and Sociobiology, 50*, 231–238.

Tooke, W., & Camire, L. (1991). Patterns of deception in intersexual and intrasexual mating strategies. *Ethology and Sociobiology, 12*, 345–364.

Townsend, J. M., & Wasserman, T. (1997). The perception of sexual attractiveness: Sex differences in variability. *Archives of Sexual Behavior, 26*, 243–269.

Trivers, R. L. (1972). Parental investment and sexual selection. In B. Campbell (Ed.), *Sexual selection and the descent of man 1871–1971* (pp. 136–179). Chicago: Aldine.

Trost, M. R. (1996, August). *"Let's stay friends" and other strategies for rejecting romance*. Paper presented at the meeting of the American Psychological Association, Toronto, Ontario, Canada.

Walsh, D. G., & Hewitt, J. (1985). Giving men the come-on: Effect of eye contact and smiling in a bar environment. *Perceptual and Motor Skills, 61*, 873–874.

Williams, G. C. (1966). *Adaptation and natural selection*. Princeton, NJ: Princeton University Press.

18

Sex Differences in the Transition to a Heterosexual Romantic Relationship

Paul A. Mongeau
Arizona State University

Mary Claire Morr Serewicz
University of Denver

Mary Lynn Miller Henningsen
Northern Illinois University

Kristin Leigh Davis
Arizona State University

Relationships change. Many changes are subtle, whereas others represent unmistakable and qualitative shifts in relationship definition. Although the development of a romantic relationship might occur in any number of ways, a simple hypothetical example might include three qualitative changes. The first major change might occur when two people meet and talk for the first time (i.e., a shift from strangers to acquaintances). A second major change might occur as the acquaintances communicate regularly over time and get to know and like each other (i.e., a shift from acquaintanceship to friendship). The final change might involve the discovery and consummation of mutual romantic interest (i.e., a shift from a friendship to a romantic relationship).

The focus of this chapter is on the third shift, specifically, what Mongeau and Teubner (2002) referred to as a *romantic relationship transition* (or RRT) between a man and a woman. Mongeau and Teubner defined the RRT as that point or period in time when a relationship changes from being either platonic or nonexistent to being romantic. By definition, then, all romantic relationships experience at least one RRT. In a vast majority of cases, relationships evolve from one relationship form (e.g., friends or acquaintances) to a romantic relationship. Even "love at first sight" involves an RRT. In this specialized case, however, the initiation of the romantic relationship and the initiation of an acquaintanceship are simultaneous events.

SEX DIFFERENCES IN RRTs

Over a decade ago, Canary and Hause (1993) asked if there was any reason to research sex differences in communication. Their answer was that communication scholars should look for sex differences only when there was a good theoretical reason to do so. We believe that an RRT, as the earliest stages of a romantic relationship, provides a context in which there is good reason to look for sex differences (particularly among college-aged individuals). Moreover, these sex differences focus on sexual interactions. First, at this age, men tend to see the world in more sexual ways than women do (e.g., Abbey, 1987; however, see also Schwartz & Rutter, 1988). Second, in a meta-analysis of studies on sex differences in sexuality, Hyde and Oliver (2000) reported that men tend to espouse more liberal sexual attitudes and engage in a variety of sexual behaviors more frequently than women do. Moreover, Hyde and Oliver reported that sex differences in sexual attitudes and behaviors are at their zenith in casual relationships and tend to decrease in size as relationships become more committed.

Even though there are consistent and important sex differences in sexual interaction, it is important to keep in mind that both men and women enjoy sex (Schwartz & Rutter, 1998). Moreover, both men and women prefer to have sex within close committed relationships (Laumann, Michael, & Gagnon, 1994). It is in uncommitted relationships (where RRTs are likely to occur) that sex differences are likely strongest. Even in uncommitted relationships, sex differences are neither qualitative nor constant. Even though Hyde and Oliver (2000) report relatively large sex differences, results suggest that men's and women's sexual attitudes and behaviors differ in degree rather than in kind.

Sex Differences, Relationship History, and RRT

Mongeau and Teubner (2002) argued that RRTs vary dramatically across cases. One important source of this variation is partners' past relationship history. For example, Mongeau and Teubner demonstrated that partner knowledge prior to the transition influenced both the speed of the RRT and the timing of dating relative to the transition itself. Specifically, partners who knew each other well tended to engage in slow transitions and dated before the RRT. These couples cherished their friendship and feared harming it by rushing into an RRT. In several cases, partners who knew each other well even broke the taboo of talking about relationship status (Baxter & Wilmot, 1985) before the transition. In contrast, less familiar partners reported a much more rapid RRT and reported dating following the transition. A typical description of this type of RRT involved meeting a stranger or acquaintance on a Friday night and being in a romantic relationship with him or her by the next weekend.

It should come as little surprise that relational history influences an RRT. Several theories posit that interaction history and partner knowledge strongly influence the nature of relationships (e.g., Altman & Taylor, 1973; Berger & Calabrese, 1975; Sunnafrank, 1986). Moreover, it is important to recognize that relationship history appears to moderate the effect of sex differences in RRT. As will become clear, women tend to vary their behavior (both sexual and communicative) to reflect social and relational cues to a greater extent than do men (Baumeister, 2000). This suggests that a couple's relationship history (e.g., whether they have just met or have a strong existing friendship) likely influences the woman's behavior to a greater extent than it does the man's behavior. It also suggests that, as partners grow increasingly intimate and close before the RRT, sex differences should be consistently less important in the actual transition.

RRTs AS TURNING POINTS

Our theoretical perspective in this chapter is turning points. Baxter and Erbert (1999) defined turning points as "transformative events in which the relationship is changed in some way, either positively or negatively" (p. 551). Bolton (1961) argued that turning points represent a particularly appropriate method that scholars could use to study relationship development. Over the past two decades, several studies have used turning points to study the development of a number of different relationship types, including those between faculty member and chair (Barge & Musambira, 1992), family members (Baxter, Braithwaite, & Nicholson, 1999), friends (e.g., Johnson, et al., 2004), and romantic partners (e.g., Baxter & Bullis, 1986; Baxter & Ebert; Bullis, Clark, & Sline, 1993).

An RRT represents a major macrolevel turning point (Baxter & Bullis, 1986) in the development of a romantic relationship. Given the combination of affective, behavioral, and cognitive components of romantic relationships, an RRT likely also includes any number of other, subordinate, or microlevel turning points. Following this logic, we further assume that a couple who is experiencing an RRT will engage in a number of behaviors for the first time (within the context of the particular entanglement, at least). In this chapter we focus on three such "firsts": first dates, first significant disclosures, and first sexual encounter. There are several reasons why we focus on these three particular changes. First, previous research has identified these events as turning points in romantic relationships (e.g., Baxter & Bullis; Bullis et al.). In addition, these events also represent important markers of the progress of RRTs. Third, these events either represent communicative behaviors (i.e., the first significant disclosure) or involve communication in important and fundamental ways (i.e., first date and first sex). Finally, each of these events has been linked in important ways to sex differences.

It is possible to gauge romantic relationship development, in part, by observing which turning points have, and have not, been reached. Some turning points likely occur early in relationship development (e.g., first meeting, activity time, and first date) and suggest a platonic acquaintanceship or budding friendship. Other turning points, such as joint exclusivity decision and living together, clearly indicate a romantic entanglement (Baxter & Bullis, 1986; Baxter & Ebert, 1999). At some point between the turning point of activity time and that of establishing exclusivity, the relationship makes a fundamental change from platonic to romantic (even though previous research has not identified an RRT as a turning point in and of itself). Although existing turning-points research delineates some of the *components* of RRTs, very little research has focused specifically on how these fundamental changes occur.

In summary, an RRT represents, by definition, a major change in the definition of the relationship (i.e., a turning point). Moreover, it is our contention that RRTs do not represent a single turning point; they are multifaceted processes that involve a number of affective, behavioral, and cognitive changes that can represent subordinate turning points. These changes lead, in complex and theoretically interesting ways, to the formation of a romantic relationship.

FIRST DATES AND RRTs

Courtship has taken on a variety of forms, depending on a large number of historical and cultural factors (Cate & Lloyd, 1992). The predominant mode of courtship for most of the 20th century in Western cultures was dating. Although dating is no longer the exclusive route taken to marriage, it remains a "ubiquitous and distinct part of modern culture" (Harris, 1993, p. 360; see also Bailey, 1988). First-date initiation and enactment has received considerable research attention over the past two decades (see Mongeau, Carey, & Williams, 1998 for a more detailed review of this research). Although this research initially assumed that first dates and RRTs occurred simultaneously, this is not necessarily the case (Mongeau et al.). Mongeau, Serewicz, and Therrien (2004) presented evidence suggesting that, in many cases, first dates preceded RRTs. Even if they are separate events, first dates are important because they are romantically charged events (Mongeau, Jacobsen, & Donnerstein, 2004; Mongeau & Kendall, 1996). Therefore, *first* dates are likely partners' initial opportunity to interact in an overtly romantic context.

First dates are likely fraught with uncertainty about both the partner and the relationship (Mongeau et al., 1998). This is consistent with the research of Messman, Canary, and Hause (2000), who found that emotional uncertainty (in part, questions about the partner's feelings) was an important reason why cross-sex friendship are maintained as platonic. Moreover, Abbey (1987) reported that about 20% of the participants in her study indicated that they had, at one time or another, disagreed with their partner as to whether an event was a date. Despite the strong levels of uncertainty that are present in first dates, direct talk about partners' feelings and the nature of the relationships is expected to be quite rare, as this represents the primary taboo topic in developing relationships (Baxter & Wilmot, 1985). Therefore, first dates likely allow partners to reduce both partner and relational uncertainty, although the relationship uncertainty reduction may have to be performed indirectly (e.g., inferring first-date goals from behaviors).

Another reason why first dates are important is that they represent an important hurdle in the development of a romantic relationship. If the first date does not go well (e.g., partners do not reach their goals for the event), it would seem unlikely that partners would make it to the point of an RRT. In order to facilitate an RRT, a first date should allow partners to reach their goals and result in a number of positive attributions and evaluations of the partner. First dates might mark the beginning of an RRT rather than their being simultaneous events.

Sex Differences in First-Date Scripts

Research indicates that first dates are both scripted and differentiated by the partners' biological sex. Several investigations indicate that college students can describe the progression of behaviors expected on first dates with "stunning regularity" (Honeycutt & Cantrill, 2001, p. 24; see, e.g., Laner & Ventrone, 1998, 2000; Pryor & Merluzzi, 1985). Honeycutt and Cantrill described the typical sequence as follows:

> The man goes to the woman's residence, the woman greets him, the man meets her family or roommates, and they engage in small talk and decide where to go. If they decide, for example, to go to a movie, the typical script includes waiting in line, buying refreshments, and getting something to eat after the movie. The man then takes the woman home and walks her to her door. The couple summarizes the evening at the end of the date. The man may ask to call again; the woman may hope he asks to call again; they kiss, say good night, and thank each other for the evening; and the man departs. (p. 24)

Honeycutt and Cantrill's (2001) description clearly indicates that the behavioral expectations for first dates are largely gender based (see e.g., Laner & Ventrone, 1998, 2000; Pryor & Merluzzi, 1985; Rose & Frieze, 1993). First-date scripts describe men as being proactive; that is, they initiate the date, provide transportation, pay for all date expenses, and initiate sexual contact (e.g., a good-night kiss or more intimate physical contact). Scripts for first dates depict women as playing a more reactive role, as they accept the date initiation, follow the male's lead, and accept or fend off the male's sexual advances.

The consistencies in first-date script research "reflect the customs and values of both the society and subculture in which they occur" (Honeycutt & Cantrill, 2001, p. 24). The consistencies of first-date scripts (and the sex differences they contain) are all the more noteworthy given researchers' varying methodological choices. For example, in some studies, participants reported their behavior or expectations from actual experiences (Rose & Frieze, 1993), whereas in other studies they reported "typical" first dates (Laner & Ventrone, 2000; Pryor & Merluzzi, 1985). Another methodological difference is that some researchers asked participants to generate their own list of date behaviors (Laner & Ventrone, 1998; Pryor & Merluzzi; Rose & Frieze) other researchers asked students to use behaviors provided by the researchers (e.g., Laner & Ventrone, 2000). In summary, there is considerable agreement at the cultural level (or at least subcultural level, as all studies used college students) concerning the nature of first dates (including a clear differentiation of expectations based on the gender of the partner).

Sex Differences in First-Date Initiation and Enactment

Several studies investigated the role that first-date initiation plays in creating expectations for the event itself (Bostwick & DeLucia, 1992; Mongeau & Carey, 1996; Mongeau, Hale, Johnson, & Hillis, 1993; Muehlenhard & Scardino, 1985). In these studies, college students were asked to respond to hypothetical scenarios or watch videotapes that varied the nature of the date initiation (e.g., the sex of the initiator). Muehlenhard and Scardino found that a woman who initiated a date was evaluated by men as more of a casual dater and more sexually active when compared with a woman who did not initiate a date. Mongeau et al. reported that a woman who made the initial romantic move (i.e., hinted that she wanted a date or asked without a hint from the man) was evaluated as being more interested in sex and more of a casual dater when compared with a woman who followed the man's lead. Mongeau and Carey reported that men's sexual expectations were elevated when a man was evaluated in the scenario following date initiation by a woman.

The accumulated research clearly indicates that female first-date initiation heightens male sexual expectations. What this research does not tell us, however, is how date initiation influences what actually occurs on first dates. To answer this question, a second set of studies asked college students to recall their most recent first-date experience (Mongeau & Johnson, 1995; Mongeau, Yeazell, & Hale, 1994). These studies hypothesized that men would report greater intimacy (both communicative and sexual) than would women, and that this difference would be particularly pronounced in first dates initiated by women.

Mongeau et al. (1994) investigated perceptions of communicative intimacy on first dates initiated by women or by men. They found no evidence of sex differences in perceptions of communicative intimacy in first dates initiated by men. When women initiated the first date, however, the results were opposite of what was expected. On first dates initiated by women, women were evaluated as communicating *less* intimacy (when compared with men). Mongeau and Johnson (1995) compared sexual expectations and behaviors in first dates initiated by men with those initiated by women. They found that men reported both expecting, and engaging in, more intimate sexual behavior than did women. Again, inconsistent with the hypothesis, participants reported *less* sexual intimacy on first dates initiated by women, when compared with those initiated by men.

First-Date Expectancy Violations

The accumulated data from the first-date initiation and enactment research presents a very interesting pattern. The first set of studies indicated that a woman's initiation of a first date inflated a man's sexual expectations for the event. In direct contrast, the second set of studies found that women were evaluated as expressing less intimacy (both communicative and sexual) on first dates initiated by women, when compared with those initiated, by men. These data strongly suggested the existence of expectancy violation processes (Burgoon, 1993; Mongeau et al., 1998). According to Burgoon, expectancies represent sets of anticipated behaviors in social situations. Subsequent interaction, however, can either meet or violate expectations. Violations, in turn, can be evaluated either as being positive or negative. Positive violations should generate more preferred outcomes when compared with merely meeting expectations. Negative violations should generate less preferred outcomes when compared with meeting expectations.

Mongeau et al. (1998) suggested that the pattern evident in the first-date initiation and enactment research (i.e., men's expecting more, but experiencing less, sexual intimacy on first dates initiated by women) reflects a negative expectancy violation. Burgoon (1993) explained that negative expectancy violations, however, likely have deleterious relationship, effects. If the pattern of data does represent negative expectancy violations, however, they were generally not serious enough to harm the relationship, as Mongeau et al. (1993) reported that first dates initiated by women generated, on average, 27 subsequent dates (although the median number of subsequent dates was only 5). It is important to remember that evidence for expectancy violations comes from the accumulated results from several studies rather than direct observations in a single investigation. Therefore, future research should look directly for expectancy violations. If negative expectancy violations do occur, how are they identified? In other words, how does the man realize that his date isn't acting in as warm and sexually inviting a way as he expected? What influence do these negative expectancy violations have on the date and the relationship following the date? In answering such questions, an important concept to consider is what Burgoon called *communicator reward valence*, or "whether a target co-interactant holds the prospect, on balance, of making the interaction a rewarding, pleasurable one or not" (p. 34). Unexpected behaviors (i.e., expectancy violations) that are performed by communicators with high (when compared with low) communicator reward valence (e.g., attractive date partners) are less likely to be evaluated as a violation. Moreover, if the behaviors are identified as a violation, they are less likely to be evaluated as being negative.

FIRST SIGNIFICANT DISCLOSURE AND RRTs

Significant disclosures of private information between partners appear to be another turning point embedded within the larger RRT. Research on turning points in developing romantic relationships suggests that disclosures are important components of the RRT, but this line of inquiry has not isolated first significant disclosure as a turning point in itself (e.g., Baxter & Erbert, 1999; Baxter & Pittman, 2004). Instead, various first disclosures appear in several other turning points such as "get-to-know time," "quality time," "passion," and "relationship talk." Get-to-know time involves relatively superficial interaction early in a relationship that allows partners to get to know each other better (Baxter & Pittman). Quality time causes tension as partners struggle between simply enjoying their time together on its own terms and using that time to discuss issues relevant to the relationship (Baxter & Erbert). Passion involves the first expression of affection, either nonverbally (e.g., a first kiss or first sexual encounter) or verbally (e.g., the first "I love you"; "Baxter & Erbert, Baxter & Pittman"). Finally, relationship talk incorporates explicit discussion of the state of the Relationship (Baxter & Erbert, Baxter & Pittman).

First significant disclosure and RRTs," seems to differ from the smaller turning points of the first date or first sex. That is, unlike a first date or first sex, many different types of significant disclosures can occur for the first time (e.g., self-disclosures of personal information, saying "I love you," and expressing a desire for an exclusive relationship). Moreover, the ordering of these events might vary. Even with variations in their order, partners likely recognize each disclosure as a turning point. As previous research has identified sex differences in self-disclosure (e.g., Dindia & Allen, 1992), in this section we consider how significant disclosures relate to sex differences and similarities in the RRT.

Sex Differences and Similarities in First Significant Disclosure

Much research has addressed phenomena relevant to sex differences and similarities in first significant disclosures between romantic partners. Baxter and Erbert's (1999) study of turning points in heterosexual romantic relationships investigated differences and similarities between men and women in their recollection and perceptions of turning points. Men and women were similar in how frequently they described turning points in general, and the turning points relevant to disclosure in particular. Furthermore, men and women were similar in how they rated the centrality or importance of various relational dialectics for the four turning points related to significant disclosure. Likewise, Morr and Mongeau (2004) found that men and women did not differ in their expectations for the communicative intimacy of a hypothetical first date. These findings give support to sex similarities in the identification and understanding of the significant events related to disclosure in an RRT.

These similarities are interesting when considered in light of the large body of research on sex differences in self-disclosure. Although men and women in Baxter and Erbert's (1999) and Morr and Mongeau's (2004) studies did not differ in their perceptions of disclosure-related turning points, men's and women's behavior during those turning points likely differ. Dindia and Allen (1992) performed a meta-analysis of 205 studies on sex differences in self-disclosure published between 1958 and 1989 (including a total of 23,702 participants). The findings of their analysis indicate that women disclose more than men, but the difference is small. When the self-disclosure occurs with an opposite-sex target, as happens in an RRT for a cross-sex couple, the difference between men and women is very small, as women disclose only slightly more than men. Taken together, this literature would indicate that women probably disclose a bit more than men during an RRT, but that men and women are similar in their perception of the disclosure event and its meaning for the intimacy and dialectical tensions related to those disclosures.

Sex Differences in Disclosure on First Dates

Research on first dates has also included information relevant to first significant disclosures. Most of these studies have included the investigation of sex similarities and differences, and researchers are also beginning to look into the influence of relational history as a moderator of sex effects. Before analyzing the evidence for sex and relational history effects, we find it important to consider some conflicting evidence about the nature of communication on first dates.

First-date script research demonstrates the importance of conversation for both men and women, but it does not indicate expectations of highly intimate disclosure. For example, Rose and Frieze (1989) found that both male and female participants included "get to know date" and "talk, joke, and laugh" (p. 264) in their first-date scripts. In addition, Pryor and Merluzzi (1985) reported "conversation with date after arrival" and "talk about common interests: 'small talk'" (p. 367) as expected on first dates. In both cases, couples exchange information that allows them to reduce uncertainty and discover common interests. Moreover, the emphasis on small talk and getting to know one's date implies that partners do not know each other well.

Given that much of the interaction on first dates comprises small talk, it does not appear that abundant significant disclosure is occurring. Conversations in more established romantic relationships appear to be equally mundane (Bradford, Feeney, & Campbell, 2002). Thus, it appears that communication between potential romantic partners is also likely to involve disclosure as an unusual event (Duck, Rutt, Hurst, & Strejc, 1991). We speculate that the atypical nature of significant disclosure increases its importance to relationship partners. Thus, disclosures identified as significant may be particularly important markers of the development of an RRT.

In contrast to the first-date script research, the limited research on communicative expectations suggests that first-date interactions are expected to be quite intimate. For example, Mongeau, Aselage, Ficara, and Hart (1997) and Morr and Mongeau (2004) both reported high levels of expected communicative intimacy. In the study by Morr and Mongeau, scores on receptivity–trust and immediacy–affection expectations scales, on average, were quite high (above 4.0 on a 1–5 scale).

How could script research indicate mundane first-date interaction even though communication expectancy research indicates relatively high levels of intimacy? A tentative answer to this conundrum might be the specific nature of the first date. We argued earlier that first dates occur before, and provide important information necessary for, the successful completion of an RRT. In this case, although the topics of discussion are not highly personal, they may be strategically chosen to allow a partner to reduce uncertainty and gauge the other's interest in, and acceptability for, a transition to a romantic relationship. Thus, it may not be the topic per se that generates higher intimacy ratings, but the implications that these topics might have for a subsequent RRT.

Sex Differences, Relationship History, and First Significant Disclosures

Data from first-date script research suggest that date partners are generally considered strangers or acquaintances. Assuming that partners are, at best, acquaintances, small talk may be necessary for individuals to get to know each other on a personal level. However, Morr and Mongeau (2004) manipulated relationship history in scenarios. When the date partners were described as friends, communication expectations reflected considerable intimacy. Thus, the difference in results from the first-date script and first-date expectations may represent different assumptions about the existing relationship between date partners.

An understanding of the complexity in the research on scripts and expectations for first-date communication helps to contextualize the findings of research on sex differences and similarities in expectations for first dates. Mongeau et al. (1997) found significant sex differences in expectations for communication intimacy on first dates. Specifically, their participants expected women to express more immediacy or affection than men. However, this difference should be interpreted in light of an interaction effect indicating that the initiator of the date, whether male or female, was expected to express more immediacy or affection than the person who was asked for the date. The difference between initiator and the person being asked for the date was greater when the woman initiated the date (Mongeau et al.). Moreover, male participants expected men to express greater receptivity or trust than would women, whereas female participants expected women to express greater receptivity or trust than would men (Mongeau et al.).

In the study by Morr and Mongeau (2004), participants put themselves in the place of the same-sex individual in a first-date scenario. In this study, there were no significant main effects for sex on communication expectations. Furthermore, although Morr and Mongeau reported relationship history main effects for both immediacy–affection and receptivity–trust, relationship history influenced women's expectations to a greater extent than men's expectations. Both men and women expected friends to experience greater intimacy than acquaintances, but women expected a larger difference in intimacy between friends and acquaintances than did men. Though the effect sizes for these interactions were small, these findings imply that women would expect to adjust the intimacy of their communication to match the nature of the relationship more than would men.

Taken together, findings of research on turning points and first-date expectations imply that men and women experience turning points in disclosure similarly. However, differences between men and women are likely to occur in their enactment of disclosure behavior (e.g., self–disclosure, expression of immediacy or affection) and encouragement of the partner's disclosure (e.g., expression of receptivity or trust). Sex differences are also likely to occur in the degree to which disclosure and receptivity to disclosure differ based on relational history.

Although there is much research relevant to sex differences in self-disclosure, less research exists on sex effects on disclosure within an RRT and on moderators of sex differences. Beyond the significant disclosures embedded within an RRT, consideration of management of the disclosed information is likely to be important for the developing relationship. When Petronio's (2002) theory of communication privacy management is applied, disclosures within an RRT contribute to the formation of a dyadic boundary around the private information shared by the dating partners. Rules for handling that private information can be explicitly negotiated, or partners may assume implicit agreement about how the information should be handled. Given the sex differences discussed relating to self-disclosure and communication expectations, a future investigation of sex differences and similarities in overall privacy management during an RRT is warranted.

FIRST SEX AND RRTs

The final behavioral event that we consider as representing an important turning point in RRTs is the first sexual encounter. Sexual intimacy is the primary characteristic of romantic relationships that is typically absent from close platonic cross-sex friendships (Hendrick & Hendrick, 2000). Therefore, the first sexual encounter between partners is likely an important indicator of, and motivator for, RRTs.

Sex Differences and First Sex

Considerable research is consistent with the notion that men and women differ in their views of the interrelationship between sexual behavior and romantic relationships. Specifically, men and women differ in motivations to have sex (Christopher & Cate, 1984; Leigh, 1989), judgments of the likelihood of sexual intercourse (Hill, 2002), and actual sexual behaviors (Mongeau & Johnson, 1995; Taris & Semin, 1997). A complete review of this research is beyond the scope of this chapter. As an example, consider the research on motivations for first sex with a particular partner. Carroll, Volk, and Hyde (1985) found that women reported emotional closeness as the primary motivator for having sex with a partner for the first time. Men, in contrast, reported sexual release as their primary motivation. Along similar lines, Leigh reported that women reported emotional expression to be a more important motivator than did men. Men, when compared with women, reported pleasure as a more important motivator.

Although considerable research is consistent with sex differences in sexual interactions, "the etiology of these differences, however, is wildly controversial" (Mongeau, Serewicz et al., 2004, p. 124). Although several theoretical positions focus on these sex differences (e.g., Eagly & Wood, 1999; Hyde & Oliver, 2000), discussions typically focus on evolutionary and social explanations. Evolutionary explanations (see, e.g., Buss, 2003) assume that humans' distant past placed different mating pressures on men and women. These different pressures caused the sexes to develop different strategies for passing their genetic information to the next generation. On one hand, men developed a strategy of mating with as many women as is possible. Women, on the other hand, faced the more demanding tasks of carrying and raising children. Consequently, they developed a strategy by which they reserved sexual access to those men who demonstrated a willingness to provide the resources necessary to nurture and raise children.

In contrast, social explanations of sex differences in sexuality are based on differential sex-role expectations. According to social learning explanations (Bandura, 1977), individuals are positively reinforced for sex-role consistent behavior (thereby increasing its future enactment) and punished for sex-role inconsistent behavior (thereby reducing its future enactment; see also Hyde & Oliver, 2000). Key to the social learning explanations is the sexual double standard (Sprecher, McKinney, & Orbuch, 1987). According to the sexual double standard, men are rewarded, and women punished, for engaging in sex outside a close and committed relationship. Thus, through their own experiences and observation of others' outcomes, women develop more negative attitudes toward, and become less likely to engage in, casual sexual behavior than do men.

The disagreement between advocates of social and evolutionary perspectives could not be wider (e.g., Eagly & Wood, 1999). Despite the well-entrenched positions taken by many advocates of these explanations, many others scholars believe that "it is hard to tease apart biological differences and social differences" (Schwartz & Rutter, 1998 p. 4). In response to the difficulty in differentiating these explanations, several scholars (e.g., Baumeister, 2000; Wood & Eagly, 2002; Schwartz & Rutter) attempted to combine the biological and social explanations for sex differences in sexual interaction. For example, Baumeister, as well as Vohs, Cantanese, and Baumeister, (2004), developed the theory of female erotic plasticity to combine evolutionary and social explanations. Vohs et al. defined erotic plasticity as "the degree to which sexuality is shaped by social, cultural, and situational variables" (p. 461). Specifically, the theory of female erotic plasticity presumes that women (when compared with men) vary more in how they feel, and express, sexual desire. The basis of women's variation in sexual interaction lies in social factors, including cultural norms and situational variables. The most important situational factor is the nature of the relationship with their partners. Biological forces, in contrast, cause men to be much more consistent in their experience, expression, and enactment of sexual desire. Social, cultural, and situational variables (e.g., the nature of their relationship with a potential partner) make less difference for men than for women.

Sex Differences, Relationship History, and First Sex

The theory of female erotic plasticity argues that social and situational forces influence sexual behavior more strongly for women than for men (Vohs et al., 2004). This suggests that relationship history, as we have discussed it, should moderate sex differences in sexual interaction. There are ample data to support the claim that relationship history influences sexual interaction to a greater degree for women than for men. Each of the sex differences in sexual motivations, judgments of the likelihood of sexual behavior, and reports of sexual behavior noted herein were moderated by relationship history. The aforementioned sexual motivation studies clearly indicate that women's reports of sexual interest were strongly influenced by the state of the relationship (as emotional closeness and expression are the primary motivators) when compared with men's motivations (highlighting emotional closeness, pleasure, and sexual release).

Metts (2004) investigated the relative timing of two aspects of the passion turning point—first sex and first declaration of love—on both positive and negative relationship outcomes. Metts argued that saying "I love you" to one's partner acted as a framing device for interpreting the relationship meaning associated with the first sexual intercourse. As a consequence, she predicted that engaging in the first sexual intercourse before disclosing love for one's partner would lead to more negative (and fewer positive) relational outcomes than having sex following that particular disclosure. Results were consistent with these predictions. Expressing love and commitment for one's partner related positively to escalation and confirmation of the relationship, and it was negatively related to regret about having had sex for both men and women. The effect on escalation–confirmation was stronger, however, for women than it was for men. Thus, the preceding passion turning point (i.e., saying "I love you") made a greater difference in positive emotional reaction for women than for men.

Finally, in a study of first-date goals, Mongeau, Serewicz et al. (2004) reported that the correlation between sexual goals and relationship goals (partially a function of relationship history) differed between men and women. Specifically, they found that the correlation between sexual activity goals and romantic potential goals was significant and substantial ($r = .43$) for women but uncorrelated for men ($r = -.06$). Moreover, the correlation between sexual activity goals and reduce uncertainty goals was significant and positive for women ($r = .21$) but significant and negative for men ($r = -.28$).

As this review demonstrates, RRT is a communication phenomenon worthy of further examination. Given the complexity of an RRT, we need to examine both macrolevel and microlevel turning points, including component sex differences. Moreover, scholars need to keep an eye on changing social norms and conditions. The social and blended explanations for sex differences predict that, as social conditions change, so too should sex differences (as women, more than men, react to social conditions). For example, as initiation of a first date by a woman becomes increasingly acceptable, it might make less of a difference to the enactment of first dates.

DIRECTIONS FOR FUTURE RESEARCH

The preceding review suggests several directions for future research on RRTs. First, research has to consider how friendships and romantic relationships differ (or blend) as an RRT occurs. Second, we need to expand our scope both methodologically (particularly in the samples that we use) and theoretically (including social influence theories). We discuss each of these issues in turn.

Differentiating Platonic Friends and Romantic Partners

The focus of our chapter is on sex differences in how relationships make the transition from friendship to romantic. One important and difficult question that has been ignored, however, is exactly how these relationship types differ. What differentiates romantic relationships from platonic relationships has been ignored, in part, because it is a difficult question to answer (e.g., Hendrick & Hendrick, 2000).

There are several ways that friendships and romantic relationships might differ. One approach to differentiating friendships from romantic relationships might focus on emotional responses like love (Hendrick & Hendrick, 2000). The difficulty is, of course, that love does not exist only in romantic relationships. Messman et al. (2000) reported that friends and romantic partners differed in liking (with friends exceeding romantic partners) but not love. Components of romantic love such as being communal (Feeney, 2004), involving reciprocal caregiving (Shaver & Hazan, 1988), and powerful emotions directed toward the partner (Kovecses, 1991) can also characterize friendships (Knobloch & Solomon, 2002).

Friendships and romantic relationships might also differ in desired personal characteristics for partners. Sprecher and Regan (2000) found that participants preferred higher levels of social status, physical attractiveness, and warmth, humor, and intelligence in romantic or sexual partners than in friendships. These characteristics are also relevant to platonic cross-sex friendships, as participants thought it more important to have cross-sex friends with higher social status, more physical attractiveness, and personality attributes, such as warmth and humor, than torh same-sex friends.

Our theoretical perspective for this chapter is turning points. Perhaps turning points among friends differ from those experienced in committed romantic relationships. Research indicates that friendship and romantic relationships can be distinguished by passion, mutual love, and exclusivity (Davis & Todd, 1982) as well as external competition and serious commitment (Baxter & Bullis, 1986). These elements, however, are not typically found in transitioning relationships. In fact, Johnson et al. (2004) found that friendships and relationships experiencing an RRT report the same common turning points (i.e., shared activity, living together, and talking or hanging out).

One behavior used to differentiate romantic relationships from platonic friendships is sexual behavior (Berscheid, 1988). Even sexual interaction does not directly differentiate relationship types. For example, some romantic relationships do not involve a sexual component; some couples abstain from sexual activity until marriage. In contrast, a relatively large proportion of platonic college relationships now involve sex (Afifi & Faulkner, 2000; Mongeau, Ramirez, & Vorell, 2003).

If emotions, preferences, and behaviors cannot differentiate friends from romantic partners, how then should the distinction be made? Monsour (2002) defined cross-sex friendship as a "voluntary, nonfamilial, nonromantic relationship between a male and a female in which both individuals label their association a friendship" (p. 26). On the one hand, this definition is not very helpful as friendships are nonromantic and, by extension, romantic relationships are not platonic. On the other hand, Monsour's definition is important and potentially very helpful because it focuses our attention on the *label* of or *meaning* assigned by partners to the relationship and the associated behaviors, emotions, and so on. It is not the sexual behavior that differentiates friendships from romantic relationships, but the meaning (personal and relational) that partners assign to it.

Future research from a turning-points perspective, then, has to consider not only the occurrence of turning-points but also the meanings that partners assign to them. The same turning point, for example, might be evaluated very differently dependent on the relationship definition. Moreover, performing an RRT might cause partners to redefine the meanings associated with previous turning points. For example, at the time, a kiss that occurred long before an RRT might be defined as insignificant and the result of alcohol consumption. Following the RRT, however, this turning point might be redefined as the first sign of impending passion between partners. It is important to consider how the sexes assign meaning to particular turning points and how the meanings associated with the progression of these changes might differ between men and women.

Expanding Our Scope

It is important that research focus on how relationships make the transition from platonic to romantic. Whether by looking at the RRT as a whole or by looking at the component turning points (e.g., first dates, first significant disclosure, or first sexual encounter), however, this research has to expand its scope in two ways. First, researchers need to expand their samples. Second, researchers would profit from considering RRTs from the perspective of social influence theories and models. We briefly consider each of these points.

Diversity of Samples

Although the research reviewed herein is interesting and sheds important light on the nature of RRTs, serious questions remain about its generalizability. A vast majority of the studies reviewed here included samples from U.S. colleges and universities. Consequently, these studies represent a relatively narrow slice of the demographic pie. There are relatively few studies on first dates, first significant disclosures, and first sexual encounters of noncollege students. For example, we don't know how various ethnic and socioeconomic groups might respond differently in, and to, these events. Research on same-sex romantic couples also lags behind that on cross-sex couplings. Finally, there is relatively little research on age differences despite the fact that senior citizens are a rapidly growing proportion of the population.

The diversity of study samples is directly relevant to the consideration of sex differences in RRTs. Baumeister's (2000) theory of female erotic plasticity suggests that variations in women's behavioral interactions vary as a function of cultural (and presumably subcultural) norms. As subcultural norms change, so should the sex differences in RRTs. As a consequence, if we are to understand the role that sex differences might play in an RRT, it is critical to study a broad array of cultural and subcultural groups.

Theoretical Diversity: RRTs as Interpersonal Influence

RRTs, logically enough, have been studied primarily from interpersonal and relational perspectives. In this chapter alone, we have discussed dialectics, privacy management, uncertainty reduction, social penetration, expectancy violation, and other theoretical formulations. It is our contention, however, that RRTs also fall within, and could usefully be analyzed from, the umbrella of interpersonal influence processes. In this section, we explore this contention and suggest several directions for future research based on this connection.

Central to the research on both date initiation and interpersonal influence is the importance of strategic, goal-directed behavior (Dillard, Anderson, & Knobloch, 2002; Mongeau, Serewicz, et al., 2004). In influence interactions, scholars have increasingly acknowledged the importance of goals in the generation of influence messages (e.g., Cody, Canary, & Smith, 1994; Dillard, 1990; Dillard, Segrin, & Harden, 1989; O'Keefe, 1988; Schrader & Dillard, 1998). Within the context of first date research, men and women have reported different goals for first-dates (Mongeau, Serewicz, et al., 2004). Thus, considering RRTs as a form of interpersonal influence should illuminate new directions for study.

Although few studies have directly linked theories used in interpersonal influence research to RRTs (for an exception, see Kunkel, Wilson, Olufowote, & Robson, 2003), theories of interpersonal influence could offer frameworks for the study of RRTs. Each of the theories of interpersonal influence, however, would highlight different features of the RRT. In addition, each of the theories would provide different contexts for investigating sex differences and similarities in RRTs. For example, message design logics (e.g., O'Keefe, 1988), the goal-planning-action model (e.g., Dillard, 1990; Hullet, 2004), politeness theory and facework research (e.g., Brown & Levinson, 1987; Cupach & Metts, 1994), research on plans, planning, and action (e.g., Berger, 1997; Berger, Karol, & Jordan, 1989), and research on resistance to influence (e.g., McLaughlin, Cody, & Robey, 1980) would all preference different features of the RRT. Importantly, reviews of interpersonal influence research tend to find that there are few consistent sex differences (Wilson, 2002). Linking the body of research on first dates with the research on interpersonal influence may offer a new direction for finding meaningful sex differences.

One benefit of the proposed marriage between interpersonal influence theories and RRTs is that research on RRTs has been criticized as largely atheoretical (Mongeau et al., 1998, but see for an exception Mongeau & Carey, 1996). The link to influence research provides new avenues for study that may offer a way to correct that flaw. The new theoretical contexts would offer a framework for interpreting the consistent sex differences in the RRT research.

CONCLUDING COMMENTS

Working from a turning-points perspective, we have used first dates, first significant disclosure, and first sex as three exemplars of turning points that compose RRTs. This research has helped us to understand important events and aspects of relationship development. Many other turning points deserve greater attention in future RRT research. It is important that we take a broader view of how relationships make the transition from platonic (or nonexistent) to romantic. It is important to consider each turning point as it occurs, the ordering of those changes, the meanings that partners attach to those changes, and how similar or different these meanings assigned by partners might be. Each subordinate turning point is influenced by previous turning points and, in turn, influences future changes. Subsequent turning points might cause a redefinition of earlier relational events. Without such a process orientation and longitudinal studies, our understanding of romantic relationship development will remain piecemeal.

Any theory of RRTs should focus on the role of sex differences and important moderator variables such as relationship history. Heterosexual men and women tend to see their sexual worlds differently (Abbey, 1987; Baumeister, 2000). Of course, future research on RRTs among gay men and lesbians would certainly be equally important and compelling. Finally, future research and theorizing about RRTs has to pay special attention to the past relationship history of the couple. The nature of previous interactions (including, potentially, past RRTs) is critically important for determining how partners understand, and assign meaning to, RRTs.

Finally, we began this chapter by claiming that RRTs were a particularly appropriate place to look for sex differences. The subsequent reviews are clearly consistent with that claim as sex differences were discussed in first date, first significant disclosure, and first sex research. Moreover, the nature of these sex differences is quite consistent across domains. In particular, research on first dates (Morr & Mongeau, 2004), first significant disclosures (e.g., Morr & Mongeau), and first sex (Hyde & Oliver, 2000) all reported that men's behavior was more consistent across situations and women's behavior was more likely to reflect the relationship context. This suggests that a complete consideration of sex differences in RRTs must also take into account the role of relationship history. Specifically, women are more likely to be mindful of, and responsive to, past relational events to a greater extent than are men.

REFERENCES

Abbey, A. (1987). Misperceptions of friendly behavior as sexual interest: A survey of naturally occurring incidents. *Psychology of Women Quarterly, 11*, 173–194.

Afifi, W. A., & Faulkner, S. L. (2000). On being "just friends": The frequency and impact of sexual activity in cross-sex friendships. *Journal of Social and Personal Relationships, 17*, 205–222.

Altman, I., & Taylor, D. A. (1973). *Social penetration: The development of interpersonal relationships.* New York: Holt, Rinehart & Winston.

Bandura, A. J. (1977). *Social learning theory.* Englewood Cliffs, NJ: Prentice-Hall.

Barge, J. K., & Musambira, G. W. (1992).Turning points in chair–faculty relationships. *Journal of Applied Communication Research, 20*, 54–77.

Baumeister, R. F. (2000). Gender differences in erotic plasticity: The female sex drive as socially flexible and responsive. *Psychological Bulletin, 126*, 347–374.

Baxter, L. A., Braithwaite, D. O., & Nicholson, J. H. (1999). Turning points in the development of blended families. *Journal of Social and Personal Relationships, 16*, 291–313.

Baxter, L. A., & Bullis, C. (1986). Turning points in developing romantic relationships. *Human Communication Research, 12*, 469–493.

Baxter, L. A., & Erbert, L. A. (1999). Perceptions of dialectical contradictions in turning points of development in heterosexual romantic relationships. *Journal of Social and Personal Relationships, 16*, 547–569.

Baxter, L. A., & Pittman, G. (2001). Communicatively remembering turning points of relational development in heterosexual romantic relationships. *Communication Reports, 14*, 1–17.

Baxter, L. A., & Wilmot, W. W. (1985). Taboo topics in romantic relationships. *Journal of Social and Personal Relationships, 2*, 523–269.

Berger, C. R. (1997). *Planning strategic interaction: Attaining goals through communicative action.* Mahwah, NJ: Lawrence Erlbaum Associates.

Berger, C. R., & Calabrese, R. J. (1975). Some explorations in initial interaction and beyond: Toward a developmental theory of interpersonal communication. *Human Communication Research, 1*, 99–112.

Berger, C. R., Karol, S. H., & Jordan, J. M. (1989). When a lot of knowledge is a dangerous thing: The debilitating effects of plan complexity on verbal fluency. *Human Communication Research, 16*, 91–119.

Berscheid, E. (1988). Some comments on love's anatomy: Or, whatever happened to old fashioned lust? In R. J. Sternberg & M. L. Barnes (Eds.), *The psychology of love* (pp. 359–374). New Haven, CT: Yale University Press.

Bolton, C. D. (1961). Mate selection as the development of a relationship. *Marriage and Family Living, 23*, 234–240.

Bostwick, T. D., & DeLucia, J. L. (1992). Effects of gender and specific dating behaviors on perceptions of sex willingness and date rape. *Journal of Social and Clinical Psychology, 11*, 14–25.

Bradford, S. A., Feeney, J. A., & Campbell, L. (2002). Links between attachment orientations and dispositional and diary-based measures of disclosure in dating couples: A study of actor and partner effects. *Personal Relationships, 9*, 491–506.

Brown, P., & Levinson, S. C. (1987). *Politeness: Some universals in language usage.* Cambridge, England: Cambridge University Press.

Bullis, C., Clark, C., & Sline, R. (1993). From passion to commitment: Turning points in romantic relationships. In P. J. Kalbfleisch (Ed.), *Interpersonal communication: Evolving interpersonal relationships* (pp. 213–236). Mahwah, NJ: Lawrence Erlbaum Associates.

Burgoon, J. K. (1993). Interpersonal expectancies, expectancy violations, and emotional communication. *Journal of Language and Social Psychology, 12*, 30–48.

Buss, D. M. (2003). *The evolution of desire: Strategies of human mating* (Revised ed.). New York: Basic Books.

Canary, D. J., & Hause, K. S. (1993). Is there any reason to research sex differences in communication? *Communication Quarterly, 41*, 129–144.

Carroll, J. L., Volk, K. D., & Hyde, J. S. (1985). Differences between males and females in motives for engaging in sexual intercourse. *Archives of Sexual Behavior, 14*, 131–139.

Cate, R. M., & Lloyd, S. A. (1992). *Courtship.* Newbury Park, CA: Sage.

Christopher, F. S., & Cate, R. M. (1984). Factors involved in premarital sexual decision-making. *Journal of Sex Research, 20*, 363–376.

Cody, M. J., Canary, D. J., & Smith, S. W. (1994). Compliance-gaining goals: An inductive analysis of actors' and goal types, strategies, and successes. In J. A. Daly & J. M. Wiemann (Eds.), *Strategic interpersonal communication* (pp. 33–90). Hillsdale, NJ: Lawrence Erlbaum Associates.

Cupach, W. R., & Metts, S. (1994). *Facework.* Thousand Oaks, CA: Sage.

Davis, K. E., & Todd, M. J. (1982). Friendship and love relationships. *Advances in Descriptive Psychology, 2*, 79–122.

Dillard, J. P. (1990). A goal-driven model of interpersonal influence. In J. P. Dillard (Ed.), *Seeking compliance: The production of interpersonal influence messages* (pp. 41–56). Scottsdale, AZ: Gorsuch Scarisbrick.

Dillard, J. P., Anderson, J. W., & Knobloch, L. K. (2002). Interpersonal influence. In M. L. Knapp and J. A. Daly (Eds.), *Handbook of interpersonal communication* (3rd ed., pp. 425–474). Thousand Oaks, CA: Sage.

Dillard, J. P., Segrin, C., & Harden, J. M. (1989). Primary and secondary goals in the production of interpersonal influence messages. *Communication Monographs, 56*, 19–38.

Dindia, K., & Allen, M. (1992). Sex differences in self-disclosure: A meta-analysis. *Psychological Bulletin, 112*, 106–124.

Duck, S., Rutt, D. J., Hurst, M. H., & Strejc, H. (1991). Some evident truths about conversations in everyday relationships: All communications are not created equal. *Human Communication Research, 18*, 228–267.

Eagly, A. H., & Wood, W. (1999). The origins of sex differences in human behavior: Evolved dispositions versus social roles. *American Psychologist, 54*, 408–423.

Feeney, J. A. (2004). Hurt feelings in couple relationships: Towards integrative models of the negative effects of hurtful events. *Journal of Social and Personal Relationships, 21*, 487–508.

Harris, M. J. (1993). Issues in studying the mediation of expectancy effects: A taxonomy of expectancy effects. In P. D. Blanck (Ed), *Interpersonal expectancies: Theory, research, and applications* (pp. 350–378). New York: Cambridge University Press.

Hendrick, S. S., & Hendrick, C. (2000). Romantic love. In C. Hendrick & S. S. Henrick (Eds.), *Close relationships: A sourcebook* (pp. 203–215). Thousand Oaks, CA: Sage.

Hill, C. A. (2002). Gender, relationship stage, and sexual behavior: The importance of partner emotional involvement within specific situations. *Journal of Sex Research, 39*, 228–240.

Honeycutt, J. M., & Cantrill, J. G. (2001). *Cognition, communication, and romantic relationships.* Mahwah, NJ: Lawrence Earlbaum Assciates.

Hullet, C. R. (2004). A test of the initial processes of the goal-planning action model of interpersonal influence. *Communication Studies, 55*, 286–300.

Hyde, J. S., & Oliver, M. B. (2000). Gender differences in sexuality: Results from meta-analysis. In C. B. Travis & J. W. White (Eds.), *Sexuality, society, and feminism* (pp. 57–77). Washington, DC: American Psychological Association.

Johnson, A. J., Wittenberg, E., Haigh, M., Wigley, S., Becker, J., Brown, K., & Craig, E. (2004). The process of relationship development and deterioration: Turning points in friendships that have terminated. *Communication Quarterly, 52*, 54–68.

Knobloch, L. K., & Solomon, D. H. (2002). Intimacy and the magnitude and experience of episodic relational uncertainty within romantic relationships. *Personal Relationships, 9*, 457–478.

Kovecses, Z. (1991). A linguist's quest for love. *Journal of Social and Personal Relationships, 8*, 77–97.

Kunkel, A. D., Wilson, S. R., Olufowote, J., & Robson, S. (2003). Identity implications of influence goals: Initiating, intensifying, and ending romantic relationships. *Western Journal of Communication, 67*, 382–412.

Laner, M. R., & Ventrone, N. A. (1998). Egalitarian daters/traditional dates. *Journal of Family Issues, 19*, 468–477.

Laner, M. R., & Ventrone, N. A. (2000). Dating scripts revisited. *Journal of Family Issues, 21*, 488–500.

Laumann, E. O., Michael, R. T., & Gagnon, J. H. (1994). *The social organization of sexuality: Sexual practices in the United States.* Chicago: University of Chicago Press.

Leigh, B. C. (1989). Reasons for having and avoiding sex: Gender, sexual orientation, and relationship to sexual behavior. *Journal of Sex Research, 26*, 199–209.

McLaughlin, M. L., Cody, M. J., & Robey, C. S. (1980). Situational influences on the selection of strategies to resist compliance-gaining attempts. *Human Communication Research, 7*, 14–36.

Messman, S. J., Canary, D. J., & Hause, K. S. (2000). Motives to remain platonic, equity, and the use of maintenance strategies in opposite-sex friendships. *Journal of Social and Personal Relationships, 17*, 67–94.

Metts, S. (2004). First sexual involvement in romantic relationships: An empirical investigation of communicative framing, romantic beliefs, and attachment orientation in the passion turning point. In J. H. Harvey, A. Wenzel, & S. Sprecher (Eds.), *The handbook of sexuality in close relationships* (pp. 135–158). Mahwah, NJ: Lawrence Erlbaum Associates.

Mongeau, P. A., Aselage, C., Ficara, L., & Hart, M. (1997, November). *Communication and sexual expectations for first dates.* Paper presented to the National Communication Association, Chicago.

Mongeau, P. A., & Carey, C. M. (1996). Who's wooing whom II: An experimental investigation of date-initiation and expectancy violation. *Western Journal of Communication, 60*, 195–213.

Mongeau, P. A., Carey, C. M., & Williams, M. L. M. (1998). First date initiation and enactment: An expectancy violation perspective. In D. Canary & K. Dindia (Eds.), *Sex differences and similarities: A handbook.* Mahwah, NJ: Lawrence Erlbaum Associates.

Mongeau, P. A., Hale, J. L., Johnson, K. L., & Hillis, J. D. (1993). Who's wooing whom?: An investigation of female-initiated dating. In P. J. Kalbfleisch (Ed.), *Interpersonal communication: Evolving interpersonal relationships* (pp. 51–68). Hillsdale, NJ: Lawrence Erlbaum Associates.

Mongeau, P. A., Jacobsen, J., & Donnerstein, C. (2004, July). *What rates as a date?: A comparison of undergraduate and non-college respondents.* Paper presented to the International Association for Relationship Research, Madison, WI.

Mongeau, P. A., & Johnson, K. L. (1995). Predicting cross-sex first-date sexual expectations and involvement: Contextual and individual difference factors. *Personal Relationships, 2*, 301–312.

Mongeau, P. A., & Kendall, J. A. (1996, July). *"What do you mean this is a date?": Differentiating a date from going out with friends.* Paper presented to the International Network on Personal Relationships, Seattle, WA.

Mongeau, P. A., Ramirez, A., & Vorell, M. (2003, February). *Friends with benefits: An initial investigation of a sexual but not romantic relationship.* Paper presented to the Western States Communication Association, Salt Lake City, UT.

Mongeau, P. A., Serewicz, M. C. M., & Therrien, L. F. (2004). Goals for cross-sex first dates: Identification, measurement, and the influence of contextual factors. *Communication Monographs, 71*, 121–147.

Mongeau, P. A., & Teubner, G., (2002, November). *Romantic relationship transitions.* Paper presented to the National Communication Association, New Orleans, LA.

Mongeau, P. A., Yeazell, M., & Hale, J. L. (1994). Sex differences in relational message interpretations on male- and female-initiated first dates: A research note. *Journal of Social Behavior and Personality, 9*, 731–742.

Monsour, M. (2002). *Women and men as friends: Relationships across the life span in the 21st century.* Mahwah, NJ: Lawrence Earlbaum Associates.

Morr, M. C., & Mongeau, P. A. (2004). First date expectations: The impact of sex of initiator, alcohol consumption, and relationship type. *Communication Research, 31*, 3–35.

Muehlenhard, C. L., & Scardino, T. J. (1985). What will he think? Men's impressions of women to initiate dates and achieve academically. *Journal of Counseling Psychology, 32*, 560–569.

O'Keefe, B. J. (1988). The logic of message design: Individual differences in reasoning about communication. *Communication Monographs, 55*, 80–104.

Petronio, S. (2002). *Boundaries of privacy: Dialectics of disclosure.* Albany, State University of New York: Press.

Pryor, J. B., & Merluzzi, T. V. (1985). The role of expertise in processing social interaction scripts. *Journal of Experimental Social Psychology, 21*, 362–379.

Rose, S., & Frieze, I. H. (1989), Young single's scripts for a first date. *Gender and Society, 3*, 258–268.

Rose, S., & Frieze, I. H. (1993). Young singles' contemporary dating. *Sex Roles, 28*, 499–509.

Schrader, D. C., & Dillard, J. P. (1998). Goals structure and interpersonal influence. *Communication Studies, 49*, 276–293.

Schwartz, P., & Rutter, V. (1988). *The gender of sexuality.* Thousand Oaks, CA: Pine Forge Press.

Shaver, P. R., & Hazan, C. (1988). A biased overview of the study of love. *Journal of Social and Personal Relationships, 5*, 473–501.

Sprecher, S., McKinney, K., & Orbuch, T. L. (1987). Has the double standard disappeared? An experimental test. *Social Psychology Quarterly, 50*, 24–31.

Sprecher, S. & Regan, P. C. (2000). Sexuality in a relational context. In C. Hendrick and S. S. Hendrick (Eds.), *Close relationships: A sourcebook.* Thousand Oaks, CA: Sage.

Sunnafrank, M. (1986). Predicted outcome value during initial interactions: A reformulation of uncertainty reduction theory. *Human Communication Research, 13*, 3–33.

Taris, T. W., & Semin, G. R. (1997). Gender as a moderator of the effects of the love motive and relational context on sexual experience. *Archives of Sexual Behavior, 26*, 159–177.

Vohs, K. D., Catanese, K. R., & Baumeister, R. F. (2004). Sex in "his" versus "her" relationships. In J. H. Harvey, A. Wenzel, & S. Sprecher (Eds.), *The handbook of sexuality in close relationships* (pp. 433–474). Mahwah, NJ: Lawrence Erlbaum Associates.

Wilson, S. R. (2002). *Seeking and resisting compliance: What people say, what they do, when trying to influence others*. Thousand Oaks, CA: Sage.

Wood, W., & Eagly, A. H. (2002). A cross-cultural analysis of the behavior of women and men: Implications for the origins of sex differences. *Psychological Bulletin, 128*, 699–727.

19

Do Women Work Harder Than Men at Maintaining Relationships?

Daniel J. Canary
Jodi Wahba
Arizona State University

The presumption that biological sex affects communication behavior all the time is not valid in the face of evidence that sex differences tend to be very small and inconsistent across interaction contexts (Canary & Hause, 1993). At the same time, men and women clearly differ. The issue is determining what behaviors differ and when. We believe that one key area to look for sex differences concerns how men and women maintain their close, personal relationships. Several reasons warrant the examination of sex differences in relational maintenance behaviors. The sum of these reasons is that women are more *relationally responsive*; that is, women (vs. men) tend to engage in thoughts and actions that protect and promote their personal involvements.

First, an examination of sex differences in relational maintenance behaviors directly tests the assumption that women are primarily responsible for developing and maintaining close relationships. This assumption has been stated by many scholars who have examined various relational processes. For example, Fincham and Linfield (1997) constructed measures of both positive and negative marital quality and examined the extent to which these would associate with attributions for events in the marriage. They found that both positive and negative marital quality indices were related to wife (but not husband) attributions of causality and responsibility for events in marriage. The difference appears to be more significant regarding causal attributions (e.g., locus). Fincham and Linfield interpreted these findings as evidence for the view that women are more sensitive to relationship events and function as relational barometers.

Second, and related to the aforementioned idea, research on couple conflict management suggests that sex differences should be witnessed in maintenance behaviors. Conflict research shows that women tend to function as relational firefighters to identify and solve relational problems, including the confrontation of their partners, whereas men tend to avoid conflict (Gottman, 1994). This pattern of engagement for women suggests that they would likewise expend energies to maintain their relationships in episodes not involving conflict. Whether or not the results regarding conflict transfer to positive and proactive behaviors that individuals engage in to maintain their relationships remains an area for speculation.

Third, an examination of sex differences in relational maintenance tests the view that women are socialized to be more communal, whereas men are socialized to be more instrumental. According to social role theory (SRT; Eagly, 1987), men and women specialize in different spheres of behavior as a result of the traditional division of labor (in which men engage in higher status, paid labor and women oversee the household). According to SRT, this traditional division of labor is the product of both the socioeconomic environment (e.g., agrarian vs. postindustrial societies) and the physical properties of men and women (e.g., upper body strength vs. ability to bear children; see Eagly, Wood, & Johannesen-Schmidt, 2004; Wood & Eagly, 2002). The implication of this theory is that women (more than men) assume as part of their gender role the development and maintenance of relationships. Additionally, most people believe that women are more communal than men, which implicates greater sensitivity and skill in a variety of relationally promoting ways (Eagly et al.; see also Burleson & Kunkel, chap. 8, and Wright, chap. 3, both this volume).

Finally, an examination of sex differences in maintenance behaviors tests the idea that women (vs. men) are more inherently motivated to engage in relationship development and maintenance. For instance, Wong and Czikszintmihalyi (1991) found that individual differences in affiliation interacted with sex to affect friendship interactions. Specifically, high school girls were highly affiliative and engaged in friendship interactions more frequently than did high school boys. Girls also spent more time than boys in terms of thinking about their interpersonal relationships. The authors interpreted these findings as reflecting greater motivational strength to maintain relationships among girls. In a related manner, Josephs, Markus, and Tafarodi (1992) conceptualized self-esteem as sex based; men and women use different criteria for assessing their self-worth. For men, self-esteem is tied to their ability to have an independent self (e.g., see themselves superior to others on different types of achievements). For women, self-esteem is related to their ability to foster positive relationships (e.g., women with high self-esteem recalled more information regarding friends and groups than did others). Accordingly, individual differences associated with one's sex might be linked to the maintenance of close relationships.

We address the question of sex differences in relational maintenance in the following manner. First, we summarize the research on sex differences in relational maintenance, emphasizing a program of research that began with Stafford and Canary (1991). This material references differences in maintenance that are solely due to biological sex (male or female). Next, we offer a theoretical account of these sex differences that emphasizes how gender is constructed through a cluster of activities that occur in two foci—division of household labor and play. Third, we offer a set of moderating factors that alter the main effects for sex that we observe in the relational maintenance literature. Finally, we offer conclusions based on this analysis. Before this project is undertaken, however, we need to define the critical term *relational maintenance*.

Relational maintenance has been defined in several ways (for reviews, see Dindia, 2000, 2003; Dindia & Canary, 1993; Duck, 1988). Dindia and Canary presented four definitions, though these are not exhaustive: to keep a relationship in existence; to keep a relationship in a specified state; to keep a relationship satisfactory; and to repair a relationship. In our view, stability is necessary but not sufficient, given that people often remain in stable but dissatisfying or otherwise dysfunctional relationships (Heaton & Albrecht, 1991). Instead, we define relational maintenance as those actions and activities that people enact in order to sustain desired relational features, such as satisfaction, love, commitment, trust, and so forth (Canary & Stafford, 1992; Stafford & Canary, 1991). This definition points to behaviors that promote such relational characteristics, or what we initially identified as relational maintenance *strategies* (Stafford & Canary). Other research has identified the nonstrategic, routine ways that people maintain feature characteristics of their close involvements (e.g., Aylor & Dainton, 2004; Dainton & Stafford, 1993; Duck). This latter line of research looks at how people use the same set of behaviors in mundane and nonstrategic ways (e.g., one might engage in positive behaviors without the intent of maintaining the relationship). Our review references both the strategic and routine ways that people maintain their relationships.

FINDINGS REGARDING SEX DIFFERENCES IN RELATIONAL MAINTENANCE STRATEGIES

Using factor analyses of existing maintenance behaviors coupled with open-ended items obtained in interviews, Stafford and Canary (1991) derived five strategies for maintaining romantic relationships: *positivity* refers to being polite, cheerful, and upbeat, and it means avoiding criticism; *openness* concerns direct talks about the nature of the relationship and disclosing needs; *assurances* refers to the manner in which a person conveys continued love and commitment; *social networks* concerns the purposeful involvement of friends and family as support systems for the relationship; and *sharing tasks* involves performing household responsibilities and other tasks. These maintenance strategies represent proactive and constructive behaviors (Guerrero, Eloy, & Wabnik, 1993). Additional types of relational maintenance behaviors have been found in research on friends, platonic relationships, and romantic involvements (e.g., Canary, Stafford, Hause, & Wallace, 1993; Dainton & Stafford, 1993; Messman, Canary, & Hause, 2000; Stafford, Dainton, & Haas, 2000). Nevertheless, the five-factor typology remains the most robust and widely used measure of relational maintenance. Indeed, Dindia (2000) noted that this typology and its measurement have "dominated" the research on relational maintenance (p. 291).

The use and perception of these maintenance strategies matter quite a bit to partners. Several scholars have independently found that these strategies predict critical relational features, such as liking the partner, love, commitment, and control mutuality (i.e., the extent to which both parties agree on who has control in the relationship; see, e.g., Canary & Stafford, 1992; Canary, Stafford, & Semic, 2002; Stafford & Canary, 1991; Weigel & Ballard-Reisch, 1999a, 1999b). Indeed, maintenance strategies have been found to predict up to 80% of the variance in these relational features (e.g., Weigel & Ballard-Reisch, 1999b), and both partners' efforts matter. In other words, both men and women engage in these behaviors with positive effect. However, there is some evidence that women tend to engage in maintenance efforts more than do men.

Most of the research using the five-factor typology and its variants has reported sex differences, with the performance of more maintenance behaviors by women than by men (e.g., Aylor & Dainton, 2004; Messman et al., 2000). However, the results are consistent for only two of the five maintenance behaviors. In particular, studies have found that women engage in more sharing tasks to maintain their relationships than do their male counterparts (Canary & Stafford, 1992; Canary et al., 2002; Ragsdale, 1996; Stafford et al., 2000). Items that represent this strategy include "help equally with tasks that need to be done," "do my fair share of the work we have to do," and "perform my household responsibilities." In this vein, women more than men appear to engage in work that is considered the joint responsibility of both partners, including household chores. In addition, women engage in more openness (Aylor & Dainton, Canary & Stafford; Canary et al., Dainton & Stafford, 1993; Ragsdale, Stafford et al.). Items that reflect openness include "encourage him–her to disclose thoughts and feelings to me," "seek to discuss the quality of our relationship," "remind him–her about relationship decisions we made in the past," "simply tell him–her how I feel about our relationship," and so forth. Accordingly, women appear to engage in more attempts to engage in relationship talk, or what Dindia and Baxter (1987) identified as *metacommunication strategies.*

We should acknowledge that men also use these proactive strategies. That is, within dyads, partners tend to engage in similar maintenance behaviors (Dainton & Stafford, 1993; Weigel & Ballard-Reisch, 1999b), and the rank ordering of the use of maintenance behaviors is very similar for men and women (e.g., Messman et al., 2000). So, it appears that both men and women engage in these proactive and positive behaviors to maintain their close relationships.

In addition to these findings, we have seen that women's assessment of equity appears to matter more than mens' assessment of equity. *Equity* as a theoretical construct is based on the principle of distributive justice, in which fairness is seen as a function of both the individual's outcomes or inputs and her or his partner's outcomes or inputs (for a review of equity theory in close relationships, see Hatfield, Traupmann, Sprecher, Utne, & Hay, 1985). More precisely, several studies have reported that women's assessments of how equitably they are treated predicts not only their maintenance behaviors but also their partners' maintenance behaviors (Canary & Stafford, 1992, 2001; Stafford & Canary, 2004). Specifically, women's assessments lead to the familiar inverted U in predicting equity outcomes (see Hatfield et al.). That is, both husbands and wives in relationships in which the wife feels equitably treated engage in the most maintenance behaviors, followed by partners in relationships in which the wife feels overbenefited, and then by partners in which the wife feels underbenefited (Canary & Stafford, 1992, 2001; Stafford & Canary). Although male-defined equity also predicts maintenance behaviors, the findings are not as strong or consistent with equity theory as female-defined equity.

Moreover, Weigel and Ballard-Reisch (1999b) found that wives' maintenance behavior significantly affected couple satisfaction, commitment, and love more so than husbands' maintenance behavior. In that study, the researchers created latent couple scores from individual-level data, and they calculated alternative Structural Equation Modeling models. The best fitting models all found that the wives' maintenance behaviors predicted couple-level experiences of relational quality. Although Weigel and Ballard-Reisch would not go so far as to say that these data reflect alternative role assignments in marriage, they did interpret the findings as suggesting that wives are more influential in terms of relational experiences. These findings are especially interesting if we consider that husbands' and wives' maintenance behaviors correlated at .61 (standardized path coefficient).

In brief, biological sex affects the use of maintenance behaviors in three ways: (a) through women's use of sharing tasks and openness; (b) through women's assessment of how fairly they are treated; and (c) through the way in which women's maintenance behaviors affect dyadic measures of relational quality. In the following section we offer a theoretic explanation for these findings.

GENDER AS CLUSTERS OF ACTIVITIES

Our interpretation of the findings regarding sex differences in relational responsiveness generally and relational maintenance specifically concerns the clusters of activities that men and women enact. Canary and Emmers-Sommer (1997) argued that men and women engage in various clusters of behaviors that are associated with each sex, and previous research supports the view that men and women vary in several routine activities. Cody, Canary, and Smith (1994), for instance, reported that men and women pursue different types of goals involving the compliance of other people. Men were more likely to initiate relationships, confront other people, and engage in other instrumental pursuits (e.g., have conflicts with teachers and bureaucrats). In contrast, women engaged in a wider variety of activities, including pursuing goals related to helping others through charity work and advice giving, escalating and deescalating romantic relationships, sharing activities with friends, seeking support, enforcing obligations made to them, and protecting their personal rights. Moreover, women were more persistent and more likely to engage in both rational and emotion-based influence behaviors.

Given the potential range of activities, one must find a way to organize them conceptually. Canary and Emmers-Sommer relied on Feld's (1981) focus theory to indicate how activities cluster: "A focus is defined as a social, psychological, legal, or physical entity around which joint activities are organized" (Feld, p. 1016). Although Feld's theory originally concerned how social networks are linked, Canary and Emmers-Sommer adapted the theory to explain how behaviors are linked to gender roles, and they identified two foci that organize activities pertinent to gender roles—the division of household labor and play or leisure. These foci function in a similar manner as Eagly's social roles, but they emphasize activities that become associated with gender roles instead of how social roles affect gender roles. That is, how boys and girls adopt household chores and how they learn to talk during play help define appropriate behaviors for each sex. Accordingly, our adaptation of focus theory holds that people learn gender roles most from the chores they are expected to perform around the house and from the sorts of leisure activities they learn and are expected to learn. Moreover, these foci are constraining because they structure social behavior by specifying different behaviors that should be done by boys and girls, and by men and women.

Perhaps the most important gender-related focus of activity concerns the division of household labor (Canary & Emmers-Sommer, 1997). Women perform more everyday, mundane, and personally unrewarding chores when compared with their male partners. Hochschild (1989) estimated that women work an extra month of 24-hour days per year doing household chores, and women who work outside the home still do approximately 70% of the household labor (South & Spizte, 1994). Of course, the division of household labor varies according to the amount of income the woman brings home, whether the man holds an egalitarian attitude, and other factors (Coltrane, 1996). Nevertheless, the mass of data on the topic indicate that men are slow learners when it comes to doing such things as planning for meals, doing the laundry, and wrapping birthday presents.

One major reason women perform more of these chores concerns the fact that the division of household labor falls along gendered boundaries. That is, women are primarily responsible for what are so-called feminine jobs that largely occur inside the house (e.g., cooking, cleaning, and changing diapers), and men are primarily responsible for so-called masculine work that mostly occurs outside the house (e.g., mowing the lawn, shoveling snow, and washing cars). Research shows that the feminine jobs, which must be done daily, take much more time than do the masculine jobs (Ferree, 1991; Manke, Seerym Crouter, & McHale, 1994). Importantly, men in dual-career couples do not tend to do more housework than their partners unless the woman makes more money than they do (Maret & Finlay, 1984). Cubbins and Vannoy (2004) summarized the research in the following way: "An essential finding of this research is that no matter how much American women work outside the home, they continue to do the majority of housework" (p. 183). Children learn this division of household labor during childhood and adolescence, such that the gendered pattern of doing chores continues *including* in dual career families (Benin & Edwards, 1990).

The inequity in the division of household labor leads to decreased relational satisfaction and stability among women, but not necessarily men (Frisco & Williams, 2003; Gottman & Carrere, 1994). One explanation for this finding is that inequity in the division of household labor overbenefits men while underbenefiting women, and the experience of being underbenefited in close relationships is personally taxing, leading to feelings of anger and depression (Sprecher, 1986). No doubt as a result of this inequity, women tend to find the division of household labor a much more important issue than do men (e.g., Cubbins & Vannoy, 2004; Gottman & Carerre). Accordingly, it is not surprising that women (vs. men) who are discontent with the division of household labor are more likely to confront their partner, which leads to competitive conflict and further dissatisfaction (Kluwer, Heesink, & van de Vliert, 1997). In brief, how men and women negotiate the division of household labor represents an important arena in defining gender roles in conjugal relationships (for a fuller treatment of how partners negotiate gender roles, see Canary & Emmers-Sommer, 1997).

The secondary sphere of activity concerns how people spend their leisure time. This is a secondary sphere in part because leisure time is usually dependent on work and household tasks (the term *leisure time* is often defined as the time remaining after paid work and household chores are finished). Research shows that women enjoy less leisure time both inside and outside the home than men (Firestone & Shelton, 1988; Freysinger, 1994). Women (vs. men) also report that "quality" time spent with the family is less leisurely (47% for women vs. 74% for men, Shaw, 1993). For instance, women might fold laundry while watching TV, whereas men would not; women might be more inclined to prepare and serve dinner, whereas men might not.

Moreover, men and women and boys and girls tend to engage in different forms of leisure time. In elementary school, high school, and college, men report engaging in more sports than do women (e.g., Vaughter, Sadh, & Vozzola, 1994). Boys tend to engage in competitive games defined by rules of play that require no negotiation between competitors (Maccoby, 1990). If the rules are not followed, then resolution can be found by referring to the codified version of them (e.g., PGA rules of golf) or by fighting. In contrast, girls tend to prefer games that require interaction and negotiated outcomes that focus on goals of relationship building over winning (Maccoby). In brief, and according to Maccoby, male games restrict interactions regarding relational development and maintenance, whereas female games promote such interactions.[1]

Drawing on this research, Gottman and Carerre (1994) argued that sex segregation during childhood play leads to differences in the ways that men and women later manage problems in marriage: Wives think about their relationships more, seek to disclose, and attempt to confront and resolve problems; husbands attempt to avoid the discussion of problems. Moreover, male inexperience in negotiating relationships during play is implicated as the reason why men experience greater negative physiological arousal during conversations about relational problems, which adds to their sense of urgency to avoid those talks (Gottman & Carrere). In contrast, women are more likely than men to pursue problem-solving discussions regardless of their experience of negative physiological arousal (Levenson, Carstensen, & Gottman, 1994).

Using focus theory to interpret sex differences in maintenance behaviors would point to the use of sharing tasks and openness as female activities. Specifically, women's greater involvement in household chores would lead them to engage in sharing tasks as means of maintaining their relationships. That is, women learn from childhood how to perform a variety of household chores, and they come to appreciate the personal sacrifice those behaviors exact. Doing more than one's fair share of the chores constitutes one way to indicate one's commitment and love. The point is not that women get stuck with doing chores; the point is that they report it as something they symbolically as well as pragmatically do to keep their marriages satisfying (Stafford & Canary, 1991).

Likewise, women's greater involvement in play and leisure activities that focus on interaction between playmates appears to groom their relational sensitivity and use of openness to define their relationships and manage problems when they arise. Men also engage in these maintenance behaviors and value them, but not as much, and what they think and do might not matter as much. In a word, we are proposing that men and women each engage in maintenance behaviors that are valued because they are recognized as being consistent with activity foci that define gender roles.

At the same time, this explanation is not absolute. Several moderating factors likely affect the sex differences cited here. In the following section we provide a tentative list of those factors.

---

[1]Maccoby's (1990) summary of the sex-segregation phenomenon in childhood play indicated that the segregation between the sexes was far from absolute. Still, the propensity for children's play to be gendered and sex segregated is clear.

FACTORS THAT MODERATE SEX DIFFERENCES IN RELATIONAL MAINTENANCE

Relational Type Moderates Sex Differences

One of the propositions made by Canary and Emmers-Sommer (1997) was that "gender role prototypes reflect in different couple types" (p. 145). For instance, the division of household labor varies according to different marriage forms. Ferree (1991) found four different types of two-career marriages: *two housekeeper*, wherein both partners performed at least 40% of the work; *drudge wives*, wherein the woman did more than 60% of the work; *semihousewives*, which involved wives who did more than 60% of the chores but worked fewer than 30 hours outside the home; and *cash paying*, wherein both partners did fewer than 20 hours of work in the home but paid others. Clearly, not all households are run the same way.

More generally, research by Fitzpatrick (1988) and Gottman (1994) has revealed three pure couple types. Fitzpatrick derived these types based on self-reports of one's traditional ideology, interdependence, and conflict. The *traditional* marriage involves conventional beliefs about gender roles, high interdependence between spouses, and moderate conflict (most of which occurs over important issues). The *independent* couple type have nonconventional beliefs about gender roles, moderate levels of interdependence, and a lot of conflict (in part because they are often negotiating their gender roles). The *separate* marriage contains conventional beliefs but little interdependence and conflict. It is important to note that each of these couple types are seen as functional, and reports of relational quality have been high for all three types (e.g., Fitzpatrick, Best, 1979). Gottman used observational analyses and derived a similar category of functional couple types (pp. 158–211). He found two types of conflict engagers and one kind of conflict avoiders. The first includes the *validating* couple, which at first tends to minimize conflict through validating each other; however, then they increase disagreement and then resolve conflict. Gottman equated validating couples to Fitzpatrick's traditional type. Second, the *volatile* couple engages in a lot of disagreement and criticism throughout their conversations. Gottman equated volatile couples to Fitpatrick's independent type. Finally, *avoiders* avoid discussion of conflict and they tend to minimize disagreement. Avoiders were seen as similar to Fitzpatrick's separate type.

Likewise, couples should not mix or change relational types, or else problems can arise. Fitzpatrick has found some evidence of this. When the husband and the wife do not agree on their relational schemata, the couple is classified as *mixed*. The most common mixed type involves a separate male and a traditional female. Research has shown that men and women in this relationship tend to respond to each other in sex-stereotypic ways. For example, men do not disclose as much as their partners who seek their disclosure, and these couples do not agree on how interdependent they should be (Fitzpatrick & Best, 1979; Fitzpatrick, Vance, & Witteman, 1984).

The research also shows that traditional couples get along well, in part because they understand their gender roles in conventional terms. In this relationship type, the division of household labor follows along traditional markers (i.e., the woman does the "inside" chores, whereas the man does the "outside" chores). In the independent relationships where egalitarian values reign, conflict can emerge over the division of household labor, especially when inequities arise. For example, Kluwer et al. (1997) found that egalitarian wives, but not traditional wives, were likely to confront their partners about inequity in the division of household labor. Accordingly, complaining about the dirty kitchen to the husband would not occur to the traditional wife, but it would occur to the independent wife.

One study examined how relational maintenance strategies vary according to couple type. Weigel and Ballard-Reisch (1999a) surveyed married couples and found that traditionals and independents engage in more relational maintenance behaviors than do separates. Traditionals and independents both used more assurances and openness than did separates. Furthermore, traditionals used more task sharing than did either independent or separate marriages. These findings comport to the view that people in separate marriages limit the amount of information they exchange. In addition, only independent types tended to reciprocate maintenance behaviors. However, traditionals' and separates' use of maintenance behaviors is relatively independent of their partners' use. These findings suggest that independents are mindful of the efforts that their partners enact, and that traditional and separate partners focus more on conventional roles to determine their behaviors. Unfortunately, interaction tests involving sex differences were not reported, so the issue of whether relationship type moderates the general effect that is due to biological sex was not directly addressed.

Increased Egalitarianism Alters Traditionally Defined Sex Roles

On several fronts, women are becoming equal partners in the workforce as well as in the home, in particular, with women becoming more instrumental (i.e., like men) in specific ways regarding their choice of education, leadership, and risk taking, among others (Wood & Eagly, 2002). In examining the division of household labor, Coltrane (1996) argued that increases in egalitarianism have led to increased sharing of household chores, with further egalitarianism and equality on the way. Coltrane noted that changes in demographics, economics, and social trends will require that men become more egalitarian in performing more chores at home, including greater involvement in raising children (e.g., as women earn more income they define themselves as providers, which requires men to perform more of the chores). Of course, recent advances made as the result of Title IX (which requires greater equality for women's sports) has lead to greater participation in team sports for women. These changes imply that the foci for gender role activities will change.

However, the change will be slow. For example, Gershuny and Robinson (1988) examined the changes in the division of household labor that occurred between the 1960s and the 1980s, and they found that women decreased the amount of chores per week by approximately 1 to 1.5 hours. Moreover, in dual-career marriages, boys and girls appear to be learning the traditional division of household labor, with girls doing more in dual-career homes and boys doing less in dual-career homes when compared with their counterparts in single-career families (Benin & Edwards, 1990). In single-parent homes, girls appear to do much more than boys in terms of the role obligations of housework (Hilton & Haldeman, 1991). The implication of these findings is that, in dual-career and single-parent households, the traditional division of labor remains entrenched. Generations will likely pass before work and play are gender-neutral activities.

Gender Moderates Biological Sex

A limited number of studies have examined the relative effects of sex versus gender, where sex references biological differences and gender concerns the psychological and social ways that people experience and express what it means to be a man or a woman. Given that one important feature of the feminine role is the importance placed on relationships, we would anticipate that psychological femininity (but not the more instrumental orientation of masculinity) would be linked to efforts to maintain close relationships. Although the results are not entirely consistent with this prediction (as we subsequently review), they do confirm that psychological gender (vs. sex) appears to have a more robust effect across maintenance behaviors. Accordingly, the personal orientation or gender role of the individual would appear to alter the sex-based effects.

To our knowledge, only two studies compared the influence of sex and psychological gender on variations of the Stafford and Canary (1991) maintenance strategies. First, Stafford et al. (2000) examined effects that were due to sex differences and psychological gender (feminine and masculine) on married couples' maintenance behaviors. Using regression analyses, these authors found that biological sex affected only two maintenance behaviors—openness and sharing tasks, as already noted. However, psychological femininity was significantly and positively associated with all seven maintenance behaviors, that is advice, assurances, (positive) conflict management, social networks, openness, positivity, and sharing tasks; psychological masculinity was unexpectedly, positively associated with three behaviors—assurances, positivity, and openness. In a follow-up study, Aylor and Dainton (2004) examined sex and gender differences in both routine and strategic maintenance behaviors by using the same factors as Stafford et al. Aylor and Dainton found that biological sex affected only one maintenance behavior, which was routine openness (with the use of more openness by women). However, psychological femininity positively associated with most of the routine maintenance behaviors (openness, conflict management, sharing tasks, and giving advice) and with three strategic behaviors (positivity, openness, and conflict management).[2] Interestingly, psychological masculinity positively associated with openness and sharing tasks. Adherence to these gender roles thus clearly appears to moderate the influence of biological sex on maintenance behaviors and diminishes the influence of household chores and play on gender roles more generally.

In a related line of research on accommodative behaviors, Rusbult, Verette, Whitney, Slovik, and Lipkus (1991) examined sex and gender differences in college students' reports of constructive and destructive accommodation tendencies (i.e., behaviors performed in response to a problem or the partner's rudeness). Using both closed-ended and open-ended measures, men (vs. women) reported using more destructive tendencies to exit (i.e., leaving or threatening to leave) and neglect (i.e., indirectly punishing the partner). However, the effects were less clear regarding the responses of voice (i.e., discussing the problem) and loyalty (i.e., giving in to the partner). When responding to a closed-ended measure of constructive behavior, women scored lower than men, but on an open-ended measure, women scored higher than men. Moreover, psychological femininity (but not masculinity) was significantly correlated with both destructive and constructive accommodation tendencies. Psychological femininity was positively correlated with both destructive and constructive responses in the zero-ordered correlations, but psychological femininity was negatively correlated with destructive responses when the simple regressions were examined.[3] In addition, psychological femininity obtained both direct and indirect effects on accommodation behaviors, whereas sex differences were entirely mediated by commitment in a predication of the accommodation behaviors of exit–voice–loyalty–neglect. In sum, psychological gender appears to predict a range of maintenance behaviors better than does biological sex.

Microscopic Analyses of Maintenance Efforts Moderate Sex Differences

We should note that maintenance activities occur at different levels of observation. The strategies we have been discussing reflect a rather global level of observation, with instructions often pointing to what one's partner has been doing recently (e.g., Canary & Stafford, 1992).[4] Of course, people define and maintain their

---

[2]The significance levels were based on the *p* values reported in Tables 2 and 3 in Aylor & Dainton. For some reason, significant effects (i.e., $p < .05$) were not marked as such in the notes for these tables.

[3]The effects that were due to psychological femininity found by Rusbult et al. (1991) change when we compare the zero-order correlations (reported there in Table 2) with the simple regressions (reported there in Table 3).

[4]We should point out that Ragsdale (1996) had married couples keep daily diaries of their maintenance behaviors. This is somewhat puzzling, because a few of the items would appear to occur only once in the day at most (e.g., "asks how my day has gone," "likes to have periodic talks about the relationship").

relationships in more precise ways during interaction. Analyses that examine more precise aspects of interaction should reveal whether women or men work more to maintain their relationships at a more microscopic level.

From a power perspective (where men's greater status requires less of them), one might hypothesize that women perform a majority of conversational maintenance work. Fishman (1978) was the first to explore this idea. She reported that women, in fact, did more conversational maintenance work. Such work was reflected in several linguistic behaviors, including the use of backchannels (e.g., "Oh, uh-uh"), less talking (as measured in talk time), asking questions, and interrupting. However, Fishman's findings are based on a sample of *three* couples, two of which involved her graduate students. Moreover, only 5 hours of over 50 hours of tape recorded conversation were analyzed. This selectivity in both sampling and analysis erodes confidence in the inferences she made.

Other studies attempting to test Fishman's hypotheses have revealed that her inference that women do all the conversational work is unreliable. For example, in a study of seven couples, DeFrancisco (1990) reported that men talked less than women and engaged in more question asking, and that sex differences were absent when it came to backchannels. In an examination of 35 roommate dyads, Kollack, Blumstein, and Schwartz (1985) reported that men and women interrupted each other equally, engaged in a similar amount of talk (though men did talk a bit more), and used backchannels equally. In a third study, Robey, Canary, and Burggraf (1998) examined 20 married couples engaged in small talk. They reported that husbands and wives engaged in similar levels of talk time, interruptions (confirming as well as disconfirming), and hostile questions. Wives did engage in more nonhostile questions, and husbands engaged in more backchannels, relative to their spouses.

Probably what occurs in microscopic studies of maintenance is that partners tend to respond to each other. As Burggraf and Sillars (1987) found, the reciprocation of behavior more strongly predicted one's behavior than did sex. That is, the tendency to exchange behavior of the same form is stronger than the tendency to engage in behavior that is prescribed by one's biological sex. Accordingly, one would expect to see very similar frequency patterns of conversational maintenance behavior at the microscopic level within dyads, which is what the research referenced herein shows. In a word, at the microscopic level, we see little evidence for the view that women engage in more maintenance efforts at the conversational level.

Negative Behaviors Combine with Positive Behaviors to Obscure Sex Differences

It is clear that the maintenance of relationships involves how partners use negative behaviors as well as positive behaviors. Support for the dual-function model of relational maintenance was offered by Rogge and Bradbury (1999). Rogge and Bradbury proposed that marital outcomes of stability and satisfaction might be alternatively predicted by physical aggression and communication behavior. These authors found evidence that aggression at Time 1 predicted dissolution 4 years later, but that positive–negative communication better predicted whether or not a stable marriage was also satisfactory. In a similar manner, Huston, Caughlin, Houts, Smith, and George (2001) found that positive features (e.g., love, responsiveness) combined with negative features (e.g., ambivalence, partner negativity) to differentiate marital stability and quality over a 14-year period. In addition, Marshall, Weston, and Honeycutt (2000) found that abusive men who use positivity (vs. those that do not) are more successful at maintaining their relationships because positivity largely mediates the effects of physical abuse on relational satisfaction.

One analogue for examining how partners maintain both positive and negative features of their relationships can be found in dual-process models that connect relationships to health. In their assessment of the literature, Burman and Margolin (1992) found that the connection between relationships and health can be positive or negative, depending on the extent to which those relationships added stress or reduced support. Likewise, Kielcolt-Glaser and Newton (2001) updated this review and termed the stress and support factors as *negative* and *positive dimensions* of marriage, respectively. Similarly, Walen and Lachman (2000) identified two processes regarding the relationship–health link as *support* and *strain*. The idea is that relationships are not defined and maintained by using only positive behaviors; negative behaviors also can be seen as functional, and not all positive behaviors are necessarily functional. Given that sex differences in maintenance only refer to positive behaviors, future research has to examine the how dual dimensions of positive and negative maintenance behaviors interact to affect relational stability and satisfaction, and whether men or women are better at balancing the negative with the positive (see also Sagrestano, Heavey, & Christensen, chap. 20, this volume).

In sum, several factors moderate the sex differences that we find in the aegis of literature referencing behaviors that people use to maintain close relationships. These include relational type, gender, level of analysis, how negative behaviors combine with maintenance strategies, how psychological gender moderates effects that are due to biological sex, and that dual-process models have yet to be examined.

CONCLUSIONS

The review given herein indicates that women are more relationally responsive, at least in terms of performing household chores and discussing the nature of the relationship. In addition, women appear to have their fingers on the pulse of the relationship to the extent that their (but not the men's) assessments of equity predict relational maintenance behavior (both hers and his). Furthermore, women's maintenance efforts (more than men's) appear to matter more to the couple's experience of relational quality. However, this conclusion does not suggest that only women are responsible; rather, men and women engage in maintenance behaviors in a similar and interdependent manner. People in interdependent marriages especially watch each other to determine what kind of maintenance strategy should be used.

The explanation for the sex differences found in maintenance behavior was derived from focus theory (Canary & Emmers-Sommer, 1997). That is, gender roles emerge from two foci, such that sex differences in the division of household labor and leisure activities affect relational maintenance behaviors in marriage. Although this theory is a macrolevel social structural theory, it also has implications for the individual experiences that partners have when communicating with each other. However, more research is needed to ascertain whether variations in work and play are reflected in variations in maintenance behaviors. Obviously, we think they do, but we must obtain more direct evidence.

As mentioned, several factors no doubt moderate the sex-difference findings, which were just reviewed. The implication of these factors is that main effects caused by sex are probably moderated much of the time, making strong inferences to all relationships untenable. These moderators probably combine with each other as well. For example, increased egalitarianism should associate with changes in psychological gender as well as relationship types (e.g., Noller & Hiscock, 1990), both of which should reduce the manner in which stereotypical sex roles are enacted.

At the same time, the way men and women maintain relationships will probably not change soon. They already are more similar than different in terms of using proactive and positive behaviors. From our view, it will be interesting to see people redefine their gendered activities, even if that requires a generation or two, and whether these changes ultimately lead to changes in how men and women maintain their close, personal relationships.

ACKNOWLEDGMENTS

We thank Heather Canary and Kathryn Dindia for their helpful comments on an earlier version of this chapter.

REFERENCES

Aylor, B., & Dainton, M. (2004). Biological sex and psychological gender as predictors of routine and strategic relational maintenance. *Sex Roles, 50*, 689–697.

Benin, M. H., & Edwards, D. A. (1990). Adolescents' chores: The difference between dual- and single-career families. *Journal of Marriage and the Family, 52*, 361–373.

Burggraf, C. S., & Sillars, A. L. (1987). A critical examination of sex differences in marital communication. *Communication Monographs, 54*, 276–294.

Burman, B., & Margolin, G. (1992). Analysis of the association between marital relationships and health problems: An interactional perspective. *Psychological Bulletin, 112*, 39–63.

Canary, D. J., & Emmers-Sommer, T. M. (with Faulkner, S.). (1997). *Sex and gender differences in personal relationships.* New York: Guilford.

Canary, D. J., & Hause, K. S. (1993). Is there any reason to research sex differences in communication? *Communication Quarterly, 41*, 129–144.

Canary, D. J., & Stafford, L. (1992). Relational maintenance strategies and equity in marriage. *Communication Monographs, 59*, 243–267.

Canary, D. J., & Stafford, L. (1993). Preservation of relational characteristics: Maintenance strategies, equity, and locus of control. In P. J. Kalbfleisch (Ed.), *Interpersonal communication: Evolving interpersonal relationships* (pp. 237–259). Hillsdale, NJ: Lawrence Erlbaum Associates.

Canary, D. J., & Stafford, L. (1994), Maintaining relationships through strategic and routine interaction. In D. J. Canary & L. Stafford (Eds.), *Communication and relational maintenance* (pp. 3–22). San Diego, CA: Academic Press.

Canary, D. J., & Stafford, L. (2001). Equity in maintaining personal relationships. In J. H. Harvey & A. E. Wenzel (Eds.), *Close romantic relationships: Maintenance and enhancement* (133–150). Mahwah, NJ: Lawrence Erlbaum Associates.

Canary, D. J., Stafford, L., Hause, K. S., & Wallace, L. A. (1993). An inductive analysis of relational maintenance strategies: Comparisons among lovers, relatives, friends, and others. *Communication Research Reports, 10*, 5–14.

Canary, D. J., & Stafford, L., & Semic, B. A. (2002). A panel study of the associations between maintenance strategies and relational characteristics. *Journal of Marriage and the Family, 64*, 395–406.

Cody, M. J., Canary, D. J., & Smith, S. W. (1994). Compliance-gaining goals: An inductive analysis of actors' goal types, strategies, and successes. In J. Daly & J. Wiemann (Eds.), *Communicating strategically: Strategies in interpersonal communication* (pp. 33–90). Hillsdale, NJ: Lawrence Erlbaum Associates.

Coltrane, S. (1996). *Family man.* New York: Oxford University Press.

Cubbins, L. A., & Vannoy, D. (2004). Division of household labor as a source of contention for married and cohabitating couples in Metropolitan Moscow. *Journal of Family Issues, 25*, 182–215.

Dainton, M., & Stafford, L. (1993). Routine maintenance behaviors: A comparison of relationship type, partner similarity and sex differences. *Journal of Social and Personal Relationships, 10*, 255–271.

DeFrancisco, V. L. (1991). The sounds of silence: How men silence women in marital relations. *Discourse and Society, 2*, 413–423.

Dindia, K. (1994). A multiphasic view of relationship maintenance strategies. In D. J. Canary & L. Stafford (Eds.), *Communication and relational maintenance* (pp. 99–112). San Diego, CA: Academic Press.

Dindia, K. (2000). Relational maintenance. In C. Hendrick & S. S. Hendrick (Eds.) *Close relationships: A sourcebook* (pp. 287–300). Thousand Oaks, CA: Sage.

Dindia, K. (2003). Definitions and perspectives on relational maintenance communication. In D. J. Canary & M. Dainton (Eds.), *Maintaining relationships through communication: Relational, contextual, and cultural variations* (pp. 1–30). Hillsdale, NJ: Lawrence Erlbaum Associates.

Dindia, K., & Baxter, L. A. (1987). Strategies for maintaining and repairing marital relationships. *Journal of Social and Personal Relationships, 4*, 143–158.

Dindia, K., & Canary, D. J. (1993). Definitions and theoretical perspectives on maintaining relationships. *Journal of Social and Personal Relationships, 10*, 163–173.

Duck, S. W. (1988). *Relating to others.* Chicago: Dorsey.

Eagly, A. H. (1987). *Sex differences in social behavior: A social-role interpretation.* Hillsdale, NJ: Lawrence Erlbaum Associates.

Eagly, A. H., Wood, W., & Johannesen-Schmidt, M. C. (2004). Social role theory of sex differences and similarities: Implications for the partner preferences of men and women. In A. H. Eagly, A. E. Beall, & R. J. Sternberg (Eds.), *The psychology of gender* (2nd ed.), (pp. 269–295). New York: Guilford.

Feld, S. (1981). The focused organization of social ties. *American Journal of Sociology, 86*, 1015–1035.

Ferree, M. M. (1991). The division of household labor in two-earner marriages: Dimensions of variability and change. *Journal of Family Issues, 12*, 158–180.

Fincham, F. D., & Bradbury, T. N. (1992). Assessing attributions in marriage: The Relationship Attribution Measure. *Journal of Personality and Social Psychology 62*, 457–468.

Fincham, F. D., & Linfield, K. J. (1997). A new look at marital quality: Can spouses feel positive and negative about their marriage? *Journal of Family Psychology, 11*, 489–502.

Firestone, J., & Shelton, B. A. (1988). An estimation of the effects of women's work on available leisure time. *Journal of Family Issues, 9*, 478–495.

Fishman, P. (1978). Interaction: The work women do. *Social Problems, 25*, 397–406.

Fitzpatrick, M. A., (1988). *Between husbands and wives: Communication in marriage*. Newbury Park, CA: Sage.

Fitzpatrick, M. A., & Best, P. (1979). Dyadic adjustment in relational types: Consensus, cohesion, affectional expression, and satisfaction in enduring relationships. *Communication Monographs, 46*, 167–178.

Fitzpatrick, M. A., Vance, L., & Witteman, H. (1984). Interpersonal communication in the causal interaction of marital partners. *Journal of Language and Social Psychology, 3*, 81–95.

Freysinger, V. J. (1994). Leisure with children and parental satisfaction: Further evidence of a sex difference in the experience of adult roles and leisure. *Journal of Leisure Research, 26*, 212–226.

Frisco, M. L., & Williams, K. (2003). Perceived housework, equity marital happiness and divorce in dual-eamer households *Journal of Family Issues, 24*, 51–73.

Gershuny, J., & Robinson, J. P. (1988). Historical changes in the household division of labor. *Demography, 25*, 537–552.

Gottman, J. M. (1994). *What predicts divorce.* Mahwah, NJ: Lawrence Erlbaum Associates.

Gottman, J. M., & Carrere, S. (1994). Why can't men and women get along? Developmental roots and marital inequities. In D. J. Canary & L. Stafford (Eds.), *Communication and relational maintenance* (pp. 203–229). San Diego, CA: Academic Press.

Gottman, J. M., & Levenson, R. W. (2000). The timing of divorce: Predicting when a couple will divorce over a 14–year period. *Journal of Marriage and the Family, 62*, 737–745.

Gove, W., & Hughes, M. (1979). Possible causes of the apparent sex differences in mental health *American Sociological Review, 44*, 59—81.

Guerrero, L. K., Eloy, S. V., & Wabnik, A. I. (1993). Linking maintenance strategies to relationship development and disengagement: A reconceptualization. *Journal of Social & Personal Relationships, 10*, 273–283.

Hatfield, E.., Traupmann, J., Sprecher, S., Utne, M., & Hay, M. (1985). Equity in close relationships. In W. Ickes (Ed.), *Compatible and incompatible relationships* (pp. 91–117). New York: Springer-Verlag.

Heaton, T. B., & Albrecht, S. L. (1991). Stable unhappy marriages. *Journal of Marriage and the Family, 53*, 747–758.

Hilton, J. M., & Haldeman, V. A. (1991). Gender differences in the performance of household tasks by adults and children in single-parent and two-parent, two-career families. *Journal of Family Issues, 12*, 114–130.

Hochschild, A., (with Machung, A.). (1989). *The second shift: Working parents and the revolution at home*. New York: Viking Press.

Huston, T. L., Caughlin, J. P., Houts, R. M., Smith, S. E., & George, L. J. (2001). The connubial crucible: Newlywed years as predictors of marital delight, distress, and divorce. *Journal of Personality and Social Psychology, 80*, 237–252.

Kiecolt-Glaser, J. K., & Newton, T. L. (2001). Marriage and health: His and hers, *Psychological Bulletin, 127*, 472–503.

Kluwer, E. S., Heesink, J. A. M., & van de Vliert, E. (2000). The division of labor in close relationships: An asymmetrical conflict issue. *Personal Relationships, 7*, 263–282.

Kluwer, E. S., Heeskink, J. AM, van de Vliert, E. (1997). The marital dynamics of conflict over the division of labor. *Journal of Marriage and the Family, 59*, 635–653.

Kollack, P., Blumstein, P., & Schwartz, P. (1985). Sex and power in interaction: Conversational privileges and duties *American Sociological Review, 50*, 34–60.

Josephs, R. A., Markus, H. R., & Tafarodi, R. W. (1992). Gender and self-esteem. *Journal of Personality and Social Psychology, 63*, 391–402.

Levenson, R. W., Carstensen, L. L., & Gottman, J. M. (1994). The influence of age and gender on affect, physiology, and their interrelations: A study of long-term marriages. *Journal of Personality and Social Psychology, 67*, 56–68.

Maccoby, E. E. (1990). Gender and relationships: A developmental account. *American Psychologist, 45*, 513–520.

Manke, B., Seery, B. L., Crouter, A. C., & McHale, S.M. (1994). The three corners of domestic labor: Mothers, fathers, and children's weekday and weekend housework. *Journal of Marriage and the Family, 56*, 657–668.

Maret, E., & Finlay, B. (1984). The distribution of labor among women in dual-earner families. *Journal of Marriage and the Family, 46*, 357–364.

Marshall, L. L., Weston, R., & Honeycutt, T. C. (2000). Does men's positivity moderate or mediate the effects of their abuse on women's relationship quality: *Journal of Social and Personal Relationships, 17*, 660–675.

Messman, S. J., Canary, D. J., & Hause, K. S. (2000). Motives to remain platonic, equity and the use of maintenance strategies in opposite-sex friendships. *Journal of Social and Personal Relationships, 17*, 67–94.

Murray, S. L., & Holmes, J. G. (1999). The (mental) ties that bind: Cognitive structures that predict relationship resilience. *Journal of Personality and Social Psychology, 77*, 1228–1244.

Noller, P., & Hiscock, H. (1990). Fitzpatricks typology: An Australian replication. *Journal of social and personal Relationships, 6*, 87–91.

Ragsdale, J. D. (1996). Gender, satisfaction level, and the use of relational maintenance strategies in marriage. *Communication Monographs, 63*, 345–369.

Robey, E. B., Canary, D. J., & Burggraf, C. S. (1998). Conversational maintenance behaviors of husbands and wives: An observational analyses. In D. J. Canary & K. Dindia (Eds.), *Sex differences and similarities in communication: Critical essays and empirical investigations of sex and gender in interaction* (pp. 373–392). Hillsdale, NJ: Lawrence Erlbaum Associates.

Rogge, R. D., & Bradbury, T. N. (1999). Till violence does us part: The differing roles of communication and aggression in predicting adverse marital outcomes. *Journal of Consulting and Clinical Psychology, 67*, 340–351.

Rusbult, C. E., Verette, J., Whitney, G. A., Slovik, L. F., & Lipkus, I. (1991). Accommodation processes in close relationships: Theory and preliminary empirical evidence. *Journal of Personality and Social Psychology, 60*, 53–70.

Shaw, S. M. (1993). Dereifying family leisure: An examination of women's and men's everyday experiences and perceptions of family time. *Leisure Studies, 14*, 271–286.

South, S. J., & Sptize, G. (1994). Housework in marital and nonmarital households. *American Sociological Review, 59*, 327–247.

Sprecher, S. (1986). The relation between inequity and emotions in close relationships. *Social Psychological Quarterly, 49*, 309–321.

Stafford L., & Canary, D. J. (1991). Maintenance strategies and romantic relationship type, gender, and relational characteristics. *Journal of Social and Personal Relationships, 8*, 217–242.

Stafford, L., & Canary, D. J. (2004, June). *Equity and interdependence predictors of relational maintenance strategies*. Paper presented at the International Conference on Personal Relationships, Madison, WI.

Stafford, L., Dainton, M., & Haas, S. (2000). Measuring routine and strategic relational maintenance: Scale development, sex versus gender roles, and the prediction of relational characteristics. *Communication Monographs, 67*, 306–323.

Vaughter, R. M., Sadh, D., & Vozzola, E. (1994). Sex similarities and differences in types of play in games and sports. *Psychology of Women Quarterly, 18*, 85–104.

Vogl-Bauer, S., Kalbfleisch, P. J., & Beatty, M. J. (1999). Perceived equity, satisfaction, and relational maintenance strategies in parent-adolescent dyads. *Journal of Youth and Adolescence, 28*, 27–49.

Walen, H. R., & Lachman, M. E. (2000). Social support and strain from partner, family, and friends: Costs and benefits for men and women in adulthood. *Journal of Social and Personal Relationships, 17*, 5–30.

Weigel, D. J., & Ballard-Reisch, D. S. (1999a). All marriages are not maintained equally: Marital type, marital quality, and the use of maintenance behaviors. *Personal Relationships, 6*, 291–303.

Weigel, D. J., & Ballard-Reisch, D. S. (1999b). Using paried data to test models of relational maintenance and marital quality. *Journal of Social and Personal Relationships, 16*, 175–191.

Wood, W., & Eagly, A. H. (2002). A cross-cultural analysis of the behavior of women and men: Implications for the origins of sex differences. *Psychological Bulletin, 128*, 699–727.

Wong, M. M., & Czikszintmihalyi, M. (1991). Affiliation motivation and daily experience: Some issues on gender differences. *Journal of Personality and Social Psychology, 60*, 154–164.

20

Individual Differences Versus Social Structural Approaches to Explaining Demand–Withdraw and Social Influence Behaviors

Lynda M. Sagrestano
Southern Illinois University at Carbondale

Christopher L. Heavey
University of Nevada at Las Vegas

Andrew Christensen
University of California at Los Angeles

INDIVIDUAL DIFFERENCES AND SOCIAL STRUCTURAL APPROACHES

In this chapter, we outline two schools of thought that have developed in the psychological literature to address the question of whether men and women are similar or different. The first approach is termed the *individual differences approach*, in which characteristics of the individual, such as biological sex, are examined to understand group differences in behavior. The second approach is termed the *social structural approach,* in which characteristics of the social context, both at the situational level and at the broader social cultural level, are examined to understand the behavior of individuals in situations. An individual differences approach focuses on between-group variability while neglecting within-group variability, which is often much greater (Feingold, 1995; Hare-Mustin & Marecek, 1988, 1990; Unger,

1979), whereas a social structural approach focuses on within-group variability but may neglect between-group differences. We first present the theoretical underpinnings for each of these approaches. We then provide empirical evidence for and against these approaches from research on the demand–withdraw pattern in marriage and the use of social influence in peer and marital relationships. We conclude with a discussion of the importance of not only identifying sex differences and similarities, but, when there are differences, understanding the underlying mechanisms that lead to these differences.

Individual Differences Approaches

One individual differences approach is a biological or physiological approach. From this perspective, men and women are biologically or physiologically different; as a result of these "essential" differences, they respond differently to certain types of stimuli, thus resulting in behavioral differences. These differences are presented as innate to men and women, residing within the individual. For example, Gottman and Levenson proposed a social psychophysiological theory of sex differences wherein men find the high levels of negative arousal that are created by conflict more aversive than do women, and therefore are more inclined to withdraw from conflict in an attempt to lower the aversive arousal (Gottman & Levenson, 1988; Levenson, Carstensen, & Gottman, 1994). Furthermore, Gottman and colleagues suggested that a subgroup of men who are violent toward their partners experience increased heart rate, which is associated with escalating violence (Gottman, 2001; Gottman et al., 1995), although this finding has not been successfully replicated in other labs (Meehan & Holtzworth-Munroe, 2001; Meehan, Holtzworth-Munroe, & Herron, 2001).

A second individual differences approach is a socialization approach, growing out of psychodynamic theory, suggesting that men and women grow up in different social worlds, develop different identities, pursue different goals, and, as a result, behave differently. Miller (1976) posited that women develop a sense of self that is organized around forming and maintaining relationships, in contrast to men, who develop a sense of self that is organized around separation from others. Building on the work of Miller, both Chodorow (1978) and Rubin (1983) posited that the differences between women and men derive from the traditional family structure, wherein women assume responsibility for early child care. Boys and girls grow up in different social environments, and although both boys and girls experience the same developmental imperatives, the tasks they must perform are different, and these differences lead to profound sex differences in personality, which are formed at an early age, deeply rooted, and are hard to change (Rubin).

Gilligan (1982) hypothesized that these differences in personality have far-reaching effects on the behavior of women and men. She argued that women and men have different ways of imagining the human condition and different values. These differences in perspective lead to differences in their ways of relating to each other; women approach issues from an ethic of responsibility and caring for others, and men approach issues from an ethic of fairness and justice. Gilligan suggests that women's development follows a different trajectory from men's development, and she notes the importance of valuing women's voices. The notion of valuing women's voices has led to further theorizing on women's ways of knowing (Belenky, Clinchy, Goldberger, & Tarule, 1986), with a focus on connected knowing, or relational development (Jordan, Kaplan, Miller, Stiver, & Surrey, 1991; Jordan, Walker, & Hartling, 2004). These theorists posit that women's ways of thinking and relating grow out of their experiences in families and schools that devalue them and their ideas, thus compelling women to work in collaboration with others in a connected community where they learn through sharing and listening to others, and women's ideas are valued. Ultimately, women have a predisposition for connection with others that affects their communication behavior (Belenky et al., Jordan et al., 1991, 2004).

Much research has focused on the notion that men and women communicate in different ways on the basis of their different orientations. Robin Lakoff (1975) began the focus on sex differences in communication styles by asserting that women's speech is overly polite, hesitant, and deferential, and, as a result, ineffective. Her analysis sparked the assertiveness training movement, designed to cure women of their poor communication styles (see Crawford, 1995, for a full discussion of the assertiveness training movement). More recently, Deborah Tannen (1990, 2002) has received substantial attention both in the academic literature and the popular media for her work on sex differences in communication. According to Tannen, boys and girls grow up in different environments that require them to use language for different purposes. Girls use language to seek confirmation and reinforce intimacy, usually in dyadic or small group situations. In contrast, boys interact in larger groups and use language to protect their independence and negotiate status in the group. These patterns of communication are learned in childhood and become a part of women's and men's interaction styles in adulthood. Similar to the analyses of Chodorow and Rubin, Tannen posits that women's language centers on connection and intimacy. Women use language to negotiate friendship networks, minimize differences among network members, and avoid status hierarchies. Men's language, in contrast, centers on maintaining independence as a means of establishing their place in the status hierarchy. As a result, Tannen argues that men and women not only use language differently, but they interpret conversations differently. What is offensive from one perspective is completely logical from the other, thus leading to conflict. Tannen proposes that the solution requires men and women to understand the underlying differences that motivate their divergent conversational styles, and then accept these differences as fundamental and nonchangeable.

Social Structural Approaches

The individual differences approach to understanding sex differences and similarities in behavior met with much criticism from psychologists who felt that sex differences were being exaggerated and politicized (e.g., Crawford, 1989;

Marecek, Kimmel, Crawford, & Hare-Mustin, 2003). Specifically, empirical psychologists argued that the consideration of sex as a biological category does not recognize social structural differences (i.e., situational and social cultural differences in contextual factors) in the experiences of women and men. Researchers were focusing on person-based causes of differences instead of examining the social, historical, and cultural forces that underlie these apparent differences, such as the uneven balance of power between women and men, which may be more predictive of behavior (Bohan, 2002; Crawford, 1989, 1995, 2001; Hare-Mustin & Marecek, 1988, 1990; Marecek et al.; Yoder & Kahn, 1992). Including social structural factors allows researchers to find possible underlying mechanisms of emerging individual differences (Fine & Gordon, 1989; Hare-Mustin & Marecek, 1988, 1990).

The social structural approach emerged to encompass sociocultural variables into theories designed to explain sex differences and similarities in behavior. Unger (1979) proposed that we use the term *sex* to refer to biological mechanisms and physiological differences between women and men, but we use the term *gender* to refer to the "nonphysiological components of sex that are culturally regarded as appropriate to males or to females" (Unger, p. 1086). However, this terminology does not solve the problem of determining which differences are due to sex and which are due to gender. At the core of this confusion is the difficulty in determining causality, as the mechanisms underlying most behaviors likely have both biological and sociocultural components (Deaux, 1993; Marecek et al., 2003; Unger & Crawford, 1993).

Power, status, and social roles have emerged as variables of particular interest in the literature on social structural approaches to studying sex and gender (Conway & Vartanian, 2000; Eagly, 1983, 1987; Henley, 1977; Sagrestano, 1992a, 1992b; Sagrestano, Heavey, & Christensen, 1999; Sherif, 1982; Unger, 1978; Wallston, 1987; Yoder & Kahn, 1992). One major theory that exemplifies the social structural approach is the social role model (Eagly, & Koenig, chap. 9, this volume). According to the social role model, men and women are differentially distributed into social roles, with men tending to occupy higher status roles than women. High status has been found to be associated with expectations of high competence, and men are perceived to be more competent than women (Conway & Vartanian; Wood & Karten, 1986). As a result of the unequal distribution of men and women into social roles, individuals perceive women as more easily influenced than men because lower status individuals are seen as more easily influenced (Eagly & Wood, 1982), and recent evidence suggests that men are more influential than women (Carli, 2001). In addition, Eagly suggests that the distribution of women and men into social roles underlies current gender stereotypes. For example, people in homemaker roles (usually women) are regarded as more communal, whereas people in employee occupations are perceived as more agentic (Conway & Vartanian; Eagly & Steffen, 1984). This hierarchical distribution leads to social norms that legitimize the unequal status of women and men. This legitimization may lead to a type of self-fulfilling prophesy in which expectancies about men and women are played out in interactions that confirm expectations and therefore maintain them (Eagly, 1983, 1987; Eagly, Wood, & Diekman, 2000). The social role model suggests that, as men's and women's roles change, sex differences will also change, such that as women gain status in society, sex differences will decrease (Eagly, 1983; Eagly et al., 2000).

The exploration of the effects of social structural variables on communication was sparked, in part, by Nancy Henley's (1977) book *Body Politics*, in which she outlined how those with power use language to maintain the social hierarchy. For example, those with power or authority often touch their subordinates, but subordinates rarely touch their supervisors. As men tend to hold higher status positions, they tend to touch others more often. When the balance of power is more evenly distributed, sex differences are reduced. Although Henley's original analysis pertained to nonverbal communication, her argument is equally relevant to verbal forms of communication (Crawford, 1995, 2001; Thorne, Kramarae, & Henley, 1983). Crawford and Henley have argued that very little evidence exists to support the notion that women and men use language differently (Crawford, 1995, 2001; Henley & Kramarae, 1991). Instead, differences can be explained as *transactional*. In other words, observed differences between men and women are not a function of sex; they are a function of situations and interactions that promote certain types of behaviors while suppressing other types of behaviors. For example, situations in which men routinely have more power than women may constrain women from touching men more than they constrain men from touching women. Therefore, these types of "sex differences" are not rooted in early socialization, as is argued in an individual differences approach, but rather in social power and how it shapes our verbal and nonverbal language. By focusing on sex, rather than other social structural variables (e.g., power relationships), social structural variables become "invisible" (Crawford, 1995, 2001).

It is possible to conduct research in which the individual differences and the social structural approaches are compared and contrasted. In the following sections, we present two programs of research in the area of communication and conflict interaction that have addressed these issues.

THE DEMAND–WITHDRAW INTERACTION PATTERN IN MARITAL CONFLICT

One of the earliest empirical studies of marriage (Terman, Buttenwieser, Ferguson, Johnson, & Wilson, 1938) found that wives often complained that their husbands were emotionally or physically withdrawn, whereas husbands complained about feeling pressured and nagged by their wives. More recent studies have indicated that women tend to be more conflict engaging and coercive whereas men are more pacifying and withdrawing (see review by Gottman & Levenson, 1988). In our own studies of the demand–withdraw interaction pattern (a pattern in which one partner tries to discuss problems, criticizes and blames the partner for the problems, and requests or demands change whereas the other partner tries to avoid discussion of the problems, defends self against the criticisms, and withdraws from the discussion), we have consistently found that women are more likely to be demanding and men withdrawing, whether demand and withdraw are assessed with self-report measures (Christensen, 1987; Christensen & Shenk, 1991) or observational measures (Christensen & Heavey, 1990; Heavey, Christensen, & Malamuth, 1995; Heavey, Layne, & Christensen, 1993).

What leads to this asymmetry in interaction and its association with sex? Why does one partner demand and the other withdraw, and why is the former usually the woman and the latter the man? To answer this question, we first need to make an important distinction between the structure of conflict and the process of conflict (Christensen & Heavey, 1993). By *structure* of conflict, we mean the conflict of interest between people (Peterson, 1983), that is, the differences between them that create a problem or dilemma for them. By the *process* of conflict, we mean the overt conflictual interaction that takes place between them. For example, a couple may have a structural conflict about how much time they should spend with wife's family of origin. She wants to spend a lot of time; he wants to spend little time with them. The process of their conflict refers to how they solve this problem through their interaction. For example, one could regularly give in to the other but pout about it, they could mutually criticize each other for their positions, either one could try to gently persuade the other, and so forth.

A frequent structural conflict in marriage concerns the amount of closeness or intimacy that spouses desire in their relationship (Caughlin & Vangelisti, 2000; Christensen, 1987; Jacobson, 1989). We reasoned that this conflict might lead to a conflict process of demand–withdraw interaction. The spouse wanting greater closeness might engage in demanding behaviors because these behaviors could bring about closeness—trying to talk to the other about the problem, criticizing the other for his or her distance, and requesting or demanding greater closeness. However, the partner wanting greater distance might naturally engage in withdrawing behaviors to achieve distance—avoiding conversation, defending one's position regarding distance, and withdrawing from any conversation about distance. On the basis of the work of Miller (1976), Chodorow (1978), and Rubin (1983) described earlier, we also reasoned that women would be more likely than men to want greater closeness and intimacy. Therefore, women would more likely demand because of women's greater interest in closeness and intimacy.

To test this idea, we developed a measure of conflict over closeness and intimacy (Christensen, 1987). In three studies, we have shown that the amount of structural conflict regarding closeness is positively correlated with the total amount of demand–withdraw interaction (Christensen, 1987; Christensen & Shenk, 1991; Walczynski, Schmidt, Christensen, & Sweeney, 1991). That is, couples who reported discrepancies in their desired closeness (more time together, more sharing of feelings) and independence (more time alone, more privacy) were more likely to report engaging in the demand–withdraw interaction pattern. We have also found that women want greater closeness, and, in spouses, but not dating couples, those who want greater closeness are more likely occupy the demanding role (Christensen; Walczynski et al.). Similarly, research by Caughlin and Vangelisti (2000) indicated that, for both husbands and wives, a desire for closeness was positively correlated with demanding and negatively correlated with withdrawing. Although we can only speculate about why this pattern appears to apply to spouses but not dating partners, it may be that the lower level of commitment generally present in dating relationships serves as a prohibition against demanding greater closeness. In other words, in dating relationships, the degree of closeness and commitment can be understood as being actively negotiated, whereas spouses are likely to feel freer to demand the closeness that they believe they were promised in the agreement to marry. It may also be that, in dating relationships, the expectation is that men are the pursuers and this pattern is a counterforce to the usual demand–withdraw pattern.

Despite its importance, conflict over closeness is hardly the only conflict that troubles relational partners. Other conflicts also likely lead to the demand–withdraw interaction pattern. We reasoned that conflicts of interest, such as the conflict over closeness, in which there was an asymmetry in dependence on the partner for resolution of the conflict, would lead to demand–withdraw interaction. By asymmetry of dependence we mean that the actor can only achieve resolution of the conflict with the partner's cooperation, but the partner can achieve resolution of the conflict without the actor's cooperation. For example, in the conflict over closeness, the person wanting greater closeness (i.e., the actor) can only achieve that goal with the partner's cooperation. However, the partner, who wants greater distance, can achieve that unilaterally. Conflicts of interest with asymmetry of dependence can be distinguished from conflicts of interest with symmetrical dependence. For example, if Marge wants to spend the Christmas holidays with her family and Joe wants to spend them with his family and they both want to be together for these holidays, then there is a conflict with symmetrical dependence. Both Marge and Joe are dependent on the other for the successful resolution of the conflict. Neither can unilaterally achieve his or her goal.

We reasoned that in a conflict with asymmetrical dependence, the actor, who needed the partner's cooperation for resolution of the conflict, would likely engage in demanding behavior. However, the partner, who can achieve need satisfaction without the actor, would likely engage in withdrawing behavior. To test these ideas, we conducted three studies in which we compared spouses' interactions under two conditions—one in which they discussed an issue identified by the wife and one in which they discussed an issue identified by the husband (Christensen & Heavey, 1990; Heavey, 1991; Heavey et al., 1993). We solicited issues in which the husband or wife wanted change in the other, because these kinds of issues represent unequal dependence. If the wife selects an issue in which she wants change in her husband, then she is dependent on him to make the change. He is not dependent on her to make a change in himself and is presumably more likely to favor the status quo of no change or is at least less invested in change than is his wife.

We tested two competing hypotheses. From a social structural approach, we would expect to find that each partner was more likely to demand on her or his own issue and withdraw on the partner's issue. However, if the conflict interaction process operates independently from the structure of the conflict but is instead tied directly to the sex or personality of the participants, then we would expect to find each partner having a similar, stable level of demand and withdraw across the two interactions. Thus, our study was directly testing a social structural versus individual differences approach.

In the first study, Christensen and Heavey (1990) examined data from 31 couples who had a boy aged 7 to 12 in a summer camp program. Because the study was conducted as part of this summer camp program, our focus was on changes in parenting. We asked each parent to rate how much change she or he would like in five areas of childrearing by the partner (e.g., being more positive with son, being more strict or consistent with son). We then asked parents to discuss the area in which they had made the most extreme rating (i.e., they wanted the most change from their partner in this area). Results on both the self-report and observational measures indicated that the nature of the discussion shifted dramatically depending on what issue was discussed. Overall, a main effect emerged such that husbands and wives were more demanding on their own issues and more withdrawing on their partner's issues. However, an interaction effect emerged in which on wives' issues, wife demand–husband withdraw was much more likely than the reverse, whereas on husband's issues, there were no differences between wife demand–husband withdraw and the reverse.

This study was limited by an exclusive focus on childrearing issues. Because childrearing has often been the primary province of the wife, perhaps wives have a greater investment in change on these issues. This disparity in the investment in these issues may have resulted in greater polarization on wives' issues than on husbands' issues. To correct this problem, we conducted a second study on 29 couples, each with a preschool-age child (Heavey et al., 1993), but we had husbands and wives both rate the amount of change they each wanted on 20 common areas of change in marriage that were not limited to childrearing issues (e.g., more affection, more time together). We selected issues for discussion that had the highest equivalent ratings of change (e.g., the husband's issue and the wife's issue had the same rating of change). In this way we hoped to ensure equal investment in change by both husband and wife. Despite this improvement in methodology, the results were essentially the same as in the first study on both self-report and observational measures. Spouses changed their interaction when they discussed different issues; they showed polarization in demand–withdraw on the wives' issues, but not as much on the husbands' issues.

In the third study in this series (Heavey, 1991), we moved from a strict focus on change in partner because, when we asked partners to talk about a specific change they wanted in the other, we may have prompted them to be demanding. Instead, couples rated their dissatisfaction with a number of content areas such as finances and physical affection. The husband's issue was identified as the area in which he rated the most dissatisfaction; the wife's issue was the area in which she rated the most dissatisfaction. When the experimenters gave instructions to the couples, they asked them to discuss these content areas but did not specifically instruct them to try to change their partners. Despite this different methodology (and a somewhat different observational coding system), the results were similar to those of the previous studies.

These three studies have consistently demonstrated an effect of conflict structure on demand–withdraw interaction. When partners discuss their own issue, they more likely demand, but when they discuss their partner's issue, they more likely withdraw. However, we found a greater polarization of demand–withdraw interaction when partners focused on women's issues than when they focussed on men's issues. That is, when discussing wives' issues, wives were much more likely to be demanding and husbands withdrawing than the reverse, whereas when discussing husbands' issues, the likelihood that husbands and wives would be demanding or withdrawing was quite similar. Furthermore, a review of the results of all three studies indicates that the effect of social structure (whose issue was being discussed) was consistently larger than the effect of gender (the general tendency of men to withdraw more and women to demand more).

Research by others has confirmed the importance of social structure. For example, Holzworth-Munroe, Smutzler, and Stuart (1998) found that partners demanded more on their own issues and withdrew more on their partners' issues. Furthermore, in violent distressed marriages, couples exhibited more demanding and more withdrawing than in nonviolent, nondistressed couples. In particular, violent couples, whether distressed or not, showed the highest levels of husband demand–wife withdraw. Klinetob and Smith (1996) found that, on men's issues, a pattern of husband demand, wife withdraw emerged, whereas on women's issues, a pattern of wife demand–husband withdraw emerged. A close examination of their findings, however, revealed a pattern of polarization similar to the findings of Heavey et al. (1993) that did not emerge in the studies by Holtzworth-Munroe et al. (1998). Furthermore, Caughlin and Vangelisti (1999) examined six "typical" relationship issues and found evidence for polarization by using both concurrent self-report measures and observational measures.

The problem remains of explaining the greater polarization that occurs in demand–withdraw interaction on women's issues versus men's issues. One explanation may have to do with amount of change desired. Earlier we described data suggesting that women want more closeness in marriage than do men. Considerable data also demonstrate that women do the burden of housework and child care, even when both spouses are employed full time outside the home (Biernat & Wortman, 1991; Hochschild, 1989). Therefore, it is not surprising that women in general (versus men) want more changes in marriage (e.g., Margolin & Weinstein,

1983, although Caughlin & Vangelisti, 1999 find no differences in desire for change on prototypical interpersonal conflict issues). Often the kinds of changes that a wife seeks are that her husband have a closer relationship with her and be more involved in child care and housework. These changes can only be achieved with the husband's cooperation. However, if the husband does not want a closer relationship or greater involvement in housework or child care, he can simply not engage in the requisite behaviors. This conflict structure is precisely the kind that our studies suggest would elicit demands by the partner wanting change and withdrawing behavior by the partner not wanting change. If women seek more change, then they would more commonly be in the demanding role, potentially establishing a stronger pattern of wife demand–husband withdraw overall (that emerges even in situations in which husbands are seeking change—note that it didn't emerge in situations in which husbands were seeking change—in those situations, demand and withdraw were used equally by both partners).

A second explanation may have to do with resources. Given that men tend to have greater resources in the marital relationship, they may be able to structure the relationship as they want. As a consequence of this difference, couples may have been more successful in resolving men's issues and accommodating men's needs over time. If women have deferred to men's wishes more often than men have deferred to women's wishes, then a pattern may have emerged in which women comply with men's desires for change more quickly and with less conflict than men comply with women's desires for change. Over time, this difference may result in women's desiring more change in the relationship, and more expressed conflict over women's issues. Therefore, a greater degree of polarization could be expected to develop as a pattern over time with women's issues.

Comparisons of our studies with those finding the complete role-reversal pattern (i.e., on women's issues, wives demand and husbands withdraw, whereas on men's issues, husbands demand and wives withdraw) indicate that, as marriage increases in length, there is less of a role reversal (Eldridge & Christensen, 2002). In other words, early on in marriage, before there has been much opportunity for patterns to emerge and become ingrained, a role-reversal pattern is common. In contrast, later in marriage, as patterns emerge and become habitual, greater polarization is evident. This explanation is consistent with a social structural view; that is, men's greater power in the social structure leads to different reactions to men's versus women's needs and desires for change. Over time, these lead to specific patterns of behavior that are replicated in future conflicts.

Similarly, if women have simply had more desires for change than have men, then couples are more likely to have had discussions around wives' desired changes than around husbands' desired changes. The greater frequency of discussion around these issues may lead to greater polarization in the stands that husbands and wives take. Thus, over time, one might expect more conflict and greater polarization over women's issues. This explanation is more consistent with an individual differences approach, suggesting that women in general want more from relationships than men, which leads to differences in behavior. However, the underlying reason for women's wanting more change and men's wanting less change in the relationship may be socially determined rather than inherent to women. Thus, these explanations are not mutually exclusive; it is possible that both may find some support. Future empirical work is needed to shed light on these questions.

SOCIAL INFLUENCE BEHAVIOR

The study of social influence is a second body of research that has examined individual differences and social structural explanations of sex differences and similarities in conflict behavior. Much of the research on the use of social influence techniques has focused on individual differences, and, in particular, sex differences (Carli, 1999; Falbo & Peplau, 1980; Kelley et al., 1978; Witteman & Fitzpatrick, 1986). For example, Falbo and Peplau found that, in a study of dating couples, men used more direct and bilateral techniques, whereas women used more indirect and unilateral techniques to influence their partners. From a social structural perspective, researchers have focused on power and social roles (Howard, Blumstein, & Schwartz, 1986; Kipnis, Schmidt, & Wilkinson, 1980; Orina, Wood, & Simpson, 2002; Trentham & Larwood, 2001), and they have typically concluded that social roles play an important part in the choice of influence techniques. However, few studies have simultaneously examined sex, social roles, and the use of social influence techniques. A qualitative study conducted by Mainiero (1986) found that men and women in more powerful positions were more persistent in their influence attempts then those in less powerful positions; however, women were less persistent than men when in less powerful positions. Similarly, in a study of visual dominance (Dovidio, Ellyson, Keating, Heltman, & Brown, 1988), no gender differences in use of visual dominance (defined as the ratio of looking while speaking to looking while listening) emerged among those in high power positions, whereas men used more visual dominance displays than did women when in low power positions. These findings, although not specifically addressing social influence techniques, indicate that influence behaviors are determined by both gender and social roles. To address this gap in the literature, we conducted a series of studies to examine sex, social roles, and social influence in peer and marital relationships. These studies were designed to compare hypotheses derived from social structural and individual differences perspectives.

In the first study (Sagrestano, 1992a), college students responded to a series of scenarios in which social power was manipulated by means of expertise, which has been shown to be related to persuasiveness in previous research (French & Raven, 1959; Maddux & Rogers, 1980). Men and women responded to three scenarios wherein they interacted with an imagined partner in situations in which they had different levels of interpersonal power: more power than their partner (expert), less power (novice), and the same amount of power (equivalent). The dyads were either same sex or mixed sex. No sex differences in the use of influence were found, and both men and women chose the same five techniques most often: persuading, reasoning, discussing, asking, and persisting. However, direct techniques were more often used when participants had expert power over their partners, and bilateral techniques were the first choice of participants in the equivalent condition.

This study provided preliminary support for a social structural interpretation of the use of social influence techniques in nonintimate relationships. However, the self-report data and hypothetical nature limit the extent to which conclusions can be drawn about actual behavior. Therefore, we next designed a laboratory simulation in which we examined sex, social roles, and the use of influence by using mixed-sex and same-sex dyads (Sagrestano, 1993). In this study, participants completed pretest questionnaires to determine their attitudes on a set of controversial issues. They were then matched into same-sex and mixed-sex dyads such that they disagreed on the topic of discussion, and they were scheduled for the laboratory portion of the study. Social roles were manipulated through expertise, such that one participant was trained to be more expert on the topic than the other. Participants spent 10 minutes discussing the topic and trying to persuade their partners to agree with them, and the interactions were coded for the use of influence techniques. Results indicated that expertise, but not sex, predicted the use of influence techniques. Furthermore, men and women in positions of high and low expertise power used techniques in similar sequences (e.g., persuading, reasoning, discussing, asking, and persisting).

Although this second study provided additional support for a social structural interpretation of influence technique use in nonintimate relationships, both of the aforementioned studies examined influence in settings depicting clear power differences. Furthermore, participants in the observational study met in the laboratory and did not have expectations for their relationship continuing beyond the experiment. We therefore designed the third study to examine the use of influence in ongoing marital relationships in which the balance of power was not externally delineated.

The third study (Sagrestano, Christensen, & Heavey, 1998) used data from two existing studies already described here (Christensen & Heavey, 1990; Heavey et al., 1993) to examine how social roles affect the use of social influence. We believe that social roles are conceptually linked to the power structure of the relationship. More specifically, we would argue that power in close relationships operates on at least two levels: the overarching balance of power and domain-specific power that is manifested at the situational level (see Sagrestano et al. for a more in-depth discussion of this issue). Given that power and social roles are not clearly defined in most close relationships, we chose to focus on a situational manipulation of social roles. However, we recognize that this approach does not allow for an examination of the effects of the overarching balance of power.

As we described herein, spouses spent time discussing two issues in their marriage: one in which the wife wanted change in the husband, and one in which the husband wanted change in the wife. This created two alternate roles for the partners. In each discussion, one person enacted the role of seeking change, whereas the partner enacted the role of being asked to change, and perhaps trying to avoid being influenced. Results replicating across both data sets supported a social structural perspective. Social roles, operationalized as who was seeking change during a particular interaction, were related to the use of influence techniques (effect sizes: $d = 0.39$–0.83; $r = .19$–$.38$), whereas sex was not (e.g., partners seeking change engaged in more explaining of behavior, defending behavior, and suggesting change; partners resisting change engaged in more questioning to clarify problems and use of self-attributions). These results suggest that men and women do not differ in their choice of influence techniques, but rather that, when men and women occupy similar social roles, they behave in similar fashion.

CONCLUSION

Research on the demand–withdraw interaction pattern supports both the individual differences approach and the social structural approach with regard to sex differences in communication. Specifically, in asymmetrical dependence situations, when partners discuss their own topics they are more likely to demand, whereas when discussing their partner's issues they are more likely to withdraw. This supports a social structural perspective in which the context of the goals of the interaction predicts demand–withdraw behavior. However, the demand–withdraw interaction pattern is more polarized on women's issues than on men's issues. That is, men and women are more likely to conform to rigid demand–withdraw patterns when the woman is requesting the man to change than when the man is requesting the woman to change. From a social structural perspective, this may reflect a pattern that has developed over time as a result of general asymmetry in the relationship. From an individual differences perspective, this may reflect a sex difference in relationship expectations resulting in women desiring more change. However, these two interpretations are confounded in that women's greater need for change may be the result of a general power asymmetry in the relationship, as well. Unfortunately, participants in marital research cannot be randomly assigned to be in the traditionally higher or lower power position (i.e., husband or wife), and, therefore, neither a social structural explanation nor an individual differences explanation can ever be ruled out. However, further research with same-sex intimate couples may help to further disentangle these effects.

The research on social influence can partially address the problem of random assignment in that two of the studies were conducted in peer relationships. By examining both same-sex and mixed-sex dyads, we could examine the role of broader asymmetry in the balance of power between women and men. The overwhelming lack of sex differences across individuals and dyads provides support for a social structural interpretation. This was further augmented by our marital studies of social influence, in which sex differences again did not emerge.

These findings point out the importance of considering both individual difference and social structural variables when conducting research. An individual differences perspective tends to neglect within-group variability, whereas a social structural perspective tends to neglect between-group variability. Inclusion of both types of variables allows researchers to avoid both exaggerating and minimizing sex differences by examining the effects of each simultaneously. In doing so, we would be better able to understand the emerging pattern of sex differences and similarities in communication behavior.

REFERENCES

Belenky, M. F., Clinchy, B. M., Goldberger, N. R., & Tarule, J. M. (1986). *Women's ways of knowing: The development of self, voice, and mind*. New York: Basic Books.

Biernat, M., & Wortman, C. B. (1991). Sharing of home responsibilities between professionally employed women and their husbands. *Journal of Personality and Social Psychology, 60*, 844–860.

Bohan, J. S. (2002). Sex differences and/in the self: Classic themes, feminist variations, postmodern challenges. *Psychology of Women Quarterly, 26*, 74–88.

Carli, L. L. (1999). Gender, interpersonal power, and social influence. *Journal of Social Issues, 55*, 81–99.

Carli, L. L. (2001). Gender and social influence. *Journal of Social Issues, 57*, 725–741.

Caughlin, J. P., & Vangelisti, A. L. (1999). Desire for change in one's partner as a predictor of the demand/withdraw pattern of marital communication. *Communication Monographs, 66*, 66–89.

Caughlin, J. P., & Vangelisti, A. L. (2000). An individual difference explanation of why married couples engage in the demand/withdraw pattern of conflict. *Journal of Social and Personal Relationships, 17*, 523–551.

Chodorow, N. (1978). *The reproduction of motherhood: Psychoanalysis and the sociology of gender*. Berkeley: University of California Press.

Christensen, A. (1987). Detection of conflict patterns in couples. In K. Hahlweg & M. J. Goldstein (Eds.), *Understanding major mental disorder: The contribution of family interaction research* (pp. 251–265). New York: Family Process.

Christensen, A., & Heavey, C. L. (1990). Gender and social structure in the demand/withdraw pattern of marital conflict. *Journal of Personality and Social Psychology, 59*, 73–81.

Christensen, A., & Heavey, C. L. (1993). Gender differences in marital conflict: The case of the demand/withdraw interaction pattern. In S. Oskamp & M. Costanzo (Eds.), *Gender issues in contemporary society* (pp. 113–141). Newbury Park, CA: Sage.

Christensen, A., & Shenk, J. L. (1991). Communication, conflict, and psychological distance in nondistressed, clinic, and divorcing couples. *Journal of Consulting and Clinical Psychology, 59*, 458–463.

Conway, M., & Vartanian, L. R. (2000). A status account of gender stereotypes: Beyond communality and agency. *Sex Roles, 43*, 181–199.

Crawford, M. (1989). Agreeing to differ: Femininst epistemologies and women's ways of knowing. In M. Crawford & M. Gentry (Eds.), *Gender and thought: Psychological perspectives* (pp. 128–145). New York: Springer-Verlag.

Crawford, M. (1995). *Talking difference: On gender and language*. Thousand Oaks, CA: Sage.

Crawford, M. (2001). Gender and language. In R. K. Unger (Ed.), *Handbook of the psychology of women and gender* (pp. 228–244). New York: Wiley.

Deaux, K. (1993). Commentary: Sorry, wrong number—a reply to Gentile's call. *Psychological Science, 4*, 125–126.

Dovidio, J. F., Ellyson, S. L., Keating, C. F., Heltman, K., & Brown, C. E. (1988). The relationship of social power to visual displays of dominance between men and women. *Journal of Personality and Social Psychology, 54*, 233–242.

Eagly, A. H. (1983). Gender and social influence: A social psychological analysis. *American Psychologist, 38*, 971–981.

Eagly, A. H. (1987). *Sex differences in social behavior: A social role interpretation.* Hillsdale, NJ: Lawrence Erlbaum Associates.

Eagly, A. H., & Steffen, V. J. (1984). Gender stereotypes stem from the distribution of women and men into social roles. *Journal of Personality and Social Psychology, 4*, 735–754.

Eagly, A. H., & Wood, W. (1982). Inferred sex differences in status as a determinant of gender stereotypes about social influence. *Journal of Personality and Social Psychology, 43*, 915–928.

Eldridge, K. A., & Christensen, A. (2002). Demand–withdraw communication during couple conflict: A review and analysis. In P. Noller & J. A. Feeney (Eds.), *Understanding marriage* (pp. 289–322). Cambridge, England: Cambridge University Press.

Falbo, T., & Peplau, L. A. (1980). Power strategies in intimate relationships. *Journal of Personality and Social Psychology, 38*, 618–628.

Feingold, A. (1995). The additive effects of differences in central tendency and variablity are important in comparisons between groups. *American Psychologist, 50*, 5–13.

Fine, M., & Gordon, S. M. (1989). Feminist transitions of/despite psychology. In M. Crawford & M. Gentry (Eds.), *Gender and thought: Psychological perspectives* (pp. 146–174). New York: Springer-Verlag.

French, J. R., & Raven, B. (1959). The bases of social power. In D. Cartwright (Ed.), *Studies in social power* (pp. 150–167). Ann Arbor: University of Michigan.

Gilligan, C. (1982). *In a different voice: Psychological theory and women's development.* Cambridge, MA: Harvard University Press.

Gottman, J. M. (2001). Crime, hostility, wife battering, and the heart: On the Meehan et al. (2001) failure to replicate the Gottman et al. (1995) typology. *Journal of Family Psychology, 15*, 409–414.

Gottman, J. M., Jacobson, N. S., Rushe, R. H., Shortt, J. W., Babcock, J., La Taillade, J. J., et al. (1995). The relationship between heart rate reactivity, emotionally aggressive behavior, and general violence in batterers. *Journal of Family Psychology, 9*, 227–248.

Gottman, J. M., & Levenson, R. W. (1988). The social psychophysiology of marriage. In P. Noller & M. Fitzpatrick (Eds.), *Perspectives on marital interaction* (pp. 182–200). Philadelphia: Multilingual Matters.

Gray, J. (1992). *Men are from Mars, Women are from Venus. A practical guide to improving communication and getting what you want in your relationships.* New York: HarperCollins.

Hare-Mustin, R. T., & Marecek, J. (1988). The meaning of difference: Gender theory, postmodernism, and psychology. *American Psychologist, 43*, 455–464.

Hare-Mustin, R. T., & Marecek, J. (Eds.). (1990). *Making a difference: Psychology and the construction of gender.* New Haven, CT: Yale University Press.

Heavey, C. L. (1991). *Causes and consequences of destructive conflicts in romantic relationships: Cognitive, affective, and behavioral predictors of course and outcome.* Unpublished doctoral dissertation, University of California, Los Angeles.

Heavey, C. L., Christensen, A., & Malamuth, N. M. (1995). The longitudinal impact of demand and withdrawal during marital conflict. *Journal of Consulting and Clinical Psychology, 63*, 797–801.

Heavey, C. L., Layne, C., & Christensen, A. (1993). Gender and conflict structure in maritial interaction: A replication and extension. *Journal of Consulting and Clinical Psychology, 61*, 16–27.

Henley, N. M. (1977). *Body politics: Power, sex, and nonverbal communication*. Englewood Cliffs, NJ: Prentice-Hall.

Henley, N. M., & Kramarae, C. (1991). Gender, power, and miscommunication. In N. Coupland, H. Giles, & J. M. Wiemann (Eds.), *'Miscommunication' and problematic talk* (pp. 18–43). Newbury Park, CA: Sage.

Hochschild, A. R. (1989). *The second shift: Working parents and the revolution at home*. New York: Viking.

Holtzworth-Munroe, A., Smutzler, N., & Stuart, G. L. (1998). Demand and withdraw communication among couples experiencing husband violence. *Journal of Consulting and Clinical Psychology, 66*, 731–743.

Howard, J. A., Blumstein, P., & Schwartz, P. (1986). Sex, power, and influence tactics in intimate relationships. *Journal of Personality and Social Psychology, 51*, 102–109.

Jacobson, N. (1989). The maintenance of treatment gains following social learning-based marital therapy. *Behavior Therapy, 20*, 325–336.

Jordan, J. V., Kaplan, A. G., Miller, J. B., Stiver, I. P., & Surrey, J. L. (1991). *Women's growth in connection: Writings from the Stone Center*. New York: Guilford.

Jordan, J. V., Walker, M., & Hartling, L. M. (Eds.). (2004). *The complexity of connection: Writings from the Stone Center's Jean Baker Miller Training Institute*. New York: Guilford.

Kelley, H. H., Cunningham, J. D., Grisham, J. A., Lefebvre, L. M., Sink, C. R., & Yablon, G. (1978). Sex differences in comments made during conflict within close heterosexual pairs. *Sex Roles, 4*, 473–492.

Kipnis, D., Schmidt, S. M., & Wilkinson, I. (1980). Intraorganizational influence tactics: Explorations in getting one's way. *Journal of Applied Psychology, 65*, 440–452.

Klinetob, N. A., & Smith, D. A. (1996). Demand–withdraw communications in marital interaction: Tests of interspousal contingency and gender role hypotheses. *Journal of Marriage and the Family, 58*, 945–957.

Lakoff, R. (1975). *Language and women's place*. New York: Harper & Row.

Levenson, R. W., Carstensen, L. L., & Gottman, J. M. (1994). The influence of age and gender on affect, physiology, and their intercorrelations: A study of long-term marriages. *Journal of Personality and Social Psychology, 67*, 56–68.

Maddux, J. E., & Rogers, R. W. (1980). Effects of source expertness, physical attractiveness. and supporting arguments on persuasion: A case of brains over beauty. *Journal of Personality and Social Psychology, 39*, 235–244.

Mainiero, L. A. (1986). Coping with powerlessness: The relationship of gender and job dependency to empowerment-strategy usage. *Administrative Science Quarterly, 31*, 633–653.

Marecek, J., Kimmel, E. B., Crawford, M., & Hare-Mustin, R. T. (2003). Psychology of women and gender. In D. K. Freedheim & I. B. Weiner (Eds.), *Handbook of psychology* (Vol. 1, pp. 249–268). New York: Wiley.

Margolin, G., & Weinstein, C. D. (1983). Areas of change questionnaire: A practical approach to marital assessment. *Journal of Consulting and Clinical Psychology, 51*, 920–931.

Meehan, J., & Holtzworth-Munroe, A. (2001). Heart rate reactivity in male batterers: A second look at the evidence. *Journal of Family Psychology, 15*, 415–424.

Meehan, J., Holtzworth-Munroe, A., & Herron, K. (2001). Maritally violent men's heart rate reactivity to marital interactions: A failure to replicate the Gottman et al. (1995) typology. *Journal of Family Psychology, 15*, 394–408.

Miller, J. B. (1976). *Toward a new psychology of women*. Boston: Beacon Press.

Orina, M. M., Wood, W., & Simpson, J. A. (2002). Strategies of influence in close relationships. *Journal of Experimental Social Psychology, 38*, 459–472.

Peterson, D. R. (1983). Conflict. In H. H. Kelly, E. Berscheid, A. Christensen, J. H. Harvey, T. L. Huston, G. Levinger, E. McClintock, L. A. Peplau, & D. R. Peterson (Eds.), *Close relationships* (pp. 360–396). New York: Freeman.

Rubin, L. B. (1983). *Intimate strangers: Men and women together*. New York: Harper & Row.

Sagrestano, L. M. (1992a). Power strategies in interpersonal relationships: The effects of expertise and gender. *Psychology of Women Quarterly, 16*, 481–496.

Sagrestano, L. M. (1992b). The use of power and influence in a gendered world. *Psychology of Women Quarterly, 16*, 439–448.

Sagrestano, L. M. (1993). *The effects of gender and power on the use of influence in interpersonal relationships*. Unpublished doctoral dissertation, University of California, Berkeley.

Sagrestano, L. M., Christensen, A., & Heavey, C. L. (1998). Social influence techniques during marital conflict. *Personal Relationships, 5*, 75–89.

Sagrestano, L. M., Heavey, C. L., & Christensen, A. (1999). Perceived power and physical violence in marital conflict. *Journal of Social Issues, 55*, 65–79.

Sherif, C. W. (1982). Needed concepts in the study of gender identity. *Psychology of Women Quarterly, 6*, 375–399.

Tannen, D. (1990). *You just don't understand*. New York: Ballantine.

Tannen, D. (2002). *I only say this because I love you: Talking to your parents, partner, sibs, and kids when you're all adults*. New York: Random House.

Terman, L. M., Buttenwieser, P., Ferguson, L. W., Johnson, W. B., & Wilson, D. P. (1938). *Psychological factors in marital happiness*. New York: McGraw-Hill.

Thorne, B., Kramarae, C., & Henley, N. M. (1983). *Language, gender, and society*. Rowley, MA: Newbury House.

Trentham, S., & Larwood, L. (2001). Power and gender influences on responsibility attributions: The case of disagreements in relationships. *Journal of Social Psychology, 141*, 730–751.

Unger, R. K. (1978). The politics of gender: A review of relevant literature. In J. A. Sherman & F. L. Denmark (Eds.), *The psychology of women: Future directions in research* (pp. 461–518). New York: Psychological Dimensions.

Unger, R. K. (1979). Toward a redefinition of sex and gender. *American Psychologist, 34*, 1085–1094.

Unger, R. K., & Crawford, M. (1993). Commentary: Sex and gender: The troubled relationship between terms and concepts. *Psychological Science, 4*, 122–124.

Walczynski, P. T., Schmidt, G. W., Christensen, A., & Sweeney, L. (1991, August). *Demand/withdraw interaction in dating couples*. Paper presented at the American Psychological Association, San Francisco.

Wallston, B. S. (1987). Social psychology of women and gender. *Journal of Applied Social Psychology, 17*, 1025–1050.

Witteman, H., & Fitzpatrick, M. A. (1986). Compliance-gaining in marital interaction: Power bases, processes, and outcomes. *Communication Monographs, 53*, 130–143.

Wood, W., & Karten, S. J. (1986). Sex differences in interaction style as a product of perceived sex differences in competence. *Journal of Personality and Social Psychology, 50*, 341–347.

Yoder, J. D., & Kahn, A. S. (1992). Toward a feminist understanding of women and power. *Psychology of Women Quarterly, 16*, 381–388.

21

Gender, Power, and Violence in Heterosexual Relationships

Julia T. Wood
University of North Carolina at Chapel Hill

- Once upon a time there was a beautiful maiden whose wicked stepmother locked her in a tower, where she stayed until a prince rescued her.
- Stand by your man.
- Elyse was beautiful but very poor when she took the job as housekeeper for Marcus Rockford, a rich, powerful business magnate.
- He will not always say, what you would have him say, but now and then he'll say something wonderful.

Do any of these sentences seem familiar? The first is a summary of the children's fairy tale, *Rapunzel*, in which a dashing young man rescues a beautiful, young maiden. The second is the key refrain in Tammy Wynett's blockbuster country song, "Stand By Your Man," which beseeches women to be loyal to men even when those men disrespect them. The third introduces the main characters in a prototypical romance novel, in which rich and powerful Marcus Rockford will sweep Elyse off her feet and save her from a life of poverty. The final line is from "Something Wonderful," a song that Anna sang in *The King and I* to explain why she would go along with the king although he was at times cruel and tyrannical.

Each of these lines reflects heterosexual romance narratives that are thoroughly ensconced in Western culture. The narratives teach us about relationships and about gendered identities—that is, what women and men are supposed to be and do and how they are supposed to relate to each other. Growing up with these narratives, we are encouraged to see men as strong, powerful, and able to rescue women from lonely towers, poverty, and other kinds of distress. The narratives also teach that a man may transgress, hurt a woman, or be abusive, and that a woman—at least a *good* woman—will "stand by" her man.

Western culture's romance narratives are not just the stuff of bodice-ripper novels, heartbreak songs, and fairy tales. They are also stories into which we may place ourselves and our relationships. They offer us characters, plot lines, and ready-made meanings for experiences that otherwise might be incoherent. They tell us what to expect in relationships, what is normal, and how we should respond to the (mis)behaviors of our partners. Although most people do not live by plot lines that include perpetrating and tolerating intimate partner violence, some do. In this chapter, my goal is to show that among the many romance and gender narratives circulating in Western culture, there are ones that allow intimate partner violence on which individual men and women may draw to make sense of violence in their relationships.

By way of further introduction to the themes of this chapter, let me offer excerpts from interviews I conducted with men who had perpetrated intimate partner violence (Wood, 2004) and women who had been targets of intimate partner violence (Wood, 2000, 2001).

Demetrius: I was the man in the relationship. I was always brought up like, a man's 'sposed to be more in control of a relationship. Things got to go my way or no way. I mean, I respect, respect a woman's opinion, but I just feel they had to go my way or no way at all. As far as a male, the worst thing you can do is hurt his pride. You just be prepared for war right there.

Ellen: I never, ever thought to blame him. I was, like, maybe I did something wrong; maybe I shouldn't have said that; maybe I just need to be quiet.... I had to be doing something wrong because nobody would just react like this for no reason.

Kordell: I punish her. I can take her to her limit 'cause she's in love with me now. She's gonna put up and put up and put up with me.

Vivian: I was raised old fashioned where you don't just walk out of a marriage. You stuck it out to the end, I don't care what you went through.

These four excerpts suggest the theme of this chapter: Intimate partner violence reflects, embodies, and reproduces codes of masculinity and femininity and gendered narratives of heterosexual romance that are deeply woven into the fabric of Western culture. Although clearly not everyone who embraces these narratives participates in violent relationships, well-established understandings of gender and romance allow for male violence against women. Demetrius makes it clear that he equates manhood with being in control, particularly of women. In five short sentences, Demetrius crystallizes a gender ideology that enables him to assume men are and should be dominant and women are and should be deferential. Ellen's statement suggests that she agrees with Demetrius about women's place relative to men. She believes that it is her fault if her partner is violent toward her, and she regards disciplining her as his right. Kordell subscribes to another aspect of gender ideology: that love is central in women's lives. Using this knowledge to control his partner, Kordell explains that once he gets a woman to love him, he can do whatever he wishes to her. As if in response, Vivian states that she is supposed to stay with her man, no matter what he does to her.

These statements from women and men reflect a shared gender ideology that claims it is natural for men to dominate women and equally natural for women to defer and remain loyal to men who harm them. The perspectives are complementary in that for some people they work together to construct men's intimate partner violence as justifiable and women's acceptance of that violence as consistent with a feminine desire to preserve relationships.

This chapter discusses intimate partner violence, a phenomenon that is widespread in Western culture. The first section of the chapter presents basic information on intimate partner violence and explains the chapter's primary attention to male perpetrators. The second section of the chapter highlights the gendered dynamics that inform intimate partner violence, arguing that dominant codes of masculinity, femininity, and heterosexual romance normalize men's domination and—in extreme cases—violence against wives and girlfriends and women's toleration of that violence. The chapter closes by identifying directions for future research.

INTIMATE PARTNER VIOLENCE: AN OVERVIEW

I begin my examination of intimate partner violence by asking what it is, whom it affects, and why researchers focus on male perpetrators of intimate partner violence.

What Is Intimate Partner Violence?

There is consensus that intimate partner violence includes physical assaults between spouses or romantic partners. Beyond that, there is not agreement on what counts as intimate partner violence. Some researchers adopt a broad definition that includes verbal aggression, psychological abuse, economic control, physical assault, and sexual violence (sometimes classified as distinct from physical assault). Other researchers and clinicians limit the term *violence* to physical acts of aggression such as beating, kicking, stabbing, and strangling. They acknowledge that nonphysical acts of aggression—verbal, for instance—are wrong and can be harmful, but they distinguish between physical violence and other kinds of abuse.

There are reasons why physical violence has emerged as the sine qua non of intimate partner violence. First, it is arguably the most severe and dramatic kind of aggression between intimates, so it compels attention. Because physical violence anchors an extreme end on the continuum of aggression, it stands out as particularly appalling. Second, physical violence exceeds and often encompasses other kinds of aggression. Whereas verbal and emotional abuse may occur without physical violence, physical violence is rarely unaccompanied by other kinds of abuse (Follingstad, Rutledge, Berg, Hause, & Polek, 1990). Third, physical violence can be more easily identified (e.g., evidence such as bruises and broken bones) and measured (types, severity, and impact) than other kinds of aggression. Because of its clarity and extremity, physical violence frequently serves as a reference point for assessing other kinds of aggression, or abuse, between intimates. Thus, researchers who claim that emotional abuse should be classified as intimate partner violence often build their argument by invoking the criteria used to assess physical violence—for instance, demonstrating that emotional assaults cause harm that is severe and measurable, albeit by different yardsticks than those used to measure physical violence. For all of these reasons, many researchers and clinicians reserve the term *violence* for physical assaults and use terms such as *aggression, domination*, *control*, and *abuse* for other kinds of harmful behaviors enacted and experienced by intimate partners.

Who Is Affected?

Intimate partner violence affects a wide range of people. Although some differences exist between groups, intimate partner violence cuts across lines of race and ethnicity (Cazenave & Straus, 1990; Holtzworth-Munroe, Smutzler, & Bates, 1997), sexual orientation (Barnett, Miller-Perrin, & Perrin, 1997), and economic class (Bachman & Saltzman, 1995; Goldner, Penn, Sheinberg, & Walker, 1990; Goode, 2001; Jacobson & Gurman, 1986). In addition, intimate partner violence is not restricted to adults. Between 12% and 36% of 14- to 18-year-old high school students report that they have perpetrated or been the target of physical violence from dating partners (Goode, 2001; Gray & Foshee, 1997).

Overall, at least 28% and possibly as many as 50% of women suffer intimate partner violence (Department of Justice, 2000; Jackman, 2003; May, 1998a, 1998b; Murphy-Milano, 1996). The number could be higher because only about 25% of physical assaults are reported (*Extent, Nature and Consequence*, 2000). National surveys report that nearly 25% of women and 30% of men regard violence as a normal and even a positive part of marriage (Jacobson & Gottman, 1998), which suggests that there is substantial acceptance of violence between spouses in our culture (Jones, 1994, 1998a, 1998b; Wood, 2001).

Why Focus on Male Perpetrators of Intimate Partner Violence?

A minority of researchers (DeKeseredy, Saunders, Schwartz, & Alvi, 1997; Frieze, 2000; O'Leary, 2000; Straus, 1993, 1999) assert that intimate partner violence is perpetrated fairly equally by men and women. That claim, however, is not accepted by a majority of clinicians and researchers (Christopher & Lloyd, 2000; Goldner et al., 1990; Holtzworth-Munroe, Smutzler, & Bates, 1997; Jacobson & Gottman, 1998; Johnson, 2001; Johnson & Ferraro, 2000).

The claim that men and women equally perpetuate intimate partner violence is particularly difficult to support when intimate partner violence is separated into distinct types. In 1995, Johnson identified two major subtypes of intimate partner violence: patriarchal terrorism and common couple violence. In more recent work, Johnson and his colleagues (Johnson, 2001; Johnson, Conklin, & Menon, 2002; Johnson & Ferraro, 2000) have modified the names for the original two types and expanded the typology to include four subtypes, which take context into account the following: (a) *situational couple violence*, initially called *common couple violence*, which occurs in the context of a noncontrolling relationship; (b) *violent resistance*, which is self-defense or fighting back against a violent, controlling partner; (c) *intimate terrorism*, initially called *patriarchal terrorism*, which is violence perpetrated by one partner who desires control over the other partner; and (d) *mutual violent control*, in which both partners are violent and controlling.

Johnson (2001) draws a particularly clear line between situational couple violence, which is more common, practiced by both sexes, and less likely to involve frequent or severe violence, and intimate terrorism in which one partner—usually the man—inflicts severe and multiple types of violence in order to control the other partner—usually a woman. A majority of those who distinguish among types of intimate partner violence concur that men are more likely than women to engage in the most severe types of violence and to cause greater injuries and deaths (Barnett et al., 1997; Christopher & Lloyd, 2000; Langley & Nada-Raja, 1997; Morse, 1995).

Existing work also indicates that men and women may have distinct motivations for engaging in intimate partner violence, and that the distinct motivations predispose men to engage in more and more severe violence against female partners than vice versa. Although both men and women may be motivated by anger and hurt, women are more likely than men to become violent in self-defense than in offense or to use violence to express fierce emotions (Archer, 2000a, 2000b; Campbell, 1993; Hamberger, Lohr, & Bonge, 1994). In contrast, men are more likely than women to become violent as a means to gain or retain control over partners (Hamberger et al., 1994; Jacobson & Gottman, 1998; Lloyd & Emery, 2000).

GENDERED PATTERNS IN INTIMATE PARTNER VIOLENCE

An increasing number of researchers assert that intimate partner violence is a heavily gendered phenomenon (Christopher & Lloyd, 2000; Goldner et al., 1990; Jacobson & Gottman, 1998; Johnson, 1995, 2001; Kimmel, 1996, Messner, 1997; Oakley, 2002; Wood, 2000, 2001, 2004). Given the greater number of male perpetrators of intimate partner violence and the greater severity of their violence, it is not surprising that researchers have concentrated on men and masculinity in efforts to understand intimate partner violence. In this chapter, I follow this tendency by giving primary attention to research on the relationship between intimate partner violence and masculinity.

Codes of Masculinity

Research on men and masculinity has highlighted intersections between men's intimate partner violence and cultural codes of manhood. Researchers highlight the troubling connection between men's efforts to control others, particularly women, and codes of masculinity that are prevalent in many societies (Kimmel, 1996, 2002; Lloyd 1999; Lloyd & Emery, 2000; Messner, 1997). Some researchers assert that men who engage in intimate partner violence identify with and embody *in extremis* widely accepted cultural ideologies that promote masculine authority and aggression (Boyd, 2002; Goldner et al., 1990).

Extending this line of inquiry, I conducted a study that highlighted two contradictory, although not entirely independent, views of manhood that are woven into Western culture and embraced by some individual men (Wood, 2004). The first narrative holds that men are superior to women, which entitles them to dominate and hurt women and to expect women's deference. The second narrative holds that men should protect and not hurt women. Interestingly, many men in my study expressed allegiance to *both* codes of manhood, creating a tension that often legitimizes violence in a particular moment, followed by remorse for having harmed a woman.

Men as Dominant and Superior

Based in patriarchal ideology, one view of manhood holds that men are superior to women and are entitled to sex and other attention from their wives and girlfriends, that women are supposed to please and defer to men, that men have the right to control and discipline women, and that women should center their lives around men, although men are entitled to independence. Numerous researchers have noted that cultural practices may legitimate this view of manhood by approving of men who are dominant, powerful, and controlling and by approving of women who stand by their man, no matter how men treat them (Adams, Towns, & Gavey,

1995; Coan, Gottman, Babcock, & Jacobson, 1997; Kimmel, 1996, 2002; Meyers, 1997).

Reflecting the patriarchal view of manhood are comments from four men whom I interviewed (Wood, 2004):

- "I was the man in the relationship. I was always brought up like, a man's sposed to be more in control of a relationship."
- "Things got to go my way or no way. I mean I respect, respect a woman's opinion, but I just feel they had to go my way or no way at all."
- "A man, he's supposed to run the household. So if you're a man, you ain't really gotta, I ain't gotta answer to my old lady. But with *her*, she wanna go somewhere, she's supposed to come to me and say 'I wanna go to such and such. I wanna do such and such.' That's the way I was brought up. It's still in me."
- "As far as like the man being the head of the household, it's kind of old fashioned, but I believe it."

However, there is a twist to the patriarchal view of manhood. Existing research has shown that male against female intimate partner violence may be equally or more likely to be inflicted by men who identify strongly with the patriarchal narrative of manhood yet feel, or fear, that they do not measure up to that narrative (Boyd, 2002; Dutton, 1998; Kimmel, 1996, 2002; Lloyd, 1999; Messner, 1997; Wood, 2001, 2004). In other words, men who endorse a view of masculinity that they cannot achieve may have "a defensive masculinity which involves adopting a behavioral pattern that is aligned with their conception of society's image of a 'macho' man" (Sugarman & Frankel, 1996, p. 31). For these men, the patriarchal view of manhood is how they see "real men," but they are not confident that they personally embody that ideal. Violence, including violence against women, becomes a means of reassuring themselves that they are powerful, in control, and otherwise real men.

Explicating the connection between male power(lessness) and violence, Oakley (2002) asserted that male "violence against women is particularly likely to happen when men feel their power is threatened" (p. 38). Using violence to compel what they perceive as women's respect and subservience seems to be a means to assuage their insecurity about their ability to meet a masculine ideal they esteem. In a wide-ranging review of research that hypothesized connections between power and violence, Holtzworth-Munroe, Smutzler, Bates, and Sandin (1997) concluded that power per se is a less good predictor of male violence than a sense of powerlessness. Faludi (1999) reported that some men who enact violence against wives and girlfriends do so as a means of claiming the power and status they see as a birthright of manhood. In sum, men who feel they are not powerful may see dominating and controlling female intimate partners as a practicable route to gaining power.

Clearly articulating the relationship between his violence toward his wife and his insecurity in his manhood, Weeks, a man I interviewed (Wood, 2004), concluded his description of pummeling his wife's face by saying, "My self-esteem was real low and that's why I put her on my level." In an even more explicit statement, Ricardo answered my question of why he beat his girlfriend by saying, "I couldn't get a decent job. . . . I didn't feel like I could take, uh, like I was the provider, you know what I'm saying. I didn't feel like a man."

The patriarchal view of manhood may contribute to men's intimate partner violence both for men who feel they are so-called real men and for men who feel they do not measure up to the code of manhood that they endorse and admire. Men who believe they personally embody this ideal of manhood feel they are entitled to control relationships and women, be deferred to and catered to by women, and use discipline or violence to enforce their male entitlements. Men who are not confident that they measure up to the patriarchal view of manhood may use control and violence to enforce women's deference, which gives them some assurance that in the realm of private relationships they are and are perceived as real men.

Men as Protectors of Women

A second narrative of manhood that is also well established Western culture is in some tension with the patriarchal view. Drawing on a code of chivalry, this code requires men to respect and take care of women and never abuse them. In a recent book, Felson (2002) argued that both the culture and individual men subscribe to a chivalrous code, which holds that men should protect women. Felson claims that "violence against women [is] not an expression of sexism" (p. ix) because "chivalry leads men to protect women, not harm them" (p. 5).

Felson's claims do not fare well against data gathered by many researchers, which demonstrate that some men who engage in intimate partner violence recognize the cultural code of chivalry but violate it in their own relationships with wives and girlfriends. In addition to men who endorse and live by a code that mandates that a man never harms a woman, there appear to be some men who subscribe to chivalry as an abstract code but who do not necessarily follow it in their relationships with wives and girlfriends. Some men may believe that men should protect women in general and mothers and daughters in particular. However, that chivalry does not automatically find its way into some men's relationships with wives and girlfriends, and it does not deter some men from intimate partner violence. Men who both endorse and violate the chivalrous code may be like those described by Stark and Flitcraft (1996) in their study of men who batter wives. Many male batterers, they observed, are "men who covet their wives at one moment as if they were unique and irreplaceable, then beat them the next as if they were disposable (and replaceable) objects" (p. 34).

Although the chivalrous code of manhood is clearly more prosocial than the patriarchal one, the two share the assumption of male superiority. Further, these two views of manhood are not wholly independent. At an abstract level, some men seem to feel it is wrong for men to hurt women as a group, but at a concrete level they believe they are entitled or compelled to hurt the particular women with whom they have intimate relationships.

Codes of Femininity

Just as there are culturally constructed and reproduced codes of masculinity, so there are codes of femininity. Clearly, femininity does not mean what it did 200, or even 20, years ago. Today women, at least in many societies, are no longer considered men's property; women have access to higher education and gainful employment; and women have legal standing, and rights and freedoms that are equal, at least formally, to those of men. These changes are important, yet traditional narratives of femininity persist and they are complementary to equally persisting traditional narratives of masculinity.

Dominant codes of femininity entail at least three themes. First, women are expected to please and defer to men. Second, women are expected to be "relationship experts," who take care of others and work to preserve relationships. Third, an intimate relationship with a man is central to a woman's life.

Pleasing Men

In her classic book, *Man's World, Woman's Place*, Janeway (1971) noted the connection between pleasing others and power: "The whole question of pleasing is central to an analysis of woman's role. . . . pleasing as a policy . . . pleasingness as an attribute commonly expected of women and other subordinates. . . . The powerful need not please. . . . Pleasing goes with dependence and subordination" (pp. 113–114). Women are expected by others and often themselves to please, care for, and defer to men. Illustrative of the centrality of pleasing to dominant codes of femininity are quotes from women who had been targets of intimate partner violence (Wood, 2001, pp. 247, 252):

- "I had to look a certain way for him."
- "I'm supposed to please him."
- "I wanted to be like he wanted me to be."
- "I kept trying to figure out what he liked and didn't like and to behave right around him."

When their male partners were violent toward them, many of the women I interviewed attributed the violence to themselves, not their male partners. Vivian told me, "I'm the one that's in the wrong, so I just lived with it" (p. 254). Similarly, Baily said that, "every time he hit me, I had gotten him started over something and I always felt like I started it" (p. 254). Explaining why it was her fault that her partner pummeled her when she was dressing to go to a party he had told her not to attend, Derise said, "if I had listened when he first said not to go, none of it would have happened" (p. 254). And Melinda reasoned that "there's something inside of me . . . that is allowing this stuff to happen to me" (p. 256).

Being Relationship Focused

Also central to reigning codes of femininity is the expectation that women will be the relationship experts. As such, they are expected to invest energy in preserving relationships by anticipating and meeting others' needs and by forgiving and being loyal to relationship partners. Far more than men, women are "subject to call by other people" (Janeway, 1971, p. 86). Socialized to notice and respond to others' needs and to provide for others' comfort, a woman learns "to identify the satisfying of others' needs and complying with others as *a need of her own*" (Eichenbaum & Orbach, 1987, p. 61).

In my interviews (Wood, 2001), women who had been in violent relationships told me again and again that they felt they were supposed to care for and take care of their abusive partners and that they felt making the relationship work was their job. "I was determined to make it work," said Bailey (p. 250). Mary's cohabiting boyfriend raped her, then threw her out of their house. The next day, she returned to get her things and "I washed his laundry and put it in a separate basket" (p. 249). According to Beverly, "it was my responsibility to keep things okay" (p. 249). After her boyfriend beat her brutally, Beverly thought, "it was over and we were okay. I didn't want to make too big a deal over it" (p. 253).

Needing a Man to be Whole

Underlying expectations to please and care for others is the nucleus of the dominant narrative of femininity, which is the belief that a woman's value is contingent on her ability to attract and hold a man. A woman who does not have a male partner is incomplete, undesirable, and unfeminine. Again, quotes from women who stayed with violent partners dramatically illustrate their internalization of this facet of the code of femininity (Wood, 2001, p. 253):

- "If something were to happen and I was not with him anymore, I wouldn't know what to do in my life."
- "I was afraid to be alone."
- "I didn't want to be by myself."
- "Everyone else always has someone and I was like, 'this is just my someone and I'm going to have to put up with what little I have.'"
- "Other men wouldn't be interested in me. I should count myself lucky that he was."
- "I felt so complete with him. He was my world."
- "I just felt like I needed to have someone."

Believing that she needs a man to have a full and good life can induce a woman to perceive staying in a violent relationship as preferable to not having a man in her life, which is to say, to not being whole.

The Interrelatedness of Gender Codes

Narratives for masculinity and femininity exist and operate in relation to each other. Male dominance makes sense only in relation to female deference; the masculine sense of entitlement to care, forgiveness, and attention requires a feminine willingness to supply these rewards. Although less overt, sweeping, and formally codified than in previous eras, patriarchal patterns persist in Western cultures. As Oakley (2002) noted, "there aren't any 'Patriarch Headquarters'" (p. 220). Yet patriarchy persists not so much as matter of laws but as ensconced beliefs and everyday practices that continue to maintain that men are more powerful than women; women should defer to and please men; caring for others, including men, is a primary responsibility for women; good women stand by their men; and men will transgress and should be forgiven by their partners. This is practical, day-to-day patriarchy, which is a system that is collaboratively constructed and sustained by individuals as they act and interact in their relationships.

Our understandings of gender and relationships are both personal and social. They are personal in that they are constructed and used by particular men and women to make sense of their experiences and relationships. They are also resolutely social because they reflect and embody culturally produced, sustained, and approved narratives of gender and romance. Both women and men are socialized in a culture that includes romance and gender narratives that tell us it is acceptable for men to dominate and, in some cases, use violence against female intimates. Attending to cultural narratives does not require absolving individuals for reprehensible actions. Men who are violent toward women can and should be held responsible for their actions. Women should be encouraged and taught not to tolerate violence from intimate partners. Yet we miss the mark badly if we focus only on individuals and ignore the larger ideologies that shape their actions.

DIRECTIONS FOR FUTURE RESEARCH

Only in recent years has intimate partner violence been studied seriously. Much good work has been done; much more is needed. I regard six lines of future research as particularly important. First, we need a fuller understanding of men who perpetrate intimate partner violence. We need to understand their reasons, their beliefs about results, and their awareness of options to violence. Second, by extension, we need focused study of educational and therapeutic efforts to stop intimate partner violence. Which ones work best, or do different ones work well in specific situations or with specific populations? Which ones work best for which groups of men? Third, we need to develop and assess forward-looking efforts that aim to prevent intimate partner violence before it happens. What strategies can best reach young children and adolescents as they begin dating? Fourth, it is important to study forms of intimate partner violence that are outside the purview of this chapter: intimate partner violence between gay partners, between lesbian partners, and intimate partner violence perpetrated by women against male partners. Fifth, we need to understand why many men do not commit intimate partner violence and many women do not tolerate it. Research that gives us insight into why some individuals resist the dark side of Western culture's gender and romance narratives would enrich our understanding of reasons why prevalent narratives are interpreted in different ways that lead to distinct personal embodiments of masculinity and femininity and distinct approaches to intimate relationships.

Finally, we need to adopt a contextual view of and approach to intimate partner violence in all research in this area. As I have argued in this chapter, it is a mistake to view or study intimate partner violence as a strictly personal or interpersonal phenomenon—one that can be explained by individual pathology or dynamics between the two people involved. Instead, in all of our future research, we need to recognize that intimate partner violence exists in particular social and cultural contexts, whose ideologies and narratives for gender and romance shape what happens in specific relationships—what is considered normal, appropriate, and acceptable.

CONCLUSION

In summarizing research on intimate partner violence, this chapter highlights cultural ideologies of gender and heterosexual romance that work together to legitimize a disturbingly coherent narrative that represents men's violence toward women intimates as expected, normal, tolerable, and appropriate.

Both men and women are inclined to allow men's domination of, and sometimes violence toward, women partners if they accept, however inadvertently, cultural narratives that portray male domination and violence and female deference and loyalty as normal aspects of gender and heterosexual romantic relationships. And acceptance is routine and generally less than conscious because the narratives are so thoroughly woven into Western culture that they become virtually invisible, undetectable. "We live in the midst of an epidemic of male violence," writes Ann Oakley (2002), "but we have difficulty naming it as such because of a deep-seated reluctance to admit that 'normal' ideas about gender and ordinary imbalances of power are both implicated as causes" (p. 45). We need to rethink what we consider normal about masculinity and men and femininity and women.

In her classic book, *The Everyday World as Problematic*, Dorothy Smith (1987) noted that the inequality of marriage (and, by extension, heterosexual relationships) "is not a conspiracy among men that they impose on women. It is a complementary social process between men and women" (p. 34). Masculinity is meaningful in relation to femininity; femininity is meaningful in relation to masculinity; each requires the other to have form and significance. The problem is not that narratives—and material embodiments—of masculinity and femininity exist. It is that the existing narratives allow and normalize inequality, domination, and, in extreme cases, violence. Although those of us who are not science fiction writers may not be ready for a genderless culture, we may well be ready for a culture in which genders are constructed and practiced differently than they are today.

Narratives are powerful in shaping social life and informing individuals' sense making. Yet, the narratives authorized by a culture are neither finite nor fixed. Existing narratives are contingent and open to revision. They can be changed if individuals and institutions decide the narratives that exist at any particular historical moment are inadequate to define and direct our lives. It is possible for us to revise existing narratives. It is possible to imagine and bring into existence new gender narratives that allow us to see and be men and women who do not dominate and defer. We also have the capacity to fashion new romance narratives that define what is acceptable, normal, and good in romantic relationships.

REFERENCES

Adams, P., Towns, A., & Gavey, N. (1995). Dominance and entitlement: The rhetoric men use to discuss their violence toward women. *Discourse and Society, 6*, 387–406.

Archer, J. (2000a). Sex differences in aggression between heterosexual partners: A meta-analytic review. *Psychological Bulletin, 126*, 651–680.

Archer, J. (2000b). Sex differences in physical aggression to partners: A reply to Frieze (2000), O'Leary (2000), and White, Smith, Koss, and Figueredo (2000). *Psychological Bulletin, 126*, 697–702.

Bachman, R., & Saltzman, L. (1995). *Violence against women: Estimates from the redesigned survey.* (Publication No. NCJ-154348). Washington, DC: Bureau of Justice Statistics, U.S. Department of Justice.

Barnett, O., Miller-Perrin, C., & Perrin, R. (1997). *Family violence across the life span.* Thousand Oaks, CA: Sage.

Boyd, N. (2002). *Beast within: Why men are violent.* Vancouver, BC: Groundwood/Greystone Books.

Campbell, A. (1993). *Men, women, and aggression.* New York: Basic Books.

Cazenave, N., & Straus, M. (1990). Race, class, network embeddedness, and family violence: A search for potent support systems. In M. Straus & R. Gelles (Eds.), *Physical violence in American families* (pp. 321–340). New Brunswick, NJ: Transaction.

Christopher, F., & Lloyd, S. (2000). Physical and sexual aggression in relationships. In C. Hendrick & S. Hendrick (Eds), *Close relationships: A sourcebook* (pp. 331–343). Thousand Oaks, CA: Sage.

Coan, J., Gottman, J., Babcock, J., & Jacobson, N. (1997). Battering and the male rejection of influence from women. *Aggressive Behavior, 23*, 375–388.

DeKeseredy, W., Saunders, D., Schwartz, M., & Alvi, S. (1997). The meanings and motives for women's use of violence in Canadian college dating relationships: Results from a national survey. *Sociological Spectrum, 17*, 199–222.

Department of Justice. (2000). Publication No. NCJ-167237. Washington, DC: Bureau of Justice Statistics, U.S. Department of Justice.

Dutton, D. (1998). *The abusive personality: A trauma model.* New York: Guilford.

Dutton, D., & Strachan, C. (1987). Motivational needs for power and spouse-specific assertiveness in assaultive and nonassaultive men. *Violence and Victims, 2*, 145–156.

Eichenbaum, L., & Orbach, S. (1987). *Understanding women: A feminist, psychoanalytic approach.* New York: Basic Books.

Department of Justice. *Extent, nature and consequence of intimate partner violence: Findings from the National Violence Against Women Survey.* (2000). Washington, DC: Office of Justice Programs, U.S. Department of Justice.

Faludi, S. (1999). *Stiffed: The betrayal of the American man.* New York: Morrow.

Felson, R. (2002). *Violence and gender reexamined.* Washington, DC: American Psychological Association.

Follingstad, D., Rutledge, L., Berg, B., Hause, E., & Polek, D. (1990). The role of emotional abuse in physically abusive relationships. *Journal of Family Violence, 5*, 107–120.

Frieze, I. (2000). Violence in close relationships—development of a research area. Comment on Archer (2000). *Psychological Bulletin, 126*, 681–684.

Goldner, V., Penn, P., Sheinberg, M., & Walker, G. (1990). Love and violence: Gender paradoxes in volatile attachments. *Family Process, 19*, 343–364.

Goode, E. (2001, August 1). 20% of girls report abuse by a date. *Raleigh News and Observer,* p. 10A.

Gray, H., & Foshee, V. (1997). Adolescent dating violence: Differences between one-sided and mutually violent profiles. *Journal of Interpersonal Violence, 12*, 126–141.

Hamberger, L., Lohr, J., & Bonge, D. (1994). The intended function of domestic violence is different for arrested male and female perpetrators. *Family Violence and Sexual Assault, 10*, 40–44.

Holtzworth-Munroe, A., Smutzler, N., & Bates, L. (1997). A brief review of the research on husband violence. III: Sociodemographic factors, relationship factors, and differing consequences of husband and wife violence. *Aggression and Violent Behavior, 2*, 285–307.

Holtzworth-Munroe, A., Smutzler, N., Bates, L., & Sandin, E. (1997). Husband violence: Basic facts and clinical implications. In W. K. Halford & H. J. Markman (Eds), *Clinical handbook of marriage and couples interventions* (pp. 129–156). New York: Wiley.

Jacobson, N., & Gottman, J. (1998). *When men batter women.* New York: Simon & Schuster.

Jacobson, N., & Gurman, A. (Eds.). (1986). *Clinical handbook of marital therapy.* New York: Guilford.

Jackman, M. R. (2003). Violence in social life. *Annual Review of Sociology, 28*, 387–415.

Janeway, E. (1971). *Man's world, woman's place: A study in social mythology.* New York: Dell.

Johnson, M. P. (1995). Patriarchal terrorism and common couple violence: Two forms of violence against women. *Journal of Marriage and the Family, 57*, 283–294.

Johnson, M. P. (2001). Conflict and control: Symmetry and asymmetry in domestic violence. In A. Booth, A. Crouter, & M. Clements (Eds.), *Couples in conflict* (pp. 95–104). Mahwah, NJ: Lawrence Erlbaum Associates.

Johnson, M. P., Conklin, V., & Menon, N. (2002, November). *The effects of different types of domestic violence on women: Intimate terrorism vs. situational couple violence.* Paper presented at the annual meeting of the National Council on Family Relations, Houston, TX.

Johnson, M. P., & Ferraro, K. J. (2000). Research on domestic violence in the 1990s: Making distinctions. *Journal of Marriage and the Family, 62*, 948–963.

Jones, A. (1994). *Next time she'll be dead: Battering and how to stop it.* Boston: Beacon.

Jones, A. (1998a). Battered women. In W. Mankiller, G. Mink, M. Navarro, B. Smith, & G. Steinem (Eds.), *The reader's companion to U.S. women's history* (pp. 607–609). New York: Houghton Mifflin.

Jones, A. (1998b). Domestic violence. In W. Mankiller, G. Mink, M. Navarro, B. Smith, & G. Steinem (Eds.), *The reader's companion to U.S. women's history* (p. 609). New York: Houghton Mifflin.

Kimmel, M. (1996). *Manhood.* New York: The Free Press.

Kimmel, M. (2002, February 8). Gender, class and terrorism. *Chronicle of Higher Education*, pp. B11–B12.

Langley, J., & Nada-Raja, S. (1997). Physical assault among 21-year-olds by partners. *Journal of Interpersonal Violence, 12*, 675–684.

Lloyd, S. A. (1999). The interpersonal and communication dynamics of wife battering. In X. B. Arriga & S. Oskamp (Eds.), *Violence in intimate relationships* (pp. 91–111). Thousand Oaks, CA: Sage.

Lloyd, S. A., & Emery, B. (2000). *The dark side of courtship: Physical and sexual aggression.* Thousand Oaks, CA: Sage.

May, L. (1998a, July 10). Many men still find strength in violence. *Chronicle of Higher Education,* p. B7.

May, L. (1998b). *Masculinity and morality.* Ithaca, NY: Cornell University Press.

Messner, M. (1997). *Politics of masculinities: Men in movements.* Thousand Oaks, CA: Sage.

Meyers, M. (1997). *News coverage of violence against women: Engendering blame.* Thousand Oaks: Sage.

Morse, B. (1995). Beyond the conflict tactics scale: Assessing gender differences in partner violence. *Violence and Victims, 10*, 252–272.

Murphy-Milano, S. (1996). *Defending our lives.* New York: Anchor/Doubleday.

Oakley, A. (2002). *Gender on planet earth.* New York: The New Press.

O'Leary, K. (2000). Are women really more aggressive than men in intimate relationships? Comment on Archer (2000). *Psychological Bulletin, 126*, 685–689.

Smith, D. (1987). *The everyday world as problematic.* Boston, MA: Northeastern University Press.

Stark, E., & Flitcraft, A. (1996). *Women at risk: Domestic violence and women's health.* Thousand Oaks, CA: Sage.

Straus, M. (1993). Physical assault by wives: A major social problem. In R. Gelles & D. Loseke (Eds.), *Current controversies on family violence* (pp. 67–97). Newbury Park, CA: Sage.

Straus, M. (1999). The controversy over domestic violence by women: A methodological, theoretical, and sociology of science analysis. In X. B. Arriga & S. Oskamp (Eds.), *Violence in intimate relationships* (pp. 17-44). Thousand Oaks, CA: Sage.

Sugarman, D., & Frankel, S. (1996). Patriarchal ideology and wife-assault: A meta-analytic review. *Journal of Family Violence, 11*, 13–40.

Wood, J. T. (2000). "That wasn't the real him": Women's dissociation of violence from the men who enact it. *Qualitative Research in Review, 1*, 1–7.

Wood, J. T. (2001). The normalization of violence in heterosexual romantic relationships: Women's narratives of love and violence. *Journal of Social and Personal Relationships, 18*, 239–261.

Wood, J. T. (2004). Monsters and victims: Male felons' accounts of intimate partner violence. *Journal of Social and Personal Research, 21*, 555–576.

Epilogue

Janet Shibley Hyde
University of Wisconsin–Madison

In this second edition of *Sex Differences and Similarities in Communication*, Kathryn Dindia and Daniel Canary have brought together authoritative reviews of what has become a vast array of research on gender, communication, and social behavior. Several issues are prominent in the field and surface across multiple chapters: the gender similarities hypothesis; the question of whether researchers should study gender differences at all; the question of interpretation, that is, what do we make of findings of gender differences; the concept of doing gender; the importance of context; the interaction of gender and ethnicity; and the interaction of gender and social class.

THE GENDER SIMILARITIES HYPOTHESIS

For decades I have advocated the gender similarities hypothesis: that girls and boys, men and women, are more alike than they are different (e.g., Hyde, 2004; Hyde, 2005; Hyde & Plant, 1995; Hyde & Rosenberg, 1980). One of the strengths of this volume is that the authors provide balanced considerations of the evidence for gender differences versus gender similarities. Typically they conclude in favor of gender similarities. It is particularly invigorating to note the ways in which a recognition of the gender similarities hypothesis can lead to major advances in a field. Wright (chap. 3, this volume), for example, details his earlier beliefs in large, dichotomized, polarized differences between men's friendships and women's friendships, and his dawning realization that men's and women's friendships instead display variations on a continuum and much similarity.

The gender similarities hypothesis does not state that men and women are similar on every psychological dimension. A few gender differences are moderate and even large in magnitude. Examples include gender differences in smiling, emotional expressiveness, and sensitivity to nonverbal cues (Hall, chap. 4, this volume; Guerrero, Jones, & Boburka, chap. 13, this volume) and gender differences in attitudes about casual sex (Oliver & Hyde, 1993).

SHOULD RESEARCHERS STUDY GENDER DIFFERENCES?

One of the most basic questions that must be asked is this: Should researchers study gender differences? Those who respond in the negative argue that continued research reifies constructions of gender as difference (Hare-Mustin & Marecek, 1994; Hollway, 1994). I have previously argued that researchers should study gender differences, but with some guidelines (Hyde, 1994). The media and the general public will continue to be entranced with the idea of psychological gender differences, so scientists have an obligation to continue research in this area to counter widespread misconceptions.

This dilemma of whether to study gender differences is exacerbated by the mass media, which are jubilant over reports of gender differences and bored by findings of gender similarities. Dindia presents the evidence for the similarities perspective well in chapter 1 of this volume. Some scholars have tried to counter the differences fascination by writing popular-press books on gender similarities, such as Barnett and Rivers's *Same Difference: How Gender Myths Are Hurting Our Relationships, our Children, and our Jobs* (2004). Allen and Valde (chap. 6, this volume) argue that we should continue to conduct gender differences research—which typically finds gender similarities—precisely because scientists are obligated to pursue research that corrects popular misconceptions. It remains to be seen whether the culture can listen to the evidence about gender similarities.

Part of the remedy is for researchers to report not only significance tests for gender differences but also effect sizes, as noted by Dindia in chapter 1, this volume (see also Hyde, 1994). This practice was recommended for all research by the Task Force on Statistical Inference of the American Psychological Association, and it is now part of the APA *Publication Manual* (American Psychological Association, 2001; Wilkinson and the Task Force on Statistical Inference, 1999). Journal editors seem not to be enforcing these guidelines, however, so the focus on significance testing, to the exclusion of considerations of effect size, continues unabated.

WHAT DO WE MAKE OF GENDER DIFFERENCES?

Imagine that a meta-analysis has found evidence that a particular gender difference in social behavior is moderate or large in magnitude. What should we make of that? Evolutionary psychologists leap to evolutionary answers. We should step back a moment, though, and recognize that studies of gender differences never use experimental designs. That is, they never randomly assign participants to be either male or female. Gender differences designs are at most quasi-experiments (Cook & Campbell, 1979). Even in research that finds a large difference, the design is confounded. The male group and female group differ not only in their sex, but in hundreds of other ways, such as the books they read and the gender composition of their friendship group in childhood, the athletic activities they experienced in high school, and their career aspirations. Any given finding of gender differences may not be about gender, but rather about being a literature versus engineering major, being employed outside the home or being home full time, or being employed in a job with much power or one with little power and control.

This design limitation means that we must always be extremely cautious in our inferences about findings of gender differences. At the least, we should demand that the finding display replicability. We should not conclude that, because men and women also differ in some biological characteristic such as hormone levels, that the biological factor therefore causes the behavioral difference.

An additional methodological flaw occurs when average gender differences on a continuous scale suddenly are translated to categorical differences between women and men. Wright illustrates this point in his chapter on gender and friendship (see chap. 3, this volume). Women's friendships have been characterized as communal and men's as agentic, which is a categorical or typological view. However, the actual research shows no gender difference in agency and a difference in communal qualities, but only an average difference. The typological view is simply not a legitimate conclusion from the research.

DOING GENDER

One of the objections to gender differences research is that it focuses on gender as a property of the individual. An alternative approach is to view gender as a social construction that is the product of enactments between people who, in essence, are "doing" gender. Crawford and Kaufman capture this model well in their chapter in this volume (chap. 10), with their emphasis on social processes and the ways in which social processes construct gender. They note that these processes can operate at three levels: the sociocultural, the level of interpersonal interactions, and the individual level in which society's constructions of gender are internalized. These processes help to create power inequities between men and women and serve to maintain male dominance.

This focus on doing gender takes research in a very different direction—away from searches for gender differences and their causes, and toward studies of the processes that reproduce gender relations from one generation to the next.

When the focus shifts away from thinking of gender as an individual or person variable, an alternative approach presents itself: the consideration of gender as a stimulus variable (Hyde, 2004). This is part of what occurs in doing gender. The gender of one person is a stimulus to the other person and vice versa. This point is well illustrated in Mulac's chapter (chap. 12, this volume). When the spoken language of men and women is transcribed and stripped of all overt gender cues, native speakers of American English are unable to judge accurately the gender of the speaker. That is, when the gender cue is stripped away, the average observer cannot tell the difference, despite the fact that members of the general public devour Tannen's books (1990) and believe that they can tell the difference. The gender of a speaker is a powerful cue or stimulus.

CONTEXT IS EVERYTHING

One principle that has emerged in social psychological research is that psychological gender differences can appear or disappear, depending on the context in which they are assessed. For example, stereotype threat research shows that gender differences in performance on advanced mathematics tests appear if participants are told that men typically outperform women on the exam, and gender differences disappear if participants are told that the exam shows no gender differences (e.g., Spencer, Steele, & Quinn, 1999). Context can operate at multiple levels, including instructions to an individual on a written exam, dyadic interactions (e.g., Deaux & Major, 1987), peer group influences, institutional influences (e.g., law, religion), and complex cultural influences. The importance of context is elaborated by Eagly and Koenig in chapter 9 this volume, articulating a social role theory of gender differences and similarities; and by Di Mare and Waldron in chapter 11, this volume, on gendered communication in Japan and the United States.

THE INTERSECTION OF GENDER AND ETHNICITY

Although the chapters in this volume focus on gender differences, as noted earlier, gendered behavior always occurs in a context—whether in an elementary school classroom, on a date, or in the workplace. In the United States, one of the crucial sociocultural contexts for gender differences is the ethnicity of those who are interacting and communicating. Most of the research on gender differences in communication has been conducted with samples of White individuals, leaving us with little idea of what the patterns of difference or similarity might be among Blacks, Asian Americans, or other groups. As an example, our meta-analysis of gender differences in self-esteem showed a small difference favoring men, $d = 0.21$ (Kling, Hyde, Showers, & Buswell, 1999). However, when studies were broken down by the ethnicity of the sample, the gender differences was $d = 0.20$ for Whites but $d = -0.04$ for Blacks. That is, this much-touted gender difference turns out to be small, and, worse, turns out to be true only for Whites; Blacks show no gender difference.

As a second example, stereotypes hold that emotional expression should be highly gendered (Plant, Hyde, Keltner, & Devine, 2000). According to stereotypes, men may express anger but women should not. However, an investigation of these gender stereotypes of emotion in four U.S. ethnic groups revealed quite different patterns (Durik & Hyde, 2005). Among Blacks, for example, women are believed to express more anger than Whites believe White men do.

GENDER AND SOCIAL CLASS

Feminist theory stresses not only the interaction of gender and ethnicity but also the interaction of gender and social class (Hyde, 2004). Again, most of the research reviewed in this volume is based on samples of middle-class individuals, often college students. This leaves unanswered the question of whether the differences—and similarities—would also be found in working-class or poor individuals. Social psychologists, like other psychologists, have typically ignored the issue of social class, leaving it to the sociologists. A trend over the next decade will be to integrate social class into our theory and research designs, including our research on gender.

REFERENCES

American Psychological Association. (2001). *Publication manual.* (5th ed.). Washington, DC: Author.

Barnett, R., & Rivers, C. (2004). *Same difference: How gender myths are hurting our relationships, our children, and our jobs.* New York: Basic Books.

Cook, T. D., & Campbell, D. T. (1979). *Quasi-experimentaiton: Design & analysis issues for field settings.* Boston: Houghton Mifflin.

Deaux, K., & Major, B. (1987). Putting gender into context: An interactive model of gender-related behavior. *Psychological Review, 94,* 369–389.

Durik, A., & Hyde, J. S. (2005). *Ethnicity and gender stereotypes of emotion.* Manuscript submitted for publication.

Hare-Mustin, R. T., & Marecek, J. (1994). Asking the right questions: Feminist psychology and sex differences. *Feminism & Psychology, 4,* 531–537.

Hollway, W. (1994). Beyond sex differences: A project for feminist psychology. *Feminism & Psychology, 4,* 538–546.

Hyde, J. S. (1994). Should psychologists study gender differences? Yes, with some guidelines. *Feminism & Psychology, 4,* 507–512.

Hyde, J. S. (2004). *Half the human experience: The psychology of women.* (6th ed.). Boston: Houghton Mifflin.

Hyde, J. S. (2005). The gender similarities hypothesis. *American Psychologist, 60,* 581–592.

Hyde, J. S., & Plant, E. A. (1995). Magnitude of psychological gender differences: Another side to the story. *American Psychologist, 50,* 159–161.

Hyde, J. S., & Rosenberg, B. G. (1980). *Half the human experience: The psychology of women* (2nd ed.). Lexington, MA: Heath.

Kling, K. C., Hyde, J. S., Showers, C., & Buswell, B. (1999). Gender differences in self-esteem: A meta-analysis. *Psychological Bulletin, 125,* 470–500.

Oliver, M. B., & Hyde, J. S. (1993). Gender differences in sexuality: A meta-analysis. *Psychological Bulletin, 114,* 29–51.

Plant, E. A., Hyde, J. S., Keltner, D., & Devine, P. (2000). The gender stereotyping of emotions. *Psychology of Women Quarterly, 24,* 81–92.

Spencer, S. J., Steele, C. M., & Quinn, D. M. (1999). Stereotype threat and women's math performance. *Journal of Experimental Social Psychology, 35,* 4–28.

Tannen, D. (1990). *You just don't understand: Women and men in conversation.* New York: Morrow.

Wilkinson, L., & the Task Force on Statistical Inference. (1999). Statistical methods in psychology journals: Guidelines and explanations. *American Psychologist, 54,* 594–604.

Author Index

E

F

G

I

N

O

R

S

X

Y

Z

Subject Index

T

V

W

Y